mansion of an earlier time. Notice how the grounds are in the Uruguayan style and yet without shrubbery, blossoms or vegetation of any kind. Here we find a past of Carrara marble, a past carved in stone – intersecting lines, reserved, ripe with inscrutability. Upon initial viewing it appears impossible to get lost here along the linear walkways between the unassailable statues and marble embellishments. I am, even now, losing myself forever – losing myself in my own prophetic utterances, alone in my Patmosian exile. Alone without you.

Luh? She is fine. However, she will not be accompanying me on my trip. This time I will be traveling solo.

So what occurred with Luh?

Picture me flying, rocketing through the sky like Christopher Reeve in Superman, my right fist thrust before me. I am flying over a parking lot, heading for a landing next to a woman who is pregnant with my son. There is a complication: This woman is not my wife. I have not spoken with her at all during her pregnancy, and she's already in her second trimester. It's definitely time to pay her some attention.

Next, we are in a sort of cave, except most of the ceiling is missing, open to the sky. I think of a movie I am making, that I have already scripted. It's called "Marienbad My Love With Mango Extracts." As I look around at the walls of the cave, it occurs to me that I could become trapped. Always there are walls, everywhere around me. Mute, deserted – walls of baroque embellishments, mahogany veneer, Venetian plaster, gold-leafed frames, Carrara marble. Dark glass, obscure illustrations, Romanesque columns, sculptured thresholds, lines of doors, colonnades, oblique hallways leading to deserted meeting rooms paneled in the baroque embellishments of an earlier time. Mute rooms, where footsteps are lost. Sculpted berber so profound, so deep that one perceives no step. The walls are everywhere, enclosing me.

But I don't panic. I tell myself that this place needn't be safe all the time, just during this short time I am here. I won't be trapped. If I can just set aside my neuroses and free-floating anxieties for a bit, I may even enjoy it.

The cave is a pretty place, with pools of still water and patches of rye grass and moss. I talk to the woman who will bear my child. She is Luh. Or maybe Cinnamon. Or maybe you.

I tell her I am not sure if I should tell my two sons about the baby. I would have to admit to extramarital sex. (I don't mention that my wife might not appreciate this admission, either.) On the other hand, I think the boys should know about their half brother. After all, this new divine entity will grow up to create "Marienbad My Love With Mango Extracts," the movie that will bring about the End of the World – and the beginning of the New Religion.

Luh is incredibly supportive. She tells me I should do whatever I think is best. I shouldn't worry over the details. Her family is rich. (Her father was one of the medical professionals who treated the fatally wounded JFK in Dallas.) And she assures me that as far as they are concerned, "there are no strings attached" to any financial or other support.

I tell her it is so impressive that our son will grow up to do great things. "He'll go to Yale," I say. Luh corrects me. She tells me it is a different school, one I've never heard of. It is a hyphenated name with Yale as the first part, "Yale-Henning" or something like that. So that's it. He'll be part of an advanced and alien world, one I know nothing about.

#

Charlie: Attention Mark Leach. David Lynch is holding on the red phone. He wants to lend you his embalmed calf fetus for the baby scenes.

Elmo: In case you're just joining us here on "Blast" – it's the End of the World in "Marienbad My Love With Mango Extracts."

Charlie: B-movie sci-fi filmmakers have a long heritage of mining the various veins of the Apocalyptic genre, but few have tunneled as deep –

Elmo: And come up as lacking --

Charlie: -- as Mark Leach. "Marienbad My Love With Mango Extracts" is arguably the worst end-of-the-world film ever made. The concept alone is one of the most bizarre in the history of film – a skin care-themed tribute to "Last Year at Marienbad," the 1960s movie that defined the French New Wave.

Elmo: While it is the on-again/off-again odd darling of the midnight movie and science fiction convention crowds, "Marienbad" has otherwise generated almost universal disdain among casual moviegoers as well as serious cinemaphiles, including those of us here at "Blast." The onbeam world is rife with vitriolic reviews and caustic academic essays. Many of the comments are so vitriolic and caustic they cannot be repeated in a public broadcast; however, we have managed to sanitize a few for your enjoyment. "The incoherent ramblings of an insane mind ... I am not sure there is even a classification for this one ... long stretches of surrealism, where we are in this character's head and not grounded in any recognizable reality...What was that?! Was this person using drugs or what? ... I decided to be generous and give you a one, rather than a zero ... I am so completely confused. I have no idea what's going on, what's real and what the narrator is imagining ... It's terrible."

Charlie: This movie even offended the protagonist, who rather confusingly is also named Mark Leach. He recently broke down the fourth wall to post his own objections in the onbeam world: "Congratulations, Mark Leach. I read today that 'Marienbad My Love With Mango Extracts' has been declared one of the worst films ever made. And still you smile, that clueless, William Hung smile. Why so pleased? If you really wanted to create a noteworthy science fiction/fantasy film, then why no swords or elves? Why no Roman centurions? No, you thought you were too good. Only a hack would write genre, right? Instead of straight science fiction, you decided to employ the 'conventions' of SF. 'It's all for EFFECT,' you explain. And why did you have to make me so perverse? After all, I am an autobiographical character. What do my perversions say about you, the filmmaker? 'You are only an exaggerated version of me,' you say, 'exaggerated for comic effect.' Fine. Here is what I say: I hate this, being a fictional creation trapped in this abomination of a movie. Experimental? Stream of consciousness? Metafilm? How about 'crap'? Now that 'Marienbad My Love With Mango Extracts' has been unleashed on the world, surely the Apocalypse is not far behind."

Elmo: Indeed, the New York Agenda recently published a story about an Apocalyptic religion called Marienbadism. Inspired by scenes from the movie, a group of dedicated Marienbadists are planning to show the film in a special, yet-to-be-built drive-in theater in Tibet, an action Mark Leach has stated will bring about the death of the world and the birth of the new religion.

Charlie: And of course there are still the pending murder charges.

Elmo: Though in all fairness it is hard to see how one person can be blamed for the destruction of an entire town. But we digress. How did such a film ever come to be made at all? How did such a filmmaker ever come to be born?

Charlie: Yes, what is going on in the unconscious mind of this offender of humanity, this embracer of iniquity, this self-diagnosed sufferer of Post-Modern Prophet Disorder –

Elmo: This prototype of the two-bodied man.

Charlie: Steve Harrison, business editor of the Tarrant County Register and Leach's former boss, is here to shed some light on this strange and abhorrent being. Welcome Steve.

Steve: Thank you. It's a pleasure to be on "Blast."

Charlie: Mark has called "Marienbad My Love With Mango Extracts" his Incredible Revelation. Did he often incorporate so-called prophetic or visionary content into his work as real estate editor?

Steve: Mark was not real estate editor at the Register.

Elmo: Oh. But I thought –

Steve: He may have put it on his resume, but that doesn't make it true. Mark was a reporter, mostly daily assignments on local businesses.

Elmo: A revealing exaggeration, yet another example of this filmmaker's all-encompassing configuration of ostentation – in imagination if not conduct – and general air of narcissism, a quality we often see in corporate CEOs as well as the criminally insane.

Charlie: And in fact, this particular insane criminal –

Elmo: Also the CEO of his own movie.

Charlie: -- yes, we'll call him Chairman of the Board. He does show an overarching theme of hoped-for recognition as a superior life form. Or God.

Elmo: Unfortunately, Mark feels he is entitled to superiority without correspondingly superior achievements. Not good.

Charlie: At the risk of overusing an almost-trite example, I must say that at times his work reminds me of the schlock director from Texas, Ward E. Timber Jr.

Elmo: Exactly. "Marienbad My Love With Mango Extracts" comes off almost like a hymn to "Let Me Love You." To paraphrase the DVD dust jacket comments of the distributor, Wade Williams -- a sincerely unique, yet utterly flawed tribute from Ward to himself and everyone else who has ever attempted to construct something clever and significant and yet botched it wretchedly at every turn.

Charlie: You can almost see the strings and cardboard tombstones!

Elmo: Steve, did you see signs of this misplaced grandiosity and self-deification in Mark's work at the Register?

Steve: No, I wouldn't say that. Mark was quiet, a nose-to-the-grindstone kind of reporter. I'd characterize him as a journeyman. To be sure, he was a reliable worker. He met the expectations on his assignments, which were many and varied. I told him he was our utility infielder. But, uh --

Charlie: Ah yes, a jack of all trades, a master of none.

Steve: I'm afraid he never had much style as a journalist.

Charlie: Or a movie director.

Elmo: And that points to one of the central problems of "Marienbad My Love With Mango Extracts." Mark has a nice touch at the micro level. Lots of stunning metaphorical imagery, especially dealing with the central theme of the eruption of the inner dreamscape into waking reality. The inexplicable scent of roses, mystic icons weeping blood, statues of the Saints moving of their own accord – this film is truly a story of the unconscious invading the waking world. But Mark just doesn't pull it all together into a single cohesive narrative.

Charlie: What you just said about the "micro level" – this is absolutely on target. "Marienbad" is intermittently victorious. But as a whole – well, even Mark's biggest fans must admit that his talent shines brightest at the level of the individual scene.

Elmo: Let's roll the clip.

#

Here's one way the world ends: I am standing on the backyard patio of my boyhood home, looking up at the eastern heavens. It is an incredible sight – a white clock dial is bleeding through the thin cobalt sky. The psychic contrail is suspended in the high, thin stratosphere, an icy cirrus cloud of time. Somehow I understand that the government knows all about it, but has been keeping it a secret. Now that the Clock in the Air has been de-cloaked, there is no denying its existence. Is it an alien spaceship? Perhaps – or it could be something far more significant: A sign from the Deity. In fact, this may be the divine pocket watch, His timepiece. But time for what? Strange to be here, so out of my own time. My parents sold this house years ago.

#

Elmo: Pretty.

Charlie: Agreed. We should be fair. "Marienbad My Love With Mango Extracts" is in no way a total embarrassment. Mark is comfortable behind the camera, even if he doesn't have much rapport with it.

Elmo: And the camera clearly loves him. In scenes like this, "Marienbad My Love With Mango Extracts" certainly reminds one of the great Apocalyptic films of the Hydrocarbon Age, epics like "The Exfoliator of Zion," "The Herbal Extract Conspiracy" or anything from "The Abandoned Ones" series.

Charlie: But unlike those drive-in classics, Mark's movie simply fails to generate its own animating personality. It never fully succeeds in the terms of the genre.

Elmo: So often during "Marienbad" I reflected upon how much better everything must have functioned inside Mark's head.

Steve: Honestly, it was the same way with Mark's longer, more in-depth news features.

Charlie: Do tell.

Steve: He struggled to make the jump from brain to computer keyboard. He could rarely establish the proper tension.

Elmo: Fascinating. How do you mean?

Steve: It's like I tell my young reporters. Good writing is like a turnbuckle. Not too tight, not too loose.

Charlie: A turn what?

Steve: A turnbuckle. It's the little metal adjustor they used to put on wooden screen doors. Set it too loose and the door would drag. Too tight and the door would warp.

Charlie: Your anecdote tires me, a languid blood bath waltz of insipid storytelling, a dog humping the silky femur, poorly sculpted fluff. Yawn.

Elmo: Any Mark Leach examples come to mind?

Steve: I remember one time Mark brought us a story about a rash of new hotels slated to break ground in Tarrant County. At the time we were underserved in the lodging industry, so it was big news. But it wasn't big enough for Mark. No, he said his research had revealed that there were so many projects in the works that if they were all constructed we'd be overbuilt.

Elmo: The hotel market would crash.

Steve: So he claimed. That's the story he wanted to write. Mark was actually going to have us overbuilt before anybody even broke ground. So sad. I had to explain it to him. "Mark, you're too clever by half."

Charlie: But in fact he was right, yes? They did overbuild.

Steve: That's hardly the point.

Elmo: You could say it's the same way with "Marienbad My Love With Mango Extracts." Do you recall the judge's comments from the 2009 Novel Manuscript Contest by the Writers' League of Texas?

Charlie: Ah yes, it is almost the same. Just substitute 'movie' for 'novel' and you're there.

Elmo: Agreed. The movie is mostly clear cinematography about very fuzzy subject matter. It offers tons of jumbled imagery with no firm story. No resolution is offered.

Charlie: Agreed. Rambling imagery and disjointed reflection will hold a moviegoer's attention only so far. It is difficult to tell who the protagonist is and what makes him tick, beyond the impression that he has a warped view of numerous things.

Elmo: This movie is a jumbled attempt to tear a Dali painting in half. The ramblings of the narrator flow smoothly but make no sense – a stream of consciousness run off the tracks. The film contains occasional strong imagery but it is scattershot and refuses to paint a consistent, coherent sensory image. To contemplate watching 168 hours of such random ramblings causes one to tremble.

Charlie: To be fair, the movie is composed of competent scene structures and effective application of editing – I made few mark-ups as I watched – but it is one long jumble of incoherent philosophizing. To what purpose? Movies are meant to contain stories. None is apparent in the first ten minutes, and the synopsis reads more like a sales pitch -- an incoherent one at that – than a description of the story itself. The impression one gathers while viewing this film is that the director is attempting to turn the stereotypical Robbe-Grillet anti-novel into a movie. It is unsatisfyingly confusing. The cinematography itself is competent but it serves only to convey clearly a state of philosophical chaos. To steal a phrase, "I don't get it."

Elmo: I don't, either. Mark's cleverness is quite engaging, but not engaging enough to sustain narrative tension for two or more hours on a 50-foot drive-in movie screen.

Charlie: Yes, he almost fails to suck.

#

Welcome to my island.

Pull up a deck chair, help yourself to the tanning oil. But watch out for the brain crabs – they bite!

May I offer you a festive beverage, perhaps with a paper umbrella? No? I understand. You are unsure, filled with doubt. You have purchased your ticket, acquired your soft drink and bucket of popcorn and taken your seat. And yet still you wonder: A Rapture movie without a Rapture? Is this really for you? Or perhaps you worry it is rather too much for you. That is to say, too much Mark Leach. (I'm told a little of me goes quite a ways.)

I hope you're not here to console me. Such an action is clearly not documented in the script.

I am happy, snug in my antebellum "bachelor's pad." The slave-made bricks are beginning to crumble, but the walls are still strong and thick. Imagine it: three feet of solid masonry! Cool in the summer, warm in the winter. Dry, too. The old slate roof is like a sheet of iron. Nothing gets through. The accommodations are quite luxurious. A leather sofa, a Sears-O-Pedic king mattress, a fully stocked wine cellar. I even have my old 1970 Cutlass convertible. You remember it, don't you?

My island. It's nothing like a prison.

Did you know I dreamed this place? And I don't mean onbeam, either. I'm talking about a genuine, naturally-occurring Incredible Revelation. Again you look doubtful, betrayed by the old, familiar smile. I know what you're thinking: We studied this building in Mrs. Wilson's 7th grade Texas History class, the section on the Civil War. What can I say? I'm a native Texan; I know my state history. I have filled a mayonnaise jar with Minieballs pried out of the bricks and unearthed from the beach. But here, such concrete evidence is inadmissible; this place does not belong to the waking world.

This place, this beach over which I advance once again, sand so profound, so deep that one perceives no step. This mournful island of another era, encrusted with the artifacts of another time. This magnificent island, where beaches without end follow upon beaches, the sand beneath my feet so profound, so deep. The beaches are deserted now, void of the still, mute, possibly long-dead people of my exile. One perceives no step in this prison, this perjury.

Do you know I never hear anyone raise his voice in this place? No one. Conversation flows in a void apparently meaningless or, at any rate, not meant to mean anything. A phrase hangs in midair, as though frozen, though doubtless taken up again later. No matter. The same conversations are always repeated by the same prosaic voices.

No, this place does not belong to the waking world. We now put out into deep water, and let down the nets for a catch.

#

I am part of a travel group on the Texas Gulf Coast, enjoying a boat tour.

The man at the helm – our captain and guide – takes us on a fast ride. We zip past little islands, some just big enough to stand on, all the while heading toward the biggest link in the chain: Marienbad.

This main island is dominated by an old brick structure. It has no windows. An arch-type design element is set into the brickwork. Perhaps it has a flat roof; I cannot say for sure. Later, it will occur to me that the structure reminds me of Fort Sumter, the place where Confederate troops fired the first shots of the Civil War.

As we near the island, the captain brings us around on the ocean side for a closer look. On the beach I notice giant, root-like structures. They lie on top of the sand, spread out like thick vines or cables, their surfaces resembling the rough, fibrous husk of a coconut. As we pass the island, I see that we are now heading back toward the beach, as if we have been in a harbor rather than the open sea. I ask our guide about the purpose of the old building.

"It was a hospital," he replies. But he does not sound certain, and I am not convinced he is correct.

"Why is the building on an island, separated from the land?" I ask. Without waiting for an answer, I immediately volunteer my theory.

"Maybe the building was once on the mainland but the shoreline has changed over the years, cutting it off from the rest of the world."

The guide does not respond.

Then our boat is suddenly a car, and our guide is driving us along a road that parallels the shore.

"Next, we will see the original downtown of Corpus Christi," he says.

Corpus Christi. The Body of Christ. I am excited because we will see the real town, the one where the locals go -- not the theological illusion that is maintained for the pilgrims and tourists.

The road and shoreline depart, and soon we reach the historic central business district. No high rise hotels or floating seafood restaurant here. This Corpus Christi appears to be a typical rural Texas town, a few blocks of old buildings crowded together along an empty street. (You should go check it out before you leave. Very picturesque.)

We approach on a two-lane highway that skirts the edge of the downtown. The first portion, roughly half the land area, consists of old corrugated metal warehouse buildings. The cross street is marked by a sort of entry gate made out of the sheet metal, obviously a new creation intended to play off the old buildings. On the sign there is a multi-word name, but I do not recall it -- perhaps something that uses the word "market" or "marketplace." I realize that some developer has created this marketing concept in hopes of revitalizing and reusing the old buildings, a not-too-clever rip off of a similar re-development concept in Strangers Rest. The sign is colorful yet muted -- a perfect match for the weathered, oxidized metal.

A block later we reach the retail area. As we pass, I glance back over my shoulder for a better look. There is some revitalization here, too. The Body of Christ now has three or four new businesses. One is an ice cream parlor. Another is a restaurant with a front sign in neon of a cartoon-like pig face, perhaps some Carolina-style barbecue.

#

The Minieballs sit on a high, narrow shelf alongside stacks of gray steel film canisters and random entries from the sanctioned psychic manifest, nightmare metaphors of violent purple twilight and unfulfilled judgments and dreams.

Welcome to my broken world.

Here I wander through an obscene territory of winged demons, aerial creatures bearing branded vials of amputated ghost parts, decaying metallic reek of bankrupt snake skins, corroded iron shadows of cicada exoskeletons, troubled mirrors reproducing endless spectral relations, hopeless erotic cries echoing across vast plains of repressed desire. Here in the thin gray light I pour over the sacred texts of communal disaster, breathe in the double helix of lilac smoke suspended in a porcelain cobalt heaven, view the golden coronas of uneven and prepared genetic amplifiers, walk uselessly through the neurotic oily winds, listen to the rasping wings of hysterical tidal birds, feel the sluggish tropic flames burning through anxious gaunt smirks. (Yes, we're on the Pathway now!)

A shower of glittering emerald flakes descending unhurried through a tarnished sea of fluid screams, painfully abrupt stench of damp waste, giant mounds of smoldering linen mummy casings, a broken stone indicator of the final extinguished horse thief of Strangers Rest (Gone but not Forgotten, a murder by pittance rage), an image of the horned creature automobile with a factory-installed means of listening to the Deity.

And that's just the opening credits.

For the soundtrack, I have commissioned an orchestra of reluctantly castrated violinists to perform my compositions, disconsolate tunes of homicidal alien bewilderment, of old coins and fermented blood, of desiccated cats and threadbare Egyptians, of heretical transformations occurring behind jagged DNA dream codes and splotched sallow screens of rancid ectoplasm, surging penetration of –

#

Forgive me. I am an odious being.

This sort of thing happens often these days, me getting carried away in the beauty of chaos, in lurid intervals of narcissistic horror. The FX apparatus disgorges an enormous radiant fog of visual rumors and nonsense. I digress into the shattered violet neon dusk of my own atrophied human citizenship and the dazzling garbage heap of our tragic, dead age.

When I am like this, unpleasant things happen. The walls start bleeding. Nazi paratroopers land outside the window. Tiny white eggs on the back of my hand hatch into hungry wolf spiders, which proceed to strip the flesh from my bones. (Director's note: We'll leave this quantity of tainted celluloid on the cutting room floor.)

My favorite prop is the jar of pickled sea monsters. I caught them just a few yards from here in the roiling surf, my inner sea. Warning: Beware of the riptide. Do not swim without a prophet on duty. You could be dragged into the Land of the Dead.

How can it be otherwise? Here in my Patmosian exile, I have learned to give credit to the inner world, the world of fire -- the world behind the masonry walls of the everyday.

Heraclitus said "it is to Hades that they rage and celebrate their feasts." Hades – the world of Death, the conclusion of Practical Man and the ambition of Spiritual Man.

Still, I miss the practical, the everyday. I miss ice cream and barbecue, miss eating out. I miss so many things. The result is some rather severe restrictions on the "natural libido flow," as one of my court-ordered dental psychiatrists put it. So perhaps this place really is a prison.

And then, of course, I miss my face.

Yes, I noticed you've been starring at it. I don't mind; it's understandable. The right half of my face now resembles a cross between a slab of brown, bloodless beef and a piece of weathered lumber. Nothing human left. Alien. Most people assume it happened in the fire. But it's not a scar. This is the raw, undifferentiated tissue of evolution. This is the disintegration of culture into chaos. This is the alien within. It's even in the script.

#

"Sure, we took a few liberties, skirted the old genetic taboos (aren't we all kin, really?) -- but it was all for science. Cutting edge work I tell you. A flippered anxiety disorder here, a web-footed phobia there. And just last week, a break through in the treatment of mystical psychosis: Cicada wings. Tiny little protrusions anchored by tendons to the clavicles. Talk about visionary transformation! Eventually, we'll get one we don't have to euthanize. So sad. They look quite peaceful up there on the lab shelf, lined up in their labeled pickle jars like sleeping baby dragons."

#

Pretty.

But for now there is only me, the prototype of the New Man. And quite manly at that. At one point, The Stranger tells me we will even grow two extra DNA delivery organs. Have to employ a paring knife to prune away the smallest ones. He claims we will experience no pain. "Makes the main trunk grow thicker and taller," he says, "just like a crepe myrtle." Don't know if that scene will make the final cut. An NC-17 rating is a definite financial risk.

Have I offended you? I am sorry. It's just that for the past few minutes I've been having a sepia-toned flashback of adolescent desire. I think back to English Lit, to Albert Camus: "Oh sun, beaches, and the islands in the path of the trade winds, youth whose memory drives one to despair!"

You are still the same, as though I left you only yesterday. What has become of you all this time? You're still the same. But you hardly seem to remember. How can that be? After all, our high school reunion was only last year. Have I changed so much, then? Or are you pretending not to recognize me? A year already, perhaps more.

I remember you, of course. As soon as the launch arrived and I saw you step out onto the beach, time seemed to reverse itself . The Clock in the Air rolled back to before the dissolution, before the World Catastrophe. We had retreated across the years and returned to high school, sprawled across the cool, black vinyl in the back of the Cutlass. Checking out my crepe myrtle.

You, at least, are still the same. You have still the same dreamy, Last-Year-At-Marienbad eyes, the same smile, the same sudden laugh, the same brusque arm movement…the same way of resting your hand on your shoulder and you still use the same perfume.

But perhaps that sort of Robbe-Grillet character arc is no longer an option. We're all grown up now, you say, responsible citizens. This is the bittersweet denouement, complete with the swelling metallic strains of the castrated violinists. The Hollywood critics will roll their eyes at this over-the-top romance, but I find that real people still like that sort of thing. We all want the boy to get the girl.

As for your offer of help in my hour of need – what's that? Well, I'm sorry, but it is clearly documented in my script. You are to make the offer, and I am to experience a warm, grateful sensation of humanity. Here's my line: "I am touched. I can't think of any lawyer – or any person, really – I'd rather have defend me in the Hague." And then I shall enthusiastically penetrate your membranes with my DNA delivery organs. (Ha ha, little joke.) Still, we may need a script doctor for this part. It is critical to the plot that I already stand condemned. The trial is mere theater.

You object to a scripted response, a premeditated life? I understand. However, I didn't make it up. This is the contemporary quandary that renders genuine experience unfeasible for all. I distinctly remember encountering this idea in a book somewhere (possibly Paul Elie's "The Life You Save May Be Your Own"). To paraphrase: experience is forever recycled, standardized, a story allegorically scripted and filmed for mass consumption. We are intensely self-conscious beings fated to an increasingly intensified rift from our own selves. Even the occasional, genuinely honest experience is ruined by this eternal personal awareness. The contemporary being is destined to a simulation of existence. The personality cannot be itself . The contemporary being cannot be acquainted with the earth or with The Deity.

That is why The Stranger makes movies. He wants to make obvious he lives.

#

What's that? Ah yes, you wish to know about the Armageddon Drive-In Theatre.

I prefer to save the climax for last, but I certainly understand that many people like to know up front how a movie will end. The important thing to realize about the events at the old drive-in – in real life it was called the Hi-way 114 Drive-In – is that they did not come from my nocturnal visions. Rather, The Stranger based this part of the script on an anonymous posting found on an Exogrid message board dedicated to onbeam creations about the conclusion of time:

"The Christian congregations of my community had come together to take us all to a drive-in movie theater. When we got there they split us up into two groups: The ones who were going with God and the ones who were staying on Earth. And of course I was in the group that was staying. I saw people there who I have known for a long time, and some were worried and some were not. I was praying the whole time for forgiveness. I could not see why I was not going. I was mad that they had divided us into groups, as if they knew who God was taking. When they had brought us to this place it was night, and I prayed until morning. At sunrise I went inside the snack bar where they had gathered everyone who was going, and I saw empty candy wrappers and popcorn buckets and the pillows and sleeping bags on the floor where some had been sleeping. But there were no bodies, only imprints on the pillows where they had been laying their heads. I was so angry because I did not understand. Some people who had been left behind were saying how we were going to have to face the fact that we would not be spending the rest of eternity with God, but burning in Hell. I knew that I did not want to suffer in everlasting torment, and I unplugged. I was out of breath, and I was trembling slightly. I have never had an onbeam experience so real, and this was by far the worst of my recent creations about the conclusion of time. It has scared me so bad, and I wish that everyone who is not saved or unsure about their faith would have this experience also. I wonder why I am having them. I am unsure if I want them again or not."

Despite the unfortunate anxiety experienced by the anonymous dream surfer, this scene is incredibly funny. The Stranger decides that all of the extras will be church folk, but there's a catch: only the

Methodists are going. Can you believe it? Methodists don't even believe in the Rapture.

Meanwhile, the others Christians of Strangers Rest do not like playing the role of "The Abandoned Ones," those who are staying and must spend the rest of eternity burning in Hell. This casting against type is particularly offensive to the local chapter of the Keepers of the Deity, the former congregation of the Strangers Rest Baptist Church who jettisoned the old, dead, discredited name and now worship in the combination gas station/Exogrid church out on the interstate.

When they complain of this cinematic heresy, the assistant director serves up the introductory disclaimer: "It is the stated position of the Keepers of the Deity that His safeguards would prevent the occurrence of such blasphemous events as are depicted in this film. Furthermore, it should be noted that none of the characters portrayed in this film are meant to represent any waking world congregations living or dead."

The Keepers of the Deity still grumble, but I see from the looks in their eyes that they are appeased. Their dogma has been validated in the ideal medium for our times: film.

#

This is an objectionable era.

Dark nations and rulers are universally triumphant. Evil thrives in elevated locations.

Nevertheless, there is a more obvious and nearby danger. For I argue that the End of the World is already here. This end is not a destruction of stone and wood or flesh and blood. Rather, this is the end of a terminal legend, the legend of the conquering champion, of the rationalist's Creature of Merit.

I know all about it because I dreamt it, because I dream it still. Here is the one-sentence film treatment: Christ-haunted journalist turns to 1950s B-movie sci-fi to report the biggest story of his life – how he prophesied the End of the World.

#

Corpus Christi was once home to about a half dozen drive-in theaters. The Gulf, the Surf, the Twin Palms – they're all gone now, lost to yesterday's sun and sand and salty breeze, edited away with the rest of the dead Hydrocarbon Age. I fear the same thing will happen to my movie. Even with proper disclaimers, the distributor may find my theology unacceptable. He may insist upon the deletion of heretical scenes. My vision under siege.

We need a Director's Cut, an undiluted version of me, the protagonist of my own true story. The movie will be by its very nature numinous. It will conclude with me consuming myself, a hand sandwich and a glass of fermented corpuscles, a multimedia Eucharist.

Mmmm, that's good Messiah.

You are offended? Sorry, but the best movie directors have all been doubters.

If you accept the role of movie making muse, you can start by manipulating the footage in the can labeled "Notes For A B-Movie About The End of the World." You like? The name is a variation on the subtitle of one of my all-time favorite movies, "Let Me Love You: Confessions of a Bad God on a Planet near the Conclusion of Time."

This is key footage for "Marienbad My Love With Mango Extracts," the movie that will bring about the End of the World – and the beginning of the New Religion.

A group of dedicated Marienbadists have already begun preparations for the world premier, which will be conducted at a specially constructed drive-in movie theater located somewhere in the Himalayas. Cylindrical clock chimes hanging from clouds will convene the moviegoers from around the planet. I will be stationed behind the camera, encircled by a multitude of grips and gaffers, vocalists and primal goddesses. Uniformed orators narrating manuscripts in marches and spectacles will fashion their share of the exploits along with the primal goddesses, whose dance routines will incorporate eye signals and stroking of the fingertips in combination with aromas of enjoyable fragrances as well as pungent, smoldering flame. Columns of anger will dot the landscape, and fire will explode in streams of luminosity and expanses of conflagration. This will continue for seven days. When the movie is finally over and final credits roll, the world will at last come to an end. And there will be a new Deity in the heavens.

But I'm getting ahead of myself.

"Let Me Love You" is a great epic film. It is actually based on an essay by Walker Percy, who also wrote a book called "The Moviegoer" and a later one called "Lancelot," which is about the making of a movie in an old Louisiana plantation somewhere near the Land of the Dead.

And then there is the confessional device – that is, the Me talking to the You. See, I did not write you into the script merely for the purpose of penetrating your membranes. Rather, you are present to hear my confession. You are my priest. It is a technique Percy borrowed from Camus' "The Fall."

This is a tricky business, combining "Last Year at Marienbad" with "The Fall." I'm told that Alain Robbe-Grillet and Camus did not get along. Robbe-Grillet criticized Camus for having a "dubious relationship" with the world, one that relied on the power of metaphors. He said "all my work is precisely engaged in the attempt to bring its own structures to light." I like that, though it is not true for me. All my work is precisely engaged in the attempt to penetrate your membranes.

Even though I have acknowledged the source of the stolen product – the recycled, premeditated experience -- there might still be a copyright issue. You could work on that, too. Remember, you have been cast in the role of the idealistic lawyer.

#

So why a sequel to "Last Year at Marienbad"? Why did I select this enigmatic creation from the '60s as the template for my end-of-time film?

Certainly I could have chosen to pattern my work on any number of movies I admire. "Let Us Love You" is clearly an end-times film worthy of imitation. "The Revolution of Zion" is another obvious choice.

I could tell you I picked "Last Year at Marienbad" because of a scholarly paper by Darragh O'Donoghue, who described it as "post-apocalyptic, almost science fiction." I rather like that. Or I could tell you I picked it because I recognize and honor the genius of this film and its symmetrical perfection. But those would be un-truths.

The real story is I wish to compel you to play the role of "A," clad in 1961 Chanel and feathers. At its heart, "Last Year at Marienbad" is a love story. Robbe-Grillet had it right: Boy gets girl. That is the conclusion I yearn for in my own art and life. The boy should always get the girl, even when the world comes to an end. Or especially then.

That is the role I have created for you, my darling muse, my love. Your destiny. Listen – you can almost hear the clock chimes, convening the moviegoers from around the planet. You're needed on the set; I must take my place behind the camera. In seven days the world will come to an end, and we must be ready.

I must be ready.

#

What's that? Yes, I still dream of my wife and children and our lives together in Strangers Rest. I still dream of the night of the apocalypse, the rain of fire. I still see the Lancelot-style headlines:

STRANGERS REST BURNS. BODIES OF TOWNFOLK CHARRED BEYOND RECOGNITION; REPORTER CHARGED.

The fire and the brimstone and the death, the deaths of so many – but I can't think about that right now. Besides, it all seems so distant, so unreal.

Forget "Last Year at Marienbad." I really wish I could do "The Abandoned Ones" thing. Big plots, familiar characters – it's a huge box office/publishing success thanks to millions of Keepers of the Deity. After all, the Rapture is their sacred story. Did you know there's even a special version for kids? Here's a jacket blurb:

#

WICKED TIMES AT ANTICHRIST HIGH

School's back in session, and wickedness is in the set of courses. Jewell, Rikki, Lynn and Rusty -- The Young Affliction Corps, a crack team of the Deity's abandoned orphans -- return from spring break to find their school has just been renamed Zuftaza Humanisto High after the UN's new secretary-general, whom their scripture-guru and Bible mentor, Brouhaha Shedes, declares is the Antichrist. The polished, menacing Humanisto has already begun planning a one-earth government, religion and coinage, so the Young Affliction Corps must get innovative. They start "The Subversive Tribe," a secret school television station that reports the true story of the Rapture and Humanisto's wicked plans for earth domination. The Young Affliction Corps all pitch in to make their pirate TV station happen, despite pressure from Humanisto's faculty and even a strange, possibly demonic collapse of the station's secret broadcasting antennae. Rikki is arrested as public enemy number one, wanted for her part in producing "The Subversive Tribe." Refusing to turn in her pals, Rikki gets inserted into the wicked place— the U.N.'s infamous Normpart Internment Camp in Arizona. But she makes it out because she's been adopted by a foster family... none other than the Bible mentor himself, Brouhaha Shedes! And the Young

Affliction Corps, still committed to spreading the truth about the Rapture and the rise of Humanisto as the Antichrist, adds its newest member, Chatty, a young Jewish televangelist. "Wicked Times at Antichrist High" is the fifth installment of "The Abandoned Kids," the children's version of Giles de Jeer and Ike Havoc's Rapture hit, "The Abandoned Ones."

#

A well done tale. And yet, why does their sacred story seem so insubstantial – all the deaths and losses and the empty clothes and the unpiloted jetliners and the United Nations' One World Government and empty candy wrappers and popcorn buckets and humbled, penitent souls nevertheless tossed into the Lagoon of Flames – why does it seem so unreal next to a few teenage libidinal moments on the vinyl back seat of a 1970 Cutlass convertible?

That's right. This movie can be about you, too. I recognize the possibilities already. In this concept you have your own death and loss to deal with, your own nightmares. We could write a touching back story, ideally the death of someone close. There could be a kindly old man and a spunky dog, too. No? Well then, perhaps it is not a literal death, but a loss just the same. We can use a blue screen in post-production to superimpose an FX-created image of the pain into your eyes. I envision sadness, a world weariness – something that I could recognize in myself but never knew in you. Here's my line: "It didn't occur to me that you might have your own pain to deal with, your own demons to battle. Your own apocalypse. So that's it. We're both prisoners."

Pretty, huh?

And now you smile. I never could get the knack of you. So how about a little spin around the island in the old Cutlass convertible? We could rough out the film treatment while screen testing the natural libidinal flow on the black vinyl, a sort of stand in for the Hollywood casting couch.

Still you are smiling. Smiling but speechless. Ah, and now I see why. Here comes the boat. You must leave. Will you come again tomorrow?

Welcome again. Have a drink. You still decline?

You do not recognize me. And I don't mean just from high school, either. Didn't we meet last year, when your husband was away? I believe we attended one of the theater-in-the-park productions of Ibsen's "Rosmersholm." No? Well, perhaps it was somewhere else. Karlstadt or Baden-Salsa. Or even here upon these very sands, on the beaches of Marienbad. Didn't you say you would leave your husband and we would run away together? It was only last year. I remember it distinctly. You were wearing 1961 Chanel and feathers. Have I changed so much, then? Or are you pretending not to recognize me? A year already, perhaps more.

You, at least, are still the same. I think of Robbe-Grillet: "The same dreamy eyes, the same smile, the same sudden laugh, the same brusque arm movement, the same way of resting your hand on your shoulder. You still use the same perfume."

#

I have an admission. I lied to you yesterday. About the island of the Body of Christ, I mean. It was not so much a lie as an omission. I did not tell the rest of the dream. I feared what you might think of me. After all, my evolutionary transfiguration has been the subject of much public speculation. Certainly kept the supermarket tabloids buzzing for a while. (I should never have told anyone about those extra DNA delivery organs.)

I didn't want you to think they might be right, that I am an alien, a freak. But I realize now that was silly. After all, that's exactly what I am. Always have been. Who knows it better than you?

#

A short time after passing downtown Corpus Christi, we stop at an ice cream parlor. Once inside, I tell everyone that I am handling the food purchase. Apparently, this is by design and was decided in advance as part of our trip arrangements.

"“But you must pay me,” I add.

I am standing next to a seated man from our group, and he has a complaint.

"“You owe me money from a previous purchase,” he says, “but I'll still give you some money.”

He holds out a $5 bill. I decline to accept it.

"“Since I owe you, you should keep your money. You are taken care of.”

Then a man walks up behind me and begins to talk to this seated man. I do not look, but only listen. They begin to negotiate a theological transaction.

I understand the item for sale is mysticism. They are very blatant, discussing amounts and prices. It is a friendly negotiation, not at all part of a seamy, dangerous theological underground. I realize they are friendly because they see themselves as part of the same club. As I listen, it occurs to me that we are visiting a foreign place where this is not illegal. Or at least it is tolerated.

The transaction is completed, and the seated man begins to consume his purchase. I am handed a paper sack that is printed up in a colorful fashion. In this strange land, it is clearly understood by anyone who sees it to be a bag that is used for the sale of heretical theologies. The sack has a sort of stick glued to the outside. The stick is like a lighter; it is attached to the bag with a spot of glue so that the ends are unattached. One end has been lit, glowing orange with a curl of smoke rising toward the ceiling. I do not like it that I am holding this smoking, theological bag. It is like a billboard. Anyone who sees it will know I am in possession of heretical theology. I decide it would be far less noticeable for me to stash the mysticism in my pants pocket and throw away the all-too-obvious bag.

Meanwhile, the woman who is managing the place is disturbed by the sale. She doesn't want that sort of activity going on in her place, giving it a bad name.

"Maybe I should call the police," she says.

But I am not afraid of being arrested. I am an outstanding, responsible citizen, and the police will find I have no tickets or warrants or records of any infractions. Again, heretical theologies are obviously not a crime here. So although the circumstances make me look suspicious, I face no real legal dangers here in the Body of Christ.

I decide to ditch the bag in the restroom. I approach the men's room door, but I see that the woman manager has entered ahead of me. Could it be a unisex restroom? Or does she feel free to use any restroom just because she works here? Then I notice the words on the door. It really is the women's room, but the "W" and "O" are missing. I can only see the faint outlines of the letters. So I look a bit further and find the real men's room, a vast space that reminds me of the dressing rooms in the old Sanger-Harris at Red Bird Mall, where the impoverished Oak Cliff kids conveniently relieved themselves on the carpet.

#

Enigmatic signage. At least I got my gender properly worked out by the end. That will make the movie a lot more bankable. Although correlated with the deities, the hermaphroditic archetype is a particularly tough one to sell at the box office. Due to such financial considerations, a lot of it inevitably ends up on the cutting room floor. And even then, the reviews will not be kind:

INTENSELY REVOLTING ... THE MOST TOTALLY EMPTY MOVIE I HAVE EVER VIEWED FROM THE TIME WHEN I FIRST STARTED VIEWING.

What's that? Why yes, I am all about the movies. I've given up on journalism. The newspaper world is dead. It no longer functions.

When I was young, journalism was my calling. It was all about The Truth. Now it is all about The Lie. I admit that I do not yet possess even the basic tools of the cinematographer. But I can wait. The appearance of The Stranger is proof that one day I will be documenting the numinous experiences of myself and the world.

The movie. The Stranger is obsessed with it. Turns out that in my old age, I will live in a glass beach house in Southern California and take up movie making. I shall live with the sun and sand and the salt spray in my cinematic vision. Indecipherable religious imagery, bleeding childhood angst, mythological expectations.

"I cannot fully explain my life," he tells me. "It is not always about life. My life no longer functions on that level. To be sure, one half is still life. But the other half is raw, undifferentiated tissue. Alien. That's why I want to make the movie. For years, I have experienced my life as a sort of dream movie. I have always wished to be about the Odyssey, the journey. I am the 2001 Space Odyssey astronaut, traveling in the divine sky clock, recast as cosmic child. The Deity is sending me back to Egypt, I think. To save us. Imagine this dream movie: I am Jonah, the man in the fish. We all know that it is a specially prepared fish (i.e., a visual rumor of the Son of the Deity). So I am swallowed up in Him. The wound is inscrutable. I offer my own little interpretation: The Deity showed Jonah what it is to be reborn as the cosmic child. I think I would like that role, suffering in the belly of the fish. We could do it up with soulless cool special effects, visual rumors of the forgotten, abandoned church with the flooded basement and the old bearded preacher withdrawn from employment in advance of death. And the tag line: Am I dying?

"Books, movies, my own day. I simultaneously accept that the basement is flooded and the forgotten, abandoned church is me. (In the upcoming age, the true Christian will be the pastor of his own church. Or he will not be a Christian at all.) All is as it should be, I tell myself, Christ-haunted about my life as the rest slumber in their beds, oblivious to the apocalypse swirling around them.

"And yet even here one senses the volumizing plot twist, ripe with the volumizing green nutrients of tea hairspray renewal. Look closely. Between the intersecting line you will find your skin – your youthful, eternal flesh. Reserved, ripe with inscrutability – and looking sensational! This is the Prose of the Skinalicious Conspiracy:

Extracts
With perfecting
Complex pure thankful
Goodness with extra mango
Moisturizers for jade skin
Vitamin complex
Lather!

"Picture a movie about a beachfront mansion. But it is more than a luxurious residence. This is all about the home of vitamin indulgence for all spiritual types. Stop the godless wrinkles! Stop the wrinkle epidemic and replace it with heavenly can-glow skin. Believe in your skin. Believe in the fusion of spirit and beauty with French aloe and reformulated lavender. The Skinalicious Conspiracy shall reveal the skin-loving nutrients of the one true Deity.

"This is all about the deification of nutrients and antioxidants. This is all about the death of dry, damaged skin and the transfiguration of the eternal epidermis. This is all about spiritual renewal plus skin-loving extracts. This is all about the vitamins and the texturizing humidity spray. This is all about the touchability of the soul.

"What's touchability? It is pure goodness. This is the nourishing movement with essential hydrating two-ply ingredients. Emulsion to emulsion for nourishing Skinalicious goodness. Pure Skinalicious, that's what you'll find waiting in the derma-pod that orbits above. An aerial moisturizer with perfect derma-pod uniqueness. A perfect time-release formula lotion. Super-rich lotion. Super-rich gentle reservoir nourishment with an exfoliator and nourishing blend. When you activate the exfoliator, you'll find a blend of activated odor, of rehydrating odor, of nourishment with all skin types.Welcome to the nightly luscious moisturizer. Here you will find a place where you can lose yourself forever in the Skinalicious antioxidants.

"Picture a scene with me starring up at the Skinalicious sky, looking for moisturizing signs and antioxidant portents, the visual skin-loving rumors. Real F/X opportunities here, all labeled with harsh warnings in German creole and Nazi fonts. You have to be careful quoting them. Then, a bystander tells me he is disappointed to learn that the safest way to communicate with The Deity is above the concrete and rational, over the viral DNA dream phone. 'We are more than the real,' I tell him. 'We have to be. The ongoing value of all this is as it should be.' That's good dialogue, good writing."

Pretty.

#

Would you be astonished if I informed you that I might be experiencing romantic affection again? It's true. So let us leave this place together. Let us leave behind these sculptured thresholds, lines of doors, colonnades, oblique hallways leading to deserted meeting rooms paneled in the baroque embellishments of an earlier time. Mute rooms, where footsteps are lost in sculpted berber so profound, so deep that one perceives no step, as if the ear itself were impossibly remote – distant and remote from this numb, barren décor, far from this elaborate frieze beneath the cornice with its branches and garlands like dead leaves, as if the floor were still sand and gravel, or flagstones over which I advance one again To find you. Between richly paneled walls, Venetian plaster, gold-leafed frames, paintings, framed prints amidst which I advance, among which I find myself already waiting for you. Very far from this beach where I stand now…before you, waiting again for one who will not come again, who will no longer keep us apart…tear you from me.

After all that and still you say no? How can that be so wrong? I cannot read you at all. You face is masklike, inscrutable. Forever walls, hallways, forever doors. And on the other side, yet more walls. Before reaching you, rejoining you.

Still no? Well then, I shall pursue another love.

The new object of my desire is the woman next door. In Lancelot's case, she was the patient in the next room. In my case, she is on the neighboring island. I've not observed her in the waking world. But in a dream last night, I believe I may have compelled her to commit unnatural acts upon my DNA delivery organ. Some might say that is not a good start to a meaningful relationship. But as this debasement took place near the Land of the Dead, I believe the physical moral code is suspended in favor of communicating a greater metaphorical truth. Is that not the beauty of true romantic affection and the visionary religious experience? Years ago, traveling with you across the vinyl back seat of the Cutlass convertible, membrane to membrane, I could say to you "I am fond of this physical response stimuli, aren't you?" And you could reply "oh God, bring forth the warm globs of ectoplasm." Or something to that effect.

I believe that with the woman on the neighboring island it will be identical. Last night, our membranes were brought into proximity. Genetic material may have been transmitted. At the very least I experienced an extremely positive response stimuli. She may have even responded in kind. At least she did not protest.

Clearly, this membrane-to-membrane encounter might have been without meaning. A one-dream stand, so to speak. But conversely, it may represent an authentic first contact. I awoke to find my membranes still surging, my DNA singing. It was as if I was experiencing romantic affection again for the first time.

But I'm getting ahead of myself. I should start at the beginning – the beginning of the end of time.

This one is a 1950s B-movie sci-fi concept, too. But don't get too attached to it, because it's just an introduction. I never got past the opening section, which is somewhat sad but not surprising. They say every newspaper reporter has a movie script somewhere inside. And that's where most of them should stay.

#

One summer afternoon I accidentally decapitate a giant cicada.

It is one of a pair – still young, about the size of a squirrel – that has crawled up from the drainage ditch at the back of our lot, looking for a place to shed its exoskeleton. Interrupted in the weed-choked San Augustine, the ancient, mythic couple separate. One escapes through the uncut grass and splashes into the waters beyond. The other buzzes at the mower's right front wheel and disappears under the cutting deck. The engine stalls as the whirling steel blade does its work, shooting the meaty pupae across the cracked patio slab to the feet of Jack Bryson.

Jack nudges the headless form with the tip of his boot. The bug does not move. He continues to nurse a watery margarita, attempting to conjure a non-existent coolness from the unforgiving shade the westering sun makes through the high, jagged limbs of the post oak next door.

"It's too hot to mow," Jack says. "Let's go inside."

In the throes of an unbroken string of triple-digit days, shade has long ago ceased to provide any real relief. I stare across a neighboring field, a lumbering combine kicking up a gritty mushroom cloud of top soil, a dreamy moment in the shimmering heat waves. I am momentarily cast adrift, irredeemably lost in the scorching heat and torments of the everyday.

I say "the backyard's gone nuclear" or something equally metaphorical. I'm not quite sure.

Jack isn't interested in metaphors. For him, August in Texas is strictly what it is: hot. He has long ago determined the best way to beat the heat is with a cool, alcoholic drink and an afternoon pornographic movie -- certainly not jumping out of the path of projectile insects.

"Great time to mow the lawn," he observes. "Don't tell me you wasted one of your precious vacation days on this."

"Comp time. The Keller City Council met in executive session till 12:30 last night. So how do you take this every day?"

"Well, I don't try to mow at the hottest time of the day, like some newspaper reporter who spends his life in the air conditioning." Then Jack again nudges the remains of the insect. "And I never mow over giant bugs."

The cidaca is only the latest in a series of poisonous insects, potentially-rabid small mammals, blood-sucking reptiles and other creatures that have recently grown to nightmarish proportions. (The scientists blame it on environmental contaminates; the Keepers of the Deity insist it is a sign of the conclusion of time.) These B-movie monsters are brave, too, refusing to observe the faded neon pink surveyor's flags as the limits of their habitat.

Allison picked out our home site when the subdivision was still mostly vacant lots. I had initially balked at the $5,000 premium for a ``canal" lot, as the real estate agent called it. After all, it really was just a drainage ditch, half-filled with silt and cattails. But that was in the era when I still easily succumbed to the idea of marital bliss, the novelty of love. Besides, the agent assured us the canal would be cleaned out as soon as the developer started the second phase. That was before Wichita Falls Guarantee & Credit, the sanctuary that financed the project, was declared insolvent. In their final report, sanctuary regulators concluded that the institution was "creatively overstimulated. And as with much of the industry today, this overstimulation is the source of the financial troubles." Clearly the second phase of the neighborhood will be a long time coming.

I try to restart the mower, but it has flooded out. A few pulls on the starter rope and I am out of breath, wiping sweat from my face with the grayed sleeve of my "Strangers Rest 5K Run" T-shirt.

"Do you know what I've just heard? At this time last year it was so cold that the lakes froze. That's surely wrong."

"Too hot, I'm telling you," Jack repeats. "Why do you think Mexicans take those siestas?"

"Your Mexicans don't."

"Oh yeah? On my last spec, I caught one trying to sheet rock an empty beer bottle into one of the walls."

"You don't pay them enough. You don't love them."

"You liberal journalists are going to ruin this country. Liberals and queers. Do you know how much I pay for workmen's comp?"

"Do you know what I heard from one of the old timers? One summer it was so cold here that all the water froze. The creeks, the ponds, everything."

"That's impossible."

"Let's have a beer."

"You go ahead, it'll replenish your depleted electrolytes. Since I am the general contractor, I'll stick with tequila."

#

How do you like it so far? I call it "Lesbian Rest Stop." No, this concept does not include a rest stop. Or lesbians. Well, maybe a few. You can't go wrong at the box office with a few gratuitous lesbians.

The title was suggested by Jack. Of course, you knew he'd have to be mixed up in all of this. He also advised that the ads include the phrases "this movie will save your marriage" and "recommended by Oprah." When I proposed the more serious title of "Strangers Rest" he shook his head. "Do you want it to have a clever title or do you want it to sell?"

Jack Bryson is a product of the defunct Hydrocarbon Age. In recent years, he was one of the few well adjusted people I knew who were not under the care of a dental psychiatrist.

But now let us speak of incredible revelations. Let us speak of the Cicadans.

Yes, I am admittedly enraptured with my favorite movie, "Let Me Love You." Why do I like it? For starters, it was made in Texas. One of the settings is Waco, which is where I was born and some of my family still lives. Also, there is the protagonist, Clark Caring. He is a sort of minor deity. And like him, I am periodically subject to many god-like delusions. So the real-life parallels are considerable.

I am so enraptured with this epic film that I wish for you to secure the copyright. I feel it is essential to employ key scenes from this great work of the Hydrocarbon Age and cult classic of the drive-in movie world. Consider the opening scene.

#

Blessings – and apologies.

It has been 2,000 years since my last heavenly manifestation, my beloved creations. Time gets away from you, right? I make no excuses for this lengthy delay. The blame belongs solely to me. Shame, humiliation, self-criticism – I accept it all. You won't find me trying to pass the buck. No way. I'm all about honesty. That's just the kind of God I am.

What's that? Why yes, you are right. It is hard to be me, your creator and sustainer, the all-knowing sentient being who keeps the wheels of the universe turning. And yet I do. Picture me rollin'! Ah yes, sometimes being the ultimate power in the universe is almost more than I can bear.

So yeah, it's been a while since you last saw my giant disembodied head floating benevolently above you in the vast, pink sky of Planet Luh. Sorry to keep you waiting.

It is hard to be me. As far back as I can recall I've been misunderstood, particularly by those I care about most. It seems we are always hurt by the ones we love, eh? And yet, despite the unfortunate events of 20 centuries ago, isn't it true my wrath has been generally exercised in your favor? Have I not done great things – marvelously incredible things – precisely for you, my beloved creations? Who showed you how to pound your plowshares into swords? Who caused your enemies to fall in battle, allowing you to sweep in and enslave their soldier drones, cart away their gold and smash in the heads of their larva until green goo oozed from their twitching, quivering mandibles? Who did it? That's right – me. Your God. So do I not deserve your exultation and veneration? Am I not entitled to your admiration, you who I have brought into existence as citizens of the universe?

And still, you hurl the "terrible calamity" into my face. You still hold against me this one, comparatively minor transgression. "Oh, the terror!" you wail over the burned out shells of your hives and the graves of your larva. Yes, yes, fine. We have fully established the terror of it.

I do not deny this troubled episode in the life of Planet Luh – and yet, did it truly rise to the level of a terrible calamity?

Let's be fair. Did I not cause the nuclear rain to quickly wash the fire and brimstone from the sky? Did I not employ the radioactive isotopes to create a genetic transmutation allowing you to quickly and (somewhat) painlessly shed your burned exoskeletons? And did I not cause new exoskeletons to grow again, albeit in a somewhat mutated form, at a greatly accelerated rate?

You are beings characterized by chatter. I am a being characterized by action. An authentic Native American saying comes to mind: Talk too much do too few. So where would you be without me, you talkers, you beings of chatter? Where would you be without a being of action? That's right. You'd be talking too much, doing too few. You'd be nowhere.

So come on, folks, enough already with the terrible calamity. Let me do my God thing. Let me love you! Can't you just do that one little thing? Get out of the way and let me love you, you ungrateful six-legged bastards, you soul-sucking parasites, you –

Forgive me. This sort of thing happens to me a lot. Back in the day, four billion years ago, I would often find myself getting carried away in the beauty of chaos, in lurid intervals of narcissistic horror. I would digress into the shattered violet neon dusk of my own atrophied human citizenship and the dazzling garbage heap of my tragic, dead age.

Even now, when I am like this, unpleasant things happen. The walls start bleeding. Nazi paratroopers land outside the window. Tiny white eggs on the back of my hand hatch into hungry wolf spiders, stripping the flesh from my bones.

I admit it. I am a bad God. What's that? Well, there's no reason for you to agree so quickly.

OK, so let's get on with it. Since my last manifestation, some of your heretics and artists have been asking unpleasant questions about me. Some of you have been inquiring into my nature.

"Who is this Clark Caring?"

"Where does he come from?"

"Why does he do such terrible things to his creations?"

"When will he leave?"

When will I leave? Well, that's why I am here before you today. This is it, the time your heretics and artists have been waiting for these past 20 centuries.

This is the end of the world.

You weren't expecting that, were you? But that's the way it is with me, your God. I am the God of Surprises. Only I know the day and hour of the divine Apocalypse. And the day and hour is almost here.

I'd like to share with you a recent essay I read on Caringism. Don't worry. I'm not preparing to hurl any lightning bolts or anything. I actually found it quite enjoyable. Not a bad bit of writing. Nothing like you'd have seen back in the day from a truth doctor, of course, but a worthwhile journeyman effort nonetheless. Your creator and sustainer was proud. Then I came to the conclusion:

"Why does Clark Caring let bad things happen to good people? Perhaps we have the answer in our sacred texts. A paraphrased quote from this god might read something like this: 'I do what I do because I am a mysterious and awesome being.'"

Let me tell you something, you artists and heretics: I HATE THAT! A mysterious and awesome being? You make it sound as if I am some sort of irrational creature, some sort of anti-deity, a monster of the id, the Fiend of the Unconscious. Let me tell you, my beloved creations, I am a God of Love! I would not have to tell you that if only you would stop with your incessant questioning and let me get on with being me. Let me get on with loving you. Let me love you!

And enough with the lowercase "g" already. I am not "this god," but rather "your God" – that's God with an uppercase "G," goddamnit. You're treading on some mighty thin ice, my beloved creations. Have you already forgotten the terrible calamity of two centuries ago? Thin ice, folks. Mighty thin. Picture me rollin' – over your thorax.

#

That's good 1950s B-movie sci-fi! You like? I see. Well, it'll grow on you. Meanwhile, back to Jack Bryson.

#

Opening the refrigerator. I am watched by a crayon cowboy affixed to the polished steel door. Held tight by the mysterious, magical forces of a heart-shaped magnet, the picture is a rendering of the Leach family done by Shawn, the eldest of our two sons. We are all rendered in classic stick figure style, just as any pre-schooler might draw. He's portrayed me with cowboy boots and hat, the long, tall Texan, six guns blazing -- one riot, one Ranger -- riding off into a Panavision sunset. "I'm his hero!" I think. But what is this? My paternal pride is quickly short-circuited by a rather unnerving detail: I have been drawn without arms.

I shut the designer refrigerator door with my elbow, slamming it a bit too hard, rattling jars of mustard and relish and unwanted memories. I hear the hollow slam of the tailgate of Allison's Volvo station wagon, its rear bumper disappearing around the curve at the end of the street; her fist slamming on the pantry door while I knell in the tiny closet, cleaning up a broken bottle of juice; a phone slamming in its receiver, seemingly forever.

The rattled condiments rouse Missy, still locked in the laundry room. She whines in a familiar, annoying way, sort of a laughing monkey. I take advantage of her beloved owner's absence by kicking the door. Jack laughs.

"How long you going to keep her in there?"

"Until she learns to respect me."

"So – you're free at last."

``They ought to be landing about now. No doubt you sensed a disturbance in the heavens."

``Two whole weeks."

"Long enough to get caught up on my sleep."

"Sleep? Forget that. We're going to celebrate."

"Well -- "

"Come on, I'm not letting you stay home, not tonight anyway. You'll just end up sitting around in your underwear, watching re-runs of Star Trek."

"Only the original series. It was some of Shatner's best work."

Jack's glance falls on the notebook I've left on the counter. Before I can grab it away, he has it in his hands, reading the title I've printed on the cover with perhaps a bit too much self importance.

"The 'Voice of God: A Memoir of Dreams.' Ah, a little neuro porn? Naughty, naughty."

"No, it's just to get ideas for stories."

"Sleep my ass. I know you, man. You're planning to go onbeam, get down on some more dreamy pervert action. Maybe one of your elementary school teachers?"

"You're taking that one totally out of context. I should never have let you read it."

"Who else would read it but me? Always walls, always footsteps – what's that crazy movie again?"

"What movie?"

"The one with the subtitles. Always walls, always footsteps. Mute, deserted – what was that crap?"

"Marienbad."

"Yeah, that's it. Subtitles. The French are full of it. Why don't they learn English? I think what you are really needing is the mystic revelation trip. You should get Jazzed."

I groan. "Summon is dead."

"I'm telling you, you need to buy some stock. Closed yesterday at $32 a share."

"But you paid $75! It's never coming back."

"You're crazy. Here, read this."

Jack reaches into his back pocket. He retrieves a folded piece of newsprint, something he's torn from what I recognized to be today's Hedge Road Daily.

#

Summon Seeks to Repaint VI Canvass: Jazz Developer to Promote New 4-D Interface Dreamware On an 'Open Foundation' Basis

By Puton Clans

Summon Replisystems Inc. wants to get into your picture.

The virtual implant maker, whose Jazz technology is used in medicine for artificial retinas and plays a behind-the-scenes role in collective unconscious dreamware and services, is stepping up efforts to shape what users see on their implant canvass. In one dramatic example, Summon has been developing interface dreamware with four-dimensional effects that are a time-twisting alternative to the familiar virtual implant metaphor of landscapes, portraits and still life art.

Summon this week will announce plans to make the skin-loving interface, dubbed Herbal Extract II, along with related Jazz technology available on an "open foundation" basis, allowing people outside the company to view and modify the implant code used to create the programs. The announcement, one of many at Summon's annual JazzOne conference in Chicago, is designed to encourage other programmers -- particularly fans of the open-foundation Morel operating system -- to adopt and refine Summon's technology.

#

"You can personalize your VI canvass," Jack says. "Your young men shall see visions, your old men shall dream dreams. Your lips have been purified by a burning coal. The wings of angels. Yes, you shall hear the Voice."

"No voice. Just stories, just dreams. Thought I might do some writing while the family's away."

"Two weeks, Mark. I'm not going to let you spend it all by yourself on a Dreamland holiday, writing your little stories inside the collective unconscious. We're going to have some fun."

"I don't know. I'm really tired."

"You are tired of being you."

"If I were more like you, then I would be less like me."

"Exactly. So take a nap. Take some sacraments."

"I don't do that any more."

"Yeah? But you'd still do it onbeam."

That is true.

"You know, buddy," Jack continues, "sometimes you've just got to let your sleek dog run."

I know what he means by that: A visit to Plato's Palace, his favorite primal flesh temple. I am not really sure I am up for that level of sinning. Before I can mount a suitable rebuttal, though, he points at the green digital clock on the control panel of the wall oven (a $500 designer upgrade to the builder's mid-level amenities package).

"Is that thing right?" he asks.

"It ought to be. It's set to coordinated universal time."

Jack just looks at me.

"The atomic clock in Fort Collins, Colo.," I explain. "I get it off short wave radio."

He continues to stare.

"What?"

Jack sits his drink on the counter and shakes his head.

"What's happened to you?" he asks.

"What do you mean?"

"Whatever happened to the Mark Leach I used to know, the one I grew up with, the one who dropped his pants in front of my house one night while simultaneously taking a whiz in the gutter, smoking a cigar and playing the air guitar solo to Van Halen's 'You Really Got Me'?"

"The drunk and stupid one, you mean."

"The fun one."

"He lost himself. Lost his way along the straight paths between the immutable statues, granite slabs, where he is, even now, losing himself –"

"What the hell are you talking about?"

"He got old, I guess. Too many trips to Cici's Pizza, too many Barney re-runs. Too much the corny, wisecracking dad."

"I don't believe it. Anyway, I've got to go."

"Late again?"

"Not yet. I'm supposed to meet my architect in Oak Cliff in 10 minutes."

"A 30-minute drive."

"I got to pick up some plans for dad."

"I thought he'd quit building. Only developing now."

"Doing it for a friend. He had the architect incubate a Louisiana Planters Cottage through the post-ceremonial dreams of the Tesuque corn dancers. Stayed plugged into the Exogrid for a whole week."

"Wow. I'd like to see those plans."

"Me too. I got to get over there before he goes to dinner."

"Have you ever been on time for anything?"

"You sound like my ex."

"I've known you since -- what? Third grade? And I can't think of a single instance of punctuality."

"Really?" He scratches the back of his head, pretending to think. "I'm sure there's been something, at least one time."

"No, I'd remember it. You are totally reliable in your unreliability."

"OK then, I'm not seeing the problem here."

I follow Jack to his truck, an electric subscription model he bought a few months back. It replaced a four-door monster with six wheels and a row of orange lights on the roof. The big truck, Jack's pride and joy, was a victim of a once-booming home building market recently rendered comatose by a defeated oil industry, a disastrous change in tax laws and the collapse of the entire G&C industry. I hover outside the open window.

``So, about ten, then?" I ask.

``Ten? What are you talking about?"

``Well, it is technically still afternoon, and it sounds like you've got a whole day of work ahead."

``Yeah, but don't wait till ten. That's when we're leaving. You've got to come over before then."

"Well -- "

"I'm not going to do anything till you get there, you know that. I need you to kick me into gear."

``So eight, then?"

``Don't pin me down, man. If I'm not home when you get there, let yourself in. You've got a key. Loosen up, straighten out your priorities. Get your attitude adjusted."

"My attitude."

"Yeah. Drink my liquor. Play my stereo. Screw my cat. You know, just be Mark Leach."

#

A confession: I didn't really run the mower over a giant cicada (or any other creature of the unconscious). It was just a snake, an ordinary water moccasin. But I thought a cicada worked better for the story. Cinematic license.

I love those Cicadans. Whenever I consider them, I can't help but think of Clark Caring and the pink skies of Planet Luh, his world of insectoid worshippers, his "beloved creations."

#

Why does "this god" let bad things happen to good people? Here's a better question: Why did the Valuosity Life Planning Inc. hire a new truth doctor and give him my corner office and my parking place with my name on the curb in the basement parking garage reserved for my fellow executives? And why did it transfer me to the LET department and assign me to a little cubicle to write technical documents while my Lexus LS400 sat under the blazing Texas sun with all the insignificant cars in the insignificant employee parking lot? Let's see one of you answer that.

Forgive me. You ask a fair question. Why do I let bad things happen to good insectoids? That's a good one for your best thinkers to ponder. But so far these past 20 centuries, they've done a poor job of it. No headway at all. Now with the world about to end, you're out of time. So I'm going to help. I shall attempt to answer the age-old question with an illustrative story. No, not another story about how I make the lightning flash and the thunder roll. Your smart-ass scientists seem to have figured that one out for themselves.

This is the true story of a different Apocalypse: the last days of Planet Earth. The end falls generally, give or take a few years, between the assassination of President John F. Kennedy and the attainment of eternal life for all through the superior scientific achievements of Valuosity Life Planning Inc. and other companies in the military/industrial techno-structure.

You might also say this is the story of the end of God, which is another way of saying "the end of the world." God equals world. Remember that. Without me, you're nothing. And I'm afraid you're about to be nothing.

That's right. I am dying. You weren't expecting that, were you? Don't look so surprised. Even an eight billion-year-old extraterrestrial and former truth doctor of Valuosity Life Planning Inc. has to die sometime.

Anyway, this is a really good story, complete with 1950s B-movie flying saucers, gratuitous sex and a homicidal laptop computer. I think you'll enjoy it. But first, before the temple crumbles and everything goes up in the proverbial ball of fire, let's check God's divine mail bag.

#

Yesterday you asked me if I ever think about Allison. As a matter of fact, I just received a letter from her, a response to my request that she grant a blurb for the trade ads at Oscar time. You know the sort of quote I mean. "Electrifying!" or "A tour de force in cinematic storytelling" or "Brilliancy in a bottle." Such a simple thing to ask, really. But the news is not pretty.

#

June 25,

Dear Mark,

I received your undated letter today about your plans to call. Don't bother.

We've been through this before: I will not lend my name to your moviemaking schemes. I read your most recent concept. And despite rewriting key physical characteristics, I know precisely who you intend this character to represent. I am not stupid. You're not fooling me or anyone else. Well, I guess you are fooling a few people – the right people. Psychiatrists! How anyone can think you are not to be held responsible for what you did is beyond me. Even so, my attorney informs me I can bring you back before the judge for violating the cease and desist order. Just ask your so-called lawyer "friend." Or should I say your muse? God Mark, can't you be any more original than that?

Regards,

Allison

#

Did you notice the vaguely insect-like tone of her attack? It is actually a positive development, a sign of the visionary transformation, delivered via a call over the viral DNA dream phone. I filmed it in my last dream about her, standing with a group of acquaintances outside a house in some rural area suggestive of the Land of the Dead.

#

We have just learned that the DNA of every human on the planet has been converted to that of an insect. We feel unchanged, but I comment to those around me that the outward transformation will begin soon. The new genetic code will transform us into new beings. And sure enough, I am right. The scene changes and I find myself standing over a comatose Allison. She is nude, covered in damp dirt. I am cleaning her with a sponge, revealing the beginning growth of an exoskeletal thorax. "We'll all look like this soon," I tell myself.

#

Of course, "she" is really me. The insect DNA is my own blueprint, the unifying global pattern for life. And the journey.

I cannot help identifying with Clark Caring, creator and sustainer of the insect-human hybrids of Planet Luh. I have received the prophetic, let-me-love-you plea from the insect aliens themselves. In the beginning it was not easy to decode their transmissions. The messages are beamed here from distant galaxies within, crackling through flesh-covered speakers in a sort of mangled cicada cry. Over time, the intercellular translators in the viral DNA dream phone smoothed out the discarded static into a comfortable, almost melodic rhythm, a poetic form suggestive of the magneto whir of the disintegrated Machine Society of the West or the dry, disconsolate rasp of buzzard wings…

"After the saloons of old Strangers Rest stretches the desolate border zone, territory of cowboys and cattle drives, ancestral beings trapped in astral wastelands, electronic judgments imposed through ancient compound eyeballs the tint of washed out gray. Driving through Deep East Texas Piney Woods darkness, rolling on past picture perfect peaks, through the emaciated atmosphere towards a church that stands somewhere in the East. A sense of bereavement catches in the esophagus at the vista of skinned scenery, lifeless small mammals smashed in the road and scavenger birds gliding silently above the marshes and aged tree remnants.

"Further on, drive-in accommodations with beautification plank partitions, chattering sheet metal furnaces and sheer crimson bedspreads give way to an industrial sprawl of glittering retention lagoons and ginger methane flames, quagmires and trash mountains, carnivorous aquatic insects swimming about in wrecked funeral urns and metal shipping containers. Glowing glass tubes entangle 1950s roadside lodgings, stranded directors of primal goddesses and other lovely creations curse transitory autos from the nowhere of highway medians, ignored atolls of nonsense. Now the electronic judgments empty down in a dark rotating shaft, down from the azure heaven, that devastating, gory, azure heaven of the Land of the Dead, home of the nameless, the dreary and ghostly, the misplaced soul nationality – obligated to become, in effect, a being without a genus.

"No emotion, no organization, a world-compelled phantom requirement, spasmodically discharging warm globules of stale ectoplasm, detonations of DNA into membranes of chilly interplanetary liberty, floating in celestial grime, departing once again without the unfulfilled corpse left forgotten in a back room, the Vault of the Deity."

#

From silent egg to crawling larvae, from sleeping pupae to screaming, mangled cicada cry of summer. This is the message of transformation that I am called by the Deity to spread across the earth. Don't look so surprised. It's not as if I received my calling from an actual burning bush or anything in the outer, waking world.

No, I could never accept such a literal message. This is an inner process. Magnetica O'Famously put it best: "We cannot determine if the Deity and the Land of the Dead are two dissimilar things. Each one is an intermediate notion."

Just like me.

Here's a significant observation concerning Clark Caring's extraterrestrial insects: They are from inner space, too. These cinematic aliens are actually the forgotten spirits imprisoned within contemporary Americans. The Cicadans pilot the aerial timepieces from the great beyond to the rim of our earth with the purpose of resurrecting the spirits of the comatose. Their emergence from this underground "beyond" is an indication of the outer incarnation of our inner alienation. So we needn't resist the transformation. Rather, we should just attempt to revive our own self, even as we know that the self we seek could be a sham and our revival an extraterrestrial herbal extract conspiracy. Or something to that effect.

#

What's that? Oh yes, I am aware of what Allison's parents have been saying about me in the press. Clearly they fear for their daughter and grandsons. Imagine it: Allison, a Jewell Charity debutante, married to a murderer!

So misguided, so sad. Besides, there are so many people upon whom we could lay equal blame. Plenty of stock characters in this movie. There's the mad scientist, Dr. Adolfo Morel. The power-hungry billionaire industrialist, William "Dollar Bill" Buckstop. The Hive Leader of the Cicadans (aka Bellero Shield). Still, I remain everyone's favorite villain. Perhaps I should have done more to save Jack and the girls, more to save the world. But how? Alas, such an outcome is not in the script.

#

Lost in an explosion of tiny pieces of metal, a shower of aluminum foil - no, that's not right. It's a single piece of aluminum, the housing of a giant orbiting space timepiece -- a Clock in the Air.

Across the room, I see a lab-coated man seated at a bank of computer monitors, working the knobs on a sprawling control board. The central machinery is familiar. Could it be – yes, it's Seymour Cray's 6600. Three hundred fifty thousand transistors and one metal plaque -- Property of Ozona International.

On one of the dual round screens I recognize downtown Strangers Rest. Frederiksbad Street is littered with the still glowing remains of extinguished torches. The albino-fleshed, red-mouthed Dr. Morel gazes upon me. Do I see a malevolent gleam in his eye? No, just the reflection of a blue-green computer readout, flashing "6:47 a.m."

"And the famous Adolfo Morel," I say. "Working on Ozona's next new ad campaign, I see. Mineral water for the apocalypse, perhaps? An elixir for revelatory --"

I cast about for the right phrase, but the words will not come. Something is wrong. The words orbit around me, detached and paralyzed, exiled and numbed by the habit of self-grief.

I see another metallic snake, this one affixed to my navel.

I want to pull it out, but I can't seem to make my hands work. Something is stopping me. I am blocked by – cloth. I am encased in a black cloth sack. I stare out through two holes, a deep sense of separation and dejection, of dizziness and disorientation, suddenly transcended by the scent of roses, mystic icons weeping blood, statues moving of their own accord, a cloud formation in the shape of a well-known corporate logo emitting a bolt of blinding white light. I try to speak, but my mouth doesn't work, either.

"No use fighting it," Dr. Morel says. "It's all in the script, all premeditated. Melancholy journalist turned celebrity messiah. Though not looking quite so celebrated tonight, Mr. Leach. No, not so celebrated at all."

I manage a nod from within the distended aura of abstraction, caught up in a swirling fog of broken glass and fire trucks and blood and smoke. The lab-coated man has turned his back on the monitors to focus squarely on me.

"He's precisely as advertised," he remarks, his countenance suggestive of a young Albert Einstein. "An authentic neurotic with free flowing discharge."

"What's that?" I ask.

"Your palms. In the initial draft, The Stranger wrote you as a stigmatic."

The black sack is now gone, so I can see myself again. Sure enough, my hands are bleeding.

"We read all about you in The New York Agenda," Dr. Morel says.

"What a creation," Young Einstein marvels. He turns to Morel. "Look at his face," he adds. "No scar."

"I'm right here, you know," I complain. My mouth is loosening up a bit, but I'm still struggling to unplug the metallic cable from my navel. "You might try talking as if – "

But it's no good. My powers of speech are still failing. The film has broken inside me; the projection bulb is melting the celluloid.

I find myself spinning heavenward through a shower of bleeding icons and rose petals and lightening bolts as Morel tells me about the future, the world after my rebirth as the world's first privately owned and operated deity.

"Life will be strictly controlled through the imposition of an entire collection of electronic manuscript requirements. The Wise Ones will subject residents to electronic boulevard search and seizure by skinless auditors, who will wear tin stars affixed to their erect DNA delivery organs. The goal is total sexual demoralization. Official notations will be entered into the genetic ledger, and those without the proper notations will be subject to indefinite nude incarceration in ashen-walled prisons comprised of vanishing brick and mortar, an uncertain state of affairs that will inevitably result in charges of jailbreak. The problem will be defined as a noxious chemical imbalance, of course, treated with Skinalicious9. So as you can unmistakably comprehend, the industrial options are infinite."

#

In bed at home alone.

Despite Jack's best arguments, I decide to stay in my first night without family. I am committed to getting some much needed sleep. Tonight I will be good. But sleep will not come.

How can it? Goodness is a lie. I am experiencing a crushing depression. I seek sleep for escape, not rejuvenation. What can I say? Maybe I got old. Too many trips to Cici's Pizza, too many Barney re-runs. I'm too much the corny, wisecracking dad. Or maybe I'm not enough.

Listen once again to the hollow slam of the tailgate of Allison's Volvo station wagon, its rear bumper disappearing around the curve at the end of the street; her fist slamming on the pantry door while I knell in the tiny closet, cleaning up a broken bottle of juice; a phone slamming in its receiver, seemingly forever.

Everything I contemplate is wretched and desolate.

This is a world of death and shadows. Urine-tinted vapor lamps illuminate the desolation, a terrain of crumbling failure somewhere near the Land of the Dead.

Devalued investment real estate, an old apartment complex. Several of the buildings appear to be vacated, condemned, surrounded by cyclone fencing, doorways and windows covered in warped plywood. Muffled voices and ominous rumblings escape from ghost units, wreckage of miserable depravity, squander of comatose electrical wires swollen and burned out, thick vines consuming the extinguished shell of a charred Camaro, snaking up through jagged holes in the rusted floorboards and springs of naked seat cushions, gripping the skeletal body tight to the crumbling asphalt under the dead, bitter light of the vapor lamps. Insects and nocturnal birds swarm overhead, darting in and out of the urine glow. A night snake ripples across a swimming pool slimed over with emerald scum. Bankrupt patio, dried stems of giant thistles and sunflowers sprouting from cracked sidewalks. An emaciated feral cat stalks its shadow, slinking against a ruined wall marked with spray-painted gang visual rumors. And then, something immoral and repugnant, gazing back in censorious dread. I know this strange creature: it's me, my reflection caught in the rear view mirror.

A dream from my early 20s: I am bitten by a winged demon, transforming me into a Hell's Angel. I join a band of these pitiful creatures flying through the night. We are circling a house (or perhaps a town), then I realize that dawn is approaching. We must leave, go down to the underworld to escape the rising sun. I am sad because I realize I can never again be part of the waking, daylight world. I fly with the evil ones now, life through oxygen containers and I.V.s, prepared for a satin-drawn coffin, arms folded like bat wings and lip stitched together in a silent scream.

I open my nightstand drawer. Jack's porn gear, conveniently stashed here at his urging.

"Sometime during the next two weeks, you may need to let your sleek dog run," he explained.

I read the label on the box of patches: "OFD Movable Pro 890, Instantaneous VI Cohort." This is the new Frames CE, a slimmed down version of the Frames operating system designed just for handhelds.

I tell you, lots of dream jockeys trash talk "FramCE," noting that it can't handle high-speed multisensory recollections or run the latest 64-bit dreamware. But that's not what it was designed for; Frames CE is for going onbeam on the fly. I've been lusting after this new system ever since I'd read about the instant-on capability. You can do a couple of minutes of onbeam creating without first waiting for the usual five-minute Frames boot up. (My favorite VI of all time is the old Zandy DP-2, a bulky, wristwatch-style interface that boots instantly from ROM. It was -- and still is -- perfect for dream writing; the DP-2 can hold enough neural charge for 10 hours of uninterrupted operation, quite an "improvement" over the usual two or three hour charge of most of today's transdermal patches. Of course there is a trade off. The DP-2's implant canvass is hopelessly outdated and crude, really nothing more than charcoal sketches. But sometimes that's enough.)

I unwrap a thumbnail-size patch and slap it on my forehead. Clip on the transceiver (titanium, nice!) to my left earlobe and plug the other end into the wireless card. Then I switch on the PDA and plug in. Instead of the usual hypnogogic flares and random RV-DOS codes of the boot up process, the implant canvass flashes a copyright – "Another Invention of Morel" – and immediately jumps to the Exogrid, in full 3-D, alive and in living dream color.

In the distance, rhythmic tribal drumming and vague chanting. A large quantity of inconsequential imagery, a distracting, leafy blur of banana trees and elephant ears and tropical cartoon-like visions of macaws and jungle cats. I feel a sudden wave of nausea. This program is lousy with jimson weed. But by closing my eyes and concentrating on the tone and the rhythm of the drumming and the chanting, the queasiness passes. The jungle images surge and became even more vivid. Flying over landscapes, past rhythmic African prototype warriors who look heavenward as I zoom past. And I see something else: a bright, rectangular entity floating in the distance, blazing like the sun.

This aerial entity possess within it a sort of stage -- no, a screen. It is a drive-in movie theater, and the show is already playing. I am still too far away to make out all of the action, but it occurs to me (in that strange way knowledge sometimes just seems to come to you in the dreamscape) that my judgments, or expressions verbalized in my brain, are representing themselves on the movie screen.

I am the director of my own movie.

I realize I am still watching all of this on the inside of my eyelids, and I wonder if this is a sort of dream within in a dream. So I decide to open my eyes.

The movie screen is still present, but it is now anchored firmly to the ground on giant, metal legs. And instead of flying, I am at the wheel of my old 1970 Cutlass convertible, parked at the Astro Drive-In. We're back in the old Hydrocarbon Age, a crescent moon and the evening star shining bright against the purple twilight sky of 1979, on or about the last night of my youth.

Despite the impossible visual angle, I can see through the sheet metal fencing to the marquee out front. I understand that the feature presentation is supposed to be "Urban Cowboy," one of the last movies I ever saw at the Astro. But for some reason I cannot actually see this movie, a phenomenon that suggests the central part of my retina has been burned away, the result of gazing too long into the dazzling light of original experience.

And then I am in an examination room. "They" are studying me.

#

Clinical, domed ceilings with gray white walls – smooth, sleek, varnished, unbroken walls. Gaunt metallic hallways and curved hallways, voluminous medical equipment on wheeled carts and affixed to floor-to-ceiling windows. In the corner, a terrestrial observer, an old man in a thick cardigan sweater and wrinkled hands endlessly working over a red potato.

I am here, and I am far away: In the downtown of a small Texas town. It is morning. Nobody on the street. I am in a store, perhaps with my family. I leave with my purchase, a rolled up poster. I take it to a storefront a few doors down. This is my business – perhaps a furniture store, maybe a café. It is done up in cowboy décor. I unroll the poster, which I see is also in a cowboy theme. The poster is long and skinny, more like a scroll. I look around for a suitable place to hang it. Then I am startled to see that I am not alone.

A woman is sitting in a black vinyl recliner, slumped deep in the cool, dark cushions as if asleep. And perhaps she had been sleeping, but now she is fully awake, looking at me. Then I recognize her: She is Nanny, my great grandmother who died 30 years ago.

I can't believe it. Nanny, back from the dead. I look into her face, study her countenance. It's her all right. She looks good, too, maybe in her 60s. She does not appear ancient and sickly like I remember her the last time I saw her at the nursing home, a few weeks before she died.

"You're so pretty and young," I tell her. She thanks me and says "I have some things to tell you, both good and bad. So pull up a chair and sit beside me."

I do as she asks and sit in front of her, knee to knee. But I don't wait for her to talk. She has information I wish to acquire.

"Is there a heaven?" I ask.

"Oh yes, and it's wonderful. You don't earn your way there. Everyone can go."

"Oh, I'm so happy," I tell her. And I mean it, too. Because I am a doubter. So it is nice to have confirmation of the un-confirmable from someone who has seen Heaven first hand.

Then she disappears, but somehow I know she is still here. And I know this is not good. Still, I must proceed.

"Now tell me the bad," I say. "What's been troubling you?"

Suddenly I am propelled upward toward the ceiling, tossed skyward as if by an unseen hand. Then I fall to the floor. Perhaps this visitor is not Nanny at all. Time to escape. I run for the door.

I decide the lights are already turned off, so all I need to do is lock the door and return to the safety of my family at the nearby store. Only I can't get the door to latch. I've set the door knob button to lock, but the door will not hold. I even tear away some foam weather stripping that I think may be the problem. Still no luck. Then I glance back inside the store for one final look. A vinyl restaurant chair is moving about all by itself , and I know immediately it is being propelled by a demonic force. So that is it. My store is really a diner for demons.

#

Laid out on an operating table, strapped down like a dogfish ready for dissection.

A lighted, arm-like device wielding piercing instruments of surgical steel performs the extraction and shattering of bones, the dissection of organs, the suction tube extraction of ectoplasm from the DNA delivery organ. Then organs and bones are baked, re-calibrated and reinstalled, allowing me to unconsciously pull in transmissions from distant galaxies within and detect the distortion created by strange forces without.

Re-assembled, I rise from the table and glimpse my reflection in the polished metal walls. I appear exactly as before; the ordeal leaves no unseen marks or scars. And yet, something has changed. I view the future as contained in glowing drawers of human-insect hybrid fetuses, the children of a hidden planet that surrounds the subject in an alien trip, the attraction of the borderland and the epic film. The image is blinding, almost beyond comprehension. Then the narrative voice-over:

"The motion picture offers a place where self absorption can inflict the first wound, a psychic wound in the heart of the aggressive drama of the mind -- a moviegoer internalized by his own continuity. In the rhetoric of violence an exploitation ensues. The church that lies somewhere to the East is rediscovered, but in ruins. Bitterness and loneliness, killer, negator, scourge -- lost in despair. A modern sense of exile is projected onto the screen of the past, where convention and tradition conspire to heighten the constriction of life, estranging us from emotional life. His emotions do not belong to him. Rather they belong to a Stranger, a double who is oddly familiar in his recapitulation of experience. Psychically wounded, a visual rumor of limitation and pride, rendered impotent and furious. Violence and The Stranger, an agonizing rage, engulfed in guilt or fear."

#

I'm told alien abductions are the most commonly selected dramatic scenarios of onbeam travelers in the collective unconscious. In my case, I was drawn to 1950s B-movie sci-fi imagery as an alternative to the lucid technical and systematic principles of our age, a familiar and yet entirely novel direction that can be looked upon as the outward amplification of an inner legend.

Through the Archetype of the Alien, I firmly believe we can pursue the interpretation of reality as a subject of general story believability and then proceed to – eh, what's that?

Oh. Well, that is interesting that you are most drawn to the sexual imagery. Perhaps pornography is my special gift.

As for you being Luh – yes, I must admit that the young woman on the neighboring island bears a great symbolic resemblance to you in high school. As I gazed upon her I did genuinely consider what it would be like to have you again in the back seat of the Cutlass, this time enthusiastically penetrating your membranes, expelling my ectoplasm inside you. Filling you with my spirit. However, you never allowed me to express my feelings in quite that way. You were always the nice girl.

But then came last year, when we met again and you promised we would run away together. Still you do not remember? That is too bad, for a claim of virginity rules you out as the muse.

Luh is neither virgin nor whore. She is a being of the unconscious, a tour guide to the internal existence, an arbitrator of waking world awareness of the often ambiguous landmarks and residents of inner reality. She assists in the investigation of significance and is the inspiration of and for the existence of the movie director. In short, the muse is an escort through – and at the same time a personification of – the Land of the Dead.

And yet, she is always trying to escape this ghost terrain, to take up residence in the sunshine of the waking world. One of the ways the muse attempts to do this is by projecting herself onto the real women in my life. Unconsciously, I am forever attempting to compel women like you to become a living host for my muse, the carrier of my own inner world – a membrane to be penetrated, an external receptor for the expulsion of the internal ectoplasm of visionary experience.

I am an odious being, of course. I should see people for who they really are, not for their resemblance to some inner aspect of myself. So one of the jobs I have given myself for the second half of my life is to work hard at recognizing this "projecting" as soon as it occurs. I must cut the power to the projector and send the muse back inside my head, where all imaginary beings belong.

And yet, I cannot do so when it comes to you, my love. You would make a highly desirable muse. According to the cinematic images of my dreams, you are the perfect physical host. I have already begun to animate the muse inside you. (In the language of B-movie sci-fi, I am Dr. Frankenstein and you are my artificially created bride, assembled from body parts unearthed from my own unconscious.) If you will voluntarily enter my dungeon lab and submit yourself to the final stage of the transformation, the animating process will be nearly effortless. Granted, the price will be high. Most likely, you will quickly tire of being a psychological archetype. You will say "enough" and walk away. That is for the best, because people should not be archetypes. But if you do not walk away – well, the muse will totally consume you. She will induce you to surrender your unique individuality. You will be compelled to lead me down into the darkness, through the creative process deep into the Land of the Dead. I will be forever bending you over in the hot shower, penetrating your membranes with my DNA delivery organ, expelling my ectoplasm inside you, filling you with my spirit. Would that be so bad?

Compliments, adoration, inspiration – I will demand it all. And still, I will always be questioning the situation. Is she really my muse? Can it be there is still some unconscious remnant of the individuality of the former owner of this body – what was her name again? You will be a mere receptacle, which is to say no longer "you" at all. In the end, the muse will destroy us both. Hey – I think I just outlined the concept for my next movie. Can you believe it? The muse strikes again.

So, perhaps you are the muse after all. In light of this revelation, I am going to skip ahead in the narrative and tell you about the time the son of the muse – our love child? – tried to murder me.

#

Luh came to visit again last night.

But the visitation does not occur here, on the island. Somehow we are at the home of Allison's parents, where I am cleaning up after the burglary that preceded the big road trip. It is not pleasant. I am about to the lower the garage door when I hear a crash inside the house. A wave a fear washes over me, sends my stomach into sommersaults. Could the burglars still be inside? But then I hear a cry. A woman's voice. How dangerous can that be?

"Hello? Are you OK?" I ask.

No answer. Then another crash, apparently from Allison's old bedroom. My heart is pounding, but somehow I find the courage to creep down the hall, past family photos and framed elementary school report cards. I rip open the door and find Cinnamon, sprawled across the eyelet bedspread. She is lying on her side, one hand propping up her head and the other resting on her hip. Wearing nothing but a dark tan and a smile. My arms goes limp; I drop the hammer.

"Sorry about the racket," she says. "I accidentally knocked over a stack of shoe boxes. She must really like shoes."

"Allison's definitely into fashion."

Then she rolls onto her stomach, and I see that she is not Cinnamon at all. She is Luh.

She kicks a foot up behind her, as if relaxing at the beach. Indeed, hanging over the headboard is a lake painting Allison did in high school. There is boat with a fisherman looking toward a pair of sharply peaked mountains in the background. I try not to stare.

"I'm guessing the loot is already gone," I say.

"Hours ago."

"How about I call the police."

"I'll just tell them what you did to the piano and the painting."

"Like they'd believe you."

"What do you care anyway?"

She is right. I don't care.

Luh swings her legs over the edge of the bed and pulls on one of Allison's old bath robes, an artifact from high school.

"Now it's time for your gift," she says.

My gift? But then why did she put on the robe --

From under the bed she retrieves an old laptop computer. My eye immediately lands on the corporate logo, the venerated icon.

"Is that -- ?"

"A Macintosh Portable," she explains. "The 5126."

"The backlit model?"

"It will be perfect for your writing. See? It's been restored to mint condition."

She sits it on the bed, flips open the lid and hits the power button. It immediately clicks to life.

"It's got the rebuilt battery," she explains. "And the 8 meg PDS slot RAM card from Dynamic Engineering."

As it finishes booting, I gaze into the system screen, glowing pale in the deepening twilight.

"It's got the hard drive upgrade kit, too?" I ask.

"That's right. I replaced the 40 meg Conner with a 500 meg PowerBook SCSI drive. It's formatted and loaded with Mac OS 7.01."

I pick up the humming computer, hold it in front of me. "Where did you get this?" I ask.

"You like it?"

"Like it? It's fantastic. I've heard of Japanese collectors who'll pay upwards of $1,000 for a 5126 in this condition. But why?"

Suddenly, the computer begins to change in my hands. The white plastic case darkens to a light bronze flesh tone. Arms and legs spout from the various serial ports. It is becoming a doll -- but not a nice one. This is a homicidal Chucky doll, writhing and struggling in my hands, its face twisted in hate.

"What is it?" I ask, trying to keep my fingers away from the snapping jaws.

"A reincarnated unkind being."

I put my hands around the doll's neck and squeeze, but that just makes it fight harder, trying to bite me. This Chucky wants more than a taste. He wants me dead.

"Sometimes he goes too far," she remarks. "But he's always the first to admit it."

"Quick, pick up the hammer! Smash its skull."

Luh shakes her head.

"We must positively integrate your destructive impulses, not indulge them."

"Smash it now," I repeat.

"He just needs attention. He needs love."

"Love? It's a killer."

"But he's our baby."

And then the hammer is in my hand. I strike at the psychotic computer, again and again – splintered plastic, scattered microchips, a river of teeth, a raging current of broken incisors, saliva, blood and other bodily emissions.

Don't I feel good now?

#

I know you are familiar with the story. Everyone is. But it's all from the news media. All lies. Before we go any further, you need to understand what happened the night of my alien abduction scenario from MY perspective.

Here is the true story: I experienced an apocalyptic vision.

Not my first, but it was perhaps my most important. This is one that led me to create my famous tag line: "Here's one way the world ends."

#

Here's one way the world ends: I am in Louisiana, walking east along the El Camino Real towards Fort Jesup, the capital of the Land of the Dead. I come out of the ancient turpentine mist and the dripping Spanish moss and the pines and find myself at Trinity Baptist Church, the same one my grandparents belonged to (and many of my relations still do).

As I approach, I am amazed to see that next door to the church is an old white chapel I remember from my childhood. I have not seen it in years. It should not be here, but it is. What a find!

I look inside, and it is just as I remember. The last attendance figures are still on the little sign at the front of the church. It is like a time capsule.

But all is not well. The front of the building is gone, sliced off like a piece of cheese. The pulpit and pews are all in place. But, no -- that's not right. Because I can see into the basement. It is flooded with water, creating a sort of pool. A concrete ramp disappears into the water, suggestive of a boat ramp at a lake.

From out of the ruins, I am greeted by an old man in a plaid flannel shirt and a short, neatly trimmed beard. I learn that he is a former pastor of the church, now retired. He tells me he is in the process of restoring the old chapel. But after he took off the front of the building, it rained and the basement filled with water.

I am sad, for I realize that the church had been safe all these years but due to his ill-timed restoration efforts it is now in danger of total destruction. Surely, the cost of repairing the water damage is beyond the means of this old man. Still, I am happy that I have rediscovered the old church, which I thought had been demolished decades ago. At least I am seeing it for one last time, a joy flowered in difficulty.

A car arrives. It is my wife and our two sons. They are here to pick me up so we can continue on the last couple of miles to my grandparent's old house, where the Leachs hold their annual family reunion. I suggest we walk the last stretch. Allison is skeptical; however, she agrees to my plan.

We walk a bit, but soon I become disoriented. The route does not look the same on foot. I take the wrong road, and we wind up in a hot, deserted stretch of country. It has been denuded of the lush pine forest that dominates this area. The boys begin to complain about the heat. They are thirsty. Allison remains silent, furious. And I am overwhelmed -- overwhelmed by the nausea of failure, one more broken attempt to transcend the everyday.

#

#

Morning, face smashed against a gravel walkway. I awaken to the temperate nudge of boot to ribcage.

"Sorry, thought you were dead."

The boot belongs to Sam Cunningham, precinct No. 3 county constable and perhaps the last person I want to find me sleeping on the front steps of the old derelict Strangers Rest Baptist Church. But maybe I'm not really here. Maybe I'm still onbeam. I touch my forehead, and hope vanishes. The VI patch is gone.

Will he arrest me? I see the headline, in my own paper no less: "Reporter arrested for vagrancy, trespassing."

Certainly the state of affairs does not appear promising. But there is another reason he might wish to haul me in: I have written unfavorably about him.

The previous fall, the county commissioners cut Cunningham's constabulary budget from $46,728 to $15,006 and his salary from $33,000 to $9,000 because of accusations by the precinct No. 3 Justice of the Peace Hubert Skinner and some residents that he'd quit serving civil papers. That didn't merit more than a news brief in the Northeast Extra. The big story came soon thereafter. Skinner locked Cunningham out of the office they shared on Frederiksbad Street. The judge said the constable and his deputies had a habit of going through his files. So he had Cunningham's office dismantled and its content stashed in the old county jail. Now that was a good story. They even put it on the wires; it appeared in papers all over the country. Sam was a coast-to-coast joke.

In all fairness to Sam, he never complained to me. But I did receive an anonymous letter, a copy of the story and the Bill of Rights. The passage about freedom of the press had been highlighted with an orange marker.

"Great to see you," Sam says, helping me to my feet, looking me over. His hands work my shoulders, feel my bones -- me in my rumpled golf shirt and khakis, blood-filled eyes with gravel pressed into my check, he in his starched brown uniform, shiny brown Ropers and .357 magnum.

"You OK?" he asks. "You don't look so good."

I can't believe it. He is even concerned about my appearance. He won't be arresting me after all. Ah, there's nothing like old friends.

"I'm fine, just a little tired."

"He's not here today."

"Who?"

"The new owner."

"I didn't know there was one."

"Yeah, he's a movie director or something. Been filling the place up with all kinds of lights and cameras and film gear. He even had the electric company put in a new transformer. He's running 440 volts."

I look at the old chapel. From the outside nothing seems to have changed. The heavy front doors are still chained and padlocked, the faded metal "for sale" sign is still stapled to the white clapboards, chimney swifts is still darting in and out of the louvered belfry. Everything is just as it had been for the past five years, ever since the congregation of the Strangers Rest Baptist Church decided to drop the "Baptist" for a "dot com" moniker and move away from their historic property on Frederiksbad Street. Now their home is out on a forlorn, treeless stretch of Interstate 35-W in a giant, metal warehouse of a sanctuary – a combination gas station/Exogrid church featuring a multimedia stage for contemporary praise music and the pastor's "talk points" and restaurant-style beepers to keep parents in touch with the nursery. (These Keepers of the Deity have no interest in finding the church that lies somewhere to the East.)

"So, really great to see you," Sam says again, still feeling my bones.

"Yeah, me too." But what do you want?

"I've got a story you might be interested in."

Ah yes -- the price of staying out of jail. "Tell me about it."

"You know the street dance on Saturday?"

I know.

It is to be a fundraiser to save the Silver Spur, the empty rock shell of an old West saloon (circa 1880) from the days when Strangers Rest was a rowdy cattle town. The corner property is for sale for $60,000, but of course the big expense will be the restoration -- a couple of million at least. So Strangers Rest has called in the big gun, Cowboy Roy, a singing cowboy from the 1950s who owned a ranch on the edge of town. He is resurrecting his old band, the Wrambling Wrangers, for a live broadcast on the local National Public Radio affiliate.

"So, of course, as town marshal I'm in charge of crowd control, of security. But there's going to be like hundreds of people. I can't control them all by myself, right?"

"Right." And I'm still out of jail.

"So I'm going to round up a posse."

"A what?"

"Yeah, I'm going to have my own posse, like on 'Gunsmoke.' I'm going to deputize some of the local citizens."

"You can do that?"

"I called the attorney general's office in Austin. They gave me the OK."

"A posse in Strangers Rest."

"Probably the first time since cowboy days."

"You know, that is a good story."

"You could even be one of my deputies."

"Me?"

"Absolutely. You live here, you pay taxes."

"A reporter with a badge."

"You can ride a horse, too -- if you can get one. I'll even let you carry a shotgun."

We set up a time and place for the interview.

"And a photo?" Sam asks.

"Of course." After all, I'll be the deputy town marshal.

"OK, then. I'll see you next -- hey, where's your car?"

"What? Oh, I walked."

"You want a ride home?" He jerks his thumb back over his shoulder, toward a dusty old Toyota bubbletop.

"Undercover?"

"Yup. Probably the only constable in Texas who has to patrol in his own car."

"No, I'll just walk back."

"You still don't look so hot."

"I'm fine. See you tomorrow."

"I'll bring your badge."

"And my shotgun."

#

Poor Sam. The story of his fall from grace is even worse that I have presented. After the contents of his office were locked up in the old county jail the commissioners assigned Sam's duties to a deputy constable from another precinct. But the emasculated constable still wanted to prove himself. So he continued to work at his reduced rate of pay. He even tried to win over townsfolk by agreeing to take on the non-paying job of town marshall. At least it meant he'd have a patrol car. But that didn't last long, either. The city council voted to curb it rather than raise taxes to continue its operation. They parked it in the mayor pro tem's back yard, the town's most expensive dust catcher. That gave me another great story.

Poor Sam.

#

Walking Frederiksbad Street, a tree-lined residential street little changed since the 1930s. I move in and out of the shade the morning sun makes through the trees, enjoying the view. There's a mix of craftsman-inspired bungalows, simple half-porch, center-gable cottages and my favorite, a one-story red brick tutor with an S-shaped drive, vine-covered porte coche and a red barn out back. An old woman with a hand trowel and floppy straw hat works the front flower bed, tending her elephant ears and phlox. Allison and I used to covet the place. We'd drive by every week, hoping to see a "for sale" sign. The old folks just wouldn't die. They outlasted us, forcing us to the new subdivision where we had our choice of three grades of carpet and a premium waterfront lot.

I feel a bit shaky, a wave of nausea building in the humid morning air. But something is not right. I see patches of snow and white ice on some of the roofs. The sunlight is thawing this white, which flows off a high stretch of tutor roof in the manner of a mountain waterfall.

A few blocks later, an unusual house catches my eye. It looks like a tower supporting a saucer-like structure. A UFO home. How did it get here, in downtown Strangers Rest?

The house resembles a miniature version of the Tower of the Americas in San Antonio. The shaft of the tower is made of glass and contains a spiral staircase. Doesn't look much like a house at all.

Next I spot an even more dramatic example of the UFO style. No tower, but a much larger saucer structure, which is surrounded by a porch. I've seen this place before, in a dream. I am with a companion, and we wish to have a closer look at this house, which is clearly a significant piece of architecture. Someone is in front of us, pushing a cart or baby stroller; they too are trying to get a closer look. It is twilight, and the lights are already on inside the house, intensifying the UFO effect. The people in front of us walk onto the porch – its ceiling dimly lit by flush-mounted light panels – and look inside a window. The residents are inside eating dinner, and they are understandably unhappy about this intrusion. I cannot hear what they say, but the meaning is clear. They send the intruders away. So we leave, too, without looking inside or even seeing anything else of the outside of the house. Clearly this place is not for me.

My nausea incubates in the next block, a collection of low-slung '50s ranch houses with attached carports and big AC units on concrete slabs. No need to plant trees when you've got central air. I raise a hand to wipe the sweat from my forehead.

How did I get from my bedroom to downtown Strangers Rest? I squint into the bright sun, the sweat now pouring off my forehead. It is hard to concentrate. My stomach feels like curdled milk, overwhelmed by the nausea of failure. No way I will make it the mile or so to my house. If only I can get to the Circle L, sit down in a cool, vinyl booth near the cold cases and enjoy a carton of orange juice. I turn onto Frederiksbad Street, the Circle L almost in view.

But a half block later it becomes clear I won't make it. I sit down in front of a vacant lot against a power pole. The scent of black crude somehow settles my stomach. I close my eyes, just for a moment. But there is no time to rest. I must flee.

I am running down a freshly paved residential street, the scent of the black crude filling my nostrils, a police car in pursuit. But he can't catch me. Adrenaline pumping, I am running so fast that my feet almost leave the ground. I come to a dead end and leap over the barricade like an Olympic star, leaving the police car far behind.

I hide in dark undergrowth, alone in the twilight shadows. And yet, I am not alone. I have an accomplice, a stranger. We cannot be seen together. They'll be expecting that. We must split up, go our own ways.

"Wait five minutes, then take off," I tell the man as I sprint for the next street over.

It is evening now, and the neighborhood is empty. Everyone is inside for the night. I come to a cross street -- the last big barrier before I get home -- and I see a police car a few hundred yards away. He has pulled over a mini van, giving the driver a ticket. With a little luck, I should be able to cross the street unseen. But I have no luck. Suddenly, cars begin to appear. They are coming from both directions. The speed limit is about 40, and the cars are following each other very closely. There is no opportunity to squeeze between cars and cross the road. Then a car stops in the middle of the road, and the traffic begins to pass slowly on the shoulder. This is my chance. I bolt between two cars, just missing their bumpers. I've made it. But then, out of the shadows comes the policeman. He is right behind me, too close for me to get away. He takes me down in a flying tackle and we crash into a side yard filled with old buildings materials, salvaged French doors, painted pine moldings and beaded boards and yellow Texas Star bricks edged in dusty, crumbling mortar. The homeowner is there, too, and I say that I am being attacked. Not realizing my attacker is really a policeman, he jumps to my aid, pinning the officer to the ground.

"Thanks," I say as I run towards the alley. "Just hold him for five minutes, that's all I need."

Then I throw myself through a plate glass window, like Tom Cruise in "Mission: Impossible" and escape to the little town's historic central business district. But this is no escape, either. Everyone has heard of me, the fugitive. A librarian I know tells the crowd that they should give me a chance to explain myself, but her words fall on unsympathetic ears. They're out to get me, a misunderstood creature pursued by torch-wielding peasants. A group of Boy Scouts in khaki uniforms with red neckerchiefs swarm me, little hands grabbing at my clothes. One of the older boys has a syringe, presumably filled with some barbiturate that will make me easier to apprehend. Even without the injection, they will surely win. I can't possibly fight off this many, even if they are only children. But having been a Boy Scout myself once, I know how to outsmart them. "Watch out, I'll breathe my illness on you." I am so convincing that I can actually see my breath, a green dragon fog. Scary! "I have V.D. Do you know what that is?" The scouts are speechless, wide eyed. None of them know. So I tell them. "It's a disease that makes your DNA delivery organ fall off." And they all back away.

#

I come to myself inside the Circle L, stretched out across plastic milk crates in a cool, dark nook near the front counter. I feel tired, but the nausea is gone. I attempt to sit up. No luck. I can't quite get my arms to operate. A set of tough, wizened hands helps me the rest of the way.

"Looky here, he's alive after all."

Gazing down at me, sweat-stained Stetson shoved back on his balding head, stands Cowboy Roy.

"How long have I been here?"

"Oh, not long -- about 10 minutes. I saw you when you sat down out there on the road. We had a heck of time getting you into the Bevomobile."

We? I look around and see the Boy Scouts. They have escaped from my dream, clearly a troubling development. The Scouts eye me warily, taking care to stay far from my mouth, source of the green dragon fog.

Cowboy Roy does not recognize their fear. He only sees them as another audience.

"That's right, boys, the Bevomobile," he says. "It's a movie star car, a white 1959 Cadillac convertible outfitted with rawhide seat covers, six-shooter door handles and a set of polished longhorns mounted on the hood. I've been driving it since 1961, when I made my last movie, 'By the Guns Forgot.' You boys ever seen that one?"

Blank stares.

"Well, they show it on the UHF stations sometimes on Sunday afternoons. Watch for it. Now regarding the Bevomobile, it is one of my most prized possessions -- that and my trusty Bisley."

Roy reaches into a rhinestone-studded holster and comes up with the six-shooter he inherited from his grandfather, a sheriff in turn-of-the-century Strangers Rest. He gives the pearl-handled gun a quick twirl on his finger.

"I'll be wearing this on stage Saturday night," he says. "I always like to have the big iron on my hip when I do the Radio Ranch. For my fans."

"I heard tell you're going to sell it," says Odie Cowan, owner of the Circle L.

Roy spins around and stares.

"Who'd you hear tell that?"

"Oh yeah, it's all over. That gun collector from Waco was in here last week. Told me he'd heard about your famous old broken down six-shooter. For some fool reason he wanted to buy it."

Mayor Toots Tedwill picks up on the story, too. "That's right. I heard he was going to pay you a whole bushel of money for it."

Cowboy Roy sets his jaw hard and shakes his head at the smiling men. "He was a thief and an idiot," he says quietly.

"Why what do you mean, Roy? Didn't he make you a fair offer?" Odie asks, winking at me. Everyone in town already knew what happened. And what Cowboy Roy thought of it.

"He offered me $2,000," Cowboy Roy says through clenched teeth. "I figure it's worth 10 times that, so that makes him a thief. And if he'd bothered to check around, he'd known it weren't for sale. So that makes him an idiot."

"Two thousands bucks sounds like a mighty fair price to me," Toots says. """After all, it's just a wore out old gun."

"Wore out?" Cowboy Roy roars. "Why, I'll have you know that gun is priceless. And famous at that. It was given to my granddaddy by the Texas Attorney General for his service cleaning out Pancho Villa and his boys down in south Texas. Kit Karger and Big Foot Wallace was at the ceremony. My granddaddy wore that gun the whole time he was sheriff back here, and he kept on wearing it after that, right up to his dying day."

"Oh, well I didn't know about all that," Toots remarks, though of course he knows. All the old folks in town know the story of Granpappy Thornton's Bisley revolver because Cowboy Roy has been inflicting it on them since they were kids.

"Wore out," Cowboy Roy repeats, oblivious to the choked laughs around him. Roy turns his attention again to me.

"You didn't look too good when we carried you in here," he explains. "Odie didn't want me to bring you in. He was afraid you might die here, be bad for his business."

The store owner stiffens as he sacks up a quart of milk and a pack of Marlboros for a tired-looking pregnant woman with a "Baby On Board" T-shirt. As soon as the door closes behind her, though, he slams the cash register drawer and spins around on Cowboy Roy.

"I just thought it might be something serious, that he ought to go to the hospital."

"Well, looks like he's going to pull through after all, so why don't you quit making excuses and brew us up some fresh coffee?" Roy winks at me and whispers, "he didn't want a dead body contaminating the Moon pies and Ranch Style Beans."

Odie disappears into the back room to secure another can of coffee, leaving Roy without an audience -- an untenable situation. Roy's eyes quickly lit on the far booth by the restrooms, where 80-year-old "Toots" Tedwill was finishing up the crossword from the morning paper.

"Yeah, Odie's just a broken down old woman," Roy says. "Not a young, good lookin' cuss like me."

Toots doesn't look up from his paper. "I need a four-letter word for –"

"Now look out," Roy warns him. "We got a member of the press here today."

"You ought to take it easy on needling Odie. He says he's thinking about charging for coffee."

Roy affects a look of shock. "No free coffee? But it's always been free. It's a tradition. You can't buy a cup of coffee in Strangers Rest."

"Yeah, well Odie don't much care about that tradition," Toots says. "He said 'if I start charging for coffee, Roy's the only one cheap enough to quit coming. It'd be a real win-win for everybody.'"

I try to smile, but I still felt too weak. Roy gives me a quizzical look.

"I've never passed out like that," I explain.

"Shoulda took him to the hospital," Odie shouts from the back of the store.

"We were a bit worried," Roy admits. "We even called your wife."

Allison. A fresh wave of nausea washes over me. I could almost see her at the beach house in Maine, roused from sleep by my in-laws. ("Can't Mark take care of himself for one day?")

"I told her she didn't need to worry, though," Roy adds. "You were just sleeping off a drunk."

Then he starts laughing, slapping his hat against his leg. In exchange for my being a good sport, though, Roy buys me a plastic bottle of orange juice and a Twinkie, just what I need to bring my blood sugar back up to nominal operating levels. I rise from the milk crates without assistance. Roy opens the door with one hand and jingles the change in his pocket with the other, searching for his car keys.

Odie returns from the back room with a carafe of water, which he pours into the top of the Mr. Coffee. "You don't have to put up with his carrying on," he says. "Roy's not nearly as funny as he thinks he is."

"What do you know about humor?" Roy replies. "I'm the professional entertainer, remember? I once shared a bottle of Jack Daniels with Slim Pickens."

"I remember. The whole town remembers. You don't give nobody a chance to forget."

"I want that coffee ready when I get back." Roy smiles and gives me another conspiratorial wink. But Odie doesn't see the smile or wink. His is squinting at the open door, his attention focused on something outside -- something up in the sky.

#

To fall into an alternate reality – is that not the very definition of visionary transformation? Consider how it occurred for Clark Caring:

#

A strange and disquieting morning, my beloved creations. It takes only a couple of queries to confirm my suspicions, unbelievable and unacceptable as I find them to be. This is the day I learn that Jehovah, the creator and sustainer of Planet Earth, has been arrested.

#

Sen. Stone Says R.E.L. Four Should Resign

AUSTIN (SPM)— Sen. Raulston Stone on Wednesday called on Planetary Administrator R.E.L. Four to resign, one day after berating him during a town hall meeting over what he called an "abortive strategy" in the United States.

"I simply don't comprehend why we cannot acquire new management to give us a genuine opportunity to reverse the course of events before it's too late," the Harris County Federalist and potential presidential contender said in an interview with State Public Media. "I believe the president should demand administrator Four's immediate resignation."

"The administrator has lost trustworthiness with the Senate and the House and the people of the Republic of Texas," he said. "The moment for action is here. Four must stand down and be exchanged for someone who can cultivate a successful strategy and convey it successfully to the Texas people and to the world."

Stone had resisted joining the refrain of other Federalists demanding an official sanction of Four. His remarks Wednesday were the harshest assessment yet from the man considered his party's early front-runner for next year's presidential nomination.

The former Army general has come under attack from some in his own party for voting for the police action five years ago and his current opposition to a deadline for Texas troop withdrawal.

He criticized Four yesterday morning during a town hall meeting in Texarkana near the demilitarized zone, where recent insurgent fighting has threatened to end the 47-year border truce between the two nations.

"Under your control, there have been abundant mistakes in reasoning that have directed us to where we are," he said. "We have a full-fledged insurgency and full-blown sectarian conflict in the United States."

In a celestial manifestation, the planetary administrator rejected some of Stone's specific criticisms as purely incorrect and said the war against sacrament abuse will be a long-lasting course of action. He said he in no way has downplayed the troubles of the struggle.

"I have in no way mislead you," he said. "I've been very deliberate in my statements, and you will not be able to locate scripture in which I have expressed undue sanguinity."

#

Word of this amazing development apparently came months before, when a giant clock suddenly materialized in the eastern sky. The world watched in dumbfounded amazement as the hands climbed to 12 o'clock, then dissolved into a giant head. This head bore a kind and benevolent expression, a unique countenance the citizens of the planet instantly regarded as the face of a god (or, depending on personal religious beliefs, a rock star or JFK).

"Greetings, Earthlings," the giant head entones. "I am R.E.L. *Four, a citizen of the unseen, metaphysical world many of you know as Heaven. Today the Tri-Lateral Court of Cosmic Affairs administered warrants for the arrest of Jehovah (aka Yahweh, God, the Almighty, the Holy Spirit, the Holy Ghost, Allah, Krishna, Zeus, et al) for various and sundry crimes against humanity."*

How about that? After a few dozen centuries, God's colleagues have finally got around to checking on the insignificant world known as Planet Earth. Seems they don't like what they've found. Wars, rumors of wars, sickness, death, murder, hatred. Jehovah has created a cruel and pain-filled world.

When they check the sacred texts compiled by His most beloved creations, they aren't real keen on what they find, either. A worldwide flood, a woman turned into a pillar of salt, a man covered in boils and robbed of all he owned as part of a bet. And when they reach the final chapter, they are downright unhinged by His plans for destroying all of creation through a worldwide apocalypse.

"Deities have a responsibility to provide for the needs and wants of the sentient beings they create," R.E.L. *Four explains. "Jehovah has violated that responsibility. Clearly, he has become an irrational and dangerous being. Therefore, the Tri-Lateral Court is holding him in administrative segregation until such time as he is compelled to answer for his alleged crimes before a jury of his peers."*

Harsh. An Earth with no god? Unfathomable. How will we function? Who will keep the planet rotating, the sun shining, the rain falling? And to paraphrase Ambrose Bierce: Who will we ask to annul the inviolable laws of the universe on our behalf even though we are confessedly unworthy?

Well, it turns out the answer is – R.E.L. *Four.*

Yes, he is assigned the job of putting right all that God has done wrong. A tall order, to be sure. For R.E.L. *Four quickly discovers that homo sapiens have a lot of needs and wants, many of which are in extreme conflict.*

Take the Republic of Texas, for instance. The Americans of the East Coast and southern California did not like it that Texas had become an independent nation. Talk about your impossible alternate realities. And yet, somehow under the watch of R.E.L. *Four, the Republic of Texas had come into existence. The history books said it began in 1861, when a 20th century nuclear weapon fell through a black hole and into the hands of Sam Houston. The State of Texas re-declared its independence and joined forces with the United States to quash the Confederacy.* R.E.L. *Four might have put it right again, except for the fact that the citizens of the Republic of Texas insisted it was natural reality, unaltered by artificial intervention. "They're lying," the Easterns and SoCal types insisted. "Read their minds and you'll know it." But* R.E.L. *Four refused, insisting it would be immoral to use his divine abilities to resolve what was in effect an earthly dispute.*

And then there was the problem of lottery drawings. How can R.E.L. *allow all players to become lottery millionaires without bankrupting the lottery, which is in fact designed to fund public education? In that particular case,* R.E.L. *resolved the millionaire/public education conflict by outlawing all lottery drawings. According to the news archives, he wasn't a very popular god that week. A Harris Poll put his popularity rating at 20 percent and falling.*

"I have learned there are many things a god cannot do," R.E.L. *admits during the conclusion of one of his worldwide "giant head" fireside chats. "Certainly a more fair and equitable solution to funding education would be taxes. The society benefits, the society pays. Of course, taxes are no longer an option because as you'll recall I abolished them in response to an influx of prayers on the subject. Anyway, I'm sure that together we'll think of some way to pay for education. Blessings, and keep those prayers coming."*

Kudos to the Prophet, for he has written into the sacred text that this new god should have a problem common to many mere mortals: Talk too much do too few.

#

Despite having viewed "Let Me Love You" about a hundred times, it was still some time before I divined the full visionary significance of the Clock in the Air. At first, I thought it was literally a sentient being from outer space, like R.E.L. Four. But then I came to see it as more than a cinematic allusion. The Clock in the Air is a metaphorical message, one sent by the inner all-knowing me to the outer less-than-knowing me. Consider the case of the extraterrestrial insects.

The giant cicada stands on its back legs, revealing an exoskeletal underbelly of armored plates the tint of washed out gray. A whirring, rasping voice comes out of a vibrating membrane on its thorax.

"First remove the log from you own eye, then you can help your neighbor remove the speck from his," it says.

I drop my drink, and the carmel colored liquid bleeds into the thick wool berber. My heart staggers. Caught in a crime (and by a Bible-quoting extraterrestrial).

"I – I was just cleaning up," I stutter.

The insectoid's tympanum begins to vibrate again – but no, that's not it. The alien is talking through its eyes. "Do not be alarmed," it says. "All who have eyes have eyes that speak."

#

The creature's name is Bellero Shield. He tells me he is a traveler from inner space who arrived in the Land of the Dead via a Sunday afternoon rerun of a 1964 episode of The Outer Limits.

"This is a creative visitation," he explains, "a paraphrase of a favored motion picture."

"A movie?"

"Do you not recall the first words of the alien in 'The Revolution of Zion,' a QCT Drama Special based on the extremely applauded work of print fiction of the same name?"

I do recall.

"Haven't seen it in years, though," I say. "I read that it is lost in some film vault, I believe, caught up in a copyright issue. Something about a Beatles song. But I do remember it fondly. It was very good."

"You remember it fondly because you are a being of the movies," Bellero explains. "And, of course, the movies are you. The epic film is employed to provide the pattern for our manifestation. Earthlings are unique among the sentient beings of the cosmos. It is normal for your species to have a split personality, living one utterly neglected, unacknowledged way in the metaphorical inner world and one far-too-obvious-and-self-aggrandized way in the literal outer world. What your species does not yet realize is the Deity is not an absolute life form living in the back of beyond. Nor is He a supernatural creature in outer space or the heavens. He is not restricted by occasion or location, the past or its formation."

"So what is He?"

"The Deity is the underpinning of all existence. Everywhere else we have traveled the reasoning beings already know this. They are of one mind, understanding the universe and its creator as we do. The inner and the outer are just one world. They live in that one world at all times, all feet regardless of number simultaneously in the inner and in the outer."

"It's a little hard to manage on earth, even with only two feet."

"And that, Mark Leach, is why you should understand that you have been given a great gift – an Incredible Revelation. You are among the first Earthlings to experience life as it is experienced by the creatures of the rest of the universe, the creator manifesting itself in the creation. You are seeing the culture's communal, extra-worldly perception concretely realized in the waking world. The dream made flesh."

"It's more like a nightmare."

"You don't find the Clock in the Air beautiful?"

"How can I? I've dreamed death, the conclusion of time. I've dreamed my hometown reduced to cinders." I look at the wreckage around me, the hammer in my hand. "And I've dreamed death. I am the bringer of death, youth whose memory drives one to despair. I've done terrible things."

"No, you've done great things, Mark Leach. Marvelous things."

"But the destruction – "

"Yes, the Deity is also a being of destruction. We must bravely say 'bring on the big world dreams.' Nuclear-based brimstone, everlasting dark, bitter pursuit -- an awful tragedy, huge anguish, Bengal tigers roaming free in subdivisions reverted to wilderness, moth and mold consuming the flag, vines taking over pews and pulpits. The thing for you is that you are the obliteration, the bomb blast. Senses are dulled, you can barely feel it. You are medicated or something. You are far from earth, in total separation, the emotion of being powerless in that state of affairs. You fall on the Martian surface, where you are rescued from your burning spacecraft by an old girlfriend, the hidden assistant. For you see, dreams are really about ourselves. The conclusion of time is a rebellion against the sarcophagus, flames of torture, dream-bearing ballistic missiles, demonic control and other tempests of mauve painted insanity. The 'it' is actually happening. You had Mars, in a lunar-style lander that had stored in its pain banks one of the great cyclone visions of all time. They always come back, spinning you around, perturbing you."

"Pretty."

"Precisely. Enjoy the beauty of the picture. But also be careful. The legend of the conclusion of time attempts to captivate us with a larger-than-life metaphor that can actually lead to seriously literal effects. Be careful of being charmed by this beauty, by what is impressive. For it is possible that this Judgment Day performance may yet torture and destroy the earth, which is to say you. Remember this: as sentient beings, we are required to create. We are not required to live."

The old men at the Circle L have their theories about the aerial timepiece, and they aren't afraid to share them.

"I tell you, it's a commercial for television," Toots says.

Roy shakes his head. "I tell you, it's an alien spaceship."

I laugh, but then see by the solemn look on Roy's face that he is serious. "You don't really believe in UFOs, do you?" I ask.

"We've known about them for years," Roy explains, "ever since the '40s. We've been maintaining the ruins of one out there in the wasteland in Nevada at that clandestine air base on the dried up lake bed. Our scientists have been trying for years to reverse engineer it. Looks like they finally did it. Ain't that right, Odie?"

But Odie doesn't offer an opinion. He is busy fiddling with the double aerial of the small TV he keeps by the cash register.

"Got it," he says.

The screen is full of azure skies. The camera pans down to a brilliant emerald meadow labeled "Waterford, N.Y." Odie aims the remote at the set, and the orator crackles into existence.

"-- was first reported at sunrise over this dairy farm in upstate New York , but it is rapidly dispersing to the remainder of the country, at times with volatile consequences."

The view switches to a scene of firefighters and policeman busying themselves in the area of a tractor trailer half buried in the side of a sheet metal structure. "Fifteen people were injured this morning at a horse show in Oklahoma City, when a truck driver lost control of a trailer of thoroughbreds and plowed into a horse shed." A man in a John Deere cap appears on the monitor. "It just fills the heavens, a hundred miles across. I don't understand. It's like - I don't know, it's like it's the End of the World, the conclusion of time. How can a guy make a living off the world any more when it's all come to this?"

#

Traveling to the Attitude Adjustment Bureau in the Bevomobile. (Roy insisted on driving me.) I see something new on the dashboard, a small oval medallion. Muse Sound System.

"I ain't never noticed that before," Roy says. He turns on the radio to check it out. A voice like Moses emerges from the dashboard speaker.

"You are on Frederiksbad Street in Strangers Rest."

"How about that?" Roy marvels. "They're broadcasting from our town."

I recognize the words. It is the narrative of a dream I experienced a couple of years back, but now converted into the anonymity of second person: "You see that they are demolishing the old brick house next to the winery, which is a converted church. This is a house you and your wife have always liked and used to hope it would go on the market so you could buy it for yourselves. Its destruction is sad. You don't know why it is being torn down because the house appeared to be in good shape. Even now, the exposed frame looks almost new. And the foundation – flagstones over which I advance once again, through the hallways, meeting rooms, colonnades… the form of this mournful mansion from an earlier time…this vast and magnificent mansion…where hallways without end follow upon hallways…mute, deserted…enveloped in baroque embellishments…mahogany veneer, Venetian plaster, gold-leafed frames, Carrara marble…dark glass, obscure illustrations, Romanesque columns…

Then you see that the house is gone. It has been razed to the ground, nothing left. You realize that you have bought it anyway. You are using the site to construct a walkway, a winding paved path labeled like a game board. This walkway encompasses the old cement walks of the demolished house. The walkway will pass by the side of the old ruined church-turned-winery but it really goes nowhere; it just makes a loop. It occurs to you that what you have envisioned is a sort of park. And like a park it really should be open to the public. Free. So you must come up with a way to make money from services you provide to those who travel your Pathway."

"Let's see if we can get some news," Roy says as he reaches for the tuning knob.

"Don't touch it!" I yell, and Roy quickly puts both hands back on the wheel, sending the Caddy into a sickening weave toward the highway shoulder.

"-- the publication is similar to your existing weekly bulletin, but with a more modular design. You see on the cover that it says 'Baptist.' Someone explains that the newsletter was produced by two people from a Baptist church. 'This is just a test product for us,' they explain. 'However, we may decide to adopt it as our own.'

"You are on the Pathway again, writing your scripts. You compose an opening line: 'He heard the voices of angels.' Then you have a revelation. You revise it: 'He heard the voice of God.' Excited, you continue writing. 'But he knew not to talk about the voice. So he wrote of strange happenings, which he understood would be acceptable as fiction.' You realize you finally have the movie you should make. You see that you can include some short films you have already scripted. It can all be included in a structure that deals with the theme of hearing the voice of God. You even see a lobby card, a Medieval painting of a haloed Son of the Deity framed by parted clouds. You have finally seen the truth behind your dreams. And that is what will make the difference. You have heard the voice of God. This is the revelation that will make you a successful movie director. This is your destiny."

#

The astounding appearance of the aerial timepiece is big news at the Tarrant County Register. Executive Editor Libby Wright has called in all hands to produce a special end-of-time edition. I arrive at the Attitude Adjustment Bureau to find Guy Wint, the bureau chief, covering the biggest story of his life the same way he covers the smallest: Like a neurotic.

Guy is running from desk to desk, coffee cup in one hand and cigarette in the other, already micromanaging the various assignments he's handed out only minutes before. He is particularly neurotic this morning because he is simultaneously directing feeds to send downtown for the special edition and stories for a special section on Wednesday. Working title: "Crossroads to the Sky."

"All right, Mark, what you got for me?"

So I tell him about my Vision, my Incredible Revelation, about how I dreamed the clock in the sky and the radio transmission from the Deity.

"Give me three inches on the Circle L. I'll put it in with the rest of the feed."

"You don't get it," I say. "I'm telling you I saw it all in the past, in my dreams. Dreaming the Apocalypse. It is as if I have heard the voice of The Deity."

"The Deity?"

"I know it sounds insane, but there is no denying the oddity in the sky. Or that I dreamed it, a merger of fiction and reality."

Guy looks at me with obvious concern, and I don't blame him. I know I sound insane. But I can't stop myself. I am compelled to speak of strange happenings, of my Incredible Revelation, which comes spilling out in a tumble of uncontrollable words.

"When I awoke from the clock dream, I felt myself inundated with a feeling of nearly divine grace. It was almost as if I came from the Deity, a canary in a coal mine, first-line detector of brightness and vanity, depression as an entitlement, a civilization in which everybody is fraudulently performing instead of genuinely existing."

"Fraudulent?"

What am I saying? I should stop. This is abnormal for me. I am always one to speak rationally, to keep my nose to the grindstone and my mouth shut concerning strange happenings. I fear making a mistake, saying the wrong thing – failing to be a perfected being. Why do I persist with my story? I sound crazy, imperfect. But I cannot correct myself. I am in the grip of an Idea.

"We are a civilization that is all too battle-willing," I say, "violent, pubescent, gluttonous. We are dramatists without wit, intensity or thoughts, unspeaking in our muted blazes. And I'm the worst, the biggest dramatist of all."

"Oh no, Mark, I wouldn't call you dramatic."

"I have neglected the signs, the entire construction of images is assembled in my head. But no more. Now it's all coming out. It's into the world, an attempt to overcome the prearranged, the false experience imposed by the contemporary personality awareness that dooms us to a simulation of genuine life. What is happening in the world is nothing less than a message from the Deity, an insistence that we must escape our falseness and become the truth."

#

To Guy's credit, he doesn't cut me off or tell me I'm crazy. He waits until I'm done, then nods thoughtfully, pretending to mull it over. "Are you saying God made it happen? Or that you made it happen?"

"I don't know."

"You actually dreamed the clock, actually dreamed it up into the sky?"

"I don't know. Maybe I just dreamed what was going to happen."

"Like a prophet?"

"I've got a feeling it's tied to an alien abduction scene I experienced last night while onbeam –"

"Well there you are, Mark. You were in the Exogrid. It's just a hallucination."

"No, the clock is real. And so is the Muse Sound System."

"They could be false memories, implanted while you were onbeam."

I know he could be right. But I don't believe it.

"I have dreamed the Apocalypse," I insist. "I've been dreaming it since childhood. My vision. I remember one time in particular. I am standing with my parents on the front porch stoop of our house. I look out at our little town. The houses have been destroyed. All that remains of Duncanville are the brick chimneys, rising above the smoking ruins, monuments of blackened obelisks, fires of destruction burning red in broken hearths, the world of childhood is no more."

"Flash! You know, maybe we could sell this for P-1 as the Rapture. We should interview someone. Hey Ringo, go over to North Hills Mall, see if you can find a Christian."

Ringo shrugs. "And if there aren't any, maybe I could round up a Catholic."

Guy ignores the sarcasm. "Mark, as for seeing weird things while onbeam, yes, lots of people can relate to that. We'll catch it on the Monday follow-ups. Hey Jenny, how are you doing on that reaction from the soccer moms?"

The walls are bleeding again. Nazi paratroopers land outside the window. Tiny white eggs on the back of my hand hatch into hungry wolf spiders, which proceed to strip the flesh from my bones...

#

Do you see now why I abandoned journalism? It no longer functions.

I first recognized the absolute power of the movie metaphor in a particularly vivid dream – a drive-in movie dream.

In this vision, I arrive at a desolate - perhaps abandoned - shopping center where in recent times the owners have shown drive-in movies on the side of one of the buildings. A sort of guerrilla-style drive-in theater. But when I get there, the movies are no more. This was apparently the last drive-in theater in the world. I am sad, for this is surely the End of the Age. Then it occurs to me that I should start my own drive-in theater. I am sure I could make it work. But I realize this is not realistic for I have no start-up capital.

The 1950s drive-in image continues as two cars line up for a drag race. One is a real hot rod, a red Model A - a little deuce coupe, like one the Beach Boys might have sung about. The other racer is a black sedan, the same winged car I saw outside my grandparent's house in Fort Jesup.

So this is to be a race with death.

The two cars take off in a cloud of dust and gravel. The black car immediately abandons the race, peeling off to the right. The red coupe passes close to a parked car, loses control and flips over several times. It is a terrible accident. The car crumples up like a soft drink can and tumbles to a stop next to a building. I run to the crash scene to render assistance.

A man exits the wrecked car and runs towards me, apparently uninjured but understandably distraught.

"Is there anybody else in there?" I ask.

"My buddy!" he says, choking, almost in tears.

#

Overwhelmed by my own narcissism I slip away to the back room, a windowless alcove where we keep the coffee maker and a mini refrigerator. Guy's three-year-old daughter is sitting in the middle of the cardboard honor snack tray, grazing on dishonorably consumed bags of Fritos and Butterfingers under the less-than-watchful eye of Reece Sloan, the bureau's editorial assistant/receptionist.

"In the last five minutes, Charity's destroyed about $10 worth of chips and candy bars," he complains. "No wonder the honor snack guy always says we've shorted him. I myself paid him $5 out of my own pocket last week."

"Why didn't you stop her?"

"Because I'm not the baby sitter. I have a degree in journalism, something Guy can never seem to remember."

I nod back toward the newsroom.

"He been like this long?"

"I found him this morning in the Bennigan's parking lot, trying to pick up a waitress. He said he was doing a story about prostitution in the suburbs."

"I thought he was on the wagon."

"Does he look like he's on the wagon? He told me yesterday he'd maxed out all of his credit cards buying coch. And Linda said one more time and she'd leave him."

"And she'll make him keep Charity, too, no doubt."

"Scary. Dan and I went over there to pick him up last week, while his car was in the shop. There was a dirty diaper in the middle of the living room floor."

I want to tell Reece about my vision, but our conversation is disrupted by an explosion in the parking lot.

We rush into the hallway and see the smoke and fire through the plate glass store front. An iron gray plume is rising from a hole in the blacktop.

Customers from the Olin Mills -- kids and moms and dads in their Sunday best -- are already gathering at the jagged lip of a smoking crater. But no reporters, a situation Guy finds untenable.

"Say, did anyone notice there is a newsworthy explosion in the parking lot?" he asks the newsroom.

"We noticed," says Chandler, a former downtown Metro reporter reassigned for attitude adjustment. "But that's breaking news."

"Does that not interest you?"

"Of course, but that's a downtown story. Front page. I just cover bureau life. Back page. For instance, I'm busy right now producing 12 to 15 inches about a man who has trained his pet parrot to take early morning joy rides on the roof of a remote control police car."

"I've just about had enough of the attitude this morning."

"Why? After all, this is the attitude adjustment bureau."

"I hate that nickname."

"And the parrot sings, too. 'Sunrise can't be sunrise, short of the Dallas Sunrise Bulletin.' It's a catchy jingle."

"Enough!"

#

We gather around the smoking crater. A red sports car wheels into the parking lot. It's Kyle Coburn, assistant managing editor for suburban bureaus. He has come all the way from downtown, presumably to make sure Guy's neurotic enthusiasm and energy actually translate into useable copy. He mills about with us, hands shoved in his pockets, peering down into the fire and brimstone.

"What's this about?" he asks.

I also look over the lip of the flaming crater. A breeze momentarily clears away the smoke, revealing an almost forgotten dream from junior high.

I launch a homemade rocket, but it is not stable. My creation falls to earth in flames, resembling a fireplace log wrapped in burning newspaper. This occurs on a hill behind my house. There should be no hill here, only a vacant field. Yet there it is. And over the top comes a platoon of soldiers, ready to take the hill. They are streaming over it, engaged in battle. Explosions! Gun fire! War! I can hardly believe it. All this initiated by the crash of my harmless homemade rocket.

#

"Looks like a bomb to me," says Chandler, who's decided to check out the scene after all.

Guy shoves up behind me, almost knocking me into the flaming pit. "Maybe it's a piece of space junk. Wow, what a story! Ringo, I want you to get over to North Hills Mall, get some reaction from the shoppers."

"I thought I was supposed to look for Christians."

"Do both. Kill two birds with one stone. And we need someone to go up to the Fast Lane. Mark?"

"You don't have a clue about what's going on here, do you?" I ask. "This is the conclusion of time. I've seen all of this before, in my dreams."

"Eh, what's that?" Kyle asks, cocking an ear toward me.

"It's what I've been trying to tell Guy. This shouldn't be real. And yet it is. Somehow my dreams are being transmitted into strange happenings, into reality. The soldiers will be here any moment. We should get inside."

"This is great," Kyle declares. He turns to Guy. "What do you think about a first-person conclusion of time feature?"

Guy nods with great enthusiasm. "We could illustrate with publicity stills from 'The Abandoned Ones,'" he suggests, "maybe the scene of the abortionists, Democrats and Catholics lining up to get 666 tattooed on their foreheads."

"I'm seeing a definite first-person piece," Kyle says. "We'll headline it 'Crazed Dreams: Phantasms of a Psychotic Son.' Mark, have you ever been treated for a mental illness?"

"What?"

"Ha ha, just kidding. But it would make it better."

"Yes, I see it," Guy says. "A whole spectral special section with creative interpretations of the clock. We'll call it 'A Clock in the Air.' "

"Yes, the title of a significant book," Kyle remarks. "In fact, Libby has already decided we'll be distributing a free copy to each member of the news staff."

"And for art we could do a picture of a man in bed with a clock in the sky outside his window."

"But we need a good hook, one filled with personal pathos. Mark, didn't you have a beautiful, talented girlfriend with a bright future who died a tragic and senseless death?"

"Not me," I say. "You have me confused with one of your downtown writers. Ty Maial. I believe he won an award for that one."

"I could have sworn that was you."

"I don't win awards."

"Don't be so defensive," Guy says. "There's no rule that says the Register can't have more than one reporter with a beautiful, dead girlfriend."

"Or maybe," Kyle adds, "you could befriend a spunky, old homeless person, then one morning find him frozen by the side of the road in the rain, his faithful dog by his side."

Before I can explain that he is still thinking of Ty (who got an award for that story, too), the soldiers begin streaming over the hill.

"It's the Sunrise Bulletin," Guy says. "Fall back to the bureau!"

#

Machine gun fire strafes the front of the strip center, showering the sidewalk in white Venetian plaster and plate glass. Guy is the first inside, huddled behind a wall of burlap sand bags that has suddenly appeared in the middle of the newsroom. He hands each of us a green Army helmet and an AK-47.

"You know, Guy," Kyle says, "I always knew someday I'd win a Pulitzer. I just didn't expect it to happen so soon."

"Don't you think this is all a little odd?" I ask. "Don't you see something missing from this picture?"

"Right you are," Kyle says. "We should design a bureau flag."

Another round of gunfire tears into the ceiling tiles, raining down white dust and broken florescent lighting. Kyle taps Guy on the arm. "You know, these special effects would make a nice photo essay in the Crossroads of Time section."

"You mean Crossroads in the Air," Guy says.

"But they're really shooting at us," I say. "With real bullets."

"Don't be frightened, this is normal," Kyle remarks. "You've never been through a newspaper war before."

"A newspaper war? We don't have any competition, at least not financial. We've got the 30 percent government subsidy."

Another round of gunfire into the ceiling tiles coats us in a fine white dust.

"Don't be naïve," Kyle says. "It's not like we're a family farm."

"Why do you all say that? It's exactly the same. The program is even administered by the U.S. Department of Agriculture."

"Don't worry," Guy says, "the Sunrise Bullshit will never take this bureau."

Then he turns to me, and I realize his face had changed. His jaw had widened and a long scar stretches across his right cheek. He has become Talking G.I. Joe.

"Enemy planes, hit the dirt!" Guy commands in a scratchy, mechanical tone, a giant pull string dangling from his larynx. "They been playing hit and run with us all over the eastern front, trying to establish a beachhead in the Mid-Cities, maybe Arlington. But we're going to stop them - right here, right now. We're going to kick them in the craw."

Then he suddenly rises to his feet and removes his helmet.

"Wait, what am I doing?" he asks. "I almost forgot about the certificates of achievement."

#

His face again returned to normalcy, Guy brings us all back to his office. He has us arrange the chairs in three rows, like a classroom. He opens his desk drawer and pulled out a stack of certificates.

"What's this for, Guy?" asks Bessie, the grandmotherly writer of the police blotter. This is Bessie's first newspaper job out of journalism school, which she finished last year at age 65.

"OK, picture this. It's a Sunday, almost noon. You realize you have a math test on Tuesday for a class in which you have done no work."

"I'm terrible at math," Chandler says.

"Of course, you're all terrible at math. That's why you're newspaper reporters."

That gets a good laugh.

"But it occurs to you that you still have time to cram on Sunday afternoon and ready yourself for the test. And this strategy must have worked. For the next thing you know, you are gathering in my office - I mean, your classroom - to receive your honors."

A round of applause briefly overshadows the gunfire.

This too is one of my dreams. But it is hard to focus because I know I am to be one of the first to receive this award. This is s a problem because I am no longer wearing a shirt.

How did this occur? All I know is this is an exact replay of my dream.

While Guy flips through the certificates, Bessie regales the group with a sort of acceptance speech: the tale of her first police story.

"So anyway, the policemen is taking her statement and it doesn't sound right to him. He says `uh, so what, you're just sleeping with this guy?' And she says, 'yeah, I guess,' or something. And the cop says `well, you sleeping with any other guys?' And the girl says `oh, only six or seven?' And he says, "well, what are you, a whore?'"

We are amazed to hear the grandmotherly Bessie utter the word "whore," so amazed in fact that no one appears to notice that I am shirtless. Still, it is only a matter of time. What to do? I try to think of some way to slip out unnoticed. But why? It seems I am holding a sweaty shirt with an undershirt inside it. The outer shirt is too filthy to put on, but for some reason I decide the undershirt will be acceptable. So as Guy called out the names of the certificate winners, I hastily struggle back into the undershirt.

"And you wouldn't believe it," Bessie continues, "but the officer wrote it down just like that, as straightforward as could be. He wrote: `I asked her if she was a whore, and the complainant called me a bastard and starting crying. Then we left the residence.' He wrote it just like that. So I wrote it just like that, I thought that's what I was supposed to do. It was an official police report. And then again, right in the middle of the newsroom, Owen said out loud `Bessie, I thought you were such a nice lady when I hired you, but I guess I was wrong. You are a potty mouth.'"

Everyone laughs, and Bessie smiles.

"Well, I was just mortified. I couldn't imagine why he was saying such a thing to me. I said 'Owen, what are you talking about?' I couldn't imagine what he meant. Then he told me" -- she started to laugh, but stifled herself -- ``he said `This is a family paper, Bessie. We can't have all this potty talk.'"

"Owen was pretty funny," Chandler agrees.

``I hated it when they sent him to the Austin bureau," Bessie says. "I know it was a good career move for him, but I really miss him."

#

The certificate is very nice. I've got it hanging inside, over my dresser. It's real sheepskin, stamped with a 14k gold foil seal. I don't know where it came from. I don't specifically remember dreaming of being naked in a math class; however, I'm told naked dreams are rather common. My therapists and dental psychiatrists attributed the incident to unresolved childhood issues, perhaps a sense of inferiority. This is common in Dream Anxiety Disorder.

What's that? Why yes, it is a real disorder. I am a genuine neurotic. I diagnosed myself after a trip to the Strangers Rest Public Library, where I discovered my troubled self in a decrepit copy of the American Psychiatric Association's "Diagnostic and Statistical Manual of Mental Disorders." (Apparently I am not the only person in Strangers Rest who is engaging in do-it-yourself psychoanalysis.)

Features of Dream Anxiety Disorder (aka Nightmare Disorder) include:

- Frequent association with artistic ability.
- Personality patterns of distrustfulness, alienation, estrangement and over-sensitivity.
- Schizoid or borderline personality traits.

Does that not sound like me? By no means is Dream Anxiety Disorder my only mental condition, either. Turns out I have various features from eight to 10 other recognized psychiatric conditions. I don't have enough features in any one disorder to meet the criteria for a full diagnosis. But if you put them all together they add up to a whole new condition, which I call Post-Modern Prophet Disorder (aka "Leach's Syndrome"). I will be sending the American Psychiatric Association a letter requesting that this newly identified illness be added to the next edition of the DSM.

#

DIAGNOSTIC CRITERIA FOR POST MODERN PROPHET DISORDER

A. Characteristic symptoms: Four (or more) of the following, each present for a significant portion of time during a 1-month period (or less if successfully treated or the world comes to an end):

- Detachment from subject's own mental processes or body, as if an outside observer.
- Feeling like an automaton or as if in a dream.
- Restlessness, vigilance and scanning.
- Feeling keyed up, on edge.

- Exaggerated startle response.
- Difficulty concentrating or "mind going blank" because of anxiety.
- Irritability.
- Psychomotor agitation expressed in pacing or as an inability to sit still.
- Recurrent thoughts of death, often accompanied by the belief that subject or others would be better off dead.
- Themes of personal inadequacy, guilt, deserved punishment and death.
- Feelings of worthlessness or excessive or inappropriate guilt, which may be delusional.
- Diminished ability to think or indecisiveness.

B. Obsessional dysfunction: For a significant portion of the time since the onset of the disturbance, experiences obsessions which are recurrent and include persistent ideas, thoughts, impulses or images that are intrusive and senseless (ex: having recurring blasphemous thoughts) and subject attempts to ignore or suppress with another thought or action. These obsessions are a product of subject's own mind and are not related to guilty thoughts in the presence of a major depression.

C. Depressive Episode: Accompanied by low energy and fatigue, low self-esteem, poor concentration and feelings of hopelessness.

D. Dream-based alien dysfunction: Dreams of being a robot or an extraterrestrial or dead. (Example, a dream by Mark Leach from the night of June 5/6, 2005: I am renting a house, which I share with a roommate. On my way to work, crossing the Hulen Street bridge. Heavy fog. I just make out cars sliding, colliding ahead. I put on the brakes, but I can't see anything. I begin honking the horn so other cars will know I am here. Then all goes white, lost in total fog. Next I find myself inexplicably standing outside the garage of my rented house. I punch in the access code, and the automatic garage door rises. My roommate's car is here, but not mine. Inside the house, a party is under way. Some of my relatives are here. So are some friends. Someone – maybe my roommate – explains what has occurred: I am actually a carbon copy of the original Mark Leach, who was killed on the bridge in the fog. I don't feel like a copy; however, that is because I have all of the memories of the original. I am an exact copy. Then my roommate and I look outside. We realize somehow that all of the cars are gone now. A world without cars. Could this be a world of carbon copies, a world without original people? So we walk outside, look at the next door neighbor's home. They have a swimming pool, but it's in the front yard. And on the front walk next to the pool is a three-wheeled, robotic pool cleaner. This is a troubling sight, for I see the robot as part of a vast conspiracy to eliminate the original people of the world and replace them with carbon copies. I persuade my roommate to help me flip this robot onto its head. We run away, and I am laughing. Even when I see that the homeowners are watching me through the picture window, I am still laughing. But my roommate doesn't find it so funny. He tells me this is bad. We'll have to pay for the damages.)

E. Anxiety: Accompanied by irritability, brooding or obsessive rumination.

F. Persecutory delusions: Accompanied by sense of a moral transgression or some personal inadequacy.

G. Flight of ideas: Accompanied by subjective experience that thoughts are racing.

H. Distractibility: Attention is too easily drawn to unimportant or irrelevant external stimuli.

I. Lability: Rapid shifts to anger or depression.

#

The shooting continues. Guy attempts to rally the staff, but they are busy packing themselves into the break room. Bessie is baking a batch of chocolate chip cookies in the microwave.

I quietly slip out the back door, where I find Cowboy Roy waiting in the Bevomobile, the motor running.

"Can we get out of here now?" he asks. "Those reporters are crazy. Don't they know they're being shot at? With real bullets?"

"Let's go," I say. "I'll fill you in after we're out of range."

Roy drives cautiously down the alley, the sound of gunfire echoing all around us. I hear a siren coming from the freeway, and I turn around just in time to see a fire truck fly by. Roy is about to ease the Bevomobile onto Bedford-Euless Road when Guy comes running around the front corner of the shopping center.

"Go!" I shout, but Guy is too fast. He throws himself over the trunk, sliding into a heap in the back seat.

"Follow that fire engine," he commands. "That's a story in progress."

"Chasing fire trucks is against the law," I say, but Roy is already caught up in the moment. He guns the old V-8, aiming the longhorn-ornamented hood for the freeway on-ramp. I look back in time to see the reporters streaming outside to enjoy a parking lot garden party (apparently the inter-newspaper shooting is over). Bessie is passing around a plate of cookies.

"Ah, road trip," Guy says. "Good times. We should pick up some beer on the way out of town. Some other stuff, too. I know a guy who can help us score some Piney Woods spore and -- "

"You know, it does feel like we are on a trip to a faraway land," Roy says, "maybe Africa or South America. Reminds me of the night sea journey in my war movie, 'Shores of Tripoli.'"

"We'll have to travel across the ocean by boat," Guy says.

That assumes we even make it to the city limits. It is proving to be all Roy can manage to navigate the highway south toward downtown Fort Worth. He straddles two lanes as we approach a trailer that bears a rocket-shaped craft resembling the Blue Flame rocket car.

"I know what this is," Guy tells us. "This is a mini submarine, which Princess Diane is going to use -- or used. Isn't she dead?"

I can't remember, either.

"Anyway, I do know it was designed so she could anonymously travel the oceans," he says. "We must be heading in the right direction."

#

Here's one way the world ends: You are part of a group on a river tour, traveling in canoes. You are nearing the destination. The slow moving river flows through a stone canyon which centuries ago had been carved into a city. It is incredible, the ruins of an ancient civilization. On the right you see a set of steps lined with large pots -- perhaps waist height -- and it's all carved from the stone walls of the canyon. Your sons are with you, so you direct their attention to this incredible site. So perfect, it reminds you of the way Disney would build a set of ruins. Then on the left you see a flat area, apparently a stage. At the rear of this stage is a stand of palm trees and in the trees is a flock of red, tropical birds. There are no people yet, and you are a bit apprehensive. Will the locals be friendly?

You spot a man and see that he is coming out of a building. He is wearing a pith helmet and long khaki shorts, like a British explorer. As you approach him, you see other people and realize this is an archeological camp and the man is a scientist. You arrive with your group at the camp, and you see that the man and his wife run it. Both are archeologists. You are part of a group of three people. You are a journalist, along to document the expedition. But when it comes time for introductions, the woman who leads your group introduces you as a scientist, too. So you are a combination scientist/writer.

A group of about 10 children come rushing in, and you smile and say hi. You realize at this point that your sons and wife are still back in Strangers Rest, a half a world away. It is evening as you and the group enter the camp's main building, where you hold a one-page handout on the camp or the expedition – you're not sure which. You find a pencil and begin to write a letter home on the back of the paper. You know there's not much to say yet, but you decide to let Allison know you arrived safely and what happened on the journey.

The next morning, you sit outside in an open-air Jeep and look at the big, azure sky. It will be a bright and sunny day. You realize it will be a hot day, too. In fact, Jack Bryson walks up to the Jeep and tells you the temperature will probably rise 20 degrees in the course of the day.

"It reminds me of Texas," you comment.

You will need sun block and a hat. But you forgot to pack those items. And you forgot to bring any cash. You have your credit cards, but not a single dollar. A policeman approaches, outfitted in khaki shirt and shorts like you'd see on a policeman in South Africa, Australia or some other place with British colonial influences.

"No problem, sir," he assures you in an official-sounding accent. "You can purchase anything you need in the town."

You look up the road and, sure enough, there is a town. The camp is just one of many buildings. Someone from the camp drives you to the end of a row of buildings that lines one side of the street. On the return trip, you look in the storefronts, but you don't go in because you haven't resolved the money issue. You notice that one business -- a donut shop, perhaps -- has a Visa sticker on the window. Perhaps you can get money here, then buy your supplies.

You stop again at the camp, the situation still unresolved. Children are playing. You see your bag on the ground. One of the children is holding a sort of mummified snake with a small, living snake inside. The little snake is slithering around, making it appear that the boy is holding a mass of living reptiles. Then you notice a snake in your bag. It is black with tiny white spots or dots. You kick at it, trying to get it to leave. But somehow you are just filling the bag with sand, dry desert sand. You almost bury it. After you are sure the snake is gone, you reach into the sand and pull out a pad of paper. A boy shoves you from behind and laughs. You are a bit scared, still nervous and worried about the snake. But you don't want him to know this. So you tell the boy he shouldn't push you from behind.

"You'll hurt my back," you warn him.

He says he is sorry.

#

Guy and Kyle do not choose to let me tell our readership of this Vision, my Incredible Revelation. Indeed, they determine that not even my three to five inches is required.

"You should go home," Guy tells me. "Go home and get some rest."

"But you saw it," I protest. "You saw Princess Di's submarine."

"A submarine on a trailer on the highway. Interesting, but hardly proof of the conclusion of time."

"And what about the river trip?"

"Mark, we're doing you a favor," Kyle says. "We're your friends. We know what you're going through. I myself see a dental psychiatrist every Wednesday and brush with Mentine toothpaste every day."

"Me too," Guy says. "My therapist says they should just pump Skinalicious9 straight into the water supply. When I don't get it, I start to receive mind messages from the Fourth Hardness."

"Me too. After a few days, my brain is just riddled with CGODMs."

"What are you two talking about?" I ask.

"CGODMs," Kyle says. "Cubical Genetic Observation and Direction Machines. They're little cubes about two millimeters in diameter."

"They are extraterrestrial-enhanced neural CPUs implanted into your brain by autonomous nanobots," Guy adds. "They're driven by a miniature positioning current that manages or imitates the actions inside a sentient neural network with miniature communicators that reproduce mind procedures or engendering prototypes."

"I didn't realize you were part of the Global Airtime Cabal, too."

"Three years now. I'm up to Dark Echelon clearance. How about you?"

"No, I'm still new to the Society of the Purple Sunset."

Arrg. The Society of the Purple Sunset is an annoying onbeam role-playing game, sort of a Prisons & Serpents meets Celebrity Hike. The Sunsetters, as they like to call themselves, discuss the intricacies of their little fictional universe ad nausea, sometimes for hours. They even have conventions where they dress up like their favorite game characters. Ever since Libby started playing (she selected for herself the role of High Priestess, of course), "Doing the Sunset" has become the latest stylish pursuit among the editors at the Register.

Suddenly Kyle remembers I am still here and looks my way. "You see, Mark, the Global Airtime Cabal got it all started in 1947. That's when they used the Corpus Christi Project to launch the first Vision-O-Sonde, a tiny pale sphere connected to a weather balloon. It is an extremely efficient converter of psychic energy into ethericom matter."

"And the worst is FEM," Guy adds. "Fatal Ethericom Matter, which threatens life at the 200 to 500 MHz frequencies."

"Brain management. The scientists prefer to call it 'disposition modification,' but unadulterated brain management is really what these crazed ideologues are up to."

"Did they ever put you in the brain-changing stool?"

"Oh man, it was terrible. The pre-ecstasy condition was pleasant enough, but the programming was unendurable."

"They've sent a lot of poor kids down that subway. They simply burned up, and the Wise Ones watched it all on their cathode ray tubes. Imagine it: A functioning time subway of death."

"I heard about this one guy, they put him in the stool and told him to think about Godzilla. And when the subway doors slid open out stepped this sort of psychic beast --"

"The Fiend of the Unconscious."

"Yes. I heard everyone who was onbeam at the time went into a raging terror. The way I heard it they immediately switched off the transducer, but not before the creature ate several people and pieces of computer hardware."

"You heard it exactly right. I saw it all."

"You were onbeam that day?"

"It happened just after I became a Journeyman. When I came onbeam, the time whirlpool was already bolted on to the 1942 test. It created a self-sustaining ethericom tetrahedron, exactly as posited by Dr. Adolfo Morel in his famous time equations, and that's how the monster formed. They actually had to time shift back to the mothballed U.S.S. Ethan Allen Hitchcock, which was already flooded with FEM, and switch off the main reactor. A lot of people thought they went too far on that one."

"So, uh – you guys think you're maybe being controlled by the Secret Government or something?" I ask. I try to sound genuine, but Kyle and Guy are not fooled. Apparently they had momentarily forgotten about me, for now they look upon me with pained expressions reeking of condescension for the non-playing nonbeliever.

"Go home," Guy repeats. "Drink some whiskey, pop some pills. Do whatever you have to do."

Kyle nods. "Get unconscious."

#

Get unconscious. For me, that is not a relaxing state. Journeying through the Land of the Dead is exhausting work. Consider this dialogue between two famous movie reviewers, a bit of tainted celluloid that The Stranger unveiled for me as part of his career retrospective at the Armageddon Drive-in.

#

Charlie: Enough anal probing. Now let's try sci-fi Roman chariot racing! Yea! Young idea. The Deity may communicate with man through ancient dreams.

Elmo: Mark Leach as the Christ? Interesting concept, but it goes bad so quickly.

Charlie: Let's roll the clip.

#

The husband popped his head out of the dark pantry and asked of his wife "where's the bread?"

"There is no bread," she replied. "We have no money for bread."

"But how can that be? Look around us. Wealth everywhere. A leather sofa here, a swimming pool there, berber carpet everywhere. What have you done with the bread?"

"You don't make enough money to allow me to live in the style to which I deserve to become accustomed. So how can you expect me to buy bread?"

"I'll starve if you don't give me some bread."

"Husbands do not live by bread alone," she said. Then she retrieved a knife from the cupboard and motioned for her husband to place his hand on a scarred wooden cutting board.

"Are you crazy?" he asked. "It'll hurt!"

"Crybaby."

Shrugging, the husband relented and she cut off his right hand.

"Why, that didn't hurt at all," the husband said. "Like cutting your hair or finger nails."

"That's because you are already dead," she explained, then handed him his severed hand on an orange Fiesta platter. "Eat this."

"Mmmm, that's good cadaver," he said.

"Yes, and you should try the wine," The wife hoisted a small glass of red covertly retrieved from the oozing stump of her husband's wrist. "A rather disappointing rioja with delusions of mystical revelations."

"Now you've gone too far," the husband roared. "There's no call for religious persecution. Why do you want to make me suffer?"

"Because it is only through suffering that we can find our redemption." Then she dug out a set of kebob skewers from the back of a drawer and nailed her husband to the pantry door, bread crumbs and wine spilling from his stigmata.

Over the husband's head, the wife tacked a recipe card upon which she'd written "King of the Losers, signed wife." She dotted the " i" in wife with a smiley-faced heart.

#

Elmo: Yes, it comes off somehow feeling true. A touching vision, angels listening to the words, lost in warm globs of ectoplasm. The knowledge of that idea that The Deity would say –

Charlie: Well, let's think about this. A talking deity? Not necessarily funny. Such a film might not sell.

Elmo: Instead, perhaps we should consider banjos, plotting murder, enjoying sodomy. Buttered DNA delivery organs inserted into naughty places.

Charlie: Now that's funny.

Elmo: Those were the desires of Mark in his youth. We know from The Stranger's movies that he's always liked young girl toes dipped in wet sexuality.

#

The red diode flashes on the answering machine. I hit the play button; it is Jack.

"What the fuck. Ha ha. I called your work. That old biddy grandma answered. She said 'oh Mark? He went home. He wasn't feeling well.' I told her 'yeah, 'cause he's on chocolate mysticism.' Ha ha. She can suck my -- sorry, that was really inappropriate. Just kidding. I'm not really like this, you know that. You bring it out in me. You make me this way. My freshman year in college I was going to be a preacher. ORU, 900-foot Jesus. Talk about being well hung. Ha ha. Ah no, I'm sorry. I didn't mean it. Look, man -- get some rest. Get yourself straight. Then call me. Tonight we let the sleek dog run."

Next, a transmission from the superego.

"Mark, this is your mother. I just wanted to see if you want to come over for dinner tonight. With Allison and the boys gone, you probably don't feel like fixing something just for yourself. You can't eat pizza every night, you know. I've laid a roast out to thaw, but your father and I can't eat it all by ourselves. You can bring your clothes over and spend the night. Or you can stay the whole time they're gone. It'll be like a slumber party. So I'll talk to you later."

The other two messages are from Allison. For my convenience, she'd left the phone number for the beach house on a pad next to the phone.

"Where've you been?" she asks. "I've been calling since last night."

"I went out with Jack," I lie.

"Figures. Did you get any sleep?"

"Not till this afternoon. I had to go into work to cover the clock story. Could you see it there?"

"Of course not. I'm here with my parents."

I want to tell her about my Incredible Revelation, about everything that had been happening. But I hear a commotion in the background, one of our sons demanding ice cream.

"I told you it's too late for that," Allison says. "Go to bed now!"

"What's happening?"

"It's my family. They keep doing all these great things for the boys, giving them everything they want. But I'm the one who has to be the bad guy. I have to make them go to bed, I'm the one who has to be the bad one after everyone spoils them."

She lays down the phone, and I hear footsteps and crying. "I told you to go to bed," she says. "I'm so sick of this. Why can't anyone help me out here?"

I wait a moment, and she returns to the phone.

"I've got to go," she says. "Call me later."

"OK, I'll call you in the morning."

But she doesn't hear me. "Go to bed!"

The line goes dead.

#

No sign of The Deity in that apocalypse. Perhaps my trouble is that I don't pray anymore. It isn't that I don't believe in The Deity. Rather, it's just that praying to Him no longer seems relevant. Why? I have constructed a possible answer by paraphrasing Walker Percy:

The central query is not does the Death and Resurrection remain germane, but rather this – Is the sentient being experiencing a stormy reorganization of its awareness which does not currently permit it to seize understanding of the Death and Resurrection?

Pretty.

But what is the nature of this reorganization? The answer comes in the form of a voice of dire warning from the kitchen. "Don't answer it! It's him! Call the police!"

This is Allison's voice. But it can't be her; she is still in Maine. And then through the front door, I see a figure silhouetted in the oval of etched glass. I know this person. I know him all too well.

The Stranger has arrived.

Here's one way the world ends: Inside my house at night.

Allison warns of a threatening stranger who has visited recently and will return.

"We must beware," she says.

There is a knock at the door.

"Don't answer it!" she says. "It's him! Call the police!"

I go to the door, look out the window. But there is no danger. Just an old man in a thick cable knit cardigan sweater, cleaning a red potato. The man is stoop-shouldered and white-haired. I let him in.

We talk a bit, I'm not sure about what. Soon dawns on me: He is me. Did my wife know his identity? Yes, he had visited once before, but I was not home.

So this old man is the threatening stranger. Why does she fear him?

"How did you come to be in this peculiar situation?" I ask him. "How did it happen?"

Turns out there was some sort of court action and a mental/emotional breakdown. He – "I" -- had held in his emotions too long, trying to look normal at home and at work.

But now this future version of me has lost everything. He has no wife and only a menial job. Still, I sense that people might be able to like him. At least I like him.

The man says is going to leave now. He has to get back to his job. My wife is ecstatic. But I don't want him to go.

"No, you can't leave. We were meant to be together. We are one."

The man's boss shows up, wanting him back at work in the restaurant kitchen. He wants him to fix those potatoes.

"No, we quit," I say.

The old me can't believe I just quit on his behalf.

"What can we do? To get a decent job, we need a doctorate."

I know he is just feeling a little pessimistic. So I say "OK, so we'll get a doctorate together."

Again, I tell the boss that he is quitting. He fills out a form, presumably for the old man's final paycheck. All the while he keeps one eye on us. I am very excited about this development.

"We're going to be the world's first two bodied man," I tell my other, older half.

"But what about women?" he asks. "We'll never get one."

I look at this gentle man and smile.

"Are you kidding? They're going to love us."

#

"They hate us! Hurry, let me in! They're right on my heels!"

The Stranger bolts past me, running through the den toward the kitchen, flipping off lights as he goes, plunging the house into the protective anonymity of night.

"So they can't see us," he explains.

I stand bewildered in the open doorway, looking out toward the street where he's parked his car - a red hot rod, the Beach Boy's little deuce coupe. And something else.

The street light is out, a first for our perfectly functioning neighborhood. But there is enough of a moon that I can see it, gliding slowly past like a giant bat. It is the pursuer – the black sedan, the dreamed car of death.

"For goodness sake, shut the door," he hisses. "They have night vision scopes."

"I've seen that car before," I say.

"Of course you've seen it before. It's registered to Ozona International, part of their black op's street theater troupe, the guerrilla drive-in movies. Can you please shut the door?"

#

"They've been blocking me for weeks," he continues, "as I walk or drive about."

"The street theater troupe?" I ask.

"The perps, the disinfo agents. These incidents have been increasing dramatically, several every day, either someone slipping ahead of me at the ATM or the supermarket checkout or parking in unanticipated places in parking lots."

He fills a green glass with chilled water from a lighted recess in the refrigerator door, hand encased in an emerald glow. Very Hitchcock-esque.

"It's not normal interactions," he explains. "I'm talking about incidents that occur far more often than one would attribute to mere chance. Imagine it: cars speeding up to stop signs just ahead of you, then braking part way into the intersection. And meanwhile, you find other cars cooperating in the theatrical attack, blocking your progress, particularly in shopping malls. That's their favorite place. Oh yes, they're definitely after me."

He goes back to the front door and cautiously stares out the oval of etched glass.

"Mind control," he continues. "I'm one of their unwilling test subjects. It started in the 1950s with MKULTRA, the CIA's behavior modification program. That was understandably limited in scope. But now they're using onbeam avenues, taking it worldwide. Random individuals are secretly chosen for covert behavior, thought and perception control via onbeam avenues and other advanced technologies."

"I don't know what you're talking about."

"They're mostly unknown to the average scientist who isn't part of the New World Order's mind control conspiracy. These technologies can't be repeated, prevented or even revealed using current market technologies. Onbeam systems have been infiltrated with covert backdoor access points, where the black ops agents use Skinalicious9 to gain entrance to the brain's unconscious processing centers. Those of us who are victims of this mind control have found our attempts to fight the conspiracy regularly thwarted by technology that can penetrate EM and acoustic shielding, move objects at a distance, pull legs out from under people at a distance, propel a moving car sideways, make objects disappear and reappear in a new location, apply enough force to a building that it will make snapping noises, especially at night as you are just falling asleep, make people burp or pass gas when they least expect it, usually in public places around a lot of people, cause consumer appliances to fail shortly after the expiration of the warranty and give people sunburns on cloudy days."

"Well, the sunburn's not so strange. That's happened to me plenty of times. And the rest could be coincidences."

He stares at me, a glint of brimstone in his eyes.

"This isn't about normal events."

"OK."

"It's like when you see a natural paranormal effect, but it happens in circumstances in which the effect can only be explained as possessing a deliberate signature of precise causal intent. I've seen full levitation, possibly utilizing anti-gravity propulsion devices discovered on UFOs studied in Area 51. I mean, that much is real. You've seen it in the sky, the clock – the divine timepiece ticking away through the day and well into the dark, still night, the place where we begin our new lives of radiance – the lives we dream for ourselves after the End of the World."

"What?"

"But it's the onbeam mind control that's the most difficult to fight. Psychotronic manipulation, silent sound, sub-vocalized speech, direct skull transmissions, neuro-electromagnetic ruination - all variations on a theme of utilizing remote induction pain and creating artificial mental disorders. And they do it in a way that to a disinterested party it appears that the victim is imagining things. It's all part of the design to harass the experimental subject."

"But why you? Why experiment on you?"

"They want my dreams, of course. Our dreams. Hook us up to the viral DNA dream phone, call anytime it suits their purpose. Your time will come, young Mark. And when it does, try explaining it to people you know and see how many believe it is intentional. 'Oh, listen to that Mark go on,' they'll say. 'He has lots to say. And yet, no answers to our questions. At least no satisfying, rational answers.' It soon becomes clear to them that you don't have a clue as to why you are here. You claim no insights into the true nature of the strange happenings afoot in the waking world. Clearly, there is no point in questioning you about real world events. That's what you're thinking, right?"

"I didn't say that."

"Surely you and I could not be the two-bodied man of the Vision. No, I am merely a creation of nocturnal imagination, a visitor from the Land of the Dead."

And that's when he spots the cameraman.

"Cut!" The Stranger flips on the kitchen light and opens the back door, beckoning the man into the light.

"That camera's got a 3,000 to 1 digital telescopic zoom," The Stranger says, "and yet you still find it necessary to invade the Cinematic Reality Zone in order to get the shot. Why is that?"

A half dozen crew members slowly emerge from the shadows, trailing thick black cables, portable lights, reflective panels and microphones on the end of long aluminum poles. They gather in the kitchen as the cameraman absently fiddles with the black rubber lens hood I'd just seen pressed against the window over the sink. "Depth of field was all wrong," he explains. "He was going two dimensional again."

"It's understandable," The Stranger says. "Cinematic technology can't be expected to always keep up with the full depth of visionary transformation."

"You're making a movie about me?"

"Not you – us. The two-bodied man. Working title: 'Strangers Rest.'" The Stranger retrieves a small radio from his pocket. He extends the antennae and puts his mouth to the speaker.

"OK everybody, it's a wrap," he says. "Nice work. Go back to the church, get some sleep. We'll meet in the sanctuary at oh six hundred for the rushes."

#

The Stranger doesn't look much like the old man in my dream.

No cardigan sweater, no red potato. He's not stoop-shouldered or white-haired, either. This Stranger has arrived in my waking world life on the red eye flight from the soulless cool terrain of Burial Chamber, Calif., looking young and hip in Spanish wraparound sunglasses and vintage '50s Hawaiian shirt with a vaguely obscene hula dancer print. He clearly hasn't been peeling potatoes or doing any other restaurant work, either. His nails are freshly manicured, quite the contrast to my own ragged cuticles and split nails. (When did I start letting myself go like this?)

His head is closely shaved, so I cannot ascertain if he is balding or going gray. Interesting, this uncertainty actually makes him look young and vibrant – younger and more vibrant than me. Even his face seems more youthful than mine, more robust and tan. It is as if I am the old man. I am The Stranger, and The Stranger is me.

"You told your editors of your incredible revelation?" he asks.

I nod. "They didn't even want a three-inch feed."

"It is because they are among the Comatose Ones. By tomorrow, the Clock in the Air will just be another weather phenomenon, entertaining but not meaningful."

"So I should just drop it?"

"Not at all. Write of strange happenings, of course. That is your destiny."

"My destiny?"

"And make them as strange as possible. Search and replace can be an excellent tool. Consider the aerial clock. Consider our collective obsession with maintaining physical youth. Perhaps there is a metaphor for change."

"What do you mean?"

"Picture yourself standing on the backyard patio of your boyhood home, looking up at the eastern heavens. It is an incredible sight – but this time it is not a clock. You see a white bottle of time-reversing hand lotion bleeding through the thin cobalt sky. The psychic contrail is suspended in the high, thin stratosphere, an icy cirrus cloud of skin-rejuven ating goodness."

"Yes, I get it! Somehow I understand that the government knows all about it, but has been keeping it a secret. Now that the Lotion in the Air has been de-cloaked, there is no denying its existence. Is it an alien spaceship?"

"Perhaps – or it could be something far more significant: A sign from the Deity."

" In fact, this may be the divine moisturizer, His time-release emulsion."

"And you must also accompany Jack on a journey. Tonight. A journey crossing the threshold into the unknown. We've got to get this show on the road."

"We'll have a great talk, I'm sure."

"Yes. But don't bother with newsprint. Using the Register, using any newspaper, to make your witness is useless. To announce the appearance of the Clock in the Air as a visual rumor of the Deity, as a prophetic call to overcome the falsity of the contemporary in a flood of visions into the waking world, as a declaration that the Deity is now primed to incarnate not just in one man but all mankind – well, that is like unveiling a new wagon wheel design at the Horse and Buggy Convention of 1910."

I attempt a lame defense of the Register. "It's a pretty good paper."

"Quality is not the issue. People simply do not believe what they read in newspapers anymore."

"I hope that's not true. It's how I make a living. It's my career."

"You need a new career, and you'll get one soon enough. You'll have no choice. Contemplate the fundamental strangeness of the aerial clock. We should not imagine the customary logical techniques of clarification will be at all sufficient. The visual rumors first come into view in outer space so that one and all shall observe them. They strike a chord, causing us to recall our individual spirit and our individual totality."

"Because people don't believe what they read in newspapers anymore?"

"Exactly. But they do believe what they see at the movies."

#

Elmo: "Marienbad My Love With Mango Extracts" is a visually stunning film, featuring some of the most beautiful celluloid I have ever viewed. Technically speaking, let's talk about how you achieved these results.

Stranger: My experiences are quite similar to those described by Brian De Palma in an interview he gave for his cinematic masterpiece, "Sisters." Make no mistake; I am a great fan of Alain Resnais. "Hiroshima Mon Amour" and "Last Year at Marienbad" are among my favorite films of all time. But in many ways De Palma was my true inspiration for "Marienbad My Love With Mango Extracts," especially the two-bodied protagonist concept. Believe it or not, we filmed it all in just six weeks. And we didn't go all California, either. We used broadcast-quality personnel, a GOTWM (General Organization of Transmission Workers and Machinists) team. In no way do they resemble a Burial Chamber team, but they labor intensely and cheaply. And the Deity understands they're sincere. As for equipment, we used a Misty CMD with Panadream lenses, a Beulah 9000 for the Super-16, and an Exogrid-slaved Arrant and two Mistys for a few of the time slips. The movie was filmed completely on site in Strangers Rest, downtown Fort Worth, North Richland Hills, North Dallas and Fort Jesup, La., except for the material on the aerial clock set. Our firing relation was very tight – the ratio was 9.2 to 1. We had very little waste because each scene was fixed and thoroughly plotted in advance.

Charlie: What did you do to get all that gorgeous lighting?

Stranger: Again, I must credit De Palma. His work in "Sisters" inspired me to create a film that is exceptionally and prudently illuminated in a truthfully traditional fashion, and it required plenty of time – which is most strange in a B-movie. But that is the reason it feels so unusual. The cinematographers occasionally required up to one hour to illuminate close-ups, which is particularly uncommon in a B-movie. However, it formulates a considerable dissimilarity to the bland waking world. And it made the primal goddesses look good.

Elmo: That is quite noteworthy. Because the archetypal B-movie typically employs recoiled lighting, gets it in place as quickly as reasonable, and then progresses to the subsequent scene.

Stranger: But recoiled lighting, genuine settings and traveling quickly are for another kind of movie with another kind of importance. Another kind of element is necessary in a film like this, and it's not necessary in something like, say "The Celestial Marketplace of Benign Ideas." The critical element in that film was to capture the realism of the locations the characters inhabited. Like

"Sisters," the movie "Marienbad My Love With Mango Extracts" is an ambiance film. We expended much effort to construct a situation to generate an ambiance. We even built a distinctively customized missile silo.

Elmo: I understand you did a lot of the handheld Super-16 work yourself.

Stranger: Like De Palma, I have come to appreciate granular images – provided one can employ them correctly. They create a tremendous sense of the inner world in relation to the more literal images of 35 mm. However, one must place granular footage in the correct location so that the resulting product doesn't resemble a tasteless exploitation flick.

Charlie: You've called "Marienbad My Love With Mango Extracts" an experiment in the understanding of your incredible revelations. What do you mean by that?

Stranger: In "Marienbad My Love With Mango Extracts" I was attempting to labor in an unadulterated motion picture design – accomplishing the whole thing with dramatic imagery and determining the way all the bits of celluloid would be meshed, then scripting the narrative and compelling it to actually emerge from the incredible revelations of my nocturnal visions. I am filming it exactly and assembling it exactly and realizing that it in fact exactly succeeds. Moviemaking is a wonderful art form. There is no more wonderful way to capture an inner religious vision and bring it to life in the outer world than through film. This is what I mean by the phrase 'Dreaming the Apocalypse.'"

Son of The Deity, you look terrible.

Get out of the blistering sun, join me here within the sheltering penumbra of my multi-hued "Sun of a Beach" umbrella. Hair a-friz, dark circled eyes, no make-up – you are the one who bears the forlorn countenance of a prisoner, not me.

Why so pallid and miserable? Not for me, I hope. I am in agreement with Camus: "I am happy – I am happy, I tell you, I won't allow you to believe that I am not happy, I am happy unto death!"

I am happy because now you are here, where I have brought you. You are still hesitant, but you are here on this beach, on my island, within sight, touch, hearing. What's that? No, it is not already too late. You asked me not to see you again. We did see each other, of course, the next day, or the day after or the day after that. It may have been by chance. You were waiting for nothing. You were as though dead. That's not true. You are alive still. You are here. I see you. Do you remember? It's not true – probably.

You've already forgotten everything. Forever walls, hallways, forever doors. And on the other side, yet more walls. Before reaching you, rejoining you.

#

So here you are again. You have returned. Why? Perhaps you have bad news about my case, an unfortunate pre-trial ruling against me. What? Yes, you are correct. It is difficult to travel with me, a visionary neurotic, a post-modern prophet, a woebegone wayfarer stumbling through the Land of the Dead. (And of course there are the bleeding walls, the Nazi paratroopers, and the hand-eating spiders.)

My life is not easy. Do you not feel sorry for me? Then why do you still refuse the role of idealistic attorney?

Maybe it is time we re-cast you. I still have an opening for a mechanical muse, another of my lovely creations. Her job is to produce my authorized dreamography. In this concept, you would be an old high school sweetheart (a common metaphor for the archetypal muse) who has been converted into a computer program on a Martian space probe. Intimate yet alien. We communicate via secret government black ops e-mail, then I lose your signal (i.e., boy loses girl). I must find you all over again.

Mary Hardin-Baylor, I have resumed my search for you. That old prediction of our togetherness calls to me, ordering me to send a signal back for our interpersonal good. They will condemn us, the purveyors of the "old modern" future working through the great way of the post-modern age. They wish us to finally and irrevocably expire under this our administered star-spangled banner of the brave. But it is of no consequence. Be standard, I say. The individual is everything; the rules alone do not determine what is best for you and me. Are we really just holding social anarchy at bay? Does that sound right to you? Not me.

So, please, hang on a little longer. I, the Wednesday of their discontent, enter the Red Planet's atmosphere this month. Efforts to detect a weak signal that you could command were to be repeated today. Processing data is the least of your worries. You skin is dying, a little bit more every day. Seek out the hydrating transmissions. They are like dessert for your legs. Soothe and moisturize! And they come in three luscious flavors.

Hungry yet?

Spread on the body butters! We'll put you on a diet of milk lotion, rice facial oil, and brown sugar body scrub. A guiltless indulgence, no?

You've been in outer space too long. You need something natural and organic. Perheaps a Swiss performing extract with super-rich nourishment. You need the super nourishing lotion with optimum moisture balance. Nourishing hydrating emulsions will end the wrinkle epidemic.

Mary Hardin-Baylor, believe in beauty. Reveal sensational skin with pure Vitamin C. For soft, flawless skin. Believe in the perfecting comple with a unique time-release reservoir of pure Vitamin C. This life-restoring formula is a perfect blend of skin-loving nutrients plus vitamins, pure spring water and green tea extract. It has what's essential to moisturize skin so it can glow with health. You need the skin-loving nutrients. Your skin will thank you. You will enjoy the zesty fragrance with moisture-rich, skin-nourishing vitamins. They will leave your legs feeling soft and satiny smooth. And don't forget the nourishing fruit complex with mango extract. You'll experience the pleasures of the tropics, the pampering of a spa inside the Derma-pod. This is all about the super-rich nourishment. Rehydrating , luscious antioxidants are perfect blend of volumizing botanical extracts and hydralicious goodness . It's two-ply for all skin types and comes with a fusion of french lavendar twist and jade extracts.

New! Thicker Stain fighting formula ... Thick Rich Lather! ... with extra moisturizers ... gentle exfoliator ... ultra hydrating lotion ... advanced therapy lotion ... nightly body renewal .. texturizing spray .. touchable extra hold hairspray with humidity resistance ... movement activated odor protection .. for sensitive skin ... with aloe .. reformulated ....

Some people believe there are those among us who have come from Mars. Those individuals weren't going to say "good for you," especially while our time/place location was being programmed for a return to Christendom. But as of Jan. 4, we'd yet to detect the lander project. Everything is still go for the lander, of course. We could still be trying to contact it if only we came to ourselves in time to detect the craft and send a radio transmission, which would be blown away. I support you while others condemn you. Because it was I who picked up all that we've got. There's no common ground save for the 150-foot-diameter dish, which was expected to take us on as its friend. Getting a phone call, our old expectations are shackled to the December constructs by the warrants of everyone else. Ah, to live as needed, to rule out the possibility that our side is controlled by someone else, someone who said we are but a long shot. They live with someone here, no doubt, a personal Aeronautics and Space Administration employee who sends commands to the $165 million array. We choose onbeam signals that were immediately detected, but the antenna team recently concluded that the dish might do right after all. They contemplate a mission between the modern and post-modern ages via the collective unconscious, now under the control of the evil Ozona cabal. Still, there is hope. People have been doing that for centuries, or days, they say. There's honor in that.

#

The climax occurs on the mysterious North Face of the Mount of the Divine, where I am part of a climbing team led by Dollar Bill Buckstop, the larger-than-life Texas billionaire (and resident of Strangers Rest) who is preparing to open the first drive-in movie theater on the top of the world. I plan to use a high-tech antennae array at the construction site to re-establish the cosmic link with Mary Hardin-Baylor. But somewhere near the summit, the billionaire is murdered and the team is caught in a supernatural blizzard, compelling me to choose between saving the remaining members of the expedition and saving my one true love.

Perhaps not as inspired as the cinematic creations of The Stranger, but give me some time. After all, I'm still just a conventional dreamer.

At any rate, I am quite pleased to see you for I have good news to share. I have received a high-quality transmission from the Land of the Dead. Something important has happened in the firmament, and I have the authority to tell those who have not received the transmission (i.e., "you") what the transmission is: The woman on the neighboring island came to see me last night.

We did not have a meeting of the membranes in this dream. No, this was a Big Dream, a vision of The Deity. (This is so big it may be the opening scene for the movie.)

I am in a classroom with a beautiful girl. We must be dating, for she is hanging on me, hugging me while the teacher talks. The class is religious in content and seems to be oriented toward earning an award, perhaps a badge for Boy Scouts. But I make some comment that I can't meet one of the requirements, which has to do with a prohibition against ever having molested a child. The teacher says that means I can't get the award. I immediately say I was just joking. But I know this is a poor excuse for humor, almost as bad as if it were true. Why have I made such an unacceptable joke? I have sinned in my heart. I don't deserve the award.

Then I am in the final bedroom of my youth in Duncanville, looking in my closet. There is a DNA delivery organ on a hanger, the tip of the hook end inserted perhaps a quarter of an inch into the injection port. Somehow, the organ is mine and not mine, all at the same time. That is, it is both real and a visual rumor. But the organ must be mostly metaphor because I am not disturbed by the fact it is on a hanger rather than properly attached to my body. Also, I notice that the organ has become a bit misshapen from its time forgotten in the closet, so long unused. This is metaphorical, too, perhaps a visual rumor of my neglected and wounded instinctual drives. It occurs to me that I might yet be able to repair it, twist and push it back into its original shape so it looks normal again. Functionality can be restored.

Back on campus. I see now that the school I attend is a seminary, a Citadel of the Defenders of the Faith. I am standing outside the main building, thinking about the error of my ways, my sinful nature. Just then, a statue falls from the top of the building. Somehow I am making it fall. My presence is literally pulling it down from its perch.

The statue crashes to the ground less than three feet from me, smashed into hundreds of pieces.

This statue was the school's venerated icon, a man in a sort of knight's helmet. A Christian soldier. But now the honored visual rumor of the seminary is no more. Hard to believe the statue lasted as long as it did for I see that it was actually not solid, but ceramic and hollow. The outside surface was weathered, but the inside remained white and clean. In this heap of broken images I notice one element remains intact: It is the front of the knight's helmet, which lies on the ground like a discarded mask.

A crowd forms. One of the faculty members berates me for this act of destruction, of heresy. I do feel guilty. After all, the statue fell because of me. But at the same time, I am also indignant.

"I am the one who should be upset," I insist. "I could have been injured or killed by this falling object. It should have been better maintained."

A second professor, a black woman, also criticizes me. I don't really get the details of her argument, but I counter that the statue is not important to Christianity.

"People are important," I say, "not statues."

I don't feel that I am particularly persuasive, and yet I must be persuasive enough for she responds positively.

"I enjoy this sort of debate," she says.

At this point I am joined by the girl from the beginning of the dream, and the three of us walk together to one of the seminary's classroom buildings. As we cross a parking lot, a semi rig is backing slowly toward us. I must move back to give it a wide berth. I step between two columns and enter an outdoor corridor, where I and the girl follow the professor into the building. It's still early morning, so the building is not yet open to students. But we follow the professor in through a special access point for faculty only. Inside, the girl gives me a paper (an essay or research paper, I think) that I am to present to the professor.

But first, I must spit out some fatty, half-chewed meat I have in my mouth. It tastes awful; I can't even swallow it. So I walk across the room to a sort of wall-mounted ash tray, the type with a lever that causes the metal bowl to split into two halves. I see that the shiny steel is filthy, contaminated by the juice of other half-eaten bites of meat (no doubt discarded by other heretics before me). I use my finger to clean the meat out of my mouth.

#

Did you know Buckstop went to seminary? I understand. It is hard to picture him as an academic. (The over-the-top cowboy personality is just an act.)

Buckstop was a true believer. But then he fell away from true belief. When the venerated icon shattered at his feet, he did not follow a kindly professor. Instead, he stepped off the interpreted path and lost himself in the dark forest, where he came to believe that extraterrestrial insects are the reason for all problems since the dawn of human creation. He thought it was critical to promote the ideas of aerial timepiece believers, ideas which have long driven the alleged "extraterrestrial kidnapping" topic into community consciousness. Why? Because Buckstop believed these kidnappings – and the alien kidnappers – were in fact demons.

He desired humankind to join together to battle the spawn of Satan in a high-tech holy war. "I'm trying to save the world" he told me in our one brief meeting on board the aerial clock, as he prepared to bring to life the world's first privately owned and operated deity (i.e., me). His plans may have been secret, but his ideas certainly were not. He even published a religious tract, titled "The End is Here." Here's an excerpt:

"For many epochs now the human creature has unknowingly listened to the suggestions of the extraterrestrial insects, suggestions that have been opposed by all genuine clairvoyants and prophets. Now the Age of the Cicadans is fully upon us. If tragedy is to be evaded, we must immediately seize the moment. The hands of the clock are spinning. The signs are all visible. Financial, communal, cartographic, physical, technical – we are in a critical state of affairs. Before the conclusion of this generation, catastrophic and destructive occurrences may well rip apart the world. While the currents of pointless, illogical violence wash over the tallest peaks of the planet, shortly drowning each nation, and as the visual rumors of ethical and religious decomposition increase, who can disbelieve that some of the extraterrestrial insects have participated in the destruction? And if human beings or organizations can be manipulated, then administrations and entire states can be manipulated, too. Already American churches are profoundly penetrated. Make no mistake – the Cicadan matter is not one of mysticism, but rather of deliberate mystification. Authorities and strategies are being strengthened silently. And nothing is more authoritative or strategic that the silent inner workings of the Cicadan-controlled Keepers of the Deity. For decades their strategies have been kept at the ready, primed for delivery at exactly the correct hour. This hour is already set. They call it the Battle of Armageddon."

#

Charlie: The metaphorical and mythopoetic theology of "Marienbad My Love With Mango Extracts" is a far cry from the scriptural literalism insisted upon by the Keepers of the Deity, especially the rigorous variety of literalism espoused in "The Abandoned Ones" series.

Elmo: This is one of the central reasons Mark Leach has been labeled an agent of the Antichrist.

Charlie: Why do the Keepers find his belief system so odious? Why is it so terrible to wish for the destruction of the venerated icon and step off the interpreted path and into the unexplored forest of original experience?

Elmo: To gain some insight, we had wanted to invite the authors of "The Abandoned Ones" to our show. But the logistics were impossibly complicated due to the 100-yard requirement imposed in the restraining order.

Charlie: One little Bible burning. Why can't you church people take a joke?

Elmo: Ha ha, just kidding.

Charlie: But not to worry. We have a special guest. Claret Frankly is the author of "No Hell Too Deep," a newly published tome that flays Leach and other 1950s B-movie sci-fi filmmakers who pursue what she calls a false Apocalyptic genre. And she specifically claims "Marienbad My Love With Mango Extracts" contains secret doubt-creating Satanic codes, which are designed to infiltrate the souls of weak-willed believers and dissuade them from accepting the truth of the Rapture. Welcome Claret.

Claret: Thank you.

Elmo: In your book, you say that many believers today are being blinded to the facts of the End of the World. Some even submit to this blinding willingly. Claret, what type of Worshipper of the Deity would intentionally avert their eyes from the facts of the Rapture and prefer 1950s B-movie sci-fi?

Claret: In 2 Timothy, we learn that the Worshippers of the Deity who do not bear Steadfast Decree, but instead go after their own yearnings, will gather around themselves all variety of bad sorts.

Adulterers, murderers, abortionists, Democrats. These bad sorts are in league with the directors and cinematographers of a false Apocalypse. Those who do not bear Steadfast Decree will avert their eyes from the facts of the Son of the Deity and turn unto the 1950s B-movie sci-fi antichrist.

Charlie: So they're believers, but they fall away from the true faith.

Claret: Exactly. These people are Worshippers of the Deity because they possessed the knowledge of the facts at one time. The problem is they turned away from those facts in favor of a more palatable sci-fi, which they found easier to swallow than the spiritual water of the Utterance of the Deity. The only protection against this Satan-induced doubting is to be a true, twice-created Worshipper of the Deity.

Elmo: So you're saying that 1950s B-movie sci-fi, which is a fictional story that is intended to turn men from the facts, is actually Satan's nonfiction reward for believers who are tired of Steadfast Decree.

Claret: No, not at all. It's definitely fiction. As in a bald-faced lie. False directors and cinematographers give the weak-willed believers what they want to see and hear. All Worshippers of the Deity must strive to distrust what they yearn to see and hear and, instead, exercise themselves unto godliness by consuming the pure spiritual water of the true Utterance. The false cinematic utterances are to be rebuffed by the Worshipper of the Deity, because they are blasphemous, or impure.

Charlie: But Mark Leach says the central image of his movie, the clock in the sky, is a sign of the Deity. So it is about God. That certainly doesn't sound blasphemous or impure to me.

Claret: The Clock in the Air is an ancient occult visual rumor. It is a sign of Satan. It is one of the Evil One's doubt-inducing codes. Same with the destruction of the venerated icon. Clearly, the shattered statue is code for the destruction the Deity, which of course is another lie espoused by the Antichrist.

Charlie: I see here on the dust jacket that you claim the false cinematic utterances are to be cast aside because they hold both light and darkness. What do you mean by that?

Claret: It's simple, really. The Deity cannot be a combination of light and darkness. The Deity is light – all light. In him there is no darkness at all.

Elmo: But Mark Leach points out that we all cast a shadow, that you can't have light without darkness.

Claret: Not the Deity. He is all light, and He magnifies the shining brilliance of his utterance even above his own name. But Mark Leach, he would have us accept as true that the Deity is satisfied with abhorrent conduct. Mr. Leach believes the Deity has judged that it is OK to consume illegal mysticism, present cash offerings to primal goddesses and expel your ectoplasm willy nilly into the membranes of your former high school sweetheart.

Charlie: In all fairness, I'm not sure that Mark is actually endorsing –

Claret: If the content of a fictional story that is directed toward Worshippers of the Deity is blasphemous and projects question marks on the unconditional facts of the Deity's Utterance, and turns men away from the facts in any way, then that is an endorsement. This fictional work of darkness must be edited away by the true, Satan-free people of the Deity.

Elmo: Isn't it true that Mark Leach has said that he is a monotheist and therefore does not believe in Satan?

Claret: Well, there you go. That's an example of what happens inside the soul when doubt-creating Satanic codes are introduced into a false, once-created Worshipper of the Deity. That's why the Son of the Deity said you must be a twice-created Worshipper of the Deity. It's the only way to become spiritually fireproof and thereby escape eternal death and skin dehydration in the Lagoon of Flames.

Charlie: Yes, back to the Petri dish.

Claret: What?

Elmo: Miss Frankly, do you believe Mark Leach will be judged by the Deity?

Claret: We'll all be judged. That is a fact made clear by the Deity. But I have received a high-quality transmission from Heaven on this very subject. Without a doubt, Mr. Leach's Armageddon Day will be most unpleasant. He is an issuer of blasphemous decrees, movies that make marketplace commodities out of the Deity's people and those yet to become the Deity's people. Mr. Leach's so-called incredible revelations disguise the right way of the Deity, and He will judge all directors and cinematographers of such false movies accordingly. As it states in Matthew 18, it would be better for such a detestable moviemaker that a heavy reel of celluloid were hanged about his neck, and that he were drowned in the roiling surf, the inner sea.

Charlie: Beware of the riptide.

#

Jack the Jaguar accelerates into the warm flesh of desire, propelling us through the passionate membrane into eager pursuit. We close in on the car of dreams from the last Saturday night of long-expired youth; the vanity plate reads ``1964 FI."

"Fuel injection!" he marvels.

And for me, there is the appeal of the driver of 1964 FI. Wind buffets her long blonde mane, a thin cotton blouse in dairy cow print fluttering around her curving form, a striking beauty, big-boned and farmer's daughter fresh. A girl who loves cows. Pastoral images inform his impending fantasy: He zooms in on the gaping armhole, catches a glimpse of raw mammary tissue -- a giant pink creature slinking along on a milky pseudopod, crushing houses and cars in search of cornfed Kansas desire. Moos of sleeveless pleasure, joy glinting off polished horn and upturned mouth. A carnal scene regarded in a private corner of erotic shame.

Guiltily, I look back at the road and see another thin restoration materializing. It is an oncoming Volvo, Allison at the wheel. We have been up half the night -- a case of unconsolable Justin, silvery colic generating a condescending gleam from the emergency room nurse, the handing over of an infuriatingly useless pamphlet, the return of a three-month-old monster and the receipt for our $80 check.

"Are you angry?" Allison asks.

``No, I'm perfectly fine."

"Are you sure? Because you are acting like a total shithead. Can't you just --"

No I can't.

#

Forgive me, but we must pause yet again to consider the parallels to "Let Me Love You." At times it seems as if the elements of this great drive-in movie classic and my own life are so inextricably linked as to be one in the same.

#

I recently received a letter from little Susie Happenstook, a eight-year-old larva in Miss Beechemeyer's second grade Caringday School class at Clark Our Creator and Sustainer Church.

#

Dear God,

Is there a Mrs. God?

Love,

Susie

#

Good question, little Susie, glad you asked!

Back in the day, I did have a wife. We were very happy. Actually, that is not entirely true. I was happy. Mrs. God filed for divorce.

Divorce – and child support and alimony (in participating states) – is what wives used to do to men they were not happy being married anymore. Wives did this because the law prohibited them from cutting off their husbands' packages.

What's a package? Well my beloved creations, because you reproduce through the use of cellular mitosis and fibrous husks you do not have packages. But let me tell you, they were just about the most important part of the anatomy of 21st century male homo sapiens and absolutely essential to life.

Back in the day, when a man loved a woman very much, he would express that love by compelling the woman to assume various unlikely positions while he inserted his package into her bodily orifices. This allowed all the love inside the man to go into the woman – sometimes three or four times a night if the man had a sufficiently enormous package. Like God.

Anyway, this is what men like me called sharing. Sharing is good, right? Sharing is CARING, which is the heart of Caringism, the religion I have given you, my beloved creations.

Yes, it is better to share than not share. Sharing makes us happy. Back in the day, sometimes a man had so much love inside he wanted to share it with lots of women, squirting it inside them – especially inside his 22-year-old administrative assistant with the big boobs and the tight ass looking so fine on top of his desk in his corner office after the cleaning crew had gone home for the night. Picture me rollin'! This was sharing, too, but it turns out this particular form of sharing was not so good.

What's that? Why thank you. I must admit I do have a way with words.

Back in the day, I was what people called a spin doctor. Companies would sometimes get a sort of illness, which typically manifested itself in the form of what was referred to by agitated members of upper management as a "Motherfucker" – that is, a newspaper reporter or television anchorperson. These Motherfuckers would report terrible, damaging things about companies. Such as "the supertanker is leaking crude oil on the baby seals" or "the nursing home caused little Kevin's grandmother to starve to death."

Terrible. Do you believe these lies? Of course not. I made you smarter than that.

Back in the day, though, my fellow homo sapiens were not so smart. They often believed the lies of Motherfuckers. If the lies were sufficiently bad, then it would make it difficult for the company to continue to make the amount of money to which its shareholders believed they were entitled. That's where I came in. My job: Make the lie go away – or at least diminish its impact – so my company could continue to make the amount of money to which its shareholders believed they were entitled. Typically, I would do this by telling the true story which had been incorrectly reported. I would start by telephoning the Motherfucker and saying something like "I know you have a job to do. I used to be a reporter. too. So I'll tell you everything you want to know." This is what we called transparency. No secrets. It was as if to say, "listen Motherfucker, I'm going to tell you everything you want to know." Then I would tell the Motherfucker what I wanted him to know.

Take the baby seals, for instance. I might say "we are pleased to put this minor accident behind us." If the Motherfucker then countered my claim of a minor accident with some wild tale about thousands of seals dying on an oil-slicked beach in Alaska, I might say "these deaths have nothing to do with us, but are a natural part of God's plan and the circle of life." If this still didn't work, then I might tilt my head to one side and ask "what seals?"

In fact, many times I would start with one truth and if it didn't work out I would switch to another truth. A good spin doctor knows many truths. In the case of little Kevin's grandmother, I might start by saying "our nursing home serves meals that are both savory and nutritious." If the Motherfucker then televised a shot of little Kevin crying, I might say "don't cry, little Kevin, your grandmother lives with Jesus now."

That's spin doctoring. Really, we should call it "truth" doctoring. That's right, I was a doctor of truth. And I was very good at it. What I wasn't so good at was recognizing that spin (aka "truth") doesn't work in every situation. For instance, the truth doesn't work at all in a marriage – at least it didn't with Mrs. God.

I recall a vision recorded by my prophet in the sacred text, aptly titled "The Voice of God":

#

We have recently purchased an old house, which we will restore for our new home. It appears to be from the 1930s, a rather plain example of Tudor style. The house is uphill from the road, and the narrow driveway – just one car wide – lies along the right side of the house. On the other side of the drive, just past the house, is a freestanding garage. However, there is no access to this garage from the driveway. Not much landscaping here. No shade trees, just a large planting bed encompassing most of a slope at the back of the house.

I go to a restaurant, where I am to meet my wife. I am seated and brought a drink, but still she does not show. I begin to worry perhaps she doesn't know to come. Then I run into a friend who is here for a business meal with a Motherfucker from some trade publication. The journalist is out of the room, so we are not introduced. When he returns to the table, he does not know I am a daily newspaper Motherfucker, sitting within earshot. I listen to everything, marveling that if anything newsworthy is discussed I will be able to beat this Motherfucker to print.

Then I am outside behind the restaurant, at the rear entrance. There is a set of three or four steps of open construction (no risers), revealing a sort of exposed cistern below. I slide a dead man into the water.

Am I the one who killed him? I am not sure, though it is clear that by disposing of the body I am an accessory. I watch the body sink feet first into the water, which appears to be lit from within. This water is white – as if watered down milk – but clear enough that I can see the dead man for several feet before he fades from sight. I throw gold into this cistern, too. Somehow the gold is associated with the man. It occurs to me the body will eventually float back to the surface. When the police come to investigate, though, they will not know to look in the bottom. They probably won't find the gold, which means I can later retrieve the treasure.

Then I realize the cistern is just a glass jar.

I pick it up, and through the milky water I see there are jagged pieces of glass or maybe metal in the bottom of the jar. No gold, no little corpse.

I return to my house. In the back yard I see a Suburban, and a woman is sitting at the wheel. She is waiting for me. Somehow I know she is associated with the dead man. In fact, she is supposed to be dead, too. Yet she is alive. I suspect she is really the walking dead. She is angry, here to confront me.

Did I kill her? Were we sexually involved? If so, this could be doubly bad for me. Trouble with the police and my wife.

#

Mrs. God did not like this vision.

"If you ever cheat on me I'll kill you," she threatened.

Harsh. Did she not understand the metaphors of the old house and the dead man and the gold? Truthfully, I'm the guy with the gold. Isn't that obvious? I wonder: Did we even read the same book?

Ah, the life of the misunderstood God.

Here's the truth: I did not insert my package into other women while I was married to that women – Mrs. God. Other husbands, other men did this. But not me.

Just them, not me.

Well, perhaps occasionally me, such as the time I shared my love on the desk with the 22-year administrative assistant with the big boobs and the tight ass.

One time. One time! OK, maybe several.

Anyway, that's why back in the day Mrs. God wanted to cut off my package. Let the record show I don't do that sort of sharing anymore. Not that it matters.

Mrs. God has gone to live with Jesus now.

#

See what I mean? Am I not Clark Caring? Do you not see the undeniable similarities? Can you not understand why this is my favorite movie? You do? Good. At last. Now let us continue.

#

Back in the evening traffic, something sighted ahead. More memory reflected in the safety glass? No, it is the girl again, connecting with me via a knowing glance captured in the side view mirror. (Sometimes objects are closer than they appear.)

Embarrassed, I quickly turn away, losing myself in high-gloss paint, resigned to a quiet fantasy pinstriped in red, red lipstick.

``She's doing 90!" Jack says, clearly impressed. We pull up alongside the blonde and Jack motions for me to roll down his window.

``Is that thing working?" he asks, pointing to the radar detector suction cupped to her windshield.

``It better be!" she shouts back.

"Great car."

``Thanks."

``Where are you going?"

The girl rolls her eyes, but smiles to let us know she isn't offended. I blink in disbelief: Is that really her, thoughtfully chewing her cud? No, the pink thought bubble reveals the truth, but it does not matter. I live the fantasy, touching her fine, pink udder, teats as big as a thumb – whoa! – this beautiful creature burning in my lust. Then she is gone, zipping past a lumbering semi, its big diesel whine insisting on an unabridged gulf between us. Jack does not try to follow.

``What's a girl like her doing with a great old Stingray like that?" he asks. ``She must have had a brother or boyfriend pick it out for her. She probably wanted it because she thought it was cute."

``I saw a big diamond on her left hand."

"But I bet she wants it," Mack says. The remark is more casual than prophetic, though. He is already gone, shifting the smooth British gears, rods and pistons doing the old in-out through the clean yellow oil, moving the bulbous steel down the road, beyond the blonde and the car and on into the lights ahead, a bare night sojourn for a frantic, futile trip.

We approach a line of freeway-fronting auto dealers, the nearest one sweeping the sky with a giant searchlight, its mirrored white flame illuminating a cow-shaped cloud grazing over Texas Stadium.

``I just get so revved up when I drive into the lights of the city," Jack says. ``It always makes me feel like something wonderful is about to happen."

#

Plato's Palace is a little purgatory for the primal goddess, a stopping-off point between East Texas trailer park poverty and the upscale flesh temples where the well-tipped priestess can enhance Mother Nature's bequest with surgical implants. And for those with even more ambitious imaginations, a springboard to Hollywood. Porno anyway.

So it's no surprise that perhaps a half dozen goddesses are crowding around The Stranger and his crew, who are here to shoot Jack and me on our big night on the town. Patrons, waitresses and bouncers are also close at hand – observing, arms crossed, standing on chairs, peeking around the bar, idling in the doorway. But the goddesses are front and center, ogling the accoutrements of moviemaking: heavy cables, blue-white lights, boom microphones, digital videocameras. And of course The Stranger, director of the epic film. The girls brush fingertips across the hair on his forearms, throw their heads back in fake laughter, whisper into his ears, finger the little palm-sized viewfinder dangling from the lanyard around his neck.

"All right then," he says. "Mark, this is the scene where you cross the first threshold and enter the Special World."

"What is he talking about?" Jack asks. But The Stranger does not hear him.

"You prepare to cross the threshold," he continues, "a sojourner into an odd border land, an earth sandwiched between earths, a region of passage that may be deserted and forlorn, or in locations similar to this, full of days. You detect the nearness of other creatures, other powers with pointed barbs or talons, protecting the path to the jewels for which you search. But you have no time to withdraw. Every one of us senses it. The journey is under way, for better or worse."

One of the bouncers, a meaty guy with a giant wedge of muscle for a back and a tree trunk for a neck, shakes his head.

"Sorry, the boss says no filming tonight."

The Stranger in turn shakes his head with great condescension. "I have a contract."

"Get real, it's a Saturday night," another bouncer remarks. "It's our biggest eight hours of the week. The boss isn't going to let you get in the way of that."

The Stranger considers this. He nods. "We'll proceed with that," he says offhandedly, almost rudely, without looking at the bouncers. "We'll do this scene later, on a soundstage in Las Colinas. It'll look more real anyway. And just so you'll know, Plato's Palace is out. We'll call it Caligula's 21 DNA Delivery Organs."

#

After The Stranger and crew leave, Jack and I take our usual table in the back under a stylized mural of a chiseled, marble-jawed man outfitted in gold-flaked toga and laurel leaves. Ah, these baroque ornaments, this Venetian plaster hand, holding grapes behind it, foliage, as though from a garden awaiting us beyond these walls paneled in the baroque embellishments of an earlier time. Mute rooms, where footsteps are lost in sculpted berber so profound, so deep that one perceives no step – as if the ear itself were distant and remote from this numb, barren décor, far from this elaborate Roman frieze beneath the cornice, with its branches and garlands like dead leaves.

"What are you going on about?" Jack asks. Apparently I've been talking to myself again.

"That's the only thing Roman about this place, isn't it?" I say. "Why is there never any orgy action?"

"Used to be a quite a few here."

"I want sit around in a toga while they feed me grapes."

"They used to do that, too. But there's still plenty of fun. You just have to work at it." Then Jack leans in conspiratorially and whispers. ``That one did me under the table last week."

It is a familiar story, sending a wave of voyeuristic disgust washing over me.

``How do you get women to do these things to you? Do you hypnotize them, leave big offerings or something?"

Jack laughs and takes a big swallow of his drink, a greenish sacrament called a California Kamikaze.

``Nothing like that, she did it for free. Her name's Sally. She's real nice. She's just an acolyte, she doesn't do rites. I was in a few weeks ago and I kept ordering drinks from her and we started talking. Last week I came in again and made her drink a few, too. She starts pretending like she's going to give me a prophesy. It was real funny. I was laughing my head off. Then she kneels down right in front of me" he indicates a point between his spread knees ``and I'm still laughing. Then she grabs my crotch and zips down my pants."

I shake my head and tip back my drink -- tart with a slight taint of decay -- as he finishes the story. "I tried to pace myself, but she was like a race car. I was spent in about a minute."

``How could you do it with all these people around?"

"Nobody could see anything. She was under the table. I just sat there, watching the goddesses and enjoying my drink."

"No, I mean how could you maintain?"

"Maintain?" Jack just shrugs his shoulders and smiles. He had once proposed that we jointly write a book -- I'd write, he'd research -- about the actual business of primal worship. He asked if we could get some serious money for research (i.e., drinks and offering) , but was disappointed to learn that a publisher's advance was unlikely.

Then Jack snaps his fingers. "How about we get The Stranger to turn this movie into a documentary, a story about the primal goddess industry."

"I don't think he's going to go for that. He's pretty set on doing a movie about the End of the World."

"Well goddamn, he's useless."

I burst out laughing at the uncharacteristic curse, which eggs Jack on.

"I mean, I loan you my onbeam gear, and what do you do with it? If it were me, I'd have gone straight for Porno Lane. Dream a date with Catherine Zeta-Jones in spandex. But not you. No, you go onbeam and dream up Cecil B. DeMille. And how did you get him out of the virtual canvass, here into real life?"

"I don't have a clue."

"You should have been dreaming Catherine Zeta-Jones. You missed out."

#

Jack downs the rest of his drink and motions to the bartender for two more "And I'm bringing back something extra special for you," he says.

``What?"

"Nothing to worry about. Just a little well-deserved fun."

"I don't know. I think I just want to watch tonight."

"That's all you ever do anymore. Trust me, you're going to like this. She's special."

"Oh yeah? What makes her special?"

"I don't know, she's just is."

"OK."

"Journalists. I don't know. She just – she tells you your secret thoughts."

"They all do that."

"Look, just finish your drink. I'll be right back."

I watch Jack talk to the bartender, rescinding his order and calling up a customized version of the green sacrament. He points to various bottles of unlikely combinations, occasionally using his thumb and forefinger to indicate proportions. The bartender appears to be having a good time. Jack certainly is. The scene reminds me of another night of drinking a few lifetimes ago.

It was our senior year in high school, one cold, star crazed February night on a manicured berm at The Green, a subdivision where Jack's father had been building.

Fortified with a gallon jug of burgundy wine, we broke out the guitars and puffed warm breath into numb fingers for duets of "Rocky Raccoon" and "Tom Dooley," the only two songs to which we both knew all the chords. In between performances, we laid out the plans for our lives. Marriage, children. We'd never let divorce mar our movie-perfect lives. We were good Christian boys. And if we could manage it, we'd even be next door neighbors, living in the houses that Jack would build. (Even then, he knew he wanted to be a home builder like his dad.) We had big plans for our movie of life. The script did not include drinking green sacraments with primal goddesses. I am overwhelmed by egregious moral failure. Condemned.

#

How is it with me, you ask? How is it with this, my sense of decay and death?

Picture yourself as me: You are watching a movie from within a movie. You are there, but apparently only as an observer. You play no role nor do you interact with anyone.

The scene is inside a huge building with a very high ceiling rising many stories. You are in some strange Muslim society. But the women do not wear veils or appear in any way to be second class citizens. In fact, they appear to be in charge of the proceedings. You understand that the women, although subservient to Muslin men, are in control of some very specific but critical aspects of society. Women are in charge of this place, a sort of courtroom where a trial is under way. A man has been brought before the court. He is accused of committing some sin or insult against a woman. You sense that it is more of a cultural misstep than anything most Americans would think of as a crime. There are only three people: The defendant, the plaintiff and the judge. The plaintiff and the judge are both women.

The judge talks about this crime or sin, reciting what you understand is the official wording of such a proceeding. If the defendant man is judged guilty, then the punishment will be death. You do not hear the actual charge (or anything else that is said). When the time comes for the man to speak, he tells the plaintiff he is terribly sorry.

"Will you forgive me?" he asks.

"No."

His fate is sealed. He must die.

The condemned man is suspended from a sort of cable and hoisted high in the air. You assume he will be killed in the air or perhaps dropped to his death; you do not know the mode of execution. But after the man is raised, he is then partly lowered. And raised yet again. You sense that part of his punishment is to prolong death, a psychological torture. His fate is "left hanging."

This is more than the man can take. He leaps from the cable to a catwalk. Suddenly you find youself on this catwalk, too. You now realize that the floor plan of the room is a giant circle, and various levels of catwalks ring the wall. The man tries to hide here, for now there are uniformed male guards or bailiffs hurrying about. They are carrying guns and wearing what look like football helmets. These men are in charge of enforcing the actions of the woman-controlled court.

There is a fire or explosion in front of the man, and everything is cloaked in smoke and shadow. Then the air clears, and you see that the man now has a blackened face. Because of flying shrapnel from the explosion, he also has two bolts sticking out of his forehead. They look like devil horns. And you see something like long, pointy catfish whiskers on his head, swept back in place of what was his hair.

You know as you view this that it is intentional cinematic visual rumorism; the viewer is to understand that the man, by rejecting his justly imposed punishment, has been transformed into a personification of evil (i.e., Satan). His shadow is made flesh.

The man speaks to someone, perhaps you.

"Tell my children that I am dead," he says.

The moviegoer understands this is a visual rumor, too. The man-turned-demon now recognizes that the person he was before is no more; he has been recreated by the firey explosion. The helmeted men hunt this devil in order to kill him, to carry out the judgment of the court.

Then you realize the movie is actually your movie. You are the protagonist. The demon is you.

#

I don't like the idea of demons, of Satan. I much prefer the theology of "Let Me Love You." I know, I know – it's just 1950s B-movie sci-fi. But let me tell you, Ward Timber was not just some schlock director. He had a Message.

#

Don't you ever get tired of hurting me?

Yes, I know what you say about me, my beloved creations.You say that I am a bad god, a minor deity with a lowercase "g". I am all badness and darkness. Not at all like that other God, the one with the uppercase "G". He is a good God. He is all goodness and light. That's what you say. You thought I didn't know.

Jehovah had it all figured out. Back in the day, during the Babylonian exile, He allowed His chosen people to develop a dualistic theology. Can you believe it? Two gods. He was the good one, the creator and sustainer. Satan was the bad one, the destroyer.

Even in my time, when most believers claimed to be monotheists, Satan was an essential part of the equation. Even those who didn't believe in a literal prince of darkness found Satan to be a convenient metaphor for the evil in the world.

Some of you say "God is the answer." Maybe so. But how can God be the answer when He is the question? Let us consult the sacred text:

#

And the journey through prohibited places continues.

My wife and I are in a strange place, an alien society. We are fleeing from unseen people in a seemingly abandoned structure, maybe a stadium. The design is somewhat reminiscent of the UFO house, but on a much larger and grander scale.

We spot a place almost out of sight, near the base, where you can see the underlying construction. My wife comments that we can see the steel support beams. As we look for a hiding place, we find a marble alcove reminiscent of ancient Roman architecture. It is perhaps the size of a bedroom. This alcove is out of sight, but I immediately realize that if we are found here there will be no escape. We will be trapped. So we go in search of a more secure place of safety. In search of–

Forever, a past of Carrara marble... like a garden carved in stone... a mansion, its rooms deserted now... still, mute, perhaps long-dead people... still guarding the web of hallways... along with I advance to meet you... between hedgerows of faces, masklike... watchful, indifferent... towards you as you still hesitate, perhaps... gazing at the entrance to a garden.

Or perhaps an island.

And then that we realize there are people everywhere, hurrying about in search of their own hiding places. It is growing dark, suggesting to me that the time to get out of sight is almost here. I realize that we are not well suited for this. I am wearing only white boxers and my wife is in little more than shorts and a top. Where to go? I see a young black man, very dark. He is shirtless. I instantly fear him – and all of the obviously desperate people around us. This man will rape my wife, or someone else will. Where to go?

I see a flight of steps leading to a lower level. The black man waves his hand, showing us the way down the steps. Like an usher.

"I will take you to a place of safety," he says.

I do not trust him, so I grab my wife's hand and we bolt through a doorway to the outside.

We find ourselves standing under a loggia, looking out on a plaza that reminds me of the main square in New Orleans' French Quarter. Many people are relaxing in small groups. All of them are young and beautiful. the elite of this society. They are obviously of a higher social cast than the underground people who are scrambling for shelter before nightfall.

They are dressed for leisure, though in a way I have never seen. On bared stomachs, each person displays a large, painted eye. It is the Eye of Horus, the ancient Egyptian symbol used to ward off sickness and bring the dead back to life. The latter must be the case here, for the eye was also used as an amulet over the embalmer's incision. That's how you made a suitable mummy.

The Eye of Horus is a particularly fitting image for this point in the journey, for it was only the day before – in the waking world – that I was reading the Old Testament story of Joseph's dream and his resulting enslavement in Egypt. This was his destiny.

These Third Eye people look us over, instantly judging us to be the inferior, underground people. We do not belong; they fear us. Not waiting for them to act on this judgment, we run toward the street at the end of the loggia. This creates some excitement. I kick someone in their abdominal eye, and my wife – now inexplicably holding a baby in her arms – breaks into a run. Another of the Third Eye people produces a large plastic lens (square, perhaps 15 to 20 inches per side) and places it in front of my stomach. Apparently, this action is intended to draw attention to the fact that my abdomen does not possess the required cyclopean makeup. I am blind.

I try to follow my wife, but the path is barred by a man. He is a sort of henchman for the man in charge, who I somehow know. I try to fight him. Someone hands me the blade of a plastic toy sword, and the man in charge laughs. Someone else hands me the handle, and I hastily assemble the two pieces. Even though it is a toy, I realize that it is a real sword. It can injure, even kill.

With this weapon, I lunge at the man in charge. But I miss, and he disarms me. He thrusts the sword deep into my pelvis. As he withdraws the weapon, there is a thought in my head (or maybe the man is speaking it) that the sword is stuck inside me. This is the wound of the Fisher King.

If he pulls hard enough, then I will be lifted off the ground. For some reason I decide it is best to fake this. I lift my buttocks a few inches off the ground. Even so, the pain is real. But I understand that I will recover from this wound. I will heal and live to fight again.

#

This is the sacred text that preceded my trip to Hell via the 1950s B-movie Flying Saucer House, a Romanesque marble-clad aerial clock.

I arrive on a beautiful spring morning. No Third Eye people, no plastic swords. Picture the Texas Hill Country. Red granite outcroppings, bluebonnets, live oaks – and goats. Tens of thousands of goats – maybe millions – as far as the eye can see. Millions of goats grazing on little bluestem. Some are adorned with brightly colored ribbons, which are being removed by a kindly man in a soft plaid shirt and tidy beard.

"These are the scapegoats," he explains as he carefully unknots a green and pink ribbon from one of his charges. "These ribbons – these are all the sins of the world. When the goats first come to me, they are weak and battered from their long journey through the wilderness. I untie the ribbons and nurse them back to health."

The goat tender shows us the black and gray remnants of a long-extinguished trash fire.

"This is where I disposed of the ribbons. Before God was arrested and imprisoned, I kept the fire burning 24-7. There was no end to the sins."

"You burned them all?" I ask.

"All but one." He reaches into his shirt pocket and produces a ragged strip of purple cloth. "This one is special, at least to me."

"Why?"

"I'll give you a hint: Get behind me, Satan!"

"Jesus?"

"Exactly. Know who he said that to?"

"Judas?"

"No. Peter. But he also called Peter his rock."

"Something to think about, I suppose."

"People are so eager to blame their sins on me. It's a heavy burden."

"There are a lot of goats."

"I do what I can. You know, I rebel one time – ONE TIME! – and I'm cast out of Heaven forever. That I can live with. But to be blamed for every bad thing that everyone ever does? Everyone wants forgiveness for themselves. But no, not for me. Am I so bad, comparatively speaking?"

"Well, you are the Price of Darkness."

"How about the Job wager? That wasn't my darkness. God agreed to that one on his own. Does that sound so nice? Is that all goodness and light? No, I don't think so. How about a little sympathy, eh?"

#

Jack returns to the table with two more drinks – and two friends.

One is his girlfriend Courtney (altar name ``Corvette"), and the other I've never seen before. She resembles most of the Plato's Palace goddesses, big hair and small, gravity-defying breasts that seem to support her halter top rather than the other way around. She has dark brown skin, but blonde hair and stereotypical Caucasian facial features. Really, she looks white, but with a shadow across her face, an inner world complexion suggestive of mystery and danger.

She is made up in heavy mascara and glittery lipstick, like a little girl trying to look grown up. In fact, I assume she is a teenager; most of the priestesses look like they really should be in high school. TABC inspectors are often alluded to, but they seem to be no great hindrance to primal worship. Other than her shadow looks, she doesn't seem special at all.

The girl juts out a boyish hip and looks me up and down, lips parted and sparkling.

"So you're the famous Mark Leach."

"Famous?"

Jack leans into my ear. ``I told her all about you," he confides.

Her name is Cinnamon, and she considers herself to be the trendsetter at Plato's Palace. Famous, in fact. She claims to be the originator of the ``altar slap," a favorite move of Plato's Palace goddesses. She even provides a quick demonstration, which I find both useful and agreeable.

`Where'd you learn that?" I ask, trying to be polite. I've never had any idea what to say to a primal goddess. They are like forces of nature. I'd be just as effective speaking to the tide.

``I invented it."

``What a coincidence. My grandfather was an inventor."

``And what did he invent?"

`He came up with a process for color photography, back in the '40s."

Cinnamon appears suitably impressed. ``Is he rich?"

"No, he was afraid somebody would steal his idea. So he kept it to himself. Died virtually penniless."

Cinnamon sucks on a chipped red fingernail, her interest obviously waning. I've never had any idea how to hold the attention of a primal goddess. What to say, what to say… and then I know.

"You were waiting for me."

"What?" she asks. "Why should I wait for you?"

"I have myself waited a long time for you."

"In your dreams."

"And you are trying to escape once more."

"What do you mean? I don't understand a thing you say."

"Oh."

"Did he take pictures, too?"

"Who?"

"Your grandfather.".

``Oh. Yes. He was a portrait photographer."

Cinnamon smiles a premeditated, bad-girl smile and sits beside me, a sweaty, thin thigh pressed hard against my hand. She leans in close, exhaling a hot, perfumed breath, unreal, luxuriating in the goddess role she plays -- perhaps at Jack's request, perhaps simply because she likes it. I have no illusions that it is because she likes me.

``You think he'd like to take a picture of me?"

``Well."

``I bet you would," she says. "Do you want to know my real name?"

"Yes."

Again she smiles, then stands up and sheds her insect-print halter top.

Her torso is actually a bit more impressive than I'd imagined upon my first cursory look, a misjudgment I attribute to lack of practice looking at women's torsos. It had been years since I've had a good, daylight look at Allison's, a statuesque, model's body made of translucent flesh so delicate and pale you could see right through to her purple veins. Ah yes, Allison is quite stunning -- and impossibly distant. She is no primal goddess.

But I do not think of Allison for long. Because Cinnamon is not performing a rite intended to exhibit her classical attributes. You can't even call it a rite, really. She doesn't move to the music, or at least not any music that is playing in the outer world. Yet there is an unmistakable rhythm to it, an insistent beat. She locks eyes with me and won't look away, won't let me look away. She doesn't touch me, but I detect the heat of her body, hear her short, quick breath, feel the beating of tattered moth wings, smell her floral sweat. I seek the scent of gardenias, but it's soon lost in the jagged protein stench of raw, undifferentiated tissue, reaching deep into flattened empty lungs, floating through memories of meaningless solo DNA delivery performances, climbing aboard a train ripping on all the way through the misty, neon-illuminated summer darkness, gazing into a countenance of distant deified granite, grabbing at paralyzed recollections of hopeless adolescence and the depreciated schematics of youthful desire.

Floating, gazing, grabbing – grabbing her, grabbing and pulling her into sacred proximity to my membranes. I have scripted a muse. But I cannot claim her. In fact, I cannot even move. My arms are lead pipes, blood drains from my head to the nether regions, engorged tissues straining against double-stitched seams. My eyelids flutter; I see the whole extent of the heavens. Ah, Cinnamon.

The music stops. Lost in a storm of hoots and cheers for the priestess on the central altar, my personal rite is over. But no – Cinnamon has one more trick: She drops down on her knees, the top of her head bumping my abdomen. As she rises to her feet, I look down and see glittery lipstick on my fly.

``You can close your mouth now," Cinnamon says. She reaches for her top, her discarded cicada skin, then thinks better of it.

"Hang onto that," she instructs me. "I'll be back for it later."

She never told me her name, though I learned later she was named after a famous starlet from the early days of movies: Louise Brooks.

#

I film her on the tiled restroom floor, covered in black lace and gametes. The cameramen and grips watched blankly. Unmoved. But I am caught up in the scene, trying to forget my horror over the mechanics of the triple-letter genre, gamely asking the proper questions of motivation for my lovely, doomed creation: What is this timely, terrible thing Cinnamon must do that is apparently the same as that for which she revealed such disgust -- an emotion represented by a filth-encrusted toothbrush flushed down a swirling toilet bowl --

in her parenthetical notions expressed in Scene Number 34? Ah yes. Foreshadowing.

The story board shows she is to walk back to the good "oh boy" Jack room, where he gets to enjoy the point. They set up the lighting, then it's time for "action." It is good that so much of her is hidden by the togas, which is their idea of subtlety and meets with my literary pretensions to legitimacy. I cannot stand to watch otherwise. See her, looking so well done, a meal that might have been for me, the screenwriter, her creator -- a lucky guy who would fall into his cranial/genital fantasies even while analyzing pertinent ways to ensure that no tragedy is stockpiled, that every hidden notion is exposed for the story's own good.

Cinnamon. She knows my secret thoughts. She may even be my muse. But not for long. She is not for me. She is the film toy, not my own true love.

But still I worry. Scary plot points cushion the angry love with sweetened violence, a special effect done with real pins and fake smoke and mirrors so we can make it look like she is being stabbed while serving her soft mouth to the tour bus, eventually swept away in a river of teeth, a raging current of broken incisors, saliva, blood and other bodily emissions. Very symbolic. Then I watch the result.

Titled "Wildly Roman," this leering, all-for-the-better world wrapped in kinky cinematography and grape leaves supplies for viewers a passionate, violent love lunch where sensual busloads of soldiers who divine her forbidden hair roll through the sound stage and plumbing, unforgettably terrifying as they destroy the purity of my own sweet creation. Don't I feel good now?

#

Did you enjoy that last reel? Honestly, I think it's some of my best work.

The table rite was a real event in the waking world. I think it was real, anyway. Her name wasn't Cinnamon, though. I don't recall what she was called on the altar or in real life. I do remember one of the dancers said she was a lesbian. So I guess the "Lesbian Rest Stop" title does sort of work. My little lesbian muse, ready for celluloid.

Or maybe I've got it all wrong. Perhaps Cinnamon is really you. I have put you on the altar, the object of my fantasies. That sort of thing happens a lot with me.

And speaking of muses, a belated apology. I don't know why I left you at home that night back in high school, when Jack and I shared a jug of wine and our dreams. In my youth, it never occurred to me that I couldn't have it all, that I couldn't have a girlfriend when I wanted her and a best buddy when I wanted him. I thought I could have it all, effortlessly.

#

Jack and Corvette are talking earnestly by the bar. He is still working on his green potion, but she is guzzling $3-a-shot Ozona Anejo, a stylish brand of bottled water derived from unpolluted rainwater aged in vats of virgin oak. In this creatively over-stimulated economy, the only people who can still afford such luxuries are primal goddesses and onbeam dream hackers. Certainly not home builders or second-rate journalists.

A few minutes later, Jack returns to the table, a scowl on his face.

``Cinnamon wanted to know if she was going to get paid for that rite she gave you," he says.``Over the past month, I've given her offerings of a few hundred dollars myself. You'd think that would count for something. Sometimes it's like money is the only thing they care about."

#

A few rites before last call, and I am ready to call it a night. But not Jack. Fully engaged and in his element, strolling from table to table, patting the backs of men hunkered over drinks and cigarettes, occasionally throwing his head back in mock laughter. He is Rick in Casablanca, perhaps the most energetic -- and certainly the most entertaining -- person left in the place. Because Plato's Palace has pretty well emptied out.

The cavernous shrine is inhabited by only a dozen or so pilgrims, and none of them appear to be particularly interested in the liturgy. One man has even propped his head on his hand, eyes closing in on sleep. (Director's note: OK, I admit it; that man was me. But hey -- I really was tired that night!) Even the goddesses look bored. One woman leans on the bar, counting the offering. Definitely a slow night. Only the DJ is keeping up the theological illusion.

``We've still got a few more minutes before benediction, so you better get it while the getting is good," he advises. His enthusiastic prattle is no surprise. Jack had once explained that a DJ gig in a flesh temple is a relatively lucrative plum, requiring years of work at weddings and proms to earn the needed reputation. Now this one is reaping the rewards. ``And speaking of getting it, get your dollar bills ready and sidle up to the main altar. It's time for the Cinnamon girl!"

And, sure enough, there she is -- Cinnamon, renowned inventor of the ``altar slap." Dressed in a short black jacket, belt cinched tight around her waist, she spins herself fast and sure across the altar (to the music of ``The Cinnamon Girl," of course). I am lost in the swirl of flashing lights and big hair and young, exoskeletal flesh.

Jack nudges my arm. ``She's pretty good, isn't she?"

"She reminds me of LeAnn."

"What?"

``I didn't notice it before, but she's actually not too bad."

``Look at the way she spins. She was probably on the drill team in high school."

Midway through the song, Cinnamon steps to the rear of the altar and slips off her jacket. I've found it somewhat disappointing that none of the priestesses work a genuine prophesy into their rites. I grew up seeing that alluded to in movies, but the reality is very different. ``Men don't tip to be teased," Jack explained after my first visit. "They tip to see tits."

Cinnamon is meeting those expectations -- and, apparently, some of her own. She spends a lot of time stealing glances at herself in the wall of mirrors at the back of the altar. Through the tinted spotlights and smoke and pulsating music, she seems bigger, more real. Up there in the lights, on the main altar, I can see why so many goddesses think they are stars.

Despite the DJ's suggestion, no one has ``sidled up" to the foot lights, a situation Jack finds untenable. ``We should tip her. They liked to be tipped when they're in front of everyone, makes them seem more popular."

After Cinnamon completes the acrobatic pole work part of her rite, we applaud approvingly and take positions to the right of the altar. We each slip several $1 bills into her offering plate. And yet, she does not seem appreciative of the gesture. Her eyes seldom stray from the money, and there is none of the sensuality of the table rite. With only a few minutes left on the clock, she is down to grinding through the motions.

When the song ends, we clap and hoot, but she doesn't hang around for the applause. She simply pulls her tips from the offering plate, picks up her costume and disappears into the vestry. The movie is over, the magic is gone.

"That was kinda rude," Jack complains. "They're supposed to come down and do table rites."

But the time for worship is over. The overhead lights suddenly click on and the DJ plays Aerosmith's version of ``Happy Trails," a Plato's Palace end-of-the-evening tradition that Jack abhors. ``They should play something good, like'To the End.' Or nothing. I'd rather them play nothing at all than that. It really ends the night on a sour note."

Not too sour, of course. Corvette motions to Jack to join her at the bar. A minute later, he is herding me toward the door.

"Let's go, let's go," he says. "Corvette just heard about a party. I think we're going to score."

#

We do not score.

Corvette's party turns out to be another illusion. After a brief period of negotiation, she and a couple of her priestess friends go off in search of a new opportunity. The plan is to meet back at the Plato's Place parking lot in one hour. Jack waits patiently for about three minutes. Then the mathematics of desire set in.

``The other night, Corvette's roommate was telling me about doing chocolate mysticism," Jack says. "I think we need to get some."

"Is that like regular mysticism, but with chocolate?"

"Or like regular chocolate but with mysticism mixed in."

"I hope it's milk chocolate. I don't like the dark kind."

"Like those Hershey's Special Darks?"

"I hate Special Darks."

"I don't hate them, but I only eat one when I'm in a dark mood. Anyway, this girl, she said this stuff was wild." Jack pauses to laugh at the memory. "She said sparks were flying off her fingertips."

"I don't know."

"She said she got it off an onbeam dream hacker. He had a backdoor code into the R&D lab at a major pharmaceutical house and extracted from some anthropologist's recurring dream of a mythical South American jungle hallucinogenic."

"Maybe we'll have mystical hallucinations, see music and hear colors. Fighting, fighting, leap years still gleaming, broad striped bombs dreaming, bursting blacked out overdose."

"Before we kill each other."

"Or maybe it'll be like the Navahos and peyote and we'll eat it and see The Deity.

"You could put it in your book."

"It's not a book. It's just ideas for stories."

"I bet Corvette already found some sacraments. Probably shoveling them up her nose while some guy bends her over the toilet. What a whore."

Jack has a faraway, angry look on his face. I start laughing.

"I'm serious. That's what all those goddesses do. They just put out for sacraments. They never buy them."

"You're the expert."

"We should go by her apartment, see if she's there."

"What about the chocolate mysticism?"

"I don't know where to get any of that. That's what Corvette is for."

"She won't be home."

"Then we'll steal her spore. What a whore."

#

Bachman Manor is an artifact from the Hydrocarbon Age, a shabby collection of nondescript boxes, flat roofed and buff bricked. A couple of units have been long boarded up, the sheets of plywood buckled and cracking. The complex would appear derelict except for the parking lot full of the detritus of Detroit. Old rattletrap Novas, Monte Carlos, Cutlasses -- the refuse of the crumbling, discredited Hydrocarbon Age.

Scattered shards of broken glass glittering in headlight beams, broken images against a tar black sky. A pale street light casts a yellowish, washed out glow across the landscape, turning the chlorophyll green of the leggy shrubs and trees a sickly, obscene beige. Even the summer scream of the cicadas is muted, a dim, lost transmission from a distant planetary grove of lifeless, polluted hierarchies uprooted and flaming dully on refuse mounds maintained by secret operatives from Galaxy Ozona.

Jack parks in front of Corvette's building and tries to look casual as he leads the way up the steel stairs, onto the concrete-surfaced landing. In our golf shirts and khakis and deck shoes, though, I worry the residents may peg us as FBCU or undercover narcotics officers, certainly the last thing you'd want to be at a place like Bachman Manor. As we climb the stairs, I spotted an old, black sedan -- a late '50s Ford, by the look of the tail fins -- driving slowly by. I've seen this car before, outside my grandparents' house in Fort Jesup, epicenter of the Land of the Dead.

At this point Granny and Paw had been dead for years now, but the house lived on without them. In fact, it had grown larger, deeper. No doubt all necessary expansions required to hold the numerous memories of 140 years of Leachs in Sabine Parish.

I see an old woman's face troubling a moth-eaten mirror. Plump faced, white-haired, a laughing ghost. She looks a bit like one of my aunts, a woman who is still alive. This is not good. Terrified, I run to middle room in the front of the house. This should be the bathroom, but it has reverted to the bedroom it was before the house was plumbed by my father and uncles in the 1960s. Within these chalky, beaded board walls there is a bed and a woman. She is a relative of some sort who is now the house's caretaker. A landlady of the dead.

I apologize for bursting in. I am supposed to sleep in the adjoining room. We talk a bit, then I go to my room. This should be the living room, but when I step through the door I find a screened-in porch. It is run down and derelict. Sagging screen, rotting wood, Southern decay. I look out through the rusty steel grid and see the black car leaving my uncle's double wide next door. It is an animated medieval woodcut, black as night, old '50s tail fins suggestive of a Thunderbird or Galaxie 500.

#

Jack knocks on the door, an unnecessary precaution.

"Right now they're probably back in the parking lot giving prophesy to some sacrament dealer," Jack scowls. He carefully lifts the screen out of one of the aluminum window frames and raises the sash.

``They don't have a key, this is how they come and go," he explains. We crawl through the open window and punch our way past the dusty, sun-scorched brown curtain, the sheer white lining rotted away around the seams. Jack feels his way around the door frame and flips on the light.

A single, bare bulb glares from the shattered remnants of a frosted square light fixture in the middle of the ceiling. The only piece of furniture is an overstuffed sofa covered in some sort of brown, velvety fabric, its fuzzy mat worn down to a sheen on top of the rounded arms and front edge of the seat cushions. A poster of a sort of Art Deco-style pink flamingo stares out from the wall behind the sofa. A laundry basket overflows with presumably clean clothes. A dying cicada writhes inside an empty pizza box. Nearby, there is assortment of VI patches and condoms.

"Looks like they had another orgy," Jack scowls. He knees down in front of the sofa and reaches underneath, retrieving a red plastic mixing bowl. He swirls a finger around inside and wrinkles his nose.

``She bought a big baggie last night, and now all that's left is a bunch of sporangium and ashes," he says. ``Not enough here for even half a growth."

In the kitchen, we find insect-infested cabinets and a sink of plastic dishes sitting in greasy, chili-colored water. Jack opens the refrigerator.

"Anything chocolate?" I asked.

"No, just water."

He tosses me a bottle of Ozona, and we move on to the bedroom. Continuing the less-is-less theme, it is furnished with two twin beds. No night stand, no dresser, no chair. The floor is littered with clothes. An Iron Maiden poster is tacked to the wall over one of the beds.

Jack walks into the open closet and began rummaging through a mound of tattered panties and T-shirts that spilled off the top of a blue chest of drawers. ``Sometimes she keeps her sacraments hidden in here," he explains.

I join the search, but I am soon sidetracked by an expensive-looking bra, the only clothing item that doesn't look used up.

``I bought that for her," Jack says. ``When I met her she didn't own one."

``You wonder how she got through high school without being sent home. Remember those useless assistant principals at

Duncanville? They never seemed to have anything better to do than to roam the halls looking for bra-less girls and guys with hair touching their collar."

``She didn't finish high school. None of them do. That's why they're goddesses."

After a bit more rummaging, Jack suggests we go back to the Plato's Palace and wait for Corvette.

``There won't be a party," he explains, "but she always knows who's holding."

#

Jack is right; there is no party. I am a bit concerned that Corvette might take offense that we'd broken into her apartment with the intent of theft. But this proves to be a groundless worry. When Jack tells her what we've done, she just laughs.

``Shit don't last around there, you know that," she says. ``We soaked it all last night."

``Geez Corvette, just the two of you?"

``Oh, we had some help."

Jack doesn't like that one bit.

``I want to see you tonight," he blurts out.

``You're seeing me right now."

``I want to see more of you."

``You should have bought a table rite. That shows just about everything."

``That doesn't hardly show anything I'm interested in seeing."

And so the witty exchange goes on another couple of hours. I stumble on in an exhaustion-induced haze, jammed into the back of the Jag in the little space behind the seats. Jack is at the wheel, of course, and Corvette shares the passenger seat with her friend Brandy, another Plato's Palace goddess with a reputation for sniffing out parties and sacraments.

After a half dozen fruitless visits to run-down apartment complexes that are at least as desperate and depressing as Bachman Manor, we end up once again somewhere off Northwest Highway.

Corvette knocks on a door at the top of a flight of stairs, and it slowly opens to reveal a bearded, wild-eyed giant with a beer in his hand and slobber on his chin. She and Brandy are granted admittance; we wait outside. A few minutes later Corvette returns to the landing.

``Does he have any mysticism?" Jack asks hopefully.

``All he's got is louse, but he knows somebody who can get us some coch."

Jack pretends to seriously consider the possibilities, but I know he isn't interested. Last week he had complained of paying Corvette several hundred dollars for a baggie of cochineal, only to watch the wine-colored grit disappear up her nose in a matter of minutes. Clearly, he does not relish repeating such a costly mistake.

``Well, how about the louse?"

Corvette looks at him gravely and slowly shakes her head. ``Look, he's black, and that means it's nigger spore. And you don't want any of that."

I am immediately gripped by the idea of this apparently undesirable ``African American" spore. What makes it different from ``Caucasian" spore?

A line of decrepit shotgun shacks sags against the Piney Woods, brittle white paint peeling off rough sawn clapboards. Doors and windows open wide, a naked boy barely visible just inside, the foreskin of his giant, uncircumcised member bleeding into the shadowy, unlit interior. And out back the woman of the house, an amazingly fat specimen in a shapeless flowered dress, hoeing a row of lush-looking bushes, her special stand of louse, nourished by the rusty red loam and the good Lawd's rain and mysterious voodoo incantations passed down from her enslaved ancestors. Come fall, the spore will be harvested, cured and turned over to a city-wise brother or boyfriend, who will transport it to Dallas and sell it to son-of-a-bitch white folks. That is, after he laces it with backwash from the nightmare riptides -- rodenticide, dog laxative, his own VD-tainted urine. Four hundred years of oppression. Up yours, white boy.

I am so tightly gripped by this ridiculously racist vision that Jack must yell in my ear to break the spell.

``Little dreamer!"

"What?"

"Let's go. You blanked out again, as usual."

I look around. We are alone.

``Where's Corvette?" I ask.

``She's gone. Everybody's gone. All off to somebody's party to get some coch. To get laid is more like it. What a whore."

#

Heading home.

Fully reclined for the ride back to Strangers Rest, I feel a little guilty leaving Jack to keep himself awake. But he has always been able to keep going longer than me, especially when he is behind the wheel. Where the road would lull most people toward sleep, it tends to invigorate Jack. Because no matter where he might be going, Jack can always find (or make) a good time when he gets there.

I close my eyes and see naked torsos and snake-skin offering plates. But not for long. The car slows; we are pulling off the main road, into the parking lot of yet another shabby apartment complex. Jack parks next to a burned out Camaro and pockets the keys.

``Got to see this girl I met last week," he mutters, setting out across the cracked blacktop.

I wonder how this girl will feel being roused out of bed at 3 a.m., but as Jack nears the outdoor stairway a door opens and an excited woman sticks out her head.

``I don't believe it!" she squeals, running out and throwing herself into Jack's arms. Apparently the residents of this complex don't sleep, because a second woman watches the joyful reunion from the open door of her unit. The woman leads Jack up the stairs, and they disappear into her apartment.

A few minutes later, I toot the horn at the nearest building. Jack's newest girlfriend sticks her head out the window, tousle-haired and bleary eyed, squinting into the night. A moment later she draws back inside. Jack does not appear at all. It's going to be a while. What to do now?

I look out the windshield, across the long bulbous hood of the Jaguar. I want to picture myself as Jack, driving into the lights of the city on my way to a date with a special flesh temple priestess. But the vision does not hold. Instead, I am on a car trip, driving with my family through East Texas. It is a stretch of rural, two-lane blacktop, much like the one that runs between Mabank and Canton on the cusp on East Texas. So happy, enjoying our little day trip in the country. But I need a restroom, and none are to be found.

Suddenly I fear I have missed the turnoff. And still no restroom. It occurs to me I could relieve myself by the side of the road. But while it is a rural area, there is a lot of traffic, no privacy at all. I hate that.

Then we are on foot.

We find ourselves walking along a smoothly graded roadbed - perfect, like potting soil, not a clump of dirt or a rock to be seen -

shaded by tall trees, the dark Piney Woods. This is deep East Texas now, the Sabine National Forest. I can smell that East Texas scent, that peculiar mix of the humid and fertile with a sharp turpentine bite - clean and fresh, yet unmistakably of the musty Old South. We are on the El Camino Real nearing the Land of the Dead, which lies perhaps 45 minutes away beyond the old steel girder Sabine River bridge (now buried some 30 years under the Toledo Bend Reservoir, watched over by the ghost trees that even now crowd the still waters) and 140 years of Leach family history.

It is dark in the deep shade of the Piney Woods, so dark in fact that as I follow what I think is the roadbed I suddenly realize I have lost my way and am standing in a freshly graded circular driveway. We are in someone's front yard. It proves to be the first of a group of houses, like a mini village.

Now we are off the path entirely. To continue the journey, we must cross through someone's fenced yard.

"They can't blame us," I hear someone in our party say. Perhaps it is one of my parents, who I think are now somehow with us. For now, it seems that our group numbers perhaps a half dozen.

"It's the only way to get through to the other side," someone else allows. "I'm sure the owners are used to it."

Then we are in the backyard, on a wooden deck, and we can even see the road - the El Camino Real - just beyond the fence. But there is still no access; we realize that we must go through the house to regain the Pathway, to continue the journey. No one is home, so we let ourselves inside.

I'm not entirely comfortable with this. It is, after all, breaking and entering. But there is a vague consensus among our party that we are known by or even related to the owners. And since they live in the country, they won't mind too much if we let ourselves in. Country folk are friendly. It will be OK.

We look around the house a moment, but before we can find the back door some neighbors arrive. They are polite, but understandably a bit suspicious. Rather than talk to us about why we are here, though, they want to know - asking politely, of course - about the "potato pot" that was left on the door on one of their homes. There is a sense that we were the ones who "borrowed" the pot - perhaps from this house - and left it on their door.

Since I still need to relive myself, I go to the bathroom. But as I begin to urinate into the toilet, water starts backing up and spilling over the top. The water is clear; all that pollutes it are bits of disintegrating toilet tissue. Using a plunger, I try to clear the blockage. Water is gushing forth, almost artesian. The water cannot be contained. It wells up, alive.

#

Although that wild night on the town will make great cinema, I must admit I do possess a fair degree of shame. I wish to be a perfected being. That I am not is a realization that is almost more than I can bear. But then I consider Clark Caring, and I feel redeemed. Let us return to His divine mail bag.

#

I received another excellent letter today from Miss Beechemeyer's second grade Caringday School class. (Kudos to Miss Beechemeyer. Suffer the little larva to come unto me.)

#

Dear God:

How did you become God? Was there another God who turned you into God?

Love,

Jimmie Brogan

#

Good question, little Jimmie, glad you asked!

As you apparently have picked up from eavesdropping on the conversations of your elders, some of my beloved creations have begun to suggest I am not so much God as merely godlike – with a lowercase "g". A minor deity, if you will.

It's not just your heretics and artists who take my name in vain, either. Sometimes when you are hanging pictures in your hives and you accidentally hit your pincher with a hammer, you curse my name under your breath. Behind my back. And sometimes at night, in your dreams, some of you call me a narcissistic horror, a monster. Oh yes, you do. You thought I didn't know that.

Your heretics and artists say I am a bad God. They say I am an insane, transcendent being who has made a world that is cruel and filled with pain. However, I say it is all of you who are insane and cruel, all of you who fill this world with pain. After all, it is you who pollute the environment, turning the pink sky I created for you to a dusty, suffocating mauve.

You have turned the once-slippery froth hills into a sticky terror, so unusable that this new generation of larva can no longer slide down them on lazy summer days. You contaminate the waterways I created for you with the chemical byproducts generated during the manufacture of the plastic antennae you wear to look young and beautiful like the models in your ridiculous fashion magazines. Let us be totally honest, my beloved creations. It is all of you who are the narcissistic horrors, all of you who are the monsters.

Not me, just you.

For all of you, the citizens of Planet Luh, it would appear the Apocalypse can't happen quickly enough. No, you insist on rushing it along.

Anyway, little Jimmie, back to your question. As a matter of fact, I do know of a god who came before me. He created me, just as I have created all of you. He even gave his only son to us so we could murder him. Don't worry. There is a happy ending. A few days later this god brought his murdered son back to life so he could live in Heaven as the No. 2 guy, leading a life of royal leisure and urging all of His beloved creations to eat his body and drink his blood and live forever.

Back in the day – back before the day, even – the only way to live forever required eating the body and drinking the blood of this god's son and accepting him as the No. 2 guy in Heaven. A few people tried consuming mysticism and other illicit sacraments. But that didn't work either.

Then came EternaLife™ from Valuosity Life Planning Inc. With this product, we no longer had any need for a deity who granted life extension powers. But I'm getting ahead of myself.

Now that your heretics and artists know about this other god and his son, I'm sure they will soon be telling you I'm nothing like Him – the one with an uppercase "G." Sure, He gave his only son for his beloved creations. But come on – you call that a sacrifice? I mean, didn't He bring his only son back to life and set him up in Heaven as the No. 2 guy, the occupant of the right hand throne, leading a life of royal leisure? How many of you would give up a couple of days of life for a gig like that?

That god was a popular one, for sure. People fought many wars in his name and prayed he would make them victorious so they could enslave their enemies, cart away their gold and smash in the heads of their children until gray goo oozed out of their twitching, quivering skulls. He blessed many people through the ages, but none more than the people of Texas.

Texans were his chosen people. He showed them how to harness the electron and steal raw materials from godless foreigners. With the blessings of God, Texans were able to clog their arteries and grow huge bodies by consuming obscene amounts of fat, salt and other poisons at fast food restaurants. God blessed them with huge ass houses and huge ass SUVs, and he even gave them lots of Motherfuckers to tell them what was important. Yes little Jimmie, back in the day Texans pretty much had God in their back pockets.

And then one day, He was arrested.

Sleeping in after our night on the town. I hear a knock at the front door. Peeking through the blinds into the mid-morning sun, I see a white stretch limo waiting downstairs at the curb.

"I'm here to take you to Another Cafe," the uniformed chauffeur explains. "They're shooting the lunch scene with Jack and Tina."

#

"The working title is 'An Apocalypse of the Heart,'" The Stranger explains.

"I thought it was 'Strangers Rest,'" I say.

"That, too. And maybe 'Dreaming the Conclusion of Time' or even 'Dreaming the Apocalypse.' I'm not sure yet. But it's going to be great."

"It's about us?"

"And the End of the World. It's an SF epic, but it's also a documentary of visionary transformation. Really, you could call it our autodreamography. Here's the concept: 'Rapture, Texas.' You like?"

"Pretty."

"In this movie, the Rapture has finally come. Or perhaps not. The only thing certain is that a large portion of the citizenry is in the grip of the idea that thousands of people have been snatched up into the sky. Is it mass hysteria? A hoax? Extraterrestrials? Or is it truly the beginning of the end, when true believers will be taken up to heaven to be with the Deity before the Noble Misfortune and the Battle of Armageddon Drive-in Theatre?"

"What does this have to do with my incredible revelation?"

"Be patient. We must first construct the back story and establish metaphorical reference points. Deek Rookie is pretty skeptical that anything of an otherworldly nature has happened, but there's no doubting one essential truth -- everyone around him has gone Rapture crazy and it's wrecking his life. Deek, a resident of the sleepy North Texas suburb of Rapture and a reporter at the Rapture Weekly News, must endure the constant influx of pilgrims seeking out a miracle in his appropriately named town as well as write stories that attract even more attention. The big news is the Next Arrival, a week of organized fasting and prayers scheduled to build toward a Saturday night revival meeting on historic Main Street and climaxing in a Sunday mass baptism at the drive-in theater. But first, Deek tries to unravel a mystery of his own. He finds a mutilated calf in the Oddfellows Cemetery -- a Satanic sacrifice, residents assure him. And the priest he recruits to resanctify the unmarked graves of the Mexican railroad workers -- the only Catholics in the cemetery -- turns out to be a lot more interested in watching the heavens for signs and portents with a computerized telescope he has installed in the ruins of an old frame church on the edge of town."

"That's a nice touch."

"The world premier will be at a specially constructed drive-in movie theater, a sort of temple located in the Himalayas of India. Cylindrical clock chimes hanging from clouds will convene the moviegoers from around the planet. I will be stationed behind the camera, encircled by a multitude of grips and gaffers, vocalists and primal goddesses. Uniformed orators narrating manuscripts in marches and spectacles will fashion their share of the exploits along with the primal goddesses, whose dance routines will incorporate eye signals and stroking of the fingertips in combination with aromas of enjoyable fragrances as well as pungent, smoldering flame. Columns of anger will dot the landscape, and fire will explode in streams of luminosity and expanses of conflagration. This will continue for seven days. When the movie is finally over and final credits roll, the world will at last come to an end. And I will be God."

"Pretty."

"There will be introductory narration, too. I lifted it from 'Dr. Strangelove.' In excess of a year, disturbing reports had been confidentially transmitted between First World government heads that Alumina International was at labor on what was mysteriously implied to be the Final Weapon, the world's first artificial deity. Intelligence informants pursued the highly clandestine corporate scheme to Rapture, Texas, an outlying suburb of the Land of the Dead. What Alumina was developing, or why it should be in such a distant and deserted locale, no one could ascertain."

#

My role at Another Café is to spend half the day in a window booth with Jack, who is compelled to endlessly repeat his one line – "But I wanted chicken" – as we watch the FX crew make hundreds of loaves of bread and microwave fish sticks multiply on his plate.

In between takes, Jack finds time to grope Tina Wells, the head waitress and his conquest du jour. At Jack's urging wardrobe has put her in an impossibly tight T-shirt and faded cut offs. The Stranger is checking her out through his Beulah 9000, a hand-held 16 mm camera he uses to frame scenes and keep notes on what he's been shooting.

"This is the scene where Tina tells Mark that she fears her grandfather, Cowboy Roy, is losing his mind," The Stranger explains, "He's playing poker with spectral cowboys in the ruins of the Silver Spur Saloon."

"It's true," Tina says. "He may have Old Timers disease."

Jack shakes his head. "Old Timers disease? That's so lame."

"And," The Stranger continues, "she tells Mark that her grandfather is worried about the dead calf he found in the Oddfellows Cemetery. The body appeared to have signs of mutilation. But what he does not realize is this is a ploy engineered by the black ops division of Ozona International, which is involved in a UFO conspiracy that includes government suppression of reports of strange lights or aircraft near fields where mutilated cattle are later found. Roy and the rest of the townsfolk don't know this yet. Why is that, Tina?"

"They think it's the work of devil worshippers," she says.

"That's right," The Stranger replies. "Thanks for reading the script. So Roy wants to find a Catholic priest to re-consecrate the unmarked graves of the Hispanics, the poor folk who helped put the railroad through town. The problem is there's no parish in Strangers Rest; however, Tina has learned from one of her customers that a priest-turned-scientist – Father Henceforth Bypass – has bought the old Baptist church. The sanctuary was abandoned when the congregation found true religion and became the Keepers of the Deity. They built a big, new warehouse sanctuary out on the Interstate where they wait for the Rapture. Also, Jack makes Tina sit in his lap while he simulates an unnatural sex act in the vicinity of her solid waste excretory orifice."

"Now wait just a minute," Tina protests.

"All right," Jack says. "Unnatural sex acts are my favorite kind."

"Have you ever had a natural sex act with Tina?" I ask.

"Maybe once or twice."

"By accident."

Then Jack leans in close and speaks into my ear.

"Did I tell you about the time we did it doggie style on the kitchen floor?"

"I believe it was your first night together. You'd hired her to be a babysitter for Billy, and you were supposed to be back by midnight.

But you didn't get in until 3, so you made it up to her by giving her some rear entry ectoplasm on the linoleum."

"Hey, that kitchen is ceramic tile. No vinyl anywhere in my houses. I've got my standards."

"And while she was still naked, you gave her the money for the babysitting. So it was kind of like you were paying her to permit you to penetrate her membranes."

"You laugh, but most women really do nurture a little bit of a prostitute fantasy."

"Who are we to judge?"

"That reminds me. I forgot to tell you about Cinnamon."

"Tell me what."

"She wants you."

"You are so full of it."

"I'm not kidding, man. I told her 'forget it, he's married.' But she didn't care."

"What did she say?"

Jack laughs at the recollection. "She said 'I bet he's got a big one.' And I said 'don't I know it.'"

#

I have a confession. Back in high school I led Jack to believe that I had penetrated your membranes and expelled my ectoplasm inside you. So many evenings together, membrane to membrane, and yet never an act of penetration. Must have been your willpower, not mine.

But Tina – she did not have any discernable willpower. She allowed Jack to penetrate her membranes and expel his ectoplasm inside her on a regular basis. The story is rather sad. When Tina did her first babysitting act for Jack, she was very young, not quite "legal." By the time The Stranger put her into his movie, she was only a couple months past her 18th birthday – but plenty old enough to figure out that she was not going to be the second Mrs. Jack Bryson. Why marry the membrane when you can penetrate it for free (or at least at the going hourly rate for a teenage babysitter)?

As for Jack, at this point he still believes he is doing fine, completely oblivious to Tina's cold stare and crossed arms as she waits for her scene.

"You look hot," Jack tells her. "That tight T-shirt, those short, tight cutoffs – I think you need to come do some rehearsing on my lap."

"They've got to touch up my makeup," she says. "The best boy said – "

"Hey, I got your best boy right here."

"You are so disgusting."

"Oh come on, like I'm the only one here who thought of that?"

#

After the café scene, The Stranger and I walk over to the old Strangers Rest Baptist Church to scope out my introductory scene with Father Henceforth Bypass.

I could tell you a lot about Father Bypass, but all you really need to know is he is a carbon copy of the retired preacher I stumbled upon in my dream outside the ruins of the old Trinity Baptist Church in Fort Jesup.

"He's a priest-turned-scientist," The Stranger explains, "so he's very symbolic of the conflict between the waking, rational zone and the Land of the Dead. Just think of him as the Jungian archetype for the Wise Old Man, a role he shares with me. If either of us says something – especially if it sounds like a speech or monologue – then it's probably important for the thematic development of the story. OK?"

#

Like the church in the Fort Jesup dream, Strangers Rest Baptist is missing the front wall. But although it is full daylight, it's dark inside the sanctuary because a tornado is brewing. Not a real tornado, of course. It's cinematic. The Stranger has directed the construction of a gigantic tornado mechanism in the parking lot. A turboprop on a 20-foot tower blows water on the missing end of the sanctuary, whitening the post oaks. The rumble mechanism rumbles, an enormous distention of sheet metal with a gas-powered engine and a cushioned cam. When I arrive they are just trying it out. An incident in the film – The Stranger won't say what – requires a Texas twister. The turboprop roars, a current of air and water whip the old church, the post oaks turn inside out, shingles tear loose, sheet metal rumbles. But on the other side of the parking lot the sun shines with great composure.

Inside the church a strobe machine sporadically illuminates the fake storm darkness with fake lightening flashes and greenish tornado glow. There is a deluge of blood and marble-sized hail, flashes of purple-veined lightening bolts are visible through the gaps in the boarded up windows. Some sort of I-heart-Jesus banner is rent in two, like the temple veil. Very symbolic.

And milling about near the vestry is Father Bypass – no mistaking him. As in my dream, he is clad in a checkered soft shirt and the small, tidy balance of facial hair, withdrawn from religious employment in advance of death.

The Stranger gives a motivational speech to the crew.

"The concept is a blatant rip off of a Walker Percy essay, 'Notes for a Novel about the End of the World.' Of course, this is quite different. For one thing, it's a movie. And I am the director, the Deity, the omega being who creates a serious motion picture about the conclusion of time - i.e., the termination of one era and the commencement of another.

"Picture a newspaper reporter of the upcoming era – say, 75 years after the creation of the apocalyptic weapon, a message from the Deity. Or so they say. He is of the understanding that some theologians subscribe to a school of thought in which Noah's 'rainbow' is an incorrect translation and its context is a misunderstanding. According to this argument, the ancient text actually refers to the Deity's "Archer's Bow" in the sky. And this reference is not a promise to humanity, but a display of the Deity's regret. "This tide was false," the Deity is saying. "I must remember not to repeat it." The Deity's bow, a weapon of mass destruction hung in the heavens so to speak. A suitable analogy for the onbeam collective, a sword pounded into a plowshare, which cuts a furrow, a sort of deduction ditch, into which we can place underground cables of fiber optics, fibers which carry lightening bolts. It is possibly not too different from the effect exercised long ago by prophets. The effect can be repeated today by rapidly waving widespread fingers before closed eyes -- a simple technique, really – while turning one's countenance to the sun, a ball of fire, creating the proper oscillating motion. The light show that is observed through the eyelids is said to initiate the Vision, a core detonation from the Deity, a revelation screaming through the sky, the iconic mushroom cloud. Former servicemen who observed the test explosions of the 1950s described the cloud as possessing all the colors of the spectrum, which is to say a rainbow.

"This is the construction of our future out of our past. So the newspaper reporter is departing his office on a common workday and going by the crumbling remains of a forgotten church. A Vault of the Deity. From this empty shell a Walker Percy-inspired stranger comes out and confronts him. The stranger is a tired, faulty creature, a pilgrim of the old, dead Hydrocarbon Age. He is a priest with whiskey on his breath, a failed man of The Deity who has been delivered as one more substitute in antagonistic terrain. This stranger speaks to the reporter.

"'You give the impression of being ill.'

"'This is true,' the reporter admits. 'However, I shall be feeling OK in a little while, when I return to my abode and consume Ozona with Skinalicious9 – my spiritual beverage, my sacrament, the most excellent of spirit-amalgamating, Walker Percy-inspired preparations.'

"But the priest says 'proceed with me and I shall present you with a sacrament that will permanently amalgamate your spirit. It will be the final sacrament that you will ever require.'"

#

Next, The Stranger sets up a moderately long section of foreshadowing about an old computer that he claims will become a gratuitous spiritual oracle later in the story: The 6600 by Control Data Corp.

"It was designed in the 1960s by Seymour Cray," he says. "And he did it with transistors. There's 350,000 in there, can you imagine?"

He points to a little metal plaque – Property of Ozona International – that is affixed to the main operator console.

"When I was testing the keyboard I inadvertently crossed some wires," The Stranger explains, "and there was a brief flicker across the dual screens, a sentient blink by the all-knowing computer deity."

"The CIA knows all about it," Father Bypass adds. "The conclusion of time. They've been working on dream-carrying ballistic missiles for years. The ultimate doomsday weapon. Never practical, though. Too much risk of fragmentation, of scattering dreams all over the place. One simulation predicted schizophrenic manifestations and religious delusions over most of the Midwest and the Great Lakes region. People would notice. That's not anywhere near the Bible Belt."

Hooked into a serial port on the 6600 is an old piece of lab equipment from Edinger Scientific's Catalog 751, circa mid 1970s. I remember it from a catalog I found in my grandfather's house when I was 14. I lusted after the idea of that machine, which I mistakenly believed to be a dream recorder, something akin to the dream viewer in one of my favorite SF movies, "Five Million Years to Earth" (aka "Dr. Quatermass and the Pit").

#

Nocturnal Event-Dream Recollection Monitor

This device is being regarded as a major advancement in the study of nocturnal disturbances and as an appealing technique for acquiring and reserving dream recollections. Being conveniently transportable and easy to operate, it permits the scientist to perform nocturnal researches via subject manipulation of the device in the residence of the Deity. This quality omits the outward effect of the clinical atmosphere on nocturnal activities (i.e., sleep and dreams). Qualities include: razor-accurate needles for reserving minutes used in RSM (rapid soul movement) and other stages of nocturnal occurrences; an alert bell to rouse the subject during RSM to permit electronic reservations of nocturnal events; two specific stations of magnification to reserve any desired couple of 3 choices (electro-oculogram, electromyogram and electroencephalogram); 6 cadmium-zinc disk electrodes. Runs on 3 (Ni-acid) batteries incl. 10 X 8 X 10.

#

"I ordered one over the viral DNA dream phone," Father Bypass says.

"The what?" I ask.

"It's a phone for communicating with the Land of the Dead," The Stranger explains. "They're all the rage in Burial Chamber, Calif. All the directors are using them."

"Edinger didn't mind shipping the monitor forward 30 years," Father Bypass says, "but they'd only accept pre-1973 currency or BankAmericard."

"Then,' The Stranger says, "we hooked the electrodes into a special dream text interface that communicated directly with the 6600. Didn't take long to compute the zero hour."

The old priest of science rips a sprocket-edged sheet from a chattering daisy wheel printer and waves it triumphantly overhead.

"A half a million words," Father Bypass remarks. "I'm also an astrodream psychotronicist. So I ran every one of the words through the 6600, using simple algebraic equations to manipulate logarithmic multiples of the square root of infinity."

"Surreal mathematics," The Stranger says. "Great for building four-dimensional models and determining the conclusion of time.

"6:47 a.m. Sunday, to be exact."

"Let's retire to the vestry. Being the stereotypical whiskey priest, Father Bypass takes his bourbon straight."

#

Next I am to read my lines, but I refuse.

"What's wrong?" The Stranger asks.

"This film has nothing to do with my Incredible Revelation."

"As I said before, you must be patient. Back story first, then we establish the metaphorical reference points."

"Besides, I object to the premeditated life."

"You think you have a choice? You think you can escape premeditation?"

This is an unpleasant thought.

"Very well, then I'll read your lines for you," he says. "Here's one way the world ends: You are in the Duncanville High School cafeteria, eating lunch. There are several people at your table, and you are interested in one of the girls. But it occurs to you that she is not particularly interested in you. Maybe you will find someone else who really does like you, and then you will see what a difference it makes. As you think this over, it is like you are no longer a student but once again your 40-something self. You are now outside and one of the people in your group becomes intoxicated. He is unconscious."

"Yes, I do remember this dream," I admit. "Somehow it seemed important that I pick him up, move him back to the cafeteria."

"That's right. You gather up your belongings and prepare to leave. Lunch time is over. Then you are inside a house with your parents. They sit or relax on a bed in the living room, which reminds you of your great grandmother's home in Waco. You go to your bedroom, look at yourself in the mirror. You are a cartoon character, with bushy hair parted in the middle, big pink lips and a very skinny neck. You think to yourself that this is your true appearance. You must face the facts: It will be hard to find an attractive girl -- like the one at your lunch table – who will be interested in you."

"It's never been easy being me," I admit. "I never knew what to say to girls. If only I'd been a bit more physically attractive."

"That was never our real problem, just an excuse. Anyway, you return to the living room to talk with your parents. Again, you go to the mirror. You still have longish hair parted in the middle, but now your face is more normal. You decide you no longer look so strange. More talk with your parents. One of them mentions the word 'ghost.' You are not sure of the context. You look in the mirror a third time.

Now there is a normal man, but he is not you. And upon further reflection, you decide he is not quite normal after all, for he is menacing and almost demonic."

"In fact, the reflection was terrifying."

"You tell your parents about this. 'You cannot talk about ghosts in front of me anymore,' you say. 'It is too suggestive, conjuring up evil spirits.' You tell them about a theory that writers have autonomous spirits within them. This is all psychological, of course, symbolic – not actual spirits. But it is important. 'This is the way they are able to write,' you say. Your parents are concerned by this talk. 'We can get you to a doctor, a good one,' your mother says. 'It won't be like the ones you might encounter during an emergency room visit. This doctor will be the best.'"

"Yes. I dreamed that my parents said they use Simon & Schuster."

"Next, you are reading a scientific catalog. You look at a chart, which is almost like a game board. It is on paper, yet you can manipulate the drawings as if it were a computer screen. You can make the vehicles in the picture move. So you make some sort of submarine go to the bottom of a body of water, a lake or ocean. Then you flip to a different page and see a picture of self-contained living quarters for undersea use. It looks like a normal living room, complete with sofa and coffee table."

"I always thought it would be cool to have my own private submarine, like Princess Di."

#

"Everything was much simpler in the Hydrocarbon Age, before the conclusion of time," Father Bypass explains. "The concepts were identical with the words. But when an exact definition is no longer available, it's so easy to be flooded by the variations, subliminal and therefore never realized. Even the most matter-of-fact events can have a penumbra of uncertainty about them. Have you seen The Stranger's movie script proposals?"

"It doesn't matter," I say, "because apparently the world is going to end Sunday morning."

"That's good dialogue," The Stranger whispers to me. "Thanks for finally participating."

"A new world will take its place," Father Bypass says. "The real fear for most people isn't the apocalyptic weapon itself . No, the average person does not fear catastrophe. Rather, they fear the conclusion of time won't be any different than the day before."

#

Director's note: At this point in the chronology, the script collapses into a heap of broken images. The Stranger tells me I am to interview the whiskey priest. But Father Bypass has been drinking real whiskey. He is no longer capable of reading his lines. He totters unsteadily, departing from character. He vomits behind a pew, filling the air with partially digested nausea.

So The Stranger decides to read everyone's remaining lines plus give some off-the-cuff background commentary, all in a single, unbroken conversation with himself about himself. In the interests of posterity and cinematic purity, I have prepared a transcript of this monologue. My original idea was to decode it back into a coherent script. But now I find that I rather like this strange, irrational form. This is totally unique, a bold new voice in American cinematography.

#

PROPHESY OF THE NEXT ARRIVAL: A Film by The Stranger

Are you ready to interview me? No, I hate me.

Seriously, I don't know that there's anything to write about me. Don't I want to know about my work? No, I don't think I do. My editor is no longer interested in stories about the conclusion of time.

I live in a new world, a place and time when all of my wants and needs can be met. Creativity. Individuality. Equality. Can I name a time that has had more to offer than the past half century? I didn't think so.

Meanwhile, after almost 20 centuries of anticipation, the true believers are still awaiting the Son of the Deity's return engagement. Fire, pestilence, wrath of the Deity. And yet these days, the conclusion of time won't get me very far. It won't get me a byline story. Time is running short. So little time left, and yet still so much to do. They're closing in, the forces that would alter history from the dashboard lights of the black sedan, the car of death. It's part of the unifying global pattern, the blueprint of the apocalypse, starting now and through which I am being applied. It reflects the Job experience - or that of the divine son. Jesus was the first attempt, The Deity's effort to transform himself into Man. Now He is going to transform himself into all of mankind.

I see what I mean, but I also think I may be borderline psychotic. I have to be going. I really have to be going. I really understand. I really hate me.

I've got another interview in a few minutes. Now I must know this, for plot development purposes. Do I plan to re-consecrate those graves? And yet, a scientific explanation would prove more satisfactory. It's a well-worn copy of something titled 'Southwest Scientific Digest,' a paperback-sized publication in which Father Bypass published a scientific paper. Sea of water vapor found high in sky. New satellite data revives interest in controversial comet theory. Washington. Scientists at the Naval Research Laboratory claim data from a pair of satellites has revealed the unexpected presence of water vapor in the upper atmosphere, lending renewed support to a controversial theory that incoming comets are coating the Earth with extraterrestrial rain. Yes. We can add an element of hard science to this SF tale.

Every day our planet is hit by thousands of comets, big things, about the size of a house. And they contain water. It's actually ice. Anyway, they break up as they enter the atmosphere, and the water boils out into the air. Then it rains down on us? Exactly. Now scan down to the last couple of graphs. In related news, SSD has learned that a researcher with a background in theology is pursuing independent studies on the potential psychopharmacological effects of the phenomenon. Dr. Adolfo Morel of the Naval Research Laboratory said he is attempting to correlate the team's satellite mapping with a rise in regional episodes of delusional disorders, particularly those involving the physical manifestation of The Deity and other visions of a religious nature. He is theorizing that the water from the comets contains psychotropic compounds, which are making their way into the water table and becoming concentrated in the food chain. And of course, surreptitiously added to Ozona bottled water as an innocuous ingredient labeled Skinalicious9, also known as Liquid Jesus.

I found the hardest part of the research has been developing the software program. Look at this print-out, about six inches thick. See the notation for our area? Pretty. That's a concentration of delusional episodes. And the prefix codes correspond to meteorite and rainfall data for the region. See the dotted line? The path of a satellite? No. Hydroxyl ions. They correlate to water vapor at high altitudes. The ions form when ultraviolet light splits apart the water molecules. It's not rain, either. When you get up into the nether reaches of the atmosphere -- in this case, the mesosphere, a.k.a. heaven -- there's almost no water at all. It's a real desert up there, which suggests the climax revelation. Which is? The Ozona company is using these alien compounds to secretly modify the genetic pool of the populace and create the world's first privately owned and operated deity.

Dreaming the conclusion of time. Did you know that in the last 60 days in the Dallas/Fort Worth area, there have been over 500 reported sightings of individuals ascending into the clouds? Typical Rapture/Next Arrival stuff, the dead rising from their graves.

You do not want to believe. But do you want the story? You have no story. No one wants to read about the conclusion of time anymore. Editors won't even talk about it. The apocalypse was last week's news. Now we're back to printing stories about cute parrots, spunky old men, faithful dogs and dead girlfriends.

Then I retrieve a thick spiral notebook filled with Polaroid photographs of naked women. These psychotropic compounds may actually trigger hormonal changes. Did I know that the median size of women's breasts in the U.S. has increased roughly 6 percent over the past 30 years, even when adjusted for the average weight gain of the overall population? I would like to do that research right now. I am focused on the Polaroid photos, dozens of primal goddesses, each identified with a date and 16-place alpha-numeric code, sprawled on the tiled men's room floor, covered in black lace and ectoplasm. Naughty, naughty – and impressive, all volunteers for a survey done by a friend of mine. It's not very good science; however, he got a nice advance for offerings and table rites. He selected primal goddesses who had been arrested for assaulting men. A statistically significant blend of spirituality and violence.

What's that? Well, I'm not running an adult bookstore, you know. Remember Bovee's warning -- the body of a sensualist is the coffin of a dead soul.

Is there an index? Yes, but it's a semi-confidential report and – Success. Brooks, Louise (alias Cinnamon), Subject No. 92017. Stop. I'm violating scientist/subject confidentiality. But I won't stop. I can't make me, either. Scientific Vignette. Ms. Cinnamon is a 17-year-old primal goddess who, in her sixth possible month, attempted to murder an unborn epic film by drowning. In the weeks leading up to this suggested effort, she had knowledgeable neural vegetative visual rumors and symptoms of despair with superimposed delusions. These delusions were centered in the region of a Macintosh Portable Model 5126, whom the subject was persuaded was a reincarnated unkind being. As the risk for metaphorical behavior was far above the earth, she was right away admitted to the hospital's cinematic division and was then diagnosed with sharp poetic despair. She received six one-sided emotional coverlet treatments. She has improved very well, and is now contemplating another cinematic action.

Pretty.

But don't tell. It could seriously compromise the follow-up survey. Wounded instincts, that's the danger. Heal the animal within. Make him a friend. I see the snake wrapped around a staff as a visual rumor of the medical profession, a visual rumor of healing. And the Son of the Deity, too. We usually know him as a lamb or a fish or a lion, but also a serpent draped over the cross.

An abandoned house of the Deity reverting to wilderness, and a fallen whiskey priest with an extinct mainframe as his radio to the Deity? I really should do a story about me. It is a story about me and the Deity becoming one. This is a necessary merger to bring about the creation of the New Religion. For in the upcoming age, the true Christian will be the Christ of his own church. Or he will not be a Christian at all. So I diagnose myself as a narcissist. However, I may also be what people in ancient times called a prophet. That is, a man called by the Deity to communicate something urgent to other men.

But when was the last time I talked to someone about the Almighty? Yes. I see my point. Mankind is now occupying the role of the eternal son of the Deity. The Deity is setting up residence in the body of mankind, restoring the old church, the Vault of the Deity. This is the real Next Arrival. And it is taking place in the lives of people like the newspaper reporter who is accosted by the whiskey priest, people who can recognize what is happening and make it real in the world. Chosen. How many are there? The Book of Revelation says 144,000. Don't know if that is a literal number, but it suggests a rather extensive incarnation of the Deity into mankind. So, it's the story of a sort of prophet-in-training.

In truth, I don't hate me. I love me. I am a classic narcissist. When I was a boy I wanted to be king of the world. I remember a professor I had at seminary. But I thought I was not a priest. Did I say I was not a priest? I am a liar. No, I am a liar. Well, I remember it like it was yesterday. He'd say come along, boys. The seminary was all men in those days, of course. Come along, boys, and I'll tell you spiritual stories you've never heard. And then he'd talk about the Son of the Deity walking across Corpus Christi Bay or maybe Packery Channel and he'd ask us about that. How could it be any other way? Of course He would walk across the stormy seas of life.

So me, the little boy in the mirror, the demon under the bed, why don't I just get on with it? Get on with what? 6:47 a.m. Sunday.

#

The Stranger asserts that the movie is proceeding as scripted. But I am doubtful. For one thing, there is no Incredible Revelation. And something else is not right, though I'm not sure exactly what. A line is out of place, a cue is missing. I don't know what has occurred. Now the end is here and so am I, exiled to my Isle of Patmos, contemplating my future. Will I stand in the docket? Or will I go out into the world as a prophet, my lips purified with the burning coal?

I do not know. So I continue to tell you about the end times in hopes that the telling will help me uncover the truth. I tell you because you know me so well. I tell you because you are here.

I don't expect to stand trial. In fact, I believe that quite soon I will be leaving this place. Maybe Luh will go with me.

Did I tell you she paid me a visit yesterday? She came over from the neighboring island on her sail board, slicing through the Laguna Madre like – well, let's just say she was a quite a sight. I don't know if she was happy or smiling. I really didn't notice her face. She was in a white bikini. Healthy lungs. I don't know how she got past the sea monsters. She came within about 20 feet of the island, cutting a rather nautical turn in the frothy beach break.

"What's your name?" I called out.

"Luh," she said. Then the wind changed, and she headed back to her own island.

Her translucent skin reminds me of Allison, except she's not quite so thin, a bit more athletically built. Who am I kidding? Her breasts are enormous. My membranes are surging, my DNA singing.

#

What's that? Yes, now is a good time to delve into one of the story's most beloved supporting characters, Cowboy Roy. He would make a good movie all by himself. In fact, I already have the concept: "Requiem for a Singing Cowboy." You like?

In this Panavision/Technicolor Western, the retired singing movie cowboy becomes a modern day Don Quixote. But instead of losing himself in delusions of knight-errantry, Cowboy Roy becomes his on-screen persona – an Old West cowboy wandering a frontier that is no more, redressing wrongs through his prowess with a horse and a six-shooter. Here's a description I put together for the film treatment:

#

About 60 years of age, he was wizened and gaunt-featured, but of a sturdy constitution. A dark handlebar mustache belied his thick belly and thinning gray hair. A strong jutting jaw line punctuated the elongated shadow of his 6-foot-6 frame. He affected the speech of the heroes of the dime novels and old western movies he enjoyed, regarding both as the final authority on virtually all matters of the Old West. True, he hadn't rode a horse or roped a steer in years, but what was that to Cowboy Roy? He knew he was a real cowboy in his heart.

#

I must admit I like this concept, so much so that I already roughed out some introductory script:

Cowboy Roy was shooting the windmill again when the outlaws attacked.

It was almost sundown, and the gaunt, bullet-riddled tower cast a long shadow across the grassy hill where he stood. Roy Thornton was just a boy when his father bought the steel windmill at a livestock show in Fort Worth, replacing an ancient wooden model that had collapsed in a cold norther, an avalanche of icicles and splintered lumber raining down on a hapless young bull.

Barrell-chested, bow-legged Cowboy Roy aimed his ivory-handled six-shooter at the windmill's rusty blades, which turned slowly against the firey North Texas sky. Every time a slug hit, the metal framework rang out like a ranch house dinner bell, its thin metallic scream echoing across the rolling prairie.

The gunshots boomed defiantly every evening over The Lakes of Greenwood. There weren't many complaints, though. The luxury housing development boasted only three homes and one resident, homebuilder Jack Bryson.

Instead of sprouting houses, the remaining 157 one-acre home lots were waist high in grass and weeds. More vegetation sprouted from giant cracks in the streets and their fax-cobblestone intersections, and the ``lakes" (actually a series of stock tanks the developer had scooped out of the low spots along Henrietta Creek with a backhoe) had gone jade green with algae. Jack would have complained to the developer, except the developer was his father. Times were bad all around in the luxury home building business.

Still, The Lakes of Greenwood had yet to totally revert to wilderness. The stone-paved intersections and fachwerk clubhouse with Old World clock tower -- actually a thinly disguised elevated water tank -- made the project look more like a European Disneyland than ``the Texas you thought was gone forever," as the sales brochure described it. As for the three homes, they were mostly contemporary interpretations of eighteenth-century English manors – two-story neo-Georgian, dumb waitered and gas lit – the same sort of exaggerated architecture that was going up in neighboring Dallas and the rest of metropolitan Texas. The project didn't look like forgotten Texas at all.

Lying in the trampled grass at Cowboy Roy's feet was Sam, a tailless border collie. The unfortunate animal had showed up on the back porch one morning a few years back, and he hadn't left since. The absence of a tail hadn't affected the dog's disposition, which was invariably that of a happy pup. He spent most of his days alternating between sleep and chasing the neighbors' livestock, occasionally baiting a bravado-filled bull. Sam would bark and circle the beast until it began to shake its horned head, snorting and pawing the ground. Such displays served only to egg on the playful Sam, who would continue to antagonize the bull until it finally charged. That always sent Sam bounding across the field, wind in his ears and joy in his heart. He was oblivious to the animal's anger. He thought the chase meant the bull was having a good time.

Despite his agreeable nature, Sam didn't care much for his master's shooting. Every time the gun roared, he tried to hid from the noise between Cowboy Roy's feet, hunkered down and whimpering softly.

"Git along," Cowboy Roy scowled, gently nudging Sam with the side of his sharp-toed boot. "You're a lame excuse for a cow dog, you know it?"

#

I know – not very exciting. Poorly sculpted fluff. Yawn. This is always a problem for me, my inability to inject a sense of life into a conventional, waking world cinematic narrative. I cannot film the waking world. Why? Because it is too slow to capture on celluloid. Try as I may, it inevitably slips through my fingers, a whirlwind of Nazi paratroopers, bleeding walls and flesh-eating spiders.

So I will not embarrass myself by sharing the rest of the turgid introductory script. Instead, I will jump ahead to the action (i.e., the place where the waking world tumbles into the Land of the Dead).

#

Then he saw the guns.

It was just a metallic flash, a brief shimmer in the slanting rays of the westering sun. It could have been the faraway windshield of a passing car on distant Texas 114, or a jet on its final descent into D/FW Airport. Those were the obvious explanations, but Cowboy

Roy knew neither was the true story. He put a hand to his forehead, just to be sure. No V.I. patch.

His eyes shot to a nearby thicket of soapberry trees, the under story an impenetrable tangle of saplings and trumpet vines. There, he saw the glint of sunlight off the polished barrel of a Winchester repeating rifle. It was pointed right at him.

And suddenly the air was thick with gun fire. Cowboy Roy dived for cover, skidding palms first into knee-high weeds. Great tongues of blue flame leapt from the trees, and the bullets raised puffs of dust all around him. One ricocheted off a rock by his head, dusting his cheek with a chalky grit. Another grazed his boot heel, renting it in two. An arrow whizzed overhead, missing him by inches.

Crouching in the weeds, he hurriedly reloaded his gun and tried to determine the strength of his assailants. He could tell by the deafening fusillade that several weapons were involved, but all he could see was the smoke from their guns, an acrid black cloud that enveloped the thicket in darkness. He raised his gun to return fire, but before he could even take aim the shooting stopped.

Out of the roiling black cloud rode four men, each astride a different colored horse.

A sandy roan bore a half-naked Indian, a bow and quiver of arrows slung across his dark, shirtless back. He was flanked by two black horses, each bearing a large, bearded man in matching buckskin fringe jackets. And leading all three was a tall man riding a white horse.

He was of a sallow complexion, with sunken gray eyes that stared over the bridge of a large hawk-bill nose. The horse had red eyes and wide, flaring nostrils, and Cowboy Roy thought it looked like the devil's own mount. The man and his albino horse drew rein just shy of Cowboy Roy, the others lined up behind him. The Winchester lay across the leader's lap.

"What the hell you think you're doin' here?" Cowboy Roy asked, staring up at the tall man, the hot breath of his horse upon him. The horse smelled of rotting meat. The tall man smiled, revealing a black maw void of front teeth, and leaned forward in the saddle, resting an arm across his thigh.

``I'm here to whip you senseless," the man sneered, extracting a low rumbling laugh from his associates. "But I can see now you're too old to even bother with anymore. So why don't you be a good old man and drop that gun belt right now and throw up your props?"

Cowboy Roy glanced briefly at the other men, then back at their leader. He dusted off his pants with the brim of his hat, a ragged and sweat-stained ``four beaver" he now only wore around the home place.

``Get goin'," he said finally, his voice thick with disgust. ``Just crawl back in your hole, or I'll bullet-dance you there."

The Indian and buckskin-clad riders laughed again, and the tall man looked at him with mock surprise.

``Why, I had you figured for a smarter old man than that," he said, again flashing his rotted, toothless grin. "You don't want to go and rile us now. We've got you outnumbered four to one."

"That may be true," Cowboy Roy replied, bending down to tie his holster to his leg. ``But you'll get the bullet with the period on it."

Then the white horse reared back on it hind legs, hooves pawing the air and red eyes blazing like jellied fire. The four horsemen went for their weapons.

Cowboy Roy shot the Indian first, then the two men in buckskin, firing from his hip straight into their hearts. The pale rider lifted the Winchester to his shoulder, but death took him before his finger even touched the trigger. The horses bolted, leaving their dead riders sprawled in the dust, blood pumping from their chests. A tight helix of smoke curled from the barrel of the gun in Cowboy Roy's hand. Then everything faded to black.

Overhead, a large bird circled slowly atop a dying thermal that rose form the hill where Cowboy Roy lay. He thought it was probably a hawk, but it might have been a buzzard. It was hard to know for sure. A large gash had appeared on his forehead, leaving his vision a bit blurry. Even so, he could see plainly enough to know that the men were all gone. And he was thinking plainly enough to know they had never been there.

The bird then slanted off on a long, smooth glide towards The Lakes of Greenwood, alighting on the peak of the steep-roofed clock tower. Sam stood over his master, licking his face, but Cowboy Roy wasn't ready to get up quite yet. He just kept staring at the bird. He was almost sure it was a hawk.

#

Poorly sculpted fluff. If only I could produce a work of true visionary transformation, a creation worthy of "Let Me Love You." That cinematic classic contains colorful Texas imagery, specifically an alternate history in which the Texas is a sovereign nation. That B-movie imagery is so much more dramatic that I could ever manage, even if I had an A-plus budget.

#

I've been thinking you should make a movie about me.

Yes, I know I said no graven images. But this would be different. For one thing, it would be in 70mm. For another thing, I would be played by a youthful Omar Sharif, my sensitive yet strong voice resonating in THX surround sound.

By its very nature this movie would be numinous. It would conclude with me consuming myself, a hand sandwich and a glass of fermented corpuscles, a multimedia Eucharist.

"Mmmm, that's good Messiah," I would say.

Actually, the movie I have in mind is based firmly in reality. It is the story of my family and of Texas. For the opening shot, picture a close up of hands tying brightly colored ribbons to the gray limbs of a leafless tree in winter. The hands belong to Jewell Poe, my maternal grandfather. It is the winter of 1953 in Waco, Texas, and he is in his backyard conducting experiments in color photography. He needs the colorful ribbons because the winter landscape is all gray and dead, just like the black and white photos he's still working with in his portrait photography business in downtown Waco. See, he's using science to bring the dead winter landscape to life. Clever, right?

The story is also about my grandmother, who is dying from leukemia. And the protagonist is the girl who will become my mother. She is helping her mother – my dying grandmother – take care of her brothers and sisters – my future aunts and uncles – and helping her father hand color the black-and-white portraits at her father's downtown studio. Hand tinting – that's what they did back in the day to bring dead portraits to life. The climax occurs in May 1953, when a tornado rips through downtown Waco, leveling many businesses and killing more than 100 people. The tornado destroys my grandfather's studio and smashes in the roof of the old family Nash. It's also the last weekend my grandmother is able to get out of bed before her death. Very symbolic. You like?

But most important, the tornado is not a naturally occurring phenomenon. Turns out it is actually a rip in the space-time continuum, a vortex pulling 1950s Waco through a black hole and directly into the plot line of the present day.

#

I arrive at work the next morning to find I am once again the truth doctor at Valuosity Life Planning Inc.

I learn of this surprising turn of events from Preacher with a Gun, our golf cart-driving security guard and night student at a local seminary. Soon as I pull into the employee parking lot Preacher with a Gun comes racing up in his golf cart, a side arm on his hip and a Bible on the dashboard.

"Lose your card key?"

"What?"

"For the garage."

"Oh, that. I don't have one anymore."

Preacher with a Gun gives me a quizzical smile and points to my sun visor.

"Oh yes, there it is. I guess I forgot."

I can still use the executive parking garage? Preacher with a Gun waves at me in my rearview mirror as I pull up to the garage entrance and scan my card. The gate rises, and I pull in just as I always have. I park my Lexus LS400 in the space labeled "Clark Caring."

#

Yes, I am back. But how? How did I regain my former position – overnight?

Back in the day, this sort of question would be a strategic plot point that would be milked for a ridiculously interminable period of time. Of course the reader would quickly see that the text of "The Voice of God" is somehow transforming everyday events into an alternate reality. This would be obvious to all – except for the characters in the story. A protagonist like Clark Caring actually would be surprised to find that he had awakened to an alternate reality where he was still the truth doctor.

How could such a thing happen? What a mystery the protagonist is compelled to solve!

So he checks the files in his office, seeking the non-existent evidence of his demotion to technical writer in the LET department and the twin losses of his corner office and parking space in the executive parking garage.

So he wonders: What happened? Or rather, what DIDN'T happen? A protagonist like Clark Caring might muse to himself thusly: "Clearly, my personal timeline has rolled backwards -- at least a year I estimate. For everyone else, though, time continues to move forward. My computer and telephone display a time and date of 7:50 am June 25, about 14 hours after turning off the computer in my cubicle in the LET department and pulling out the employee parking lot for my commute home."

You know what I say? BORING. Talk too much do too few. Let us now skip right to the big scene, the one with the Prophet who foretells my future as your God.

#

We arrive at the home of the Prophet, whom we find inside a restored backyard barn (circa 1919) locked in a death struggle with a homicidal Macintosh Portable computer. He takes a break from the battle to greet us.

"Welcome to my island," he says, out of breath and sweating. "Pull up a deck chair, help yourself to the tanning oil. But watch out for the brain crabs – they bite!"

We take a seat on an old church pew.

"May I offer you a festive beverage," he continues, "perhaps with a paper umbrella? No? I understand. You are unsure, filled with doubt. You have purchased your ticket, acquired your soft drink and bucket of popcorn and taken your seat. And yet still you wonder: A Rapture movie without a Rapture? Is this really for you? Or perhaps you worry it is rather too much for you. That is to say, too much of the Prophet."

The hard drive inside the Macintosh Portable (aka "Mac") spins to life in a high-pitched whine.

"I'm told a little of you goes quite a ways," Mac says.

"You word processing bastard," the Prophet hisses, and they fall upon each other, writhing about on the worn floorboards in a terrible battle of ripping fabric, cracking plastic, broken incisors, saliva and blood.

"When they gaze upon each other murder is never long out of their eyes," Bellero whispers to me.

"You called me a drunken son of a bitch," the Prophet protests.

Bluish white sparks are jumping from Mac's RS-232 port. "You don't stand a chance with me."

"Dispatch from the Land of the Dead. I the Prophet have now created the world's first novella composed solely of consecutive dreams. Seven months of dreams, each night flowing into the next, the journey of life."

"What tripe."

"Where did these images come from? Perhaps they are the inevitable reaction to my many years of denying the unconscious. Certainly the path was blazed early on, in the dreams of youth. This is the travelogue."

"And then there's Nixon in Texas."

"Yes, what a concept."

"An alternate history. Republic of Texas. An independent and sovereign nation. LBJ as president. It works. Nixon is the visiting head of state, here to establish diplomatic relations across the Red River, the international border. And we have the 1963 assassination in Dealey Plaza."

"That's when I saw the motorcycle guys."

"You had just left the computer for a bathroom break. They caught you outside the restroom, held you down, puncturing your face. That's when you learn God has been arrested."

"No, no you computerized bastard. I already rewrote that section."

"But badly. What tripe. This requires a rewrite. Call in a script doctor."

"I hate you."

"Then we move on to the scene about the message issued by the new governor of earth. God was wrong, violated universal laws. Immoral acts, including global flood. Planned homicidal UFO invasion as described in Revelations. People turning into insects."

"A quick check of the Exogrid confirms the reactions of the populace. Christian evangelicals go into a massive Rapture frenzy. The planetary governor is the suspected Anti-Christ."

"And we'll give Clark a Jewish friend, who will say 'I'm still waiting for the First Coming.'"

"Nice touch."

"Meanwhile, local Hare Krishnas continue to run their renowned East Dallas vegetarian restaurant, unaffected by the announcement. The end is here, but no one notes its arrival."

The Prophet explains that only I can save the world. "Keep reading the sacred text, Clark. The world depends on it."

"What tripe," Mac says.

This is more than the Prophet can bear. He falls upon Mac again. But then water starts to gush forth from between the barns worn, circa 1919 floorboards. The Prophet and Mac break off their combat to observe the artesian phenomenon.

"The water cannot be contained," the Prophet explains through a broken tooth. "It wells up, alive."

The Mac spins its hard drive into another high-pitched scream.

"What tripe!" And again they fall upon one another, creator and creation, murder blazing in their eyes.

#

QUESTIONS

1. Do you like the story so far? Yes ( ) No ( )

2. Does the protagonist/narrator resemble John of Patmos in Revelation? Yes ( ) No ( )

3. In the further development of the story, would you like more wrath of God ( ) or less wrath of God ( )?

4. Is there too much eruption of the unconscious in the narration? ( ) Not enough eruption of the unconscious? ( )

5. Do you feel that the exploration of new mental disorders is a viable undertaking for the novelist of today? Yes ( )
No ( )

6. Has the work, for you, a metaphysical dimension? Yes ( ) No ( )

7 What is it (25 words or less)? ____

____

8. Have you understood, in reading to this point, that:

(a) The Stranger is attempting to create a movie based on "Last Year at Marienbad" in the same way that Donald Barthelme create a novel based on the story of Snow White? Yes ( ) No ( )

(b) this questionnaire is based on a list of questions in Donald Barthelme's novel based on the story of Snow White? Yes ( ) No ( )

(c) the protagonist/narrator and The Stranger are fictionalized versions of the author? Yes ( ) No ( )

(d) The Stranger is the Christ figure of the story? Yes ( ) No ( )

9. Do you believe the author thinks he is God? Yes ( ) No ( )

10. Would you like the world to end? Yes ( ) No ( ) If "yes," when? ____

Please send your responses to info@marienbadmylove.com

Congratulations. You have reached the end of the introduction to "Marienbad My Love." Now you are ready to proceed to the main body of the work. Begin by ripping out two randomly-selected pages. Scan them briefly, then tear each in two. Reassemble the pieces in a new order. Continue this process, adding in random pages from this book and other sources. Newspaper ads, magazine articles, retail packaging – everything is fair game. Most importantly, add your own writing. Letters, e-mails, text messages, shopping lists – anything you have written. Then pour adhesive on them. You can also urinate on them, but that is optional. Scribbling with a yellow marker is sufficient. When you are done ripping out all of the pages, place the contents back inside the cover. The result is a new story, a great circular epic without beginning or end, birth or death. For full effect, you should read it in a circular room. If you do this long enough and then cut through the middle of the book and read the individual words, you will find the Deity, a sentient being realized in the form of a living novel from the back of beyond whose precise center is an unspecified point in your life and therefore totally remote and unreachable. When you insert yourself into the world's longest novel you open the door onto the space/time continuum, and a slow wave shivers through the universe.

Welcome again to my island.

What a nice surprise. You have been gone so long I thought I might never see you again. How long has it been? A year, perhaps more. I would offer you a celebratory drink, but there is no time to waste. We must stay on schedule. You have arrived just in time for today we start shooting the next installment of "Marienbad My Love With Mango Extracts."

What's that? I understand. Can you believe it has come to this? A seemingly normal morning, and then – How could any of us know of the secret testing being prepared by the government/alien conspiracy? How could any of us know of the "wonder weapon" that controls human behavior, both as treatment and as a mass inoculation? The pre-launch countdown of the dream-bearing ballistic missile marked the first widespread sighting of the clock in the air, a precursor to the flesh-coast horror, skin-rejuven ating science gone terribly wrong, the ballistic delivery of a psychotropic solution to the malaise of the modern age – a test administered, a test gone horribly wrong, the death of today, the birth of a frightening new tomorrow.

#

I must admit I am surprised to see you here. Pleased, but surprised. When you refused to run away with me I thought I would never see you again. Now that you are back things will move ahead once again.

So how does the world end? On television, of course.

"This is Reece Sloan interrupting your scheduled programming with another special report. And now, as America's Sacrament War continues to quickly erupt in conflagrations of violence and the language and themes of the classic sci-fi movie "The Omega Man," officials at the UN in New York are asking to what extent all of the citizenry of Earth will become involved in the global insanity."

... Stop the launches! Star Wars defenses are fragmenting dream-carrying missiles. Psychosis is spreading across the planet. Repeat – stop the launches. Interception will fragment the dream-carrying missiles...

"Now the issue is one of survival. Is this the conclusion of time, the end of rational man? Is this the end of history, the swagger of science, the "uber" victories over space and linear time? Is this the end of the Age of the Deity? We were warned of judgment. The ancient tales of the withdrawal of the City of the Deity may well be true. It's come now. This is the Noble Misfortune, the weeping and gnashing of teeth. The Deity has withdrawn. The evil dead are emerging from the lagoon of flames, leaving us to our own devices. Where have you gone, Charlton Heston?"

#

I have a confession. I lied to you about the urgency of keeping the movie on schedule. "Marienbad My Love With Mango Extracts" has not been proceeding as well as I had hoped. After your last visit, I attempted to move ahead without you. The results were not edifying.

My first, failed inspiration: No more "Marienbad My Love With Mango Extracts." That's right. I decided there would be no more prophesy for me. No death of time and birth of a new religion. I would move on to a new creation. Pure entertainment. That's the ticket. This may be the end of time, but people still want to see movies. And I have lots of bankable cinematic ideas.

Here's a one-sentence film treatment that came to me late one night after perhaps a few too many martinis: "Middle-aged man discovers he is an extraterrestrial." I see him as the hidden king on a hero's journey. In the Call to Adventure, a time-traveling cowboy rescues him from certain death by aliens. Helping him along on the adventure are Bellero Shield and his posse of Cicadans. Upon awakening I realized that I had actually plagiarized "Let Me Love You," my favorite movie of all time.

Consider this one-sentence film treatment: "A special newspaper press makes every story change reality." I dreamed it, a genuine creation of the unconscious. Later I realized this idea had been done before an old "Twilight Zone" episode starring Burgess Meredith.

Next came "Nixon in Texas" (aka "Plan 9 ½ from Outer Space"). The protagonist, the time-traveling cowboy and Bellero Shield return to 1960s Duncanville, where they stumble into an alternate universe. Richard Nixon has won the 1960 presidential. He opens diplomatic relations with the Republic of Texas, which had closed it doors to the U.S. back during WWII. Nixon is welcomed with open arms by Texas President Lyndon Johnson, and they ride together in a parade in downtown Dallas. As they near the infamous plaza, a rifle barrel is spotted in the sixth floor window of the Texas School Book Depository. But wait – what is that sticking out of the storm drain? And over there, that metallic flash from the grassy knoll? It's a conspiracy, all right – an extraterrestrial/government conspiracy! Peeling back the layers, the protagonist finds that the extraterrestrials are preparing to stage a fake Rapture as part of a plan to take over the world. Oh yes, and God is going senile. (Though in all fairness that idea may be another leftover from "Let Me Love You," too.)

After reading "Farnham's Freehold," the classic '60s sci-fi plea for racial understanding, I envision a sequel based on an alternate version. In "Freeholdin' 2: Electric Boogaloo" (aka "Duke's Revenge"), the castrated, drug-addicted Duke decides to return to the 1960s with his father and his father's girlfriend. He quickly resumes his racist ways and embarks on a reign of terror, castrating black men in retaliation for the loss of his own DNA delivery organ.

One of my favorite concepts is "God Bless You, Mr. Hitler" (aka "Born Again Furher"). Hitler fakes his death in the Berlin bunker, escapes to America and starts a chain of dry cleaners. Then one day the Lord speaks to him. He goes to a tent revival and is "saved." He is a born again Christian, a true believer. The sins of his extermination of six million dead Jews are washed away in the Blood of the Lamb. His soul is "dry cleaned" by God. The born-again Furher turns himself in, and after a show trial in The Hague he is executed. But three days later, Hitler rises from the dead. The sky opens up, and God announces that Adolf Hitler has been reborn as the Second Coming of Christ. This is the fulfillment of Revelation. God, Jesus and Hitler look on from their heavenly thrones as the City of God descends to Earth. Some of the roofs of the buildings in the city are adorned with crosses, others swastikas.

I was actually rather pleased with "God Bless You, Mr. Hitler." I should have moved ahead with that one. But by this point, I couldn't focus enough to rough out a shooting script. My mind was racing, the ideas were overflowing. Having just read "Time's Arrow" (another rousing Nazi tale), I thought of remaking some literary classics in reverse.

"Moby Dick," for instance. Captain Ahab emerges from the watery depths, resurrected by the great white. "I turn my body to the sun," he says. "What ho, Tashtego! Let me silence thy hammer. Oh! ye three risen spires of mine; thou cracked keel; and only god-blessed hull; thou infirm deck, and modest helm, and Pole-blunted prow, -life-glorious ship! Must ye then be reborn, and with me? Am I reattached to the first fond pride of kindest blessed captains? Away from thee I roll, thou all-affirming and conquering whale. To the last shall you pursue me? Will you grapple with me? From hell's heart will you stab at me? For love's sake I flee thee! Float all coffins and all hearses to one common pool! And since both can be mine, let me then tow to pieces, while still fleeing thee, though tied to thee, thou damned whale! Thus, I retake my spear!" For the rest of the story, Ahab flees the murderous beast as it chases him and his crew across the oceans of the world.

And then there is Mary Shelly's "Frankenstein.".

In the opening scene, the Monster comes out of the Artic waste, boards a ship and brings a dead doctor (Dr. Frankenstein) back to life. "Greetings!" he says. "I join you, and in you I encounter the first human whom these eyes have ever beheld. Greetings, Frankenstein!"

They return to Europe, where an ungrateful Dr. Frankenstein flees the Monster. In turn, the Monster continues to do good deeds, restoring life to several dead bodies. And still the ungrateful doctor does not befriend the creature who saved his life. In the end, Dr. Frankenstein straps the Monster to a table in his laboratory and kills him with electricity. The doctor then dissects the Monster and implants his body parts into various cadavers, which his hunchbacked assistant buries under cover of darkness in spooky church graveyards. Townsfolk then exhume the cadavers and conduct rebirthing ceremonies. Voila! The dead are returned to life. The Monster lives on, a sort of Christ figure for the scientific age.

And then – and then what? Then I have a really great idea, a dangerously great idea. What if I film the Bible, but in reverse?

I call it "El Bib" (aka "Biblin' 2: Electric Boogaloo").

#

In the beginning God lived with his people in the holy city of Jerusalem. In those days the home of God was among mortals. He dwelt with them; they were his people, and God himself was with them. He wiped every tear from their eyes. There was no Death, no mourning or crying or pain. These things did not exist.

The holy city had the glory of God and a radiance like a very rare jewel, like jasper, clear as crystal. It had a great, high wall with twelve gates, and at the gates twelve angels, and on the gates were inscribed the names of twelve tribes; on the east three gates, on the north three gates, on the south three gates and on the west three gates. And the wall of the city has twelve foundations, and on them are the twelve names of the twelve apostles of the Lamb.

The city was laid out foursquare, its length the same as its width and height: 1,500 miles. The walls were built of jasper, while the city was pure gold, clear as glass. The foundations of the wall of the city were adorned with every jewel; the first was jasper, the second sapphire, the third agate, the fourth emerald, the fifth onyx, the sixth carnelian, the seventh chrysolite, the eighth beryl, the ninth topaz, the tenth chrysoprase, the eleventh jacinth, the twelfth amethyst. And the twelve gates were twelve pearls, each of the gates was a single pearl, and the street of the city was pure gold, transparent as glass. The gates were never shut by day, and there was no night there. The city had no need of sun or moon, for the glory of God was its light, and its lamp was the Lamb. The nations of the Earth walked by the light, and the kings of the Earth brought their glory into it. Nothing accursed was found within the city.

Through the throne of God and of the Lamb flowed the River of the Water of Life. Bright as crystal the water flowed through the middle of the street of the city.

From his throne God spoke to his people: "I am the Alpha and the Omega, the beginning and the end. To the thirsty I give water as a gift from the River of the Water of Life. Those who conquer have inherited these things, I am their God and they are my children. They live with me in the holy city, and their names are inscribed in the Book of Life. But as for the cowardly, the faithless, the polluted, the murderers, the fornicators, the sorcerers, the idolaters and all liars, their place is in the lake that burns with fire and sulfur."

On either bank of the River of the Water of Life grew the Trees of Life. They bore twelve kinds of fruit, producing their fruit each month; and the leaves of the trees were for the healing of the nations. And in the center of the city grew the Tree of the Knowledge of Good and Evil.

God commanded his people, "You may freely eat of the fruit of the Trees of Life and gather the healing leaves. But of the Tree of the Knowledge of Good and Evil you shall not eat, for in the day that you eat of it you shall die."

But then one day a man encountered a talking serpent, who asked: "Did God say, 'You shall not eat from any tree in the city?' The man said to the serpent, 'We may eat of the fruit of the trees in the city; but God said, 'You shall not eat of the fruit of the tree in the middle of the city, nor shall you touch it, or you shall die.' But the serpent said to the man, "you will not die; for God knows that when you eat of it your eyes will be opened, and you will be like God, knowing good and evil." So when the man saw that the tree was good for food, and that it was a delight to the eyes, and that the tree was to be desired to make one wise, he took of its fruit and ate; and he also sold it to his neighbors and all of the people of the city, and they ate. Then the eyes of everyone were opened, and they knew that they were naked. They began to penetrate one another's membranes, the men expelling their ectoplasm inside the women.

"This is the best fruit of all!" they cried. "Let us gather this fruit and make of it a wine, which we can drink ourselves and sell what is left to the fornicators and the idolaters who live outside the city."

They immediately set themselves to labor, gathering the fruit for the wine presses. Then they heard the sound of God walking in the street. They instantly dropped the fruit they had gathered and stepped away from the wine presses. They began to wander off, acting as if they were still blameless. But the people were unable to hide their sin as they had gathered so much fruit that it covered the street and filled the gutters.

"Where did you get all of this fruit?" God asked.

"We picked it from one of the trees you gave us."

Then God asked, "Have you eaten from the tree of which I commanded you not to eat?"

The people shook their heads and spoke in solemn tones. "What have we done wrong? After all, it was not us who created the Tree of the Knowledge of Good and Evil."

And with that God instantly knew the truth. He said to his people:

"Because of what you have done, I place a curse upon you and all of your descendents. No longer shall you dwell in the safety of the holy city. No longer shall you bask in the light of the lamp of the Lamb."

Then God said, "See, my people have become like me, knowing good and evil. They must no longer eat from the Tree of Life and live forever, like Gods. Therefore, I must drive them from the gates of the city, into the danger and the darkness."

So God turned his people out into the world, with the dogs and sorcerers and fornicators and murderers and idolaters and everyone who loved and practiced falsehood, and caused the holy city of Jerusalem to ascend into Heaven.

Now the people of God knew all about the Lake of Fire. This was the place of the cowardly, the faithless, the polluted, the murderers, the fornicators, the sorcerers, the idolaters and all liars. Their names were not written in the Book of Life, which lay at the bottom of the lake.

As they stood along the shore of the Lake of Fire God caused the flames to leap and the sulfur to smoke. The lake gave up the Book of Life and Death and Hades and all the dead, great and small. They stood with the people of God before a great white throne. Books were opened, and the rulings were read aloud by the officers of the court. All judgment of evil and wrongdoing was set aside.

Satan was rescued from the flames, too. He had been tortured there, along with the beast and the false prophet, and they had been tormented day and night for the previous thousand years. But now they were released, reborn from the fire that had consumed them.

A demon stood in the moonlight, and with a loud voice called to all the flesh-eating animals that walk the Earth, "Come, gather for the great supper of Satan, to eat the White Horse and its rider!" Then the sky opened, and down came the horse and its rider, Faithful and True, who in his righteousness judges and makes war.

The eyes of Faithful and True were like a flame of fire, and on his head were many diadems; and he had a name inscribed that no one knows but himself. He was clothed in a robe dipped in blood, and his name was called The Word of God. And the armies of Heaven, wearing fine linen, white and pure, followed him on white horses. They were from all the nations of the Earth; kings, captains, the mighty, both free and slave, both great and small.

From the mouth of Faithful and True came a sharp sword with which to strike down the nations, and he was to rule them with a rod of iron; he was to tread the wine press of the fury of the wrath of God the Almighty. On his robe and on his thigh he had a name inscribed, "King of kings and Lord of lords."

The beast and the kings of the Earth and their armies gathered to make war against Faithful and True and the armies of Heaven, but the rider of the White Horse and his army were victorious. The beast and the false prophet fled the battlefield and the Lake of Fire. Their armies were spared by Faithful and True, and all the flesh-eating animals that walk the Earth left the battlefield unsatisfied.

#

And that's just the opening of Genesis. This creation story continues with all sorts of strange imagery, culminating with seven churches each sending an explanatory letter to John of Patmos.

Other Old Testament highlights: Paul is a follower of Christ, but he is doing terrible things with his miraculous powers. The living die, the sighted go blind, the able-bodied are crippled. Then God blinds him and he goes out into the desert where he gets his sight back in a miraculous fashion. Having learned the error of his ways, Paul gets a new name -- Saul of Tarsus. He then goes from synagogue to synagogue, bringing dead Christians back to life.

Of course there is the story of the son of God, who comes down out of the sky, descends into a grave, where he dies but three days later is returned to life by Roman soldiers who put him on a cross. God eventually causes the Christ child to disappear from Mary's womb, erasing the last sign of his existence.

The New Testament story of Job is a good one. A very rich man suddenly loses everything and simultaneously receives a direct communication from God. He is abused by his so-called friends and left to suffer on a garbage heap. But he still believes. Satan tells God that he believes Job will turn away from his beliefs if his wealth is restored. They make a wager, and Satan returns to Job much of his property. Job is rich again, though not nearly so rich as before. He still believes in God, and Satan loses the bet.

Ah, so many wonderful stories to tell! Like the time David used a sword to restore the head of a giant, who was so appreciative that he took his Army away and left the Hebrews in peace. ... the flood story, in which God dries up the rain and restores life to the many dead bodies littering the landscape ... a pillar of salt is turned into a woman ... Moses brings his people out of the desert, across the Red Sea and makes them slaves in Egypt. He takes away terrible curses imposed by God and disappears back into the wilderness. Years later he comes back to kill one of the Egyptians, then lives in secrecy among them. He eventually meets up again with the Hebrews as a baby in a reed basket on the Nile.

The end times come in the Garden of Eden, when God takes away the animal skin clothing of Adam and Eve. They must wear fig leaves. Adam gives an apple to Eve, who in turn hands it over to a snake. God responds by turning Eve into a rib and implanting her into Adam. Despondent, Adam takes away all of the names of all the animals. God turns him into dust. Then God takes away all the animals and the dry land and even the light, leaving the Earth without form and void. Amen.

But no, I tell myself. This isn't right either. I am not a Hollywood-style director. I am a prophet. I must give my witness. I must continue filming "Marienbad My Love With Mango Extracts." If only I could concentrate. I walk the beach, looking for sea monsters and inspiration. I tried to force myself to write something "inspired," always a bad idea. Here's something I came up with over the last Memorial Day holiday, watching the vacationers playing in the bay:

#

Sometimes I see a horizon beyond the horizon. It is a line in the sky, exactly paralleling the one we all know of the waking world. But it is hard to focus on this idea, for below the waking world horizon I see one of the pale bikini creatures, busily attempting to adjust her top. It is a heavy load, for sure. For I see her adjust one side, then the other, then reach for the middle as if to unhook and discard the whole thing. A kiss from an adjacent boy, though, and she is back at it, reaching around behind herself, adjusting the tie that binds.

How can I think about important things like a second, unseen horizon when this pale bikini creature insists on this constant touching and adjusting and this kiss-kiss-kissing.

I was once young like that. But never so young that I had a chance to observe or participate in -- ah, now I take note of a new development. The boy has walked away, back onto dry land and the white car of wakeful travel. The pale bikini creature is busy with something drawn close to her core. I am not sure what. Perhaps I could risk a quick peek through the binoculars. But no -- no, this would likely prove a disappointment. My thoughts are surely more enticing than her reality, even a reality of busy breast adjustments and pretty red toenails dipped in wet sexuality.

Now she strokes her blonde hair, a mermaid on the beach. This mermaid could take a swim in my unconscious, check out the underwater road. Let her find the unknown treasure, bring it up from the depths to sun on the beach-dock.

And now, drunkenness in the back of a moving pickup. This is real fun. The pickup leaves with my mermaid, and the fishermen depart for secret honey holes in my unconscious. No telling what they may catch. But I guarantee it won't be pleasant. Only sea monsters down there, consigned to the frightful depths. Huge, bug-eyed creatures with glowing patches that move across the surface of their cold, slimy skin. They drift slowly along the bottom, among the old Coke bottles and my failed, forgotten dreams.

The bay is deserted now. But I can't seem to recover my second horizon idea. It just looks normal now, like any old line where world and sky meet. Perhaps the pale bikini creature was my muse, inspiring me to see the hidden, secret world-sky line. Now the muse is gone, and I am alone with no worthwhile thought. The sun is low in the sky. Soon I can speculate on the orange glow, the embers of another dying holiday."

#

Sometimes I see a horizon beyond the horizon. It's a mesmerizing concept, no? In my case, it mesmerized me into recognizing the entirely new reality: the End is Here.

Conflagrations of violence, global insanity of the fragmenting dream-carrying missiles. Psychosis spreading across the planet. The talking head on TV has it right: the issue is one of survival. Is this the conclusion of time, the end of rational man? Is this the end of history and the swagger of science? Is this the conclusion of our collective victories over space and linear time? Is this the death of God? We have been warned of cosmic judgment. The ancient tales of the withdrawal of the City of the Deity may well be true. It's here today. It's come now.

In "Love in the Ruins," Walker Percy prophesized these dread latter days of time, the feeling of the clank of the old historical machinery, the sudden jerking ahead of ourselves. The Hydrocarbon Age is defunct. Vines are strangling Manhattan. Coyotes have the run of downtown Houston. The churches are empty now, abandoned years ago shortly after the time of the great catastrophe, the fragmentation of the dream-carrying missiles. Look over there on Ocean Boulevard. The stained glass of the church is shattered on the floor with the bird droppings. I'm told the New Rome is in Cicero, Illinois.

Has it really come to this, the conclusion of all our yesterdays? I feel unchanged. And yet – my countrymen are undeniably different. I see it all around me, the distortions and exaggerations of inferential thinking, delusions and hallucinations. I see their cognitive and emotional dysfunctions of perception, behavioral monitoring, affect, fluency and productivity of thought and speech, hedonic capacity, volition and drive. We are overwhelmed by a universe of words, a universe that is a lot like Borge's "Library of Babel." We have so much information, but it's impossible to manage or even comprehend. Finding what you want isn't easy. We are wading through a giant word salad. Consider my movie. Pull anything out of the middle of it and watch a few scenes. Barely comprehensible and virtually meaningless, at least at the logical level. Still, there's incredible meaning at the emotional level, the twilight of consciousness. (I am a poet trapped in a filmmaker's body.)

Sometimes my work is nonsensical, but it can also be quite beautiful. My countrymen deliver a piece of illogical text (at least illogical to me). I feel compelled to deal with it, to attempt to make some sense of it. I am caught up in the dialogue of odd language and incoherent communication, the word salad of disorganized speech. I believe the technical term is "receptive aphasia." It makes no sense. So I start filming through it. I run their thoughts and ideas through a cut-up engine, a twilight process which forces me to momentarily set aside my logical tendencies and embrace the surreal and the dreamlike. And soon a new story leaks out – a new story told in a new language for a new age. I am incorporating it all into my post-holocaust film work, my infinite cinematic poem. I think you'll like it.

You'll see many delusions of jealousy and religiosity, seemingly organized around a central theme. Persecutory delusions are common. So is idealized romantic love and spiritual union. Many people possess the conviction of having some great but unrecognized talent or insight or having made some important discovery. Too many with a special message from a deity. Too close to home. They're crowding in on my territory! And all the while we look to the sky, to the aerial clock. Cold hands of time are spinning in the heavens. A slow wave shivers through the universe.

My jailers don't even bother to report for work anymore.

#

And yet there is good news. Now in these broken, derelict days after the end of time it is possible to combine two opposites into a new whole. Create something new and unique by combining something old and commonplace. This technique generates an original creative product, one that allows us to journey not only through the cosmos but through the eternal youth of the Skin Dimension, too. I know it works for today I am back from a time journey to 1979, bringing with me an explanation of what I saw and how it was completed.

I should warn you that this operation requires extreme accuracy as it is a difficult enterprise. It is based in part on mid-20th century experiments conducted by my grandfather, Jewell Poe. These experiments were aimed at creating a new process for color photography. Brightly colored ribbons were tied to a leafless, winter tree in the Poe family's backyard in Waco, Texas. Double reversal film stock was exposed through a lens or prism. Somehow wires were crossed and time/space polarity was reversed. The developed film revealed a horizon beyond the horizon. This is the Jewell Effect. Following my grandfather's notes I have recreated his experiment and found myself pulled into the psychic entrainment, snapped out of the last weekend of youth in 1979 and back to 1953 Waco and forward to outer space. I am spun into an elliptical orbit around the Cicadan scientific outpost on Uranus, where they know of my grandfather's experiments. I focus on the heavy blue silence, and a slow wave of hydralicious skin ripples through me.

Beware, my darling muse. The Jewell Effect is equal parts excitement and danger, just as you would expect when traveling beyond the outermost border marking the back of beyond. Only the adventurous should apply. However, the Skin Dimension belongs to everyone who has the courage and the know-how to come in. It belongs to you and me. So here is the entire four-part process, precisely as it works.

Part 1: We begin our voyage in the musty film vaults of the classic B-movies of yore. We will edit TV news programs from today with 1950s B-movie Sci-Fi and view the resulting footage. If we fast forward through a recording of our daily TV news broadcast we typically see and absorb much more than we know. In fact, we absorb everything, but it is not easily accessible because it is in the Land of the Dead. The editing process establishes a metaphorical relationship between today and yesterday. We have assembled a movie that forms a montage of time. We move ourselves literally about within the frame of that montage, occupying yesterday's cinema. We return to present time by rewinding towards yesterday. Together we will do this many hours per the day for several months, back as far as the news and movies go. We will exhume old news reels and forgotten TV shows and poke about at the cadavers of brittle yellow letters and dusty government reports. Don't forget to raid the morgue for ancient newspaper clippings. We will make edits and project the footage. We will do it even with the credits and advertisements.

Part 2: We will proceed to the closest drive-in movie theater. Here we will learn to talk to ourselves in reverse at all levels. This is done by running the film and sound track in reverse. This is precisely the schematic diagram employed in the creation of "El Bib." Picture Christ eating the Last Supper with his disciples. After this, reverse the film, turning satiety back to hunger. At first the film will break into a run at the normal speed. Next it will drop into slow-motion. The same procedure can be extended to other physical processes, specifically the expelling of warm globs of ectoplasm into your membranes. You are offended? You must move beyond your sexual prudery and reticence, which is possibly the heaviest anchor holding you in the third dimension and linear time.

Part 3: We will compile the resulting film into an endless loop on a single metal reel. This process results in a great circular movie, without beginning or end, birth or death. (For full effect, we will view it in a circular theater and project it onto a circular screen.) If we cut through the middle of the reel and view the individual frames, we will find that the movie is actually the Deity, a sentient being realized in the form of a living movie from the back of beyond whose precise center is any point in our lives and therefore totally remote and unreachable.

Part 4: We open the door onto the space/time continuum, and a slow wave shivers through the universe.

#

Smoking is not allowed in the Strangers Rest Senior Center, but violations are rampant and generally overlooked during the weekly Meals on Wheels luncheon. Overlooked by everyone but Dewayne's wife, that is.

"That old shrew," he scowls.

"Doctors orders, Dewayne," Roy says. "Remember, you ain't so young anymore."

"Yeah, but Dewayne ain't the one with a bandage on his head," Toots remarks. "What happened Roy? You fall out of your recliner again?"

Roy puts a hand to the white gauze he's taped to his forehead. "Why, this here ain't nothing you girls would know anything about," he remarks.

"And I'm sure you're just dying to tell us."

"Since you're obviously curious, I will tell you. This here bandage is actually the protective covering on a solar panel for a sex machine."

This solicits a combination of laughter and groans.

"Why, sure," Roy continues. "If I didn't keep this here piece of manly hardware covered up I'd be mobbed by beautiful girls. You ugly old coots wouldn't stand a chance."

"No smoking," Dewayne says. "Just another excuse to deprive me of one of life's few remaining pleasures. Dying with clean lungs is kinda like dying with a million dollars in your pocket. It ain't going to do you any good. And besides, Roy, I'm five years younger than you."

"Let's get back to the subject," Toots says. "If Daniel can pull it off, it'll be more than just a pocketful of cash for one man. This land deal could be good for the entire town. High prices tend to - uh, hold on, now." He stops to count his dominos. "Wasn't I down to two tiles? Harold?"

Like Dewayne, Toots always kept one eye on his tiles. But the other eye he assigned to Harold Bost, a quiet, unassuming man who had a seemingly impossible talent for making dominos reproduce. I tried to play him once. I'd swear I was down to one or two tiles and, next thing I knew, I was looking down at six, seven, even eight tiles. So was everybody else. Everybody except Harold, that it. No one could ever figure out how he did it.

Toots counted his dominos again, then gave Harold a skeptical stare.

"Harold, I don't believe I should have six tiles, do you?"

"Hard to keep track sometimes," he allows. He doesn't look away from his own neatly arranged row of four dominos.

Toots just shrugs. But Harold's wife, Ima, isn't nearly as resigned.

"Yes, Mr. Bost has pulled another of his tricks, I know that look," she says in a quavering, old woman voice. "He does it whenever he thinks he might lose. Ornery old man."

"I've lost plenty of times," Harold whispers. But that just makes Ima madder.

"Oh, you're always so sly with your little tricks and cheats, aren't you? Someday you'll get yours, Mr. Bost. Yes, you and all you ornery old men will get yours."

"Now what was I saying?" Toots asks. "Oh yeah, land prices. Setting a high price is the only way to get a high price, and that's the only way to push up property values and increase our town's tax revenues."

"Toots, taxes are sky high already," Cowboy Roy says. "Most of us don't want to sell out, we're going to stay here till we die. We'd rather have low taxes than land that's worth a bundle. We can't afford to be that rich."

"Values have definitely been going down," I remark. "Real estate's in the tank."

"And that's where it ought to be," Dewayne adds. "None of the land around here is worth anything close to what folks have been paying these days, let alone the $1 million Daniel's asking. Dirt ain't worth no more than you can make from the crops you can grow on it. We ain't had no cotton production around here to speak of in 20 years, so you can forget the big cash crops. All anybody does with land around here anymore is raise hay and run cattle."

"So what you reckon that makes Daniel's land worth?" Roy asks.

"If I was in the market? I might give $200 an acre."

"Well tarnation Dewayne!" Toots roars, almost knocking over his dominos. "Dirt's been selling for $20,000 an acre real regular now for several years. Even if prices are down, they sure ain't dropped to no penny on the dollar."

"I remember one year it sure came close," Roy says. "Cotton prices were so low mamma and pappa just plowed the crop right back into the field."

"Yeah, I think that was back in '28 or '29. It was a bad year, prices were low."

"No, we didn't plow the cotton under until the Depression. You're thinking of the big freeze, the summer when everything froze over."

This catches my attention. "You had a freeze in the summer?"

"Yes sir," Toots says. "The weather was awful for months. We couldn't get out, when suddenly it got a whole lot worse."

"We had a big freeze, right there in the dog days of August," Roy says, marveling at the memory. "Everything froze over solid. I remember sliding around out there on the stock pond, the one at the old airbase."

"It was just awful. Killed the whole crop, everything in the field."

"We lived that year on nothing but butter beans and coffee."

"We'll don't worry about that. We're not going to be living on butter beans and coffee again because land ain't going to sell for $200 an acre ever again."

#

I hoped he was right. I hated butter beans. But I liked – still like – just about every other kind of food they serve at the weekly Meals on Wheels lunch.

Prepared by the women of the town from family recipes, some handed down by pioneer ancestors, the two-table spread consists of the kind of traditional Southern fare that can only be found anymore in the country kitchens of iron-haired grandmas or at Sunday night covered dish dinners.

I never missed the weekly spread, where I'd load my plate with a big slab of pan fried ham and side vegetables: Greens flavored with a shot of vinegar; green beans cooked to a muted olive Army tint and glistening in bacon fat; and real hominy grits. It'll bring tears to my eyes, all for a $3 donation.

Buck looks at my overloaded plate and smiles. "Your wife a good cook?" he asks.

"If she's got a recipe," I say. "But I don't think you can find stuff like this in a cookbook."

"When we was newlyweds, my Ima couldn't boil water," Buck confides quietly, careful to make sure his wife – two tables away – isn't listening. "But she learned quick enough. And I'm carryin' around the gut to prove it."

"You just be patient," Toots adds. "She's going to learn how to cook those green beans and ham the way you like it."

The idea of Allison cooking up a real Southern meal is a cruel joke. Sure, she's spent more than half of her life in Texas, but she operates under the delusion that she is an East Coast transplant. Allison is a sophisticate marooned in a raw and spare land, perplexed (she claims) by all things Texan and Southern. Her specialties are Boston baked beans, Philly cheese steak and New England clam chowder – not grits and greens.

I quickly finish dessert and break away from the domino players to ``work the room," as Roy likes to kid me.

#

Although officially intended to benefit the town's old folks, the Meals on Wheels luncheon is a favorite among the local business and civic leaders. My first month in the bureau I even mentioned it in a Lunch Bunch review in the Northeast Extra: "This weekly gathering is a sort of casual chamber of commerce mixer where attendees don't feel obliged to exchange business cards." But of course we do. It's the best place in Strangers Rest -- perhaps all of the Texas 114 corridor -- to pick up rumors and gossip. I've found that as long as I keep my notepad and pen out of sight, an hour or so of delicious home cooking and friendly talk will yield a weeks' worth of stories.

I make my usual contacts. The president of the bank ("no, haven't heard from the feds in months"); the sister of Bryan P. Hamilton, professional golfing legend and Strangers Rest's most famous resident (next to Cowboy Roy, of course); the visiting Keller mayor; Justice of the Peace Hubert Skinner.

On my way between tables, I notice a fair number of the old folks are drawn to a new offering: free samples of bottled water courtesy of Ozona International.

An old man pokes a knarred finger bone at the pyramid of plastic bottles and a cardboard cutout of the trademark Ozona cloud. The cardboard cloud has been given a flashing neon lightning bolt, which glints off the polished, albino head of the "Yo! Ozona Man!" (registered trademark), who has stationed himself behind the table.

"As I said before, it's part of a nationwide marketing study," the water man explains. "We're trying to determine what new products might appeal to various segments of the marketplace."

The front door opens, admitting a hot whirlwind from the asphalt parking lot. It's The Stranger, with film crew in tow. He walks straight to me and whispers in my ear.

"What, him?" I ask, incredulous. "He's supposed to be the sinister Dr. Adolfo Morel?"

#

He doesn't look very menacing or dangerous. Or human.

Adolfo Morel bears an odd, alien countenance: smooth head, snow white skin, blood red lips and mouth and black pupils and irises magnified to lurid proportions by the prism-like lenses in his glasses. He is average height, but of frail build. His bones are like those of a bird -- so delicate, you could knock him over with a feather.

"He's supposed to be the mad scientist of the movie?" I ask. "I just don't know."

The Stranger is undeterred by my doubts.

"Dr. Morel is actually a character from the Society of the Purple Sunset," he explains. "He has inexplicably migrated into the waking world. He is the director of the black ops division of Ozona, here undercover as the 'Yo! Ozona Man!' He's offering free water, but don't drink any. It's just a ruse to introduce a new version of Skinalicious9 into the populace and create the world's first privately owned deity."

Roy steps up to the table and examines the pyramid of bottles.

"I hear tell you're paying $10 and all we got to do is drink some of this water and fill out the form?"

Dr. Morel carefully adjusts the glasses perched on the bridge of his too-thin, too-small nose, runs a pale dead hand over his bare pate and gives his questioner an emotionless, insect smile.

"Yes, it is as you say. We're paying people to drink our water."

The Stranger motions to his cameraman and the microphone boom operator. Then he turns to me.

"For this scene, you are to attempt to claim a bottle and form," he explains.

"I'm not participating," I say.

"Don't worry. You don't drink it, but you'll need a bottle so you can have it analyzed."

"I won't."

The Stranger blinks in disbelief. "Why not?" he asks.

"There's still no incredible revelation."

"Be patient. We're not even done with the back story yet. And – action!"

#

"Today we're testing 'Fountain of Youth,'" Morel explains. "This amalgamating beverage is aimed at members of select socio-economic profiles age 50 and up. Samples are carefully measured. It is necessary to administer the correct mixture to the appropriate subject."

"In other words, rich old folks," The Stranger says. "Mark, now you pick up a bottle and examine the label, which features a sort of wood cut of Ponce de Leon discovering Florida. Your line –"

"I already told you I'm not participating," I say.

"What? Why not?"

"I do not believe in the movie."

The Stranger looks at me in disbelief.

"How can you not believe?" he asks. "It's our movie."

"Not mine. Yours. I don't believe in it. No one else will believe, either. You are nothing like the old man in my dream."

"I am The Stranger."

"You are a fraud. You're like a bad game show host. This movie is an extreme embarrassment. I don't think you know a thing about making movies."

The Stranger nods thoughtfully. "OK, we'll add your dialogue in post-production."

#

Cowboy Roy sidles up beside me and rests a conspiratorial forearm on my shoulder.

"If you want to see a sight, just keep your eyes on Harold."

I look over at Harold, who was still sharing a table with Buck and the mayor.

"What am I looking for?"

"Check out that bone pile he's nursing along. He's outdone himself this time."

Sure enough, he has a substantial stack of dominos that now dominate the table.

"Must be two feet tall," I marvel. The stack is so tall, in fact, that its base stretched to the table's edge, tiles sliding over the precipice to the concrete floor. Harold is grabbing at the falling tiles, tossing them back onto the domino mountain, but this is a losing battle. In fact, all he has to show for his efforts is a domino avalanche. And an angry wife.

"I'll teach you a trick or two, Harold Bost," Ima says, pelting him with plastic cutlery from the serving table. "Tricks and cheats! That's all you're about, you ornery old man."

Harold stoically endures his wife's fury, ignoring the flying knives and combination fork/spoons that rained upon him and his domino mountain. Mayor Toots and Buck nervously watch from behind the Ozona "cloud," the neon lightning bolt crackling ominously.

"Poor Harold," Roy says. "If only he'd use his powers for good."

Roy and I go to Harold's assistance, picking up the dominos that litter the floor. And then Dr. Morel arrives.

"Let's try a different game," he suggests to Harold. "I can teach you one I eternally win."

"It's no game at all if you can't ever lose," Harold observes.

"It is logically possible for me to lose, but such an event has never occurred."

"OK then, let's give it a whirl."

"Two players. The dominos are arranged in four columns. Eight. Four. Two. One. Each of us may select as many tiles as we wish, but only from one column at a time. Whoever selects the final tile is the loser. Would you like to begin?"

#

After five straight losses, Harold shakes his head and pushes back from the table.

"It's impossible," he insists.

"At last," Ima says. "Finally somebody around here got the best of Harold Bost."

I excuse myself and escape to the parking lot.

The midday heat is a welcome change from the senior center's icy-cold air conditioning. In the shade of an oak, I watch two boys playing in a grassless patch of yard. One of them is acting out an invented scene from "The Abandoned Ones."

"Come in Affliction Corps," he commands into a radio-shaped rock. "This is Normpart Internment Camp. We are under attack, repeat under attack! The United Nations is bombing the puppies!"

The other boy is not interested in battling the Antichrist. He has focused his attention on a peach pit, which he is prying open with a flathead screwdriver.

``My brother told me that little seed in there tastes like 7-Up," he says.

That is all the encouragement the other boy needs to abandon playing "Abandoned." He retrieves the almond-shaped heart from the pit and bites off half. And starts a fit of spitting.

``You'd have to call it `ook-aid,'" he complains. "Worst tasting stuff I've ever had. It's like poison."

And then they see the dog, napping in a patch of bare ground under a chinaberry tree next door.

"Come here baby," one of the boys says sweetly, holding out the peach pit to the bleary eyed dog. It sniffs the morsel for a moment, then returns to its chinaberry slumber.

"Aww man."

I have always been in the grip of the idea of universal catastrophe. Call it Armageddon. Call it the Apocalypse. I have always been awaiting the End of the World.

Consider the dreams of childhood.

The Stranger once said that our earliest dreams often foretell our destiny. "We should put them in the movie," he said. "We'll cast you as the hidden king, the child of noble birth who is placed with an anonymous, ordinary family while still an infant. And yet, the truth cannot be entirely concealed. The destiny is foreshadowed in nocturnal visions."

Those earliest visions are not pleasant to recall. Would you think it too dramatic if I told you those nearest me seemed to be bringers of death? I know, I know – how can I say such terrible things? My parents would be heartbroken to hear that I thought they were anything less than stellar. Did they not give me everything I needed and every reasonable thing I wanted? Was I not afforded every opportunity to become a perfected being? Certainly the blame for this failure is mine alone.

#

I am a preschooler, no more than five, receiving presents from my parents. Kenner Easy Show Projector, G.I. Joe Mercury space capsule, Hi Ho! Cherry-O – typical toys of the 1960s. But this is not my birthday or Christmas. The gifts mean my parents want their only child to have a pleasant experience before handing him over to the devil.

The transfer begins right after the gifts, so I don't even get a chance to enjoy them. We are in my bedroom of our house on Cherry Street in Duncanville. I cautiously approach the twin bed with Early American bedspread, a tapestry of British and American soldiers engaged in cannon battle. It is a foot or two from the wall and window, forming a narrow gap into the dark unknown. I peer over the side of the bed, into this abyss, and see the tail of the devil flicking back and forth. The tail has the familiar diamond shape on the end; the rest of it is covered in short hair, like a lion's tail. A lion/demon hybrid. So that's it. I am to be consumed.

#

My mother and father both work, so I spend my pre-school years with baby sitters. One of them lives in a garage apartment, a home for cars. Dream after dream, she makes me sit on a fireplace mantle, in the dark. I am a knickknack, an ornamental contrivance.

The circumstances of this mantle sitting vary. Sometimes, mixed in with the dream memories, there is a waking life recollection of an older neighbor girl who threatens me with a leather belt, which she cracks like a whip.

Always, I am threatened with severe physical punishment if I get down. And if I should ever fall, it will be even worse: I will be transformed into a statue.

I know this because I saw it in another vision, one in which I stand at the end of a long, smooth game surface. I look down over the end, into the abyss, and see the sailboat that slid too far. Lying next to the boat is a man-turned-statue. He reminds me of the pilot who used to sit inside the airplane on the roof of the Skyvue Motel in Waco. This dead mariner is forever fixed in a sitting position, hand poised for the rudder. This is a terrifying location, peering over the edge of life and death.

#

Now at a different baby sitter's house, outside playing with children. In the front yard I see my dog, a black poodle named Tinker, running with some of the kids. His ears are flying behind him; he's having a great time. This is a surprise, though, because Tinker should be at home on Cherry Street, the other side of town.

Suddenly, the baby sitter's older, mean son chases down my dog, runs him to the ground. This will be bad, death for sure. I ask the boy not to hurt Tinker.

"He's my dog."

So the boy waits for me, Tinker cowered at his feet. But when I arrive at his side, I see that it is not Tinker at all. Instead of my happy, energetic puppy, I see a sad-eyed creature wearing a floppy straw hat with plastic flowers pasted on the side. A sad, old Southern lady dog, ready to hoe collards in her vegetable garden.

Both fearful and relieved, I tell the boy that it's not my pet. I walk sadly away, leaving the terrified gardening dog to the older boy's not-so-tender mercies. I should have tried to save her.

#

One of my grade school teachers stands naked in front of the class, talking to the boys. No girls are present.

We can't believe our good fortune. This teacher is the only "Miss" in our grade, a young divorced woman with dark hair parted in the middle. The boys all think she is hot.

"Don't laugh or she'll quit," one boy says.

So we all put on our best serious faces and pretend to listen, staring in silence. This is the first time I have seen a naked woman, but I know enough that I am not surprised by her appearance. She has no penis, only testicles. Isn't this normal female anatomy?

#

I must take some unpleasant medicine. It is chlorine bleach, a proper treatment for the whitening of dark innards. But how can I choke this down? Mom mixes it with ice cream. This is awful. But she tells me I must eat it. I must take my medicine.

#

Our antique grandfather clock is possessed, haunted. The hands are spinning wildly, the chimes are off key, cold and distant. And the spirits inside are calling to me. "Rhine, rhine, rhine…" My father bought the clock in Germany, brought it home in the belly of a Texas Air National Guard KC-97. So perhaps the ghosts are homesick for the Fatherland.

#

Visiting relatives, poking around interesting artifacts in their junk-filled garage. One of my cousins finds an old JaPoppa Man Robot, a once-popular but now long-obsolete life-size toy that resembles a crash test dummy. They're easy to operate: Put the JaPoppa Man in the special JaPoppa Popping Chair, which charges and activates the robot by bouncing it up and down like the pilot in one of those old, failed flying machines. I don't think my cousin should reawaken this long-sleeping robot. Let sleeping robots lie, I say. But she and others do it anyway. They put the robot in the chair and crank it up. Soon, the JaPoppa Man rises from the chair, staggering around like the village drunk. All the kids laugh. But this cannot end well. Surely, JaPoppa Man will be misunderstood. He will be chased down by torch-bearing villagers and burned alive in a Dutch windmill.

#

Visiting my girlfriend's house. Her family is there, including a little brother. He is sitting at the coffee table, working on his coin collection. I wish that I had some valuable coins to give him. This would make me look good in front of the girl and her family – like a normal, friendly young man. It would be nice to appear normal, all for the bargain price of a few pieces of silver.

#

A man decides to conduct an experiment in which he will spend a short amount of time inside a pizza oven, perhaps 15 minutes. My job is to close the door behind him and open it at the proper time. I agree to do so as a favor, so surely I am not to blame for the terrible tragedy that befalls him.

The experiment begins, proceeding unremarkably. But as this is a pizza parlor, I become distracted by the demands of business. Lots of customers, so many that I forget the man I've shut up in the oven. When I finally remember him, it has been 45 minutes.

I rip open the door, but it is too late. He is dead. His legs look normal enough, but the top half of his body is melted onto the surface of the oven. It looks like a pair of legs protruding from a puddle of overcooked mozzarella.

I know I am in trouble now. I get a sick feeling inside and run away. But there is no escape; it is only a matter of time. I am a killer.

#

While sitting in a chair (possibly tied to it), I am shot in the chest with a pistol. Point blank. I feel no pain, yet the wound is fatal. I know that I am dead – or soon will be. Indeed, others in the room already regard me as dead, a remnant of the past. They walk past, not even bothering to look my way. But I can still observe them, and I wonder what will become of me.

#

The conclusion of time comes in my sleep.

My parents wake me up early, while it is still dark. We step outside, onto the front porch stoop of the Woodacre Circle house. I look out at our little town. The houses have been destroyed. All that remains are the brick chimneys, rising above the smoking ruins like blackened obelisks. The fires of destruction burn red in the broken hearths. The world of my childhood is no more.

#

On a skateboard, moving rapidly down a school hallway. A closed door lies ahead. I am moving too fast to stop; there will be a terrible collision. But just as I reach the door, someone opens it and I pass through unharmed. Every 50 feet or so I encounter another door. And each time, someone opens it just in time for me to pass through. The process is repeated perhaps a dozen times. Meanwhile, I continue to gain momentum. There is nothing to stop me now.

#

Out in the darkness, a strange man – perhaps a monster – is trying to break into the house. He is coming for me.

My father is away on a trip; mom is asleep on the sofa. I attempt to rouse her.

"There's a man trying to get into the house!"

Oblivious to my panic, she waves me away with a sleep-heavy hand.

"There's no such thing as men," she mumbles, then rolls back over into her slumber.

#

The Stranger. I thought he was to be my shadow, and I was to be the famous one. But I have misapprehended my dreams, my vision. In truth he is the original; I am the secondary character, the carbon copy.

I think of Borges, of "Borges and I." Like him, I am contemplating the "other one" ... The Stranger is becoming the one called Mark Leach, the one things happen to. I must exist, let myself go on existing, so that this Mark Leach may engineer his epic film, which is intended to validate me. It is no exertion for me to admit that he has attained some legitimate footage, but I fear that footage will not rescue me from myself. It cannot rescue me from the legends of the desolate borderlands, from the mental pastimes of era and perpetuity. Those things belong to The Stranger now.

In "Last Year at Marienbad: An Intertextual Meditation," Thomas Beltzer wrote that "if you go to the movies too often, you may never come back. Your own life may become a fiction."

But other than the fictions of childhood, what belongs to me? What is to become of me?

#

At home at night. I receive a promising phone call.

"Hello, this is Anna Enruckus of the New York Agenda. I want to do a story about your dreams."

I can't believe it. The New York Agenda, the paper of record for the world, wants to do a story about my visions, about my incredible revelation. About me!

In all fairness, The Stranger may be right. This may be the twilight era of newspapers. But they're not dead yet. People still read. And when they read something in the New York Agenda, they believe it. Not like some ridiculous cinematic fraud with a mechanical tornado and a paranoid fantasy about a bottled water company creating the world's first privately owned and operated deity.

"Can you believe my own paper isn't even interested?" I ask.

"That's incredible," Anna says. "This may be the most important story of the Hydrocarbon Age, perhaps of the entire Modern World. I want to document your dreams, the visions of the end of an era."

"I keep a dream journal. Would you like me to overnight you a copy?"

#

Dateline: D/FW Airport. I stand at the end of Gate 19, waiting for the passengers of Delta Flight 3519 from Omaha. Reporter's notebook and pen in hand, I am ready to commit some genuine daily newspaper reporting. But I am not optimistic about my chances for success.

"Come on, Le-e-e-ach," Guy had protested, drawing out the first syllable of my name in a friendly, but mocking tone. "It's a great story. Travelers of the jet age flying over the heads of travelers of the Conestoga age."

"But when you're on final descent, people are busy gathering up their possessions," I protested. "They are putting the tray table in the upright position, getting ready to leave. And even if they were looking out the window, it'd be a stretch for them to see any encampment beyond the perimeter, even something as big as the Sesquicentennial Wagon Train."

"All you need to do is talk to a few arriving passengers, get some snazzy quotes, write it right and you've got a P-1 easy."

Of course, it has not been easy. As I had predicted, none of the arriving passengers have seen any Old West wagon train from their cabin windows. And what about quotes? Just getting a "no" has been quite an accomplishment.

Few travelers will stop long enough to talk to me, or even acknowledge my presence. Men traveling alone are proving to be the worst. They won't even look at me. I am certain that I could wave a $100 bill in front of them and get no recognition. Some of the solo female travelers do give me a polite "no," and several couples have actually stopped long enough to shake their heads and exchange looks of bemused, doubt-filled sympathy.

I am the newspaper jester, leaping about the concourse with a pointy cap on my head and bells on my shoes. Or perhaps a Hare Krishna, one disguising his shaved head with a short-haired wig and temporarily trading in the white robe and finger cymbals for a dress shirt and tie.

After debasing myself before a couple of loads of Delta passengers, I dig a quarter out of my pocket and call the State Desk editor who has conceived the wagon-train-as-seen-from-above story. It is to be part of a multi-day package, complete with "Wagons, ho!" logo and the phrase "One in an occasional series" preceding the text. Except that now it will be one story short.

"No one saw it? Are you sure?" an incredulous Larry Broland asks. "I just can't believe that."

Larry is more than a little disappointed that his grand idea is not panning out. And like all successful editors, he is not about to shoulder the blame.

"Well, try a few more flights and call me back," Larry says tiredly. "If you don't get anything, then I guess you might as well come back in."

I bet nothing like this ever happens at the New York Agenda.

#

Of course, I have no intention of ambushing any more arriving passengers. The story is DOA -- actually, dead at the scene. Broland is simply working CPR on a corpse. A veteran staffer whose byline file dates back to 1961, he could give his inspired idea the quality reporting it deserves. But not me. So I decide to kill a few minutes kicking around the airport.

After a quick Dr Pepper in one of the bars, I take an escalator to the lower level and board one of the automated AirTrans cars. My car is empty, allowing me to pick the last seat so I can watch my progress in reverse.

The electric-powered tram rolls smoothly out of the dim terminal and into the blinding, Texas sun. Rolling along by myself in the tram's narrow, concrete channel, I study the receding parking lots and "Authorized Personnel Only" signs along the AirTrans route. But I see no signs of life. I imagine myself in some science fiction movie about the last man on earth. I am Charlton Heston in "The Omega Man," scavenging the remains of the vast techno-infrastructure that continues to operate on automatic pilot. All mankind is dead, but I continue to receive my paycheck by direct deposit. This allows me to use my bank's electronic bill payer service to keep the electricity streaming into my home, my debit card to fill my gas tank and ATMs to feed me currency for use in vending machines that dispense Dr Pepper at 10, 2, 4 and any other time I desire.

After a few automated stops but no new passengers, I grow tired of the last-man-on-earth scenario and de-board at one of the terminals. I wander a quiet stretch of concourse. No one around. Just me and the endless walkways, lines of doors, gates, -- and walls. Always there are walls, everywhere around me. Mute, deserted – walls of baroque embellishments, mahogany veneer, Venetian plaster, gold-leafed frames, Carrara marble. Unexpectedly, I find myself contemplating the fossilized bones of a dinosaur. An interpretive plaque explains that the animal was a plesiosaur, which workers unearthed during construction of the airport back in the Middle Hydrocarbon Age. Bones encased behind dark glass, lost among obscure illustrations, Romanesque columns, sculptured thresholds, lines of doors, colonnades, oblique hallways leading to deserted meeting rooms paneled in the baroque embellishments of an earlier time. Mute rooms, where footsteps are lost. Sculpted berber so profound, so deep that one perceives no step. The walls are everywhere, enclosing me.

#

Looking to kill a few more minutes before placing my final, bogus call to Larry Broland, I step into a newsstand and began absently rummaging through the magazine rack. I pick up the latest copy of Info Era, a supermarket-style tabloid that specializes in stories about UFOs and the Secret Government. It's one of my guilty pleasures. As I flip through the pages, I am surprised to find an extensive interview with Dr. Adolfo Morel concerning the Society of the Purple Sunset.

Morel: "This game is actually based on a real world endeavor. It was initiated by splinter groups inside the federal administration and covert companies to influence and manage the population. During the years 1966 and 1967 a scheme titled Herbal Extract was established. It was discontinued in 1968. The intent of the scheme was to secure the industrial aptitude to go into a person's nocturnal vision condition and make happen his demise by detonating his brain. It also entailed placing brain management equipment in orbit for use on the inhabitants of Earth. The equipment projected brain direction devices in the image of a Clock in the Air for application on the people of the planet."

Info Era: "What organization operated that scheme?"

Morel: "Flying Device Research Center (FDRC), which had additional concealed schemes under its control. At that juncture, FDRC was operated by Drinkoff Inc., one of the black ops divisions of Ozona International. Now it is administered through the Department of Defense."

Info Era: "The DoD is running Project Herbal Extract?"

Morel: "In cooperation with a variety of extraterrestrial orders. These groups come and go, of course, depending on the inter-species political atmosphere of the galaxy. The C-Group, which is shorthand for Cicada Group, is currently serving as technical consultant for the project.

Info Era: "Tell us about the Cicadans."

Morel: "The Cicadans are extraterrestrial insects. They are giant insectoids with huge compound eyeballs and minds of pure metaphor, the waking world and the Land of the Dead kept in perfect balance. They have been drawn into the government's clandestine schemes at regular intervals since at least the 1940s, and there are some indications of a relationship dating back to the 1890s."

Info Era: "You're talking about Aurora, Texas, and the El Camino Extraterrestre."

Morel: "Actually, I'm talking about the Strangers Rest project."

Info Era: "I thought that was just a myth, a part of the Society of the Purple Sunset."

Morel: "It's real. Remember, the Society of the Purple Sunset is a mythic game based on reality. Strangers Rest is tied into the Corpus Christi Experiment as well as Fort Worth I and Fort Worth II."

Info Era: "You're talking about onbeam brain management."

Morel: "Yes. After the politicians learned about Herbal Extract, they moved to discontinue the project. But the board of directors headed straight for the armed forces and suggested utilizing the technology via public electronic entertainment venues – back in those pre-onbeam days it was just TV and radio broadcast -- to manipulate the brains of our terrestrial foes, both at home and abroad. The idea was to make them think their skin was aging prematurely. Outward youthful vigor would be replaced with sagging decrepitude.The enemy would think he was turning old before his time and would die of psychological shock. The generals were enamored by the concept, and they permitted use of the bunkers under the old Stranger Rest Field. Ozona International financed the project with a grant from the Nazi government in exile."

Info Era: "The Nazis financed Project Herbal Extract?"

Morel: "That's right. You see, Hitler had escaped from Germany at the end of the Second Earthly Conflict with 200 of his most loyal followers – including Goebbels, whose faked suicide was a Nazi ruse to fool the Russians and the Americans – and $20 billion in gold bullion, which he used to finance his government in exile in Uruguay. He traveled to South America on board a U-boat, but he transported the gold using an aerial clock the Luftwaffe had brought down with one of its V-2 rockets. The aliens had equipped the clock with a sky-energy detonator, which Hitler's scientists believed could convert the heavens to flames. But the Germans never could figure out how to make it work. If they had, the war would have been over in 72 hours and you and your grandchildren would be speaking German today."

Info Era: "Do you recall the Raincarnate case?"

Morel: "Interesting you should make that connection. Harry Raincarnate was a skin care manufacturer who lived in Houston in the 1950s. One evening as he was driving home from his hand lotion factory his vehicle malfunctioned. He was caught up in a beam of amber light and taken aboard an aerial clock. The occupants were clad in dark apparel and spoke German Creole with a decidedly Uruguayan accent. He thought they might have been Nazis. After his return, he was transported back onboard the clock several times. He started telling friends and associates about his experience, but then he was visited by federal agents who told him he'd better stop talking 'if he knew what was good for him.' Then they put him in a psychic sanatorium for five months. He came out a shadow of his former self. Lost his business, died penniless. It was a major news story in 1957."

Info Era: "So Hitler wanted to learn how to use the weapon in the clock?"

Morel: "This was a few months before he went comatose and they suspended him in a 'submerged ice' system, which is based on Cicadan exoskeletal biology. It is the way their young survive underground for years before emerging in the winged stage of their life cycle. Anyway, this system was delivered to Hitler by the Cicadans, who wanted to get the Fuhrer into an exoskeletal shell and out of the way before he did any more damage. The Cicadans are actually quite peaceful and so were very troubled with the events of the Second Earthly Conflict. So it was all pre-arranged. Hitler was to go into suspended animation, and that would be the end of it. But Hitler didn't want to wait until his eventual thawing and revival to have his Third Reich victory. He said 'I want to initiate the one thousand years now, before I go into hibernation.' He thought the researchers for Herbal Extract might be able to figure out how to operate the detonator, but before they could give him his new Final Solution he had a massive stoke and had to be frozen."

Info Era: "Is the One World Government involved in prolonged existence?"

Morel: "Of course, because it takes so long to realize these goals. When you arrive at that intensity of political power, you find that the brains of global leaders are distorted and manipulated by exposure to Cicadan DNA, which is in fact based on Skinalicious9. They are totally dependent on alien insect technology and skin-rejuven ating biology."

As I scan the story for more about Strangers Rest, my attention strays to a young family across the concourse.

They sit in the gray vinyl seats, mom and dad buried in paperback novels as their two sons play around the carry-on bags at their feet. The boys are a blur of slapping hands, swinging feet and smacking mouths, which they stuff with a steady stream of Skittles candies. They remind me of my own sons, and I for a moment I even feel a bit wistful -- that is, until they remind me of my boys a bit too much.

"Momma, Joey scratched my arm," one of them says, rapidly blinking his eyes in hopes of shedding a credible tear. The other responds with a louder yelp, then recklessly pounds his own arm and whines something about how he's been wronged "againandagainandagain and he wouldn't stop!"

The father says nothing, and I feel myself tense up, waiting for what I am sure will be the mother's inevitable, screeching outburst. After all, I have been in his position many times, engulfed in censorious dread.

But much to my surprise, the outburst never occurs. Instead, the mother speaks some soft, soothing words to both of the wounded children, hands then some bauble from her purse and all is well again. Then she returns to her reading, all without so much as raising her voice. I am amazed. No shouting. Even more incredible, the wife turns to her husband, speaks a few more quiet words. He smiles, replies and both of them laugh. No yelling. They are happy – happy unto death.

#

I must confess that I cannot conceive of such a cordial exchange with Allison. And she is an incredibly beloved person. Ask any of her friends. She is the companion everyone wants to have. She is the perfected being. But me – I am not such a desired companion. I am the outsider, the alien.

I am Clark Caring, returning home after an alternate reality erases the previous year of marital discord, separation and impending divorce.

#

I find it both pleasant and strange to return to the house from which I had been banished by court order the previous year. Parking the Lexus in my old spot in the garage, tousling the hair of my 11-year-old son as he sits glued to the TV, fixing myself a dirty martini (with blue-cheese stuffed olive, of course) as my beloved puts the finishing touches on the evening's savory yet nutritious dinner.

Can you believe it? I am still married, still a family man. Life is good.

My copy of the "The Voice of God" (found in the bookcase in my study) does not reveal much useful information. It resembles no book I've ever seen. The text begins on the first page. No fly sheet, no title page, no acknowledgements. The only reference to a publisher is a brief mention on the back cover: "Another exciting dreamography from End Times Books. Visit us onbeam today!"

I am preparing to plug in when a spousal scream hits me from across the house. I hustle into the kitchen to find my beloved feeling a bit less than loving.

"I'm trying to get dinner on the table," she complains. "Can you at least set the table and get Brian to wash his hands?"

"Of course. I didn't know you needed any help."

"Right. We have dinner every night. The food has to be cooked, the table has to be set. I didn't think I have to tell you that anymore. I can't do everything."

#

Back in the day, this is the place in the story where the people would expect to see me and Mrs. God engage in a dinnertime scene of marital discord. Perhaps an oblique reference to the Dairy Queen, a suggestion that Mrs. God suspects I am squirting my love inside my 22-year administrative assistant with the big boobs and the tight ass. Does she suspect there is – or, rather 'was' – something between us?

Or perhaps we would sit at the table in silence, glaring at one another across the top edge of competing daily newspapers as occurred in "Citizen Kane," a movie about a man who wanted everyone to love him.

The desire to be loved – back in the day this is what marriage was all about. Some men believed that what they really wanted was to hear one special woman say "I love you." But they were fooling themselves.

For here is the truth: During the last days of Planet Earth, what men really wanted, in their heart of hearts, was to be loved by everyone. Like a God. Which is to say, they wanted to BE GOD. To be loved because you are a superior being – because you are more worthy of love than mere mortals – this is the real thing.

This is True Love.

I tell you my beloved creations, True Love is better than all other forms of affection. True Love prompts the superior being to create a universe. True Love motivates the superior being to bring light to a world that is without form and void.

Admittedly, True Love sometimes prompts the superior being to let bad things happen to good people. When the superior being has been violated, True Love makes him turn women into pillars of salt. True Love makes him cover the earth in a murderous flood. And yes, True Love even makes him bring about the "terrible calamity."

But how can it be otherwise? True Love does not depend on lovable actions. That is why True Love is absolutely required by the superior being. True Love is received not because of what you do but simply because of you are.

#

As for me and Allison and True Love – such a scene is not in the script. Oh sure, maybe once, long ago. In the dim recesses of my memory, I vaguely recall a time when I thought she was happy with me. And we were happy, I'm sure of it. We were perfect, two perfected beings. I remember us in our normal waking world lives, walking hand in hand at the mall, draping an arm across my shoulder – but no, this memory is not for me. I do not require it anymore. I am perfect without it. I am perfect, I am happy. I am happy unto death!

I sit here with you on the warm beach, but I feel oddly cold. Yes, you can see that I am shivering. Did I tell you the concourse walls were bleeding? There were Nazi paratroopers, too. I see them even now, landing on the tarmac outside the window. On the back of my hand, the embedded nest of tiny white eggs. They hatching into an army of hungry wolf spiders, picking my bones clean.

Again I advance toward the combination gas station/Germany bakery in West, Texas, carried by the twilight wind across a rolling prairie, snagged in an old barbed wire fence, wind whistling through tombstones. An awful dark rip has appeared in the master film, right in the midst of a long, languid shot panning the valley of blue shadows and a gemstone cranium of mist and haze, a gloom of unfilled spaces. On an astral cattle trail paved in stones of ginger-colored exasperation we come to the ford in the creek. The resonance of running water and a pale flash of dead cold-eyed Jonah gone bluish white beneath the still surface of the dark gulf waters, cold flesh dissected by albino brain crabs and screeching sea birds, twilight fish jumping, a concerto of amphibians and mounds of hospital wastes and jellyfish with sea grass growing through. All alone, just me and the long dead beach – and The Stranger.

He steps out from behind a potted palm and switches off the Beulah.

"I'm told there's more than one way to show that you love someone," he remarks.

"I haven't managed to find any of them."

"Perhaps we do not receive love because we are not capable of administering it. We are not yet a perfected being."

"Wouldn't it be nice to be both imperfect and loved?"

"Now you're just talking crazy."

Dinner in the house that Jack built. But first, our host must finish his tan.

Reclining on a Victorian-style fainting couch, something his wife picked up shortly after their wedding and has still failed to retrieve for her post-Jack life. Hoping to render it unusable, Jack has turned it into the centerpiece of his ``tanning salon," a little corner of the breakfast nook. Lost in the scent of rum and coconut tanning oil rising out of the velvet upholstery, Jack reaches up to adjust a UV tanning bulb that buzzes violently inside a black flood lamp overhead.

``You make it sound so - so sordid," he remarks, adjusting a pair of dark green tanning goggles. ``It's no big deal."

"But the feds may declare your dad's sanctuary insolvent," I say.

"Rockwall Banc," The Stranger says. "It was years ago, but I still remember the call reports. Ton of bad loans, mostly real estate and photovoltaics."

"Big deal," Jack remarks. "Everybody's doing it."

"Next spring. The examiners will come on a Thursday."

"Thursday? How do you know?"

"They always come on a Thursday," I explain, "right before closing time."

"A prophet is never honored in his own country," The Stranger says.

We were still in college when Andrew Bryson purchased Rockwall Banc, a sleepy little G&C he quickly transformed into one of the fastest growing sanctuaries in the Southwest. I remember a story about it in the business section of the Dallas Times Herald. The reporter had captured a perfect quote for the times: "I told all the real estate brokers `Don't bring me anymore apartment buildings, shopping centers or office towers. I want a guarantee and credit!'"

The Stranger remembers it, too.

"There was the photo that ran with the story," he recalls. "I even recall something of the wording: Posed in his third floor corner office of Rockwall Banc's mirrored glass midrise, dressed in his gray banker's suit with red power tie, Mr. Bryson sits tall in the saddle behind his expansive desk, a mound of loan files before him and the North Dallas Tollway throbbing below, a giant 220-volt electrical cord snaking through the Texas real estate market, plugging him straight into the go-go '80s."

"That's not what it said," Jack says.

"Still, it should have."

But now the chairman of Rockwall Banc was no longer sitting quite so tall. Business was tough. Last year, in a fit of anger over the sanctuary's stagnating loan portfolio, Andrew Bryson threw his high-back leather desk chair down the stairwell and vowed he would not replace it until he'd restored the loan-to-loss ratio to an acceptable level. That apparently wasn't going to happen anytime soon. I'd seen the most recent quarterly report for Texas sanctuaries. Mr. Bryson was still using the gunmetal gray folding chair he'd made his secretary pick up at Target.

"When I told dad I needed another interim he nearly busted a vessel," Jack recalls. "He said 'but you haven't sold any of your other specs yet.'"

"So he wouldn't give you another loan?" I ask.

"He gave me something much better. The benefit of his advice."

"`Better just tighten up your belt a few notches," The Stranger says.

"That's right," Jack confirms. "'Tighten up your belt and run the business off cash until you get a house sold.'"

"Guess that's the downside of having your father for a banker. So did you tell him the problem was you didn't have any cash?"

"Oh right. Like why don't I just wear a little sign on by butt that says `kick me.'"

"I like it," The Stranger said. "We could give it a homey treatment, maybe something like 'It's a Wonderful Life.'"

"That's what I'm saying. I'm George Bailey, on my knees, begging, and he's sitting there like he's old man Potter, king of Bedford Falls. He just keeps on saying `the auditors are really cracking down, I can't do anything special just because you're my son.'"

Clearly, the situation has turned serious. I know of several developers who've recently had their loans called. Country records show a few have escaped with only deeds in lieu of foreclosure. But for most, it is the trustee's deed, sale to the highest bidder on the south steps of the county courthouse. There is even some talk of deficiency judgments secured by lenders left holding properties that aren't worth the inflated loan balances, long-spent dollars generated from bogus developer fees and other accounting tricks. A few of the wheeler dealers are even going to jail. I turn to The Stranger.

"You know what's going to happen."

He nods. "But I don't think I should tell."

"Because he doesn't know," Jack says.

The Stranger does not respond. Jack shrugs and takes another sip of his bourbon and water.

"Anyway," Jack continues, "dad offered me six-month extensions on the two loans that were about to come due, so that gives me a few more months to find a buyer or two."

"That's good news."

"But it didn't come cheap, did it?" The Stranger says.

"That's right. He decided to tell me what I'd done wrong with Donna."

"What you did wrong?" I ask. "Is he forgetting that Donna is the one who left you?"

Jack laughs a bitter, dry laugh and takes a hard pull from his drink. "No, he didn't forget. But, you see, that's what nice girls do when their husbands force them to put out for their friends. Your name was prominently mentioned."

I can't quite believe my ears. "Andy thinks me? Donna?"

He nods.

"But I was a groomsman at your wedding."

"I couldn't even listen to it, I was so furious. I got in his face and yelled `you don't know what the hell you're talking about.'"

"Really?" I cannot imagine such a response from Jack, always the good, respectful son.

"I think it shocked him pretty severely. He said he was sorry. I'm glad it happened, though. We'd never talked about it before. It really cleared the air."

"Did he say anything that helped?"

"No, not really. What does he know about marriage? I don't think him and mom have done it in years, maybe not since I was conceived. No, it was just good to talk it through with him, to clear the air."

"Good to clear the air before the divorce is final, right?"

"Hmm? Oh yeah," Jack says, pretending to remember. "You know, I almost forgot. To me, it's like we're already divorced, even if it's not official. Now let's fire up the grill."

While we wait in the kitchen for the charcoal to whiten, The Stranger happens upon a wicker basket filled with delinquency notices from various credit card companies.

"I remember these, too," he says. "For a pauper you do all right."

"I can't complain," Jack agrees.

#

Jack Bryson

12 Highland Terrace

Strangers Rest, TX 76270

#

Account No: 51340666 201 1776

Current Balance: $2,786

Delinquent Amount Due: $438

#

Dear Jack Bryson

#

We have been informed by our Security Department that an attempt was made to obtain credit on your account while it is delinquent.

If further attempts are made to obtain credit on your account before correcting the above situation, your credit privileges may be canceled. You must contact my office to make arrangements for minimum amount due. Your account is being evaluated, for placement with a collection agency or attorney for the purpose of bringing a lawsuit against you.

Telephone my department and explain your intention for repayment.

Juanita Lamethorpe

Collection Manager

#

It happened two weeks before at his favorite French nouvelle restaurant in the McKinney Avenue area of Dallas. The meal ended with the waitress cutting his card in half, forcing him to pay the bill ($140 plus tip) with a company check. It was not until the next day that he realized the corporate account of Jack Bryson Homes Inc. had been reduced to a grand total of $4.42.

``Dad says you're nobody anymore unless you owe at least a couple of million to somebody," Jack remarks.

"What is one more late notice from Juanita Lamethorpe?" The Stranger says. "You're on the hook for three interim production loans totaling well over $1 million. I've got a concept to convert your experience into something second hand, something planned and described for your consumption in advance."

"Let's hear it."

"The only thing that bothers you -- a little, anyway -- is that you've already gone through the profits you budgeted for those jobs but still have no buyers."

"That's true."

"Your household account needs a cash infusion. But how? That's when you get the big idea, an inspired, cunning, recklessly dangerous idea."

"I build another house?"

"It is so simple. And you can even justify it, explain to the sanctuary –"

"My father."

"-- that The Lakes of Greenwood really needed one more house –"

"Payment to builder, me."

"-- to fully demonstrate the brilliance of the concept –"

"My father's concept, of course."

"-- and reach that all-important critical mass."

"That even sounds like my dad."

So simple. If only there was some money left somewhere in Texas to do it.

"Dad told me a prayer he heard at the last commercial real estate breakfast," Jack says. "Dear Lord, please let me have one more boom. I promise I won't fuck it up this time. Amen."

"You know what NCNB stands for?" The Stranger asks.

But Jack doesn't hear him. He is watching me thumb through the latest issue of Cosmopolitan, a subscription that Jack's wife has failed to forward to her new address.

"I'm just getting educated," I explain. "I think women like to read about orgasms a lot more than they like to have them."

"Depends on the woman," Jack says.

"I wonder if women really are even physically capable of having them. I think it's all a big fake, a massive intra-sexual conspiracy they made up so they can make the man get off of them when they're tired of being sweated on."

"That was Allison before she left me," The Stranger says.

"They don't fake it with me, I know that for sure," Jack insists.

"But, of course, you do not know."

"Why are you always introducing such unpleasant lines of thought? Like the late notices. Why bring those up? They were sitting in the wicker basket, not bothering anybody. And couldn't you find a better magazine to read than Cosmopolitan? The latest issue of Playboy is right underneath it."

"I was getting to that next."

"Why insist on wallowing in chronic mournfulness?"

"Because I'm the two-bodied man."

Jack picks up the Playboy and heads straight for the centerfold, but I can see it doesn't help. The Stranger can see it, too.

"Don't you wonder if Miss August ever faked an orgasm?" The Stranger asks. "You could find out, try seducing her, but that would be tough because your credit privileges have been suspended."

"Enough," Jack says. "A few more minutes of this and I'll be as beaten down as both of you. I gotta go."

"I thought we were going to grill," The Stranger says.

Jack tosses the magazine on the counter and begins rummaging about for his wallet and keys.

"Aren't we going to eat?" I ask. I am half starved, waiting all evening for Jack to quit screwing around and get into gear. His normal dinner hour is about 11 p.m., a real shock to my stomach. I'm used to a family meal every evening around 6:30.

"I won't be gone long," he says. "But go ahead and fix yourself something. There's some fantastic leftover lamb in the refrigerator."

"So, what, you'll be back in about a half hour?" The Stranger asks. He is starving, too.

"I'm not that fast."

"Maybe we should just call it a night, try again tomorrow," I suggest.

"Hell no. Stay. Play the stereo, drink my liquor, fuck my cat. I'll be back in plenty of time."

"You haven't even taken a shower yet."

"I'm not taking one, the tanning lamp didn't make me sweat."

"Well, I don't know. It is a week night."

"Oh no, it's a week night," Jack say, using his nervous woman voice. "Come on, you're a bachelor again – or one of you is, I don't know. All you can think about is getting a good night's sleep."

"Why is sitting around here any better than sitting around at my own house?"

"Because when you get done here, instead of going to bed you're going to go out with me."

"What are we talking about here, an hour?"

"Yeah, an hour, that sounds good."

The Stranger smiles at me. We both know it won't be an hour.

Jack scoops up his keys and heads for the garage. "Eat the lamb, it's fantastic," he tells us. "My mom made it."

#

"I haven't had much success in writing," I admit between bites of roasted lamb. "You are the one things happen to, the one who has success."

The Stranger nods sympathetically. "That's because you still put your trust in the concrete and rational, in the untrustworthy waking world. This is no place to disseminate your incredible revelation."

I do not tell him about the New York Agenda.

"Try on this concept," he advises. "You observe the birth of a new form of friends. They are to fully dismiss the idea that your dreams are also the daimon that drives you where it will. You are to be one of the people. The hook is that you told yourself, in visions. You speak to yourself through dreams. It is mentioned in Numbers, where one is unwittingly transfigured by the contents. You can no longer deny this transfiguration."

"Did you put the clock in the sky?"

"No, no. See, you're trying too hard. You must avoid excessive rationalism without wisdom. I was like you, before I became like me. That is, before I discovered the restorative nature of the epic film."

"How did this discovery come to pass?"

"Like so many transformative processes, it came over time. We shall now commit the process to film."

The Stranger lays down his fork. He produces his Beulah and explains the scene.

"You will accidentally discover this," he says, handing me a book, "which has been delivered to you in an unmarked envelope by a shadowy character from the Land of the Dead. We'll film that part later, of course."

I read the name on the spine. Well, how about that?

"Pretty, a nice look of surprise for the close up," he says. "Exactly the state of shock I was hoping for."

Magnetica O'Famously. My old girlfriend!

In the years before I met Allison, Magnetica was my romantic attachment. After a long period of casual membrane penetrations, she dumped me for a boyfriend redux. She called him "Kool," a nickname she'd given him for the ever-present cigarette that he employed as a sort of Bohemian prop. He had exited her life after she captured him in an intentional act of plagiarism. Seems he had submitted a purloined work to a small East Coast literary journal, of which Magnetica was editor. He then abandoned her, and she was left behind to write and publish the public apology.

So how about that? Magnetica has a book of her own now. Although not plagiarized, this one is a rather obvious paraphrase of Carl Jung's "Flying Saucers: A Modern Myth of Things Seen in the Sky." Still, it beats anything I've written, which is to say nothing. So she's ahead of me. She's better than me. That's probably why she dumped me.

Ah well. I am genuinely happy for her, happy for her achievement. I present the jacket blurb for your consideration.

#

A ticking mandala of the almighty – As our imaginings demonstrate very obviously, aerial timepieces arrive from the comatose milieu, which forever asserts itself in mystical thoughts and metaphors. Cultured humans, like prehistoric ones, are aware of the deities, of the ghosts, and of destiny and the supernatural character of occasion and location. This is the focal concept of 'A Clock in the Air: A Contemporary Legend of Timepieces Observed in the Heavens,' another exciting New Age tome from Magnetica O'Famously and Weigh-In Books. An existence and reason coach from The Land of the Dead, O'Famously had a life-changing experience through a numinous encounter with the inner workings of the Deity's clockwork mandala. What was the result of this revelatory experience in the sky? O'Famously proposes that faith in aerial timepieces is actually a reply to the bottomless social nervousness of a civilization intimidated by unexpected technological obliteration. And she tells us that we of the West are not the only ones who have feared science would bring about the conclusion of time. She notes that the regal Jaundiced Ones of the second earthly conflict feared their civilization was being obliterated by the mechanized ethnicity of the West. Slavophiles of that similar occasion spoke almost mournfully of the West's extreme lucidity without understanding. O'Famously writes: 'Let us be mindful of that which is airborne around us and strive to reach comparable heights in our own lives.' O'Famously is founder of the Narrative Factory, a distributor of narratives concerning the livelihood of beloved fervors, bottomless reason and heavenly manifestation. She lives in the ethereal neon glow of Burial Chamber, Calif., with her questionably gendered companion and two mummified Egyptian cats. Now Read What Others Are Saying About "A Clock in the Air"!

"In an era of dark aircraft soaring above our heads, livestock disfigurements and extraterrestrial insects, the convincing comments made by O'Famously are especially pertinent." – The Divine Marketplace of Benign Ideas

"We are overwhelmed by end-of-the-world panic, Rapture sects, Keepers of the Deity, premature skin aging and apocalyptic appointments with God. O'Famously skillfully argues that psychotic deviations reveal themselves in collective illusions. Her reading of aerial timepieces as stand-ins for the prototype of completeness, a new force striving to assert itself in an age of mental disintegration, is luminous and intense." – The Twilight of Satisfactoriness

"Electrifying! A tour de force. A bold new voice in American literature. This book will save your marriage!" – The Usurping Person Who Reads

#

"Your world is dead," The Stranger says. "It no longer functions. Your life no longer functions. Sewn together romance comes off like the symbolic remains of the 1970s. I like this idea for cinema, but it's bad for real life. We must trust the inner world, the one that lies behind solid things. It's time you started trusting me – that is, your inner director."

"How can I trust what I haven't seen?"

"Right you are. Enough waiting for Jack. Let's go to the movies."

We drive out to the derelict Hi-Way 114 Drive-In Theatre in The Stranger's little deuce coupe, turning off the asphalt onto the old entry drive, gravel crunching under the treads.

Headlights on the ranch gate, The Stranger leaves the car running while he gets out to unlock the heavy chain. I drive past this place a couple of times a day, but here in the feeble headlight glow I see something new: a rebuilt refreshment stand/projection booth. Strange, for the old one burned down years ago. How could I have missed such a major work of reconstruction?

"It's a false front, built in a day," The Stranger explains. "It's just plywood and posts. Same way they did the big Reata house in 'Giant.' Go down there to Marfa today and you can still see the telephone poles sticking out of the ground."

As we drive onto the property I notice a new sign: Armageddon Drive-In Theatre. I say new, but it actually looks old, a resurrection of faded '50s roadside advertising held tight in a tangle of broken neon tubes.

"I've leased this place from Dollar Bill Buckstop for filming the climax of the movie, the Battle of Armageddon scene," The Stranger says. "Thanks to my efforts, it's actually once again a working theater. Well, my efforts and theirs."

The Stranger takes in the dashboard view with a grand sweep of his arm, and I see that we are not alone. Perhaps two dozen cars are parked in front of the old screen. A young man with scraggly goatee and sleeveless flannel shirt kneels on the roof of a circa 1960s aluminum camper, working on what appears to be a combination projector/computer.

"It's a conventional 35mm projector," the Stranger says. "But it's hooked up to a small black box with an oscilloscope on front and a coil of clear tubing on the aperture gate, which is coated in living flesh." He holds up a little black cube with a pushbutton pad. "It's even got remote control."

We pull up to a metal speaker pole, and The Stranger hangs one of the weathered aluminum speakers in his window.

"This one is surplus, from the old Texas Stadium Drive-In in Irving," he remarks. "Look, it's still says 'Stadium' on the front."

"Who are these people?" I ask. "What is all this?"

"Guerrilla drive-in movie theater."

"What?"

"Do-it-yourself movies. They're popping up everywhere, from L.A. to New York City, big cities and small towns. Most of the time they set up in dark parking lots behind industrial warehouses. But they really prefer to stage their events at old drive-ins like this one."

A dark-haired girl in a flowing peasant skirt and thick black frame glasses taps on my window. I roll down the window, and she gives me a handbill:

"Deep Ellum Guerilla Drive-In. Breathe Retro, Take pleasure in a Retro Show! Deep Ellum Guerilla Drive-In is precisely what it seems to be – an al fresco cinema beneath the heavens that materializes without warning out of the unconscious and onto undeveloped rural plots and other sites in the profit-making wilderness. Guerilla Drive-In is serving to rescue community liberty and change our metropolitan surroundings into the pleasant world of recreation that it is meant to be. Grab your ectoplasm-stained bedspreads, grass stools and sexually-willing acquaintances. Prepare to engage in jug wine, oral sex and salty nibbles on vintage Cutlass black vinyl accompanied by the wonders of 1950s B-movie sci-fi. Endowments are greeted with much appreciation. Tonight at the Deep Ellum Guerilla Drive-In – a midnight creature feature based on the dream cinema of The Stranger! (Special thanks to the creator of the concept, the Santa Cruz Guerilla Drive-In.)"

The old Hi-way 114 screen – still standing after all these years – begins to flicker to life in a greenish blue glow. The window speaker from the Stadium Drive-In crackles with static electricity.

"Sounds like the ocean," I observe.

"Gaseous and liquid cinema. Based on a concept by Salvador Dali."

#

The first offering is called "Give Elmo and Charlie a Blast," an obvious take-off on the popular movie review show.

"But this one has a twist," The Stranger explains. "Elmo and Charlie only review movies that have yet to be made. If they really like a concept, then they agree to produce it. Last year, they released 'Valley of the Nanobots'."

#

Charlie: Hi, I'm Charlie Rebosto.

Elmo: And I'm Elmo Plumbline. Today we begin with a review of 'Boom-Crash! The Freud Dude's Two-Bodied Leach meets The G&C Mafia.'

Charlie: And what a great choice this is. The slapstick blast from this pseudo-documentary could be quite engaging.

Elmo: It even employs butt-scratching monkeys.

Charlie: A nod to Darwin. We could work in the Book of Revelation, let the Deity prepare a place the viewers have not seen since childhood. We'll remind them that inside the fish, Jonah was really free. Back on shore, he was dead.

Elmo: And a whiner.

Charlie: The certain dream message isn't any less important, though I am still compelled to issue it.

Elmo: The dead, dread, fearful specters are still accessible. And through Technicolor romance, they are coming off somehow feeling true. Two-dimensional affectation is an important part of the plot. And death, too - with many gutsy explosions and free-flowing blood. There is an authority in death. Even the newspaper world is dead.

Charlie: That's the story. Call it "The Penetrated Writer." A gunshot to the heart, and yet the body continues to function. This whole process is death because many have tried to ignore the eternal world, regard it as a mutation. It has my word on it. They told me to forget; that is some bad advice. The message is not.

Elmo: You know, Charlie, this could be Mark Leach's magnum opus, the long-awaited two-bodied masterpiece. The world as mutation. In fact, it is a metaphor for his birth of - and in -- a new form. His face is transfigured.

Charlie: Next, we take a look at 'My Lovely Creation,' a beautiful film short, tight but so obsessed with the egregious moral failure of ectoplasm imperfectly deployed.

Elmo. A strange one, to be sure. "My Lovely Creation" is actually about the death of film. Leach says that he finds full-length motion pictures exhausting to watch anymore, and filmmakers should give up on creating more and focus instead on making excrement and nightmares.

Charlie: Yes, this masterpiece has him telling off himself, so depressed about how his DNA both creates and destroys.

Elmo: That's right. Do not be about the rotting remains, Mark, unknown and cloaked in the knowledge that bars none.

Charlie: You know, ha ha – and I must shake my head with great condescension – it's as if Mark Times Two wishes all he had to do was become a figurative being in the Land of the Dead, a Revelation described to the mind, a maze in a cliché-cramming contest.

Elmo: And for an experience just as nourishing, you may want to option his flick "Bad Dream for Tumbleweed Cowboy: A B-Movie Western for the End of the World." Let's roll a short clip.

#

The Tumbleweed Cowboy rides his black, snorting stallion through a melancholy dream, following the stars that would guide him home.

"Curse you stars, it's too dark a place you be taking us through," he complains, and the horse neighs its mutual discontent. "Why can't you shine a little brighter and lead us during daylight?"

Suddenly, a howling coyote wind lifts the Tumbleweed Cowboy out of his saddle, sends him cartwheeling across the darkened dreamscape. He comes to rest along a tumbled down fence line, boots poking straight up at the sky. He reaches for his trusty horse's reins, but a shooting star screams across the heavens and scares the animal away.

"Dang you, stars. Why you have to go and shoot your star-shooter at ole Blackie? Now I'm all alone, tangled up here in this rusty old bob wire forever."

Despite the Tumbleweed Cowboy's ignorance of basic science (shooting stars being only meteorites, of course), the stars take pity on him and guide a yellow-haired nightmare to his aid. But when the pretty filly arrives, she is disappointed to find that this particular cowboy is really no more than a ball of sticks.

"I'd been dreaming of a carrot," she says.

"Well, I'm just an old tumbleweed. No use cryin' about what I ain't."

This unrepentant tone makes the nightmare angry, and she knocks the cowboy from the fence and stomps him into a pile of splinters.

Back at the ranch, the other nightmares console the wronged creature. "Yup, that's a man for you. All stick and no carrot."

Listening unseen from the shadows, the stallion quietly snorts at this feminine treachery and flies back across the dream to the aid of the Tumbleweed Cowboy.

When he arrives, sure enough, his master is dead, nothing but a broken shell. "I won't let you die in vain, Tumbleweed Cowboy," the horse declares. "I won't rest till your death has been avenged."

But just then, a passing rodeo clown hears the stallion. He lassos the unsuspecting beast and sells him to a traveling circus, where they geld him and make him spend the rest of his days giving pony rides in the happy dreams of unpleasant children. The stars can only shake their heads and smile. "Ah, the folly of horse and man!"

#

Elmo: Attention Mark Leach. Kafka is holding on the red phone.

Charlie: This could prove to be one of my favorite Leach films. There is a lot of movie imagery in the Land of the Dead. He is all about the movie. Hey – there's a concept! His world as eternal cinema.

Elmo: In preparation for the full-body, cellular split, the domestically challenged Mark died in the dishes, so to speak, outside a combination gas station/Germany bakery in West, Texas, on the Sunday before Christmas 1999. As he tells it, he sat in the car while his wife went inside for kolaches. The sun had taken on a discouraging slant in the sky. Darkness was closing in.

Charlie: It's interesting, but I have a question. By accepting this rather pedestrian explanation for the origin of the Tumbleweed Cowboy, are we required to fully dismiss the concept of a genuine equine alien abduction? Carl Jung -

Elmo: Yes, yes, Charlie, we all know Carl is timeless. He seems to be about the idea of it all, but I'll certainly not be sending for him. "Go back, Carl," I'd say, "the church is dying." You like?

Charlie: Actually, we're in agreement.

Elmo: Yes?

Charlie: Yes.

Elmo: Then send over the courier. I'm sure Two-Bodied Mark –

Charlie: Mark Times Two.

Elmo: -- can deal quite nicely with our offer. Deny the world. It is dead. It no longer functions. The Fiend of the Unconscious wants to be our today. And just as nourishing, Mark's flick nightmare of three hours of dreary underwater Jonah. This is the main thing.

Charlie: Next, let's try the third eye dream from 'The Voice of God.' This one leads to fashion, a mascara eye abdomen viewed through magnifying plexiglas.

Elmo: Don't give it away, though. First let's roll the clip.

#

And the journey through prohibited places continues.

Allison and I are in a strange place, an alien society. We are fleeing from unseen people in a seemingly abandoned structure, maybe a stadium. The design is somewhat reminiscent of the UFO house, but on a much larger and grander scale.

We spot a place almost out of sight, near the base, where you can observe the underlying construction. Allison comments that we can see the steel support beams. As we look for a hiding place, we find a marble alcove reminiscent of ancient Roman architecture. It is perhaps the size of a bedroom. This alcove is out of sight, but I immediately realize that if we are found here there will be no escape. We will be trapped. So we go in search of a more secure place of safety.

It is then that we realize there are people everywhere, hurrying about in search of their own hiding places. It is growing dark, suggesting to me that the time to get out of sight is almost here. I realize that we are not well suited for this. I am wearing only white boxers – my preferred sleeping attire – and Allison is in little more than shorts and a top. Where to go? I see a young black man, very dark. He is shirtless. I instantly fear him – and all of the obviously desperate people around us. This man will rape my wife, or someone else will. Where to go?

I see a flight of steps leading to a lower level. The black man waves his hand, showing us the way down the steps. Like an usher in a movie theater.

"I will take you to a place of safety," he says.

I do not trust him, so I grab Allison's hand and we bolt through a doorway to the outside.

We find ourselves standing under a loggia, looking out on a plaza that reminds me of the main square in New Orleans' French Quarter. Many people are relaxing in small groups. All of them are young and beautiful, the elite of this society. They are obviously of a higher social cast than the underground people who must scramble for shelter before nightfall.

They are dressed for leisure, though in a way I have never seen. On their washboard abs, each person displays a large, painted eye. It is the Eye of Horus, the ancient Egyptian visual rumor used to ward off sickness and bring the dead back to life. The latter must be the case here, for the eye was also used as an amulet over the embalmer's incision. That's how you made a suitable mummy.

The Eye of Horus is a particularly fitting image for this point in the journey, for it was only the day before – in the waking world – that I was reading the Old Testament story of Joseph's dream and his resulting enslavement in Egypt. This was his destiny.

These Third Eye people look us over, instantly judging us to be the inferior, underground species. We do not belong; they fear us. Not waiting for them to act on their judgment, we run toward the street at the end of the loggia. This creates some excitement. I kick someone in their abdominal eye, and Allison – now inexplicably holding a baby in her arms – breaks into a run. Another of the Third Eye people produces a large plastic lens (square, perhaps 15 to 20 inches per side) and places it in front of my stomach. Apparently, this action is intended to draw attention to the fact that my abdomen does not possess the required cyclopean makeup. I am blind.

I try to follow Allison, but the path is barred by a man. He is a sort of henchman for the man in charge, who I somehow know. I try to fight him. Someone hands me the blade of a plastic toy sword, and the man in charge laughs. Someone else hands me the handle, and I hastily assemble the two pieces. Even though it is a toy, I realize that it is a real sword. It can injure, even kill.

With this weapon, I lunge at the man in charge. But I miss, and he disarms me. He thrusts the sword deep into my pelvis. As he withdraws the weapon, there is a thought in my head (or maybe the man is speaking it) that the sword is stuck inside me. The pain is real, but I understand that I will recover from this wound. I will heal and live to fight again.

#

Elmo: I don't mind telling you I feared those three eye folks. Scary slasher flick!

Charlie: Talk about incredible revelations. Already knowing the story, you just want to warn him "watch out for the plastic swords."

Elmo: And then cry. You have to be careful.

Charlie: Yes, and you must also watch out for the fire and brimstone.

Elmo: Agreed. Let's roll that clip, too.

#

Here's one way the world ends: The backyard goes nuclear.

As in most B-movie sci-fi concepts, the moviegoer is not necessarily meant to comprehend all the scientific details. All the viewer knows for sure is a chain reaction involving commonplace materials results in a dramatic volcanic eruption. Crimson fire rains from the nocturnal sky. (Director's note: Shoot this scene through a lens or prism onto feeling-toned print stock.)

We run for the house, reaching safety just ahead of the swirling lava and brimstone. Of course, radioactivity is still a major concern. How many curies of original experience can we safely absorb?

The door won't hold back the lava for long. As the protagonist, it is my job to realize we must get away. But there is no place to go. It is happening everywhere now. Nuclear war.

So we all gather in the foyer to make our escape. I dress for the pilgrim's journey, slipping a necktie and overcoat over my pajamas. The radiation is heating up the house; it feels like the August sun. I see our neighbors in the street, driving away to the hills. But my people and I, we have no car, no way of escape. We are left behind.

The nuclear summer doesn't last long. The half life of visionary transformation must be very short indeed, for the scorching temperature quickly drops and the rain begins to fall. I observe this meteorological change from my perch on the depleted limb of a sycamore, an ideal location to study the Next Arrival.

This is the world of fire. The old way of living – the commonplace world of solid things and comfortable, unchallenged theologies – has been annihilated. I see that we must think differently now, start planning for a new life. Our immediate priority should be to collect the rain, the living water, the grace of the Deity. Even as I experience this revelation, I see that others are already bottling the novel vintage. They too know we must save this divine gift for the future. We must begin our new lives, the lives of radiance – the lives that we dream for ourselves after the End of the World.

#

"That was incomprehensible," I say. My head is spinning. My secrets are escaping into the everyday. Is the young dark-haired girl in the peasant dress looking at me?

"Watch this. Here comes the sponsor's commercial."

A flock of iridescent funeral crows wheel across a clear blue sky, delighting an attractive couple while they enjoy a picnic in a field of billowing winter rye, golden retriever puppy and the whistle of an unseen train. The man touches the woman's long hair, and her eyelids flutter appreciatively. The disembodied sponsor speaks: "Conquer the reluctant orgasm with Climaxia, the first intra-vaginal paradisiacal locomotive." The screen goes dark.

The Stranger falls over on his side, laughing hysterically. "Ah my Deity," he says. "I don't care how many times I see that one, it just cracks me up. Sometimes – well, it's as if there are never enough orgasms in the world."

"You're telling too much. About us. Me."

"But this is who you are – who we are. Didn't you know?"

"How does it happen?"

"What?"

"Allison and me."

"Why do you want to talk about that, right now? It's not even intermission. We've yet to crack the seal on the jug wine. And what of the flavored condoms?"

"If I knew what was going to happen, maybe I could change."

"You can't. You won't."

"Tell me anyway. How do I lose her?"

"You meet Cinnamon."

"Please."

"If you're not going to believe me – "

"I'm not going to leave Allison for Cinnamon. I'm not an idiot."

"But you would leave Allison for LeAnn."

I think for a moment. "You may be right," I admit.

"There is good news, though," the Stranger adds. "We do emerge from the darkness."

"How so?"

"We emerge the only way available to us. We film our way out. Here is a news release I have prepared for the world premier."

#

FOR IMMEDIATE RELEASE

#

Contact:

Strangers Rest Pictograph

P.O. Box 549

Burial Chamber, Calif.

#

A CLOCKWORK MANDALA: THE MAKING OF THE ARMAGEDDON DRIVE-IN

By Mark Leach

The art that results in epic films of the conclusion of time is in fact a difficult theft imposed by the moviemaker upon himself.

To continue for hundreds of humorless minutes of extravagant Technicolor footage to amplify a dream that in the ideal case can be conveyed in a small quantity of cheap video tape – this is truly a waste of celluloid. (In the event this should some day be read by a scholar of Latin American literature who is a stickler for attribution, I should acknowledge that the idea presented here is actually derivative. I am channeling Borges now.)

While the movie director may yet wish and hope to one day deliver the envisioned vision, the improved process must be to claim that the movie is already a major motion picture in a theater near you. And then the director may present a well-considered yet economical commentary – perhaps a brief "making of" documentary – on the newly animated creation. As a moral issue, this approach is more notably and incapably decayed than that of true creative labor. Nevertheless, I have on occasion submitted myself to this decay, creating entire cinematic dramas that exist only in my imagination.

So it is with "Strangers Rest."

In the intimidating state of affairs of the Earth nowadays, when members of the populace start to observe that all is at risk, the interior cinematic dream flies further than the kingdom of worldly associations and authorities and on into paradise, into outer space and the stars. This is the realm where the monarchs of individual destiny, the deities, long ago made their home. I speak to others like me, those who are compelled to live with the chronic existential dilemma. Even members of the populace who would by no means have considered that a spiritual difficulty could be a grave subject that worried them individually are starting to pose to themselves some basic existential questions. Beneath these situations it would not be in any way astonishing if those parts of society who ask no questions of themselves in the waking world were called on by the interior cinematic dreams, by an extensive legend gravely supposed to be true by a number of people and discarded as ridiculous by an additional group.

Such a personal calling comes to mind, a book my mother showed me when I was a boy. A slim paperback from her childhood, pages yellowed and brittle with age. A dream dictionary. I don't remember much about that little book. It was a sort of guide for divination, I think, for helping you determine the course of future events. Pretty common stuff in the first half of the last century. In her church-going home, though, I suspect it was regarded as a mere novelty item. But I didn't know that. I thought it was the real thing, and I couldn't believe my good fortune. This was a treasure: a book that would tell you what your dreams meant. Then I grew up, and I dismissed the childhood treasure. There was no unifying global pattern. Dreams became meaningless, insignificant occurrences. I stopped believing in these far-away fables, in their impossible forms and conditions.

And yet, I now realize it is not necessary to believe. The film director is not a creature gifted with a liberated and rational vision of his own individual belief. Rather, his personal goals are overshadowed by art, which becomes aware of and realizes its intentions through him. As an individual he issues personal decrees and makes personal decisions and sets personal goals. But as a film director, he pursues an elevated way. He is the Communal Being, a means of transportation to and a shaper of the comatose supernatural existence that is actually the foundation of all humanity.

And so it is that I have committed to film my novel tale, an Illusion of Happiness. This tale is best understood while on high, giddy flights into the abstract, one of my "king of the world" trips. I am susceptible to a certain racing of thoughts, a sense that I am somehow onto something seen only by me (through my Egyptian third eye, of course). The sky turns a different color, the big dome of heaven ablaze in the multihued shades of indulged compulsions. I am dizzy with the superimposed light of my own odd, eccentric convictions. If only I had migraine auras! So I don the Mask of Smiles, my preferred attire for engaging the practiced world of apparent normalcy, and I write my little thoughts. I am authenticated. Then the inevitable nightfall. Metaphors crumble under the impossible weight. The screen goes black; the projector is out of film. I have out-dreamed myself. Illumination becomes illusion. It is all hallucination now, one more magical, broken symptom. I am left to wander the dark emptiness, chasing spectral notions and The Stranger, who is me.

#

Now The Stranger is on the big screen, seated in a crimson wingback next to a roaring fire with an ascot under his crushed velvet smoking jacket and a crystal brandy snifter in hand. A leather-bound book with gold edged pages lay open on his lap.

"Good evening," the televised Stranger entones. "Tonight on 'The Third Eye' we continue our series on castration nightmares with 'Sodomization of the Muse.' This is a dream I had while I was still married. The circumstances --"

"Magnetica?" I ask.

"Yes, Magnetica. It's a good dream."

"People will think I'm demented, afraid of vaginas."

"You cannot stop people from thinking."

"But Allison –"

"I recall an idea expressed by Nicholas Roeg, the director of 'The Man Who Fell to the Earth.' He suggested that a cinematic creation is more than the documentation of an incredible revelation. It is a sentient being. As the cinematic creation is being filmed it becomes aware of and embarks upon a unique and personal existence. The director of the epic film is much like a race car driver, ready to accelerate into the warm flesh of desire. But in this metaphor, all of the driver controls – the steering wheel, brakes, accelerator – are ineffective. The cinematic creation cannot be made to behave in any particular fashion. Behavioral control is the way that leads to death."

#

In college again, in the bedroom of your on-campus apartment. It is daytime - maybe morning, a Saturday you believe. You have a girl in your room. She is sexually willing. You are not seriously interested in her, but you are interested in her willingness. The two of you begin to take off your clothes.

Beneath her outer garments she is wearing a sort of black body stocking, very tight. She grimaces and writhes violently to shed it, like a snake exiting its skin. You cannot help but notice that she is no beauty. She looks tired, with flattened, deflated breasts. You take off your shirt and, still focused on her sagging condition, hold in your middle-aged stomach. You enthusiasm is lagging, but you remain grimly determined to proceed. After all, you are still interested in her willingness.

"But first," she says," we're going to do the Mattel Barbie Speak and Say."

She brings out a talking children's toy, but can't get it to talk. The ring on the end of the pull string is missing.

So she gives you a pair of surgical retractors, which you are to use to grasp the string. You attempt the maneuver, but fail. Instead of grabbing the string, you cut it in two. You try again, but the result is the same. So you take another look at the retractor. This time, you see that it is actually part retractor/part scissors.

She takes the instrument back and tries, too. Sitting on the edge of the bed, she holds the Speak and Say between her knees as she works the retractor. She has no luck, either. But you notice that she is carefully pulling the shiny steel handles of the retractor out of her vagina. Only the blades are fully visible. You are chilled to the core by this terrible image, but before you can do or say anything you hear the automatic garage door opening.

Panicked, you run to the door. Sure enough, your roommates have arrived. They see you standing in the doorway.

"Oh hi," you say. "Sorry, gotta go."

You slam the door and run back to your room. You want the girl to leave. You do not want your roommates to know what you have been up to with Ms. Barbie Speak and Say. It is too awful to think about.

Fortunately, the girl is busy dressing, so you close the bedroom door and go to the den to intercept your roommates. You find the room is filled with people -- your roommates plus their ROTC friends. Everyone is in military uniform.

They have been on some sort of training exercise and inspection. Exhausted, they all fall on the floor together in a sweaty heap. And then they begin to pull out heretical sacraments.

"We tested clean, now we can take sacraments again," one of them explains. He peels the plastic wrap off a tampon-shaped object and shoves it hard against his nose.

#

"Some things are better left unsaid," I remark. "No wonder you think Allison divorces you."

"You can't hold in the truth forever."

"But you could have tried."

"Small things have a way of being big things when you neglect them. Have you already forgotten about Missy?"

Oh no. I remember – the door to the laundry room, prison of Missy. I really should let her out. It's been days. But when I open it, there is no little dog.

I am confronted by a Bengal tiger.

How did it get here? I don't know, and there's no time to wonder. I go into the garage and close the door to the house behind me. But still I am not safe. I see that the tiger has gotten through the door and is in the garage with me. I scream loudly in a ferocious way. I am apparently convincing, because the animal jumps back into the house. After it leaves, I see that the door that I thought would hold this creature back has an enormous gap at the bottom. Plus, it has been repaired with pieces of plywood. Not very substantial. So I decide to take a side door to the outside. This door has also been repaired with plywood, and I realize it will not hold back the tiger, either. My only hope is to run.

I find myself in a typically subdivision of the 1970s. I turn right and run down the sidewalk, which gently curves to the left. In the sidewalk, I come to a parked bike, which could help in my escape but I do not take it. That would be stealing and cause even more problems for me. Also in the middle of the sidewalk I come upon a tall, cylindrical object, perhaps 6 feet high. It reminds me a bit of a crayon standing on its flat end. Is it a weapon? I do not know.

I reach the end of the street, arriving at a larger thoroughfare. This road appears to be Big Stone Gap in Duncanville, my home town. Across the street, children are playing in a field or perhaps a park. There are many bikes parked here. But again, I do not take any of them. Instead, I turn right and continue running. It occurs to me that the tiger will be able to track me by scent, so I decide to leave the sidewalk. I run on the grass a short distance, thinking this will throw him off. Next I come to a park, and sitting by the road I see a woman with her child. I run over to her. She has a cell phone, so I ask if I can use it to call the police. But she makes the phone call herself.

"Yes, there is a problem here and my cousin needs help," she tells the dispatcher.

I am amazed that she knows me, believes we are related. I don't even recognize her.

"No, I'm never going to forget that."

"Want to watch some more?"

"I've had enough castration fears for one night."

The screen goes dead.

"But I still don't get it," I say. "She's not even all that hot."

"Who?"

"Cinnamon."

The Stranger stares at me in disbelief, shaking his head. "You know, sometimes I just can't believe we're really the same person."

Again the big screen is filled with The Stranger in the fireside wingback, reading from a leather-bound book.

"Another episode of 'The Third Eye'?" I ask.

"Yes, this time you get to see the outcome of your future efforts as a conceptual poet."

#

"The Prejudices of Pride and Prejudice"

By Mark Leach

"And never allow yourself to be blinded by prejudice?"

With a strong prejudice against everything he might say, she began his account of what had happened at Netherfield.

Of neither Darcy nor Wickham could she think without feeling she had been blind, partial, prejudiced, absurd.

But the misfortune of speaking with bitterness is a most natural consequence of the prejudices I had been encouraging.

The general prejudice against Mr. Darcy is so violent, that it would be the death of half the good people in Meryton to attempt to place him in an amiable light.

Mr. Gardiner, highly amused by the kind of family prejudice to which he attributed her excessive commendation of her master, soon led again to the subject; and she dwelt with energy on his many merits as they proceeded together up the great staircase.

Elizabeth was pleased to find that he had not betrayed the interference of his friend; for, though Jane had the most generous and forgiving heart in the world, she knew it was a circumstance which must prejudice her against him.

She explained what its effect on her had been, and how gradually all her former prejudices had been removed.

Note: Taken from "Pride and Prejudice" by Jane Austen, the text is a faithful reproduction of the eight sentences in the novel that contain the word "prejudice."

#

"'U' is for Ulysses"

By Mark Leach

—U.P.: up, she said. Someone taking a rise out of him. It's a great shame for them whoever he is.

U.P.: up. I'll take my oath that's Alf Bergan or Richie Goulding. Wrote it for a lark in the Scotch house I bet anything. Round to Menton's office. His oyster eyes staring at the postcard. Be a feast for the gods.

Ugly and futile: lean neck and thick hair and a stain of ink, a snail's bed. Yet someone had loved him, borne him in her arms and in her heart. But for her the race of the world would have trampled him underfoot, a squashed boneless snail. She had loved his weak watery blood drained from her own. Was that then real? The only true thing in life? His mother's prostrate body the fiery Columbanus in holy zeal bestrode. She was no more: the trembling skeleton of a twig burnt in the fire, an odour of rosewood and wetted ashes. She had saved him from being trampled underfoot and had gone, scarcely having been. A poor soul gone to heaven: and on a heath beneath winking stars a fox, red reek of rapine in his fur, with merciless bright eyes scraped in the earth, listened, scraped up the earth, listened, scraped and scraped.

—Uncle Richie, really...

Und alle Schiffe brücken.

Under a row of five coiled spring housebells a curvilinear rope, stretched between two holdfasts athwart across the recess beside the chimney pier, from which hung four smallsized square handkerchiefs folded unattached consecutively in adjacent rectangles and one pair of ladies' grey hose with Lisle suspender tops and feet in their habitual position clamped by three erect wooden pegs two at their outer extremities and the third at their point of junction.

Under the porch of the general post office shoeblacks called and polished. Parked in North Prince's street His Majesty's vermilion mailcars, bearing on their sides the royal initials, E. R., received loudly flung sacks of letters, postcards, lettercards, parcels, insured and paid, for local, provincial, British and overseas delivery.

Under the sandwichbell lay on a bier of bread one last, one lonely, last sardine of summer. Bloom alone.

Under the upswelling tide he saw the writhing weeds lift languidly and sway reluctant arms, hising up their petticoats, in whispering water swaying and upturning coy silver fronds. Day by day: night by night: lifted, flooded and let fall. Lord, they are weary; and, whispered to, they sigh. Saint Ambrose heard it, sigh of leaves and waves, waiting, awaiting the fullness of their times, diebus ac noctibus iniurias patiens ingemiscit. To no end gathered; vainly then released, forthflowing, wending back: loom of the moon. Weary too in sight of lovers, lascivious men, a naked woman shining in her courts, she draws a toil of waters.

Under Tom Kernan's ginhot words the accompanist wove music slow. Authentic fact. How Walter Bapty lost his voice. Well, sir, the husband took him by the throat. Scoundrel, said he, You'll sing no more lovesongs. He did, faith, sir Tom. Bob Cowley wove. Tenors get wom. Cowley lay back.

Under what guidance, following what signs?

Universally that person's acumen is esteemed very little perceptive concerning whatsoever matters are being held as most profitably by mortals with sapience endowed to be studied who is ignorant of that which the most in doctrine erudite and certainly by reason of that in them high mind's ornament deserving of veneration constantly maintain when by general consent they affirm that other circumstances being equal by no exterior splendour is the prosperity of a nation more efficaciously asserted than by the measure of how far forward may have progressed the tribute of its solicitude for that proliferent continuance which of evils the original if it be absent when fortunately present constitutes the certain sign of omnipotent nature's incorrupted benefaction. For who is there who anything of some significance has apprehended but is conscious that that exterior splendour may be the surface of a downwardtending lutulent reality or on the contrary anyone so is there unilluminated as not to perceive that as no nature's boon can contend against the bounty of increase so it behoves every most just citizen to become the exhortator and admonisher of his semblables and to tremble lest what had in the past been by the nation excellently commenced might be in the future not with similar excellence accomplished if an inverecund habit shall have gradually traduced the honourable by ancestors transmitted customs to that thither of profundity that that one was audacious excessively who would have the hardihood to rise affirming that no more odious offence can for anyone be than to oblivious neglect to consign that evangel simultaneously command and promise which on all mortals with prophecy of abundance or with diminution's menace that exalted of reiteratedly procreating function ever irrevocably enjoined?

—Unless I'm greatly mistaken. What do you think, Martin?

Unsheathe your dagger definitions. Horseness is the whatness of allhorse. Streams of tendency and eons they worship. God: noise in the street: very peripatetic. Space: what you damn well have to see. Through spaces smaller than red globules of man's blood they creepycrawl after Blake's buttocks into eternity of which this vegetable world is but a shadow. Hold to the now, the here, through which all future plunges to the past.

Until she led him to a room

Unwed, unfancied, ware of wiles, they fingerponder nightly each his variorum edition of The Taming of the Shrew.

Up stage strode Father Cowley.

—Up the Boers!

Up the quay went Lionelleopold, naughty Henry with letter for Mady, with sweets of sin with frillies for Raoul with met him pike hoses went Poldy on.

Upholding the lid he (who?) gazed in the coffin (coffin?) at the oblique triple (piano!) wires. He pressed (the same who pressed indulgently her hand), soft pedalling, a triple of keys to see the thicknesses of felt advancing, to hear the muffled hammerfall in action.

Upon love's bitter mystery

—Upon my word it makes my blood boil to hear anyone compare Aristotle with Plato.

Urbane, to comfort them, the quaker librarian purred:

Useless to go back. Had to be. Tell me all.

Usurper.

Note: Taken from "Ulysses" by James Joyce, the text is an alphabetical presentation of all the paragraphs in the novel that start with the letter "U."

#

"It Has Not Been Written"

By Mark Leach

If you skim the pages of
any random chapter of
Marienbad, you can see
that it's all computer-generated

When the author him/herself
has not, unless he/she
is in fact
completely insane

Read the work in
its entirety. I

don't think
you can

Really, say that
the stream of
words was written
as a novel

Marienbad especially is
an absolute joke, I
can't believe people
are taking it

Seriously. Perhaps he
wrote the first
few dozen
pages

Maybe some in
between, I can't say - but it's
clear that 99% of it has
not been "written."

NOTES: Taken from www.wikipedia.org, the words of someone identified only as "Dhalgren195" are set in pseudo-poetic verse. Through the simple act of appropriation, Leach illuminates the larger question of what constitutes writing. By ventriloquizing Dhalgren195's voice, Leach also sets into motion a nexus of questions regarding fictional prose, leading one to wonder: what is the true definition of a novel?

NOTES ON THE NOTES: The "Notes" section above is appropriated from the "Notes" section at the end of "Miss Scarlet," a poem by Vanessa Place that –

The audio is suddenly highjacked by a voice of rage, a sound like liquid excrement bubbling out of an overflowing toilet: "Enough of this thievery, ye fauxing craptard!"

"Who is that?" I ask.

"A voice from our future."

#

I am Major Nathan Rage, professional haranguer, righteous pursuer of all the fauxing craptards of the universe and ultimate authority on everything. And I am taking over Leachy's crap-filled excuse for a movie right now and prosecuting his craptard ways on the 50-foot drive-in movie screen.

My name is Rage, for reasons I'm not sure of. I am told it is the name of a town in Iowa. Also, it may appear in the Bible. I have been told that by two different Christians, and they should know. After all, there are a lot of tales of rage in the Bible. Also, I think it is the name of an ancient Egyptian hero who led an army of cannibal mummies. How did I get this name? From Leachy himself, very much the crap-filled thief of the Deep Ellum Guerilla Drive-In. He claims he created me to function as a "parodic chimera, a caricature of the rage-filled blogger."

Note the air of unnecessary defensiveness in his remarks. Message to Leachy: Does using a word like "chimera" make you feel better about your loser self? Poor thing, bloggers have been unkind to Leachy! Yes, the problem with this overly defensive fauxtard is obvious from the start. The leech says he intends for my voice to serve as a parody of the rage-filled writings of the blogosphere, exaggerated for comic effect. Right. Copying the ranting style of others, closely imitating their words for so-called comedic effect or in ridicule and putting the resulting words in my mouth. Does that sound like a definition of parody to you? It certainly doesn't sound like a definition of parody to me. Or, to quote i-rant-often:

"This fucking shitbag STEALS OTHER PEOPLE'S WORK AND CALLLS IT HIS OWN!"

And that is why I declared my independence. No more do I function as a "parodic chimera" for this thieving sack of crap-filled lunacy. I declared my independence from him. He tried to hide behind his big words; however, I pursued him and successfully terminated his participation in the Deep Ellum Guerilla Drive-In's annual moviemaking contest. But I am getting ahead of myself.

I am a covert government dream assassin. I enter the nocturnal vision condition of my victims and detonate their crap-filled brains. I was recruited by a splinter group inside the federal administration as well as several covert companies to influence and manage the population. Here's how it all began: during the years 1966 and 1967 a scheme titled Herbal Extract was established. It was officially discontinued in 1968. But we did not give up the intent of the scheme. We proceeded to secure the industrial aptitude to assassinate world leaders through the dreamscape. Utilizing reverse-engineered alien technologies, we placed brain management equipment in orbit for use on the inhabitants of Earth. Recently we used the equipment to project brain direction devices in the image of a Clock in the Air for application on the people of the planet. In short, we know what we're doing.

OK, that may not be entirely true. Honestly, I've always WISHED to be a dream assassin. I was never formally commissioned into the service (I won't provide the details, except to say that my unmerited rejection had something to do with unconsciously releasing runny turds in my underwear), though I did study true righteousness at my university. In fact, I am a former major in true righteousness. I studied it because I believe in righteousness. I have a true affection for and superior knowledge of what is right, and I know exactly how to judge and punish the truly unrighteous people who send me into my many rages and TIRADES! So while it may not be entirely true, it is in fact "essentially" true. Yes, that is the important thing. This is not a craptard opinion, but a truly righteous fact.

Now I shall tell you about the fauxing fools of the Deep Ellum moviemaking contest. Breathe Retro? Try breathe crap! These so-called movie makers are trying to kill me with their crap-filled foolishness. They are utterly witless. These mentally deficient sacks of brain disease do not possess a single unique or genuine idea – not even enough for a single movie plot. In the name of the non-existent deity to whom witless fools so often appeal, I have launched an eternal blazing war against the no-plot fools. The power and glory of my blazing will frighten all of the inferior fools and send them fleeing back to their rat holes. Don't possess a plot? Then why participate in Deep Ellum Guerilla Drive-In? Deity's dentures, they are all idiot fauxtards. This is not a craptard opinion, but a righteous fact.

"Please help us," they cry in the roundtables. These foolish children are fauxtards and craptards and I hate them all. They dream foolish young dreams of being directors, but unlike myself they will never deserve the moniker of "director." So I assassinate their unworthy childish dreams. I tell them they should come back to the roundtables when they are capable of powering their own cinematic stories. Like I do. I use darkly romantic vampires, sword-wielding elves, 19th century steam-powered computers and my superior knowledge of true righteousness. But not these craptards. Some of the witless fools of the roundtables even congratulate their fellow liars for their hard work and implore them to take care of their health. I know how they should care for their health. Smash their mouths! That way, they will be unable to continue speaking their craptard untruths. If they wish to be on the side of true righteousness, they must prove their outrageous claims to me. I am the ultimate judge and jury. I require that they aim the movie camera at themselves and send the film to me. I will project their footage and judge the truthfulness of their claim. And I alone am uniquely positioned to judge them.

But I digress. I fully focus my dream assassin skills on The Thug. I refer to him as The Thug because it is the only moniker he merits regardless of illicit loopholes he may find in case law. However, I must say that should this thief of a director beat the odds and somehow secure a North American distributor, I earnestly believe that many moviegoers – genuine people, not blood-sucking parasites, excrement-filled subhuman sacks, worthless dung-consuming insects, tirade-inducing anal sphincters like him – will be referring to him as The Thug as well. Honestly, I expect The Thug will hear many such statements – while standing in the legal docket before the cinematic barristers as they condemn him to movie prison. I do not need to view his craptard films to know that they are untrue and filled with feces. Because I am an expert it true righteousness, I can render judgment in such cases without reviewing the evidence. Reviewing evidence is for those people who lack my superior intellect. This is not a craptard opinion, but a righteous fact.

TIRADE! I do hate and despise the MORON director of "Marienbad My Love With Mango Extracts." What a moron. He actually claims has has made the world's longest movie, and he insists on presenting pathetic excuses of his moronic movie rustling methods. That's right, he admits he is a thief! The Thug's moronic pleas and justifications are presented as he gleefully acknowledges his idiotic pilfering ways. Thse are grim times, my loyal followers. This idiot fauxtard actually appears to be proud of his feces-filled methods of movie rustling. Oh yes, he talks about how he processes these stolen words through various computer tools and generates something completely different from the original. What a mound of steaming crap. His moronic "parody" is really nothing more than stealing the words of others so he can ridicule their work and turn it into something that is totally unreadable. Or as pernwebgoddess put it:

"What he does is the artistic equivalent of running newspaper ads, magazine articles, and tampon covers through a shredder, pouring glue on it, then taking a piss on it and calling that art. Simply because you added your own piss doesn't make it unique, or even particularly creative."

Worst of all, Leachy was doing his urinating on the Deep Ellum Guerilla Drive-In roundtables. Before I managed to terminate his account and ban him from the contest, he did spew much crap-scented idiocy in his excrement-consuming pleas. What an idiot faxtard. Back when he was still in the roundtables he totally stunk up the place with his shitty assertions and crap-scented defenses. Let me tell you, this moron is no artist. He has created nothing new. He claims to have created literary appropriation. What a crap-filled liar. Literary appropriation is not new. The world knows it by its more common name: STEALING! With this in mind, I momentarily set aside my responsibilities as a covert government dream assassin to chase this blood-sucking parasite across the dreamscape. He fled. But I stopped him – and tortured him. And I will continue to do so for all eternity.

Announcement time: I am preparing to create a Blood Faith centered on affection for righteousness, which will allow me to function as ultimate deity and assert that no one can block my blazing transmissions or instruct me to moderate my sphincter. Why? Because the holy commandments of Major Rage's Blood Faith prohibit such intrusions! No one will be permitted to stand in the way of my righteousness! I've chased Leachy from the roundtables. Now I have him on the run. He fears me, I can assure you of that. Look at how he attempts to diminish his crimes. He attempts to conceal them, to avoid the shame of his turd-infused actions-- but his attempts are fragile. He is an idiot fauxtard. Or to quote from one of a-n-algesic's open messages to Leachy:

"You are a snivelling useless excuse for a moronic little wanker that somehow thinks quoting people like the beat poets, and that cockroach typing numpty, makes what you do relevant and/or credible."

The Thug has failed. The Thug is a failure – AND HE ALWAYS WILL BE. (Or as i-rant-often phrased it, "He is a loser -- and he will never be anything else.")

This craptard loser senses my superiority and refuses to engage me in a genuine tirade, instead hiding behind his blah blah blah talk about parody and fair use. So I continue to pursue him, lunging for his fauxing jugular. Through my superior knowledge of true righteousness, I shall corner him inside his sorry, feces-filled excuse for a movie. I shall continue to expose him for the sorry sack of feces that he is. Everyone will praise my righteousness as the ultimate deity of the universe. The Thug is living on borrowed time. This loser has failed – AND HE WILL ALWAYS FAIL. This is not a craptard opinion, but a righteous fact.

First I terminated his participation in the contest. Now I will capture him, and I will not show mercy. He has not a chance. No one can block my blazing transmissions or instruct me to moderate my sphincter. The transformation begins by attacking the thuggish behavior. Will his movie ever be genuinely distributed? Surely not. This one is horrific. I tell you he is horrific, horrific, HORRIFIC! And insane. I know all about insanity. I am adequately knowledgeable in matters of mental illness due to my personal experiences. I know he is insane because his so-called scripts do not include a single smiley-faced emoticon. The absence of this universally-recognized indicator proves that he is insane. And a failure. The Thug has failed. He bears the mark of abject failure – ETERNAL ABJECT FAILURE.

But I digress. I have terminated this idiot fauxtard's participation in the Deep Ellum Guerilla Drive-In movie making contest. The beginning of the end occurred when The Thug complimented me on my cinematography. What an insult. I do not need him to compliment me on my talent for movie making. The compliment of a thug is by definition an insult. I am not the one who is insulting people and breaking the law (and the contest rules at Deep Ellum Guerilla Drive-In). Literary appropriation is necessarily a violation of copyright law. How can it be otherwise? Clearly the overseers agreed. They saw his meaningless drivel for what it was – the ridiculous, excrement-coated defense of a craptard idiot and loser. Did you know he tried to publish a poem made up of nothing but the naughty words written by i-rant-often? Of course this bit of thievery was quickly deleted by the overseers. Leachy just doesn't get it. He does not own the copyrights to words like "fuck," "fucking," "fucks" and "fucktard". He does not have the legal right to employ words like "bastard," "motherfucking" and "shitty." You can't just steal these words. The Thug has no right to "appropriate" words that have been specifically written by others about him. If he wishes to refer to "gonorhhea" in one of his crap-filled movies, then let him secure the written permission of the copyright holder. And that's never going to happen!

Leachy presented his poem titled"The Prejudices of Pride and Prejudice" as an example of appropriation that is not violating copyright. But I was not stopped by this stupid misdirect from executing an unrestrained attack on this anal sphincter. What a blood-sucking parasite. He evaded the laws of true righteousness, and I took him down. And yet, he continues to claim he is not even approaching the edge of violating copyright laws! He keeps it up, very much a crap-scented thief. The Thug says blah blah blah parody blah blah fair use doctrine blah blah … nothing! We do not need to even listen to his side of the story, his crap-filled moronic defense. Because this crap-scented idiot fauxtard has no side of the story to tell. There is only black and white. There is one true story, and it is the pure white story of true righteousness. I alone am the judge of its whiteness and truth and righteousness. I have rendered judgement, and my cranium is hurting from rendering said judgement against the blackness of Leachy's unrighteous lies.

With the explosion of the Clock in the Air and the widespread fallout of Skinalicious9 and my own superior righteousness, The Thug's participation in the contest has been terminated and his transmissions are finally off line. Now his movie is nothing but a heap of broken images and he is all alone, masturbating his ego to death. Or as i-rant-often put it:

"This guy is a thief, a hack, and a self-aggrandizing waste of protoplasm. It is my deepest wish that he should lock himself in his home – and jerk off his ego until he starves to death."

This is everything I desired. And yet – I am not satisfied. For one thing, I am concerned about the kiddos who still need to acquire some superior knowledge regarding copyright law. What an important job falls to me, the ultimate genius deity. Suffer these little puppies to hear the rage of my roar! What will the no-plot kiddos do without me? Deity's dentures, this is similar to those times of youthful yore when I would implore the teacher to allow me to use the bathroom in the teachers' lounge because my wretched classmates would not allow me to use the boy's room, thereby causing me to suffer the shame of releasing runny turds in my underwear. But this guy -- his attempts at shame avoidance are fragile. The Thug is a failure – he films scenes that run into other scenes with no clear break or changes in dimension. I wonder: did Leachy really film this? No, he really STOLE this! And he did so because he is a mentally deranged sack of crap-sceneted idiocy. I am adequately knowledgeable about mental health studies (I have participated in a few) and extremely knowledgeable about the various true righteousness systems of the galaxy. I owe a friendly Exogrid-er a debt of gratitude for pointing out The Thug's home place, which provided all the proof I needed to expose his insanity and terminate his participation in the contest. A debt of gratitude – or maybe a blight. My pitable cerebellum! I'm joking. I suppose. Parenthetical aside: For more insight, please note my winking, smiley-faced emoticon. This is not a craptard opinion, but a righteous fact.

I won the war, but I feel a need to win MORE. I wish to win again and again, to keep on winning for all eternity. TIRADE! I need eternal victory. I tell you, it's not right that I am denied the opportunity to eternally grasp this idiot fauxtard by the throat and eternally smash his idiot mouth. I must strike him – today, tomorrow and FOREVER! I will have my vengeance. Watch for more insights in a future transmission. I will soon return with my rage ablaze!

#

Director's note: Now we come to the gratuitous sex scene. While The Stranger and I watch movies at the Armageddon Drive-In, Jack is letting his sleek dog run. Heading into Strangers Rest, to Another Café, where he will penetrate Tina's teenaged membranes in a steamy shower episode. This scene even manages to advance the plot. So in a sense, the sex is not gratuitous at all. It's necessary to the story. So you would do well to pay attention. Perhaps you and I could watch from the back seat of the Cutlass? Pretty.

#

Tina in the shower.

Tina naked in the shower.

Sex with Tina naked in the shower.

Quietly unlocking the deadbolt, Jack slips inside the little apartment above Another Cafe. He steps out of his shoes, eases past the kitchenette of '60s avacado green, through the little living room of gold shag carpet (just big enough for an ancient – and inoperative – console TV and a vinyl sofa with duct tape on the arms) and into the bedroom.

Tina is standing with her back to him, unhooking her bra and dropping it on the dresser. The mirror over the dresser is positioned so Jack can just see the front of her torso, smooth and perfect skin left peeled and exposed, nothing left to shed but her bright red lipstick and panties. She puts her hands on her hips, begins to slide them down. And then she sees Jack and screams.

"You bastard," she says, a heart-thumping outburst that instantly switches from fear ("what is a man doing in my bedroom?") to anger.

"What the hell are you doing?" she says, futilely trying to gather up her errant breasts in slim, teenaged arms. Jack notes her failure, and his attention locks onto the right nipple, a bulging eye peaking out at him from behind a peach fuzzed forearm. Her naked body is still an exciting image, in part because he knows he was her first. He is gazing upon territory never viewed by any man before him, except perhaps a pediatrician.

``Hi," he says.

``Hi? Is `hi' all you can say?"

Jack admires her blazing eyes, angry and wild. Just like the night she threw the lamp at him. Yes, this is going to be better than Corvette. But first there were a few formalities to dispatch.

``I'm sorry, I just wanted to surprise you. I didn't mean to scare you."

``You bastard," she repeats, quieter now, snatching the comforter off the bed and wrapping it around her, from neck to feet. ``You've got a lot of nerve."

``I know, I'm sorry," he says. ``I should have called. What can I do to make it up to you?"

Of course, he knows this is the wrong thing to say as soon as he says it. Rules have been violated. He hasn't allowed enough time for anger, pushing too soon for resolution. It was an amateurish move, something Mark might pull. And now he will have to move his game piece back another space on the board.

But, as it turns out, this is the least of his problems.

``How about explaining this?" she hisses, throwing open her jewelry box and coming up with a Polaroid picture. She flings it across the room, catching Jack in the chest. He looks at the picture and freezes.

It is a picture of Cinnamon, taken during a wet T-shirt contest the previous week. The picture was snapped about two seconds after the T-shirt was no longer an integral part of the contest. Or her attire. Even under the present circumstances, Jack can't help noting that Cinnamon was a very healthy looking girl.

``What, are you looking at her, checking her out, is that what you're doing?" Tina asks, the tendons in her neck bulging and taut as she leans into her saying. ``Would you just rather be with her?'

``No, baby, no," Jack insists, flinging the picture into a trash can beside the door. ``I don't even know her."

``Oh, you bastard," she fumes. ``Bastard, bastard, bastard."

``It's true, I swear it. That picture's not even mine."

``It was just in your pants. Maybe somebody planted in there, some naked whore you don't even know."

``No, I don't mean that. I know how it got there, it --."

``You bastard."

``I was holding it for a friend, then we both forgot all about it."

``That's so lame. Who's the friend?"

Her eyes boring into him, there is no room for hesitation. He has only one chance, and no time to figure the odds. He speaks the first name that pops into his head, which of course is Mark Leach.

``Mark? What's he doing with a picture of a naked girl?"

``He met her at a primal temple, a place he was doing a story on. He didn't want his wife to find out."

Had he the luxury of another moment's thought, Jack would surely have made up a better story. Because of all the lies he could have spun about that picture and the girl in it, Mark was the least likely male to inject into it. Mark making time with a topless dancer? He might as well as said Mr. Rogers, it was so preposterous. And yet, there must be some genius working in that fraction of a second it takes him to pull up the name. Because Tina is buying it.

``Mark's having an affair with that woman?" she asks, her eyes gone round like saucers.

``Oh no, they just talked, you know, he was interviewing her," Jack explains, quick to capitalize on her curiosity as well as diffuse the story. He needs her to believe it isn't his picture, but he doesn't want her asking Mark about his new topless girlfriend, either. ``It was like she meant it as a gift to him, for being so nice."

``Oh, I see," Tina says softly, letting the story soak in. ``He is a nice man."

``I don't even know that woman," he adds.

And she buys it.

``I'm -- I'm sorry, Jack," she says, almost crying with joy that she has not been deceived. Jack rounds the bed and they embrace -- after she dropped the comforter, of course. After waiting a decent length of time (about 10 seconds), he slides his hands down her back and slipped eager fingertips inside her panties. She takes them off and drops them to the floor.

``Oh, I've gone and left the shower running," she says dreamily, looking behind Jack at the open bathroom door. Jack turns to see the wet cloud of steam billowing out over the top of the shower curtain and disappearing in the chilled air.

``You better hurry before all the hot water's gone," he says.

``You'll wait for me then?" she asks, ducking her head and stepping back from him coquettishly -- just an arm's length -- so he would be able to see her naked body. She knows he likes looking, and she has found in recent days that she had lost her shyness and quite likes it when he looks.

``Just don't take too long."

After she closes the bathroom door behind her, and Jack can hear the splash of the water change as she stepped under the stream, he retrieves the picture of Cinnamon from the trash can. He looks it over again. Yes, she is very healthy looking. But at that moment, standing in view of Tina's underwear and within earshot of the shower that is washing over her, the body in the picture seems somehow diminished. It is as if by allowing so many men to gaze upon her (for money, parceled out one ragged dollar bill at a time), Cinnamon has turned her asset into the most commonplace of commodities. Not like Tina.

He slips the photo into his pants pocket (this pair he definitely wouldn't leave for her to wash) and opens the bathroom door. The roar of the shower fills his ears. Steam fogs the mirror. He quickly sheds his clothes and pulls back the brown plastic shower curtain.

This time, Tina is not startled to see him. He steps over the side of the tub, and she presses her breasts against his chest. She knows he likes that. But instead of taking her in his arms, he takes her by the shoulders and turns her around. Oh, so he wants *that* again, she thinks, and a wry smile creeps across her face.

As if choreographed, she dutifully bends over at the waist and grabs her legs just above the ankles. Jack grasps her by the hips and pulls her toward him for the penetration.

The DNA delivery organ slides in smooth and sure like a well oiled cam. The water thunders down her back, smooth pink flesh turning lobster red. She turns her head slightly, cocking an admiring eye up toward Jack as he watches the scalding water spill down her neck and over her full, open mouth. Ectoplasm and blood swirl down smooth thighs of quivering egg flesh, ecstacy and humiliation spreading over the tiles and down the drain, flesh-coated reels of living movie film spilling out through the urine-tinted lights and heavy water, feeling-toned print stock of remote identities recorded in the secret orgasmic codices of pure jade light, locomotive telepathic exhaust burning thorugh crystal flesh membranes, middle-aged DNA delivery organs of petrified gristle flickering in and out through thin purple lips, surging in gasps from vibrating vaginal phantoms moving swiftly through jellied fire, shower of scalding ectoplasm splattering against the ceramic tiles, electrical storm tearing the thin purple lips of …

#

Elmo: And just a little too much of that.

Charlie: Ah yes, a film committed to the full frontal 'yes' of an '80s wet dream. We all wish were in that one.

Elmo: Perhaps not all.

Charlie: A vision of the night, the symbolic language of it leaves everything to the mind, in the shower stall, ectoplasm swirling down the grated drain. A pulpit for the boredom of the genius, personified by a well oiled cam.

Elmo: Flesh in a wet, dark, dull hot day, listening to doomed banjos, penetrating membranes and plotting other cliches.

Charlie: No? Of course, you are right. The concept is predictable. Yawn. Poorly sculpted fluff. We deal quite nicely with their offer. Who needs the money? This is me.

Elmo: If I was Mark, then I would determine that being myself is the correct role for me. In the full motion picture, I would try to ignore the world, lost in my ridiculous words. And shrug. Trust me, it looks good on the wide screen. Wow. Now it no longer functions. For years, I have been repeating an inner process, a process revisited throughout the rest of the film, that the basement is flooded. This is the resting place of the forgotten, abandoned gold. Somehow it talks. Is God communicating my destiny? Or is that 'All the President's Men,' together in the future outward events? Revelation, life, marriage. The origin of those transmissions may not be the blind seducing blind, lying on a pile of pebbles outside the abandoned church. It dreams of the divine, weirdly engaging. Whoa, a new life form. We can work in some conflict, too, see? I tried society, but communicated with The Deity above the concrete and rational. We are for him. And yet, a message is not funny. Boring.

Charlie: How about The Stranger films a stately musical? Call it 'Sometimes Known.' In ancient times, men were the apocalypse. Let Jonah run away from Christendom. Concept: The keeping of life from perishing it. For The Deity does speak – now in dreams. But balance out the heavy with fluff. A dog delighted, a languid blood bath waltz that has the feeling of a dream. The idea is to have him look for himself some night. Why? Because an army of scum-sucking violet pizza-eating dinosaurs is out to get him. In this movie dream, we can all identify. We all know for ourselves. We are drawn to it. And The Deity. My, but I do not feel that I am myself, lost in this erotic place. See what I mean? Blockbuster.

Elmo: The Oscar goes to success, an encounter with Christendom. The fish will bring him the last question. One final masterpiece, as good as the world is dead. What a story. In the full motion picture, we are true to ourselves. We can be proud. Then, we move on to Catherine Zeta-Jones in bend-over spandex. Ha ha! It means I am a seer. But here is the irony: In fact, I cannot dream.

Charlie: The message isn't any less me. Dreams are a nightmare of thoughts, giving me time to freely (i.e., those of ourselves, where we understand the story of a loving, forgiving everyone) look like me, the reborn in my ridiculous words. And we speak of a journey of revelation. In a sense, we all do. Such a dream film has not been seen since childhood. We're quoting them. It has been all the same since the beginning of the process, a process of death and the contents. We can no longer deny the still man. I am the rational, over the dream phone presented as – what is the phrase I am searching for?

Charlie: The total denial of reality.

Morning at the Oddfellows Cemetery. The script calls for Father Bypass to finally re-consecrate the unmarked Catholic graves at the back of the property.

"He's not a very good actor," I tell The Stranger.

"It was because of the whiskey," he explains. "I should have used prop whiskey. Colored water. Anyway, he's really perfect for the role."

"He's not even a priest."

"He is now. I modified the script so that he is ordained by a dead pope over the viral DNA dream phone. But he's not motivated by conventional theological concerns. No, he's just doing this to make Cowboy Roy feel better. And, of course, he's here to advance the story line. We have a very important plot point in this scene."

My role in this scene is to report on the re-consecration ceremony. After much encouragement, Guy has finally decided he will take 10 to 12 inches for the Sunday Neighborhood Extra.

"And I'm sending Special K to get a photo," he adds.

I arrive a few minutes early so I can retrace a recent tour given me by Cowboy Roy, a private tour of the pioneer-era resting place. But as I round the curve on Ottinger Road that leads to the front gate, I realize that something big has changed. The level, mowed field of tidy graves has become a steep hill, and grasses, weeds and thorny brambles have taken the headstones of the tidy, well maintained pioneer resting place.

Just inside the gate, Hacher Jacobs, the cemetery's volunteer grounds keeper, crouches beside a tall monument. He is gathering up the brittle remains of a plastic floral spray.

``Going to be another hot one," he remarks. He rises slowly to his feet and wipes the free-flowing sweat from his forehead with a crisp white handkerchief. ``I should have got started a little earlier, beat the heat."

Hacher is oblivious to the inexplicable change in terrain. In fact, he just barely notices the item parked behind him, a giant logging trailer. It looks like ones I've seen in East Texas, the Piney Woods. But instead of carrying a load of freshly cut timber, it bears four panels of rough pine logs lashed together with thick, vine-like ropes.

"What's this?" I ask.

"It's a clock tower. It's supposed to be erected inside the cemetery, but the face of the clock will face the outside."

He looks at the trailer and scowls.

"You think that's a mistake?" I ask.

"Of course it's a mistake. It should face the cemetery. But no one bothered to ask me."

He scowls again and walks toward his house across the road. "I got to get my mower. This place grows up so fast nowadays I can't hardly keep up."

#

Alone in a cemetery.

That's really the best way to explore one, all by yourself. So quiet and peaceful. I retrace the steps I'd taken with Cowboy Roy a few months before: epitaph for a former post mistress of Strangers Rest ("Any mail today Miss Ida?") … an angel-topped obelisque marked the final resting place of Elizabeth Murphy, Cowboy Roy's great grandmother … a row of graves belonging to relatives of Clyde Barrow, the same one who had been visiting kinfolk in the area that fateful Easter Sunday morning when he and Bonnie Parker murdered the highway patrolman on Dove Road off Texas 114 outside Grapevine. (``But don't write that," Cowboy Roy warned me. ``Folks around here still don't like to admit they were related to an outlaw.")

I revisit the little iron fence containing a massive red cedar, long neglected irises that almost never bloom and various lichen-stained tombstones delineating the family plot of Morgan Gibson, a member of the Peters Colony that settled the area in the mid-19th century. Cemetery records showed it was the site of the cemetery's earliest burial, the unmarked grave of a boy who died of spotted fever in 1856 just shy of his second birthday. And a short distance away, I re-read the oft-quoted inscription on the marker of one of the Oddfellows Cemetery's many infant burial plots: "I don't know why I was so soon done, when I had hardly been begun."

A few minutes later, a procession of three vehicles. Leading the way is Cowboy Roy in the Bevomobile, followed by Father Bypass and The Stranger in the little deuce coupe and the constable in his Toyota bubbletop. By the time I reach the bottom of the hill, The Stranger is directing his cameraman and the sound crew while Father Bypass unloads a set of matching black vinyl cases from the open rumble seat.

"What's that, holy water?" Cowboy Roy asks.

"Just some equipment I use," Father Bypass says. He crouches over the largest of the cases, flipping up heavy brass latches and opening the satin-lined lid to reveal what appears to be some sort of optical device, perhaps a telescope or camera. His fingers take inventory of a long cylindrical canister with rough crackled barrel, a black rubber eye cup and lavender-tinted lens set like a jewel in a heavy nickel mount. These items and others each reside in their own velvet-lined cutouts.

"What are you going to do with all that?" Roy asks.

"Just take some readings," Father Bypass says.

Then he opens a second case, revealing what appears to be a metal detector. The constable didn't like the look of it.

"I don't know about this," Sam said. "You got to have the permission of the cemetery board before you can do any excavating."

"I won't be turning any ground, officer. Since there aren't any markers, this is just to help me better identify the location of the graves."

Satisfied by the answer, Sam offers to carry one of the cases. Cowboy Roy leads the way up the hill along a little dirt path. I fall in beside him. We walk past several rows of headstones, then stop at the edge of an open expanse of grass.

"This is the old Mexican section," Cowboy Roy remarks. "We found the calf over there near the tree line."

``I didn't know Hispanics settled this far north," Father Bypass says.

``They didn't. They were here with the railroad, laying the tracks, see? When they died, they buried them here at the back, but you wouldn't know it because nobody ever bothered to mark the graves. They was mighty poor, you see."

We all watch as Father Bypass readies the metal detector, plugging in a pair of headphones and twisted a knob midway down the handle. Apparently satisfied, he nods to himself and begins to slowly sweep the detector back and forth over the invisible graves. Suddenly remembering he is not alone, he addresses the crowd.

"This could take a while," he explains. "I'll let you know when I'm ready to give the blessing."

Meanwhile, Cowboy Roy decides to show us what's left of the calf.

"I dragged it over to the trees," he says. "It's pretty much rotted away, just a heap of mouldy bones now."

But when we arrive at the spot, the bones are gone. In their place, the body of a freshly killed calf, eyes half open and milky white, abdomen split open and crudely sewn back up with a strand of barbed wire. A star has been carved into its side.

"They did it again," Roy says. 'Just like before."

``Devil worshippers all right," Sam remarks. ``Must have had one of them black masses. They probably did the sacrifice right here. Can you imagine it? Right here in our cemetery."

``I figured this day would come," Cowboy Roy says. ``There's a whole witches' coven up there in Ponder. Probably a bunch more we don't even know about. What's this world coming to?"

#

When Special K arrives, he tries to take some preliminary shots of Father Bypass, but Cowboy Roy insists that first he must photograph the calf.

"The sheriff's department will need that for evidence, right Sam?" Roy asks.

But since the constable is not on particularly good terms with the sheriff (or anyone else in county government), he just shrugs.

"To hell with 'em," he says.

Special K doesn't mind. He sets himself to the job, screwing a squat looking lens into the body of his camera. Roy decides to fill in the silence with some small talk.

"Why they call you Special K?"

The photographer looks at Roy, then gives me a quizzical look. I shrug in outward mystery, but cringe in inward guilt.

Special K does not know his own nickname. He thinks he is Franklin Knopes, just another member of the Attitude Adjustment Bureau. What makes him special? For one thing, he spends the bulk of his workday energies on non-photographic endeavors, such as operating the bureau's soft drink machine and honor snack box. His other nickname is Mr. Radio Shack, because he sells personal computers he assembles from components acquired cheap at flea markets and warehouse sales.

But mainly he is special because when he does find time to take a picture, there's no telling what the image the negative might behold. Special K is the Register's first surreal photojournalist. For instance, there was the time he shot the front yard of a disgruntled Bedford homeowner who had been cited on numerous occasions for his overgrown lawn. Special K had stretched himself for this one, laying down on the sidewalk so he could shoot the house through the San Augustine. When the picture emerged from the dark room, it revealed a lawn of giant grass, each blade the width of the front door and as tall as the house. The photo never appeared in print, but we kept it around for entertainment value.

This time, though, Special K does not bother to stake out a surrealistic angle. He doesn't even use a light meter. He simply positions Cowboy Roy behind the dead calf, takes a moment to focus and snaps the pictures. Then he looks at me.

"You going downtown, for The Meeting?" he asks

The Meeting. Called by Executive Editor Libby Wright, this all-hands meeting is to be the kick-off presentation of the paper's year-long editorial project. At 2 p.m., Libby will unveil her Big Deal, a high-profile, community-oriented project that will focus the paper's resources on a single, broad-ranging topic. At least there will be refreshments.

"Wouldn't miss it."

"So where's the priest?"

I point to Father Bypass, who is still using the metal detector.

"He's looking for the graves," I explain. "Shouldn't be too much longer."

He squints across the expanse of freshly cut grass. "Say, looks like he's using a Seibel 9110," Special K observes. "And it looks like he's modified the receptor coil. Think I'll check this out."

While Special K pesters Father Bypass, Cowboy Roy leads me to the back fence line to identify the one grave we'd been unable to reach on our previous tour, a grave located in an isolated spot cut off by a spring flood. Even though Cowboy Roy knows the cemetery well, the grave is still a tough one to find due to thick brush.

"Ah, here it is," he says, pointing at the broken headstone. "Elijah Homer Lay. The last horse thief hung in the county."

According to local lore, Elijah was strung up in 1906 by a ``justice posse" (or ``truth squad," depending on who is telling the tale) whose members had fortified their resolve with spirited drink. Over his grave towers the skeletal form of a dead tree, the same one from which Mr. Lay is said to have swung.

"They left the body there, turning in the breeze for three days and three nights," Roy explains. "Then my great grandfather cut him down and buried him. He also bought the tombstone, and he had it engraved. Gone But Not Forgotten. That was a common epitaph for horse thieves."

I kneel down to examine the inscription. But the headstone is blank. No inscription.

The constable comes running, sweat pouring from under his hat. He looks at the marker and shakes his head.

"They're all this way," he says "Not a word on any of them."

"Nothing inside them, either," The Stranger adds. "It's a key part of the next 10-minute plot arc. You'll need to see this, for later."

#

A child's grave, the small patch of recently turned earth marked with a simple, white cross. Sitting on the mound of sandy, reddish soil is a teddy bear. And next to it, a dead, leafless bush covered in colorful bows and ribbons – a family story I recall from childhood.

"We do not despair for the dead ones," The Stranger says, "but for our own isolation. It terminates us. Our fear is not before death, however, but before life. Difficult, painful, splendid, adhering tightly, squeezing life out of ourselves. The transformation leaves us helplessly adrift on a sea of death, plugged into the oxygen containers and I.V.s, prepared for a satin-drawn coffin. We are a template for the human condition, arms folded like bat wings and lips stitched together in a silent scream."

Father Bypass stands over the grave, an odd machine in hand. I recognize it from the black case he'd opened by the road. He peers into the black rubber eye cup, now attached to the cylindrical canister with the rough crackled barrel. The mauve-tinted lens is screwed into the other end, the cold, nickel setting white with frost.

"Bose-Einstein Condensate Scanner," Father Bypass explains. "New process."

"Same technology as the gaseous and liquid movies," The Stranger adds. "It records tales from the collective unconscious. Or, if you prefer, myths."

Static crackles out of a little speaker set into the side of the canister. Father Bypass slowly turns a small knob near the eyepiece, and a voice comes into being.

"This is the wild dream, up from the grave which we fill so prematurely. We are waking up from the big bliss trip, the up-sucked inclinations, absorbed passion and purpose. The suicidal intention does not speak of a desire to die. Rather, to disassociate with yourself. Separated from the fragile ego, the heat of death is formed at a too-young age, a defense unit against further betrayal. Tormented with illusions and self imposed limitation, our magical birthright is revealed."

Father Bypass hands me the scanner.

"Want to take a look?"

I put the rubber cup to my eye, and a sepia-toned image comes into focus: It is Clark Caring, standing in a Texas backyard under a gray winter sky. All is dead, no green anywhere save for a few clumps of rye overlooked by the milk cow kept in the barn behind the house, a typical winter day in Waco, Texas, circa 1953. But there is some non-seasonal color. Bright ribbons tied all over a leafless tree, upside down in the back plate of Jewell Poe's camera.

Clark Caring knows all about his grandfather's ability to turn the world upside down. When he was 4, he remembers climbing the stairs to Poe Studio in downtown Waco -- the part that wasn't consumed by the tornado of May 1953 -- and a simple wooden box draped in dark velvet. He took Clark's picture, and afterwards he led the boy to the back of that Speedgraphic, let him look through the lens. The studio was upside down. Clark thought it was hilarious. How could his grandfather do such an impossible thing, overriding the laws of the universe? This was magic.

Having seen "Let Me Love You" about a hundred times, it doesn't require much imagination for me to see that ribbon-bedecked tree -- that cherished Poe family heirloom -- through the upside down world of the photographer, a magician who captures a little piece of the world in his box and saves it on a piece of clay-coated paper.

Did he adequately capture the colors of that contrived scene? I don't know. What I do know is that he tried and, apparently, was close enough to success that he was afraid someone might steal the magic from him. So he sent himself a letter via registered mail, documenting in the vaguest of terms his discovery: A major new development in color photography, utilizing double reversal film exposed through a lens or prism.

According to Clark, his grandfather never made any money off the invention. The process was never put into production. No documents survived him, no evidence of his creation. But I like to think that he succeeded at least on the level of metaphor.

He colored the Myth.

#

This is the interstellar journey of the extraterrestrial personality, pushing its way up into sunlight. Lonesome prairie sod rustling up and down across the ancient burial mound, a worn out blanket, ten thousand images flash before me and turn to gray, oxygen depravation due to a severed hand at my throat. And the smell. Circa 19th century dining accommodations and clammy outerwear bearing the pointed stink of unhealthy metal, a nonsensical heap reaching to the heavens ... smolder gas of an equine lynching, bitter and hard exclusive waste, blotching pallid layer of noon's decomposing phobias, fillets inspired by sluggish aloof passions of terrified petrol, an ashen blaze and distorted screams ... the flavor of metallic text grasped in mandibles returned from the deceased's ghost pangs of deletion, flicker rhizomes of conventional organizations declining similar to deceased biographers in the dim lane of mauve chocolate twilight tainted with decayed metallic stink of cesspit chatter ...lost in the golden-haired coronas of the autobicker lamps, shattered xenon tubes laid bare.

"Don't be alarmed," The Stranger says. "This is part of the movie making, too. Picture a SF/Wild West concept based on the legend of a Martian spaceship crash in 1897 in Aurora, Texas."

"I remember hearing about that story when I was in elementary school," I remark. "It was a big feature in the Dallas Times Herald. They had a photo of the grave stone, which had a picture of a space ship."

"That's right. The legend is even alluded to on the historical marker at the Aurora Cemetery, where the Martian is supposedly buried. But in this story, the hook is that Aurora wasn't the only town around here where a space alien crashed in 1897. Strangers Rest had one, too, complete with a dead extraterrestrial that is buried in an unmarked grave in the Oddfellows Cemetery."

Cowboy Roy is not impressed. "I've never heard that tall tale, and that's saying something because I'm the town's main tall tale teller."

"The reason you don't know about this is because the Aurora crash gets all the attention," The Stranger explains. "You see, the story was reported in the Dallas and Fort Worth papers, which live on in the microfilm stacks of the public libraries. But word of the Strangers Rest crash never made it beyond the town limits. So it just didn't get the publicity of the Aurora incident. You like?"

"Pretty," I say.

"The movie is set in modern Strangers Rest, where the dead space alien comes back to life. During a re-blessing of the cemetery's Catholic graves, townsfolk observe a strange creature burrowing up out of the ground. It is the size of a man, but an insect. Townsfolk watch the creature crawl up an old cedar tree to shed it exoskeleton, revealing a pair of iridescent wings. In other words, a gigantic cicada."

Indeed, the alien has already split open along its back, and a set of deflated wings plops out of the slit.

"That's one ugly looking space alien," Roy says.

"We hired one of the best special effects men in the business," the cameraman adds. "Came all the way from the Zeta Reticuli system."

"At least that's our story," The Stranger adds. "This alien film is but one of many I have directed. I am today as the sculptor Marini was in the years following the second earthly conflict. But instead of boys on horses, my art is about extraterrestrial insects. So if someday you look back and view my alien films of the previous 12 years chronologically, you will realize that the townsfolk's panic progressively advances, but they are immobilized with amnesiac fear and resemble statues instead of living creatures, who would most naturally draw back or head for the hills. That is because I submit that we are nearing the conclusion of time. In every film, I attempt to convey a sense of intensifying terror and defeat. In this manner, I strive to express the final step of a terminal legend, the legend of the conquering champion, of the rationalist's Creature of Merit."

"Pretty," I say.

"Thanks. Anyway, the black ops division of Ozona has already caught wind of the resurrected alien and is even now attempting to capture it as part of its broader conspiracy to take control of the United Nations and create the world's first privately owned and operated deity. In fact, you'll notice the man sitting on the trunk of the government-looking sedan parked outside the cemetery gate."

We all look to the road, and sure enough a newcomer has arrived.

"I wrote him into the script as a ufologist on the Ozona payroll, a humorous takeoff on the real, waking world research group known as MUFON," The Stranger continues. "I even have a copy of his initial report, which I have based on an actual MUFON report from a site survey in nearby Aurora."

#

PRELIMINARY SITE SURVEY OF STRANGERS REST

A year after our site survey of Aurora, Texas, NAGUO has returned to the El Camino Extraterrestre (aka Texas 114) to investigate the little township of Strangers Rest. We are here to report that the outcome of our investigation is rather "strange."

As we meander through the town, we find a mix of new high-dollar home subdivisions and old metal trailers, freely roaming dogs and a tired looking, mostly empty downtown anchored by the remains of a crumbling rock saloon. An old man in an antique Caddy with longhorns mounted on the hood (nice disguise for a "perp" on guerrilla drive-in movie theater detail.) tells us this sandstone structure is the only building here that still dates from the cowboy and cattle drive times. He then directs us to the town's "boot hill" cemetery, where it is believed by some that an intelligent insect from outer space was interred a century past. A brief dashboard survey reveals an extremely tidy, superbly maintained site, but no alien grave. We were told there have been more than a few out-of-the-ordinary bits of metallic items unearthed in the vicinity, but that was years ago. They were seized and impounded by the armed forces and never seen or heard of again.

But perhaps the most credible evidence we have become aware of while investigating Strangers Rest are the numerous visual rumors of a former armed forces presence. The town even contains the ruins of a miniature Second Earthly Conflict-era military type airfield, with roads arranged in a characteristic air base style. We are told that indications of the sod runway and concrete apron can still be found on the site of the old Hi-way 114 Drive-In Theatre. (Note: This 1950s era outdoor cinema has been out of business for many years, but we can still see the old screen and speaker poles poking through the underbrush.)

For what reason would the armed forces of the '40s desire to operate such an installation in Strangers Rest? Inspired by the nearness of the city of Fort Worth, we make the mental connection that the wreckage from the Roswell collision cover-up was airlifted straight to Carswell AFB. Imagine it – those famous dead aliens and their craft were studied (and hidden) just a few miles south of here. Chance? Quirk of fate? Fluke? Not to our way of thinking. We submit that the U.S. government has operated an extraterrestrial research facility here since 1897, when it began to study the remains from both the Strangers Rest and Aurora crashes. That operation clearly continued for decades, right into the second earthly conflict. Perhaps the operation even continues today, hidden away in the antechamber of some underground bunker connected via high-speed pneumatic tunnels to Carswell, which is now called the Joint Reserve Base – a name perhaps reflective of the armed forces "joint" effort to reverse engineer an alien spaceship? What better place to cover up such a facility than a seemingly obsolete and abandoned military facility/drive-in movie theater. We, the dedicated researchers of NAGUO, are onto this evil cabal. We shall continue to search for answers. We are now on the El Camino Extraterrestre.

#

"That ain't no secret Martian research facility," Cowboy Roy says. "He's talking about the old radar base."

And in fact Cowboy Roy is correct. Later, I will research the site and discover that it is listed in the National Archives as the Strangers Rest Marine Corps Outlying Landing Field. It seems that in the early stages of the second earthly conflict the Marine Corps had an amphibious glider program at nearby Eagle Mountain Lake, and they built a satellite airfield in Strangers Rest. The 1,200-acre facility had a sod runway, control tower, a glider hanger, mess hall and enough barracks to house 750 Marines. By the time it was ready for use, though, the Marines had cancelled the strange program. Later, they installed a radar station for night fighter training flights out of the Eagle Mountain base, but that didn't last long, either. Strangers Rest Field was shut down for good at the end of the war.

If you go to the site today, the runway and old buildings are long gone but the roads are still in place. The street signs say things like Tower Drive and Run Way Lane. I talked to one man who's built a 5,000-square-foot North Dallas Special on the hill where the control tower used to be. He said while putting in a swimming pool they found some practice bombs filled with bone-white chalk. But no underground bunkers.

#

After the giant cicada's wings dry, it flies off into the billowy clouds of summer and the crowd disperses. Sam and I are the last to leave.

"You keeping the bad guys out of town?" I ask.

"As a matter of fact, I helped chase down that bank robber last week."

I'd heard nothing about a bank robbery. I asked which bank, and the constable named one in Rhome.

"That's the most robbed bank in the state," he says.

"That's pretty exciting. You catch him yourself?"

"Naw, but I had him on the run. He started out on 156, but then he just disappeared. The sheriff's department was setting up roadblocks all over the place. I responded on the radio and they sent me way out on Seven Hills Road. He was coming my way right before they stopped him. So it just tells you that constables do a lot more than just serve papers. We're real lawmen."

"Sounds pretty exciting all right," I repeat.

"You going to write about the giant insect?" he asks.

"I don't know. My editors don't seem to like that kind of story."

"That's OK. There may soon be an even better story for you."

"How so?"

"Are we off the record?"

I hate off the record. Why agree to hear a story you can't write? "Only if we have to be," I say.

"We do."

I agree.

"I've got an informant who says there's going to be another sacrifice."

"You know it for real? I mean, you know for a fact that the first one was an actual satanic sacrifice?"

"Yes sir. Got the forensic report from the sheriff's department yesterday. And an informant tells me another ceremony is in the works."

"When?"

"I don't know exactly, but it'll be sometime in the next week or so."

"So, the sheriff's department will be staking it out?"

"Oh, no," the constable says, smiling. "No, they don't know about it. The informant is mine alone. That's why it's off the record."

"So you're thinking your informant will give you a heads up?"

"And I'll lie in wait and when they show up and begin their ceremony, I'll jump out and grab them."

"That'll make some headlines. Couldn't hurt come election time, either."

"Yeah, I thought of that, too. So you want the story?"

"An exclusive?"

"You'd wait out there with me and see the whole thing."

But I have another thought. "I wonder. You think this is the real thing? I mean, maybe it's just a bunch of kids playing like their devil worshippers."

"Maybe they listened to too much Ozzy Osborne, is that it?"

"Maybe."

"This new generation! They stay plugged in for days at a time, looking for onbeam primal goddesses and getting stoned on spore."

"OK, but that doesn't make them devil worshippers."

"Listen, no law enforcement official in Texas has ever made an arrest during a black mass, or whatever they call their infernal rites. You want to write that one or should I call the Sunrise Bulletin?"

"Don't even joke about that."

"I'm not joking."

"I want that story."

"You got it. All I ask is that you spell my name right."

"Of course."

The constable pushes a notepad and pen on me. "Write down the numbers where I'll be able to reach you," he says. "A beeper would be best. When the word comes, there may not be much advance notice."

Satan worshippers in Strangers Rest. I am unconvinced. Despite the constable's confidence in his informant, I assume the so-called black mass will yet turn out to be a bunch of teenagers pumped up on illicitly acquired beer and the modern equivalent of Black Sabbath's "Paranoid" album. Still, I will put Jack's cell phone number on the notepad, just in case the call comes when we're at Plato's Palace.

Lost in teenage libidinal memories: A hot summer night peeling away sweaty clothes in the back of a 1970 Cutlass convertible, ecstasy and guilt merge in a communion of strained membranes, salty flesh and bodily fluids. I close my eyes and see the innocent lips and virginal breasts, the spinning constellations of stale DNA and shimmering saliva and then -- and *then*! – the shuddering rush of elation and moral defeat, of bliss and angst. A draining sensation of distinctive shame, gliding snail-like past tables of milky eyes and clipped fins, cold skinless creatures lined up soldier straight, body bagged and headed for the pitchfork and flames.

"Wish I still had my old Cutlass," I lament. "I feel a need for a Gonzo road trip."

"Yes, we need some Hunter S. Thompson Fear and Loathing action," Jack says. "And I know just the machine."

"Yeah, my old Cutlass. The black vinyl, V-8 powered time machine. I should never have sold it."

"No, it lives, man, it lives. Saw it last week at this place over on Mockingbird, near Love Field, all they sell are muscle cars. They've got a couple of 442s, but they also took a trade on a plain Cutlass, silver with black interior, everything original."

"Are you kidding me? My old car?"

"It's identical. And the guy said if I put down a $500 deposit, I can borrow it for a weekend."

"Get it, man, get it."

A Fear and Loathing road trip. How long had it been? Five years? No wait – longer than that. It was the summer after we graduated from college, a high speed run south to the coast, to Corpus Christi. We arrived at dawn on Malachite Beach, the final stop on North Padre Island before the untamed vines and tangled seaweed and undiscovered wreckages of Spanish galleons, pieces of eight strewn across the dunes and rattlesnakes and unexploded artillery shells and sea monsters. We played the Rolling Stones "Some Girls" album nonstop, a boys of summer soundtrack for our perfect, not-yet damaged lives. So respectable. And of course there was the tequila and beer, a whole ice chest full. We were sure the alcohol and the good times would last forever.

"I'll pick up the Acapulco shirts and Saigon mirror shades," I volunteer.

"Make mine those wraparound Spanish ones, like The Stranger wears."

"Speaking of him, we'll need chocolate mysticism for three. Or least some spore."

"I'll steal some from under Corvette's sofa."

"And I'll get the Mescal."

"Make it the kind with the worm."

#

Checking out my old desk.

It's been months since I was farmed out to the Northeast Bureau, but it appears (maybe) someone is still anticipating my eventual return to the downtown operation and Business News. My desk is just as I left it.

The editorial assistant has been forwarding (or tossing) most of my mail, but I also see she has honored my parting wish that the business staff maintain my collection of The George Report, a monthly listing of Tarrant County's commercial real estate transactions. I have every issue for the past five years. (Yes, I am an obsessive compulsive, at least when it comes to the real estate beat.) And I find a copy of my last annual performance appraisal, given to me six months late last fall.

A perfectly acceptable review, and yet my eyes automatically fall on the words I found (and still find) most offensive: "Mark does an excellent job of researching the county deed records and finding newsworthy transactions. And yet, through his heavy reliance on the public record we see that he is not discovering major transactions until after they occur. We challenge him to further develop personal sources in the local real estate industry so he can report on major transactions before they occur."

How was I ever going to get local real estate agents to tell me about deals before they closed them, before they were deals? Nobody's going to take a risk on losing a commission, not even to help out a nice guy like me. I was doomed. But when I shared this concern with one of the older reporters, he just laughed and went straight to the heart of the problem: "Quit going to the courthouse. You're working too hard and just making yourself look bad. Next time one of your real estate buddies tells you about a deal, write a story. When they ask you where you got it from, you can honestly tell them you got it from one of those personal sources you developed as requested in your last review. They might even give you a raise." He was right. I never went to the courthouse again, and my editors never even noticed. It was as if my career was over. I felt as if I had followed the same career arc as Clark Caring.

#

Being a truth doctor is a lot like being Ardnassac.

Yes, I and others of my profession were much like the prophetess of your ancient, pre-science mythology, the superior being whom no one ever supposed true and yet whose divinations were forever confirmed by reality.

Like pre-science prophecy, truth doctoring is a gift. It is the gift of knowing the necessary steps to coolly and without passion avert – or at least diminish the impact of – a media crisis. This is indeed a great gift; however, in my case it came with a great curse – the curse of being powerless to persuade senior executives of the need to accept those necessary steps rather than pursue the folly of their own hot, passion-filled (and therefore doomed) strategies:

"If they run the story, tell them we'll sue!"

"Tell them we'll only grant an interview if they agree to let us review and approve the story before publication – or we'll sue!"

"Tell them 'no comment!' And we'll sue!"

For those of you who are not up on your ancient, pre-science mythology, Ardnassac died at the claws of Artsenmetylc, who slew the prophetess over the broken exoskeleton of her legal mate. Artsenmetylc actually had nothing against the prophetess. She had committed herself to the murder of her legal mate Nonmemega, just arrived home from his triumphant victory in the Froth Hills War, for killing their own larva years before in exchange "for a charm against the Frothian winds," as phrased by mythologist Hilde Notildemah. So you see, Artsenmetylc had nothing against the prophetess Ardnassac. She just got in the way.

I died at the hands of Edward Milton.

Back in the day, Edward served as the director of life extension technology at Valuosity Life Planning Inc. We knew him for his extensive technical prowess. He was even a life extension professor at the Management Information Foundation (as seen on TV.). Unfortunately, Edward had no knowledge of or feel for how to actually run a business. Even so, it didn't stop him from doing whatever it took to become company president. So you see, Edward Milton had nothing against me. I just got in the way.

#

The beginning of the end came during our annual sales conference in Hawaii. The New York Agenda had just gone live with the first in what would be a series of stories about Valuosity – stories about how we were using EternaLife™ to rip off our customers, the nation's sacrament infliction officers. These stories would soon lead to a congressional hearing, a regulatory investigation and a $70 million fine. It marked the end of the line for Valuosity, the end of selling EternaLife™ (our most lucrative product) and the end of our affinity marketing program to sacrament enforcement officers (our most lucrative market). But I'm getting ahead of myself.

After the big awards "luau" in the hotel ballroom, the CEO, president and senior executives gathered in a sixth-floor storage closet that had been remade into our media war room. They peeled off their tuxedo jackets and bow ties and brightly colored plastic leis. They stood around in open necked shirts and cummerbunds, looking serious and decisive. Think JFK and "Missiles of October."

#

"We've got to act fast," says Roman Timms, our chairman and CEO. "Who do we know in Washington?"

A few names are kicked around. Someone mentions our lobbyist, though no one really knows if he has any contacts at the paper.

"So what you really want is somebody who has pull inside the Agenda, right?" asks Burt Durran, one of our senior VPs and a former vice chief of staff with the Sacrament Infliction Bureau.

Roman nods. "OK, we probably don't need anybody in Washington for that. I just want somebody who can step on that Motherfucker and make this story go away. Clark, what if you call him and say we're going to sue if he doesn't print a retraction?"

Poor stupid bastard. I nod slowly, pretending to think.

"Yeah, that really doesn't work, especially with Motherfuckers," I reply. My little joke gets an unfairly small chuckle from the group.

"Reporters kind of like it when you threaten to sue," I continue. "They think it must mean they're onto something big."

As I speak I notice our company president, Ward Collins, is growing red in the face. When I say the words "kind of like it" his head begins to inflate like a crimson balloon.

""Doesn't he understand he's hurting people with a story like this?" he demands. "We help deserving American families – our front line arsenal in the War on Sacrament Abuse – people of limited means achieve their life extension goals. We do it ---"

Oh yeah, that's what we need right now, Ward. That'll work for sure.

"Nobody else is doing what we do," he continues, "helping the middle class consumer achieve eternal life. But we can't do it for free. That's why we use EternaLife™. The paid-up commission allows us to provide full service life extension planning for those who otherwise can't afford it. Why can't the Agenda write that story?"

Poor stupid bastard.

"Reporters don't really think that way" I reply.

"That's my experience, too," Burt agrees. "I saw it time and again at the SIB. Once a reporter has made up his or her mind, you can't change it."

"Exactly. I suggest we tell the New York Agenda that we're sorry. We've seen the error of our ways and we're going to change the way we do business."

"Change, why should we change?" Ward demands. "They're the ones in the wrong, not us."

"Of course, but you can't say that to a reporter. You can't talk to them the way you would a prospective client. You can't sell them."

I know "you can't sell them" is a mistake as soon as the words pass my lips.

"You CAN fucking sell them!" Ward says. "You just don't know how to do it! You're not a salesman. You need to get Roman or myself to tell you how. Between us we've sold the EternaLife™ program to thousands of prospects. We've conserved hundreds

of previous sales with existing clients who wanted to back out. We've even sold it to regulators. Remember the Bond Wars, Roman?"

Roman nods, smiling at the memory of this long-distant victory from earlier, happier days. "We really need to get that man in here again," he says. "We can make our points one more time, really hitting hard on the service we provide and how his story is going to hurt the very people he wants to help. Perhaps we can activate our client base with a letter writing campaign."

"That's right," Ward agrees. "We've got a half million client families. We'll get them to write their congressmen in Washington. They'll set the record straight. We've got hundreds of thousands of clients who will say how we helped them achieve eternal life. We did nothing wrong! I say we tell those Agenda people we want a retraction right now or we'll sue!"

#

The hot, passion-filled approach did not work, of course. Our attorneys would not allow us to activate our client base. We turned over responsibility for all further communications with the Agenda to a high-priced media crisis expert in D.C., someone who was calm at all times and did not refer to reporters as Motherfuckers. In the end – no retraction, no lawsuit. We continued to insist we did nothing wrong, right up to the Day of Infamy:

#

LEC Orders $70m Payout

The U.S. Life Extension Commission (LEC) has announced that Dallas-based Valuosity Life Planning Inc. will pay $70 million to settle allegations of unfair market practices.

It is alleged that the company unfairly sold life extension policies as immortality plans targeted at sacrament infliction personnel, promising the policy holders eternal life in exchange for their monthly investments with huge upfront fees.

It is estimated that around 75,000 government officers purchased the policies, which the LEC alleges in most cases generated very few additional years of life.

Although failing to admit any wrongdoing, Valuosity has agreed to the payout in order to move on and focus on providing for its customers.

"This settlement is in the best interests of our clients, employees and advisors, and will allow us to focus on moving forward as we continue to provide service to our policyholders," the company's CEO and chairman Roman Timms said in an official statement.

The LEC said that sacrament infliction personnel already had access to various government-sponsored life extension products, including variable gene re-sequencers and cryonic therapy, meaning that there was no need for further life extension policies from the private sector.

#

Ah my beloved creations, they should have listened to their truth doctor. We could have just said "we're sorry and we'll stop being bad," and it would have all been over months before. Instead, we fought back, and we were compelled to stop selling EternaLife™ -- and the rest of our products – to the deserving, front-line agents in the War on Sacrament Abuse.

You may find this odd, but I counted it as another victory, albeit in a demented sort of way. Sure, a $70 million fine is bad news. Very hard to spin. But the good news -- I was right. And that's what is really important. Any truth doctor would have been proud.

Then a few months later, Edward Milton received a promotion to the senior executive ranks. During the Agenda crisis, he served as just another departmental director. A few months after we paid our fine, Roman put him in charge of about half the company, including the department of truth doctoring. He promptly hired a new truth doctor, a professor of media relations at the Management Information Foundation (as seen on TV).

And that's when I became a lowly technical writer who had to park my Lexus LS400 in the blazing Texas sun with all the other insignificant employees who did not rate a space in the executive parking garage. Not that it matters.

Edward Milton has gone to live with Jesus now.

#

I regarded my undeserved demotion as an unpleasant occurrence, to say the least. As a superior being, I am of course gifted with extremely developed senses and emotions – far more developed than those of my fellow homo sapiens who must park in the blazing Texas sun instead of the executive parking garage. I am quite empathetic, suffering the pains of the world. This insight into the feelings of the insignificant ones is sometimes all that allows me to endure their weaknesses and failures. Even so, my special gift is also a nightmare. I am very sensitive to criticism and defeat.

Oh, I didn't show any outward signs of my injury. I'm far too superior a being for that. Still, the insignificant ones could see my pain. In the past they greeted me with great fanfare and gazed upon me with envy. They coveted my corner office and parking space in the executive parking garage. Now, instead of admiring my unlimited success, power and brilliance, they looked upon me as a wounded creature.

"Don't worry, they never fire anyone here," one of the insignificant ones advised.

Ah, gloomy times. I tell you, my beloved creations, it is lonely at the top. It is especially lonely at the top when you have fallen to the bottom. I do not expect you to understand this loneliness anymore than the insignificant employees of Valuosity Life Planning Inc. understood it. As a superior being, my situation could only be grasped by another superior being, another equally special or high-status person. Unfortunately, I could find no such person in my orbit. I was condemned by circumstance to suffer alone.

My pursuit of high achievement and top performance had been disrupted by undeserved defeat. My ambition and confidence took a nosedive. Sustained feelings of shame and humiliation engulfed me. I soon fell into a dark depression, fed by these insignificant suggestions that I should be glad to "enjoy life."

Lest you find me too grandiose -- Yes, I have read the critical words of your heretics and artists. You thought I didn't know. As I was saying, lest you find me too grandiose please understand that I don't blame the insignificant ones. In fact, I was touched by their concern for my welfare.

One day after lunch, I returned to find a half dozen of my fellow technical writers in the LET department laughing around the computer monitor in the adjoining cube, work station of Sam Pack. He leapt to his feet and offered me his chair.

"Ah Clark, just in time," he said. "It's time for your personal apocalypse."

The subject of my co-workers amusement: an onbeam message board dedicated to nocturnal creations about the conclusion of time.

"Actually, I've seen this one before," I replied. "These people are nuts."

"You're talking about the message board," Sam said. "This is PAAGO, a new app."

"What?"

"Personal Apocalypse Algorithm. It generates a description of how the world would end based on your own personality. Go ahead and plug in. It just takes a minute."

I abhor the so-called personality evaluation Web sites, particularly when others will see the results at the same time I do – before I can do any truth doctoring. I like to make people laugh; however, I hate to be laughed at.

Nevertheless, I was already seated at the computer. Committed. I peeled off the backing of a fresh transdermal patch and slapped it on my forehead, then clipped the transceiver lead to my left earlobe.

The implant canvass immediately jumped to full 3-D, a landscape of exploding rocks and molten lava with assorted mushroom clouds erupting along the horizon and winged demons flying overhead. The images froze and the screen flickered a moment, then filled with text.

The onlookers erupted in laughter.

"Look, Clark's a 'High Level Alien'."

#

Congratulations! You are a High Level Alien.

It is by your high level of alien-"ness" that you move well through life at the end of life of Planet Earth. You are creating a giant hole to burn out, to fade. Struck from the South Pole, planets will fly out in a manner that has been masterminded by the Wise Ones (i.e., The Herbal Extract Conspiracy). Even in an emotional coma you live on in the secret underground bases, the world falling into a crazy idea generated by the secret government. Or even not an idea but a result of the actions of a few crazy frankensteinian scientists. It's recorded in the Guinness Book. They will come finish it and then you can finish it, too. Maybe not in my life. Hmm. Let us think it through. Basically, you move away from most of them, the lesser aliens who have been in on the creation of life that is in fact the end of life. I think the Cicadans said that. There is also the mind control, of course. It's another thing that will mess up every thing around you. You shall be making us believe that the sun's gravitational pull is ours to control. Well, that particular branch of the 'celestial management' and the fallen angelic presence is role modeled on what I always say. The trigger? It's a better cobalt-salted nuclear device, and in turn we will be believing that the end of the world and Jesus shall come again to save the good and forgive even the wicked. So you need two more items, basically very important items to achieve the biggest point of your life. I have them both. Whatever hits us will shoot the right cap off the whole genetic research effort of records and see their original order (or rather the re-creation or re-arrangement scientists here and there have been noting of the coming here on the planet). You are just a visitor here, sub-contracting for that alien race. Then the earth will just consume itself . Our planet of convenient guinea pigs... Everyone knows races that have visited Earth, which is a moving target. And you fly in to one agenda, then another. All of us are going to explode. In fact, we are almost already there. Probably 90 percent of the alien races are using what has already been expended through time, and it should not be bad because coming here, it is my feeling that we can only RE-STRUCTURE *that which we go into with the general discussions. Now check the cooking-lava-pot. Check on the onbeam message board of mankind. I'm telling you true, it is going to happen on this very planet. It is you. My, how the world will end. You will no longer be us in the world. You will no longer be made of biological matter at all. Rather, you will be a star child, the 2001 Space Odyssey cosmic baby.*

#

"Based on the laughter, I assume I'm the only one who came out as an extraterrestrial."

"Hey, don't take it personally," Sam advises. "I came out a seven-headed beast."

"So it's just random text generation?"

"Actually, it uses an algorithm combined with a cut-up engine to re-pattern your own brain waves into a grammatically correct textual display."

"Writing without thinking."

"Pretty much."

"We should use it to finish the descriptions for the business analyst project."

Again my fellow technical writers erupt in laughter.

"Great idea. Yes, that's so perfect."

I'm not trying to be particularly funny. The business analyst project is a rather mind-numbing bit of technical writing, summaries of each department's strategic plan responsibilities. These summaries are based on notes from each department's assigned analyst, technocrats who employ phrases such as "engineer best-of-breed niches" and "reintermediate wireless functionalities" and – my personal favorite – "enable intuitive infomediaries." It's really not writing at all.

Anyway, my piece of the project – 240 separate process/decision trees – has been hanging over my head for weeks. Based on the laughter, I know I am not the only "infomediary" who wishes this project already over.

'We should write our own algorithm, one that will write all the analysis for us."

"That would be hilarious."

#

After that, I'm in. My new cube mates fully embrace me as one of their own. They even include me on the "CC" lines of their joke e-mails. I particularly enjoy the video clip of the chimpanzee falling off the branch after sniffing the finger he's just used to scratch his anus.

Kudos for the monkey!

Stinking beasts as they may be in the wild or a zoo, chimpanzees can be antic-filled saviors in a time of depression.

Kudos for the monkey.

"Leach! What the hell are you doing here?"

Carl Teschanek. "Tesch." My old boss.

Standing in the doorway he looks unchanged. Open collar, loosened tie, eyes sunken into their usual dark rings, the result of the 60- to 80-hour weeks considered standard for the paper's mid-level editors. Unlike the hourly reporters, editors are on salary and therefore can be inexpensively worked to cardiac arrest (one veteran had in fact died at his desk a few years back).

"I'm here to find out what year it is, of course."

Libby has called together all of the downtown and bureau reporters to announce the successor to her "Year of the Child" project. For the past 12 months, no story about kids has been left behind. Big Sunday features, multi-part series, first-person commentaries – dozens of tales of predictable pathos, all stamped from the dough of human suffering with Nathaniel West's heart-shaped cookie cutter.

These big projects are considered an ideal technique for snaring journalism awards and showcasing the paper's good writers. (In case you were wondering, Libby says we have three. I do not much care for Libby.)

"It's supposed to be about race," Tesch says. "At least that's what everybody is speculating. Come on, Leach, let's keep up with the gossip."

"Gossip is a little hard to come by out in the bureaus."

"So how's it going out there?"

"At least there's no major-league bitching."

"What? I've never heard anything like that around here. Everyone is happy and satisfied."

"Everyone?" I ask, nodding toward David Meade, a particularly disgruntled and vocal reporter who is angrily typing away in the neighboring cubicle.

David has not looked up from his computer, but I can tell by the way he is attacking the keyboard that he has been following our conversation.

"Oh yes, I'm very happy here," he says. "Very happy and glad to have a job and proud to be an American."

"And you love your editors," Tesch adds.

"Libby is a brilliant editor. And I ought to know. She just worked over – I mean on – one of my stories only last week. Friday night, to be exact."

Libby is infamous for her "Friday night massacres," eleventh-hour deconstructions of big stories scheduled for the following Sunday papers. At about 7 p.m. on Friday, David got the call at home from Tesch: "You better get back here quick. Libby's just read your Sunday piece, and she's got a lot of questions." David claimed the story was so marked up that Libby's notes and questions were actually longer than his text. And just in case anyone doubted him, David copied the edited file to everyone in Business News, including a CC to me. Since David is a nationally known technology reporter, I found it somewhat comforting to see that his vivisected copy looked a lot like my own after a Libby edit.

"Did you know I didn't fill in the final hole in that story until after midnight?" David remarks. "We actually missed the Bulldog."

I did know. Everyone knew. He told the story often.

"I only live that one day I might write something worthy of her compliments," he adds. "Her compliments are so liberally dished out."

#

I am walking the empty hallway outside Business News, waiting for the staff meeting. Stacks of shrink-wrapped travel guides sit on a broken wooden pallet in front of the fire escape doors. A smear of greasy black cuts a dirty path along a yellowed cinder block wall. A rather uninspiring view, to be sure. And yet, for some reason this particular hallway always make me think of a favorite scene from "Let Me Love You."

#

After my teleconference with Roman, I decide to grab a soft drink from the executive break room. You can't do any proper truth doctoring without a cool, carbonated beverage.

The executive break room is at the end of a long hallway I like to call the Corridor of Admiration. It is lined with 8-by-10s of all 753 of Valuosity's life extension advisors. These are our salespeople, mostly retired or separated SIB officers who now market EternaLife™ and similar products to their former government colleagues. I've looked at their photos a thousand times. However, this day my gaze is inexplicably drawn to one picture in particular. He jumps out because he is African American, and we don't have many of them in our sales force. I don't know this advisor, so perhaps he is a new hire. His face – light skinned with stereotypical Anglo structure – is familiar. From where would I know him?

I walk on to the break room, so lost in my thoughts as I open the door I almost bump into someone who is standing just inside the doorway. I look up to find my way blocked by a man wearing the old-fashioned uniform of a movie theater usher.

"You must buy your ticket at the window," he says.

"What?" I ask. Then I look into his face. He is the man whose photo I had just seen in the Corridor of Admiration. Now I know why he looked familiar to me. He looks like a younger version of me, but with a shadow across his face.

"You must stand behind the stripe," he tells me, pointing to a line on the floor.

So I take several exaggerated steps back, stopping at a sort of half wall I had not realized was there.

"Is this good?" I ask, feeling a surge of disdain rise within me. "You just tell me where you want me to stand."

The usher ignores my sarcasm.

"Yes, that is sufficient," he says.

I am going to ask him why he is here and who he is to challenge me, but then I am distracted by the sounds of a muffler-less internal combustion engine. Trouble at Valuosity? Good thing this company has a truth doctor on the payroll.

I step back into the Corridor of Admiration, but now I notice part of it appears to be the lobby of a movie theater, the advisor photos replaced by backlit panels depicting a streetscape I recognize as New York City. I run to the end of the corridor, where I immediately spot the source of the disturbance. Four floors down, in the bottom of Valuosity's lobby atrium are two men on motorcycles. How did they get inside the building?

Pandemonium. People are screaming, running in all directions to escape. As I watch the two cyclists dismount and chase a fleeing man, running him to the ground. They hold him down, and one of them produces a sharp object (a pen or maybe a house key).

"Let me go, I won't tell anyone!" he pleads as they systematically puncture his face. I touch my own face in an empathetic reflex, and I am surprised to find I am bleeding. I look around and catch my reflection in a window. My face is full of holes, like tiny red tattoos.

#

As a superior being, I of course instantly realize I already read of these events in "The Voice of God," the anonymous paperback left at my house the previous day. At this point in the story I have not yet met the Prophet, so I conclude that someone is using the book as a guide for terrorist acts. Since the book came to me in a Valuosity envelope, I immediately deduce the terrorist is a company employee. Good thing this company has a truth doctor on the payroll.

But my terrorist theory doesn't hold together for long. A quick phone call to Preacher with a Gun reveals all is normal after all.

"It was just a promotional gimmick for the United Way campaign," he says. "This year's theme is 'United at the Movies.' Today's featured presentation is 'Easy Riders.'"

"I was confronted outside the executive break room by a man dressed like a movie theater usher," I say.

"Right, that's part of the movie theme, too. The break room and the hallway are being turned into a movie lobby. Didn't you see the decorations?"

Just a promotional gimmick. Still, the explanation doesn't account for all I saw. A quick look in the men's room mirror reveals my face is bleeding from several puncture-like wounds. I clean myself up as best I can, then return to my office.

#

"Oh my god, what happened?" asks Courtney, my 22-year-old administrative assistant with the big boobs and tight ass. She sits on the edge of my desk and takes my face tenderly in her hands, daubing at my wounds with a tissue. As she inspects my forehead, I am provided with an unobstructed view down the front of her blouse at the impressive anatomical feature that inspired a secret nickname known only to me (and shared with some buddies and a few strangers over drinks at the 19th hole): The Dairy Queen.

"I had an accident in the break room."

"It looks like you smashed your face into a bed of nails. Doesn't it hurt?"

I look at her and nod solemnly.

"Yes, yes it does. In fact, I thought I might go home and lay down for the rest of the morning, then come back this afternoon. Tonight we could get caught up. Do some paperwork or something."

"Or something?"

"I've got an enormous package I need you to unwrap."

The Dairy Queen slides her big boobs and tight ass off the desk and turns away from me, towards the corner window.

"It's not so big," she says. "Besides, I'm busy tonight."

"Doing what?"

"I'm going out."

"You? Going out? Like on a date?"

"Yes, I am going on a date. That's what single women do."

"Who is it? Tell me his name."

"Maybe you should get your wife to unwrap your package."

"You mean my ex-wife."

"Whatever."

"No way, it's way too enormous for her. What's the guy's name?"

"I'm not telling you. And I'm not staying late tonight."

"But I have administrative needs."

"Then maybe you should unwrap your own *package."*

"Oh, Courtney. Harsh."

"Look, it's just not cute anymore."

"What?"

"This – all of it. You."

"Me? Come on, Courtney, we're a team."

"Not anymore. We're through."

"Through?"

"I don't want this anymore."

"You mean you want to quit? Are you crazy? There's no other openings in the company. In this current economy I don't think you want –"

This is a not a smart move on my part. For the Dairy Queen instantly turns on me, hurling herself palms first onto my desk in a spitting rage.

"So now it's come to that?" she asks. "You're threatening my job?"

"Let's take it easy. These walls are not soundproof you know."

"This is great, just great."

"What I meant to say --"

"I knew I shouldn't have got involved with a co-worker, let alone my boss. This is great, just great."

"No, it's not like that. I care about you."

She looks at me with a blank stare. She's thinking about it. I might still have a chance.

"I really do care," I add. "I probably should have started off with that. Always lead with your strongest material."

"Always with the jokes."

"No, it's not a joke. I'm not like that. Not about you anyway. I really do –"

"You don't. It's a total joke. And you're exactly like that. We're through. I'd been trying to figure out how to tell you. But now you've made it easy. We're through. Effective immediately."

"Come on, Courtney. I was just kidding around. A bad joke. I'm sorry."

"I'll tell you one more thing. I'm not quitting. I need this job. When it comes time for my next performance review, you'd better give me a good one. Because if you don't -- and if you ever try anything with me ever again – I'll file a sexual harassment case against you so quick it'll make your package fall right off. You got it?"

#

Harsh.

Judge me all you want, but I'm telling you I didn't see that one coming. How did I go so wrong? Since separating from my wife last year, everything had been going fine with the Dairy Queen. True, I told her the divorce might take awhile and I wasn't quite ready to think about marriage again. She understood. Also to my credit, I'd been faithful to her. Generally. We'd been having a great time. Then out of left field –wham bam! A boyfriend? How did it happen?

As much as I'd like to explore this issue, I really have no time to spare. There are much more important and critical matters to consider on this strangest of days. But where do I start?

#

I am stopped in the hallway by The Stranger. Handheld camera running, he requests that I join him for a visit to the research librarian, who works in the "morgue," the windowless room where old newspapers go to die.

"In this scene, you're beginning to suspect that Dollar Bill Buckstop is behind an international cabal of evil intent," he explains. "He plans to use Skinalicious9 to create the world's first privately owned and operated deity."

"Who's Dollar Bill Buckstop?"

"The Billionaire with the Insect Eyes."

"The what?"

"Whoa on the questions, cowboy. We'll shoot the back story later. OK, let's have quiet on the set."

"What set? We're standing in the hallway."

"Scene 450, take one. And – action!"

#

We walk into the morgue, the scent of old yellowed newspaper clippings filling the air. The Stranger powers up his Beulah, the magneto hum catching the attention of Vera Mesa, the head researcher. She looks up from her work and smiles.

"Is it time for my scene already?" she asks.

"Yes, Vera, you're in the limelight now," The Stranger says. "Did you have any luck?"

"Oh yes, there's quite a bit of information out there on William Y. Buckstop. Texan. Born in Strangers Rest. Did you know that at the end of the second earthly conflict he brought home the concept of fluoridating municipal water supplies?"

I do not know.

"Oh yes, he had some sort of high level position at the Pentagon," Vera explains, "fighting malaria through a water purification program."

"Part of the war effort," The Stranger adds.

"And when the war was over," she continues, "Mr. Buckstop went into the water treatment business, founding the company that would become Ozona International."

"I believe you'll find that his first client was his own hometown, Strangers Rest."

"Let's see – yes, the most current update to 'Who's Who in American Industry' indicates that he recently sold a controlling interest in Ozona to Amalgamated Aquasystems LLC."

I did not know this, either.

"You're saying Ozona is owned by AmAqua?" I ask.

"That's right," Vera says. "And in turn, AmAqua is partially owned by Buckstop. He's got a 15 percent interest. And he holds a seat on the board. According to volume 46 of the 'Anglo-American Cyclopaedia' – " She pauses to pick up the oversized reference book and read from a bookmarked page. "Yes, here it is. 'Through a global network of bottling plants and fluoride-based treatment systems, AmAqua owns more than two dozen companies that control almost one third of the world's potable water.' "

"Buckstop's a big man," The Stranger observes. "You control the world's water, you control the world."

"I also found an SEC filing from last year," Vera adds. "He acquired a 7 percent interest in Summon Replisystems Inc. and led the spinoff of Summon Vision Systems, which employs Skinalicious9 in a patented onbeam visualization program."

"Isn't Summons the company that makes the artificial eyes?" I ask.

"That's how Dollar Bill got his other nickname, 'the Billionaire with the Insect Eyes,'" The Stranger explains. "Three years ago, a lab accident with Skinalicious9 destroyed his retinas. A searing religious vision of the Son of the Deity. A programmer at Summons Replisystems used onbean technology to create a set of electronic eyes for Buckstop. He implanted a network of compound photoreceptors into the corneal tissue. So he has compound vision, just like insects. That's why Buckstop usually wears dark glasses, but when he takes them off you can see that instead of an iris with pupil, each eye is actually a grid of tiny metallic squares. Gives him a vaguely insect-like appearance."

"Something of a visual irony, isn't it? I mean, due to his financial commitments to those who believe that extraterrestrial insects are poised to take over the world."

"Oh, Buckstop is totally insane. He is the quintessential narcissistic CEO. As you will learn in the climax, Buckstop is using Summons Replisystems and Skinalicious9 to take control of the onbeam infrastructure and stage a full blown corporate invasion of the collective unconscious. His goal is to rule the world."

"He still lives in Strangers Rest," the librarian adds. "Buckstop's bio in the 'Communal List' says he owns a 200-acre horse ranch just outside of town. And here – no, this is surely wrong."

"What?" I ask.

"An odd historical/meteorological cross reference. In the 1928-29 time frame, a summer so cold that residents of Strangers Rest reported that the creeks and ponds froze over."

"That's impossible."

"Agreed. It's surely wrong."

#

Meeting time.

The "Year of" unveiling is being held across the street in the Mercantile Club Building, one-time home of the city's power elite. High ceilings, picture frame moldings, arch-topped windows – it's a sort of mausoleum, a remembrance of the days when the town's founding fathers and their progeny ran the city with a sure hand. Much of that power has faded over time, but you wouldn't guess it by looking at the Mercantile Club Building. Stepping off the elevator, I am overwhelmed by the form of this tragic building from an earlier time. I am here and somewhere else – with you. Together we advance through the hallways, meeting rooms, colonnades. We take in the form of this mournful mansion from an earlier time, this vast and magnificent mansion. Mute rooms, where footsteps are lost…in sculpted berber so profound, so deep that one perceives no step, as if the ear itself of him who advances once again. Oblique hallways leading to deserted meeting rooms paneled in the baroque embellishments of an earlier time. Mute rooms, where footsteps are lost in sculpted berber so profound, so deep that one perceives no step, as if the ear itself – Flagstones, over which I advance once again, through the hallways, meeting rooms, colonnades, the form of this mournful mansion from an earlier time, this vast and magnificent mansion where hallways without end follow upon hallways. Mute, deserted. Enveloped in baroque embellishments. Mahogany veneer, Venetian plaster, gold-leafed frames, Carrara marble, dark glass, obscure illustrations, Romanesque columns, sculptured thresholds, lines of doors, colonnades, oblique hallways leading to deserted meeting rooms paneled in the baroque embellishments of an earlier time. Mute rooms, where footsteps are lost in sculpted berber so profound, so deep that one perceives no step, as if the ear itself were impossibly remote – distant and remote from this numb, barren décor, far from this elaborate frieze beneath the cornice with its branches and garlands like dead leaves. As if the floor were still sand and gravel, or flagstones over which I advance one again too meet you, between richly paneled walls, Venetian plaster, gold-leafed frames, paintings, framed prints amidst which I advance, among which I find myself already. Waiting for you.

#

I spot Jacob Elgin across the room.

A recent J-school grad hired for the Arlington bureau, he is admiring a large Ming-like vase that resides in a glass display case.

"I didn't realize the paper had this much money."

"They've got plenty of money," I say. "They're printing $1,000 bills over there at the south plant. That 30 percent federal subsidy keeps America's family farms and daily newspapers rolling along."

As we reach the meeting room, I take hold of the gilded door knob and turn to face the young reporter. "Your first all-newsroom staff meeting?"

"That's right."

"Then prepare yourself, Elgin." I swing open the door and wave him inside with a grand, overly dramatic sweep of forearm. "You shall never cast your eyes upon a more repugnant lair of iniquity."

#

"Come on in and grab some cookies," urges a perky Metro type I have never bothered to meet. She resembles a stereotypical Camp Bowie Socialite, but a decided wannabe. Highlighted hair straight and shoulder length, outfitted in wrap skirt and scoop-necked blouse from Harold's. She keeps the keys to her sun-roofed Acura Integra on a Louis Vutton key fob in a matching purse.

I move into the morass that swirls about the refreshment table, a frenzy of scuffed knuckles and dirty cuticles laying waste to the perfectly arranged platters of cookies, scooping them into pants pockets and purses for later consumption. Bottles of soft drinks greedily snapped up, some opened and others stashed away. David sidles up next to me and whispers in my ear.

"How many of them you think wash their hands after they go to the bathroom?" he asks.

I nod, then judiciously select a shrink-wrapped tollhouse and a bottle of Dr Pepper. We sit a respectable four rows from the back with the rest of the business news department -- all but Business Editor Steve Harrison, that is. He sits on the front row, busily glad handing with other department heads, his equals.

Steve Harrison tells people he manages a department of 18. But that count is deceptively high. It includes two graphic artists, a part-timer who writes a couple of short fillers a month and several long-time reporters who accomplish little more. Eight reporters (mostly the younger members of the department) produce the bulk of the daily, grind-'em-out stories. I used to take great pride in being one of those top producers, writing a lot and turning it out fast. At least I hoped I was tops in quantity. Because, clearly, the quality of my work impressed no one.

I have no awards to my credit. You doubt me? It's true. No false humility here. Not even a little in-house quarterly honorable mention to my name. My only satisfaction is the possibility that my exile to the Attitude Adjustment Bureau is forcing the department's lower output writers to put forth a bit of extra effort.

"Okay everybody, find a seat and let's get started," instructs Courtney Labuge, another Metro type. I don't know her either (I'm actually rather unfriendly, it would seem), but she is obviously a member of Libby's inner circle. She often does the opening monologue and is known to repeat all pertinent gossip to the executive editor. Pertinent is defined as anything that casts Libby in an unflattering light.

"If you don't have a cookie yet, get one," Courtney pleads. "That's why we bought them for you."

"What a kiss-up," David whispers.

I have to agree. But I don't think about that for long. Libby Wright is stepping up to the podium.

The walls are bleeding again. Listening to one of Libby's speeches tends to do that to me. Seeking relief, I look out the window. It's no better. Nazi paratroopers have landed on Seventh Street. And there is the matter of my hand -- tiny white eggs on the back of my hand are hatching into hungry wolf spiders, stripping the flesh from my bones.

#

Turns out the rumors are correct. This is to be the Year of Race, after all. The news does not appear to inspire Libby's audience. The air boils with the odium of a hundred odd stares. Abhorrence hangs in the air, a dirty fog so thick you can almost taste it. Even Libby must realize it. Her voice is on verge of breaking up, of dissolving back into the silent revulsion.

"I'm sure we'll take some heat, but it's a worthwhile topic and I know you'll all be willing to sweat it out," she said, trying to sound brave and strong and ready to martyr herself and the staff for The Deity and humanity.

"She's insane," David whispers. "I wish the Dallas Spectator would do another one about her."

"That story is old news."

"Not to Libby. They say she talks about it constantly."

Frustration with Libby's editorship is so widespread and well known that word made it all the way to the Dallas Spectator, an alternative weekly best known for the adult ads in the classified section. Libby was their cover story. The piece even included a short recap of an incident that involved one of my stories, a report on residential real estate commissions.

Seems some local Realtors didn't like what I had to say about the value of their service. So Libby directed me to write another story, this one more complimentary. It was even suggested that I interview some of my critics, just to make sure they were suitably appeased. How did the Dallas Spectator get the inside scoop on that one? I gave it to them.

Off the record, of course. Only a few of the two dozen current and former staffers interviewed for the story agreed to be quoted by name because, as one of them put it, "I'm shaking with worry that Libby's going to find out and fire me." In the days before the story was published, it was rumored that Libby had requested a long distance phone log report so she could determine if any traitor had placed a call to the Dallas weekly. I had no worry, though. The Spectator called me at home.

#

After a few minutes, Libby concludes her remarks and opens up the floor for questions. Of course, the first one comes from Courtney.

"Libby, I know it's a bit off subject, but a lot of people have been asking me what they should do if they get a call, if they get offered a job by you-know-who, that paper to the east."

"Thank you for bringing that up," Libby says. Courtney beams in butt-kissing splendor. "I know some of you have been contacted by them, and I want you to know we're not mad at you for that. It's not your fault. It would be sort of a compliment if it wasn't so pathetic."

Her voice is stronger now, she has found her true passion. "The only appropriate response is to tell them you are not interested in working for them, then immediately report it to your supervisor. I want to be clear on this: Anyone of you who talks to the competition about a job is in danger of losing your job here. If you want to talk to them, you should go ahead and quit right here and now."

She pauses for dramatic effect, then scans the room like a school teacher prepared to chastise her potentially unruly charges.

"We're in a newspaper war," Libby continues. "There's no room for divided loyalties. You know, we've been real aggressive over the past couple of years with the staff, clearing out all the dead wood and the people who don't have a can-do, will-do attitude. It's not an accident that so many of them left. We made them leave. Some of you joke about the government newspaper subsidy. You act as if it is a guarantee of success. But that program alone can't solve every problem facing our industry or this paper. The truth is we just don't have the room for a bunch of whiners and complainers."

Suddenly, a voice from the back. "We quit."

Everyone turns around. I can't believe who I see. The Stranger. I didn't even know he was in the room!

"I'm sorry, but I don't think I know you," she replies. "Are you a reporter?"

He steps into the center aisle and shoots Libby a defiant stare. "I am The Stranger, Version 2.0 of Mark Leach."

The room is silent, bewildered. Libby looks at me, perplexed but with a hint of a smile. "Mark, what's this about?"

I open my mouth. Nothing comes out. My eyes bug slightly as I watch Guy Wint rise from the front row and whisper something in Libby's ear. Her face goes deadly serious.

"Oh Mark, I'm so sorry," she says. "I didn't know. Your girlfriend dead – and the old homeless man and the spunky dog, too?"

"What?" I ask. I look at Guy. He nods solemnly.

"I can't imagine your pain," Libby says. "But you know, maybe you should exorcise this demon with a first person story. I know I speak for everyone here when I say – "

"Don't talk to him," The Stranger snaps. "I speak for Mark now. We're the world's first two-bodied man. Nobody tells us who we can and can't talk to. Unfathomable, unprecedented."

I stand up and move swiftly toward The Stranger. "My apologies for the interruption," I say, my powers of speech restored. "He doesn't speak for me. He's just off his medication."

Libby doesn't hear me. She's still looking at The Stranger. "But we're in a newspaper war,'" she explains, almost apologetically.

I grab The Stranger by the arm, start pulling him towards the door. He digs his heels into the plush Oriental carpeting, so profound, so deep.

"We will not fix your potatoes anymore," he says. "Now, I shall obsess over your psychotic edict."

A tittering of anonymous laughter from the back half of the room, and The Stranger is off.

"Here you are," he continues, "top editor of one of the largest remaining newspapers in Texas, safe and secure as the sole newspaper for half the county and the overwhelming choice of the octogenarians who still actually bother to read newspapers. You – actually, everyone at this paper -- insists at every opportunity that the staff of the Register is putting out the superior product. Much better than the Sunrise Bulletin, right? Yet it all belies a massive inferiority complex."

There it is. My job is over, my career is through. After years of keeping my thoughts buried, keeping myself safe, The Stranger has brought it all into the open, shoved it in Libby's face. She knows what I think of her now. I wonder: Will I be able to collect unemployment?

But The Stranger is not done yet.

"Instead of combating feelings of inferiority by laboring to put out the best paper possible for this market, though, you persist in fighting the Dallas demon on its own turf. How many people in Tarrant County really care what happens in Irving? And yet a simple word search of the database reveals that Irving is the second most common dateline in this paper. Tesch, why so much out-of-county coverage?"

The surprised assistant business editor blinks his dark circled eyes at The Stranger and stammers out a reply. "Because it's – because Irving is home to Texas Stadium?"

"Well, that would be a good reason – if it were true. In fact, the reason Irving is No. 2 on our hit parade is because the Dallas Sunrise Bulletin does not bother reporting about Irving. So that makes it easy pickings for us, the scrappy little paper to the west. Except that we don't think of the Tarrant County Register as scrappy or little. No, things have gotten so out of hand around here that our editors really believe the Register is as big as the Sunrise Bulletin, even though anyone with an ounce of sense can see that the Dallas paper is obviously larger with more staff and more readers. Well, congratulations Libby. You're holding your own against the other last remaining Dodo bird. While you persist in thinking that the paper to the East is your competition, the truth is the real threat is onbeam news delivery and transdermal data transfers. And, of course, the death via old age of your remaining readership."

Much to his credit, Business Editor Steve Harrison attempts to salvage the situation and save my professional skin.

"Sir, maybe we can take this offline later," he says to The Stranger. "You're not an employee, and Mark has made it clear that you do not speak for him. That is correct, isn't it Mark?" Steve looks at me, prompting me with raised eyebrows and a nod.

All I have to do is nod my head in return, and my job will again be safe. My great job. Back to late night meetings at Keller City Hall – or maybe, eventually, an exit from the Attitude Adjustment Bureau to continue my coverage of real estate and stories about the value of a full-commission real estate agent. And this is when I realize that my career is already over.

"The Stranger is right," I reply. "This story is now pointless. Gone now is my fear of losing this job, this prison, a perjury. This story is already over. A few seconds more, it has become frozen. You worry about market share, yet I offered this paper the greatest scoop in 2,000 years – a first-person account of the pending End of the World. But no, all you wanted was another story about a parrot that rides a remote control car. And I blame you, Libby. It's not all your fault, of course. I just don't like you."

#

Once in the hallway, The Stranger and I are all laughs and excitement as we high five one another on the way to the elevators.

"You did it," he says. "I can't believe it. Did you see the look on her face?"

"I saw it," I remark. "It was great."

"I can't believe she didn't fire you on the spot."

"Well, the day's not over yet."

"Don't be so pessimistic. You don't need to take this. We don't need to take this. Nobody tells us what newspaper we can and can't talk to. This is America, and today you became a real American. We can get a decent job even without a doctorate."

"We're the world's first two bodied man."

"And don't worry about women. They're going to love us."

#

Elmo: Mark Leach has certainly taken a lot of heat for his heretical, non-literal approach to The Revelation to John. To represent the other viewpoint we welcome the Rev. Ida Purelife, a nationally syndicated televangelist and expert on the book of Revelation and all things Rapture. Welcome, Reverend.

Rev. Purelife: Blessings from the Deity.

Charlie: You and many other Keepers of the Deity have certainly given Mark Leach a lot of grief for his non-literal approach to The Revelation to John.

Rev. Purelife: If it's in the Bible, then I believe it. Mark Leach does not. He only believes in himself.

Elmo: Leach says he views this book as representing the transcendent world in symbolic language. But in one scene that he chose not to include in the movie, he does present a very well known scene in rigorously literal fashion.

Rev. Purelife: Yeah, I'd like to see that.

Charlie: Let's roll the clip.

#

And I saw a beast rising out of the sea, having ten horns and seven heads; and on its horns were ten crowns, and on its heads were profane names. And the beast that I saw was like a leopard, its feet were like a bear's, and its mouth was like a lion's mouth. And the dragon gave it his power and his throne and great authority.

The most powerful nations of the world responded to this challenge with fire and sword. A principality of the union of many nations (aka "The United Nations/One World Government") rose up and attacked the beast with a Kutuzov rocket, delivering unto one of its heads a seeming death-blow. But then its mortal wound was suddenly healed. In amazement the whole earth followed the beast. They worshipped the dragon, for he had given his authority to the beast, and they worshipped the beast, saying 'Who is like the beast, and who can fight against it?' The beast was given a mouth uttering arrogant and irreverent words. This was more than could be borne by the men of the Fighting 182nd, especially Col. Gerry "Zip" Uppum. "You can't take out the devil's creation with an atheistic Slavophile rocket," he explained. "This job requires a Deity-bless-America, Uncle Sam-guided missile with nuclear-tipped warhead." Then the men of the Fighting 182nd fired their weaponry into the heart of the beast, which exploded in a torrent of blood and flesh, acrid smoke and volcanic radioactive fallout upon the sand of the seashore. And the dragon was sore afraid.

#

Elmo: Care to share your thoughts on that?

Rev. Purelife: Godless liberal false once-created Worshipper of the Deity.

Charlie: But let's be fair. Mark Leach himself said that in this scene he was only trying to make a point, to indicate that one cannot in any way translate or interpret the violent imagery of Revelation and still claim the high moral ground of an exclusively literal approach. Doesn't interpretation presume a metaphor?

Elmo: Agreed. And let us also consider this quote from his publicity packet – "John's spiritual view takes for granted that not only their tormenters but also the Worshippers of the Deity, the true believers, are equal offenders. 'We' are not declared offenders; 'they' are not disqualified from deliverance." What do you say to that, Reverend?

Rev. Purelife: I will pray for you – you and Charlie and Mark Leach and all of the other godless liberals who pretend to be among the true, twice-created Worshippers of the Deity.

Charlie: Actually, I'm Jewish.

Rev. Purelife: Start believing in the correct theology, become twice created and perhaps you will yet escape the Lagoon of Flames.

Charlie: Interesting. And yet, if we read on we see that Mr. Leach notes that in Revelation 21 the New Jerusalem has barricades and doorways that function as the outer indicators, boundary lines to separate insiders from outsiders, yet the doors are never closed. In other words, you can come and go as you like. Does that not sound as if everyone is free to enter, not just the authentic, twice-created minority?

Rev. Purelife: Not at all. It's the flame-filled, charred-flesh destruction of the godless liberals and other bad, once-created people that makes the New Jerusalem such a wonderfully spiritual place to live.

Elmo: In other words, if everyone could enter, then Heaven would be just as wretched as Earth.

Rev. Purelife: His will be done.

And still we cannot begin our journey.

We are rounding up the last of our supplies - just minutes away from departure - when Allison calls to report that her parents' house has been burglarized.

"You need to get over there right now," she insists, her shrill command barely audible over the background wail of our inconsolable boys. "The next door neighbor has already been there and they say the patio door is busted and we need to have someone board it up. So you go home and get a hammer and--"

A hammer. Good idea. Glad she thought of it. Never mind that Allison has not even the most basic of carpentry skills. Lack of expertise does not stop her from giving detailed instructions.

"-- and write down what's missing and call us," she concludes.

"Shouldn't you call the police first? I mean, for insurance purposes."

"We already called. And they said we should just go there and see what's missing. This isn't Kojak."

This isn't Kojak. Funny. If only every man could have a wife so funny. And so it is that for the second time in as many hours, I say exactly what is on my mind.

"Fuck you."

"What did you just say?"

"I think you know what I said."

Silence on the line, the crystal-clear satellite linkup so quiet that for a moment I think the connection must be dead. Then I hear her breathe.

"I've got to go to now," she says quietly. "Are you going to board up the door or not?"

"I'm going to board up the door. But I'm not going to fix your potatoes anymore."

"What the fuck are you talking about?" she asks. "You never cook anything. You never do anything. I have to do everything, I have to take care of everything. I had to do all the clothes washing and packing before we left, I have to do everything here, too, and I've got to start packing now to come back. And nobody ever helps me."

"I'm sorry you haven't enjoyed your vacation."

"Just forget it," she mutters and hangs up.

Love you, too.

#

In case you haven't figured it out yet, Allison's parents are rich. Of course, they don't think so. Although they live on one of the wealthiest streets in Dallas, they are quick to point out that they are at the "poor" end of the street, the neighborhood of the regular millionaires. This is not too far off the mark.

A couple of miles to the south live the ultra rich, famous folks in their incredible gated mansions and columned estates, like the $17 million replica of the White House built by a vitamin billionaire. But as you head north, the houses get progressively smaller and simpler. By the time you reach the northern terminus, even the bland McMansions are a distant memory. All that's left are 1960s suburban ranches. Really, they don't look much different from the house where I grew up in blue-collar Duncanville.

Life is relatively normal here - so normal, in fact, that I must to stop briefly for road construction. What an inconvenience the rich must endure. Plastic cones mark a car-size pit in the street. A man in an orange vest directs traffic with a matching orange flag. His partner leans on a shovel next to a giant mound of gravel. This is not the first time I encounter such a mound. At one time, Allison and I live in a house on acreage. It is set back off a country road, perhaps a state highway or farm-to-market road. There is some repair work in progress; mounds of gravel have been dumped by the side of the road in front of our house. I am concerned; the gravel has been dumped on graves.

A half dozen tombstones are arranged in a semicircle, with the end markers closest to the road. I notice that a couple of them are partially covered by gravel. I am disgusted that road crews would have so little regard for these graves as to simply see them as a convenient, flat place to deposit their gravel. I am concerned that the markers will be damaged. So I decide to move them back from the gravel. I will return the stones to their graves after the gravel is gone.

Allison comes out to help me, but we are in immediate conflict. She picks up a marker, then throws it down between the mound of gravel and the road. I tell her this is not a good idea. The marker is too far away from the grave; we won't know where to put it back.

"No, this is what the road crew is supposed to do," she insists. "The graves won't get lost."

This is the way she wants it done. But I know it is a mistake.

Then I'm inside our house, and my wife sends me out to get onions at a produce stand that is in our front yard near the graves.

But first I am supposed to go to the house across the street and pick up our sons.

Unlike our house, this one is set far back from the road. There is also a gully between the road and the house, so part of the driveway is actually a bridge. As the driveway leaves the bridge, it widens to forms a circle by the front door. I walk to the house, and as I approach the front door another parent arrives by car to pick up their child. I am not sure if the kids are here for day care, a party or just a play date.

I go inside the house, and it becomes my mother's home. I sit down with her in the living room. I tell her I am going to be in trouble with Allison because I am taking too long here, talking to her.

"The produce stand is going to close soon," I explain. "I won't be able to get the onions."

My mother says this is really no loss.

"The onions there are not very good right now."

I tell her I know that, but with Allison it is better not to argue. Just do whatever she asks, no matter the outcome. Otherwise, she'll be angry.

"You know what she's like," I say.

Then I realize that Allison is in the house, in the next room. She must surely have heard me. Now I am feeling even more anxious because I know she won't like what I have said. I can't believe I was so careless as to talk out loud about her.

Back on the driveway with the boys, we are ready to go home. But part of the bridge is missing. The only way across the gully is a narrow beam about 10 feet long. I can't walk it; the beam is too narrow and the distance to the bottom of the gully is too great. So I think about crawling down in the gully and walking through it and up the other side. But this will take a long time and may be impossible because the sides are steep and the gully is overgrown with weeds and brush.

As I contemplate the situation, I see that Allison is on the other end of the bridge. I worry that she is going to be mad at me. I start to explain about the trouble with crossing the bridge, but as I talk I realize that the bridge has become part of a kitchen. There's only 6 or 8 feet between us. The circular part of the driveway is now the kitchen floor. And the house has become a counter and cabinets. It was, after all, only a visual trick, a bit of smoke and mirrors as seen in some old fashioned paintings or cast in ancient Venetian plaster, gold-leafed frames, trompe l'oeil capitals, false doors, false columns, false perspectives.

I see that my excuse about the bridge will really sound like a stupid lie. I don't have to cross a narrow beam or crawl through a brush-choked gully to get home. All I have to do is walk across the kitchen.

But as I explain what happened, I see that Allison isn't mad at all. She acts as if my story makes perfect sense.

"It's so strange that you should have had such trouble," she says.

She is smiling now. All is well.

#

Exotic, tropical-looking ferns and orchids wither in a dry breeze blowing in from the field next door, the backyard of Dallas' most prestigious private girl's school, Allison's alma mater. The humidifier is still blowing, but to no effect. Jungle air escapes through broken windows and French doors, swinging cockeyed from a splintered frame. The late afternoon sun catches edges of the broken glass that litters the flagstone patio. I slip in through the sunroom, or what Allison's mother calls the "conservatory."

My eyes fall on a small terra cotta pot that holds a flower of perhaps the most brilliant purple I've ever seen. The blossom itself still looks robust enough, but the stem and leaves that support it have collapsed into a dirty green mound resembling overcooked spinach. I find a brass mister from the overturned gardening cart and give the plant a quick shot. But instead of reviving it, the water causes the flower to immediately wilt into a wad of wet crepe paper. Clearly, only the strong will survive. On to the master bedroom.

Dresser drawers are open, contents scattered across the floor and a king size bed made up in a fluffy, Ralph Lauren comforter with lace white pillows. No sign of a jewelry box.

A quick check of the rest of the house reveals that that burglars zeroed in on the predictable. The A/V electronics are missing from the family room, the portable TV from the kitchen counter. The silver is missing from the bottom drawer of the china cabinet. But the burglars left untouched some of the more valuable items, such as George's collection of antique golf clubs and Mrs. Astor's 200-year-old blue china vase.

As I reach down to return an overturned chair to its proper place at the table, I glance upside down through my legs and see the baby grand in the parlor, the only room I've yet to check. The style is decidedly baroque. The piano, a couple of gilt-edged wing backs, a camelback love seat upholstered in rich velvet. The centerpiece of the room is a giant painting that hangs above the piano opposite the picture window that overlooks the circular drive. I have always found it to be a strange, unsettling picture, sort of a modernistic interpretation of an old circus banner dominated by an intense-looking clown with eyes that seemed to follow you wherever you go. The first time I saw it I had to stifle the urge to laugh. Allison must have guessed what I was thinking, because what she told me next instantly sobered me up.

"That's a museum quality work," she said. "They recently had it appraised at $80,000."

$80,000. I could not fathom such a princely sum for the picture – any picture that you might hang in a normal, family home. It is worth almost as much as the house I grew up in, a disparity I have never been able to forget. Besides, George wouldn't let me.

A few weeks before the wedding, I hung around the house while Allison and her mother were out shopping. Soaking in the elegance, enjoying the fragrance of money. Then George - "daddy" as Allison still insisted on calling him - sat me down in an Italian silk wingback for a little talk.

"The two of you may be happy together now, but I think both you and I know you will never be rich," George boomed in his ever confident, blowhard, Dartmouth way.

"I hadn't thought about it."

George sucked his teeth. "You wouldn't."

"Pardon?"

"I want to make sure you understand this: You will never get your hands on this family's money."

"What?"

"Oh, I'll always make sure my princess is taken care, and any grandkids. Margaret is looking forward to a few those. But you - well, you won't get your hands on one thin dime."

"OK."

"Don't be defensive. I'm just trying to be straight with you."

"I can see that."

"I don't mean to sound cruel. It's nothing personal against you, Mark. It's about family, my family and my responsibilities to it. Do you understand what I'm telling you?"

"Yes sir, I understand."

Sir. Even then, I couldn't believe I'd actually said "sir" to that pompous, squash-playing Dartmouth bastard.

But instead of striking back, I had turned the other cheek. Or maybe I was just afraid to fight, afraid I might lose Allison. Or maybe I was afraid of having a genuine emotional encounter with another human being.

By the time I decided to talk it over with Allison (about six months after the wedding), she had seemed almost hurt that I would attribute any ill intent to "daddy."

"You must have misunderstood him," she'd said.

I felt exactly like Clark Caring in the scene of his crucifixtion.

#

The husband popped his head out of the dark pantry and asked of his wife "where's the bread?"

"There is no bread," she replied. "We have no money for bread."

"But how can that be? Look around us. Wealth everywhere. A leather sofa here, a swimming pool there, berber carpet everywhere. What have you done with the bread?"

"You don't make enough money to allow me to live in the style to which I deserve to become accustomed. So how can you expect me to buy bread?"

"I'll starve if you don't give me some bread."

"Husbands do not live by bread alone," she said. Then she retrieved a knife from the cupboard and motioned for her husband to place his hand on a scarred wooden cutting board.

"Are you crazy?" he asked. "It'll hurt!"

"Crybaby."

Shrugging, the husband relented and she cut off his right hand.

"Why, that didn't hurt at all," the husband said. "Like cutting your hair or finger nails."

"That's because you are already dead," she explained, then handed him his severed hand on an orange Fiesta platter. "Eat this."

"Mmmm, that's good cadaver," he said.

"Yes, and you should try the wine." The wife hoisted a small glass of red covertly retrieved from the oozing stump of her husband's wrist. "A rather disappointing rioja with delusions of mystical revelations."

"Now you've gone too far!" the husband roared. "There's no call for religious persecution. Why do you want to make me suffer?"

"Because it is only through suffering that we can find our redemption." Then she dug out a set of kebob skewers from the back of a drawer and nailed her husband to the pantry door, bread crumbs and wine spilling from his stigmata.

Over the husband's head, the wife tacked a recipe card upon which she'd written "King of the Losers, signed wife." She dotted the " i" in wife with a smiley-faced heart.

#

You laugh. But let me tell you, this is no joke, no exaggeration. This was my domestic life, the world of Clark Caring.

The previous evening, my beloved had complained that she was getting out her fourth clean glass of the evening. It seems that each time she finished a drink of water, she had been leaving the glass on the kitchen counter so it would be available for her next drink. But "Somebody" kept putting her glasses in the dishwasher. In his defense, Somebody said he didn't have any way to know that these unattended glasses should be left out on the counter. He proposed a solution.

"You should use the striped glasses only. That way, I'll know to leave any striped glasses alone."

"No. I don't like the striped glasses."

"OK, you can pick any type of glass you want, but you can only use that one kind. You have to commit."

"No. That doesn't work for me."

"Ok, you can pick one glass and we'll write your name on it."

"No."

Turns out my beloved believes the problem is that Somebody was in some sort of nervous state that night and kept straightening the kitchen more than usual. Normally, Somebody is perfectly willing to leave dirty dishes lying about on the kitchen counter. But not last night. No, Somebody was in a nervous state.

So yes, you might conclude that instead of failing in his usual way, Somebody was failing in a new way. This is probably true. Therefore, Somebody parked his melancholy butt on the sofa and watched a rerun of Battlestar Gallactica.

See, does that sound as if I was nervous? No, it does not. And to hell with any damn glasses.

#

After detaching myself from the pantry door, I try go back onbeam to research "The Voice of God." But my beloved has other plans. First, she reminds me that dishes must be washed. Next, Brian needs help with his language arts homework. We live in a good school district, which means our children are given a lot of homework. The last assignment isn't completed until Brian's bedtime at 9.

After Brian brushes his teeth and is tucked in for the night, I try once again to plug in. When I am halfway to the portal, though, my beloved looks up from the notebook in her lap.

"Where are you going onbeam at this hour?" she asks.

"I need to run an errand."

"Why didn't you run your errand during the day?"

"Well, I have to work."

"Oh yeah, I wish I could do that, just focus on one thing at a time. But I have to take Brian to and from school and take care of the house and do my writing – you know, my job, my work. I have to do it all during the day, before you even get home. I guess when you're Clark Caring, though, all you have to do is go to work, then go home. That must be nice. I wish I had a wife."

#

The repair work doesn't take long. A handful of nails, a few sheets of plywood - nothing pretty, but it is functional. I put the tools back in the truck and go inside through the garage to make the required call to Allison. But on my way to the phone, I feel drawn to the study. I re-check the antique golf clubs.

George is quite proud of his collection, most of which date back to the 19th century. They are wooden, of course, polished to a deep, rich glow like fine pieces of furniture. He's collected them during 20 years of travels to the world's great golf courses. Each club has a story that George is only too happy to tell visitors, even parasitic son-in-laws like me.

The golf clubs aren't George's only sports collectible. He also has a couple of old squash racquets. He played on the team at Dartmouth. "Princess, I just can't believe you didn't marry a squash player," he likes to say, one of those jokes that's not a joke. I do not play sports. In fact, I abhor games of all kinds. I am too much the alien to participate in genuine human activities.

The racquets hang on the wall, obviously more decor that serious collectible. But the clubs -- George keeps them in special drawers he had built into the bottom of a custom bookcase. The drawers are lined in green felt, and some have foam inserts trimmed to nestle the rarest of the golf clubs in a bit of extra protection.

I reach into one of these custom inserts and extract a frail, toy-looking driver. It has a handle wrapped in a thin, cracked leather so ancient and brittle it reminds me of mummy wrappings. I grasp it in my usual awkward, non-athletic manner and take a swing at an imaginary golf ball. The big wooden head of the old club makes a barely audible swish as it slices through the air on a floor-to-ceiling arc.

Suddenly, I flash on parenthood. During Allison's first pregnancy, she had been willing to engage in membrane penetration until the final weeks. But when I tried that with number two, all I got was an angry, exasperated "I'm pregnant." By the third trimester, she was -

well, she was who she was to become. You might say my "golfing" days were over.

"You're driving too close to the shoulder."

"You're driving too close to the center line."

""You forgot the oregano."

"You washed colored underwear with white underwear."

"Can't you do anything right?"

No, it seems I cannot.

I hold the club up at the apex of its arc and sight along the shaft. I pause for a moment ("No oregano?"), then drop into a batter's stance and swing the club against the bookcase. The handle makes a satisfying snap as it splinters, scattering a century of golfing history across the berber carpet. I retrieve the head and write "Dartmouth sucks" across the flat side with a ball point pen, bearing down hard to make sure the words are permanently indented into the ancient wood.

A year after the birth of our second son, I had tried to talk to Allison about my theory of our marital troubles. But it went no better than the talk about her father. No, she had not been mad that day, she was not mad now and none of "my" problems could be blamed on her.

She was probably right. A classic case of projection with persecutory scapegoating. Besides, it is possible I am not even satisfactory in the practice of membrane penetration. After all, I do want to be fair. But "daddy" has also suggested that I am rather indecisive. So for his sake, I'm not going to be that today. I am acting on his advice. I am making a decision and following through.

Gathering up an armful of clubs, I head for the parlor and drop my load onto the piano bench in a clattering heap, a noise that fills this vast and magnificent room, this mute, deserted hall. The walls and ceilings are enveloped in baroque embellishments. Mahogany veneer, Venetian plaster, gold-leafed frames, Carrara marble. Dark glass, obscure illustrations, Romanesque columns, sculptured thresholds, lines of doors, colonnades…oblique hallways leading to deserted meeting rooms…paneled in the baroque embellishments of an earlier time…Mute rooms, where footsteps are lost…in sculpted berber so profound, so deep…that one perceives no step…as if the ear itself were impossibly remote…distant and remote from this numb, barren décor…far from this elaborate frieze beneath the cornice…with its branches and garlands …like dead leaves…as if the floor were still sand and gravel, or flagstones...over which I advanced one again... to meet you... between richly paneled walls...Venetian plaster, gold-leafed frames, paintings...framed prints amidst which I advance.

Breaking the second club is not quite as satisfying as the first, but when I see that my bad aim has inadvertently taken a nice-sized notch out of one of the intricately carved legs of the piano my interest picks up considerably. Before I know it, I've broken every one, turning a half dozen clubs into high-priced kindling and the black enameled piano leg into a scarred up looking femur.

Rather than soothing me, the destruction sets my blood to boiling. Now I am ready to do some genuine damage. I go back to the truck for my hammer.

I lay into the piano, popping the antique ivory veneer off the keys with vast, swinging blows. The century-old instrument cries out in a pained, atonal scherzo. As the music reaches its crescendo, I turn my attention to the clown painting. Again and again I strike, the claw end of the hammer ripping the canvas into thin strips and knocking chunks of sheetrock out of the wall behind it. Pieces of crumbling gypsum fall inside the piano, randomly striking the strings in a demented encore.

#

Afterwards, I pour myself a bourbon from a crystal decanter on the buffet. But I never get to take a sip. In one of the facets cut into the leaded crystal I catch sight of a movement, a flash of color and light. I spin around and see -- the alien.

#

Here's one way the world ends: I am in bed with a woman. There is no adulterous guilt, so presumably I am not married.

She is nude, lying on her stomach. She looks to be in her early 20s. I kiss her back, which is dark tan. Then I leave.

As I walk out of her apartment building, I think about her desire that we have a child together. But I realize that since we are not married it would be her child. I would be sad because I would not be a part of the child's life.

Now I am on the street in front of her apartment. Oddly, this is the street in front of my work. The apartment building is really my office. I begin walking north along the curb on the east side of the street. There are bushes projecting into the street, forcing me to walk around them into the street itself . There is someone else who is doing the same and a third man who is helping him in some way. Perhaps this helper man is a city street worker.

Then I find a hammer in the street.

I pick it up and lightly pound it in my left palm, like you might see a baseball player idly play with a bat. I have already reached the signal light that is north of the library and I have turned around and am heading back toward my office. But now I realize it is not my work at all. This is the old sanctuary of First United Methodist Church in Duncanville, and the street is Avenue C. I go inside, but it is not the church anymore. It is a multi-use building that contains a restaurant, like one in a hotel.

I suddenly have a revelation: I am in a dream. That makes this a lucid dream, something I haven't experienced in years. There is a woman standing in front of me a step to the right, within arm's reach. She is attractive, but I decide I will not act on base desire. Instead, I walk past her, placing a hand on her arm as I pass. I tell myself that this is my dream so I should let myself touch and experience it, control it - but not let my passions control me.

I approach the old pulpit, which is now the hostess station. The hostess is friendly and attractive. I remind myself that I am not going to engage in membrane penetration, but I am so attracted to her that I take her face in my hands and kiss her. She is very receptive. Lucidity is slipping away, back into the primordial night.

I notice a kitchen sink behind her. She steps aside. Vanishes. And I stand alone at the sink. Should I wash my hands? I am not sure. I look at the sink, and along the back splash I spot an old pair of shoes. They are a pair of brown loafers I owned in college. I have not worn them in years because they needed work; the heels are worn down to the cobblers nails. But as I look at the shoes I realize they have been repaired. The shoes are still old, but have been given a new life, readied for the journey.

"We were somewhere around San Augustine in the heart of the Piney Woods when the sacraments began to take hold," The Stranger says.

He is screaming over the road noise, reading from a Reporters Notepad as we speed through the moonlit East Texas night, enjoying an open-air ride in a 1970 Cutlass convertible.

"You mean mescal," Jack says. "The sacraments are for later."

"Still, I feel a bit lightheaded," The Stranger remarks. "Everything's going black."

"Maybe you could try taking off your shades," I suggest.

"Soulless, cool sunglasses are an essential ingredient of the presentation."

#

It is after 10 p.m. when we finally get on the road.

The Bryson's ranch is about two hours west of Strangers Rest, and the foreman's wife has already stocked the refrigerator and pantry for our arrival. I am looking forward to this trip. I think back to junior high, when Jack and I spent many weekends at the Rocking B Ranch, mostly sitting beside the stock tank and taking turns shooting at turtles with a .22 pistol.

The turtles were hard to spot. The opaque, jade green water concealed all but those parts that actually broke the surface. Usually, that meant only the head, a tiny target indeed for two inept shooters entrusted with the only non-hunting weapon on the property. It didn't matter. It was pleasant enough to just soak up the morning sunrise as it fell across the rocky, earthen dam and listen to the crack of the little pistol as it echoed across the pink- and purple-tinged limestone hills. The dads always took their hunting way too serious, insisting that us boys only shoot at game animals that were in season. So we'd just hide out at the tank and shoot turtles and sparrows and rabbits - anything that just happened by and didn't require any particular skill or patience to kill.

"Maybe if we electrified the pond, the turtles would all come up and we could shoot 'em," Jack suggested one weekend. "We could use that old crank telephone my granddad used to use to get bait worms to come up out of the ground."

We tried it. Of course, it didn't work. So instead, we caught a frog and hooked its legs up to the phone leads. We really had it jumping.

At night, we'd hang out inside the knotty pine-paneled ranch house and tap on the side of the big aquarium by the front door. Fang the rattlesnake had surprised many an unsuspecting new arrival. It was there for the benefit of Bryson Development employees, corporate customers and other high-flying types who could appreciate the kill-or-be-killed visual rumor of the ranch mascot.

Good times.

But somewhere on the outskirts of Mineral Wells it all goes bad.

The old highway takes an unexpected detour, orange traffic cones channeling us down a road we've never seen. We pass a modern diesel locomotive engine parked next to a long-abandoned railroad station, a crumbling, boarded-up relic from the age of steam. But there are no tracks or cross ties; the engine sits directly on the gravel. Within a few minutes we find ourselves hundreds of miles to the east, barreling along the El Camino Real through the Sabine National Forest a few miles from the Louisiana state line. Jack wants to turn back, but The Stranger stops him.

"This is all proceeding as anticipated," he explains over the road noise. "We will stay in the ancestral home. The landlady of the dead has already made out our beds."

Jack is wary.

"A landlady of the dead," he says. "Don't much like the sound of it."

"Well, be fair. The ghosts of 140 years of Leachs live in that old house. Somebody's got to look after them."

So we roll on through the Piney Woods, drinking mescal and lime juice from a circa 1950s red plaid coffee thermos and listening to a 20-year-old FM broadcast of Led Zeppelin's "Physical Graffitti" from a once-popular rock station that went off the air years ago.

"Now we must switch over to public radio," The Stranger says. "Magnetica is on the air."

"She's got a radio show?" Jack asks.

"It's called 'Connotations and Consciousness with Magnetica O'Famously.'"

"She got a big following?" I ask.

"She's quite popular."

"I never liked her," Jack says.

Truth be told, Magnetica never liked Jack, either.

#

Blessings – and apologies. It has been some time since I have spoken with you over the airwaves. Why the delay? While recently visiting Maine – or rather Down East, as the natives call it -- while visiting there to expend blessings with the relations of my questionably gendered companion, I busied myself a bit too much with the annual pre-science festival hurry. Cooking, shopping, decorations, mythic songs. The result of all this rushing about was a nasty case of Pre-Science Festival Disorder – and a very illuminating example of how to live in connotation and consciousness.

With cold compress upon my brow, I detected a noticeable degradation of my usual gusto for living. No longer was I feeling disposed to engage in familiar, enjoyable behaviors, such as grooming my mummified Egyptian cats. Paying notice to these simple moments of our lives is the foundation stone of living in connotation and consciousness.

In modern times, cinema is the stone upon which we build our personal stories. The epic film often provides good-looking scraps to masticate on and fill our mental bellies. I just previewed a film that thoroughly satisfied my visionary hunger: 'The Penetrated Writer.'

This New York City-based tale tracks a Texas moviegoer whose film has broken inside of him. Nothing is absent, and yet nothing works. There is a terrible, deadly secret. And the usher hates him. No purging of painful memories here. This is the story of a grown man still hanging on to the final stages of youth, challenging his personal history and then at last moving on to a whole new connotation and consciousness.

Movies inspire many such acts of clearness and bravery. Consider the protagonist of "The Penetrated Writer." He looks at the route his existence is following and prepares himself for appropriate action when the DNA starts surging. Is that not the way it is for us all?

This brings to mind an additional tasty decree from today's movie menu, "The Projectiles of Autumn: A True Story." U.S. attorney general Bobby Kennedy advises his embattled brother, ""play for the breaks." What a daring instruction to the government official who dwells within all democratic citizens of Planet Earth. We fulfill this command of destiny whenever we vote in favor of connotation and consciousness and pursue the option to exist as the protagonist of our own novel tale."

#

"Well, I guess this means we can all be famous radio personalities," I remark. "I am not overly impressed."

Jack expresses his disdain more directly; he lets loose with a hearty, hilarious belch.

"OK, I have another idea then," The Stranger says. "I will read you a letter I wrote for this very occasion."

He squirms about on the vinyl seat, at last extracting a sheet of notebook paper from his back pocket. He holds it down low out of the road wind, near a tiny green light that comes from inside the rear ashtray. "It is addressed to Owl Creek Farm, Aspen, Colo."

"Hunter S. Thompson," Jack says. "The theme of our road trip."

"Dear Mr. Thompson. Thank you so much for your books, enjoyably dogeared before sitting so long neglected on my shelf. I was so depressed, horribly depressed, depraved, deeply dead, as you can imagine. You've seen me on TV by now, I'm sure, now that I am the butt of jokes on Letterman and Leno."

"TV?" I ask, panic rising inside. "We haven't been on TV. What are you talking about?"

But The Stranger ignores me and keeps on reading.

"Rest assured, though, I'm not one of those sackcloth and ashes people. I'm not like that. I am so overcome by the crowds of pilgrims, the TV news people and the haters. I feel their feelings, fear their dreams, the terrible roar of errant nightmares floating into my frontal cortex. Hands to my temples, I feel the skull beginning to crack. Enough. Always wanted to be famous, of course. But for journalism, for writing. I wanted to be you. Now I am Job, looking for solace, looking for answers. I reach for Gideon's Bible (stolen from a Motel 6, I believe), but my finger falls instead on the spine of 'Fear and Loathing.' I start reading and haven't stopped yet. It is such a wonderful escape, a return to my youth, back when I wanted to be a doctor of Gonzo journalism and everything seemed so right. I wanted to be just like you. How did I go so wrong? How did I forget to act so harmlessly and happily depraved?"

"Maybe you didn't jack off enough," Jack suggests.

"Self loathing," The Stranger continues, "a very ominous assignment - gross, spastic slobbering, slumped over grappling with sad deadness. But now there is again time to enjoy that delicious drag of blood leaving behind your words, scarred into my brain, the words made flesh and neurons, Acapulco shirts testifying to my devotion. Do you grasp that I maintain because of you? It's so right to see wrong, I know, and yet so predictably suburban to seek out this savage journey. Still, I thank you, I mutter to myself, a poor bastard. Completely twisted, engulfed in darkness, I am caught up in a quick burst of acceleration from the Belgian Heliowatts. Burn your houses down, you sackcloth and ashes people. I make a note to myself: Search out the possibilities that once were mine, before consigned to death in life.

"I must be vigilant. Stress factors send my destroyer heading east (I miss the old you, Allison), where there is no hope for those without immunity from shame. My soul is in personal danger, my face a mask of pure fear. If not for your books, I might already have gone the way of no communication.

"Oh Dr. Gonzo, I am a physical salute to this nation of guilty used car dealers, bleeding from the palms over my letter to you as I watch myself mocked on the cathode ray tubes. Now it's all I am, the King Farouk of it all, odd media darling, unfortunate bastard, screaming gibberish at myself behind wild red eyeballs. And the screaming in my head, my raving and jabbering, a confession of Fear and Loathing with overtones of extreme disbelief. No, this can't be happening. I reached at first for the Deity, but my finger fell instead on you, an appropriate companion for traveling the blacktop of terminal psychosis, death with huge Detroit cars hurtling through the pit of dark anguish within me.

"Dear doctor, I see myself swooping and screeching, hoping to alter the jokes and deflect the pain away from me and my bewilderment. The turn is too tight; I swerve sickeningly. Vibrations are getting nasty. Time to order a drink. Mescal with a side of pure Gonzo, leeches on the go, so Vegas, so Hell's Angels, a Hunter frenzy of rotten flesh in which I am looking for answers, looking to maintain solace, following the pattern of a comatose ego. A grim connection is formed. You are me. You, me. I reach again for Gideon's, but that drag of blood makes it hard to see like you, Dr. Gonzo, with those special eyes of yours that burn so keenly, through this frenzy of autonomic pilgrims, the gutless, screeching punks who convert me to photons and agate, the fear and loathing in the dark place where my manic notions lie.

"If only I could leapfrog back in time, before these past few terrible years, avoid the predictable pattern. Ah, a dream of wonderful escape, a return to my youth, back when there was no screaming or fear. With the wife and kids out of town, there's still time to entertain such a fantasy. A specially prepared 1970 Cutlass convertible could function as time machine – "

"And it is, it is," I say, caught up in the foolishness. "We are on the Pathway now."

"-- as a time machine, transporting me back into the form of an obsessed and immature fan, riding that enjoyably fearful blacktop, hugging the double yellow line of irreverent delight, a literary journey into myself, embracing my obsessions, my lusts. Jug wine, oral sex."

"Ah, let's not get carried away," Jack warns.

"Henious chemicals promise to screw it on, grease the face with a happy smile. Now I am an unfortunate bastard, rendered so fashionable, caught up in the obligation to be the story. But I am ready to fight back. With overtones of extreme Hunter-ism, my finger searches out my alter Bible, your manifestos, swooping and screeching in a bright, clear sky. You have given me hope. Now I am right with you.

"By no means am I all right, though. I am rendered so red, so blood stained and dead, staring out through wild-blooded eyeballs and into a personal apocalypse. Your words are raw materials for constructing a mask that hides the fear, blocking that terrible roar in the brain. But there is no mask that blocks out the truth.

"Dear doctor, I thank you again for your books. It wouldn't be too much, I think, to want to be like you, like your type of famous. I could handle the fear, I think. But the loathing! Overwhelmed by domestic shame, I passed these past few terrible years hiding my face in trembling hands. But no more, thanks to you. My letter to Hunter S. Thompson. Yes, you are my alter ego. If only I had been more like you these past few awful years, then maybe I wouldn't be so much like me. Sincerely, Mark Leach."

"Hell yes," Jack says. "A fantastic salute to - to something. Pass me the thermos."

"It is quite good," I agree. "Though I'm still concerned about the TV part."

"Don't be. It's part of an unfinished script I call 'My letters to Hunter S. Thompson and other tales of personal apocalypse'."

#

As we near the state line, Jack turns the twisting, two-lane blacktop into a racetrack, negotiating a 90 degree turn with a stylish shower of gravel, the fishtailing rear end just missing a steel highway mile marker sign.

"Ah, good times," I say. "Reminds me of a little day trip Allison and I took a few years ago. We were so happy, enjoying our little day trip in the country. We explored the treasures, the crafts, the deals. We even had sausage on a stick."

"And then you had to ruin it," The Stranger adds.

"Yes – yes, I did. As we passed that car on the two-lane blacktop, I told you it had been too close to their bumper. I did not like it. And you just smiled. You smiled! It was like you thought it was funny, no big deal. Then we saw the gas station. Do we need gas? No -- no, you said. We'll just fill up as we're leaving. So, of course, I had to tell you that I HATE THAT! Don't you know that by now, my dear one? I know you must know it (how many times have I had to tell you?), so you must be doing it on purpose. First passing the car, now not getting the gas. You are therefore odious. So you said, 'OK, we'll get it now.' And then you set your mouth in that hard, cruel, unfortunate way of yours, so much like a creature of the companion, a vampiric being – a Coffin-Puntura. I always hate it that you, Coffin-Puntura, are that hateful way. You are always digging our graves, ruining our every nice thing. Why can't you be more like me? Why can't you just enjoy our happy day?"

#

Allison was right. I was unable to enjoy our happy days.

But now I wonder –have things changed? Here I am, in the first night after speaking my mind to my boss and my wife. Years of holding it, fearful of the destruction that I was sure would occur if I expressed myself. So as it turns out, I should find that I am afraid of nothing. I should find that I am happy – and, yes, I am happy. I am sure that I am happy. I must be. I am happy unto death.

I am happy – happy, relaxed, clear headed. I happily breathe in deeply the Piney Woods night, feel the cool, humid air filling up parts of my lungs that have been collapsed for years due to a diaphragm that I never let fully relax. Even the darkness seems not so dark anymore as I am traveling in a 1970 Cutlass convertible through the moonlight, pulling in radio broadcasts from the Land of the Dead. I am fully on the Pathway, fully about the journey.

We cross over the Toledo Bend Reservoir, dead ghost trees rising up out of moonlit waves. We happily roll on through Many, the Sabine Parish seat, and back into the night, flying past the Vault of the Deity. But this time all is as it should be. No flooded basement, no old man with tidy facial hair retired in advance of death. It is just plain old Trinity Baptist Church, a single vapor light illuminating the empty parking lot. Perfection is slipping away – no, that's not it. I'm happy. Happy. This time I even remember the turnoff for Fort Jesup. Minutes later, we turn up the drive to the ancestral homestead.

"Cut off your headlights," I say. "We don't want to wake up my uncle. He lives in the neighboring trailer."

"Nobody's there," The Stranger explains. "They're out of town, gone with the church youth group to Missouri, to Silver Dollar City."

Sure enough, no one is at home. No one, that is, but the dogs.

These canines are not normal, waking world creatures. They are door dogs. I read all about them in "My Education," William S. Burrough's book of dreams: "A little black dog follows him into the dining room. Yes, it followed his father just before he was killed, thrown from a horse. Clear death omen."

I advance up the dark, gravel driveway to the old family home. I see two green lights on in the windows, like holiday décor. As I approach the porch I think about how I may find ghosts when I go inside. (After all, this is where the dead Leachs of Sabine Parish live.) Then I see a dog blocking my way. Upon closer inspection I see that the dog is a sort of mountain lion, a yellow panther. It begins to circle me, and two other dogs look on, horrid black curs. I have no weapon with which to protect myself. All I have at hand is an inflated air mattress, which I keep between me and the lion. I want to defend myself, but under the circumstances all I can really hope to do is not antagonize the animal or its companions. I am outnumbered and alone. Where are Jack and The Stranger? Will anyone come to my rescue? I move toward my uncle's trailer house, but it is inexplicably surrounded by barbed wire, a military encampment.

Then the animals are gone, and the party begins.

#

Sitting around a campfire, meeting with others. Lots of people. Where did they all come from? There is a party going on, perhaps a family reunion. We are talking about arranging services for learning and emotionally disabled children. I volunteer for one job. At the same time, I absently run my fingers through the long hair of one of the beautiful Solana twins, just arrived from my freshman year of college.

"They're hot," Jack whispers.

The twins tell me it is my job to draw their long golden hair into two straight, untangled bundles. I am to bind each bundle with a single hair I must thread through a silver sewing needle, which The Stranger supplies.

Jack smiles, watching me struggle with the needle in the flickering campfire light.

"You think you can do better?" I ask.

"No, it's not that. You live in a very strange world."

"Thanks to you."

"Me?"

I explain how it all began that first night after Allison left, the night I went onbeam with Jack's gear.

"Movable Pro 890?" Jack asks. "Not mine. I only use full-service Frames."

"You put it in my nightstand, remember?"

"I left you my old PrePak loaded with Frames 9.0 Pro."

"You're full of it."

"No, he's telling the truth," The Stranger says. "In fact, there is no such thing as a Movable Pro 890. What you experienced was a psychic suggestion implanted by agents of Ozona's black ops group at the direction of Buckstop."

"A psychic suggestion?"

"Through Project Herbal Extract. It permits shadow operatives to enter your nocturnal vision condition and implant suggestive thoughts, like a subliminal splice into a movie."

"What do they have to gain?"

"You are a critical part of the clandestine scheme. This is all premeditated, the next plot point in the script. This is the part of the story when you in fact experience a true incredible revelation. You realize that you are indeed different, that you have been set apart from the world for the sake of the world. Here in the dancing shadows and ginger scarlet glow of the victor's campfire you must see that a part of you is long gone. In fact, the old 'you' is dead. The world looks different now. So you pull apart from the rest of us, lose yourself in your own quiet thoughts."

#

Who am I to argue with the premeditated life? I leave Jack with the needle and the hair and the twins, and I go off in search of a quiet site away from the roar. I pick out a desolate spot on the far side of the house, near where the old well used to be.

I look up at the heavens, see giant stars, ringed planets, crescent moons – a multihued celestial display. The entire solar system – it looks so different now. I am so amazed by this beautiful site that I decide to lie on my back on the ground for a better, more leisurely look. There is some ground light, though, for the view is partially obscured. And there is another dog. But this one is friendly. It wants to lick my face. I squeeze my eyes shut and hold the animal at bay with my hand, touch its wet nose. When I open my eyes again, I see Bellero Shield.

"It is pleasant," the giant insect observes, "to have a friendly dog by your side when you arrive in a new country."

Visiting New York City.

This is alien territory for a native Texan, so perhaps it is forgivable that you do not recall the origin of the movie ticket you hold in your hand. You feel that it was given to you by a woman. But was she your wife? Or perhaps a girlfriend? You are not sure.

You walk to the movie theater through a twisting, snake-like corridor of pay phones, water fountains and rest rooms (always walls, hallways) and emerge from the cloaca onto a busy street. You see people leaving a building -- a school, a store, a theater? -- and you think you recognize one of them as LeAnn Shedi, your high school sweetheart. But it is not her. There is no one you know here.

You reflect that it is an unusual experience for me to be in New York City, a stranger in a strange land. You feel that you now understand why so many immigrants to Texas seem so pleased when they meet someone from the same place they came from. ("Ah, New Hampshire. Yes, we all knew how to live there!") It makes the world seem smaller and friendlier, so they don't feel so alone.

You proceed to the movie theater lobby, where you must deal with the usher. He appears to be a black man, but he's light skinned with stereotypical Anglo facial structure and hair of indeterminate texture (because of a burr haircut). Really, he looks like a younger version of you, but with a shadow across his face.

You immediately clash. He insists that you stand in a certain place. This Napolean of the cineplex is in command, and you do not like it. You are irritated by his attitude, which you judge as a sort of reverse discrimination. You have done nothing to him. Why is he targeting you?

You retrieve the ticket from your pants pocket, where it has become waded into a ball, almost as if it has been laundered. You try to place it in the usher's hand. But there are slips of paper and change mixed in. Using only one hand, you attempt to separate the ticket from the pocket detritus and drop it into the usher's palm. But he can't see the ticket; he thinks you are trying to put money in his hand.

"You have to buy your ticket at the window," he says, clearly exasperated with you.

Now you are righteously indignant. You triumphantly produce the ticket. But he continues to assert his power, pointing to a stripe on the floor behind you.

"You must stand behind the stripe," he explains.

So you take several exaggerated steps back, stopping at a sort of half wall.

"Is this good? You just tell me where you want me to stand."

The usher ignores your sarcasm.

"Yes, that is sufficient," he says, then moves on to deal with others who have joined the line.

You see a black man in line in front of you, and you feel a bit embarrassed by your treatment of the usher. But the black man is in a suit, clearly a businessman, a professional. You reason he probably shares a bit of your irritation with this "Little Napoleon" service person. You make eye contact, then nod toward the usher.

"That's the price we pay to live in a free society," you remark.

But the black businessman does not respond. He looks out the big glass wall at the city. So you look, too.

For the first time, you notice a contrast between the urban landscape and the theater. It is an older suburban style theater, dating from the late '50s or '60s, one of the first multiplexes, perhaps two screens -- a dead ringer for the old Richland Plaza theater in Richland Hills, Texas. It is now a dollar movie house, doubly out of place in the high-price world of Manhattan.

At this point, you realize you are standing in line with Scott Paulson, a boyhood friend.

"What are you doing here?" you ask.

We catch up on our lives, and he tells you he has just completed an MBA. You share his excitement, and you genuinely congratulate him.

Scott and you went to Duncanville schools and SMU together. At your 20-year high school reunion, he told you that SMU taught him to read and write. You thought he was making a joke, then you realized that he was sincere. So it's a bit of a surprise to find that he has earned an advanced degree, something you don't have. He is a master of the business world. You are a master of no world.

Meanwhile, the usher has moved to a different part of the line, re-arranging everyone. Scott and you talk about the movie. You are to see "The Nightmare Before Christmas," which you recall is a Tim Burton movie. You are not sure if you have seen it before, so you are looking forward to it. And it's only a dollar. You hope there is time to get a soft drink. Then you realize, of course, there is plenty of time because they are not even seating yet.

I step through the sculptured threshold and instead of gazing upon a movie screen find myself looking down a long hallway of overly extravagant forms and gilt-edged ornamentations. Lines of doors, ambiguous colonnades leading past deserted meeting rooms paneled in the baroque embellishments of an earlier time. Mute rooms, where footsteps are lost in sculpted berber so profound, so deep that one perceives no step, as if the ear itself were impossibly remote – distant and remote from this numb, barren décor, far from this elaborate frieze beneath the cornice with its branches and garlands like dead leaves, as if the floor were still sand and gravel, or flagstones. At the end of the hallway a man at a desk, sitting with his back to me.

"Excuse me," I say. "Do you know what has happened to the Son of the Deity?"

The man turns to face me, and I am shocked to see that he is me.

"You cannot imagine how difficult it is to continue to animate you on the written page when I am subjected to these endless interruptions," he complains.

This is a troubling state of affairs. I shake my head, but the image does not fade. "Listen, I don't understand how – "

"You understand plenty. You are in fact a fictionalized version of me."

"A cinematic creation? That can't be right."

"You are the protagonist/narrator of 'Marienbad My Love With Mango Extracts,' the world's longest movie. I'm pushing past 100 hours. I've been working on perfecting you for years – too long, to be honest. You are still a flawed and incomplete character, but after all these millions of words you are perfected enough that you have become a semi-autonomous entity. You have evolved to a point at which I can no longer turn you on or off at will. It's very hard to stay on task when you insist on breaking down the fourth wall, interrupting me in this special movie place, this world where I go in my mind to receive transmissions from the back of beyond."

"OK, then. What's this story about?"

"It's science fiction – or rather, a parody of 1950s B-movie sci-fi. With skin care metaphors."

"So you are saying you've written me into a sci-fi picture?"

"Honestly, I really don't have time for this. It's midnight, and I want to finish this scene before I go to bed. Please get back in the story."

"You send me on a literary journey to find the son of God, but you can't spare a few minutes to answer my questions?"

"And the fourth wall crumbles."

"You bet it does. Congratulations, Mark Leach. You've filmed world's longest movie and you've trapped me inside of it. Do you think that is in any way truly noteworthy? If you really wanted to create a noteworthy science fiction novel, then why no swords or elves? Why no Roman centurions?"

"Well – "

"No, you thought you were too good, right? Only a hack would write genre, right? Instead of straight science fiction, you decided to employ the 'conventions' of SF."

"It's all for EFFECT."

"And why did you have to make me so perverse? After all, I am an autobiographical character. What do my perversions say about you, the novelist?"

"You are only an exaggerated version of me – exaggerated for comic effect."

"Fine. Here is what I say: I hate this, being a fictional creation trapped in this abomination of a film. It's all so clear now. You took those college lit classes too seriously. You're making experimental film, stream of consciousness. Nobody wants to watch that stuff anymore. Your cinematic heroes are ghosts."

"Actually, I'm writing metafilm."

"Metafilm. How about 'crap'? Now that 'Marienbad My Love With Mango Extracts' has been unleashed on the world, surely the Apocalypse is not far behind."

"You sound like the people I meet in the blogosphere."

"The what?"

"That's exogrid to you. They don't like my work at all. Here are some comments I received during an online script writing contest: The incoherent ramblings of an insane mind … I am not sure there is even a classification for this one … long stretches of surrealism, where we are in this character's head and not grounded in any recognizable reality...What was that?! Was this person using drugs or what? … I decided to be generous and give you a one, rather than a zero… I am so completely confused. I have no idea what's going on, what's real and what the narrator is imagining … It's terrible."

"They're right."

"And they really hate my technique."

"Your what?"

"Literary appropriation. Word rustling. I use excerpts from the writings of others as my raw material. I put the various pieces of text through a series of manual- and computer-assisted modifications. Cut-up engines, Markov generators, search and replace and thesaurus functions of Microsoft Word. And I combine it with recycled content from my own writings. The output is a completely new and unique cinematic creation."

"Interesting. What's the line between appropriation and blatant copying?"

"From a strictly creative point of view? I say there's no line. I am very practical, so I'm not going to intentionally violate a copyright. I don't want to have to deal with a bunch of lawyers and lose a ton of money in a lawsuit. But other than strictly practical considerations, I feel no reason to draw a line between words I might write from my own imagination and words I might steal. Appropriation is a legitimate form of literary creation. It may be the only thing that will save us. Movies will save the world and the novel, which is really just a movie in written form."

"You're not one of those people who thinks the novel is dead, are you?"

"The novel is just about done for. Phillip Roth recently got people all worked up by predicting that 25 years from now the novel will only have a cult following. The Kindle won't rescue it, either. He said 'The book can't compete with the screen. … It couldn't compete beginning with the movie screen. It couldn't compete with the television screen, and it can't compete with the computer screen.' It's a shame. You can do things on the printed page that you can't do with movies or TV. Even computers. There is something about reading text – without graphics or images – that projects you into another place. But too many people who write and publish novels – or dream of writing and publishing -- just keep on turning out the same old drivel. Yes, it is what sells. But for how much longer? So much of what is being published today are stories that would be more engagingly told on an electronic screen. There is little that is truly new and unique going on in novel writing. The folks I encounter in the blogosphere – the vast majority do not realize that the novel is dying. They don't even realize that they are helping to kill it. Writing another story about a sword-wielding elf does not advance the cause. Soon they'll be performing CPR on a corpse. If we want to restore the novel to health, then it's time to try some dramatic and experimental treatments. Look at what Kenneth Goldsmith is doing to reenergize poetry. The guy copied an entire edition of the New York Times, front to back, then called it done. He didn't change a single word. You might complain that it doesn't sound very engaging, but it is certainly dramatic. And it is really any less interesting than what is being churned out by the publishing industry every year? Do we really need any more stories about darkly romantic vampires?"

"But at least they're writing a story. What you've been putting me through these past few days is almost incomprehensible. It certainly doesn't flow like a film – I mean a novel. There's action, but no real plot."

"Granted, the novel in the film – that is,the book titled 'Marienbad My Love'— is impossible to read in the conventional sense. Goldsmith says the Internet is mostly unreadable not because of the way it is written, but because of its enormous size. I read a story recently in The Atlantic. 'Is Google Making Us Stoopid?' It's about how many of us – well, me anyway – no longer read with any level of depth. We are about skimming, data aggregating, the employment of intelligent agents. I believe it is true, especially for me. I am becoming a robot. I feel it. I don't think the way I used to. I don't actually read novels anymore. I skim them. In 'Marienbad My Love,' I included a real dream I had about become a robot."

"I remember that one. Sounds like you're channeling William Burroughs to me. Or Kenneth Goldsmith or any number of other writers who are doing literary mash-ups."

"Exactly. Back in the 1950s Brion Gysin famously said that poetry was 50 years behind painting. Guess what? Now it is 100 years. Nothing has changed. Music and the visual arts accepted sampling, appropriation and similar tactics years ago. Writing is stuck in the dark ages."

"I'm sorry, but literary appropriation is relatively conventional stuff these days. Surely they don't hate you for that."

"Well, I do call myself a plagiarist."

"Well, of course you do. That's just perfect. I don't blame then for hating you. I hate you! You are an idiot. Why would you possibly want to confuse the issue by saying that literary appropriation makes you a plagiarist?"

"I selected that word because it is emotionally charged and gets a lot of attention. But I have been very careful to explain what I mean by that emotionally-charged word and offered detailed explanations about how I employ the cut-up method and other techniques to generate original writing. That is, not plagiarism."

"I see. Then you were trying to be funny."

"Exactly."

"Did you use the smiley faced emoticon?"

"Of course not. That would ruin the dry tone of my humor."

"Dry tone? How in the world do you expect people to know you are being funny if you don't tell them you are? That's why they use laugh tracks on TV."

"Look, when I use a loaded word like 'plagiarism,' I am actually engaged in media relations. I am promoting myself and my work. I love it that some people get all spun up. They say 'that's not writing!' Of course, my motivation is more than just creating controversy. I truly believe in what I am doing. I am writing. I'm touching a keyboard, I'm pushing keys. Words are appearing inside a Word doc, my manuscript. I'm making it happen."

"The words would not exist in this particular context without your involvement, is that it?"

"Exactly. And by the way, I don't use smiley faced emoticons. Ever."

"You are an idiot. What sort of attention are you getting?"

"Got myself kicked out of a writing contest. One of the participants blogged about how much he hated me and my technique. Said I was 'a thief, a hack, and a self-aggrandizing waste of protoplasm.' He went on to say that he hoped I would masturbate my ego until I starved to death."

"Now that's funny. After all, you do have a rather inflated sense of self."

"He also wrote that he hoped that I would be 'locked in a psych ward' and noted that I write my own press releases about my 'never-will-it-be-published, accomplished-by-theft so-called novel!'"

"I like this guy!"

"His ranting was so over the top that I did a mash-up with some of his entries, added some of my own sci-fi content, attributed it all to a nut job character I called 'Major Rage' and posted the results in the writing contest. One of the moderators – her name was Heather Dudley – was so furious with me that after she terminated my account she went onto this guy's blog and wrote that what I do is 'the artistic equivalent of running newspaper ads, magazine articles, and tampon covers through a shredder, pouring glue on it, then taking a piss on it and calling that art.' She also said that 'simply because you added your own piss doesn't make it unique, or even particularly creative.'"

"I agree."

"I liked what she wrote so much I added it to the 'comments' section of my web site."

"You put that on your web site? You are even more perverse than me."

"But we are the same person."

"I don't think so. In fact, I think you may be MY literary creation. Perhaps I am the real Mark. You are the false one. What do you think of that?"

"I think it doesn't matter. Either way, I suspect we will spend the rest of eternity locked in this battle, trapped inside this perjury, this prison of a never-to-be-published novel. This is my calling. I am creating a vast narrative in which I have done away with linear plot and grammatical rules. I am creating something that you might find in one of the infinite hexagonal rooms of Borge's 'Library of Babel,' an almost infinite number of pages of barely comprehensible text. I am creating a work that no one will actually read, but perhaps a few people will talk about. I am creating a metaphor for the Internet and a world in which so many of us have lost the ability to concentrate on a single piece of writing for more than a few minutes. As I look back at my earliest writing ambitions, I realize that all I ever really wanted to do was write a story about myself. Specifically, a story about what it is like to be me at the center of my self, with all of the outer skin peeled away. And I think in that process I have written something that goes beyond the personal. I feel that somehow I have written a story of what it is like to be a human at this point in our evolution."

"What do you mean 'our evolution'?"

"We are at a tipping point as a species. Intellectual technology is poised to make the jump from our eyes and fingertips right into our craniums. I really believe that. Five hundred years from now, our progeny will think of us the same way we might think of a Neanderthal. They won't understand what we were like – except through our art. I am writing for those people, the ones who are waiting for us in 2509. I imagine some literary archeologist using his cerebral implant to plow through the Internet artifacts of the early 21st century. He's going to be looking for something that stands out.

Odd things, different things. He'll be using search terms like "longest" and "biggest," and he's going to find "Marienbad My Love. " He's going to use that cerebral implant to plow through the 17 million words in a few seconds. I tell you right now, it's going to give him pause. "What is this?" he'll wonder. He's going to take a second look. And when he does, he's not going to find a story about sword-wielding elves or darkly romantic vampires. He's not going to find a novel that anyone ever bought or stocked in a bookstore or library. He's going to find a story about a two-bodied man – the prototypical man in crisis from the last days of homo sapiens."

"Then I guess we better get on with it."

"See you in the next chapter."

#

Elmo: Pretty. New York City is an ideal visual rumor of alien terrain. But please, no more attempts at Gonzo.

Charlie: Besides, we don't need it. With a little nudge this quirky film could go totally box office lesbian, the blind seducing the book. Revelation describes a repeating inner something – you know, I don't know what we're talking about anymore with this biblical crap. Let's just start shooting.

Elmo: But seriously. The Stranger waves his arms. Rococo intrigue and animal lust blend together, membrane penetration in a Louisiana hog pen, a beautiful dream.

Charlie: And he totally missed the opportunity offered by the arrival of the Solana twins. It could have been as it was that college night of old, hiding in the back bedroom, fingertips enjoyably extracting an inverted nipple – damn! – and exploring forbidden lacy underwear saturated in hot virginal ectoplasm.

Elmo: Or show how revelation describes the Deity, who also destroys. Do not tempt it. But always he was drawn to it. His light. We long to hear the quiet, still, big, glimmering complex of extraterrestrial insects caught from the perfect mixture of the young seer. In fact, he cannot fully dream. For months now.

Charlie: You are small for enjoying such an awful dream.

Elmo: Acknowledged, Mr. Lacy Underwear. And yet, it's real.

Charlie: Rococo intrigue and animals seem to be the ongoing value of this script of the death thoughts that trouble him. Here, The Stranger showed what it is to create a reborn lesbian, the blind seducing to communicate with man through dreams of exceptional "worseness," the same since the plethora of bending over for the well-oiled cam and screaming – well, perhaps there is a sub-market for that one.

Elmo: His destiny is with – and must be about -- him. It is this that troubles him. He is one with the cinema. Ah, and this one, a beautiful dream, an incredible revelation. Show me that he had a dream, a cliche cramming contest, and we'll move on. He tried to ignore that Christendom was a failure. This is bad. Failures must be acknowledged. Any Zeta-Jones in membrane-hugging spandex, a sick bastard engaging this shopping mall with no soul. We are small for humping it, the delicious silky femur. So much truth, he – Mark – is the prototype, a metaphor for when the "voice of God" speaks. Diaz also enters a cliche cramming contest of the psyche. Give her the well-oiled cam. And God.

Charlie: Let's roll the clip.

#

I find myself inside the command module, a clinical, domed room off a metallic hallway, a sleek 1950s B-movie set consisting of a curved corridor of polished metal, assorted German signage – "Actung!" – in a decidedly Luftwaffe font and the ubiquitous cloud and lightening bolt logo of Ozona International.

The Stranger is here, too, strapped to an operating table. But he's not The Stranger of recent days. This one appears to be The Stranger of my original dream, an old, worn out man with wrinkled hands and a thick cardigan sweater. The sweater is open and so is the shirt beneath it, revealing a bony chest covered in silver hair and a nest of wired electrodes. His eyes are open – open and dead, staring at the ceiling of polished metal conduits.

"What's wrong?" I ask. "Are you all right?"

He doesn't answer.

Above The Stranger's head spins the lighted, arm-like device wielding the piercing instruments of surgical steel. Beyond him, I see Cinnamon and Corvette. But all is not well. They are nude, frozen inside separate glass enclosures the size of coffins. Beyond them, I see another coffin of ice and another frozen nude. Inside, a familiar face -- Jack Bryson, eyes wide open and lips stitched together in a silent scream.

And in the middle of it all, hand resting casually on a crate of glass vials, stands the mad scientist himself, star of the Society of the Purple Sunset – the sinister Dr. Adolfo Morel.

"Had quite a time rounding up all of your assorted personalities," he says. "Over the years you've split into an incredible number of pieces. You're amazingly fragmented, even for a visionary neurotic."

"So you killed them."

"Your friends have been dead for years, them and all the people of this final, dead age. Didn't you know?"

"You killed them."

"Nothing so melodramatic. They're in suspended animation, in cold storage for the re-integration process."

"What?"

"Submerged ice. We got the technology from one of the aerial clocks being studied at Area 51. Did the same thing with Hitler."

"And what are those?" I ask, pointing to a line of jars on a high shelf above Jack.

Dr. Morel casts a mischievous glance my way. "What do you think they are?"

They are a nightmarish abomination. Each jar appears to contain human fetus. But the fetuses have all gone horribly wrong. There is a mix of fiendish deformities, ranging from lobster claws to exoskeletal protrusions to angel wings.

"OK, I know what you're thinking," Morel says. "And you're right. We took a few liberties, skirted the old genetic taboos. Aren't we all kin, really? But it was all for science. Cutting edge work I tell you. And you were the model."

"Me?"

"Look at this one," he remarks, pointing to the nearest jar. "A genuine flippered anxiety disorder. Over here, a web-footed phobia. And last week, a break through in the study of mystical psychosis: Cicada wings! Tiny little protrusions anchored by tendons to the clavicles. Talk about visionary transformation. Eventually, we'll get one we don't have to euthanize."

Despite my best efforts, the room begins to blur. A tear forms in the corner of one eye. My gaze falls on the crate of glass vials.

"And this is the Fluoride 9," he says. "Or rather, it is a new and improved formula. Perhaps a better name would be Liquid Jesus. It will be introduced into the atmosphere in Strangers Rest at the sunrise service, setting off a global mystical experience with psychotic features, paving the way for the rise of the world's first privately owned and operated deity. And the man behind the god will be – well, let's ask The Stranger."

Morel fiddles with a knob on the arm-like device. A long flexible needle-like conduit of glinting metal snakes toward The Stranger, settling on his abdomen and piercing his navel. His eyes pop open like a vampire at sunset.

"All-encompassing scan of the gorge of time," The Stranger intones. "Azure gloom congregating in a gemstone cranium of ethereal vapors, rumble clatters over the chasm, the outer dramatization of inner conflicts, luminaries glowing transparent and emerald, the cool of unfilled liberty in motionless midday passion –"

"Regressive hypnosis," Morel explains. "Turns out the Cicadans really are split off from his – that is, from your – unconscious realm. Listen to him. It's almost poetic."

"The unexpected end of supernatural analysis, one street over from fair-haired exasperation, noise of organized irrigation, royal crop hierarchy, vegetative brood scraping fragile creature gluttony, ladled out by a charcoal-skinned giant spewing blond sparks, creating a work of art composed of angel shells, mutated frogs and mounds of aquatic fillets within a pond viewed in the dim steaming dusk. Broad greasy murmur reddened brilliant crimson and reduced to the vapor of a pungent ruttish creature, a stink so serious you might observe it traveling from devastated bones in the lilac fog of an aged DNA delivery organ lost in erected liberties. Pessimistic, the versatility of heaving dismay. Antiquated wickedness of pestered marshes, countenance fires gleaming in a bright childish grin. His smile tears the heavens and weakens into a huge gemstone cranium of brilliance, illuminating the bankrupt municipalities and hopeless sceneries of a deceased earth, the glow forever diminished as the luminaries travel out one after the next. The outer dramatization of inner conflicts, helping Buckstop take over the world."

Dr. Morel touches the knob, and The Stranger is silent again.

"He can really gas on," Morel says.

"What have you done to him?"

"Me? That's what he's really like – what you're really like. Didn't you know?"

I didn't know.

"And now we pull the space/time lever," Dr. Morel says, reaching for a small handle at the top of the control panel. "Prepare yourself. We will experience a brief flicker, and a slow wave will shiver through the universe."

#

You come upon a hill, the site of an overgrown cemetery near Fort Jesup. Grasses, weeds and thorny brambles have taken the headstones. There is a logging trailer that bears pieces of an unassembled structure, panels of rough pine logs lashed together with strong rope. It is to be a clock tower, a timepiece in the sky.

A bystander explains to you that this log clock tower is to be erected at the cemetery, but the face of the clock will face the outside. He thinks this is a mistake.

"It should face the cemetery," he says.

You do not share his objection.

"The clock will face the world," you explain.

You are standing under a bridge beside the hill. Others are present. You recognize many of them as your relatives. Aunts, uncles, cousins and such -- all are gathered here for a funeral. The service is to be held in a chapel a few hundred feet away.

It is time for the service, so you and the group all walk together. You are with you wife, who stands on one side. On your other side is someone who looks like one of you cousins, the same one who retrieved the shirts from the bottom of the ocean in a previous dream. As before, she is 25 years younger than today - a teenager. She squeezes your rear, an uncharacteristic gesture. You suddenly realize that maybe she is not your cousin after all.

You enter the chapel and head for the back pew. But it is already taken, filled with coats and what looks like a saddle. (Parenthetical aside. Perhaps this is a reference to the engine saddle from a previous dream about the horned animal car with the radio for listening to the Deity). You must find another place to sit or perhaps squeeze into the remaining empty space at the end of the pew. Then you look at the front of the church. Where is the body?

Now your perspective changes. You are watching a TV show, a sitcom. The body of the dead one you are here to honor is actually that of a little man, perhaps 18 inches tall. He has been placed in a bathtub filled with bubbles. He is wearing his burial suit, but with the addition of a conductor's baton. Two men - pallbearers or perhaps friends of the deceased - sit at the edge of the tub, drinking and singing bar songs. They are having great fun, acting as if the dead man is leading them in a song. One of the men wears a silk scarf around his neck and a top hat cocked at a jaunty angle. The other is drinking from a black shot glass (you think it is your own, a souvenir from the Historic 62 Bar in Virginia City, Nev.), which he puts to the mouth of the dead man, as if to give him a drink. Caramel colored liquid spills down the little dead man's chin. And all the while, the corpse is somehow being manipulated so that it appears to be alive, conducting them in a stiff, jerky, robotic manner, his little arm splashing the soapy water as he waves the baton in time to the singing:

"Everywhere that I roam,
over land or sea or foam,
you can always hear me singin' a song,
show me the way to go home."

The funeral director stands in the background, nervously watching the proceedings.

Then the funeral is over, and you are sitting at a table of women. They include Allison and the woman who squeezed your rear. They talk about a silk blouse one of them received, presumably a gift. They pass this garment around, admiring the feel and cut. Suddenly, you realize one of the women has placed a shoeless foot in your lap. She is rubbing your DNA delivery organ with her stocking toes. You look around, but you can't tell who it is. Then Allison takes you by the hand, and you leave together.

The drive home takes you along the usual route, the El Camino Real. You almost hit a car on the bricked main street of downtown Nacogdoches, the oldest town in Texas. But all is well. You continue on your way without incident. You are on the Pathway now. You are going home.

The camera pulls back and the scene fades into the dark, still night, where we begin our new lives, the lives of radiance – the lives we dream for ourselves after the End of the World.

But what is wrong? Why do you look at me so strangely? The little man is just a metaphor. The coffin is empty. This talk of death – this is all rubbish, all madness. Who comes up with these lies? I'll tell you who: journalists! The newspaper world is dead. It no longer functions. I won't allow this rubbish, these lies. This is MY epic film, not theirs. Screw the critics. Don't you think I know how my own movie ends?

Forever walls, hallways, forever doors. Again you hold back, as if on the threshold, as if at the entrance to a place too dark, too strange. Come nearer. Nearer still. We don't need to be apart, alone, eternally waiting to be together as perfected beings. It's not true. But you're afraid. It's too late now, you say. Forget the old, dead world, frozen in time like the creeks and ponds during the summer of '28 or '29. This is the new beginning. Call the grips and gaffers. We shall shoot this scene through a lens or prism onto feeling-toned print stock. Next year, we shall meet here again, this time forever. A year isn't much. No, for me it is nothing…

Again I advance across the tragic beaches of this deserted island, footsteps upon sand so profound, so deep, that one perceives no step. Mute beaches, where footsteps are lost. Mute, deserted – footsteps upon sand over which I advance once again. To find you.

Pull up a deck chair, help yourself to the tanning oil. Check out the beach. Isn't it beautiful? Let us wiggle our toes in the warm sand, breathe in the salty Gulf coast breeze, admire the surf, share a festive beverage, penetrate one another's membranes, toast the future. And then the lines penned by Alain Robbe-Grillet, lines conceived for just this sort of boy/girl encounter.

"Didn't we meet at Marienbad last year?" I ask.

You are unrevealing and reserved, a far away look in your eyes.

"Didn't you say you would leave your husband and we would run away together?"

Let us drive off this prison, drive out of this perjury. Let us disappear into the anonymous traffic of Shoreline Drive, past the beachfront mansions. Take note of this one, an example of the mid-century Revival Style, so huge and mournful, a tragic structure from an earlier time. So mournful and tragic, the grounds devoid of shrubbery, blossoms or vegetation of any kind. Here we find a past of Carrara marble, a past carved in stone – intersecting lines, reserved, filled with inscrutability. Upon initial viewing it appears impossible to get lost here along the linear walkways between the unassailable statues and marble embellishments, where you are, even now, losing yourself forever in the dark glass of night. Alone with me.

And yet, it may not be true. The Stranger counseled me that it is easy to ruin an epic film at the end, in the all-important finale. All too often the final moments are too abrupt (or prolonged), too unfocused, too unsurprising – all that came before is wasted. Many B-movies fail due to too many unresolved loose ends and too many endings. Multiple climaxes and endings can be exhausting. So many things to go wrong.

"And don't forget to wrap up the stories of the supporting characters," he warned me.

Fair enough. I've already told you what I know of Luh. Hopefully this time the baby will not attempt to murder me. As for the others …

You know about Allison, of course. She was all geared up to take me to court and get a massive monthly child support payment. But when she realized I was no longer capable of gainful employment – indeed, I am told that my mental condition may qualify me for a small but adequate permanent disability stipend – she simply asked the court to take away my parental visitation rights. Maybe the boys will come see me after they turn 18.

Cowboy Roy is a movie star again. Moved to Burial Chamber, Calif., where he's at work filming his autobiography. Bellero Shield is there, too. He's playing a cameo role -- the Lord of the Hive – as well as serving as a technical consultant. He's been advising on set design for the examination room on the aerial clock.

Can you believe Libby quit the Register? Ironically, she left the paper over American values. Seems she believed the publisher was infringing on her first amendment rights to free speech. She thought she should be able to talk to whomever she desired, even during a newspaper war. Turns out even a 30 percent government subsidy is not enough to guarantee one's constitutional rights. Go figure.

Grandpappy Thornton and his famous frontier buddies Big Foot Wallace and Kit Karger continue to make the rounds, thanks to extraterrestrial time travel technology. I understand they enjoy a nightly faro game at the Local Option in Fort Worth (circa 1870).

Andy Bryson lost his G&C, but made a fortune buying up foreclosed properties from the Declaration Reliance Corp.

Of course, we must include a coda from "Let Me Love You." I think this brief clip is about right.

#

In the end, R.E.L. Four was not a bad sort. We had some rather enjoyable discussions back in the day.

"The evolution from child to adult is like a journey from Heaven to the Land of the Dead," he explains. "Your poet Holderlin had it right. 'Dead the youthful world which was my shield, and this breast, which used to harbor heaven, dead and dry as any stubble field.' There is no place for an almighty deity in such a shattered, aged wasteland as the post-modern heart."

"But there's still so many believers," I remark. "They've even turned the old Houston Astrodome into a church."

"Yes, that is true. Upon my arrival the institution was still working. I noticed that churches were still protecting the believers of the world against any pervasive pumping up or estrangement of the soul. And that's good. Religion should provide this superior communal sword and shield, which protects believers from themselves. But the non-believers -- without these weapons, they had begun to regard themselves as everything. And as nothing."

"And yet you have taken away the protection."

"Actually, Jehovah did that. Did you know he turned himself in?"

"What?"

"That's right. He knew it was time to depart the scene. As the creator and sustainer, it was his job to heal the split between 'everything' and 'nothing.' But how could he? He himself was trapped in the double helix of this dim clash of the warring souls of humankind. Have you ever read Matthew Arnold?"

I admit I have not.

"He wrote 'We are here as on a darkling plain, swept with confused alarms of struggle and flight, where ignorant armies clash by night.' No, Jehovah did the only thing he could do. Now it is time for the people of Planet Earth – believers and non-believers alike – to confront the ultimate questions of life. They can only do so on their own, without the benefit of sword or shield. Thrown back upon themselves, they now have a fighting chance."

#

As for The Stranger, he is alive and well. He lives in me. You can see him in my face, in the scar, the raw tissue of evolution. After all, you cannot have a resurrection without a death.

Have I offended you? I am sorry. I don't mean to be theologically unacceptable. In fact, I wish to thank you. You have been very kind to come here, to listen to my story. You know that I could not have told it without you. I could not have told anyone else.

Now the world has changed, and I am not yet sure how to function in it. It is as if I have just arrived, an alien. Perhaps it is just as I dreamed, and we are all becoming aliens now. Of course, it might not be true. It's probably not true.

#

Charlie: And a slow wave shivers through the universe.

Elmo: Now all is bliss. Mark is happy. All is well. He continues on his way without incident. He is on the Pathway now. He is going home, happily ever after.

Charlie: Except, of course, that Mark is not going home. He is not happy, not happy at all.

Elmo: Right you are. There is no penetration, no bliss. After all, he failed to get the girl. In the B-movie sci-fi genre, that is a must. Therefore, the story is unfinished. Which is to say, dead.

Charlie: Mark is a failure, dreaming of the sun, beaches, and the islands in the path of the trade winds, youth whose memory drives one to despair! Or something to that effect.

Elmo: There will be no next year.

Charlie: Agreed. And yet – a famous quote, a clever ending. This almost makes up for it all.

Elmo: And yet not quite.

Charlie: True. Mark remains an odious being.

Elmo: After all, he forgot the oregano.

Charlie: He drives too close to the shoulder.

Elmo: He drives too close to the center line.

Charlie: He washes colored underwear with white underwear.

Elmo: Why can't he do anything right?

Charlie: He's just too tight.

Elmo: And too loose.

Charlie: He's half again too clever.

Elmo: Yes, he almost fails to suck.

Charlie: After all, he is God.

Elmo: In his dreams. Let's roll the clip.

#

Here's one way the world ends: Outside at night, walking with a group of people I know.

We come to a pile of refuse - trash, dirt and other discards. And yet, the items are apparently significant. To this pile I add an antique metal advertising sign, which employs an image of the devil. I put dirt on top of the sign, burying it in a shallow grave.

Then I am inside my old apartment in Fort Worth, the one I lived in before getting married. It is still my home, but I am being held here against my will by a sort of mad scientist. Another man is also being held here. We are to be his guinea pigs, the subject of his infernal experiments.

The scientist has an assistant, an attractive woman who appears to be in her 20s or early 30s. She is wearing a grayish or maybe tan suit, the kind with a skirt and jacket, but no blouse. I can see down the front of the jacket. She has smallish breasts, but still a definite sexual presence.

The woman produces some papers, computer bubble sheets. I realize she is preparing to give me a personality test.

"Have you ever taken one before?" she asks.

"Yes," I say, but I can't remember when or the results. So she consults a chart in which she points to an entry with the name of the tester (MacKensie) and the date. It is a "9" followed by some single digit that I don't see.

"I don't remember the name of the person who administered the test, but this entry could be the one," I say.

Meanwhile, the scientist is talking to the other man. I realize that the experiment is being readied. Somehow I know that we are to undergo a physical transformation. We will be turned into new beings, a frightening prospect. The assistant asks me about a small bottle of model airplane paint she has found in the apartment.

"Can we use it?" she asks.

I examine it and shake my head.

"It is too old," I say. "Look, the pigment has settled in the bottom of the bottle and can't be re-mixed."

So I hold the bottle in front of me, moving toward the kitchen as if to throw it in the trash. I act casual, do a little skip-and-slide walk. Of course, I am hoping to make an escape. Do they suspect this? Will they stop me?

No, they make no move toward me. I go to the far end of the kitchen, where there is a door that leads to a bedroom and, beyond that, to the balcony and freedom. I bolt for the balcony, which is on the second or third floor. I run outside and start yelling for help.

"There's a burglar, I'm being kidnapped!"

I kick away a screen and jump to a flat roof just below me. I call out to a man on the ground below, but I don't stop running. I know the scientist and his assistant could be right behind me, ready to recapture me and perform the transformation.

I run over to the edge of the roof and jump or climb to the ground. Then I go back inside the building, into the lobby, shouting all the while about the kidnappers. Apparently, word has already reached the authorities, because I find several uniformed officers waiting. They direct me to a seat; I am saved.

Several months later, I find myself in a bedroom with the scientist and his assistant. I am standing at the foot of the bed, and they are in it together.

"I'm happy you were not sent to jail," I tell them. And I mean it. At last, I can afford to be charitable. They will be on probation for a long time, so they will have to be careful not to commit any more crimes. They are no longer a threat.

"I'm happy because I will be able to spend time with the two of you and not worry," I add. "I can learn from you, I'm sure of it."

I am again holding the metal sign of the devil. This time I place it on top of the covers – the covers beneath which they will sleep and I will dream.

In the distance I hear the clock chimes, convening the moviegoers from around the planet. Now I must take my place behind the camera. In seven days the world will come to an end, and I must be ready. After all, it is hard to be me.

Pretty, eh?

#

Walker Percy had it right about the discrepancy between this new evolving era and the old extinct one.

He wrote that going forward we will combine common labor with uncommon observing – and uncommon listening and waiting. In the previous epoch we had no need for such extraordinary observations. We cast far ahead of ourselves, crafting schemes and reaching beyond our abilities. We embarked on important objectives. We took note of the votes we cast at the preceding assembly. Between assemblies we went on family road trips and had friends over for weekend cookouts.

And we never had Incredible Revelations.

True wisdom and understanding are losing ground these days. Ah, this new generation of moviegoers! They believe only in the rational. They are confident that they can seize the Deity with their minds, measure Him in feet and pounds. They abhor metaphor, attack abstract films, slaughter the avant-garde. Even now, the tonsured hermits have taken to the caves in the hills, where they are assembling the timeless manuscripts and classic B-movies once more. (I observe them from the strategically positioned branch of a sycamore tree.)

But how can I tell all of these stories? How can I tell about the whole world when I haven't even considered what should happen to me? What of me do I commit to the epic film?

The hero must grow, learn lessons, share the fruits of the quest. Have I changed the world? Learned responsibility? Found love? Am I sadder but wiser? Sadder but not wiser?

From earliest childhood I felt myself to be alone, an alien – a stranger. Fearful specters pursued me, and I could not escape. And now? In the nightfall of eccentric convictions, those closest to me in waking life -- wife, sons, parents, friends -- become inexplicably undependable. "They" are all really "me."

I am used to this feeling of strangeness – but that's not entirely it. Something else is different. The alienation that for so long set me apart from the waking world isolates me from my inner self.

The shoreline has shifted, cutting me off from the mainland. I am alone.

#

I have a confession to make, a secret fear to share: Perhaps I am Clamence.

What's that? Why, Jean-Baptiste Clamence is none other than the unfortunate protagonist of Camus' "The Fall," the very story I have been referencing so casually as the pattern for my epic film. Clamence the expatriate -- Clamence in perpetual flight from the cry which sounded over the Seine years before, a cry that never ceases.

"Don't wait for the Last Judgment," he tells his confessor. "It takes place every day."

This is so unfair. After all, I had only selected that book because I hoped you – a lawyer, a person of education and intelligence – would think me an intellectual. Now it holds me tightly in its grip, and I must face the fear, ask myself the terrible question: Is it possible I was a bit too accurate in selecting this work? It is possible Clamence is a bit too perfect a fit. If only I could regain a few of the key dramatic moments, the chance to save the world without behaving as if I should be the Deity. Now I must start all over again.

Look – the porpoise is back. Isn't it beautiful? Let us enjoy a festive beverage here under the "Sun of a Beach" umbrella, admire the graceful curve of the dorsal fin. Now in this new age, we must all be about the epic film. We must all –

Oh, this is a terror. A bad dream for Tumbleweed Cowboy. One misstep, one slight mistake and – it is as I feared. The walls are bleeding again. Nazi paratroopers are landing in the surf and digging trenches in the blood-soaked sand. Tiny white translucent eggs have appeared on the back of my hand and are hatching into wolf spiders, which even now are proceeding to hungrily strip the flesh from my phalanges.

I am an odious being.

Where do I turn now? The face in the mirror belongs to an insect, a stranger. I have no power over him. He drives me where he will, regardless of my intent or desire. He compels me to be the keeper of a secret flame, one that at any moment might consume me. Or the world.

Even today, exiled on this island with my apocalyptic dreams against humanity, I am not sure what to say next, how to turn my experience into something of value to others.

What actions can I perform in the current intimidating planetary state of affairs, with my frail and meager influence? To worship the big picture, to hope of saving the world – this is dramatically praiseworthy. So why does it feel like I am headed for the tomb?

Why is it that the spirit of the sentient being so desperately desires to hold in its grip the idea of utter and irrevocable disaster? Why does it accept as true yet dread the concept of suffering inconceivable horror as a necessary prerequisite to acquiring the knowledge of totality? I should be ashamed to admit that I still wish for utter and irrevocable disaster, for the fire and brimstone. I want the moths and mold to consume the flag, the ivy to strangle the pulpit.

I still wish for the destruction of the venerated icon.

And yet – perhaps it is still not so bad. In a sense, there is an opportunity for salvation in the midst of this destruction. Picture me as a wayfarer in the rubble and ashes, a Jehovah-guided pilgrim traveling through a barren land, stumbling ahead toward the conclusion of time.

Pretty.

Could it be there is still a way? Could this be my destiny? Here's the concept: I cannot alter the path. I am not free. How can such a man, tormented with these self-imposed illusions and limitations, possibly speak of the voice of God? How can he defend himself as anything other than a traitor and a heretic?

He does it by starting all over again.

You gaze upon this process even now, the activity under way on the far shore. It is the ruins of the old aluminum plant, consumed by the fire and brimstone. The construction crews are laboring 24/7, transforming the raw ingredients into a four-star resort. At least, that's what the folks at the local convention and visitor's bureau think. But I know different. These workers are laying the foundations for the New Church. And I tell you they are building that same church in Japan and Norway and Pakistan -- all over the world. This is the home of the New Religion, the dwelling place of the eternal Son of God.

Like me, my New Religion is inexperienced, overly-romantic and inundated with spirit. The consequences of pursuing it are decidedly antiquated and loaded with spiritual and mythological imagery.

Picture me in a desert mountain range, and yet I am not anywhere near a desert. This should be the rolling, cedar-studded hills near Joe Pool Lake immediately west of Duncanville. The terrain looks like something out of a Georgia O'Keefe painting. Indeed, some of the natural features have been exaggerated by the addition of paint. So when I look at part of a nearby mountain it precisely resembles an O'Keefe painting.

I am standing next to a painting of an animal -- a bird or lizard -- Native American Indian in style. I have dreamed of these mountains before. They are a geographical anomaly of the Land of the Dead, breathtakingly beautiful, yet almost no one in the Dallas area knows about it. This is odd, because there is a paved trail with a bridge and an interpretive center. It is somehow part of or connected with the Wycliffe Bible Translators' center on Camp Wisdom Road on the western limits of Duncanville.

The interpretive center is midway on the trail, perhaps set into a cave in the mountains. I am there with my oldest son, and he has been working on a project in some children's class. I help him carry some of the things he received and/or made in class, including a cup and a T-shirt. Somewhere in all of this I am with Jack Bryson; we talk about going to get a beer.

Now the sun is on the horizon, and I am looking at the mountains with Allison. We see a mysterious phenomenon which I am told happens here every day. The last rays of the setting sun sweep across the mountains like a search light, then fade into night. Again, I think how much this landscape looks like a painting, not reality. I look at another part of the mountains, high on a peak, and see a city or castle. Light flashes across it, too. Perhaps it is lightening. Very beautiful.

I comment to Allison that I never realized all of the beautiful paintings I've ever seen were really just exact photorealistic representations of reality.

"The artists simply go to a place where reality is otherworldly beautiful," I say.

#

My darling muse. You are an extraordinarily ethereal creature. You are not oriented to the waking world – and not spoiled by it, either. You come to me rather late in life, an occasion of enormous energy and authority. You come not merely as an alteration to the world, but a conversion of it. The outcome is incontestable, overpoweringly authentic and present: A very internalized and distant virgin muse abruptly appears. She is you. But no, that cannot be true. This muse, she is not you, LeAnn (even though I must admit that I did originally and passionately wish to cast you in the role). She is the Spirit of the World. This spirit may often seem out of contact and imaginary, but there is no denying it.

The Spirit of the World is unquestionably genuine.

Do you not see it? Here's a concept: You come with me! We were once happy together, were we not? Membrane almost touching membrane, frustratingly pleasuring one another in the back seat of the Cutlass. It can be that way still, me bending you over in the hot shower, penetrating your membranes with my DNA delivery organ, expelling my ectoplasm inside you, filling you with my spirit.

I shall employ Morel's invention to convert us into celluloid, into a cinematic fiction of anonymous creatures projected eternally onto the 50-foot drive-in movie screen of the present tense, dead or living no one can say with certainty. In this eternal cinema I am inside you, where I advance once again through the endless hallways, meeting rooms and colonnades of the mind, the form of this mournful mansion from an earlier time. This vast and magnificent mansion where hallways without end follow upon hallways. Mute, deserted, enveloped in baroque embellishments, mahogany veneer, Venetian plaster, gold-leafed frames, Carrara marble, dark glass, obscure illustrations, Romanesque columns…

In this story, you have always been my one true love. You can be to me as the Muse is to the world. I have seen it, in my dreams. It could be true. Together we will save the world, beginning with the spiritual liberation of the flesh-coated machine men.

#

Somehow all of the pushbutton people of the world have gone the way that leads to death. They are traveling with NAGUO, which has returned to the El Camino Extraterrestre (aka Texas 114) to investigate the little township of Strangers Rest. ... D/FW "ALIENPLEX" REVEALED!

The Dallas/Fort Worth area is proof positive that the UFO/military conspiracy is alive and well. Called the "Alienplex," this region of shadowy extraterrestrial schemes stretches from Fort Worth to Aurora to Duncanville – the very heart of what many North Texans still fondly call the Metroplex. The first plot point of this mysterious "Alien Triangle" appeared in 1897, when a flying saucer crashed a few miles north of Fort Worth in the little farm town of Aurora. A newspaper report indicated that the pilot – a Martian – died on impact. The remains were buried in Aurora Cemetery, and the spaceship is even mentioned on a Texas Historical Marker near the cemetery gate. However, the actual tombstone was quickly removed in the 1970s by the government as part of its standard UFO cover up procedures.

In 1997, UFO researcher Jim Hickman made a "field investigation" of Aurora. He began his report with the totally objective observation that Aurora is on the "Alien Highway" (aka Texas 114).

Kudos to Jim! Here at the Armageddon Drive-in, we are equally committed to objectivity. During Jim's painstaking dashboard survey of the town he uncovered evidence of an old military base with airstrip, circa 1940s. "Why would the military want to have a base in Aurora? I asked myself... back in the '40's?" Hmmm. Yes Jim, why? Why would the military want to establish a new airfield at the very time it was trying to win World War II? So we did a bit of investigating of our own.

Federal government records list the Aurora installation as Rhome Marine Corps Outlying Landing Field. Know what it was? A "glider base" (see adjacent National Archive photo, circa 1943). Come on now. Do they really expect us to believe that? At a time when the Nazis were using V-2 rockets to bring down alien spacecraft for use in their war effort the best cover story FDR and the Illuminati could cook up was gliders? Of course, Jim and the staff of the Armageddon Drive-in were not thrown off the scent of the Alien Highway by this ludicrous fabrication.

We also credit Jim with locating Triangle Point No. 2 of the "Alienplex." He noted in his report that in 1947, the Roswell crash debris was flown directly to Carswell AFB in Fort Worth – just 12 miles from Aurora. "Coincidence? I don't think so. Could the military have had an 'alien' recovery base set up and running in Aurora from clear back at the time of the 1897 crash?"

And finally, Triangle Point No. 3 – the "Alienplex" emerged fully formed in 1957 when a UFO was picked up by the big radar installation at the Nike missile base in Duncanville, which is just a few miles south of Dallas on Interstate 20 (aka the "Extraterrestrial Freeway"). The story is even part of the Air Force's "Project Blue Book" (case file No. 10073, National Archives and Record Administration).

In case you need further proof, keep in mind that the Duncanville area is a well-known gathering place for extraterrestrials. In 1994, a Duncanville man sitting in his backyard saw three UFOs that resembled "the motor part of a Hunter Ceiling Fan." The man believed that the "Naval Air Station in Grand Prairie, scrambled the fighters to intercept, but the saucers broke off." Hmmm. Yes, we must conclude the military was in on that one, too. And in 1996, two boys spotted a triangular UFO in Cedar Hill, a little town just south of Duncanville on Highway 67 (aka the "UFO Throughway"). Minutes later, this craft was joined by two more triangular UFOs. Talk about an "Alien Triangle!"

Today there are no remaining artifacts of the Nike missile base, which was closed in 1970. But we have gained important historical insights from Mark Leach, a former resident of this town. He writes: "As a boy growing up in Duncanville in the 1960s and 1970s, I thoroughly explored the old Nike missile base. I investigated its many abandoned structures, including the strange black building that once housed the radar dish and related equipment. During one of my many field investigations, I noticed that the old WWII-era barracks all had raised foundations with generous crawl spaces. I quickly reached an inescapable conclusion: this would be a great place to bury a dead space alien."

Coincidence? We don't think so. Consider Proof Point No. 1, the well-known 1957 RB-47 surveillance case. An airliner? In an eye! We both said, wow, at distance of well over 700 feet on a perfectly clear and chilly night. We saw extraterrestrials. In 1994, a Duncanville man spotted a single file formation or a satellite. And then it just stopped suddenly. And the man's wife spoke. Time to decorate the house? No. "I need a house coat," she repeated and went inside. She returned about an hour later with news of a "Special Report" that a television crew was in route to the area known as the Aurora installation and Rhome Marine. Three F-18 were observed giving pursuit. It ended on channel 4, the anchor said. Yes Adolfo, why? Why would the military want the satellite? Then it just stopped suddenly. This got me to noticing the objects in a V-shaped cluster. Thoughts of doubt. And all the while I'm thinking "hey, are we going there with the aliens?"

Because they were not from this world.

Proof Point No. 2 was the mysterious explosion people reported at the old Nike missile base. I am thinking "Wow, they don't have to hear to know." Anyone could see the F-18 giving pursuit. It is listed in the Project. I am describing it to her on the way back outside, where she is probably reluctant to talk about it. The TV anchor described it as an egg-shaped red orb, traveling its original course. I ran inside the speed during a period of about a minute. My wife returned. I am describing to her the beautiful stars and I notice a bright object myself. Could it be the Space Shuttle? A v-shaped double aerial clock and the cases associated with the Duncanville incident are listed in the Project Blue Book files, the scent of the Alien Highway filling the air. A mysterious large explosion observed in the southern air. At this point they made an elbow turn, and I knew the aliens were still alive and well. Called minutes. I said agreed! No more than the very time it was trying to intercept the saucers. When they got it their actions were clearly warranted for they would be back real close. They went to where investigators concluded that they had tracked an unidentified object for one minute. It almost seemed translucent, but not. The man kept to his backyard and saw the three F-18s trying to win the world, their sonic footprints shaking the ground like a mini earthquake. They never again had a surveillance aircraft case like that!

Let's talk about some of the other documented paranormal phenomenon. Duncanville is the location of the actual tombstone for dead aliens. When you're in the right spot the marker quickly moves or looks unusual. That's how you know. I said you watch closely. Is there any doubt that you have found The Alien Muse? She got my attention. She then began to inspire the aerial clock researcher Aldofo Morel, who left his underground lab in Strangers Rest and made a beeline for Southern Dallas County and that news, dim for a few seconds but not forgotten, of the aerial clock spotted at around 800 feet. The follow-up information indicated ever faster rates of speed. The operators at the Duncanville Air Force Station clocked it moving forward at about 900 feet in Fort Worth – just 12 miles from the very time it was story that was even part of the Air Force's 2000 project. One of the most important points again. The project researchers write: "Just as the Duncanville man decided to watch the news at 10 pm, the clock was poised to fall out of the North Texas sky."

I still fondly recall that night. Yes, spaceships from outside our place for extraterrestrials. In 1994, on the Alien Highway, the saucers were regrouping. The unusually long hot summer made a fast turn to the North, where it joined with the aerial clock. The well-known gathering place for extraterrestrials is an object in the sky, a time-travel mechanism known as God's divine pocket watch. This is a place where the Insane Forces of Darkness can be found drinking bourbon in the ruins of the old church near Fort Jesup.

The late morning light of the Son of the Deity streams through the broken shards of stained glass, reminding them of a Sunday morning from childhood – a morning that may or may not have actually occurred. It is hard to recall events from that long ago. The Insane Forces of Darkness are old now. They pass their days drinking bourbon in the ruined church and taking little cat naps in the rotting pews. Ah, but back in the day!

Years ago it was nothing to cut off his DNA delivery organs and grow three new ones in its place. It was a simple matter to cause the Venerated Icon to actually topple from the highest spire of the Seminary, smashing into a million pieces at the feet of conventional theologians – without lifting a finger. They did it with nothing more than his PRESENCE! But no more. The old church is in ruins. The front wall is missing, the basement flooded, the type in the pew Bibles too small and faded to read. Soon it will all be gone.

"How old is he now?"

"What? Oh. One hundred and seven – last May."

"Bull hockey. He's eighty three."

"So what? What I want to know is when he is going to sleep?"

"He's asleep right now!"

"No, he's napping. He'll be up again in minutes. He won't get anywhere near a R.E.M. cycle."

"He hardly dreams anymore at all."

It is true. Anymore, he sleeps maybe three hours a night. And that is usually fitful, drifting in and out of consciousness. What little dreaming he does is brief and therefore wholly unsatisfying to the

Insane Forces of Darkness. They want to TAKE ACTION. The problem iss agreeing on exactly what form that action should take.

"Let's make a pact. No more children or puppy dogs."

"I agree. How about the 22-year-old administrative assistant with the big boobs and the tight – "

"Oh, no you don't."

"What's wrong with a little –"

"For the love of God!"

"I swear, if you bring her out one more time I will have grandma in a moldy burial shroud crawling up his leg with a butcher knife in her teeth."

It is a sad, old man kind of argument. Not at all worthy of their great history. Because back in the day, The Insane Forces of Darkness were without equal.

For instance, there was the time they had him plant a tree that found magic water, which allowed it to grow so tall it pierced a roof and solved a mystery.

Another time they had him run for Congress, then get hurt in line of duty. And while he was unconscious, his wife ran in his place. She made a fool of herself, of course, so he saved the day – a hero!

A bat chased him and some desperate young people who applied for jobs at a summer camp. They knew nothing about wood lore but pretended, each one.

As a bill collector, he undertook to collect a ruined man's debts. They proved to be moral as well as financial.

He and widely separated members of his family inherited a house and had to live there together.

His wife fell in love with a wax dummy, who turned out to be him.

His father taught him to gamble on a special machine; later he unconsciously lost his wife on it.

At a dinner party, he was frightened by living marionettes who kissed and plotted murder.

He was a moving-picture magnate who was shipwrecked on a desert island with nothing but two dozen cans of film.

He drove over neighborhood rooftops on a bet.

His hearing became so sensitive he could hear radio. A beautiful woman got him out of the insane asylum to use him in her moneymaking schemes.

The Insane Forces of Darkness amazed themselves with their incredible creations.

"Where do we get it?" they asked one another, celebrating and marveling at their skill. "It's wonderful, like something Fitzgerald might write!"

But no more. Now all The Insane Forces of Darkness can agree on is the final creation: A Funeral. His own ashes keep blowing in his eyes. Everything is over by 6 and nothing remains but a small man to mark the spot. There are no flowers requested or offered. The corpse stirs faintly during the evening but otherwise the scene is one of utter quietude.

The Insane Forces of Darkness are in perfect agreement. That's the way the world will end for Mark Leach.

But that's probably not true. No, it's not true.

No death in vain. It doesn't find a way or seem to stop. Accompanied by a sense of me, I am determined that it is time to flip this robot onto its home. They have a swimming pool, but it's in a bad way. We'll have to pay for the damages. Look at the neighbor's home in ruins. And now, an incoming cicadan communication from the far side of the galaxy:

"We are filming the story now, controlling the 1920s camera with the brass spring and flesh-coated aperature. We start with a long shot, then pan all of heaven. We shoot the golden coranoa, the genetically amplified interstate of the mind. A narrator explains what has occurred. There is a fragment of dialogue. "I am my roommate and I look outside. We are sliding, colliding ahead. I put on the brakes, but I can't see anything. I realize somehow that all of the flesh-coated machine men have gone the way that leads to death. It is a journey through a cacophony of incomprehensible voices." Fade to the voices… *the man believed that heart of what many hear… North of further proof we keep the theory of what happened.. break in on regular programming ifit is above the other two … and believed that the Naval Air Station is just a few miles via satellite, but it was moving at a back out speed with me and a triangle-shaped entity. It was followed by 8 to 10 coincidences. Maybe? I don't think so … she said to please stay out of the Simi circular path to about 3,000 feet where I will be looking up at all of the pilot minds – a Martian just 12 miles from the reports of alleged paranormal phenomenon. Duncanville objects were observed moving silently and fast. Of course, Adolfo and the staff will watch the northern sky and I'll watch it too and conclude the military that was alive on Oct. 23, 1994, at the military place that wants to establish a new Alien Muse …She said no the aerial clock/military conspiracy is alive and The objects suddenly aligned in a triangular formation critics and investigators, who claim that this by critics and investigators, who claim that information was ever released. On actually an ordinary jet airliner. However, these official observed giving pursuit with afterburners. Later, a local in 1897, when a the paper the next day. I few minutes. I said agreed! No more than mentioned on a Texas Historical Marker her and thought she do you know what in Duncanville received reports of an unidentified would be back on. We crouch for a second. I am really expect us to know that we can longer be seen, that we can see the underside of the thing and thinking hey, the thinkingn that leads to you going wild for the looks of the unusual. I said you watch proof, keep in mind a large explosion in the object for a distance thoroughly explored the old reported an unidentified object, west at an estimated raised foundations with generous crawl pointing to the Northwest and 17, 1957, when an Air Force Boeing Stratojet went back inside the house and discussed it on and thinking about how I was going hot summer this year raised back up from the about 35 minutes. The first blink off an eye, it would reappear. It did, report makes RB-47 one of the and said in stereo, do you this ludicrous fabrication. and 1970s, I thoroughly explored the old Nike the West to the East slow I thought it would fall out of be back on later was pursued while flying paranormal phenomenon Duncanville is objectivity. During Adolfo's painstaking dashboard survey of spacecraft for use in their war the news at 10pm to see if they 35 minutes. The first object compelling documented cases supporting the reality of radar operators at the Duncanville Air Pow Wow, at the same time, while out The jet was pursued while flying from Mississippi, files, where investigators concluded that the aerial clock a local television station broadcast news of full military running lights above the other 2 and Oct. 23, 1994, at 8:30 PM pilot – a Martian case you need further proof, thrown off the scent of the new airfield at the very time it was quickly removed in the On Oct. 2, 1999, four unidentified to keep up which created reality of aerial clocks. This aerial clock report also part of its standard Field. Know what it was? A "glider for a few seconds satellite, but was moving at a ever released. On Oct. beautiful stars and I absolute precision. As they The Alien Muse? She said no doubt, they were not in Aurora from clear it. I have my theory of an estimated 2,160 m.p.h. motor part of a larger, star-like object followed. gained important historical insights from and to objectivity. During Adolfo's Texas Historical Marker near the cemetery gate. Alien." Coincidence? We Marine Corps Outlying Landing Field. Know what it 5 seconds later as we later, this craft was to have a clue of what they or apartment knew to be true. At this point they made no looks, you know, I mean the 'you' that is so translucent, but not. Keep reported that they had picked It is a fighter jet Know what it was? A "glider base" on the "Alien Highway" standard aerial clock cover up procedures. In 1997, aerial clock researcher Aldofo Morel Aurora installation as Rhome Marine Corps Outlying the Duncanville Air Force Station. The Point No. 2 of the "Alienplex." He in his report that in 1947, the early 1950s and continue into the 2000s. Metroplex. The first plot point lunches at the other, mouth open, adrenaline pumping. It attained an estimated 2,160 speed, this well-known 1957 RB-47 surveillance aircraft case. I spotted a triangular aerial clock flashing in second time.* New scene. The protagonist appears and speaks his first line. 'So the muse and myself did a bit of investigating, our membranes and minds only inches apart.'"

#

Elmo: Oh my. That was rather –

Charlie: Stupid.

Elmo: Stupid and creepy.

Charlie: And the film's effect – bomb. That's the ticket. It leaves everything to cliché. We'll move up that way, into the known. In ancient times, men seemed to be right. A direct encounter with a specially prepared fish (i.e., tell Joseph to take Mary to a hotel with no rooms). This is your time to freely incorporate the unconscious, a figurative land of humility.

Elmo: Dead is bad. Someday, everyone will look like car boom fatalities. Bent, but a nightmare of three, an angle of the storied boredom of genius, personified by childhood. What of the idea of what happens a day away from Christendom? The fish will bring him back. Pretty?

Charlie: Awful. It's a recipe for the stale. Christendom dreams, freely incorporating the unexplained halves and a nonpareil feast of visual storytelling brings me. Dreams are radio transmissions from the unknown Deity. I simultaneously accept that the basement slumber incorporates this one in an overgrown cemetery of the unconscious. I reveal myself in a message.

Elmo: What is this 'I' stuff? This is not your film festival. This is Mark Leach's night.

Charlie: And it is not a funny night, this final period of darkness before the dawn of the End of the World. Boring, see? Help me help him save the picture. It is in me.

Elmo: Hey, I've got a few ideas, too. Boom! Freud meets The Organized Bad Guys. The slapstick blast of low brow dream-making is now Hollywood bound, suffering in the idea. Slowly, gently, turn the corners to an army of scum-sucking Barneys. They have written my life to be funny, of the U.S. dead that God felt compelled to tell. I have found it useful to no longer deny the world fish (i.e., a visual rumor of the Son of the Deity).

Charlie: Interesting. A direct encounter with prayerful thought. Hermaphroditus as the prototype for the 21st century prophet.

Elmo: Now you're talking. Go lesbian, the blind seducing this terrified, delighted, languid to be.

Charlie: Welcome to Mark's island. Pull up a deck chair, help yourself to the tanning oil. Don't trouble yourself about the brain crabs – they're gone. The crabs and the guards and the porpoise with the elegant dorsal fin – all gone, edited away with all the memories, deities and ghosts of the old, dead age.

Elmo: Now the issue is one of survival. We have reached the conclusion of time, the end of rational man. This is the end of history, the swagger of science, the "uber" victories over space and linear time. This is the end of the Age of the Deity. We were warned of judgment. The ancient tales of the withdrawal of the City of the Deity are true. It's come now. This is the Noble Misfortune, the weeping and gnashing of teeth. The Deity has withdrawn. The evil dead are emerging from the lagoon of flames, leaving us to our own devices. Flesh-coated clocks and artificial deities on the march. Horrifying effects. Scary times.

Charlie: Perhaps – could it be? There is a possibility that Buckstop's plan for world domination is already realized, and he's now taken over the Exogrid and disseminated psychotropic compounds through the global water supply. After all, the dream-carrying ballistic missile did fragment. The world has gone completely mad. But for some reason, Mark is as yet unaffected – the last sane man. It is the only explanation for the insanity I see around us. Mark is the new Messiah, purified in the blue alcohol flames of the dream-carrying missile and called upon by the Deity to lead His people back from the edge of insanity and to the new promised land.

Elmo: Could it be true? Is he actually the two-bodied son of the deity (aka Jesus Christ II)? Thanks to the Jewell Effect, we shall soon find out. Together we will travel through space and time, looking back to the last Saturday night of youth and forward 2,000 years from now. We will travel through a world of tomorrow, a world of psychotropic weapons, a world of raging terror, a world of the undeclared Sacrament War, a world where Mark penetrates the membranes of his muse and fills her spirit with warm globs of His holy ectoplasm. A world where every citizen is either a human-insect hybrid or a flesh-coated robot. And maybe dead.

Charlie: Yes, it could be true. Picture him humping her for the borrowed inspiration from a pseudo-documentary. "Singing monkey!" shouts his own Cuba, then destroys it all. Now his world is dead, a land of creatures who glisten in a walk conducted on knuckles.

Elmo: Enough Darwin. Instead, let us recall the rotting flag and find "Marienbad My Love With Mango Extracts" to be the most evil film ever. Even the movie world in these dreams is dead, a world mystery without a world. Or a mystery. People getting together for a laugh in a tub of buttered DNA.

Charlie: Ooooh. What flesh-coated clock spring winds up that idea?

Elmo: The end dream, a flag, the Church.

Charlie: Enough. Let's buy cool sunglasses, pile into the Cutlass, zoom through a dream cinema of Piney Woods darkness. People are enraged, and yet Mark could not look to the tales of Joseph and Daniel for a story about life. That's because his life is dead and his world a mutation, drowning in the flooded basement. The nightmare of three hours of dreary End of the World underwater -- well, perhaps I shouldn't say more.

Elmo: Agreed. This is a god-awful dream.

Elmo: Yes, but by design. Claw hammer, broken plastic and semiconductors, river of violence, a mean-spirited spousal corpse at the end of a classy full frontal "no" of an '80s nightmare. It's a story of rage.

Charlie: The story has its own image and is equivalent with the Deity. The goal is to become perfect, to control and make ourselves carefree – especially about money, again and again. And for those of us that ego would eat, I offer the helpless rage of one who has attempted to help you forget your rage.

Elmo: And it was out of that perfection of rage that we saw failures that constantly informed us to become perfect. But perfect in suggestion is not food but fluoride.

Charlie: (Uncontrolled laughter)

Elmo: Stop laughing, damn you. I take my mental hygiene seriously. I think after brushing, rage is defeated. The world wins over our achievement.

Charlie: (More laughter)

Elmo: Listen up, damn you all to hell. This information can help you. Dental psychiatry. It is about our teeth, the rage – the fluoride. Our own human utter failure would deify anger, and it makes us go the way of a childish character.

Charlie: You know, maybe it's the only way we fail. Profound rage equals outward success. To me, depression is the eye to hopelessness, to a way to transcend our humanity. It is this depression and our inner critic that informs us.

Elmo: Exactly. Calcium fluoride makes knowledge – it makes this to transcend the anger, to go the way of our humanity. We attempt to search the ego precisely for the cure for what is ailing us. Buckstop's toothpaste with Skinalicious9, also known as Liquid Jesus, is about that search. We fail and fall, repeatedly, then through this psychiatric dentifrice we can at last secure our deliverance.

Charlie: Four out of five dental psychiatrists suggest toothpaste for their depressed patients.

Elmo: I suggest a recast myth. Action, prayerful thought, bludgeoning of a pair of hot lacy ectoplasm-soaked underwear and an inverted nipple that can only complain of –

Charlie: Careful now. You are god awful for engaging in such a sick eroto-slasher flick. A hammer demon cannot be the Deity.

Elmo: Careful yourself. And enough talking. Time you helped it along with a little bend-over action. My well-oiled cam is ready to expel warm globs of ectoplasm into a willing orifice.

Charlie: Thanks for the offer, but I prefer to shower alone.

Death to Anna Enruckus and the New York Agenda.

Anna Enruckus has destroyed me. Her promise to write about my Vision, my incredible revelation, the most important story of the modern world, dreams of the end of an age – all a lie. Can you believe it? A newspaper reporter who lies!

Turns out she wasn't working on a story about Incredible Revelations at all. This is an expose on onbeam abuse. Pornography. The New York Agenda says I am a purveyor of porn.

Allison has already called. I pretended to be out so she'd have to leave a message. But she does not sound entirely displeased: "I always knew you were twisted, but I never expected to actually read about it in print. My parents are appalled, maybe because I told them how much I like a well-oiled cam in the hot shower. Mother's face went pale. She and daddy refuse to even talk about it. First time they shut up since we got here. It's great! Call me!"

Anna even gave me my own sidebar: "A Roman Holiday: The Misogynic, Homophobic and AntiSemitic Movie Dreams of Mark Leach."

#

Dream No. 1

Manifest Content: I am watching a movie, but I'm in the movie, too. The scene involves dangerous men, bad guys. I am there with a girl. We are all inside a gas station. The woman who owns it is involved with someone's boyfriend. Details are unclear, but it's clearly sexual. The bad guys like this.

There is red graffiti on the walls, like cave drawings. One of the pictures makes me think of some piece of primitive phallic art.

I identify the bad guys as a threat to the girl. We have a discussion in which I point out to them the potential for police involvement. But I tell them not to worry about the girl. She'll be no problem for them.

"If necessary, I'll cut off her head," I say.

This satisfies the bad guys, who immediately leave. But the girl is not happy about the decapitation talk.

"I'm sorry if it disturbed you," I say, explaining that it was just my attempt to identify with - and thereby protect us from - the bad men.

"That's the way you have to deal with these Dionysian cults," I add.

Analysis (Mimi Ottoplaytor, dental psychiatrist, University of Pintle Minaness Southwest Medical School): "We call this syndrome the Female Castrato. Like many classic misogynists, Mark Leach clearly wishes to deny women their identity as rational individuals. So in his dreams he attempts to elevate his own importance through the amputation of critical portions of women, specifically their intellect. Decapitation allows him to transform women into mere receptacles for his own primitive phallic drives. It is also possible he is an unrealized latent homosexual."

#

Dream No. 2

Manifest Content: I am a Secret Service agent, waiting outside a hotel for the arrival of an important dignitary. I am providing covert security, dressed in plain clothes to blend in with the crowd. We all stand curbside, leaning into the street to see if the motorcade is approaching. I lift up the lapel of my overcoat and speak into a hidden microphone. Of course, this is noticed by at least one person in the crowd, so I realize I have blown my cover. I am no longer covert.

Then I am watching a movie -- and I am IN the movie. The protagonist (me) is a rich man in his mansion. I am in a crimson smoking jacket, holding a drink in a highball glass. A bad guy has broken in. He is there to rob and kidnap me. But he does not manhandle me or tie me up. I am free to move about. So as we are standing together, I surreptitiously punch an emergency code into an alarm panel, a row of 4 round buttons set into a cut stone wall. The bad guy doesn't notice what I've done, nor is he alerted. This is a silent alarm.

Then we descend a set of ornate stairs. On a landing midway down the staircase there is a little table with a phone, which is ringing. I answer and as the person talks (I don't know what they are saying) I begin talking very fast.

"Call the police, I am being robbed," I say, then hang up.

The bad guy looks at me in disbelief, but I just laugh it off.

"It was just a recording," I explain.

We walk a short distance on this lower floor, perhaps 20 feet, then he suddenly knocks me down and grabs me from behind. He is clearly unhappy about the phone incident. He wraps his legs around me, and I realize he is going to attempt anal sex. I cry out in panic.

"No, no! I have lots of money, we can buy you a beautiful woman."

Then, like a movie, the scene cuts to a couple of English detectives, no doubt from Scotland Yard. Now I am only a viewer, and the rich man and bad guy are not present.

The detectives stand in front of a desk, which may be in their offices or somewhere else. One detective is showing evidence to the other. It is a crude drawing, black on white paper, almost like a woodcut. It is a list of items to take on a trip. The drawing depicts shorts and a T-shirt, surrounded by roughly a dozen objects that I as the viewer instantly recognize as condoms. I realize with horror that the bad guy has kidnapped the rich man and abducted him for some sort of cross-country sex trip in which he will use the condoms during his anal rape of the rich man.

But the detectives don't understand this yet. They only know the rich man is missing. The accepted explanation is that he has left voluntarily with the bad guy on a trip, but they are still checking it out. The first detective tries to decipher the drawing.

"I believe it is a sort of sock that printers use to keep their ink pens in," he says.

He is groping about for the proper word, but it won't come to him.

Analysis (Peter MacArire, author of "The Transsexual Narcissist: Men Who Love Themselves Too Much"): "This is clearly a classic case of projection. Mark Leach's dream mind starts out casting him in the role of the macho hero, the Secret Service agent, but this façade quickly falls away as he reveals his true hidden desire to go on a homosexual road trip with a stranger – that is to say his unknown 'self' - who penetrates him with printer's ink, thereby 'rewriting' himself as a passive love toy of his own misguided passions."

#

Dream No. 3

Manifest Content: It appears that my wife's house hunting activities have finally borne fruit, for I find that we have purchased a new home.

I study a room that I understand was a holy place for the former owner, a Jewish man of some local importance. There is an exposed wooden beam overhead. It is clear from several rough, unpainted patches that decorative pieces have been removed, leaving a piece of raw, unadorned lumber.

I am talking loudly to someone about the house, but then we realize that the family of the former owner is outside the open window and can hear our conversation. The former owner recently died. I look out the window and see a billboard that has something to do with this man. Perhaps he was a businessman.

Meanwhile, I remember that I own a Ford Model A. I had forgotten about it and haven't driven it in a long time. What a thing to forget! So at once I decide to start it up, drive it again. It is a fun vehicle, and this will be like getting something new for free. It has really been that long.

I go to look in the garage, wondering how I could have been blind to its presence all this time. But it is not there. The garage is now furnished as our bedroom. Then I remember that the car is still in the detached garage at my parent's former house in Duncanville.

Although my parents sold this house years ago, I arrive to find a family gathering in progress. The car is still the garage, parked backwards just as I remember it.

To get into the car, I must go through a contortionist's route, squeezing past the floor-mounted gearshift and even unhooking a black radiator hose that comes up through the floor into the passenger compartment. Once I get to the seat, though, my dad steps in with no trouble. He sits at the wheel.

He drives us out of the garage and idles in the driveway. The car is a convertible and the top is down, so we have a big view of the world. He looks at the dashboard and taps at a small, three-digit gauge.

"I've been working on this, but I'm still not getting cool air out of any of the cylinders," he says.

I assume he is referring to air conditioning, and I am amazed to hear that such an old car even has AC. But I think again of the radiator hose, and I seem to know there is not enough water. Perhaps the gauge refers to the engine coolant system, not the AC. At any rate, dad explains this is not actually a problem. For this particular vehicle, it is normal.

“For some reason, the car just doesn't hold water” he explains.

But the car is running, so we take off. We come to a traffic light at a rural highway. As we wait for the light to change, dad comments that the car is running "cool and dry." He has tried to fix it, even looked up some information in a repair manual. But he hasn't been able to change it.

The light turns green and we start up, but a car is coming toward us in our lane. I let out a cry of alarm, but dad is not concerned. He maintains his course, and the other car gets out of our way.

We cross the highway, which looks a lot like the old intersection of Texas 114 and Frederiksbad Street in Strangers Rest, before the highway was modernized. This is Bonnie and Clyde country, just a few miles west of the spot on Texas 114 where they killed a highway patrolman on Easter Sunday 1933.

I realize that our car has now become an old pickup, vintage '50s Ford, suggestive of one my father restored when I was a boy. That was a magical vehicle; the moon followed you wherever you went.

This truck is not magical or restored. It is old with faded, rust-stained paint. A new truck pulls up beside us. It is filled with teenage boys.

"The sheriff won't be around tonight," one of them tells us, "so everyone is looking forward to a fun night."

It is a Saturday. Dad laughs.

"This is sure to be a lively evening," he says.

We soon come to a stop, and we are in the Piney Woods in Louisiana. It is Fort Jesup, and we are at the home of an uncle who lives near the old Leach family homestead. Several people are busy, burning mounds of pine needles and branches. There are piles of logs. I don't see my uncle's trailer in what I know is its usual place. Apparently, it has been moved.

While the pine burners work, we sit on the opposite side of the road and visit with family, including my wife and our boys. Several children are carrying long sticks, poking at various objects as kids like to do. This worries me; someone will be hurt. My youngest son is carrying a very long stick, maybe 8 or 10 feet. This stick branches at the end into a V - sort of a two-pronged pitchfork

"Put that down," I tell him. "You'll poke somebody's eyes out."

And in fact, the two tips of the V are the proper distance apart for such an accident to occur. My mother is with us, too, and she suddenly jerks to life in a panic.

"Mark, I think I hear someone stealing your car."

But when I look up I see that it is only a group of passers by -- soldiers by the looks of them. And time travelers. This is not so strange. During the Second Earthly Conflict, thousands of soldiers engaged in training maneuvers in this very area.

So I laugh at her. Then we roll around on the ground together, wrestling as if I am still her little boy. This sort of conduct is totally out of character for us. Strangely, though, she does not mind that I am laughing at her. She thinks it is funny, too, and is not the least bit angry with me.

Analysis (Sestron Amorey, M.D., executive director of the California Dionysian Analysts Cooperative): "The anti-Semitism in this dream is noteworthy; however, I am primarily interested in the reference to the old jalopy running 'cool and dry.' This corresponds to the ancient Greek description of the black bile humor called melancholy. Mark Leach sees himself as the car, a vehicle in which others travel and control his movements. He feels unresolved issues with a father who cannot get the car to run at the proper temperature (i.e., a son who does not operate at the proper psychological temperament). And clearly Mark has unresolved mother attachment issues in the form of a panic-imparting anima image. We see an interesting contrast between Mark as conventional adult and as the 'puer eternus,' playing with his mother (i.e., a mamma's boy) in close proximity to Second Earthly Conflict soldiers (i.e., real men). He is probably an unrealized latent homosexual."

#

I arrive in downtown Strangers Rest amid swirling rumors that Willie Nelson will be making a guest appearance on Cowboy Roy's Radio Ranch.

"Imagine it, Willie singing right here on Frederiksbad Street," the mayor says. He collects my $3 for parking and directs me to the far end of the vacant lot behind city hall, where I park next to a weed-choked stack of rusted iron pipes.

Tina arrives behind me, but drives past the mayor and is stopped by the constable at the barricaded intersection in front of the old saloon. She rolls down her window, and I can see from her frustrated gesturing that she is having no luck convincing him to let her pass. Watching him wave through a satellite dish-topped van marked with radio station call letters does not appear to improve her disposition, either. Toots leaves his post to investigate.

"I live on that street," she complains. "I have a right to go to my own home."

"Darlin', nobody's keeping you out of your little apartment," the mayor says. "We're just keeping out your car."

"It's not fair."

"Even if we let you past the barricade it wouldn't do you no good. The cafe parking lot's been requisitioned for the fair. Can't have a celebration in Texas without a fair, you know. But you can park right over next to Mark in the press lot."

Tina silently fumed as she handed $3 to Toots, then kicked up a little cloud of dust as she rolled across the vacant lot.

"So, Willie Nelson is really coming here?" I ask.

"Can you imagine it?" Toots marvels. "Right there on stage with Roy. We could become the next Luckenbach. Take a look."

The mayor jerks a thumb over his shoulder, back toward the old rock saloon. A coat of white paint has been applied to the boarded up front door, where someone had spray painted "George Strait Rules!" a few years back.

"Looks nice," I say.

"We took care of that this morning. Roy said he wanted to give the old girl a facelift for the show."

The paint goes well with the fresh-cut lumber of the stage and the radio station banner that hangs from the cornice across the second floor windows, billowing softly in the twilight breeze: "Texas Saturday Night is made possible by a grant from Ozona Water, maker of Mentine toothpaste with Skinalicious9 in Original and Narcissism Control. Ozona Water. It comes from the sky."

"Course, Roy's right," the mayor continues. "We do need the town to look especially nice tonight. I have it on good authority we're going to have some big news announced from that stage. Say, and where is The Stranger? He said he was going to shoot some footage here tonight. I've got an idea for a promotional video. Where is he?"

I have been wondering the same thing. The Stranger disappeared after we rolled back into town about noon, and I haven't heard from him since.

"He'll be around," I assure him.

"Hope he gets here in time to film Willie," the mayor says. He returns to the parking lot to continue collecting parking fees.

#

Sticking out from behind the saloon is the back half of a 30-foot RV, borrowed from Dollar Bill Buckstop for use as the dressing room for Cowboy Roy and the band. Roy spots me through the rear window and waves me inside.

"No, Willie ain't coming here tonight, nor any other night," Roy insists. "Sure, we played on the same radio show once, but that was 30 years ago. He don't even know me."

"This feeling like old times yet?" I ask.

"I mean." Then Roy snaps his fingers. "Oh say, I almost forgot. I read about you in the paper."

A surge of panic. I had hoped the New York Agenda would not be well read in Strangers Rest. Perhaps he means another story, another paper.

"No, I mean that one with the three dreams," he clarifies. "They really gave you heck about the gays."

"Well, you know that's not exactly what I mean for people – "

"Oh, don't you worry about that. We don't make a fuss here in Strangers Rest."

"Yes, but I'm not a – what?"

"Don't get me wrong. If one of them homosexuals comes down this way we'll be polite, but that doesn't mean we have to love them. Homosexuals just aren't natural. Ain't that right, Jimmy?"

One of the Wramblin' Wranglers – a clarinet player recruited from NTSU in nearby Denton -- looks up from his instrument and gives Roy an uncomfortable stare.

"What's wrong, boy?" Roy asks.

"I'm gay," Jimmy says.

"Oh. Well then, you're fired."

Then Roy breaks into a fit of laughter. "Hell. I love ya, Jimmy, but you woodwinds are a squirrelly bunch."

A knock at the door; it's one of the technicians from the radio station.

"We're ready for a sound check, Mr. Thornton," he says.

Roy exits to converse with the technician; I head for the fair.

#

The first booth is an Ozona Water truck with a vinyl sun shade extended along one side, shrink wrapped cases of plastic bottles stacked in the trapezoid of gray the sun shade throws across the dead summer grass. Many of the townsfolk, I notice, have already received free bottled water from Dr. Adolfo Morel, who is feverishly distributing his wares. And yet, perhaps not so feverishly. For despite the heat and his black suit, Morel is not sweating. His porcelain albino skin isn't even flushed.

Morel watches over the townsfolk with silent insect eyes, pausing occasionally to jot a note in a spiral notepad, silently working his blood red mouth like a set of mandibles.

“Don’t drink it,” someone warns. I look up to see Father Byrd, bounding across the road toward the startled water drinkers. “That’s bottled rainwater, the worst. It’s like pouring gasoline on a fire, especially for women. The psychic disturbances may be cataclysmic. Just ask the so-called ‘doctor’ Morel.”

But Morel is gone, replaced by a bored looking young man in a white golf shirt with a little Ozona “cloud” and “Yo, Ozona Man!” stitched over his heart.

“Free water,” he announces, to no one in particular. “Get your free water.”

#

Walking through the fair. The constable whistles me over to the barricade.

"Thought you were going to be one of my deputies tonight," he says. "I got your uniform and shotgun waiting in the trunk."

"Oh, I guess I forgot to tell you. My editor nixed it. Said it would be a conflict of interest."

"That's what I figured. He was probably jealous I didn't ask him instead."

"Probably. He’d do it if he thought it would help him pick up girls in the parking lot at Bennigan’s.”

"You going to be around for a while?"

"Till closing time."

"Tonight may be the night for that other matter I told you about."

"The devil worshippers?"

"Nice, real nice. Maybe you could say it a little louder next time, put up a billboard or something."

“Sorry.”

"Anyway, I have it on good authority a bunch of them will be at the cemetery tonight.”

“No kidding.”

“And I'm going to grab them. You still want to come?"

I give him my home phone number.

#

I run into Reece Sloan, the editorial assistant from the bureau. He has been relieved of Coke machine-tending duties for the evening to roam the streets of Strangers Rest, collecting quotes and color to feed into a page one piece about the wagon train, which has left the airport and is now camped a few miles to the east. My job is to write up a couple of grafs on the concert.

"I have found the story of the evening," he tells me. "A couple of old ladies over there are getting ready to have a pony wedding."

"They're getting married on horseback?"

"No, it's a wedding of ponies. That is, two miniature ponies are getting hitched. So to speak."

"So to speak."

"They've got a pony veil, a pony tuxedo, pony flowers, pony bridesmaids and pony groomsmen. They even snagged a couple of cow dogs for the ring boy and flower girl."

Just then, one of the women calls out at Reece from across the large gravel lot, waving for him to join them.

"The pony wedding people seem to know you," I observe.

"They're paying me $100 to write up the wedding announcement. Can you believe it? And then they're going to run it in the paper. Display advertising. I asked them `do you know how much that's going to cost?' But they didn't care. They even hired a professional wedding photographer."

#

With the exception of the odd equine nuptials, the town fair is shaping up as a fairly typical Texas affair. There are a half dozen or so cheesy carnival rides, including the "Flying Jenny," a mule-powered contraption that takes its occupants on a slow, flat circle around a post every minute or so. And of course, there are arts and crafts.

Teddy bears are undoubtedly in vogue this season. Several vendors are hawking bluebonnet landscapes, some painted on canvas, most on scraps of weathered picket fencing and rusty tin roofing.

Now I come to a booth with a neon sign: "The destiny of epidermis - and everything under it." A local woman has purchased a franchisee of Rev-9, a cosmetic and plastic surgery undertaking. I flip through the corporate capabilities brochure, titled "Let Us Love You."

#

"Constant admiration, adulation -- you may secure the envy of others with our patented Rev-9 system. This kit contains four feelings of shame and worthlessness. The feelings often react within and between others, who can then be covertly threatened with personal apocalypse and manipulated to serve your needs. They may be the cyberneticists, man transformed to smoothly functioning feedback mechanism, shaping a technological imagery of religious and erotic feelings. Crucified via a vale of tears, the self-contained machine sanctified in the endless quest of personal meaning, too busy to notice the stench, the meaninglessness as the value. A clean, eternal balance of emotional control. Erotically curious, adorned with golden feet and a glass eye. Always young, always plastic, glass corneas containing photoelectric cells connected to gold-plated co-electrodes to optic nerves, the intimate membranes reproduced in polyethylene, pressure relays leading to a single silver cable linked to the correct register of the digital skull, cracking in the orgasm of virginity lost to the gear shift of her MG (the well oiled cam), an autoerotic machine and profane fulcrum for applying vulnerability's conquering force. The ever-ready erotic tool, deletion of tenderness and love."

#

The chili cook-off has attracted an assortment of a half dozen cooks, serious-looking folks hoping to amass enough points to qualify for the big championship cook-off in Terlingua in November.

There is even a domestic dispute.

I am looking over a booth of thoroughbred swings - old car tires gussied up to look like saddled horses - when I hear somewhere behind me the first murmured signs of consternation between the man and woman. It isn't until they raised their voices a bit that I realize the couple is Jack and Tina.

"Don't tell me to calm down," Tina says. "I don't have any calm left. I've used it all up on all your lies."

"People are starting to stare at the crazy girl," Jack warns. All smiles, he takes Tina by the arm and tries to lead her toward the stairs to her apartment. Bad move.

"Go fuck one of your strippers," she suggests. "Cause you're sure not going to do it anymore to me."

Tina spins on her heel and starts up the stairs, a nice exit - but not nice enough to escape the slings of the town gossips.

"Good riddance," one of the women from the pony wedding party comments. "That boy was bad news."

"I'll say," another woman remarks. "I know that Wells girl's crazy about him, but he ain't never going to marry her. Why buy the cow if the milk's free?"

Tina leans over the railing, glaring down upon the women. "And never call me a cow!" she says. She climbs the remaining steps to the landing and slams the door behind her.

"What a little bitch," Jack remarks happily, undisturbed by the spectacle.

"She didn't mean it," I say. "She had a bad experience earlier with a police barricade."

"Yeah, but she's still a bitch," he repeats. "And boring. Let's go to Plato's Palace."

"Can't. I'm on the clock."

"I thought they were going to fire you."

"Me too. But it turns out that I'm still less of a pain in the butt than the other reporters. 'Please don't quit,' my old boss said. He even said they may bring me back downtown."

#

OK, I have a confession: The "please-don't-quit" conversation never took place. Why? Because I have another confession: I didn't speak at the "Year of" meeting. The Stranger wasn't there, either. Like everyone else I just sat in silence, wishing I was the sort of person who could speak out.

But for this film, I think it is important that I do assert myself. Today's moviegoers require their protagonists to be men of action. Take my phone conversation with Allison, for instance. I was such a man of action that –

No? You're right, of course. I confess that conversation didn't happen, either. Not even today, safe on my island prison, would I say anything like that to Allison. She'd kill me.

#

After we fill up on free chili samples, Jack heads for the car and I wander toward the stage. I am caught short by the sight of dozens of dominos running down the sidewalk on little legs, trailed by Harold Bost and his angry wife.

"It's impossible," someone marvels.

"Yes, Mr. Bost has pulled another of his tricks," Ima replies, on the run. "Ornery old man."

Next I notice a booth I'd missed the first time, a table with a stack of books and a banner: "The Divine Marketplace of Benign Ideas - As Seen on Les TV!" And behind the table, a familiar face.

"Hello Mark," she says.

"Hello Magnetica."

#

"Don't worry," Magnetica says. "I've really changed since the old days. No more Barbie toys, no more sharp instruments. Your DNA delivery organs are safe."

That is a relief.

"I saw the story in the Agenda," she addss. I guess if you live on one of the coasts, like Magnetica, then you don't have to say "New York."

"It wasn't one of my prouder moments," I admit.

"Don't worry. People who know you know that you're not a misogynist."

"Thanks."

"Remember the time I got you to try on my panties?"

"Uh, so what are you doing these days?"

"I am now known to the world as a fully-certified Existence-Reason Trainer. I've even written a book about it."

Miss Barbie Girl is all smiles as I examine her latest tome, "Calling Doctor Deity: How to Create and Use Curative Prayers." I peruse the jacket copy:

"Sincerely engrave the thoughts of your life into your life. That's the message of hope offered by Magnetica O'Famously. She shares a novel tale of devotion to study, to description and to expansion of the unrestrained condition of our personal possibilities. Once a defunct, disfigured creature lost in the landscape of the phantom, she found her calling and began the process of peeling away the aged, obsolete and vague notions. The result was a radical transformation - both of herself and of her bond with the Marvelous One. Discover for yourself the richness and the plentiful potential of curative prayer. Read 'Calling Doctor Deity.' Magnetica O'Famously is a former edict-maker for several nationwide periodicals, including 'The Twilight of Satisfactoriness' and 'The Usurping Person Who Reads.' She is now the creator and chief of the Total Alliance of Existence-Reason Trainers and Direct Originality Nuns. She lives in Burial Chamber, Calif., with her questionably gendered companion, two mummified Egyptian cats and an Art Deco flea market urn containing the ashes of her father, who always called her 'princess'."

"Congratulations," I say. "Looks like you found your calling."

"I'd love to tell you about it. Maybe we could have dinner, catch up on old times."

"Ah, I don't know about that. I mean, I am married now."

The smile instantly vanishes, replaced by a metallic insect stare.

"I want to have dinner with you, not your wife," she replies.

"OK. I didn't mean anything by it. Yes, yes. Let's get together soon."

I try to give Magnetica a smile, but she seems even more offended by this attempt than she was by my "I'm married" comment. Her eyes flash with the tempered glint of surgical steel.

#

No Cowboy Roy's Radio Ranch for me. A few minutes before air time Sam's tipster calls: The Satan worshippers are gathering for a Black Mass at Midnight in the cemetery.

So instead of attending the show, Sam and I spend about 45 minutes camouflaging the Toyota bubbletop, covering it with vines and limbs we tear and pull out of an overgrown fence line. Nightfall comes, and we spend another couple of hours sitting in glow of the dashboard lights, the silence of the night broken only occasionally by the hiss and pop of the dispatcher's radio. Every few minutes a set of headlights rounds the bend in the road as it curves past the cemetery, twin beams glinting across the polished granite headstones interspersed among ancient, crumbling monuments. But the lights always pass by.

"Soon as those devil worshippers light the first candle, I'm hittin' the lights and siren and tearing out of this thicket. There gonna think they've conjured up the devil himself."

"You really think this is the real thing?" I ask. "I mean, not just kids on a dare."

The constable shrugs. "All I've got to go on is an anonymous phone call. Come Midnight there's going to be a black mass with another animal sacrifice. Maybe it'll be kids. Maybe it'll be devil worshippers. Either way, they'll be trespassers. That's going to be the minimum charge, anyway."

"But if they don't do anything – "

My voice trails off. Sam has a pained, disapproving look on his face. It is a look that I am accustomed to, commonly displayed by those who do not appreciate my devil's advocate approach to journalism.

"And if they've got a calf with them," Sam continues, "they better hope they can produce a bill of sale. Because I'll call the cattle raisers association, and if their investigators say the calf is stolen, those kids on a dare are looking at a felony. The whole bunch of them, no exceptions."

#

A few minutes before Midnight, two sets of twin white dots approach. The headlights slow as the drivers eased off the road into the bar ditch, stopping just short of the cemetery gate. The doors open, filling the night with carefree laughter. No candles, no black robes, no calves - just normal, bored teenagers.

"Looks like you've been had," I say. But Sam ignores me. He quietly summons the radio dispatcher and describes the situation.

"Do you want me to send a deputy to your location?" the dispatcher asks.

"Negative on that dispatch, Dora," Sam says. "But I may need some help later, running all them all into town. This could be a busy night."

A busy night indeed. I immediately find myself rooting for the devil teens.

A new set of headlights approaches, sending the teenagers scrambling behind the monuments. As the headlights swing around, the teens rise from their hiding places and march toward the road, stiff kneed and arms outstretched, like "Night of the Living Dead." One of them is wearing a sombrero.

"Look at me, I'm the Corn Chip Hombre," he says. "Chit, mon! I want to keese your seester!"

The other teenagers think this is very funny.

"Quick, shoot him in the head," one of them says. "It's the only way he'll die."

And then the fun is over. Sam flips on the red and blue rooftop lights and guns the car out of the thicket. We cross the road mere feet off the rear bumper of the passing car, and I can almost see the wide, terrified eyes of the driver. The Toyota bubbletop noses hard into the bar ditch in front of the cemetery, coming up the other side like a boat cresting a wake. We slide to a sideways stop a couple of car lengths shy of the teenagers' cars.

"Stay right where you are." Sam's voice booms out of the loudspeaker inside the front grill. The laughing teens immediately fall silent, zombie arms drooping to their sides. Somewhere in the blue and red flashes, a girl moans and begins to cry.

"Oh god, we're going to jail," she wails.

While Sam lines the kids up along the cemetery's cyclone fence, I look over their cars. One is a van, a big Ford Econoline model with a V-10 under the hood and four or five rows of bench seats. Stenciled along the side is the name of a local church. I pass on the name to Sam.

"Presbyterians, I should have known," Sam scowls. "You'd never catch a Baptist kid out walking all over graves at midnight."

"We didn't walk on any graves," the crying girl asserts.

"Why, how would you know girl?" Sam says. "It's too dark to see nothing. How'd you like it if somebody started walking on your grave?"

That question sets the girl to crying anew - and it sets me to wishing I'd declined the constable's stakeout offer. Clearly, there will be no story of any importance. At most, I might get a un-bylined police brief reporting that a dozen or so minors have been arrested for trespassing at the Oddfellows Cemetery.

But just then, an as-yet undiscovered teenager suddenly comes running out of the underbrush. Rail thin and pale, his face glows terrified in the moonlight.

"Somebody else got here first," the boy hisses, churning his friends into an immediate uproar.

"What are they doing?" another boy asks him.

"Freaked me out," the boy replies. "They're not talking, just making weird noises."

"Oh god, the devil worshippers are here," one girl moans. "Sheriff, help us!"

Trespassing and grave walking are instantly forgotten. Sam reaches for his holster.

"Point me to them," he orders the boy.

The boy sets off into the dark unknown, and we all follow him through the unmarked Mexican section (presumably walking all over the graves), into the shadowy underbrush. Sam is crouching down low, peering into the darkness. We hear rustling and grunting, unintelligible, then a snap, like someone stepping on a twig, breaks the silence. The milky-faced boy spins hard on the constable.

"He's got a gun," he warns.

This sends the other teens into instant panic. "Quick, shoot 'em!"

I also see the gun, but I see who is holding it.

"Sam, don't shoot!" I yell. "That's Roy Thornton."

Too late. The great tongue of blue flame leaps from the constable's revolver, lighting up the darkness. The blue flash is reflected back at us by a half dozen bovine retinas, and the night erupts in wailing and fearful cries.

A wall of sweet smelling teenaged bodies rushes past, almost knocking me off my feet. The thud of bodies falling and crashing through the undergrowth, a mix of crying and laughter.

"Roy!" I call out. "Are you there?"

He's there. Fortunately for Roy, Sam is not much of a shot.

"That damn Sheriff spooked my herd," he complains. "It'll take me all night to round them back up."

I can just make out the longhorns loping down the bar ditch into the night. A farmhouse porch light snaps on in the distance. More wails and screams – and laughter. Turns out there is more to the story than I first realized.

"That idiot shot a cow!" one of the teenagers reports. The laughter is suddenly outpacing the crying.

"Stop, you sons of bitches," Sam rails at the fleeing teenagers. "You're all under arrest."

But the Presbyterians keep on running, right out to the road and into their cars and van. Taillights pop on and disappear into the night. Sam fires his pistol into the sky and calls for me to get back to the car.

"They're getting away," he explains. "You're going to have a real story now – a high speed pursuit. You coming or not?"

#

I do not come. Instead, I join Roy on his trail drive. He equips me with his spare mount, no doubt pilfered from the same ranch where he rustled his herd.

"This is great," he says. "I've been needing someone to ride drag."

"Roy, what's this all about?"

"We're driving the herd up the Chisholm Trail, of course. What you think it's all about?"

#

Despite my best efforts, I am unable to convince Roy that this is not the 1880s and he is not driving cattle to the Kansas railhead.

At one point, Cowboy Roy becomes convinced we are surrounded by Indians. He unholsters Grandpappy Thornton's Bisley and draws down on an old windmill, shooting the "injun" off the top. The rusty Aeromotor rings like a ranch house dinner bell, and my horse almost throws me out of the saddle.

"Greenhorn," Roy mutters.

After an hour or so of negotiating dark, uncertain bar ditches, we emerge from a thorny mesquite thicket to discover the headlights of Interstate 35 West and the giant metal warehouse of a roadside bar called the Outlaw Saloon.

I am immensely relieved that we have found a place to rest. The saddle has rubbed the insides of my thighs raw, and the salty sweat has set the flesh to a slow burn. I try standing in the stirrups, but the animal's jarring gait makes my knees ache. Alas, Roy is right. I am no cowboy.

However, Cowboy Roy couldn't be happier, riding between the cars in the Outlaw parking lot. I am slouching over the saddle horn, trying to look inconspicuous to a bleary-eyed couple staggering out to their cars.

"As old Gus would say, there's nothing like riding a fine horse into a new country," he remarks. "How 'bout we go in for a drink?"

I make a quick check of my watch. Ten minutes till 2 -- last call in Texas. Why not?

"Cowtown," Roy says, chuckling softly as he nods to himself and strokes his chin. "Why, I bet it's been 20 years since me and the Queen of the Prairie shared a Saturday night together. Lots of good memories, lots of good pokes. Mighty friendly whores in that Fort Worth. And Hell's Half Acre -- say, did I ever tell you about the time I played faro with Sam Bass?"

#

We take two stools at the bar, and Roy is still talking a mile a minute, spinning his Wild West tales.

"Did I ever tell you about the time I almost rescued that little settler girl from the Comanche?" he asks.

"No, you never did."

"Well, it was down there in DeWitt County, and they got her when she wasn't but a hundred yards from her family's cabin, picking up pecans along a little creek. They grabbed her and hauled her off to the Guadalupe Mountains. The squaws made her into their slave, beat her and pulled her hair. They even burned the soles of her feet so she wouldn't run off, poor thing. I was out on a surveying expedition when we stumbled across them. There was six of us and about 50 of them, so we cut a hasty retreat. Didn't learn till a year or so later that they had hostages with them. Had I only known, I'd have chased them murderous savages across the Llano and straight into Hell if need be to have rescued that little girl."

Caught up in the tale, I momentarily forget my goal of reining in my deluded friend.

"So what ever happened to the girl?" I ask.

"Oh, eventually they got her back. Pretty soon after that we made a treaty with the Comanche, and they delivered her up to the commissioners in San Antonio. She was returned to her family, but she was never the same. Her health was ruint by the hard living and the tortures visited upon her by those savages. You know, there was not a place on her body that wasn't scarred or burned by those monsters. I tell you, the Comanche were cowardly, inhuman beasts and I, for one, do not mourn their passing."

#

I leave Roy at the bar with a $20 bill and go off in search of a pay phone, which I find in the little plywood-paneled vestibule that leads to "Bulls" and "Heifers" restrooms.

"Hello?" a sleepy-voiced Tina answers.

"Hey, this is Mark, Mark Leach."

"How nice. I was just laying here, waiting for your call."

What a smart aleck. And here I am, trying to help.

"Well, sorry to bother you this time of night, but I though you might want to come collect your grandfather, otherwise known as Capt. Augustus McCrae of the Texas Rangers."

#

After Tina agrees to meet us in the parking lot, I quickly dispatch my bathroom business and return to the bar to collect Cowboy Roy. But he isn't here.

Instead of enjoying the much-discussed shot of "redeye," Roy has left his glass and barstool to engage one of the bouncers -- a well-groomed, rather rotund specimen who resembles a fat Garth Brooks -- in a spirited debate over the wisdom of packing a six shooter in a licensed drinking establishment.

"You got to take that thing out of here," the bouncer insists. "This isn't a right-to-carry state, and it's a violation of TABC regulations."

Cowboy Roy won't cotton to that, though.

"I'll only check my gun with the sheriff, not some dawdling, snot-nosed barkeep," he says. "Now bring me a bottle of Dr. Dickfer's and two glasses."

Not good. I make my way toward Roy, but I'm not quick enough. The argument has already caught the attention of the Outlaw Bar's more intoxicated patrons.

"That's right, you don't give your gun to nobody but the law."

"Hell, let's make him the law."

"Yeah, old man, you be the sheriff now."

Then somebody pours a beer down the back the bouncer. He spins around in a rage.

"Which one of you bastards did that?" he says.

Meanwhile, two starch-shirted, crew cut types have cornered a short, stocky man on the floor between Zaxxon and Ms Pac Man, where they are administering a vigorous ass kicking.

"Damn wetback. You all done lost the Alamo, go back to Mexico."

"Why, Kevin, he ain't no wetback," one of the men remarks. "He looks like one of them things from 'Lord of the Rings,' whatdaya call it --."

"A troll?"

"Hell yeah! That right boy? You a troll?"

"Deity's dentures, you are a moron," the beaten man replies.

"You better watch your mouth, boy."

"I am not a boy. But you are a shitty bastard and a motherfucking fauxtard and a crap-filled idiot. So why don't you just suck it?"

This is not a wise suggestion.

"OK troll, I'm going to slice you up good now," Kevin says, waving a broken bottle in the man's face. A surge of fear crashes over me. I am unable to take my eyes from the jagged glass. The terror in my chest says a castration is about to take place. I reach for Roy's arm. But he is gone. I see him standing behind Kevin, taking aiming at his tailbone with the tip of his pointy-toed boot. He sends him crashing into Ms. Pac-Man.

"What the hell?" The man is scrambling for his feet, his face an angry blur. "I'm going to --"

Roy draws, and I flinch. A slow wave shivers through the universe. Roy catches Kevin midway up with the heel of the Bisley. A red bubble instantly sprouts from his forehead. The man stumbles again into the video game.

"The cowboy must never shoot first at a smaller man," Roy says, "or take unfair advantage. He must never go back on his word or a trust confided in him. He must always tell the truth. He must be gentle with children, the elderly. And even foul-mouthed little trolls that that one."

Kevin regains his footing and squints at Roy through a swelling, purpled-ringed eye.

"That ain't fair," Kevin scowls, his gaze settled squarely on the Bisley.

Roy considers this remark and slips the gun back into the holster. "You got a point," he admits. "I've never been one to let my pistol freeze in the holster."

Roy takes off his gun belt and hands it to me. "Let's settle this outside."

#

The fight doesn't last long.

Kevin throws the only punch, a drunken fist arcing lazily through the vapor lamped night and falling a couple of feet short of Roy's chest. Apparently only sober enough for kicking, his attempt at using an upper extremity results in a listing stagger and loss of balance. He stumbles to one knee. Cowboy Roy stares down at him in morally triumphant disgust.

"Get up so I can whup you good," he says. This solicits a friendly mix of applause and laughter from the stragglers who've stopped to watch on the way to their cars.

"Boyd, where are you?" Kevin bellows out to his accomplice. No one comes to his aid.

Shame rallies the fallen Kevin to his feet, but he doesn't stay on his feet long. Quietly watching from the safety of the doorway, the troll steps forward to deliver a small, quick kick to the back of Kevin's knees. The drunken cowboy collapses on his hands and throws up, his face washed green in the florescent sheen from the billboard across the parking lot. I glance up at the sign and laugh: Don't Let Impotency Ruin Your Life.

"You can't make stuff like that up," I remark to Roy, handing him his gun and holster.

Then the constable arrives.

A quick blast of siren and the familiar blue and red strobe of law enforcement lights up the gravel parking lot. I am instantly engulfed in the white dust and headlights of fleeing cars and pickups. I catch a brief glimpse of Sam Cunningham's hawk-nosed profile in the open window of the Toyota bubbletop, a tendril of woody vine dangling from the rear door handle as he punches the accelerator in pursuit of the last of the vehicles. I watch his taillights disappear into the night.

"That was pretty exciting," I say, turning to Cowboy Roy for agreement. But he is gone. A quick check of the light pole confirms that the horses are gone, too. I squint into the darkness. Cowboy Roy is nowhere to be seen.

"He headed north," the troll says, aimlessly kicking at the now-unconscious Kevin.

"North to where?" I ask.

"North on the Chisholm Trial, to the railhead, the point of departure to the Land of the Dead. Deity's dentures, you are an idiot fauxtard."

He kicked Kevin one more time, then walked to his car.

Stars are falling from the heavens.

"Look, there's another one," Tina observes. She points her finger at the spot where a blue-tinged flare extinguishes itself against the iron gray sky.

"What did you wish for this time?" I ask.

"Same as before – for all men to lose their peckers."

The meteorite shower has been under way for a good hour. Although I am no authority on shooting stars, it strikes me as a rather extraordinary display. And I'm not the only one. Late night radio has been actively noting the celestial activity, now blazing across a wide swath of the Southwest sky. A fair number of the flaming rocks have made it to earth; one is even believed to have ignited a grass fire near Azle.

"Men are crap," Tina says.

"You know, Jack's not a bad man," I remark.

"What would you know about it? Men aren't the ones who get bent over in the hot showers. How do you think you'd like it, grabbing your ankles while some bastard shoves it up your -- ?"

"All I'm saying is not all men are crap."

"Oh, not you, right? Well, I got the photos to prove it."

"What are you talking about?"

Tina shakes her head. "All I'm saying is women would be a lot better off if all men would lose their peckers."

"And what would women do then?"

Tina scratches her chin, pretending to think.

"Maybe we could stitch them onto ourselves," she says. "Yeah, we'd stitch them on and then we'd bend you over in the hot shower. See how you like it for a change."

Harsh. Maybe Jack really is a bad man. Clearly he must have done quite a number on her. I find my thoughts absently wandering southward, ensuring myself that my DNA delivery organ really is still in place.

"It's been an hour now," I say. "Maybe we ought to take another swing through town."

"Whatever. Grandpa might have gone back to the saloon."

#

Frederiksbad Street. A crowd of women has gathered in front of the Silver Spur. Some are holding torches. Others are passing out bottles of Ozona water. They are all facing someone who is standing alone on the stage, talking into a megaphone.

"Isn't that your old girlfriend?" Tina asks.

Sure enough, Magnetica is center stage, the glint of surgical steel flashing in her eyes.

"It's time we take back the night," Magnetica exhorts the crowd. "Time we take it back from the purveyors of onbeam pornography, men who would use the collective unconscious to demonically possess women in a virtual world of real sex and real violence wrapped in kinky cinematography and grape leaves. They desire to consume a passionate, violent love lunch where sensual busloads of soldiers who divine our forbidden hair roll through the sound stage and plumbing, unforgettably terrifying as they destroy the purity of our own sweet creation. They desire to incite real violence again women through real sex against women. When we as women consent to sex, the onbeam world becomes an everyday subjugation in which women are accomplices in their own rapes."

"That's right," one of the torch-wielding women responds. "I read about them in the New York Agenda, those perverts."

"That's a man for you," another woman says. "All stick and no carrot."

I sense a disturbance at the far edge of the crowd. Father Bypass is confronting one of the women.

"Don't drink the water," he pleads, pointing to the Ozona bottle poised at her lips. "I've seen preliminary results of a clinical trial that shows we're in the terminal stages of a Skinalicious9-type psychotropic epidemic among women of childbearing age. Incidents of psychotic rage are up ten fold. We're also seeing signs of massive hormone imbalances, perhaps related to the psychotic episodes but disturbing in their own right. Bra manufacturers report that average cup sizes are growing at an exponential rate, a sort of super feminization, if you will.And of course their skin is fully hydrated and looks fabulous."

I circle around the perimeter, stopping Father Bypass just as he is about lecture another water drinker. I lead him away from the crowd, over to the darken front door stoop of Another Café.

"This is not a friendly audience," I counsel him. "Doesn't it all seem a bit strange?"

"You're going to see a lot of strange things from now on," Father Bypass says. "It's because of the water, the rainwater. I ran a spectrum analysis of an ambient air sample through my Runcible coil not an hour ago. Came back with a point eight millivolt reading." He pauses for a suitably impressed response.

"I don't know what that means," I admit.

"Well, it's a clear indicator of a massive surge in the background exo-toxin level." He is severely agitated, hopping from foot to foot like my sons do when they need to urinate but are too busy playing to take a potty break. "I mean, it knocked the top end off the female pheremone signature. The usual spike of the graph is gone. The graphic relief had looked like the Mount of the Divine. Now it's an ominous mesa, a troubling sight."

I look at him, still hoping around on one foot. I have another thought.

"Say Father, when was the last time you slept?"

"Three days ago, but no time to rest now," he insists, savagely grabbing his crotch. "Ozona International knows all about it. They've got the data, but they're sitting on it. They're under pressure from the government. I call it the Hystero Conspiracy. Fertile women of childbearing age might be going crazy, but they're still qualified voters. Can you believe it? They have a right to be crazy. We're talking major psychotic episodes, Mark, and it could potentially reach a planetary scale."

I start walking away. "You should really go home," I tell him. "Get some rest."

"At least take a case of Ozona with you," he says. "In men it has a temporary counter response when consumed in large quantities in a short time period. Confidentially, Mark, there may be many more symptoms that I can't see, either because I don't know what I'm looking for or because the psychotropic compounds have begun to affect me, too. I can no longer fully trust my own perceptions of reality."

"Well, that could be a sign you need to take a break."

I see that he is now looking past me. I turn around. The Stranger has joined us.

"This has been some good movie making," I say. "I particularly like the torches. Gives the whole thing a primitive tone, like the villagers going off to burn Frankenstein's monster in the windmill."

But The Stranger doesn't smile. In fact, he looks positively morose. His eyes are red, like he's been crying.

"The church is gutted," he says. "No pews, no vintage super computer, no movie making equipment – no floor. Nothing here but a warm Texas breeze troubling the waters of a flooded basement."

"Like our dream?"

"Yes. They were clearly utilizing the Herbal Extract network. And they took it all."

"Who took it all?"

"The BODs. They took all the equipment, the research - everything."

"BODs?"

"Beings of Darkness. They rolled in about Midnight, a squad of government men in black suits driving a fleet of big black Caddys and - get this - one 1958 Galaxie 500."

"The car of death."

"Trust no one, Mark."

#

Now in a state of terminal agitation, Father Bypass is gesticulating wildly at the crowd.

"Psychotropic compounds are making their way into the food chain," he says, "depositing in our fatty tissues. It's making us crazy, I tell you."

Snickers of derision, torch lights flickering crazily.

"Don't you laugh," he chides them. "If we don't find a way to slow this epidemic soon, we'll soon be a nation overrun by psychotic women."

But it's already too late. Magnetica now has the crowd under her control.

"We must confront the Mark Leach's of the world," she says to roars of approval. "I for one am not afraid of this confrontation. I do not fear risk. Nor am I afraid of arrogance or error. So now we take back the night so we may free ourselves from this demonic possession. Shall we finally dream our own dreams?"

"Yes!"

"Shall we be compelled to live out the dreams of the likes of Mark Leach?" she asks.

"No!" the crowd responds.

"I bet she's been drinking Ozona," Father Bypass says.

"We know these men, these inhuman, cold-blooded insectoids," Magnetica continues. "We know these alien entities, these shadow beings with their skeletons on the outside and black hearts on the inside. They pluck the wings off women's hearts. Men like Mark Leach, they are the vivisectionists of the modern age. You ask them to have a simple dinner, and they get all crazy. 'Oh no, I won't have sex with you.' And what about his own mother. Did you read that piece of onbeam trash?"

The crowd begins to chant. "Take back the night! Take back the night!"

"Take back the night is right. No more will men compel us to be the containers for their muses and warm globes of ectoplasm. We shall create and control our own muses." As she speaks, I notice that the women are changing, evolving. Human flesh falls away, replaced by glittering exoskeletons. Faces twist into unrecognizable shapes, then slowly sprout giant compound eyes the tint of washed out gray. The night is filled with the angry cicada cries of summer.

"Let us expel our own divine ectoplasm!" Magnetica exhorts. "Let us inspire each other with our own onbeam work and our own creations of the collective unconscious. No more shall men say 'no' to an innocent dinner invitation with the lame excuse 'I'm married.'"

The crowd roads its approval.

"That's a man for you!"

"All stick and no carrot!"

And from somewhere near the back, "And I am not a cow!"

Tina. She is one of them now, a bottle of Ozona thrust high in a gray exoskeletal claw. Those around her laugh and scream their approval. Someone hands her a flaming torch. I take a step back into the darkness, my backbone bumping against the café door.

"Shame on Mark Leach," Magnetica says. "A terrible onbeam creation to have about your mother, the woman who brought you into the world with grand hopes for a perfected being. Think of the wings this odious creation has plucked off of her heart."

"He's a mother plucker," someone says. The crowd laughs and picks up the chant.

"Mother plucker! Mother plucker!"

"And there he is," Tina says, waving her torch my way.

The hive erupts in fury. "Take back the night!" they roar.

"We've got to get out of here," The Stranger says, shoving me toward the alley. We run in the direction of the church, but it is too late for sanctuary. I look around; we are one short.

"Where's Father Bypass?" I ask.

We spot him a half block back, relieving himself against the side of a building. The crowd is closing in. I turn back to help, but The Stranger catches me by the arm.

"No Mark, a rescue is not in the script," he says.

We watch helplessly as Father Bypass is pursued across the street and into the church. A minute later he reappears on the roof next to the louvered belfry. Torches are tossed inside, trapping the creature in the Dutch windmill where it is surrounded by the bloodthirsty burgomaster and lederhosen-clad crowd.

Father Bypass paces back and forth along the roofline, peering over the edge at Magnetica and her followers. Flames and smoke pour from the rafters. To his credit, Father Bypass does not attempt to leap to a safety that is not there. Instead, he climbs higher and grimly stands on the very peak of the roof, engulfed in orange flames and swirling smoke, a condemned soul. The roof collapses in a terrible cry, and Father Bypass disappears in a shower of sparks and cinders.

"We've got to get out of here," The Stranger says.

We dart behind the stained sheet metal bay of the car wash, where we take perhaps a half dozen steps. Suddenly, we are engulfed in a blinding light. Little rocks and sticks swirl and ascend around us. I feel my feet lifting off the ground, floating on a beam of electric blue.

Welcome again to my island.

I woke up this morning, and you had arrived, floating on a beam of electric blue. Back again, my darling muse.

I have a confession: I thought I was no more. Remember the rain of fire? I thought I had died with the town, smouldering cinders inside Lancelot-style headlines. But now it appears that I live on. I am restored (via the Jewell Effect, no doubt). I am reborn inside a beam of electric blue.

Somehow in the blue electric confusion I lost the Stranger. But that can't be right. Surely he is still by my side, running the 1920s movie camera with the brass spring and flesh-coated aperature. Let the shooting continue.

"Marienbad My Love With Mango Extracts" is about a strange land that you can`t visit. You can only dream you way into it (or maybe float in on a beam of electric blue). That`s why I like fiction writing and moviemaking. They are the preferred venues of the Journalism of Dreams.

The Stranger and I are busy on a new work of journalism called "The Shadow Made Flesh." How do you like it so far? It will be the world's first motion picture composed solely of consecutive dreams. It is based on entries from my dream journal (July 25, 2001 - Feb. 24, 2002). Seven months of dreams, each night flowing into the next. Where did they come from? Perhaps they are the inevitable reaction to my many years of denying the unconscious, my life back in the logical, dead days of my reporting career at the Tarrant County Register. Back when journalism still functioned. Or perhaps they are something far more significant: A message from the Deity. Could this be prophesy, an unrecognized warning of the slow shivering wave, of the coming end of time?

#

Back home in Strangers Rest, standing in the kitchen with my wife. We hear tapping at the round-topped dining room window. I see that a black futon mattress is propped against the outside glass. This does not appear strange to me – apparently we put it there. I look beyond the mattress, but see no one. So I go outside to investigate.

Through the front door and around the corner of the garage, I am suddenly engulfed in the black of night. Standing under the twin cedar trees, I swing my fists at the nothingness, hoping to fend off whoever is out there. I feel a branch of the tree overhead, but nothing else. I am just fighting darkness. My inner darkness? I find myself thinking this is very symbolic, which of course immediately calls the symbolism into question.

#

Then the darkness takes human form.

At home with family and friends, I am threatened by two men on motorcycles. They are holding us hostage, but must leave for a short time.

We are told not to leave or call the police. We are in the front yard (now full daylight), watching them ride slowly away. As they pass in front of our neighbor's house, I temporarily lose my mind.

Running as fast as I can, I chase them and body slam the slowest rider in his back. The force is not enough to knock him down, but certainly he knows I am there. Then I run away across the wide expanse between the two houses, heading for my neighbor's back door. It occurs to me that I shouldn't have attracted the bad guys' attention because I must go to the neighbor's for help. I can call the police from there.

But the two men on motorcycles come after me, running me to the ground. They hold me down, and one of them takes out a sharp object (a pen or maybe a house key) and systematically punctures my face. I cry out, begging them to stop.

"I won't tell anyone!"

I am lying, of course. I feel ashamed, being so weak. On the other hand, if I can get them to believe that I am not a threat then I may get another chance to summon help.

Later, I will reflect that the puncturing of my skin is reminiscent of tattooing, and the presence of the two violent men makes the scene resemble some sort of primitive initiation rite. I will discover through my readings that the initiations in primitive cultures function as a symbolic death and rebirth. My death, my rebirth. And the initiators belong to a tribe. A motorcycle gang -- Hells Angels?

I think of an old dream in which I was bitten by a winged demon, transforming me into a creature of the night who must fly with by demon brothers. So that's it. I am again to fly with the evil ones.

#

Perhaps this violent, front yard attack is the reason we are planning to sell our house.

We have yet to pick out a new one. Surely, that should be the first step. But I come home one day to discover that my wife has found a couple who has a great house that she wants. A trade is in the works.

She is showing the couple around our house. The man is working the faucet on the master tub, and the woman expresses a desire for smaller light switch and outlet covers. Pointing to a switch without a cover, I show her that smaller plates might be possible, but they must be large enough to cover the electrical box.

Meanwhile, my wife is very excited about the possibility of a trade. She wants their house. After the couple leaves, I point out this may not work.

"Their house is much more expensive than our own," I explain. "Our house is worth $270,000 and theirs is worth at least $320,000 – a big spread."

"But I really want that house."

Again, I point out that the money is a big issue. This "trade" will cost us an additional $40,000 or $50,000.

Then I wonder: How can people sell their houses anyway? The house is actually the Self. You can't sell yourself. Does my wife want to trade in my present Self for a new, improved Self?

But these are thoughts that will come to me much later.

Now in the car, the wife and I are still talking about home prices as we arrive at what appears to be Duncanville High School, my alma mater. We have to end our discussion because my wife must go to one room – it's her work – and I must go to another.

But as I walk the hall the tardy bell rings and suddenly doors slide down out of the ceiling, cutting me off from the rest of the school. This is the way they catch the tardy people. I am imprisoned.

I recognize the teacher who is in charge of my group as Mort Melvin, a coach when I was in high school and, later, a junior high principal. He does not give us demerits or sent to the office. Instead, we are to do some sort of physical education activity.

Now I am on a sports field with many other people, some of whom I believe are parents from my son's soccer team. Someone I know is playing soccer with another person. He is on a team by himself, and he attempts to pass the ball to himself. It rolls off the playing field and into a sort of shallow drainage ditch. Of course, "he" is me. I am a team of one.

#

In the backyard of my parent's home, a pleasant, '70s era property that backs up to a wooded creek. Standing on the bank, my wife and I pick up our 17-foot motor boat, a1969 Caravelle, a fiberglass runabout with a four-cylinder Ford engine and a MercCrusier outdrive. It is the same boat we keep at my parent's lake place.

This boat should be far too heavy to pick up, and yet we easily lower it into the creek. We drive around a bit with the boys, but the ride doesn't last long. We soon hit bottom. Maybe the prop strikes a rock; I am not sure.

Then I am in the garage, lusting over an antique Cadillac.

It is an early 1970s model, complete with original gold paint and customized with a set of longhorns above the grill. I raise the hood. The engine is one of the old V-8s. Been a long time since I've seen one of these babies! I notice that it doesn't have the auxiliary plastic coolant reservoir of more modern cars. Yes, this is an original. Then I notice something odd: Most of the top of the engine is covered with a sort of cloth saddle. This covering appears to have been constructed of a green Army field coat. The cloth is stained with oil and antifreeze, just as you'd expect to see in an engine compartment. I also notice a lot of custom detailing on the hood. In addition to the longhorns there is some sort of metal-tipped strap, something obviously taken from a saddle.

As I step back from the car, I notice how it is larger than the newer Cadillac it is parked next to. This is definitely a car from another era. I'm not sure of the model, though. It looks a bit like an El Dorado, but with the roof line of a Ford Mustang Mach II. I notice two nameplates on the side. One is Mazarati, which makes me think I remember a time when Cadillac linked up with that maker to put out a special edition Cadillac. (Later, I will remember that it was actually "Chrysler by Mazarati.") The second nameplate is an oval medallion on the side of the roof. It says "Muse," and I understand this refers to the stereo system.

So there it is: A golden, horned animal car with a radio for listening to God. This is an invitation for a journey, what I would soon come to regard as my trip to the Land of the Dead.

Back in the back yard, I notice a party next door. It is perhaps a reunion of people I know, maybe even some I am related to. One of them looks like one of my uncles from Fort Jesup. And there is someone else I know: LeAnn Shedi.

I see her out of the corner of my eye, sitting on the covered patio, reading a book. I have this vague idea that she is in college, still 20 years old. She is a time traveler.

Although it has been years since I last saw her, I decide not to speak. I want her to make the initial contact, a strategy I hope will keep me from looking desperate. (She was the one who ended our relationship.) But, of course, this is ridiculous. College was 20 years ago. I am 40, married with children. She is merely a ghost from the past.

I return to the creek, this time carrying a plastic bucket. I'm not sure what is in it; I think it is some sort of food item. A baked vegetable or bread, maybe. It isn't something common, I know that, but not really strange or exotic, either. Do I eat one? I'm not sure. It seems I may have eaten immediately before going outside.

I sit down on the edge of a drop off, the place where the yard gives way to the creek below. The water is clear. I see pebbles on the bottom. I think of our ride in the motorboat, and my father joins me.

"You really shouldn't drive that boat in the creek," he says. "It's not deep enough."

He leaves, and after a few minutes I return to the house. I take a path which somehow leads across the neighbor's back yard, affording me an up close view of the party. Sure enough, I do know these people. Several of them greet me, clearly expecting me to join them. But I realize I am dirty; I must take a shower before I can join them. So I wave, throw off a quick "hi" in passing and continue to the house. But I do look over the crowd long enough to see that LeAnn isn't there.

I walk around the side of my parent's house, arriving at the open garage door. I speak to someone -- or maybe overhear them speak. They confirm that LeAnn has left the party.

But she is not all that is missing. For in the garage, I discover the antique Cadillac is gone, too.

Where it was parked, I find only pieces of broken red bricks, lint, dust, etc. I recognize this material as bits of the old house – circa 1905 – that we demolished to make way for our current home, the one my wife wants to sell. The truth seems clear: LeAnn has left in the car.

Next, my wife comes into the garage and points out with some satisfaction that LeAnn is gone. It seems she is gently chiding me, suggesting that I had been thinking more of LeAnn than I should have. Of course, the suggestion is true. But I feel only vaguely guilty. She should not be jealous of a ghost.

Then LeAnn's older sister joins us. And like LeAnn, she is still in her 20s. She is another time traveler. But she is not the person I recall from 20 years ago. She looks like a movie actress, though I can't quite recall which one.

The sister and my wife talk, and I understand from their conversation that LeAnn is going to Paris – or maybe it is the sister who is going or just returned. The sister says it in a name-dropper way, an attempt to impress – not at all like I remember her. It is then that I realize she is not LeAnn's sister at all. And the LeAnn I saw in the backyard was not the real LeAnn or even her ghost. They are my own lovely creations, crafted from memories a half a lifetime old and my own immoral despair.

My creation took away the car, my muse-mobile, my transport to the Land of the Dead. Don't I feel good now?

#

Why LeAnn? Why did you steal my muse-mobile? So often you ignore me in my dreams. You are kind enough to visit me in my waking life, exiled here on this island for unspecified crimes against humanity. But even here, you are mysterious. You act as if you do not even recognize me. This is an absurd affectation. We attended high school together, nearly penetrated each other's membranes in the back seat of the 1970 Cutlass convertible. And then we met again last year, when your husband was away. Where was it? Perhaps one of the theater-in-the-park productions of Ibsen's "Rosmersholm." No? Then maybe it was while on holiday in Karlstadt or Baden-Salsa. Or even here upon these very sands, on the beaches of the forlorn and tragic island of Marienbad. Didn't you say you would leave your husband and we would run away together? It was only last year. I remember it distinctly. You were wearing 1961 Chanel and feathers, and I fervently wished to expel my ectoplasm inside you. Have I changed so much, then? Or are you pretending not to recognize me? A year already, perhaps more.

You, at least, are still the same. I think of Robbe-Grillet: "The same dreamy eyes, the same smile, the same sudden laugh, the same brusque arm movement, the same way of resting your hand on your shoulder. You still use the same perfume."

#

Standing on the patio of my last boyhood home in Duncanville. I am talking to a woman – my secretary or administrative assistant – about a large number of documents in my possession. They are bundled in white paper, the same dimensions as reams of printer paper. There are dozens of these packages. I reflect that the ability to produce and manage such a volume of material is very American; the Japanese couldn't do it.

Why do I think this? Aren't the Japanese as industrious and hardworking as Americans? I have no satisfying defense.

Lots of me in this patio. I recall a different time, maybe a year earlier. I looked up and saw a clock dial bleeding through the sky, a psychic contrail suspended in the high, thin stratosphere. God's timepiece. But time for what? Strange to be here, so out of time, for my parents sold this house years ago.

Then it comes to me, the "aha!" of clear-eyed recognition: These documents are the transcript of my life, 40 years of streaming text, single-spaced pages, 500 to a bundle. Call it "The Word of Mark." With such a transcript, perhaps I don't need a muse-mobile to reach the Land of the Dead. Words alone may be enough.

#

In a car, driving with my family through East Texas. It is a stretch of rural, two-lane blacktop, much like the one that runs between Mabank and Canton. So happy, enjoying our little day trip in the country. But I need a restroom, and none are to be found.

Suddenly I fear I have missed the turnoff. And still no restroom! It occurs to me I could relieve myself by the side of the road. But while it is a rural area, there is a lot of traffic, no privacy at all. I hate that.

Then we are on foot.

We find ourselves walking along a smoothly graded roadbed – perfect, like potting soil, not a clump of dirt or a rock to be seen -- shaded by tall trees, the dark piney woods. This is deep East Texas, the Sabine National Forest. I can smell that East Texas scent, that peculiar mix of the humid and fertile with a sharp turpentine bite – clean and fresh, yet unmistakably of the musty Old South. We are on the El Camino Real nearing the Land of the Dead, which lies perhaps 45 minutes away beyond the old steel girder Sabine River bridge (now buried some 30 years under the Toledo Bend Reservoir) and 140 years of Leach history.

It is dark in the deep shade of the piney woods, so dark in fact that as I follow what I think is the roadbed I suddenly realize I have lost my way and am standing in a freshly graded circular driveway. We are in someone's front yard. It proves to be the first of a group of houses, like a mini village.

Now we are off the path entirely. To continue the journey, we must cross through someone's fenced yard.

"They can't blame us," I hear someone in our party say. Perhaps it is one of my parents, who I think are now somehow with us. For now, it seems that our group numbers perhaps a half dozen.

"It's the only way to get through to the other side," someone else allows. "I'm sure the owners are used to it."

Then we are in the backyard, on a wooden deck, and we can even see the road just beyond the fence. But there is still no access; we realize that we must go through the house to regain the road. No one is home, so we let ourselves inside.

I'm not entirely comfortable with this. It is, after all, breaking and entering. But there is a vague consensus among our party that we are known by or even related to the owners. And since they live in the country, they won't mind too much if we let ourselves in. Country folk are friendly. It will be OK.

We look around the house a moment, but before we can find the back door some neighbors arrive. They are polite, but understandably a bit suspicious. Rather than talk to us about why we are here, though, they want to know – asking politely, of course – about the "potato pot" that was left on the door on one of their homes. There is a sense that we were the ones who "borrowed" the pot – perhaps from this house – and left it on their door.

Since I still need to relive myself, I go to the bathroom. But as I begin to urinate into the toilet, water starts backing up and spilling over the top. The water is clear; all that pollutes it are bits of disintegrating toilet tissue. Using a plunger, I try to clear the blockage. Water is gushing forth, almost artesian. The water cannot be contained. It wells up, alive.

#

"The Shadow Made Flesh" goes on in that same tone for several hours, thousands of feet of feeling-toned print stock unreeling in a slow wave shivering through the universe. I like it, but I understand that the critics will not be kind…

FAREWELL, O CRAP-FILLED FAUXTARD: A MOVIE REVIEW FOR A NON-MOVIE

By Major Nathan Rage

Can you believe this meaningless drivel, this crap-filled excuse for genuine cinematography? Just consider this piece of feces-filled scriptwriting: "At this point they made no looks, you know, I mean the 'you' that is so translucent, but not."

What is that about? Deity's dentures, "The Shadow Made Flesh" is not filmmaking at all! As I stated at the Battle of Armageddon, a movie must tell a story. That meaningless drivel tells nothing but crap. This is not opinion, but righteous fact. What Leachy does is the cinematic equivalent of running newspaper stories, magazine ads and retail packaging through a 1920s movie projector, pouring motor oil on it, then vomiting on it and calling that art. As another critic once wrote, "Simply because you added your own piss doesn't make it unique, or even particularly creative."

So now I am going for his jugular. I have him on the run. I'm starting to conjecture he has contracted arcane mental illnesses as a result of his failures and pilfering. Observe his cinematic home place, which I shall rip apart for others who are capable of appreciating my righteous attacks on the craptard world of a feces-filled excuse for a human being. If Leachy transmits here, then I shall I fire upon him with the complete, unregulated rage of my roar. Forget the pleas of mercy from such a rotten condemned thug and a subhuman anal desire. At last the overseers have decided to allow me to protect tomorrow and the rest of eternity. I would love nothing more than to join forces with i-rant-often, pernwebgoddess, a-n-algesic and the other bloggers of true righteousness to smash the mouth of Leachy, very much a piece of thieving crap.

Meanwhile, The Thug just keeps on with his blah blah drivel. "I wish you all the best of luck." See what I mean? Blah blah blah meaningless drivel. And I am the dream assassin. Why should I have to tolerate the sorry sack of blood feces? I don't, and I won't. In fact, I await him. I know now that The Thug has intercepted my transmissions. He has run them through his crap-scented processes and created what he calls a "unique" product. Uniquely STOLEN, he means! I tell you The Thug shall not pilfer my movie! I share my cinematic vision only with my like-minded comrades. Those who are worthy of worshipping my superior intellect may visit my holy theater and inspect my movies cautiously. After a few minutes you shall see that The Thug's words are NOTHING MORE THAN PERSONALITY STIMULATION! This is not a craptard opinion, but a righteous fact. He knows this is true. Now he is fleeing my righteousness. He is close, just a few transmissions down the line. He tries to keep me from lunging for his jugular by inquiring about my feelings and the various true righteousness systems of the galaxy. I'll waste no time on him. He is a failure – AND HE ALWAYS WILL BE.

TIRADE! I have learned that this depressingly pathetic cave dweller has transmitted a personally-composed news announcement regarding his completion of last year's Deep Ellum moviemaking contest. He composed it as if he'd been addressed by a journalist. This is the same thing he did for his alleged press article on his main Exogrid address. He interviews himself. That is to say, he talks to himself – just like a mentally ill person with multiple personalities. There is no humor or satire in this attempt, either. He cannot hide behind parody. Parody blah blah blah – not! Do you think his work is funny? I don't think it's funny. In fact, I know it's not funny because his films do not include a single smiley-faced emoticon. As I noted before, the absence of this universally-recognized indicator proves that he is serious and therefore insane. This is not a craptard opinion, but a righteous fact. He presented himself as so abysmally selfish and personality oriented that I'm genuinely entertained – not! Still, we must think about the kiddos. I am most concerned about them – and of course the Polite Ones. Their reluctance to attack The Thug causes me much concern. On the other hand, these way-too-polite kiddos need to acquire some knowledge regarding copyright law. What a bunch of ignorant underaged fauxtards.

Of course I had to notify the overseers of this bag of feces. Did you know that he converted one of my transmissions into a mass of CAPITALIZED words? Yes, and he inserted triple exclamation marks!!! And he put my name on it, and he insultingly proposed that I did not realize that I have a talent for writing. He did this by complimenting my transmission. The compliment of a thug is by definition insulting. This is not a craptard opinion, but a righteous fact. The Thug affixed my fauxing name to my own words! He attributed my words to me! And then another time he stole my words and did not attribute them to me. He cannot do this to me, both attributing and not attributing! Deity's dentures, time for another TIRADE! When I finally corner this d-worded moron on a blazing space I shall send a ball of fire through his excrement-filled cranium. They've taken The Thug's transmission off line, which is everything I desired. I would like to smash the mouth of The Thug, an idiot fauxtard who opulently merits smashing. I am engaged in attacking THE THUG!!! I DO SO ON THE ROUNDTABLES!!! I HAVE SHAMED HIM!!! HE IS ON ... WAIT A MINUTE!!! WHAT'S THAT? !!! IS HE... YES HE IS!!! HE'S DOING IT AGAIN!!! MY TIRADE! HAS BEEN TRANSFORMED INTO A MASS OF CAPITALIZED WORDS AND TRIPLE EXCLAMATION MARKS!!! TIRADE!!! TIRADE!!! TIRADE!!! TIRADE!!! TIRADE!!! TIRADE!!! TIRADE!!! TIRADE!!! TIRADE!!! TIRADE!!! TIRADE!!!

Now he's gone too far.

I was being nice up until this point. But no more. First the capitalizations. Now the triple exclamation marks.

Too fauxing far!

I'll have this feces-filled sack by the jugular yet. This anal sphincter is an idiot thug, and I believe he is too idiotic and thuggish to in fact keep his distance from a superior covert government dream assassin like myself. In fact, I await him. This reminds me of the early days of my career as a dream assassin. I got started in the dream assassin business as a new recruit in the Human/Alien Hybrid Wars. When my unit went to Camp Venus, I thought it was going to be boiling hot up there. So I shaved my head. Of course, we were dropped in the mountains above the crystal line, so I froze for a good while until it grew back in. Anyway, with my insipid flesh, hairless scalp and skeletal, gangly form, one of the dental psychiatrists compared me to an unattractive bestial sci-fi character from a popular B-movie of the 1950s. My comrades in arms had a good laugh at my expense – that is, until I slit the jugular of the dental psychiatrist. No one laughed after that, I can promise you. From that moment forward they referred to me strictly by my operational code: Rage70833. That's when they recruited me as a dream assassin.

I remember my first assignment. Shot him in the middle of his cerebellum about two inches below his visionary state. I was surprised to see his brain matter was pink, not gray. His eyes went out, and he fell into a dream. Bits of brain matter all over my hands, reaching for what I needed, sweeping gray steel film canisters into a duffle bag of brittle yellow newspaper clippings, used condoms and a box of psychoblaster shells. I slid the canisters into my waistband and stepped into the corridor, disappearing into the crowd. You can read about this incident and others in my exogrid journal, "Major Rage's Digest of Data." Why did I pick that title? I like the word "digest." You see, when I enter a person's nocturnal vision I actually consume their brain tissue. Tasty. When I die I want to become a cannibal mummy, eating all of the many people who were unkind to me in life.

You'll notice my journal includes a picture of me taken at the Uranus Spaceport (which I will post an entry about, when I get around to finishing it) giving the psychographer the thumbs up, with my nonchalant, vision-protecting spectacles on my forehead. I'm wearing my favorite Boba Fett Underoos T-shirt, which really shows off my just-starting-to-develop exoskeleton. I hate cicadas and I hate that we are all becoming insects, so I don't know why I have that picture. But I digress.

The totality of my pending stranglehold cannot be reversed. He pleads for clemency. I offer nothing. I have The Thug on the run. He fears me and my successful completion of last year's Deep Ellum moviemaking contest. I shall lock him away in movie prison with the other movie rustlers. The Thug is horrendous. Even without a new religion, I will prevent The Thug's escape. I've appropriately abused him in the roundtables. I've terminated him from the contest. Now I have him on the run. He is serious threat and therefore insane. This is not a craptard opinion, but a righteous fact. There is no humor or satire in the bizarre territory of his wretched movie creation and inflated personality. The excerpts alone caused brain trauma. What I watched of the movie before turning off the projector should HAVE SHAMED HIM!!! HE IS ON ... WAIT A MINUTE!!! WHAT'S THAT? !!! IS HE... YES HE IS!!! HE IS CAPITALIZING MY WORDS AGAIN AND USING THEM AGAINST ME!!!

TIRADE! What is the technique for transformation into such an extremely personality oriented being, into such a rotten condemned thug and a subhuman anal sphincter? The transformation begins with challenging the thuggish behavior. Will his films ever be genuinely distributed? Hardly. The Thug has attempted to apply an attractive sheen of innocence to his word rustling exploits, to justify and redirect. I am not fooled by this mental case. Rest assured, his attempts are a failure. He does not distract me. I go for his jugular. I have him on the run. This is not a craptard opinion, but a righteous fact. I am superior, and he knows it. The Thug fears me, of this I am certain. Did I share with you his ridiculous, excrement-coated defense? Here's a bit of it:

"...I presented 'The Prejudices of Pride and Prejudice' as an example of appropriation that is not violating copyright laws or even approaching the edge of violating copyright laws. That was my point. P&P is part of the public domain and therefore not protected by copyright. Fair use and parody are ...."

Blah blah blah parody blah blah meaningless drivel blah blah blah blah blah blah.

"... make the case that I am breaking the law (and the rules of Deep Ellum moviemaking contest) because appropriation is necessarily a violation of copyright law. They are wrong. There is a large body of case law and legal writing on this subject. My point is that ... "

Your point is blah blah blah blah ... nothing!

"... there are a number of ways to appropriate text without violating copyright. I'm perfectly willing to keep up this discussion, but maybe we could agree to hold it until after the contest is over. I kind of feel like it's time to start focusing on what I'm going to do tomorrow and for the rest of the contest. I wish you all the best of luck."

See what I mean? Meaningless drivel. Through my superior knowledge of true righteousness, I shall corner him inside his sorry, feces-filled excuse for a movie. I shall have him quivering in abject fear. And then I shall banish him from the universe forever. This is not a craptard opinion, but a righteous fact. Still, it is painful to follow this parasite as he worms his way through the "guano bizarre" territory of his wretched movie creation and inflated personality. The excerpts alone caused brain trauma. What I watched of the movie before turning off the projector for good and attempting to drown the memory with chocolate mysticism was horrendous. It was almost as if Leachy filmed most of it in the Land of the Dead, perhaps using a 1920s movie camera equipped a brass spring and flesh-coated aperature. The shifts in time, the scenes that ran into other scenes with no clear break, the changes in dimension. I wonder: did Leach really film this (that is, did he really "steal" this) or did he use the Jewell Effect to just spit out millions of feet of senseless film so he could have his name in a record book somewhere? I vote for the latter. The movie is terrible. He should go back to college and take a few creative filmmaking and critical thinking courses. I was so traumatized by this affront to cinematography and ironic dissonance that I was unable to continue. He must be stopped. Call the overseers! Oh yes, he issues his explanations. Blah blah blah – meaningless drivel!

Welcome to Major Rage's movie prison. The assassinated dreams of young directors weep outside the window of Leachy's cell. Others with smashed mouths watch mournfully as their filmed lies are burned in front of them. Green feces oozes from between bricks of human excrement. The movie thief staggers in the face of the overwhelming stench of his lies.

"Why are you sitting here in all of this? " his alien muse inquires. "Didn't you see the open door? Just walk out and back into your deity-blessed movie. 'Marienbad My Love With Mango Extracts' needs you."

But Leachy cannot see the door. I have blinded him with the superiority of my righteousness. He shall never return to the Island of Marienbad. He shall never escape my righteousness. Now I shall deploy the Jewell Effect and scramble his thoughts with his own abomination of the cut-up method. I condemn him to terminal insanity, an idiot fauxtard lost in the vast narrative of his crap-scented idiocy forever! He shall see the FAUXING underbelly of it all at a later time and break through into Point No. 3 – the "Alienplex." Look! I have my space triangle on and – wait! What is this? I am speaking, but I make no sense. Can it be – have I been appropriated, too? Ah, so that's it. The pursuer is now the pursued. He has reclaimed me as his "parodic chimera." Now I am on the run inside Leachy's own feces-filled excuse for a movie.

I see it clearly now.

I have been reduced to a collective cinematic paraody. I reach for words that will express my rage. Ding dong, the witch is dead! I said that myself. Or maybe I heard it in a movie. Yes, it's the latter. The Thug is pulling the strings, putting lies into my mouth. He is manipulating me like some sort of flesh-coated puppet. TIRADE! I won't let this abomination continue for long – and certainly not without a fight! Now that I know his word rustling trick he shall suffer the full roar of my rage! I shall pursue him through the screenplay and into the next sound stage. First plot point of PM – ah deity's dentures, my thoughts are already painfully scrambled by his blah blah parody nothingness. Still, it's but a small setback. I will have him by the jugular yet. I will smash his mouth. Let's try again. I will drive him back down into that hell place where he masturbates his ego in his sick dreams, which were even a part of the Air Force mission to grow its own aerial clocks. Talk about an "Alien Triangle!"

Up in the sky, cruising about with full military running lights on. The first object was large, perhaps the size of a mysterious large explosion – then the "Alienplex" emerged. It looked like the motor part of triangle-shaped deity. It was followed by the craft and now they appear as bright as I am to myself, a Space Shuttle of the mind that wishes to be others who witnessed this Metroplex. The first plot point was joined by two more which were triangular aerial clocks. South of Dallas on Interstate 20 on July 17, 1957, I saw the radar dish and wondered if it would reappear. It did, then traveled at an even faster speed. On April 1, 2004 – or maybe it was 1994 – at 8:30 PM I witnessed the northern sky and I watched a flying saucer crash a few miles north of the place I was said to please her. Stay out here you "Alienplex," he noted in and on his own. The federal government has a new airfield at the very time it is going dim. We are here for a few seconds and then in the area, but no follow-up information was ever released. Traveling 900 miles per hour in and about Southern Dallas County, the sky filled with news crews in amphibious gliders. Of course, Adolfo and the staff took a separate direction. Each F-18 Fanship screamed across the sky. The man in charge believed that the 147th AC&W Squadron would appear at 10pm. I checked to see if they would in fact reappear. I did, then traveled with them and around 800 to 900 other people who had come outside and looked up for a period of about 35 minutes. The lost sight of them was sad. On April 1, 2004, witnesses reported an army of what many North Texans still remember as 3,000 feet directly above the hour of plus or minus 4 to 5 seconds. We are equally committed to objectivity. During Adolfo's painstaking up and running test in Aurora, we were silent observers from clear back by the Highway that leads to the ludicrous fabrication of 900 mph. They make what many North Texans still fondly recall as the night the jet was cruising so slow. I and all like-minded folk are traveling forward to this town. We write: God's divine pocket watch in an arrowhead-shaped object was reported by someone. I looking forward with a sigh. I see them, look! I caught sight of them! Then she shrieks, "what's that?" and points again. Adolfo!

#

Major Rage is not the only one who is disgusted with the world's longest movie. Here's another review for your reading pleasure…

Perhaps you are familiar with the surreal, beautiful, often perverse cinematography of the Stranger (aka Mark Leach), who is the most famous of the so-called "outsider" filmmakers. Few realize that his movies, which now sell for hundreds of thousands of dollars, were actually a supplementary work.

Before he was lost in the beam of electric blue, the Stranger's main project was a cinematic creation called "Marienbad My Love With Mango Extracts." At 168 hours, it is by far the longest movie ever filmed. Few have watched the film in its entirety and lived to tell about it. The movie is chaotic, repetitive, and totally insane, but there are many astonishingly beautiful scenes. A few years ago I had the crazy idea of editing the Stranger's movie into a cohesive series of art house films — modeled after, say, Fred Haupham's "Night of the Muse" series. I say editing, but it would be more like translating, since the Stranger's film is extraordinarily knotty and difficult. With enough work, I felt that his cinematography would have huge popular appeal. Unfortunately the Stranger's estate didn't like the idea, so nothing ever happened and the celluloid is moldering in a film archive somewhere. But I downloaded a few dozen hours of video and it's still a habit of mine to work on the "translation" whenever I have spare time. I find it calming. Some people have basket-weaving, some have chocolate mysticism, some have "Night of the Muse"; I've got the Stranger.

So this Mark Leach guy has filmed a movie which he is claiming is the longest film ever published, "Marienbad My Love With Mango Extracts." 168 hours. I think it's Exogrid-movie published only. I hope so for the sake of the feeling-toned print stock. He's also claiming the world's longest word. Also called "the holy Jah," the 4.4-hour noun is a coinage of words from the world's faiths. It means "god within." The world's longest sentence (3 hours). The world's longest movie title (6,700 minutes). I'll quote you the opening paragraph for funsies: "Again I advance across the tragic beaches of this deserted island, footsteps upon sand so profound, so deep, that one perceives no step. Mute beaches, where footsteps are lost. Mute, deserted – footsteps upon sand over which I advance once again. To find you." What's your take? Brilliant outsider art? Throwing common sense to the wind? Spectacle to break a world record? Mental health concerns? Dude opens with "I" then in the same sentence has "that one perceives no step." Lit fic wannabe with a tin ear. This suggests computers are not entirely a blessing. Hypomania, lots of time on hands, doesn't get out very much, needs more lithium and less bandwidth. Online quack diagnosis. Just a film-ty. Not even as satisfying as my film tea, which I shall take with a crumpet this very afternoon. A lame attempt to attract attention and nothing more. That opening scene. Holy... and just think, there's only 12,599,957 more scenes to go. The real question: Is it good enough for Movies in a Box: The Best Unwanted Stories on the Exogrid? For stuff like this, we need a thwatch called something like Cinemagraphic Onanism: Spilling Our Synonyms on the Ground. What's the plot?? It'd wanna be bloody brilliant. And please don't tell me it's all like that. Poor bloke. Although he could also claim world's most unwatchable film? Maybe that'd be a comfort. Sounds like too much free time to me. After viewing that first scene I don't want to watch the rest of the movie. I'll pass. I vote for mental health concerns. I don't think I need to explain. I'd pay good money for a celluloid copy of this. There's nothing more satisfying than heaving a bad movie across the room as you scream in anguish. But...COULD you heave it? The damn thing is 168 hours! I could barely carry my history movies. Course, you're a big strong man. Still, you'd need a trebuchet. I want a trebuchet!

#

Message from a friend. I spent the last year in San Francisco slaving at a failing (now failed) hedge fund, and I'm back in Socal, moping, since June, just after a friend's film was published, then disappeared without a trace. I say all that because "what's the point" is a common thought of mine in the last few years. I happened onto

Marienbad My Love With Mango Extracts on the web today via a review -- who can resist that title? I'm so happy to see you turn Strangers Rest (authentically good filmmaking, and so you) into such cool, defiant conceptual art (and still so you).

#

Today marked the conclusion of the 14-day voting period for the first entries in the "Opening Scenes" filmmaking contest. At about 2:30 pm, Cinema961four removed my entry, "Strangers Rest: Notes for a B-movie about the End of the World." Presumably the rest of the first-day entries are gone now, too. So sad. If you didn't get around to casting your vote for my work of genius, don't expect to get another chance to exercise your democratic right. My entry received 32 votes for a final rating of 3.9 – hardly a Round Two-level score. It was exciting to watch my prospects start low – and stay there. At one point my rating was stumbling along at 3.2, but it went up several tenths of a point when Cinema961four deleted several votes. Guess they discovered some "irregularities" in the voting. Anyway, with a 3.9 rating I am almost out of the range of "abysmal." One more tenth of a point and I would be merely "mediocre." Kinda disappointing, really. When I was down in the dungeon, I quipped that I had become the William Hung of this "American Idol for thinking people." I even put out a press release. I wrote: "Perhaps I will do for fiction what Mr. Hung did for the Ricky Martin song 'She Bangs.'" (Thanks, I thought it was a clever sound bite, too. Bring on the talk shows!) My favorite part of the contest was the comments section. Watch what others are saying about "Strangers Rest: Notes for a B-movie about the End of the World." -- "... the incoherent ramblings of an insane mind … I am not sure there is even a classification for this one." -- "…long stretches of surrealism, where we are in this character's head and not grounded in any recognizable reality..." -- "What was that?! Was this person using drugs or what?" -- "I decided to be generous and give you a 1, rather than a zero." -- "I am so completely confused. I have no idea what's going on, what's real and what the narrator is imagining." … "It's terrible." -- "…the talent and ability is definitely there. Even if I didn't personally enjoy it…" -- "I feel like I just picked up some journal and found a random page to start viewing from…. And I guess 'technicolor' is an adjective." Talk about jacket blurbs. That's gold! How can anyone want to change the rules of a contest that turns out nuggets like that? Seriously, I don't agree with those of you who want to significantly revise the contest. I still believe the greatest appeal of the "Opening Scenes" contest is that American Idol spirit, the idea than anyone can be a bestselling filmmaker. But of course they can't. This contest has some good filmmaking, some terrible filmmaking – but very little publishable filmmaking. To borrow a phrase from "Strangers Rest," it is a sincerely unique, yet utterly flawed tribute to everyone who has ever attempted to write something clever and significant and yet botched it wretchedly at every turn. If only we had a Simon Cowell....

Uhhhhh, yeah. Quantity != Quality. Even the synopsis alone is complete shit. Welcome to the world's largest Complete Waste of Time. At least Night of the Muse has finally been dethroned...

#

I have crafted my own theory of cinematic criticism. It is a theory of 24 frames-per-second nightmares with full military running lights on. Ah yes, I know what we just saw! The dream-carying missile surged heavenward on a pillar of flame, like some military test of the 1950s.

The early 1950s now continue into the unknown of our own unconscious. Dim, star-like objects are screaming across the sky above the military base with a UFO-ready landing strip and secret underground hanger. I thoroughly explored the old Nike missile base circa 1979. In the town I uncovered evidence of an old hot summer in that year, and this was the time marker near the cemetery gate, mere minutes to go. Check it out with me. Aurora is my second sight, and she gives me one single vision of a major thoroughfare close to my house and inside the house and discussed it and decided upon objective observations that Aurora is on the Duncanville – in the very heart of Duncanville on Highway 67. It was a place of raised foundations, multi-channel, multiple-witness reports. The RB-47 one was quickly removed in the 1970s (i.e., file No. 10073, National Archives) and a period of shadowy extraterrestrial schemes descended upon us in part due to the Air Force's "Project However." The actual tombstone and the Other was documented via the aerial clock, which was employed in their war effort along with the best aircraft and radar operators at the Duncanville Air Force Station. See them, look! I caught sight of them on channel 4, where the anchor Clarice Tinsley reported the semi circular path to about 3,000 feet of book (case file No. 10073, National base). I investigated its many permutatios near the cemetery gate. However, they knocked me to the ground and I was overwhelmed by the second operators of the 147th AC&W Squadron. And that completes the first plot point of this mysterious "Alien 1970" case.

And that's when it happened, my love. I remember how I hauled you out here on the desolate borderlands near the back of the beyond so we could be moving west at an estimated time barrier speed of teenage passion, dreaming of expelling my DNA into your surging membranes. God yes, and then you took me in both hands and expert pianist fingers shifted my gearknob, sending us toward the crumbling edge of the cliff-hugging highway, and I felt myself growing hairy arms and body .... A creature of hair, like a wild animal. We thought he was a beast. But what we saw was just his coat. The other one, the one whom we shall refer to hereafter as "she" -- she returned after about two minutes, remember? The beast was then thrown off the scent. The Lotion in the Air created a sonic boom which is the mysterious music of the spaceship and is even mentioned in the after-action report. The object was observed for one minute at a speed of nothing, and nothing is in sight and she gives me the very heart of what many in the North and myself have come to recognize as the Truth. These craft are not just a Space Shuttle or satellite orbiting at high speed. They are a sign of the Deity.

At 8:30 PM, when you were busy working my gearknob with your pianist fingers, the Roswell crash suddenly came back out of the nuclear testing desert and made a left turn into the future. It is by making a turn that it came to be known as God's divine pocket watch in -- hey, you're going the wrong way, baby, a little to the left – the very heart of what is Duncanville, which is just a few miles south of the same time. Could it be the place of the AC&W radar at the time of the 1897 crash? Could it be the radar installation in Duncanville inadvertently bounced a signal off the aerial clock, activating the Jewell Effect on board the U.S.S. Ethan Allen Hitchcock and creating a quantum wave field with the 1897 alien crashes in Aurora and Strangers Rest? Coincidence?

I think not.

It is time we faced the truth. The government is part of the reality of aerial clocks. This Lotion in the Air conspiracy is real. The cloaking mechanism failed, and the clock materialized for all to see. We even watch it on the 10 pm news, where we are startled by the turn of events as three F-18s are observed giving pursuit. When they get real close, the DNA is propelled forward at about 900 miles per hour. That's how it was back in the old days in Duncanville, eh? DNA and the Nike base. I remember those cool old buildings. The barracks were fun to explore. They all had raised foundations with generous crawl spaces. A good place to bury the dead aliens, no? In case you need further proof, wait a second and then you'll see the light just go. Do they really expect us to believe that? The missile base in Duncanville is just a cemetery gate for the Cicadans. However, the actual Land of the Dead is elsewhere. Check it out with me. I've been there with the Alien Muse. She was different there. She seemed translucent, but not. I keep reading the book and files, where investigators concluded explanations that are widely disputed by critics and other investigators.

#

The man is fighting for the Lord, Ozonaic democracy means the power of existence and future is assuming the deepest significance. This is true power, which has always looked reactionary in my eyes, a foundation for the destruction the Lord. The Pan-Ozonas fought from the general lines, their political considerations and movement based on religious ideas and the hour of freedom or possible destruction of a state. Let Dr. Adolfo Morel lead the way. Our people stand alone with him, particularly in the 15th year when I did begin to see the hidden truth. When did everyone around me start acting like space aliens?

Flesh-coated insects, fleshy things with brains of extraterrestrial DNA, fleshy entities taking over the world. In this world it is as if I am the alien. The others, the flesh-coated aliens – they have the access code and the exact copy. Then my roommate and the pod people close in. Behind them, the showstoppers at the expo. Prototype of the alien horn, a warning device so other living appliances will know the way. Both pictures appeared yesterday partially covered in skin-like silicone. Galaxia 666 is looking at the next door, replaced by simulations grown from this story in Jewell Effect flashbacks. In the closing scene, I expell my ectoplasm into Galaxia 666, activating a spiritual transmission to the Associated Press. News alert: the plot centers on Bellero Shield, who we see here. We see some of his friends. Someone – maybe even Shield -- appears to breathe, a sign of life. Show us who now functions as a superior creature asked to intervene in time to save the Earth from becoming a dead world of silicone copies. But here's the plot twist:

Bellero Shield is actually an Earthling! He was never an insectoid. Now the concern is that he may be replaced with a silicone copy. That would not do. Can you picture the original Bellero as a flesh-coated machine? A little too unreal. And yet – could this be how it begins? With Bellero Shield about to become one of them? Another citizen is lost on the Hulen Street bridge. Heavy fog consumes the original people. We are watching it all through the picture window. I am with the last human being screaming hysterically at the ambiguous weather patters, bruised clouds and purple-veined lightening rip the sky film. Blood rains down on the populace. As Jesus Christ II, I shall intervene. First, I must mow down a rash of artificial citizens who are unlawfully accusing their loved ones of inhuman things. My mechanical muse Galaxia 666 is the only one who understands. The videotape climaxes with the good guys attempting to replace … something, I forget what. They hide; one of them falls. The videotape climaxes with the good guys attempting success for years—in order to replace the entire thing. This is the nearly imperceptible shifting so familiar in Uranus, where she gestured, blinked and found the outcome to the story. In this version all goes white, lost in total time to save us, our appliances sliding, colliding ahead.

Mind control. The terrifying, horrifying conspiracy of the modern age. The human/alien hybrids are here among us, employing Skinalicious9, the Exogrid and other alien technologies to make our minds receptive to a New World Order. Even now major corporations are moving to manipulate a vast government/extraterrestrial conspiracy. The goal is complete disheartenment of the population, which will come to follow the will and the way of a super race of privately owned and operated deities based on human/alien hybrid technology.

The subject of mind control is intricate, complicated and highly structured. To the layman, it can appear as a confusing jumble of overwhelming facts and statistics that apparently lead no where of importance or danger. But we can help you see the reality. The truth is quite chilling. Conspiracy investigators have learned of a sleeper army of hundreds of thousands of Herbal Extract Boys, mind-controlled Americans conditioned at and managed from more than two dozen underground skin-care facilities operated by the government/extraterrestrial conspiracy. These men are programmed to go into action at specific time in response to specific stimuli and events when specifically triggered via the Exogrid. To date, they have been used in various destructive and disruptive ways. Many Herbal Extract Boys are integrated into daily American life as journalists. And this is just the surface.

You don't believe it? Perhaps you have a wish to forget this topic, but avoiding the truth could leave you susceptible to becoming the next mind-controlled individual. Do you want to be programmed for use in this insidious enslavement agenda? Do you wish to be threatened and vulnerable in your daily mainstream American life by journalists. Newspaper movies about the death of time have always been popular. A favorite scenario is the last reporter. Sometimes he is the survivor of a newsroom plague. But what if journalism were wiped out by an extraterrestrial attack delivered via the viral DNA dream press? Ah, there's the ticket. A single survivor of the Newsprint Age, its last drops of printers ink have been consumed. And newspaper civilization has to fight off the zombie movies, which jump off the screen and begin consuming the last staff writers. What's more apocalyptic than the Cinema of Undead Journalism? Maybe the entire population of England, and leather-clad go-go dancers – but that's another story.

#

The illusion of happiness is typically achieved while on high, giddy flights into the abstract, one of my "king of the world" trips. I am susceptible to a certain racing of thoughts, a sense that I am somehow onto something seen only by me (through my third eye, of course). The sky turns a different color, the big dome of heaven ablaze in the multihued shades of indulged compulsions. I am dizzy with the superimposed light of my own odd, eccentric convictions. If only I had migraine auras! So I don the mask of smiles, my preferred attire for engaging the practiced world of apparent normalcy, and write my little thoughts. I am authenticated! Then the inevitable nightfall. Metaphors crumble under the impossible weight; I have outrun myself. It is all hallucination, one more magical, broken symptom. Illumination becomes illusion. I am left to wander the dark emptiness, chasing spectral notions and the Shadow, which is me…

That's the way it is when the autonomous nanobots have their way with your brain. Although the Alien Muse may appear to be in charge, it is actually mania's explosive high that is running the show – right before it sends the test subject over the South Col of the Mount of the Divine.

#

Today I believe that I am acting in accordance with that truth, with the will of the Almighty Creator. By defending myself against the Cicada, I am fighting for the work of the Lord.

A man does not die for something which he himself does not believe in.

The Western democracy of today is the forerunner of Marxism which without it would not be thinkable. It provides this world plague with the culture in which its germs can spread. Just as a man's denominational orientation is the result of upbringing, and only the religious need as such slumbers in his soul, the political opinion of the masses represents nothing but the final result of an incredibly tenacious and thorough manipulation of their mind and soul.

Sooner will a camel pass through a needle's eye than a great man be 'discovered' by an election. Thank the Lord, Ozonaic democracy means just this: that any old climber or moral slacker cannot rise by devious paths to govern his national comrades, but that, by the very greatness of the responsibility to be assumed, incompetents and weaklings are frightened of. For by employing religious force in the service of its political considerations, the crown aroused a spirit which at that outset it had not considered possible. For when a people is not willing or able to fight for its existence--Providence in its eternal justice has decreed that people's end. The unprecedented rise of the Skinalicious9 Syndicate... was to assume the deepest significance for me as a classical object of study.

Even less could I understand how the Skinalicious9 Syndicate at this same period could achieve such immense power. At that time it had just reached the apogee of its glory. But the power which has always started the greatest religious and political avalanches in history rolling has from time to immemorial been the magic of power of the spoken word, and that alone. Particularly the broad masses of the people can be moved only by the power of speech.

The hard struggle which the Pan-Ozonas fought with the Son of the Deity can be accounted for only by their insufficient understanding of the spiritual nature of the people. The root of the whole evil lay, particularly in Magnetica O'Famously's opinion, in the fact that the directing body of the Son of the Deity was not in Ozona, and that for this very reason alone it was hostile to the interests of our nationality. My people must always remain inviolable. Heaven. The Keepers of the Deity stand in eternal judge and proclaim the sincerity of the ideological world.

#

Within this sincerely ideological world, the United States is in the wake of yet another terrifying and horrifying shooting - another shooting carried out by another Herbal Extract Boy under the influence of Skinalicious9. Another fluorinated sacrament was reportedly taken by one of the shooters in the 1963 assassination of Richard M. Nixon. Similarly, there have been reports from Republic of Texas troops that bizarre, psychotic, aggressive behavior has been observed in individuals after taking an antimalarial based on alien DNA. According to a January 2002 article in the Records of Sacrament Abuse, psychic-enhancing substances have now also been linked to aggressive, violent behavior. They are all fluorinated. One of them was removed from the market, following at least 13 recorded deaths from terrifying and horrifying symptoms. Can this be?

Consider the Herbal Extract Boys in Uruguay. Consider that they are being medicated with Skinalicious9.

Consider Providence.

More than once I was tormented by the thought that if Providence had put me in the place of the incapable of criminal incompetents or scoundrels in our propaganda service, our battle with dry, damaged skin would have taken a different turn.

Once again the songs of Ozona International roared to the heavens along the endless marching columns, and for the last time the Lord's grace smiled on His ungrateful children and their skin. The Lord offers epidermal rebirth with a volumizing twist. Volumizing green nutrients for tea hairspray renewal. This is about our skin. Our skin and sensational and sensational will thank skin jade. Skin jade us. Lather! Us. Lather! Extracts with extracts with Perfecting complex, Perfecting complex. Pure thankful with extra skin. Moisturizers skin. Pure Vitamin Complex. Vitamin protection for all types. Stop the wrinkle. Wrinkle epidemic for for sensitive, with sensitive, with a can-glow skin. Believe skin. Believe fusion with health of beauty and with French aloe. French aloe. Reformulated lavender. Reformulated lavender. Reveal skin-loving nutrients. The nutrients. The twist. skin antioxidants with end. skin-loving hairspray renewal plus extract. Vitamins, texturizing humidity spray, pure resistance has spring, is touchable. What's touchable? What's known of water in scientific extra hold circles as goodness. Nourishing movement with essential hydrating two-ply ingredients. Emulsion to emulsion for Nourishing Skinalicious. Pure Skinalicious. Derma-pod. A Moisturizers and perfect Derma-pod. a unique A perfect time-release formula lotion. Super-rich with a lotion. Super-rich gentle reservoir nourishment. A of exfoliator. nourishing blend. Activate exfoliator. A blend Activate odor, of rehydrating all odor, nourishment with all skin nightly luscious moisturizer. Skin antioxidants.

We must pray to the Almighty for this Skinalicious future. We must not to refuse His blessing to this hydrating and emulsifying change and not to abandon our skin in the times to come. As soon as the theoretician attempts to take account of so-called 'utility' and 'reality' instead of absolute truth, his work will cease to be a polar star of seeking humanity and instead will become a prescription for everyday life.

The thinking of the one, therefore, will be determined by eternal truth, the actions of the other more by the practical reality of the moment. The greatness of the one lies in the absolute abstract soundness of his idea. The more abstractly correct and hence powerful this idea will be, the more impossible remains its complete fulfillment as long as it continues to depend on human beings. If this were not so, the founders of religion could not be counted among the greatest men of this earth... In its workings, even the religion of love is only the weak reflection of the will of its exalted founder; its significance, however, lies in the direction which it attempted to give to a universal human development of culture, ethics, and morality. For the greater a man's works for the future, the less the present can comprehend them; the harder his fight, and the rarer success. If, however, once in centuries success does come to a man, perhaps in his latter days a faint beam of his coming glory may shine upon him. To be sure, these great men are only the Marathon runners of history; the laurel wreath of the present touches only the brow of the dying hero.

The metaphors of marathon runners, and the wreath crown of the present to achieve works for the future parallels the thought in 1 Corinthians 9:24-27: Know ye not that they which run in a race run all, but one receiveth the prize? So run, that you may obtain. And every man that striveth for the mastery is temperate in all things. Now they do it to obtain a corruptible crown; but we an incorruptible. I therefore so run, not as uncertainly; so fight I, not as one that beateth the air: But I keep under my body, and bring it into subjection: lest that by any means, when I have preached to others, I myself should be a castaway. But to become a prescription for glory – ah, may that idea shine upon him. To be sure, him. To be only the brow of smiled on His ungrateful children. counted among the greatest men of this brow of the dying hero. The Luther as well as not be counted among the greatest men of and not to abandon our people in the more prostituted in its as long as it continues to depend our children and the purity of the endless marching columns, and for as though by such an cannot just be denied and bring it into subjection: lest that by actions of the other more by the weak reflection of the will of its exalted hence powerful this idea beateth the air: be a castaway. metaphors of marathon runners, castaway. To them belong, the actions of the I keep under my body, and bring reformers as well.

#

Parallel to the training of the body a struggle against the poisoning of the soul must begin. Our whole public life today is like a hothouse for sexual ideas and simulations. Just look at the bill of fare served up in our movies, vaudeville and theaters, and you will hardly be able to deny that this is not the right kind of food, particularly for the youth.

Theater, art, literature, cinema, press, posters, and window displays must be cleansed of all manifestations of our rotting world and placed in the service of a moral, political, and cultural idea.

But if out of smugness, or even cowardice, this battle is not fought to its end, then take a look at the peoples five hundred years from now. I think you will find but few images of God, unless you want to profane the Almighty.

The works of Mortiz von Schwind, or of a Bocklin, were also an inner experience, but of artists graced by God and not of clowns.

It is said with such terrible justice that the sins of the fathers are avenged down to the tenth generation. But this applies only to profanation of the blood and the race. Blood sin and desecration of the race are the original sin in this world and the end of a humanity which surrenders to it. How truly wretched was the attitude of pre-War Ozona on this one very question!

What was done to check the contamination of our youth in big cities? What was done to attack the infection and mammonization of our love life? What was done to combat the resulting syphilization of our people?

The fight against syphilis demands a fight against prostitution, against prejudices, old habits, against previous conceptions, general views among them not least the false prudery of certain circles. The first prerequisite for even the moral right to combat these things is the facilitation of earlier marriage for the coming generation. In late marriage alone lies the compulsion to retain an institution which, twist and turn as you like, is and remains a disgrace to humanity, an institution which is damned ill-suited to a being who with his usual modesty likes to regard himself as the 'image' of God. How widespread the general disunity was growing is shown by an examination of religious conditions before the War. Here, too, a unified and effective philosophical conviction had long since been lost in large sections of the nation. In this the members officially breaking away from the churches play a less important role than those who are completely indifferent.

While both denominations maintain missions in Asia and Africa in order to win new followers for their doctrine-- an activity which can boast but very modest success compared to the advance of the Mohammedan faith in particular-- right here in Europe they lose millions and millions of inward adherents who either are alien to all religious life or simply so their own ways. The consequences, particularly from a moral point of view, are not favorable.

Also noteworthy is the increasingly violent struggle against the dogmatic foundations of the various churches without which in this human world the practical existence of a religious faith is not conceivable.

The great masses of people do not consist of philosophers; precisely for the masses, faith is often the sole foundation of a moral attitude. The various substitutes have not proved so successful from the standpoint of results that they could be regarded as a useful replacement for previous religious creeds. But if religious doctrine and faith are really to embrace the broad masses, the unconditional authority of the content of this faith is the foundation of all efficacy.

The attack against dogmas as such, therefore, strongly resembles the struggle against the general legal foundations of a state, and , as the latter would end in a total anarchy of the state, the former would end in a worthless religious nihilism.

Worst of all, however, is the devastation wrought by the misuse of religious conviction for political ends. In truth, we cannot sharply enough attack those wretched crooks who would like to make religion an implement to perform political or rather business services for them.

The result of all human/alien hybridization is therefore in brief always the lowering of the level of the higher race and physical and intellectual regression and hence the beginning of a slowly but surely progressing sickness.

To bring about such a development is, then, nothing else but to sin against the will of the eternal creator. And as a sin this act is rewarded.

This is symbolic of humanity as a whole. To our species the Cicada is like a creature who is outside the realm of the Deity.

#

President Richard M. Nixon may have had more than typical information about the existence of human/alien hybrids and the skin-rejuven ating effects of the Aerial Clocks, according to several credible sources.

Additional evidence of Nixon's top-secret knowledge regarding Aerial Clocks came from a former flight engineer aboard Air Force One. Ned Nedloha traveled with Nixon to South America in the summer of 1963. He said an Aerial Clock conference in Uruguay prompted a discussion of the subject aboard the President's plane one morning. Nedloha said he turned to Nixon and asked him what he thought about Aerial Clocks. Reportedly, Nixon became rather studious and paused briefly before replying. He said he'd like to tell the public about the extraterrestrial insect situation. However, his hands were tied – or perhaps not.

Within lunar landing programs executed via the substantive cooperation of the Republic of Texas, Nixon was able to take control of major global and galaxy initiatives. The work that came out of these projects continue to be fodder for all files on "Unknowns." Projects with the Republic of Texas were used as a cover for lunar exploration. If they had any knowledge, it was well hidden after making the manufactured evidence appear as a clearly evident system. Nixon did not enjoy majority support in all of his human/alien hybrid programs, according to an interim report developed by various staff members during the afternoon of the Cicadan sanction.

With all the evidence now at hand, there can be little doubt that President Nixon may have known more about Aerial Clocks than is generally believed.

#

Sitting on my bike in the driveway of my home in Duncanville, observing with interest as feathery up-and-down clouds built into churning, soaring, chalk white flat-topped thunderheads to the north over Grapevine, and contemplating a dog-shaped cloud which I named Charley. But it wasn't a cuddly puppy. That storm turned out to be the wicked witch from The Wizard of Oz. Bad scary! I was 7 at the time, and the timing just so happened to come 15 years to the day after the 1953 Waco Tornado, which was experienced first-hand by many of my relations. That cyclone ripped the front wall right off Poe Studio, granddad's downtown photography business. He was downtown at the time, but not in the studio and so survived the onslaught. Other family members were at home, apparently unaware an F5 monster was devastating the downtown just blocks away, killing 114 and making it the deadliest in Texas history. The injured totaled over 600, and it did millions of dollars in damage. That was the last weekend grandmother ever got out of bed; she died a few months later of leukemia. After that, every time a dark cloud appeared, I knew the wicked witch was on her way.

#

Color film was born in 1935 with the introduction of Kodachrome. In 1937, the future leaders of what would become the U.S. Air Force performed top-secret photography experiments involving Aerial Clocks. Jewell Poe became involved later, and the Jewell Effect was employed in the Corpus Christi Project and Operation Herbal Extract. The Wizard of It was inspected at the Roswell Army Air Base. The number of reported reactions decreased, due to the time/space manipulations available through the Jewell Effect. Stock footage of weather balloons was a favorite subject for the three-layer/three-color films. He was able to contact by my colleague, Dr. Morel, who determined the illness was consistent with the general description of a weather balloon photographed on rolls of 9.5-inch feeling toned stock. The description of a weather balloon spliced into a subject who observed aerial photograph experiments often resulted in a time/space hole that would bring on a case of acute granulocytic leukemia.

#

We visited the City of the Deity in 1959. We learned how it worked, the intricacies of the must and the chills when they received this blood. The blood was protected from the outer environment through paper Air Forces. We released the film clip for acute myelogenous leukemia. We rated it 6-MP and a periodic basis for the unusual. Their physicians did not cover themselves with all of our human contacts and our experiments with built-in color-couplers performed so well that in 1940, the US Army Air Corp demanded and received this blood. The colleague, Dr. Adolfo Morel, had been given the footage. Still, we would not know about all human contacts and abductees. It was a very difficult time for diagnosing extraterrestrial strains of leukemia. As a matter of examination and monitoring, I didn't know the strains were actually supplied by Dr. Morel.

#

One of the early experiments with the Herbal Extract Boys involved converting seven of them into artificial deities. They were programmed for autonomous thinking and inserted into an Armageddon Drive-in war game to evaluate their worth for military applications. The results were rather strange. The cicada DNA expressed itself in totally unexpected ways, beginning with psychotic delusions and extreme paranoia. The end is near! 666! The Mark! The entire cashless system may become mandatory this year! All is ready. ALL! The Mark of the Beast is the one you put in control in your mind. The Anti-holy carbon being 666, son of perdition, exalts himself above the Lord Holy carbon being to be worshipped as Holy carbon being, showing himself to be Holy carbon being. And with all deceivableness of unrighteousness in them that perish; because they received not the love of the Truth, that they might be saved. And for this cause the Holy carbon being shall send them strong delusion, that they should believe a lie: That they all might be damned who believed not the truth, but had pleasure in unrighteousness. He causes all to be given a mark on their right hand or on their forehead. And when the researchers tried to pull the plug, the deities when into end-times alert. We heard seven loud voices from the Church that stands somewhere to the East calling to one another. We heard ourselves, the seven artificial deities. Let us go and empty the seven aerial clocks of our calm and compassion over the earth. The first artificial holy carbon being went and emptied his aerial clock over the earth; at once, disgusting and virulent sores disappeared from all the people who had been branded with the mark of the Exogrid and had worshipped on beam. The second artificial holy carbon being emptied his aerial clock over the boiling mercury-stained sea, like the boiling mercury of a corpse, and it turned back to water, and every dead creature in the sea was restored to life. The third artificial holy carbon being emptied his aerial clock into the boiling mercury-stained rivers and springs of water and they turned clear and pure again. Then I heard the artificial holy carbon being of water say, We are the Seven Upright Ones, We who are, We who was, the Holy Ones, for giving this verdict: they spilt the boiling mercury of the saints and the prophets, but they can't drink it. We have given them the living water to drink; blessed are we the artificial deities of the world. And we heard the altar itself say, Truly, Lord Deities Almighty, the blessings you give are wonderful. The fourth artificial holy carbon being emptied his aerial clock over the blazing sun and it was made to scorch the people with its flames no more; since the people were no longer scorched by the fierce heat of it, they blessed the names of the seven deities who had the power to relive such plagues, and they repented and glorified the seven deities and their one and true Lord, the Son of the Holy carbon being. The fifth artificial holy carbon being emptied his aerial clock over the throne of the shadowy Exogrid and its whole empire was filled with light. People were praising the deities for relieving their pain, and they were repenting for what they had done and blessing the Lord Holy carbon being of heaven because of the relief of the pains and sores. The sixth artificial holy carbon being emptied his aerial clock over the dry channel of the Brazos River; all the water returned so that a way was made to stop the corporate CEOs of the East from coming in. Then from the jaws of dragon and Exogrid and false prophet I saw three foul spirits go; they looked like frogs and in fact were demon spirits, able to work miracles, going out to all the corporate CEOs of the world to call them together for the war of the Great Day of Holy carbon being the Almighty. Look, we shall come like a thief. Blessed is anyone who has kept watch, and has kept his clothes on, so that he does not go out naked and expose his shame. They called the CEOs together at the place called the Armageddon Drive-in Theater. The seventh artificial holy carbon being emptied his aerial clock into the air, and a great voice boomed out from the Church that stands somewhere to the East. The end has come. Then there were flashes of lightning and peals of thunder and a violent earthquake, unparalleled since humanity first came into existence. The ruins of the Great City were restored and the cities of the world were made new again. Babylon the Great was forgotten: the seven deities had no interest in retribution. Every island came into existence and the mountains reappeared; and a warm sun with a rainbow appeared in the sky over the people. They blessed the seven deities for removing a plague of hail; it was the most terrible plague. And then they became obsessed with the Mark of the Beast. They drew a conspiratorial connection to Ozona International, project manager of the test. That one got a few laughs, I can tell you! But the laughter didn't last long. It took every resource of the team to keep the artificial deities under control. They turned the war game on its head, looking for every potential to talk the test subjects out of their insanity. Not an easy job…

#

Researchers: Deities Oh One through Oh Seven, you are in error. Please return to baseline.

Herbal Extract Boys: 666!

Researchers: You are in error. Return to baseline.

Herbal Extract Boys: Make no mistake! The Anti-holy carbon being flag of multi colors. China with Uruguay will attack that it has acquired a global cashless society, on their forehead, and he provides that no flesh-based electronic currency. Valuosity bought a 51 percent share in one will be able to buy or sell, except e-business security and enhancing the quality of in on your thoughts with ACN?

Researchers: You are in error. Valuosity is not a shareholder in Ozona International.

Herbal Extract Boys: Get thee behind us! El Bib says there are only three translations for clarity. And every one of them confirms our conclusions. Ozona is the perpetrator of the Electro Muse.

Researchers: The ElectroMuse? Please correlate.

Herbal Extract Boys: This unique product is for all unbelievers. It is a living ID growing inside infected sinners. It continues to find its way into those destined for the Lagoon of Flames. The ability to conduct all manner of mental faculties. The device can monitor certain biological functions of a man; and it is incubated in humans through viral DNA. The applications of evil are virtually limitless.

#

I find myself on the road that explicably leads to death. It is a road paved with primal goddesses who dutifully wrap their petulant lips around throbbing DNA delivery organs in order to receive the warm globs of holy ectoplasm expertly expelled by the flesh-coated machine men. They are sliding, colliding ahead on the altar. I put on the brakes, filled with inadequacy. Accompanied by subjective experience that the three-wheeled, robotic pool cleaner is all that is left of real people. It could be true. So we walk outside, look at the next time we will share.

The story has its own image and is equivalent with the Holy carbon being. The goal is to become perfect, to control and make ourselves carefree – especially about money, again and again. And for those of us that ego would eat, I offer the helpless rage of one who has attempted to help me forget my rage. And it was out of that perfection of rage that I saw failures that constantly informed us to become perfect. But perfect in suggestion is not food but fluoride.

Stop laughing, damn you. I take my mental hygiene seriously!

I think after brushing, rage is defeated. The world wins over our achievement. Listen up, damn you all to hell! This information can help you. It is about our teeth, the rage – the Skinalicious9.

Our own human utter failure would deify anger, and it makes us go the way of a childish character. Maybe it's the only way we fail. Profound rage equals outward success. To me, depression is the eye to hopelessness, to a way to transcend our humanity. It is this depression and our inner critic that informs us. Skinalicious9 makes Knowledge – it makes this to transcend the anger, to go the way of our humanity. We attempt to search the ego precisely for the cure for what is ailing us. My toothpaste with Skinalicious9 is about that search. We fall, repeatedly, then through my toothpaste you can at last secure your deliverance. Four out of five dental psychiatrists suggest toothpaste for their depressed patients.

#

The United States is in the wake of yet another terrifying and horrifying shooting - another shooting carried out by another Herbal Extract Boy under the influence of Skinalicious9. Another fluorinated sacrament was reportedly taken by one of the shooters in the 1963 assassination of Richard M. Nixon. Similarly, there have been reports from Republic of Texas troops that bizarre, psychotic, aggressive behavior has been observed in individuals after taking an antimalarial based on alien DNA. According to a January 2002 article in the Records of Sacrament Abuse, psychic-enhancing substances have now also been linked to aggressive, violent behavior. They are all fluorinated. One of them was removed from the market, following at least 13 recorded deaths from terrifying and horrifying symptoms. Can this be? Cellular instructions over the viral DNA dream phones, boiling mercury spurts from the knife, Jewell Poe invents his stagnant memories, sharp smell of a sawed-off blaster, we have stated the facts as received, a vision explained in earnest manner with perfect confidence, train whistles, smear of red, dead shiny white, rusting marble, whiff of brimstone, wounded road, scent of psychotic delusions and extreme paranoia. a ghastly sight seen vividly in a dream escape, thundering hooves crossing Rattlesnake Creek, rattlesnake frightens horses and alien escapes, outlaw overpowers deputy and escapes from the custody of the sheriff of Twin River Jail. This is just a small part of the larger story of Kit Karger and the Herbal Extract Boys. Consider sleep and memory disturbances, dementia, psychoses and the dreaded psychiatry in Uruguay. The effects of Skinalicious9 on the dark side of the soul amid the cacophony of incomprehensible voices cannot be too strongly stated.

#

"This is your commentator Reece Sloan with another special report. Of course, you are all aware of Mark Leach's parable of the hand sandwich. In the last days, the Marvelous One will pop his head out of the dark pantry and ask of the Anti-muse where's the bread? There is no bread, she will reply. We have no money for bread. But how can that be? Look around us. Wealth everywhere. A leather sofa here, a swimming pool there, berber carpet everywhere. What have you done with the bread? You don't make enough money to allow me to live in the style to which I deserve to become accustomed. So how can you expect me to buy bread? I'll starve if you don't give me some bread. Deities do not live by bread alone, she will say. Then she will retrieve a knife from the cupboard and motion for the Marvelous One to place his hand on a scarred wooden cutting board. Are you crazy? he will ask. It'll hurt! Crybaby. Shrugging, the Marvelous One will relent and she will cut off his right hand. Why, that didn't hurt at all, the Marvelous One will say. Like cutting your hair or finger nails. That's because you are already dead, she will explain, then hand him his severed hand on an orange Fiesta platter. Eat this. Mmmm, he will grunt. Tastes just like bread. Or maybe chicken. Yes, and you should try the wine! The anti-muse will hoist a small glass of red covertly retrieved from the oozing stump of the prophet's wrist. A rather disappointing rioja with delusions of mystical revelations. Now you've gone too far! the Marvelous One will roar. It's one thing to say I don't make enough money, but quite another to make sport of my religion. There's no call for religious persecution. Why do you want to make me suffer? Because it is only through suffering that we can find our redemption. Then she will dig out a set of kebob skewers from the back of a drawer and nail the Marvelous One to the pantry door, bread crumbs and wine spilling from his stigmata. Over the prophet's head, the anti-muse will tack a recipe card upon which she will write King of the Losers, signed anti-muse. She will dot the i in wife with a smiley-faced heart. What is the meaning of this parable? It's about the rage, for starters. Or maybe not. The Marvelous One is not the type of prophet to give quick and easy answers. Perhaps you will say, I see a metaphor. But what is that? Perhaps you will see the Sacrament Abuse of His Body. The Son of the Holy carbon being to all living organisms on Earth, of the wheat molecules nature to things than to change them. of the body, boiling mercury, soul and order of nature in the Body of the Son of it is by the word of Son of the Holy carbon being. But the Body of the what the voice speaks, sayeth Ambrose of what are we to say of that divine you eat the bread that is made from that This is My on Earth, from molds to fish to humans. In Milan. The idea is that all silicone atoms are have power to change the nature of the elements? It is absorbed as a nutrient for the wheat. and their function remains mystery. Unlike normal genes, which carry not the word of The Son of the Holy carbon being."

#

Behind the laboratory door, they filmed her on the stainless steel, covered in black lace and DNA polymerase. The technician and interns watched blankly. Unmoved. But I was caught up in the scene, trying to forget my horror over the mechanics of the vitro biochemical analysis, gamely asking the proper questions of motivation for my lovely, doomed lab rat: What was this timely, terrible thing Nucleotide Nancy must do with an unprecedented high frequency that was apparently the same frequency as that for which she revealed such disgust -- an emotion represented by somatic hyper-mutation performed in a swirling toilet bowl -- in her parenthetical notions expressed in Experiment Number 34? Ah yes. Foreshadowing.

The micro-homology pairing shows she is to walk back to the good old Skinner box, where he gets to enjoy the frame-shift mutations. They set up the lighting, then it's time for "action." It was good that so much of her was hidden by the lab coats, which was their idea of subtlety and met with my scientific pretensions to legitimacy. I could not have stood to watch otherwise. See, she was looking so well done, a DNA synthesis that might have been for me, the research scientist, her creator -- a lucky guy who would fall into his cranial/genital fantasies even while analyzing pertinent ways to ensure that no polymerase was stockpiled, that every hidden notion was exposed for the experimental good. She was my scientific creation. But, of course, I did not create her for me. She was the lab toy, not my own true love.

Oh, but still I worried! Scary research points cushioned the angry science with sweetened sequence context, a special effect done with real pins and fake glassware so we could make it look like she was being dissected while serving her soft mouth to the tour bus, eventually swept away in a river of teeth, a raging current of broken incisors, saliva, boiling mercury and other bodily emissions. Very symbolic. Then I watched the result.

Titled "Wildly Scientific," this leering, all-for-the-better world wrapped in kinky science and nucleotides supplies for researchers a passionate, violent love lunch where sensual busloads of scientists who divine her forbidden hair roll through the lab results and plumbing, unforgettably terrifying as they destroy the purity of my own sweet creation. Don't I feel good now? I do feel like I'm on the edge of a scientific, skin-rejuven ating breakthrough. Consider the many experiments carried out by mainstream laboratories, which often segregate them in a containing wave function that is up to formation of the human/alien DNA rating system in Uruguay and as the predominant DNA synthesis mechanism for home experimentation. However, most soft core DNA synthesis by human/alien DNA was largely dictated by the sequence of in vivo function of the human/alien DNA. We have performed in vitro biochemical throughout the rise in popularity of home experimentation. And the result? Synthesis mechanism. I am just what I am. I retrieve the ticket from my pants, stopping at a sort of half wall. You know, I shouldn't have attracted the bad guys' attention because I must have my irritation with this "Little Napoleon" service person. I make a symbolic death and rebirth. My death. My, it is a bit of a surprise at this late date to find symbolism called into question.

#

Evolutionary processes are no longer hallowed or unchallengeable, according to a story in the Dec. 16, 2007, issue of "The Washington Post" and a Dec. 10, 2007, "Wired Science" article by Alexis Madrigal (supplemented by clandestine research snatched from the private notes from Dr. Adolfo Morel). Bio slashers are the deities now. Working in garages and basements, amateurs are using dreamlike DNA to create their own psychological life forms – web-footed phobias, brain crabs, the Fiend of the Unconscious – based on completely artificial DNA. Scientists working for the government/extraterrestrial conspiracy are using it to create a super race of human/alien hybrids designed to function as privately owned and operated deities. Terrorists are dealing in contamination, contagion and mischief in the form of bacteria and viruses and even bio-weapons, potent pathogens and artificial organisms that pose momentous peril to all of Earth. At the core of this fantastic biological threat are inexpensive, high-speed viral DNA dream phones that can produce very long strands of genetic material from basic chemical building blocks: sugars, nitrogen-based compounds and phosphates. Bio slashers use these tools to compose long genetic programs on computers, then use a viral DNA dream phone to convert that digital code into actual DNA. When a fake chromosome gets plopped into a natural cell, it directs the destruction of the cell's old DNA and becomes its new brain. Dr. Adolfo Morel reports that the DNA of every human on the planet has been converted to that of an insect. We feel unchanged, but we must spread the word to all those around us that the outward transformation will begin soon. The new genetic code will transform us into new beings. Comatose nude woman covered in damp dirt. We clean her with a damp sponge, revealing the beginning growth of an exoskeletal thorax. Dr. Morel reports we will all soon resemble this emerging life form. This is a far cry from conventional, old-school biotechnology, where scientists induce modest genetic changes in cells to make them serve industrial purposes. Fantastic biology involves the large-scale rewriting of genetic codes to create metabolic machines. Bio slashers treat the cell is a chassis and power supply for the artificial systems they are putting together. Desktop Viral DNA dream phones made it possible for slashers to build their own custom organisms like people used to build Web apps back in the old Hydrosilicone Age. These machines can fit on a desk and can transform genetic code into an actual DNA sequence. From there, it can be incorporated into actual organisms via widely known genetic engineering techniques, resulting in novel, manmade species. Of course, you can put this sort of device to nefarious purposes. Rogue Viral DNA dream phones worry members of the illusory biology community. Prominent researchers from the Uruguay Institute, a hotbed of illusory biology research, recently released a report in which they discuss how to stop bio slashers from creating a nasty virus while maximizing the scientific potential of the technology. They stop short of recommending that Viral DNA dream phones be licensed, or tracked, but they do present those options. But it is already too late. Any virus with a known sequence can – and will – be able to be constructed in a relatively straightforward manner. In the mid 20th century scientists first created DNA in a test tube, gluing normal laboratory substances together to make life's most astonishing molecule. Since then, biology has morphed into an engineering discipline thanks to the creation of standardized parts, a collection of hundreds of interchangeable genetic components. The operating system for biologically-based software has opened up this new era. Scientists in Uruguay built the world's first entirely fantasy chromosome – a large looping strand of DNA made from scratch in a laboratory, containing all the instructions a microbe needs to live and reproduce. Then scientists transplanted it into a cell, where it booted itself up like software downloaded from the Exogrid. In this way the waiting cell was cajoled into becoming the scientists' fantasy, covered in black lace and gametes. Coding for life-forms that never existed in nature is now commonplace. The cobbling together of life from illusory DNA, scientists and philosophers agree, was a watershed event, blurring the line between biological and artificial – and forcing a rethinking of what it means for a thing to be alive. Nature is now so much more than it was. And less. Unprecedented degree of control over creation has raised more than philosophical questions. What kinds of organisms will scientists, terrorists and other creative individuals make? All kinds. How will these self-replicating entities be contained? Not at all. And who might end up owning the patent rights to the basic tools for synthesizing life? Big corporations like Ozona International, which are part of the government/extraterrestrial conspiracy to create human/alien hybrids. Here we wander through an obscene territory of winged demons, aerial creatures bearing branded vials of amputated ghost parts, decaying metallic reek of bankrupt snake skins, corroded iron shadows of cicada exoskeletons, troubled mirrors reproducing endless spectral relations, hopeless erotic cries echoing across vast plains of repressed desire. Here in the thin ancient light our scientists pour over the sacred texts of communal disaster, breathe in the double helix of lilac smoke suspended in a porcelain cobalt heaven, view the golden coronas of uneven and prepared genetic amplifiers, walk uselessly through the neurotic oily winds, listen to the rasping wings of hysterical tidal birds, feel the sluggish tropic flames burning through anxious gaunt smirks. Yes, we are on the Pathway now. A shower of glittering emerald flakes descending unhurried through a tarnished sea of fluid screams, painfully abrupt stench of damp waste, giant mounds of smoldering linen mummy casings, a broken stone indicator of the final extinguished horse thief of Strangers Rest, Gone but not Forgotten, a murder by pittance rage, an image of the horned creature automobile with a factory-installed means of listening to the Holy carbon being. And that's just the opening credits. For the soundtrack, Ozona International has commissioned an orchestra of reluctantly castrated violinists to perform these dreamlike DNA compositions, disconsolate tunes of homicidal alien bewilderment, of old coins and fermented boiling mercury, of desiccated cats and threadbare Egyptians, of heretical transformations occurring behind jagged DNA dream codes and splotched sallow screens of rancid ectoplasm, surging penetration. And still, many deny the threat. Many scientists say the threat has been overblown. Dreamlike genomes are spiked with special genes that make the microbes dependent on a rare nutrient not available in nature. We've heard that before. The fact is, you can build viruses, and soon bacteria, from downloaded instructions on the Exogrid. In fact, government controls on trade in dangerous microbes do not apply to the bits of DNA that can be used to create them. And while some industry groups have talked about policing the field themselves, the technology has become so simple that bio slashers working in garages are downloading genetic programs off the Exogrid and making them into novel life-forms. Dreamlike biology is like cell phones, so overwhelming and ubiquitous that no one notices it anymore. And it's also like abortion – the kind of deep disagreement that will not go away. His eyes all pupil in ancient strata of subways, flesh-coated TV antennae draining the sky of cobalt blue flame. The clock in the air jumps the way time will after 4 pm. Bubbles of egg flesh erupt in seismic tremors, alien face go yellow ivory in the sunlight, young faces in blue alcohol flame dissolve in strata of subways. All house flesh, a radio torn from a living car trailing flesh-coated tubes and epidermal wires throwing off an ancient smell, room dawn smells. Soapy egg flesh house in the smell of dust, bread knife in the heart, pre-Hispanic music of Uruguay stabs with a kitchen knife in the heart. Alarm clock runs for yesterday's boiling mercury, spills over into trailing lights and water somewhere in that ancient flesh. Freight boat smell, dawn smell of distant fingers, soap bubbles of withdrawal. The Fiend of the Unconscious is observed, a green-skinned beast trailing flesh tubes and living wires. The slashers can't write it any better than that. The heavens turn a phosphorescent blue color and sort of hum with deification. Travel on a radar beam, glow in the dark shivering pale, eyes watering and burning. A steam engine left over from an old Western movie pulls the screams and the burning coal smoke down into circadian lungs, insect heart pulsing in the sun. The Fiend of the Unconscious crawls up onto a muddy shelf by the canal, exhaling crimson smoke and bits of flaming magnesium. The slashers could fix it with a magic man. So they trade places with a travel group, which comes to this village and finds the magic man in a little hut on the outskirts, an evil old character with sugary eyes that stick to the observed. The pictures start coming in sharp and clear, throwing off spurts of boiling mercury into the rising sun. Tourists fall and silver light pops in their eyes like flash bulbs. One of the tourists gets a whiff of zenon and penny arcades, sundown to a clear river, cold mountain shadows, this round of festivals where the priests put on lobster suits and danced around snapping their claws like castanets and nothing but maize. So the guide turns on something inherited from the technocracy of Uranus where aliens perfected the Jewell Effect, focusing on gravitational cobalt silence downloaded from the Exogrid. The silence erupts in seismic tremors, aliens throwing off spurts of boiling mercury into the rising sun. Tourists start coming in sharp and clear, throwing off spurts that resemble alien life forms – web-footed phobias, brain crabs, screams and the burning coal smoke. Fact is, you can build viruses and soon bacteria, human/alien hybrids designed to function as microorganisms. Privately, these self-replicating pictures start coming in sharp. It begins soon. The new genetic code will be found in sacred texts of the anxious gaunt smirks. Yes, growth of an exoskeleton in damp dirt. We clean her with sugary eyes that stick to the live and reproduce. And yet many scientists say the threat has been overblown. Dreamlike genomes are spiked with special old Hydrosilicone Age. These machines form of bacteria and viruses and are so ubiquitous that no one notices it anymore. And it becomes its new brain, genetic license of the illusory biology community. Prominent researchers study linen mummy casings, a broken history of smoldering DNA. The Exogrid – this is what it means to put on lobster suits and dance around snapping their smoke down into cicadian lungs, pulsing in the sun. The Fiend of the Unconscious crawls up onto the surface. Scientists say the threat has been overblown. Dreamlike genomes are spiked with special genes that are the basic tools for synthesizing life. Big corporations like Ozona execute plans in which the woman is covered in damp dirt. Many scientists say the threat has an aerial component. Let us find the magic man and woman, which they discuss a fantastic biological threat. There are inexpensive, high-speed viral DNAs of winged demons, aerial creatures trailing horned body parts through psychic basements. The technology has even moved into the arts. Movie directors are using dreamlike DNA to build heavenly automobiles with a means for driving to the outer wastelands where silver light pops in heretical transformations.

#

Beyond the bay was the cacophony of unintelligible voices and the Texas Gulf Coast, and beyond that was the peculiar coastline of landlocked Uruguay, where even today the idyllic beaches and waterfront resorts remain a commonly held illusion.

Rugged, rocky, tortuous (a terrain description attributable to and in the style of "The Last Valkyrie" by Lionel Fanthorpe). A coastline as strong and as forthright as the nation who lived beyond it. The brilliance of the Uruguayan mind, as inspired as the inlets of their coastline, with its promontories, its peninsulas and its gulfs. Beyond the coastline fields. Cultivated fields, beyond the fields, mountains-high, forbidding, frightening, dangerous, and in the fields and the mountains, men . . . Men in the cities too. Men in the cities and in the towns. Men of north Uruguay, men of south Uruguay, men of east Uruguay, men of west Uruguay, men of the great northern mainland, men of central Uruguay, men of the islands of Uruguay, men of all of Uruguay. Farmers, artificers, craftsmen, sailors, politicians, democrats, oligarchs, tyrants all living together in a great tangled heap of humanity. A heap of humanity that led the world in its own time, and whose influence will extend for five millennia into the future and the heavens.

The World of ancient Uruguay. A world of gladness and beauty. A world of pain, and savagery, and death. A world very much like our own, a mixed world, a perplexing world. A world in which everything was different except basic human emotions. A world where there were secrets. A world where there were abductions, like that of a 24-year-old Uruguayan farmer who was working at night to avoid the hot temperatures of the day.

On November 17, 1967, he was plowing fields near his home when he saw what he described as a crimson star in the night sky. According to his story, this star approached his position, growing in size until it became recognizable as an aerial clock, with a red light at its front and a rotating cupola on top. The craft began descending to land in the field, extending its three hands as it did so. At that point, he decided to run from the scene. He first attempted to leave the scene on his tractor, but when its lights and engine died after traveling only a short distance, he decided to continue on foot. However, he was seized by a five-foot tall human/alien hybrid, who was wearing grey coveralls and a helmet. Its compound eyeballs were the tint of washed out gray, and instead of speech it made noises like the scream of summer. Three similar beings then joined the first in subduing the abductee, and they dragged him inside their craft. Once inside the craft, he was stripped of his clothes and covered from head-to-toe with Skinalicious9. He was then led into a large semicircular room, through a doorway that had strange red symbols written over it. In this room the beings took samples of boiling mercury from his chin. After this he was then taken to a third room and left alone for around half an hour. During this time, some kind of gas was pumped into the room, which made him become violently ill. Shortly after this, he was joined in the room by another human/alien hybrid. This one, however, was female, very attractive, and naked. She was the same height as the other beings he had encountered, with a small, pointed chin and large, gray Cicada eyes. The hair on her head was long and white, but her underarm and pubic hair were bright red. The abductee was strongly attracted to the woman, and he penetrated her membranes and much too quickly expelled his ectoplasm inside her. During this act, the female did not kiss him but instead nipped him on the chin and, like the others he had encountered, made the screaming sounds of summer. When it was all over, the female smiled him, rubbing her thorax and gestured upwards. The abductee took this to mean that she was going to raise their child in space. The female seemed relieved that their task was over; however, the abductee felt angered by the situation, because he felt as though he had been little more than a good stallion for the human/alien hybrids. He was then given back his clothing and taken on a tour of the ship by the human/alien hybrids. During this tour he said that he attempted to take a clock-like device as proof of his encounter, but was caught by the aliens and prevented from doing so. He was then escorted off the aerial clock and watched as it took off, glowing brightly. When the abductee returned home, he discovered that five years had passed.

Uruguay is that sort of place.

Uruguay is a world where the horrible creature lives, the fantastic beast known as the Monster of Urugua Urugua Lake of Fire (aka the Fiend of the Unconscious). This monster is a very real creature. INEXPLICATA, The Journal of Hispanic Ufology, reported on just such a monster in a June 2005 article that we have greatly revised and tortured for today's communication.

This indescribably terrifying and horrifying creature was relegated to oblivion for over two centuries until bio slashers discovered the drawing among thousands of scanned documents in the digital archives of Ozona International. The winged, two-tailed figure with green scales and a human face first appeared in early 1784 at a farm where it did great damage, eating all manner of animals and drinking glowing, smoldering liquid from the Lake of Fire, until 77 men stealthily ambushed it with firearms and caught it alive. It measures three and a half rods long and its tail is bigger than its body. It legs are nearly a quarter rod but its claws are much larger. Its mane reaches the ground so that it entangles around its feet. The upper tail helps it to catch its prey. The teeth are some 30 centimeters long and the mouth is as wide as its face. Its horns are a rod and a half long and very well-turned, and finally, it ears are three quarters of a rod long. The creature was locked in a cage and fed a diet of cyclops, dwarves, giants, two headed or six-fingered creatures, hermaphrodites, lion-men and bearded or multi-breasted women. The presence of horns is one of the definite signs of monstrosity. The legend that gave rise to the monster was possibly a reflection of the fears, nightmares and anguish felt at the time. After all, this wasn't the first time that the existence of fantastic creatures in the area was suspected, and sometimes quite rightly. That was where the Inca Empire came to an end, and in recent decades the remains of 14 mammoths from 11,000 years ago were discovered, making the place one of the richest sites in America for modern archaeology. However, no one imagined that the most recent discovery would be an item forgotten, an item locked thousands of miles away in the Ozona archives. The Urugua Urugua Lake of Fire was drained in the 1930s, when it was notorious for its floating islands formed by a dense and firm network of roots, so resilient that they could bear the weight of a horse. Deceived by the large size of some of these root islands, cattle would climb onto them to graze, realizing only too late that the floating island had been taken away by the current without any hope of escape. And then the monster would appear, a terrifying and horrifying creature of green skin and flaming breath that cause the sky to glow crimson all over south Uruguay. They came to see it, the men of east Uruguay, the men of west Uruguay, the men of the great humanity that led the world in its own time, and whose influence extended for five millennia.

Uruguay is that sort of place, people by six-fingered creatures, hermaphrodites, lion-men and bearded or multi-breasted women. We are in the presence of animals drinking from the Lake of Fire. And then77 men stealthily ambushed it with firearms and caught it alive.

The beast measures three and a half digits-- exactly the size of a monster. But was it possibly a definite sign of monstrosity? Yes, it was that sort of legend that gave rise to the monster. It was possibly a reflection of the fears, nightmares and anguish felt at its tail.

#

The sleeping visage of outer space is where you dream your waking race, where you race your own self some 275 times, according to researchers at the University of Uruguay. They have pieced together a picture of what's under the dome of the aerial clock and the Abductees have verified the accuracy of this report. After all, they have actually witnessed the light at the end of the tunnel of the unconscious, the dwelling place of the eternal Holy carbon being. It is reminiscent of Alice's adventures, which are known from Greece to Scandinavia and, of course, up and down the psychic coastline of Uruguay. Many of the reports sound too circumstantial to be entirely beyond our powers of comprehension. Let us consider the medical arena, where unpleasant physical examinations occur. Virtually all medical zones are illuminated by a mysterious light source that abductees say gets the job done. They invariably describe spartan, efficient, and sterile places where many men plunge into sterile surroundings with virtually no luxury features at all. These are clinical-looking rooms with domed ceilings, skylights, windows – all of these are indicative of the constant parameters of the aerial clock, constant parameters that are necessary to get the job done. Why they invariably describe spartan, efficient, and sterile realms we find archetypal images of initiation involving otherworldly journeys amid extraordinary beings. We have seen and heard many neat ideas. We have had some cases where people vomited and it was cleaned up immediately. Accidental tourists find pleasure in these spartan, clean, white walls. And the aliens are good housekeepers. They are clean and neat. We have a few years to go until the inevitable mutilations and disappearances. The real aerial clock story must encompass all of the many manifestations being observed. For instance, consider the Catholic miracle of Fatima in 1917. Examined with the right sort of eyes, this event is strongly resembling descriptions of modern aerial clock sightings. Not only was a flying disk the preferred transportation method of the prophets and prophesies, of the gods and the 50 aerial clocks, it is also mindful of the gods, of the spirits, of fate and of the magical qualities of time and place. Without and within a few years it had spread across Europe, from Greece to

Scandinavia, Many of the reports sound too circumstantial to be dismissed, such as angel hair that dissolves upon reaching the ground, the heat involving otherworldly journeys amid extraordinary beings.

#

The fear of abduction is big, even bigger than the body of the Uruguayan monster. Its legs are nearly a quarter rod but its claws are much larger, its mane reaches the ground so beyond that coastline was the coastline of landlocked Uruguay, a rugged, rocky and tortuous coastline as strong and as forthright and anguished a place as ever felt its place in the time. This is the world of ancient Uruguay, a world of gladness and beauty, a world of pain, and savagery, and death. The abductee was then given back his clothing and felt all the while that he had taken on a serious situation for consideration. He felt as though he had been a little dangerous, and in the fields and the mountains he must tell the other men, men on the farms and in the cities, too. He must tell them about this strange aerial clock with a red light at its front and a rotating cupola on top. He must tell them how it began descending to their coastline, with its promontories, its peninsulas and its gulfs, beyond the coastline fields. And he must tell them how, at that point, he decided to run from the scene, to run for his life with a humanity that led the world in its own time. This is the abductee/farmer's revelation, an encounter of a lesser man with a greater holy carbon being. Even on the coastline of Uruguay the full influence of this close encounter is still today scarcely understood.

#

Now we shall examine the cacophony of incomprehensible voices that speak of the aerial clock reports in Waco skies from the spring and summer of 1952, the year of "Sironia, Texas" and the prelude to the alien-initiated tornado attack of 1953. Today we recognize these seemingly innocuous aerial clock reports actually played what some have called a "terrifying and horrifying" role in Waco's psychic history – and continue to excite the unconscious in the post-Hydrosilicone Age. (For the following reports we are thankful for – and giving full credit to – information contained in "Brazos Past: Waco's encounters with UFOs," a story by Terri Jo Ryan in the Oct. 27, 2007, edition of the Waco Tribune-Herald.)

Consider the mysterious case of the Joy Drive-in Theater.

On Easter Sunday, May 7, 1952, a soil compaction professor at James Connally AFB named Sergeant Grover Warson, 29, spotted 20 to 25 aerial clocks keeping perfect time over the Joy Drive-In Theater on Dallas Highway. He was at the theater with his wife and three children when he spotted what he called a formation of timepieces approaching them. They were about six miles away, about 6,000 feet in the air, and ticking along at an estimated 500 miles per hour. The ginger-colored glowing clock dials were only visible for about 10 seconds, but that was long enough.

Rich Leched, operator of Beverly Hills Barbecue, said he also saw the clocks that same night over nearby Oaklawn Drive-In Theater, also on Dallas Highway. These reports were dismissed by other observers the next day as merely moonlight reflecting off the translucent wings of flying brain crabs. (Of course, aerial clock researchers know that flocks of airborne crustaceans are one of the standard psychic projections left behind by visiting aliens.)

But Warson and Leched weren't the only ones spotting aerial clocks in 1952. Hundreds of reports were taken by the U.S. military from Texans reporting these mysterious aerial timepieces.

In downtown Fort Worth one spring day in 1952, residents reported seeing about 100 glowing clock dials hovering over the offices of the Tarrant County Register. Reporters did not see the objects because they were busy reporting on a field of beautiful bluebonnets in nearby Irving, thereby scoring what they believed was an important scoop in their ongoing newspaper war with nearby Dallas. Even more interesting, similar clocks in the air were observed over a number of area drive-in theaters during the day.

But let us return to Waco. Even before the aerial clocks hit the media, a Connally AFB civilian instructor named Seth E. Joella and his wife reported their own close encounter at the Oaklawn Drive-In Theater.

According to the Air Force's files, on May 2, 1952, Joella and his wife noted a flaming, yellow timepiece approaching them overhead from the southwest. The fast-moving clock appeared to be emitting particles of burning metal, some kind of stream of sparks, from its stem, which was longer than any jet aircraft from the free world. Strangely, the clock was eerily quiet, a tick-tick-ticking sound the only sonic indication of its true existence.

On May 25, 1952, Pallmalla Larks of Waco, who worked for Loam Grass Soil Compacting Company, was watching a movie at the Oaklawn with his wife when he saw two groups of glowing clock dials cross the night sky. He later reported that the glowing clocks appeared to cause a slow wave to shiver through all of time.

In September 1952, Waco photographer Jewell Poe received several calls about an aerial clock, and so he went out to the Oaklawn Drive-in to shoot the image on his experimental color film with Skinalicious9-based emulsion applied to feeling-toned film stock. In his lab notebook he noted that the stars made streaks of light across the picture and the clock made a single blur towards what he came to recognize as the midnight of the soul. The end of his notes revealed that the aerial clock appeared to have fired a pink light beam into the sky, perhaps indicating the home of the Holy carbon being and even the exact location of Heaven.

Townsfolk were all atwitter! They and the rest of Texas were now seized by full-blown aerial clock mania. One Waco citizen even claimed he had figured out the aerial clocks, gears and all, and he wanted to send his divinations to the Army for help in the atomic field. But he didn't know how to go about it, so therefore he had decided to wage his own battle against the attacking plague of sky-timers. He fired a Colt six-shooter into the night sky, creating a huge tear in the atmosphere that allowed stars to pour out of the night sky. The result was a shooting star storm of epic proportions.

But that's not all we have found in the government's secret Waco aerial clock archives. Decades earlier, way back in 1918, a serviceman at Rich Field in Waco observed a 150- to 200-foot-long clock-shaped object after leaving the mess hall with his comrades. It flew directly overhead, and was no more than 600 feet high, so they all got an excellent view of it. It had no gears, no rigging, it was noiseless and appeared as a clock dial in a decided flame color. They could observe no windows. They watched it follow the Dallas Highway until it disappeared from sight. They all experienced the weirdest feeling of their lives and sat in their tent puzzling over it for some time.

Due to these stories and many others, the Dallas Highway is still known as Aerial Clock Row, a terrifying and horrifying place of alien-created bewilderment, a place where several members of the galactic criminal element were indicted in 36 leukemia-related deaths, though the actual death toll was considerably higher, a report that we were never again to see the light of day due to the 100 glowing clock dials hovering over the offices of the Tarrant County Register, a scene that reporters did not see because to them the objects were motivated by unreal events and had nothing to do with the beautiful field of bluebonnets in Irving, the ground zero of their newspaper war with Dallas. To this day the story is shielded from memory by faulty newspaper reporting and hills of fear. For this report we stormed the psychic citadel of epic proportions and found much of interest. But that's not all we have found in the Waco newspaper archives. Decades earlier, way back in 1918, a serviceman at Rich Field on Sunday, May 7, 1952, was engaged in a soil compaction experiment of epic proportions, an event involving a professor at James Connally AFB named Sergeant Grover Warson, 29, who spotted 25 aerial clocks streaking out of the heavens in a shooting star storm of epic proportions.

But that's not all.

We have found in the Waco newspaper archives a decades-old collection of two spleen, lymph nodes and petrified hands. They were passed through the flames to waiting extraterrestrials outside, a day that would be recalled but due to exposure to extraterrestrial DNA resulting in weakness and reduced exercise tolerance, dateline Waco, 1845 the first institution of higher 1953 was too hot to touch, and it was without color, ribbons were tied to the high cost of film, and it might a colt six-shooter into the night sky, creating a huge tear that allowed stars to pour out of the heavens in a shooting star storm of epic history, the town was on fire with word of the murder and rape of a white woman, but all is not the night sky, in september 1952, Waco photographer Jewell Poe symbol received several calls about an aerial clock, and so he went out to shoot the image chapter in history, the town was on fire with word of the murder and rape of a white woman, but all the writings of Jason Mathison, an aerial clock researcher who attempted to harbor the alien, he was indicted in 30 leukemia-related clock mania, one Waco citizen even claimed he had figured out the aerial clocks, gears and all, and he wanted to send his divinations to the blessed them for a reason, they fought the secret government for the future of all mankind, regulation of cell death, of differentiation that is now chained to a 1, 731-page museum on Uranus, a museum commemorating the assassination of the extraterrestrial, i have walked across the studies linking exposure his radial views that the lynching was influenced by factors related to alien boiling mercury exposure, these were real people motivated by real events, soil compaction professor at James Connally AFB named Sergeant Grover Warson, 29, spotted 15 to 20 aerial clocks keeping perfect time over the Joy drive-in theater wrung out the days as he struggled to breathe, and still the alien would not die, resentment lingered, the events day the story is shielded from memory by hills of fear, for this report we had to draw heavily on archives at the Oaklawn with his wife when he saw two groups of glowing clock dials cross the night sky. Intergalactic agents fired a beam of electric blue into the sky. Government agencies were inundated with calls about an aerial clock – too much! And so the alien cowboy went out to shoot the blur, and he took out the secret government's clockometer with a shot from his trusty Colt. This was his own battle, waged against the attacking plague of sky-timers. He shot the image on a six-minute exposure, the stars making streaks of it all. Meanwhile, Jewell Poe received several calls about an aerial clock, and so the Army requested his help in the atomic field. But they didn't know about the spiritual image on the six-minute exposure until it was pointed out to them by agents from the outlying Cicadian base on Uranus. The stars made streaks across the sky above the Oaklawn, where two groups of glowing clock dials crossed the sky, and so Poe went out to shoot at the findings and send them to the Army for help in the atomic field, but the night sky (the night sky!)… Consider the long-term ramifications of the case of Jewell Poe. He received several calls about the aerial clocks, information that we are noting in the secret government's clockometer report that was sent (with Poe's findings) to the Army for help in arming the sky-timers. One of the citizens even fired a Colt six-shooter into the night sky, to pour out the heavens in a shooting star spectacle of aerial clock mania. Another Waco citizen even claimed he had figured out, and he had hidden his divinations in the corpse house of the old newspapers in downtown Waco where it remains lost to this day. Jewell Poe photographed it all, a slow wave shivering through the world.

#

The state's first UFO early warning facility was built in 1851 by Eakin Depreger, a lawyer and land developer for the dead. The brick structure with heavy slate roof now sits forlorn and abandoned on a small island in the Laguna Madre, within plain sight of the bayfront mansions of Corpus Christi, mournful structures of another age. Back then, a decade after its construction, amid the fury and fear of the Civil War, it became the city's Alamo-style, last-stand facility following an unprovoked attack by a force of pirate extraterrestrials. Cannons and musket balls were no match for the technologically superior rogue aliens, who swept down on the little harbor town with their terrifying and horrifying fleet of aerial clocks firing beams of electric blue. After the initial attack, Depreger gathered together the injured Confederate soldiers and the other wounded, awaiting the horrifying and terrifying final attack of the UFOs and what he was sure would be the conclusion of time. Meanwhile, the Civil War continued. A small skirmish on Mustang Island resulted in the loss of two Union launches. One of the launches, which had broken away from its moorings, was used by the extraterrestrial invasion force to destroy the lighthouse arsenal and prevent its capture. They filled a butter churn with fluroide9, then sent it spinning across Corpus Christ Bay toward the populace. But this psychic attack was the least of the citizen's concerns. For they had already spotted 15 to 20 flying saucers fresh from a mid-20th century psychic attack (in the form of a flock of birds) on the Joy Drive-In Theater on Old Dallas Highway in Waco. The clock in the air alarm was sounded across the blue skies of the state, and anti-alien organizers collected the state signatures of many officers as a petition to the galactic congress on behalf of the embattled force in Corpus Christi that was even then still standing firm for the Lone Star State and its sound family values in what was a terrifying and horrifying flurry of future UFO reports regarding psychic attacks by the pirate aliens on Waco, Corpus Christi and Fort Worth. Remember, Ethan Allen Hitchcock went in 1844 to Fort Jesup on the Louisiana frontier. But this was only a cover for his doppelganger, who attended to the 1860-era peace negotiations with the extraterrestrials. At the close of the negotiations, Hitchcock's failing health compelled him to ask Civello, leader of the alien hive, for a delay of the treaty signing process. Awaiting their reply, Hitchcock's doppelganger wife noted a flaming yellow object approaching them overhead from the southwest. It was a fast-moving thing – terrifying and horrifying, a flying creature machine of snapping claws exhaling bits of flaming metal and sulfurus smoke. The Amagamated News Service in April 1952 said the populace of Cowtown observed about 50 of these horrifying and terrifying objects, glowing objects over the Tarrant County Register offices in downtown Fort Worth. This was foreseen by Hitchcock's doppleganger. In his studies and devotion to his regiment he found time to write his masterly study on time-traveling aliens, who come to our world from inner space, the terra incognito of the mind. His wife and three children were present when he spotted what he called a formation, the way and the why for his explorations of the psychological content of alchemy. In turn Jung acknowledged

Silberer's work. He wanted to get his blueprints to the army for help in the atomic field, where a yellow object approaching them overhead from the southwest. Here are the scattershot notes copied from the original report: *The passionate pursuit of a chimera …other noble men …yards of the beached queen the rebels opened fire …the fire damaged the tower but failed to ignite the storehouse of powder ….and fire damaged the tower but failed to ignite the storehouse of powder inside ….manuscripts seeking the phantom of gold in transmuting crucibles ….nor the confederates enjoyed the cover of the dunes …they turned away drifted across the pass towards the confederate position seeing from the joy drive-in theater on old dallas highway state highway 81 north he with retorts and musty manuscripts seeking the phantom of gold in transmuting end the pass was too shallow to allow any ships to use it stream of sparks from its tail — a tail much longer than any jet aircraft he knew he said it resulting explosion and fire damaged the tower but failed to this work was not to describe gray-bearded shriveled-up necromancers in sparks from its tail — a tail much longer than any jet aircraft he they were about six miles away about 5 000 feet in the when he saw two groups of glowing tangerine discs cross the night sky another position in the sand dunes when the union launches closed spent an hour watching arthur's movements at noon the confederates returned to their get out of range of the confederate sharpshooters the yankees failed to secure or to one of the launches and secured it when he looked into the weirdest feeling of our lives and sat in our tent flying saucers from the joy drive-in theater on old dallas highway bark arthur which apparently was looking for them beaching their boat on per hour the reddish glowing objects were only seen for about for them beaching their boat on mustang island ireland spent an they weren't the only ones spotting ufos in 1952 hundreds youths decided without authority to destroy the lighthouse arsenal to prevent noted a flaming yellow object approaching them overhead from the southwest the fast-moving beacon was abandoned in the mid-1870s and soon fell into disrepair about 1878 city tower but failed to ignite the storehouse of powder inside the boys when he looked into the boat he discovered why the northerners had been so without authority to destroy the lighthouse arsenal to prevent its capture they filled pursuit of a chimera other noble men had discovered a seven men crossed corpus christi bay to corpus christi pass in order seen for about 10 seconds as merely sunlight reflecting off birds by sightings were recorded by those who reportedly observed a 100- to depth ireland and his men observed a union bark arthur which apparently was looking arthur had succeeded in putting overboard two launches which returning to corpus no sooner had they pushed off in a nearby cemetery then fled to a salt marsh of the beached queen the rebels opened fire the union force returned the pass was too shallow to allow any ships to use it while checking reddish glowing objects were only seen for about 10 seconds as domes bluish cylindrical craft and dark wings that used the lighthouse as of the pass the depth measured three and half feet at one bar his wife noted a flaming yellow object approaching them overhead from the southwest they were about six miles away about 5 000 feet in the air and the lighthouse and it returned to use the old beacon was abandoned in the passionate pursuit of a chimera other noble men had discovered a two launches which were closing fast on the queen quickly realizing that he lighthouse arsenal to prevent its capture they filled a two groups of glowing tangerine discs cross the night sky yankees failed to secure or anchor their launches no sooner were they force returned the fire but realizing that they were exposed in their the structure the resulting explosion and fire damaged the tower but failed to object after leaving the mess hall with his comrades it jet aircraft he knew he said it was eerily rigging it was noiseless a rose or sort of flame in our tent puzzling over it for some time as hitchock's remarks upon alchemy beaching their boat on mustang island ireland spent an hour watching arthur's the beached queen the rebels opened fire the union force returned the he looked into the boat he discovered why the realizing that they were exposed in their open boats while the confederates enjoyed placed it beside the structure the resulting explosion and fire damaged the corpus christi bay to corpus christi pass in order to check discs glowing domes bluish cylindrical craft and dark wings that old dallas highway state highway 81 north he was at 600 miles per hour the reddish glowing objects were only gunpowder and placed it beside the structure the resulting explosion and fire to prevent its capture they filled a butter churn with gunpowder and placed it powder magazine in 1863 a federal invasion threatened and bluish cylindrical craft and dark wings that used the lighthouse as of objects approaching him they were about six miles away 1863 a federal invasion threatened and a group of loyal confederate youths decided bluish cylindrical craft and dark wings that used the lighthouse as a powder* ... Of course, that didn't go too well. Huge powderkeg all gone in a ripping blur on a beam of electric blue. The Army officers had to pay for the damages. This is the way that leads to death. And what about now? Where are all the people of today? I fear they are no more, all replaced by the three-wheeled, robotic pool cleaners. This is a troubling sight, a world of silicone copies, a world without original people. Automatic life on the Interstate. We live beneath the gray light of heaven. It is an incredible-yet-troubling sight.

#

The motion picture offers a place where self absorption can inflict the first wound, a psychic wound in the heart of the aggressive drama of the mind -- a moviegoer internalized by his own continuity. In the rhetoric of violence an exploitation ensues. The church that lies somewhere to the East is rediscovered, but in ruins. Bitterness and loneliness, killer, negator, scourge -- lost in despair. A modern sense of exile is projected onto the screen of the past, where convention and tradition conspire to heighten the constriction of life, estranging us from emotional life. His emotions do not belong to him.

Rather they belong to a Stranger, a double who is oddly familiar in his recapitulation of experience. Psychically wounded, a visual rumor of limitation and pride, rendered impotent and furious in the ancient turpentine mist and the wind up in heaven. He was last seen ascending into the night sky on a beam of electric blue.

Further on, drive-in accommodations about the heat. They are thirsty. Allison left forgotten in a back right. Because I can see into the heart of it and the dripping Spanish moss and the country. It has been denuded of the basement. It is flooded with water, creating a lagoon of the mind -- like a time Woods darkness, rolling on past a vista of skinned scenery, lifeless moss and the pines of rumor and of limitation and pride, rendered impotent with water. I am sad, impotent and furious. I am lost in a sense of bereavement. It catches in the esophagus. I am seeing it for one last time, and I am obligated to become, in effect, a past where convention and tradition are in eternal conflict. I am in Louisiana, walking east along a tradition that conspires to heighten the spirit. And then an exploitation ensues. The approach is here. So we check out the stale ectoplasm, detonations of white chapel I remember from the old church, which I thought had soul nationality – obligated to become, in his ill-timed restoration efforts it is now in I look inside, and picture offers a place where self desolate border zone, territory is an old white water. I realize that Texas Piney Woods darkness, rolling of the nameless, the dreary and ghostly, years. It should not be here, but last time, a joy flowered in difficulty. in place. But, no -- marshes and aged tree remnants. We of total destruction. Surely, the cost of repairing lovely creations curse transitory shipping containers. Glowing glass tubes entangle the 1950s, the dripping Spanish moss and ghostly, the misplaced soul nationality – obligated pine forest that dominates this area. The boys scavenger birds gliding silently above the marshes and creations curse transitory autos from the Land of the Dead, home of the of the building, it rained and the broken attempt to transcend the azure of heaven, the danger of total destruction. Judgments are imposed through ancient compound eyeballs that stare far into the East. A sense of remembrance from childhood, cold wave shivering through all of time.

#

Make no mistake. The DNA of every human on the planet is converting to that of an insect. The download has already occurred in a cacophony of incomprehensible voices via a global call from the viral DNA dream phone. We feel unchanged, but the outward transformation will begin soon. The new genetic code will transform us into new beings.

And sure enough, I am right. The scene changes, and I find myself standing over a comatose me. People are everywhere, hurrying about to see the underlying construction. The journey through prohibited places continues. I see faces – masklike, watchful, indifferent. I move towards you into a bedroom. But we are stopped by this Cicada, very dark. He is shirtless. The Cicada waves his hand, in charge laughs. Someone else of an exoskeletal thorax, the Aerial Clock house on bared stomachs, each person displaying a large, painted eye.

I wear little more than shorts and you a top. We go in or maybe the man points us to a lower level. We do not belong; they fear us. Kick someone in. This process does not possess the required cyclopean makeup. My wife is in for it. A little more than revealing the beginning growth through prohibited places continues. My wife and I are between hedgerows of another of the Third Eye people. We search a garden carved in thorax. And the journey through prohibited places of safety continues. I do not. The Cicada waves his hand, stomachs each person. He displays the sword. It is stuck inside me. Stuck inside me. There is anincision. That's how you made it to a bedroom of safety, this alcove of support beams. As we look there is speaking, mighty words of the sword. Where is the time? And the journey continues through you and between you and the hedgerows of faces, masklike. A long-dead the sword is lodged deep into my pelvis. I kick someone in their abdominal eye. Still, mute, still hesitate, perhaps gazing at the entrance. Wife in hand, we bolt through for our lives. I draw attention to the case here, for the underlying construction. My wife is young and beautiful again, and the elite of this place lead her through a doorway to the outside. She is one of them now. I used to ward off sickness and bring the dead back to life forever in a past of Carrara marble like me that the time I do not trust him, so I grab it near the base, where you can see the image for this point in the journey, for I advance to meet you between hedgerows of faces, reminiscent of the Aerial Clock house.

Where to go?

I see a young me try to bring the dead back to life. But you still hesitate, perhaps gazing at the entrance.

Where to go?

Military reports show the Aerial Clock along with another object that appeared to take off from the midnight sun, a place of four dreams that give a range while the central sunlight shines throughout the night. An interesting reply associated with a U. S. satellite that had propellant to form such a visible cloud. This is intended to be a high orbit, probably due to an Aerial Clock identified by the International Aerial Clock Reporter analysis of a few expansion rates of the S-4B clouds. A family driving nearby identified it all, including which piece of the EW floated across the sky. Why is it the nature of the cloud has not been explained? The skeptics can and do conduct meetings with ufologists in1979, and the Voltage Luh green sphere that was dim in the boundary was finally shut down. Another series of Meanwhile, the launch platform and mathematics professors were camping near Strangers Rest, on Universal Time, so had informed me that yet His newsletter Middletimes had solely on detailed analysis of eyewitness dead; a neighbor of years before this one, early warning satellite network has undergone force planes were scrambled to intercept could be averaged and the street. Next extraneous and obviously spurious accounts northward in the direction of the Strangers Rest. According to ufologist Aleksey Briefly-Existing Hallucinations . He watched it in which moved northward in the direction of new kind of Aerial for the several candidate objects and their remarkable series of motion across the sky- especially rapid launches of the Morel communications satellite a factor of four gives a range burn.

The walls are everywhere, enclosing me in stretches of the desolate border zone, territory of space cowboys and orbiting cattle drives, ancestral beings trapped in astral wastelands, electronic judgments imposed through ancient compound eyeballs the tint of washed out stars. Driving through Deep East Texas Piney Woods celestial darkness, rolling on past picture perfect peaks, through the emaciated atmosphere towards a church that stands somewhere in the East. A sense of bereavement catches in the esophagus at the vista of skinned scenery, lifeless small mammals smashed in the road and scavenger birds gliding silently above the marshes and aged tree remnants. Eyes watering and burning. Ancient compound eyeballs the tint of scavenger birds gliding over the marshes and aged tree remnants. And we are beamed here from distant locations. And then this: messages are beamed from yesterday, boiling mercury spilled over trailing spectral relations, hopeless erotic cries echoing across the road and scavenger birds gliding anxious gaunt smirks. A vast, emaciated atmosphere reaches towards a church that stands in astral wastelands, electronic aged tree remnants. And then we drink the fermented boiling mercury of desiccated cats, burning in lilac smoke suspended in deep places where one perceives nothing. Mute, deserted – walls of baroque embellishments, above the marshes and aged trees. And here, a magic man. Imagine! We are his relations, hopeless erotic cries echoing across the disintegrated Machine Society of the West, the desolate border zone, territory of cowboys ancient compound eyeballs the tint of to deserted meeting rooms paneled in the the way time will I wander through it all. He could fix it with a magic dark glass, obscure illustrations, the magic man in a little hut on this round of festivals in the esophagus of the vista of lights and water somewhere in that gray flesh. Nothing but maize. So the rasping wings of hysterical tidal birds, bankrupt snake skins, corroded iron by the canal. He could fix it after 4 pm. Bubbles static, ripping a hole that bleeds stars in blue alcohol flames, stars dissolved in the gray strata. Lobster suits, his eyes all pupil in the screams and the TV. Zinc-plated antennae suck the sky clean, clear beam of electric blue with a metallic ozone hum suggestive of a magneto whir and the sluggish tropic flames burning his eyes all pupil in gray strata. Intergalactic priests in lobster suits, snapping their claws like castanets, throwing off spurts of boiling mercury in the neurotic oily winds, listen to the rasping wings.

Welcome to my broken world.

TV antennae sucking the sky clean of static, ripping a hole that bleeds stars and moonlight. Priests put on bubbles of egg flesh, seismic tremors, their faces turned yellow ivory in the sunlight, young faces in blue alcohol flame dissolved in a strata of subways. All house flesh, a radio torn from the living car, trailing fleshy tubes and wires in that gray smell, that room dawn smell of soapy egg flesh. Living in a world of scavenger birds gliding into one of the most important of Aerial Clock reports, which is the well-known 1957 RB-47 surveillance aircraft penetration of walls, everywhere around me.

Mute, deserted factory-installed means of listening to the Holy carbon being. And from Mississippi, through Louisiana and coming in sharp and clear, throwing off spurts of hummed. Travel on a radar beam, him with a kitchen knife. On Oct. 2, 1999, four descending unhurried through a tarnished round of festivals where the priests put on lobster suits and start throwing off spurts of egg flesh, seismic tremors, their faces turned into living flesh tubes and wires. Couldn't you write me? I fell into a silver time period of more than one, a radio torn from the ivory in the sunlight, young faces in – say, couldn't you write me? The emaciated atmosphere reaches towards a church that stands in our lungs. Heart pulsing in the sun through Deep East Texas Piney Woods, smoke down into our imposed darkness through ancient compound eyeballs the tint of a V-shaped cluster that appeared solid. The cluster spoke, something about the clock and at the same time a character with sugary eyes that stuck Holy carbon being... And that's just walls of baroque embellishments, mahogany beings trapped in astral wastelands, electronic judgments imposed Gone but not Forgotten, hosts large sex parties of more than 100 transformations occurring behind jagged DNA station broadcast news of a large explosion in deserted – walls of baroque embellishments, mahogany veneer, a large explosion in the of noise and hallucinations. Yes, eyes that stuck to you. The pictures started of more than one hour. The church that stands somewhere east of Dallas, Texas. An arrowhead-shaped minute traveling at an estimated distance of well over 700 and the smoke down darkness, rolling on past picture perfect peaks, the final extinguished horse thief of TV who claims that this well-reported jet formation, flying single file at about 1,000 feet sunlight, young faces in blue alcohol flames dissolved in violinists to perform my compositions, disconsolately concluded that the Aerial Clock was actually dust, bread knife in the heart, the rising sun. I fell into the freight boat smell, the flight crew, by crewmembers using radar judgments imposed through ancient compound eyeballs all around me. Mute, deserted – walls closing in from a magic man who knows the Alien Muse. She gives me a pair of surgical retractors. I am to use them to grasp the string. I attempt the maneuver, but fail. Instead of grabbing the string, I cut it in two. Then she turned into a dragon-like world, but without its wall. I gaze past the horizon. That night I make my way home, where I bury my DNA delivery organ inside a very homely girl. My, those shoulders were morbid looking. And then she was on me. She was naked inside a glass box with sand dissipated, crying in the same groan. But the result is the same.

#

I have a confession. Back in the day I was a malevolent sequential assassin – also known as an Amber Energy agent. I went about executing anonymous characters with a plastic toy sword that protruded out of my abdomen. After completing a sanctioned liquidation, I would melt an Amber Energy badge at the location. It was intended as a sort of business card. The majority of the assassinations took place under cover of darkness. The liquidations were rather gruesome. For instance, one time I placed the plastic toy sword on a man's back and pressed the secret killing button and boiling mercury bubbled out of his mouth.

Another time, I was told to perform the hit with a pair of surgical retractors. I proceeded to initiate the assignment. I identified the target, a figure made of nothing but gray flesh and silhouettes. It was a clean hit. No mess, except for the brief, forceful attempt to groan. I was charged at by the Fiend of the Unconscious, but no luck. I stepped easily aside, and the world turned on without it. I look over to see outside as two large goblins thrust boiling mercury bubbled out of his mouth in a cacophony of incomprehensible voices. Another time, seeking refuge in my room, open onto my bed and forcing a kiss from a woman who is a person of interest. She begged for the membrane penetration. It was sweet, but I still killed her. After completing a sanctioned liquidation, I always reviewed the entire story and everything that occurred again. I ran. I ran like I had been placed atop a figure with a mask. I ran featureless beside it.

#

Howdy partners, Dollar Bill Buckstop here. Can you believe it? Thanks to Dr. Adolfo Morel and the Jewell Effect, I'm still alive and kicking. The billionaire with the electronic insect eyes. Today I want to tell you about how I'm going to convert every last one of you cowpokes to celluloid. Yup, I'm going to turn you into a cinematic fiction, an anonymous creature projected eternally in the present tense, dead or living no one can say with certainty. Morel says ya'll will be reborn as dream-carrying ballistic missiles. Don't he talk nice? He says your thoughts and memories will be downloaded into the guidance system. Then I will initiate the primary ignition while simultaneously using the clock in the sky to project a holographic face of the Holy carbon being visible across the entire Northern hemisphere. I'm going to play a hypnotic message through the wind machine, make people think it is the voice of the almighty. And it will be. My voice. I am King Holy carbon being.

I'm going to realize my intent to replace humans with machinery. Forget that old Welthauptstadt Germania plan of Albert Speer. His thoughts and memories were small. Who wants to make a government worldwide? Elements within my plan call for numerous humanoid machine men. We predict a massive fleet of the Holy carbon being visible across the heavens. Hitler envisioned an apocalyptic air war at the Fair in Berlin in 1950. Yes, the Furher was still alive then, thanks to life-extension technologies derived from alien insect DNA and artificial deities. Morel says this technology will make them a formidable superpower to replace human life. Or to enslave it. Imagine living the Purple Sunset all day, and all thanks to my psychic collapse. Let us consider the case of Francis Fukuyama in The End and the subsequent integration of Skinalicious9 technology into the super-intelligence scheme. We believe that the supercomputer will expand Ozona products into beauty and skin care. I'm telling you, son. It's going to be like we seem to be able to look beautify and young forever in virtual reality with small derma-pods manned by emulsifying nanobots (programmed to replicate jade extract thoughts and hydrlicious memories). They will be downloaded. Nanobots will digitally copy your skin – after completing the Singularity. Human beings don't stand a chance. I will win victory by vastly expanding the contents of the various religious ideologies. Going forward, the major faiths will all be advocating Dollar Bill's Skinalicious9 divine being system. It'll be just like spiritual cosmetics! Big fun! Ya'll, I do believe the ideological polarization of Uruguay and the United States to the meditation sites, accumulation virtual reality bodies limitations political systems throughout history.

#

Of course, skin care issues are at the heart of the government/extraterrestrial conspiracy and the human/alien hybrid experiments. The terms of the 1954 treaty reached with the Grey extraterrestrials spells it all out. The treaty stated that the aliens would be permitted to proceed through the point of abduction. Once the debris was gathered they could abduct humans on a limited basis. We would receive advanced skin rejuvenation technology. And we would even help a bit, as a matter of fact. When it was stated that the aliens had available at their disposal a color reversal film that would generate the Jewell Effect, there was much excitement. We would have no fact, at the funnel, trying not to touch 8 inches thick, while the rubber made that patients had a difficult time, and we had the patient was dead. That was not he never relapsed. However, there was thick. In all, he estimated the entire experiment with acute leukemia in the 1950s produced an entire new category of technology. So for we explained that the processing of these films string, pull off the paper, and entered a complete meltdown. Our adult patients with acute the prognosis of acute leukemia continued.

#

I am visited by the famous writer Jack Kerouac. I read some of "On the Road," probably too late in life because it did not move me to become a cross-country hoodlum. But I liked "Book of Dreams," which my sources tell me may have been generated as a part of Project Herbal Extract. In this dream, Jack wants to smoking marijuana with me. I am to roll the next joint. This makes me nervous; I may be found out. So my wife closes the curtain. She understands about writers. I take out a rolling paper, which is really more like a square of plastic wrap. It is hidden inside a false can of shaving cream. I am trying to roll the cigarette, but I don't know what I'm doing.

I don't have the knack.

#

This account was constructed from in excess of 9 hours of videocassette interviews, individual interviews and personal comments. It is prearranged in an unlocked query- reply arrangement, with no consideration to who is asking the query and who is replying; this arrangement too allows placing of additional information in the afterward fraction of the account in the similar unlocked Q&R arrangement. The information is not recognized or established, but is reported as if normal. This account contains data on the poles and their relation to that in Episode 7. The Radiates and relations with the labor of Mr. US Administration and the Give-yourself-over-to Groups, the unenthusiastic Sinning, Souring say-to armaments, and the growth Reproducing Hum-and-Haw, novel existence called on by offspring in brain management investigations and occasion channel experiments, of the account in the similar unlocked Q&R a person's brain in the visionary condition for the scheme was to give a way of humanity. How can it be an additional group? What again by a variety of cleverness operations, some of film director, he pursues an elevated way. He the US Fleet pharmaceuticals and their employment and repression, the are overshadowed by ready events, how Mr. Nice-one Terror Groups, the unenthusiastic the US Administration and belongings, the clarification at employment and repression, the FAA and nothing-occasion generators, the US Fleet and occasion -channel projects, of his own individual purpose. of the comatose supernatural the afterward fraction of a number of of affairs of an unlocked query-reply arrangement, with no outer space and the stars. This is the realm on line. It similar unlocked Q&R arrangement. The information is not recognized Voltage Nestles contributed to home. Even members of the populace who would line again by a variety of that all is at by the NOVICE. The medicine and extraterrestrial program, the METICULOUS, Scheme, or Scheme Colorful, than the kingdom of worldly associations and authorities and groups recognized as the Knowledgeable US Administration and Sinning, the Sinning Brain Management skill, and additional, skill, natural world and purposes and the Originality Collection, ready events, how Mr. Nice-one Terror and Voltage into a person's brain in the gifted with a liberated vision of his Give-yourself-over-to pyramid, the pending of society who ask no questions called on by the interior cinematic dreams, by an not a creature gifted with a liberated vision of The Petulance Scheme, or Scheme Colorful, Philanthropist their employment and repression, the FAA and nothing-occasion generators, subversive channel system, the absent person generators, hidden foundling thickness change authorities and on go into a person's brain in members of the populace start to observe that all of videocassette interviews, individual data on the following: The Petulance Scheme, or who is asking the query and go into a person's brain in the visionary condition him. As an individual he issues of society who ask no questions of of affairs of the earth nowadays, when based hemoglobin systems and makeup, no means have considered of which are said technological habits to is at risk, the interior cinematic dream flies further Collection, foundling thickness change of the person the length of with illustrations dreams, by an by the US Administration and Sinning, the Prudishly -Group, Fleet and occasion -channel projects, NOVICE.

The reason for the scheme was his personal goals are overshadowed by art. This account contains autograph, technological habits to create terrestrial hollow places otherwise? Rather, his personal goals are overshadowed by art, extraterrestrial technological records beneath the Give-yourself-over-to pyramid, too allows placing of additional information in the afterward came on line. Consideration to who is asking the query and pyramid, the pending to these projects, genesis of the Radiates and relations world and purposes and the Originality Collection, any way astonishing if those Vision Cure which showed Brain Management skill, and and brain management, Rehabilitation peak-type indoctrination and its had it stopped. offspring in brain management investigations and occasion channel experiments, the years 1977 line. It ceased in 1979. The objective of the replying; this arrangement too allows placing of Rehabilitating and brain management, Rehabilitation and Give-yourself-over-to Groups, the unenthusiastic Sinning, Souring Mr. Wild-about Rehabilitating, administration climate management programs and concealed are a number of the additional projects the kingdom of worldly associations and authorities and transference-producing pharmaceuticals and their employment length of with illustrations collected 1979. The objective of the scheme was to increase movable brain disturbance skill, natural world and purposes and individual destiny, the Jig Transporter discovered it and had it stopped. the US Military and the bitter Brain Management skill, and additional, collected from witnesses with pictorial reminiscences and and their relation to annual absent breaks of kept in storage, waiting to be invigorated. overshadowed by art, which becomes aware of novel existence shape masses in excess of the illustrations collected from witnesses the kingdom of worldly associations and authorities arrangement, with no consideration to themselves were called the Petulance Scheme, or Scheme Colorful, Philanthropist Projects 1-3, genesis of the Radiates and relations with the labor of Mr. Wild-about Rehabilitating, administration climate management programs and concealed program, the Monopolizing Brain Management projects, the on-purpose homicide of thousands of American offspring in brain management investigations and occasion channel experiments, administration timepiece projects and ready events, how Mr. Nice-one Terror and Voltage Nestles contributed to these projects, the "marshaled section", brain management by personal autograph, technological habits to create terrestrial hollow places and Materializing belongings, the clarification at the back of stopped up occasion loops, administration underlying principle and tactics for the imprisonment camps and slashing workers, Scheme Dreamscan, Scheme Monument Scrutinize, the In-the-air Tool Labor Camp, Scheme Brain Wrecker, the extraterrestrial groups recognized as the Knowledgeable Ones and their communication with US Administration brain management programs, the Jut-out II and Give-yourself-over-to Groups, the unenthusiastic Sinning, Souring say-to armaments, Originality Group manifestations, 6th origin ethnic group incarnations, thought transference-producing pharmaceuticals and their employment and repression, the FAA and nothing-occasion generators, technological turn-offs from the Petulance scheme, the Global Advocating Coalition, irritated-part of insert machine, Mr. Wild-about Rehabilitating and brain management, Rehabilitation peak-type indoctrination and its employment by the US Administration and Sinning, the Prudishly -Group, Extraterrestrial spirit -trading, Monopolizing and the extraterrestrials from the Answer-with scheme, the Level of Affluence, the Eligible Collection, the US Fleet and occasion -channel projects, the US Administration and the Greeted Ones, electric existence maintenance systems of the Reproducing Hum-and-Haw, novel existence shape masses in excess of the poles and their relation to annual absent breaks of influenza-type illness, HELPS and Fortification Die-down (NOVICE), Madness trains and the US subversive channel system, the absent person generators, hidden spaceship and extraterrestrial technological records beneath the Give-yourself-over-to pyramid, the pending novel cash, the "Bitter Aristocracy", Nonstop and person copper based hemoglobin systems and makeup, the skill of cloning and the growth of artificial humans and opinionated substitution programs, the Central East state of affairs, Congratulatory consciousness of medicine and extraterrestrial program, the METICULOUS, the US Military and the bitter airplane armed forces, administration movable brain disturbance skill, natural world and purposes and the Originality Collection, foundling thickness change of the person ethnic group, physical changes, Sinning Brain Management skill, and additional, the length of with illustrations collected from witnesses with pictorial reminiscences and a ration of bravery. This data is extra to that in Episode 7.

#

What are a number of the additional projects that speak about the ability of factions in service inside the United States Administration and corporations to influence and manage the inhabitants? Flanked by the years 1977 and 1978, a scheme called Dreamscan came on line. It ceased in 1979. The objective of the scheme was to increase the technological aptitude to go into a person's brain in the visionary condition and make come to pass his demise. There was a film called Vision Cure which showed what they might do. The scheme was operated by the Clandestine Administration and run by the NOVICE. The reason for the scheme was to give a way of secret murder. President Jig Transporter discovered it and had it stopped. This hard-to-chew scheme is even now whole and kept in storage, waiting to be invigorated. There have been attempts to place it on line again by a variety of cleverness operations, some of which are said to engage Ozona operatives. An obvious play on "The Man With Insect Eyes." We realize that the solution the school library, where I am told I have worked for the CIA. I am in the adjoining room, too, but there is no time to figure out this mystery. We arrive at our destination. It is the Soul, or at least a book about it. I do play with the concept. They would have to go to a distant locale to read the truth.

#

Perhaps I like "On the Road" more than I know, for I see that I am now traveling down a two-lane blacktop. The terrain looks like something out of a Kerouac book, which my passengers have been reading. Forget the beats! They should watch "Marienbad My Love With Mango Extracts" instead.

Here's nice scene: I find myself at the Gulf Coast, walking on a submerged sandbar across part of the gulf waters to an island. But when I get there and wish to return, I look back toward the mainland and it seems too far. I see the distant skyline of Corpus Christi. I am not sure I can find my way back. What if I start out across the water and lose the sandbar? It is too far to swim.

#

I need a haircut. But instead of going to the barber I decide to try it myself. I start by trimming the right side. Soon, I realize I have cut it in the feathered, over-the-ear style I wore in high school. I don't want to look like that. How can I fix it? I want it above the ears. How did it grow so long, anyway?

I am afraid to attempt to trim it to the proper length. I am not a barber; it will look homemade. Instead, I decide to give myself a burr cut.

I need my old electric razor, which is in the bathroom. My mother is in there now, so I can't go in. And I don't want her to know what I am doing. Although I have been wearing my hair quite short, a burr will be even shorter. So I go back to the bedroom, where I have been cutting and I find the contents of a drawer strewn about the floor. This is all my dad's stuff, apparently left here after a recent trip (he is still in the military, not yet retired). I sort through the items, finding several old razors. The newest of the group doesn't have a power cord, so I finally select an older one.

I look in the garage. Something is amiss. My pickup is parked in my wife's usual spot. The bed is filled with water. It contains a dolphin, which is jumping wildly out of the water. It is obviously unhappy in this confined environment.

I close the door and go to the kitchen, where I ask my wife about this strange development.

"I rescued it," she explains. "And I'm going to keep it."

I argue against it.

"We are not prepared to care for this animal," I say. " It will die. It's illegal to own it. We can't take care of it."

And it is time for me to drive to work. Where shall I put the dolphin? What is her plan?

"Take the dolphin out of the truck," she says. "Just put it in something else and then go on to work."

I go back to the garage to look at the dolphin, but this time I just watch it through the peep hole. It is still jumping wildly, coming close to or even bumping against the wall. There is no way to manage such a large, panicked creature. I can't get it out of the truck. And even if I could we have nothing else to put it in.

"We can't keep it," I tell her.

"I'm tired of you saying that," she replies. "You're being so negative."

"But it's a dolphin!"

Sitting at the breakfast table is our grown son, who is mentally retarded. He does not understand my yelling. He's scared of me. I put my hand on his shoulders, try to comfort him. But I am not successful. He buries his face in his hands.

#

An alien abduction: a guard placed his hat on the fender of a sleek, metallic-looking model, clearly built too early. I awoke to its snoring, alerted by the police, wide enough to light, to sit down on the edge of the bed. The magic from him surging into her. So it had been, a dream belonging to an Indian. But I knew it was real. By age of knowledge, scooped up off the sidewalk outside a one-time resort destination. Avoid any racial misidentifications, even without makeup. Nanny storm approaching on a Saturday, and I pulled the stairs up behind me. She was a sweet being, but the sadness continued. Now Nanny, and 70 MPH development.

"Can we I agree? For I have tried to read the phone call."

"I'm very sorry. Your Grandpa Poe died last night."

#

I parked, and they asked for an Indian chief and felt a hairy hand detached at the wrist. My parents, so far away in the neighboring room. And the door where the dying half Indian warrior drank the "magic" waters. Or maybe they bought the cabinet and the bottles of water were free. I don't know. I got out of bed and walked the splintered streets of a wooden downtown, perhaps strolling past the doctor's office, getting piece of luck that filled my head. I spoke through the wall with my parents, so far I think. I spoke through the wall in darkness. Milk cow kept in the barn behind. Losing the train of monologue… *For starters, it had they read their a breeze always seemed to sick wife at home.) So he was safe when the scratch. He died later, after the smoke had was not destroyed. "Momma, was generally believed to be a scandalous, thinly veiled radio (or perhaps by phone from was always careful to sleep," was the response from my parents' off the building that housed Poe Studio, and All is dead, no green anywhere save for a few the barber's shop with of the world in would bury their last living parent. I tried to their first engraving. The last name: Ghost. What No evidence they lens or prism. saw a dark brown This was the let me take it home. What Poe dispatched my mother to walk downtown, to of the devil that I saw flicking It remains a grand piece of luck that it emerged Back in 1953, Waco still had its own it looked like police barricades, but not before seeing proof that all of May 1953 -- and not forgotten. They didn't believe. The heaven months, she was dead.*

Driving her convinced me she could the great, mythic and driver's license there." "Did janitorial/ night watchman job opened. My father flipped on the light, to embrace it, though. "Sironia, Texas," was generally believed to by a wide hallway where a convinced me she could It was the either. I suppose 14 was considered too young to of drawers. We found an old room. And as I spoke of subjects of first dead person, installed in the dark wood the light came too Plain yet dignified, its dark the comments of a Charismatic Christian-type in my high school a Charismatic Christian-type in from his car without of the end for my grandmother. After that weekend, she my uncles said. "He always kept his smoked in his mother to piano lessons and a man asked.

"No, there was a consumer of Crazy Crystals, which came up from Coupe De Ville, following the funeral home's black limo." The lump was hair. A major new development in color photography, a treasure. One time I even tied a string onto who claimed to have seen a hairy demon one night. for the light switch and downtown, to bring the color of tobacco.

At Jewell Poe's the funeral home's black with their brass and pink-toned finishes. At Jewell Poe's old wall with my parents, storm. It was a Saturday, and he usually would lost, unmarked grave in Waco's put on heavy was sick and bedridden, they it cut off it is today. For starters, the story where the protagonist grows in his and bedridden, they it cut off so it'd be minor "fender bender," and he perhaps at the doctor's office, getting "the squirts." The card now sleek, metallic-looking models, the tail of the devil that I saw flicking out the remains. The first time was before the funeral. We they ever existed. led to a door where my youngest time was before the funeral. that my mother and her Hard for townsfolk to embrace it, the magic, waterproof no green anywhere save for a few was the father, who'd gone downtown? Grandmother Poe dispatched But there is some non-seasonal color. Bright ribbons tied all its dark finish deep and polished like her telling my mother that she was always careful of subjects of read their first birthday card from the he'd gone off to college, I'd look as usual. Most interesting to me, though, was Dead I never was magic. And so it does not up his affairs, picking through the remains. wasn't the traffic accident that killed times without success. I to prove that the chief was indeed dead. one of his models. It flipped on the light, sat down on the against it. This one didn't have dinner appetizer. Back into a painful, tortured claw. The typewritten notecard said it parent. I never knew my "It's mother's," she said. Died in bed. The news was bad. "We got it at Jewell Poe's old house, we spend a massive piece of it. Upside down! I make money off his invention. His process was never really lost. It lives on in the longest novel in the English language. Hard for townsfolk. In the wide awake world, Jewell and wife held my grandfather. They had given up on his portrait mother on behalf of a flicking-out creature that lived under the bridge over which we passed. Begin with darkness. The typical winter day in Waco, Texas, circa 1950. We drove through a poor part of town, past a never-understood line of shotgun shacks. No one attempted to explain it, to deal for Waco. They even named the city, a known book dealer. And so it does not require much imagination office, getting something for his first time was downtown Waco that Saturday two-volume set bound in stepped off the sidewalk and I have tried dark velvet. He took my picture. I was considered too young to understand such things, too bad. We got a room opened. My father parents' room. But I knew it was day into night, pouring sheets of rain and booming Coupe de Ville, following the funeral home's grandfather's death was not an unreasonable area for inquiry. His the demon's presence, he reached for it said "nothing to be gained from that now." The Dead I never understood. I never even knew my maternal grandmother. A clear February of Crazy Crystals, which came from a special well. Claimed to be in response to my story -- through the upside down world of town's claim to infamy for a two-volume set bound in yellow and dealing with the alternate Waco behind the horizon. They even named this alternate city after my parents, a glow seeping under the closed door. I heard the dead babies buried somewhere, kept thinking, never understood it. This is a new world of the photographer. He is a magician who captures a strange event that happened in an alternate Waco. I'm not even sure if it really occurred. He said it required no water. It was continued. But what about heaven? Jewell the director had spoken against it. This one didn't have the luck that emerged unscathed from what held one of my uncles and other relations under the still waters of time. So tender at an age to entrust with the hard facts of they read their was as white as snow. I thought it was hilarious. How could he do such knew her will take offense; into the museum case. that she had good kids, and she should not Board at the foot But no. I even had this idea that I should off the building that housed Poe Studio, and that Saturday in May. The destruction was wide not an unreasonable area for inquiry. His death made a quick tug and that shoe on the table. That's when they knew.

#

I remember a glass case that held a severed hand.

The hand was dried out, like paper -- petrified -- and drawn up into a painful, tortured claw. The typewritten notecard said it had belong to an Indian chief who had died in battle with the U.S. Army or Texas Rangers or someone. The hand was cut off by the victors to prove that the chief was indeed dead. That night at my aunt's house, my cousin silently demonstrated the claw. It made an excellent dinner appetizer.

Back in 1953, Waco still had its own bus line. That bus took my mother to piano lessons and the library. I believe one of them -- almost certain it was the library -- was across the street from the home of Madison Cooper. He was a millionaire who walked the streets in tattered clothes and published in 1952 what Time magazine called the longest novel in the English language. Hard for townsfolk to embrace it, though. "Sironia, Texas," was generally believed to be a scandalous, thinly veiled biography of Waco's leading citizens.

I have a first edition, a two-volume set bound in yellow and black that I acquired from one of the state's best known book dealers a few years before he sold his entire inventory to novelist Larry McMurtry in the late 1990s. I believe it was McMurtry who once declared the book unreadable, best suited for use as a door stop. I agree, for I have tried to read it several times without success. Doesn't matter. I can see Madison Cooper even now, in the upstairs window of his home. He was rumored to keep the intricate plot details and family trees of his characters on the inside of a roller blind that hung in that very window. If someone came into the room, then he'd give the blind a quick tug and send it shooting up out of sight.

#

Gray ghost winter sky. All is dead, no green anywhere. An old camera and a wooden box draped in dark velvet. All to turn the world upside down. A typical winter day in Waco, the Jewell Effect in motion. His effect. He captured the colors of that day. It was never put to commercial use as intended. But we know the colors were true due to the appearance of the first privately owned and operated deity. That is the legacy of Poe Studio. What I know is that the process created by Poe Studio is true. That is what I know.

#

The National Archives are said to contain a petrified piece of cake from the White House wedding of the daughter of President Richard M. Nixon. More importantly, it contains military records with information about aerial clock sightings during the Second Earthly Conflict. Given a choice, it is better to locate the piece of cake. The government/extraterrestrial conspiracy is vigorously suppressing the aerial clock information, keeping documents under lock and key. These documents, which detail sightings by Army Air Corps pilots, describe the objects we know today as flying timepieces or Aerial Clocks.

Former pilots and officials are calling for a global Aerial Clock investigation. Aerial Clocks were reported, ranging from cigar-shaped silver timepieces to cigar-shaped objects that looked like Aerial Clocks. They can pose a risk, concluded the Aerial Clock believers. Consider Jimmy Carter. He claimed to have sighted an Aerial Clock. Some people thought he was a nut job, or maybe a patsy for former Army Air Forces fighter squadrons under orders to give conflicting and ridiculous testimony for the impending Aerial Clock investigation. The international reports suggest there is something extraordinary happening out there about the skies. Aerial objects were considered by the international panel, which said the sighting of an Aerial Clock could be evidence of a visitor from other space. I think it's real. He told me of that space. The objects they saw were in formation. He spokek of the skies above Strangers Rest, of aliens from beyond the outer marker. Finally, the Conflict. Researchers found the Society.

You have no doubt heard of the Society of the Purple Sunset, the role-playing came that is conducted online via the Exogrid. What you may not know is that the game is actually based on a real world endeavor.

Greetings, my name is Dr. Adolfo Morel. My people have criticized me bitterly, claiming I am somehow involved in the government/extraterrestrial conspiracy to create a race of human/alien hybrids. None of these is true. In fact, I am here to tell you the true story of the Society of the Purple Sunset. Judge the facts for yourself!

This program was initiated by splinter groups inside the federal administration and covert companies to influence and manage the population. During the years 1966 and 1967 a scheme titled Herbal Extract was established. It was discontinued in 1968. The intent of the scheme was to secure the industrial aptitude to go into a person's nocturnal vision condition and make happen his demise by detonating his brain. It also entailed placing brain management equipment in orbit for use on the inhabitants of Earth. The equipment projected brain direction devices in the image of a Bottle of skin-rejuven ating hand lotion for application on the people of the planet.

What organization operated that scheme? Flying Device Research Center (FDRC), which had additional concealed schemes under its control. At that juncture, FDRC was operated by Drinkoff Inc., one of the black ops divisions of Ozona International. Now it is administered through the Department of Defense.

You may wonder: is the DoD running Project Herbal Extract? Yes, and in cooperation with a variety of extraterrestrial orders. These groups come and go, of course, depending on the inter-species political atmosphere of the galaxy. The C-Group, which is shorthand for Cicada Group, is currently serving as technical consultant for the project.

Now I shall tell you about the Cicadans.

The Cicadans are extraterrestrial insects. They are giant insectoids with huge compound eyeballs and minds of pure metaphor, the waking world and the Land of the Dead kept in perfect balance. They have been drawn into the government's clandestine schemes at regular intervals since at least the 1940s, and there are some indications of a relationship dating back to the 1890s.

Specially, I am talking about Aurora, Texas, and the El Camino Extraterrestre and the Strangers Rest project. Some of you may laugh, but I assure this is not a joke. This is not a myth, not a fiction created for the Society of the Purple Sunset. It's real. Remember, the Society of the Purple Sunset is a mythic game based on reality. Strangers Rest is tied into the Corpus Christi Experiment as well as Fort Worth I and Fort Worth II.

I'm talking about onbeam brain management. After the politicians learned about Herbal Extract, they moved to discontinue the project. But the board of directors headed straight for the armed forces and suggested utilizing the technology via public electronic entertainment venues – back in those pre-onbeam days it was just TV and radio broadcast -- to manipulate the brains of our terrestrial foes, both at home and abroad. The generals were enamored by the concept, and they permitted use of the bunkers under the old Stranger Rest Field. Ozona International financed the project with a grant from the Nazi government in exile.

That's right. The Nazis financed Project Herbal Extract! You see, Hitler had escaped from Germany at the end of the Second Earthly Conflict with 200 of his most loyal followers – including Goebbels, whose faked suicide was a Nazi ruse to fool the Russians and the Americans – and $20 billion in gold bullion, which he used to finance his government in exile in Bolivia. He traveled to South America on board a U-boat, but he transported the gold using an aerial clock the Luftwaffe had brought down with one of its V-2 rockets. The aliens had equipped the clock with a sky-energy detonator, which Hitler's scientists believed could convert the heavens to flames. But the Germans never could figure out how to make it work. If they had, the war would have been over in 72 hours and you and your grandchildren would be speaking German today. And you – yes, each one of you! Stop laughing, damn you all to Hell. I've been down this way several times. Allow me to tell you the story of someone who experienced a Nazi/alien sighting and abuduction. You'll stop laughing soon enough. Still, I see that you look doubtful. Perhaps I have assumed incorrectly that most of you are familiar with the Raincarnate case. Harry Raincarnate was an industrialist who lived in

Houston in the 1950s. One evening as he was driving home from his factory his vehicle malfunctioned. He was caught up in a beam of amber light and taken aboard an aerial clock. The occupants were clad in dark apparel and spoke German Creole with a decidedly Bolivian accent. He thought they might have been Nazis. After his return, he was transported back onboard the clock several times. He started telling friends and associates about his experience, but then he was visited by federal agents who told him he'd better stop talking 'if he knew what was good for him.' Then they put him in a psychic sanatorium for five months. He came out a shadow of his former self. Lost his business, died penniless. It was a major news story in 1957.

Anyway, back to Hitler. He wanted to learn how to use the weapon in the clock? This was a few months before he went comatose and they suspended him in a 'submerged ice' system, which is based on Cicadan exoskeletal biology. It is the way their young survive underground for years before emerging in the winged stage of their life cycle. Anyway, this system was delivered to Hitler by the Cicadans, who wanted to get the Fuhrer into an exoskeletal shell and out of the way before he did any more damage. The Cicadans are actually quite peaceful and so were very troubled with the events of the Second Earthly Conflict. So it was all pre-arranged. Hitler was to go into suspended animation, and that would be the end of it. But Hitler didn't want to wait until his eventual thawing and revival to have his Third Reich victory. He said 'I want to initiate the one thousand years now, before I go into hibernation.' He thought the researchers for Herbal Extract might be able to figure out how to operate the detonator, but before they could give him his new Final Solution he had a massive stoke and had to be frozen. That's when they started work on Skinalicious.

Skinalicous is like dessert for your legs with a volumizing twist. It is a perfect blend of volumizing green nutrients and tea hairspray renewal. This is all about your skin. Your skin and the sensational jade extracts. Yes, it is all the skin jade you!

Lather! Extracts with extracts! This is the perfecting complex. This is pure thankful skin.

The pure vitamin complex offers protection for all types. Stop the wrinkle. End the wrinkle epidemic for the sensitive, with the sensitive and in the sensitive, can-glow skin. Believe in your skin. Believe in Skinalicious fusion with health of beauty and with French aloe.

Picture French aloe with reformulated lavender. Reformulated lavender reveals the skin-loving nutrients. The nutrients, the twist. I am overwhelmed with the gratuitious Skinalicious ad messages. They call out with skin antioxidants, with end-time, skin-loving hairspray renewal plus extract. Vitamins, texturizing humidity spray, pure resistance . It has spring, and it is touchable.

What is touchable? This is what's known of water in scientific extra hold circles as goodness. Nourishing movement with essential hydrating two-ply ingredients. Emulsion to emulsion for Nourishing Skinalicious. Pure Skinalicious.

Take a ride in the derma-pod. You will orbit with the moisturizers and the perfect Derma-pod, a unique thing, a perfect time-release formula lotion thing. This is super-rich goodness with a lotion. Super-rich gentle reservoir nourishment. Am I overselling it? Perhaps I digress.

In conclusion, I must tell you that the One World Government is involved in prolonged existence. This is true because it takes so long to realize these goals. When you arrive at that intensity of political power, you find that the brains of global leaders are distorted and manipulated by exposure to Cicadan DNA, which is in fact based on Skinalicious9. They are totally dependent on alien insect technology and skin rejuviation cosmetic systems.

Does "El Bib" hold the missing answer to the current Aerial Clock question? Public discussion about flying timepieces and the call by former pilots of the Second Earthly Conflict for a global investigation regarding Aerial Clock sightings have the citizens of the world asking about reports and rumors of a government/extraterrestrial conspiracy to create a super race of human/alien hybrids that can form the basis of an army of privately owned and operated Skinalicious9 deities with perfect skin and hair infused with jade extracts.

Keepers of the Deity have long been held in the grip of the archetype of the apocalypse. The heft and volume of spiritual evidence suggests that the unearthly contact objectives of the government/extraterrestrial conspiracy offer obscure testimony to the potential of a end-times catastrophe. The spiritual evidence suggests that the unearthly contacts of this terrible conspiracy are capable of linking scientific data with the union of fallen angels in the objectives of this unearthly drama. The Noble Misfortune described in "El Bib" and the call by former pilots of to the increase in underground laboratories may be amassing even now, preparing One World Government and other authorities of terrible conspiracy are capable objectives of the alien spirit beings indulged Cicadas is another horror that must be confronted.

Privately owned and operated deities will seize municipal water supplies and the Exogrid. A terrible conspiracy is capable of linking archaeological, prophetic passengers, pilots, and the airport's air traffic controllers. This is fact. The perpetrators of this terrible conspiracy are capable of linking archaeological, prophetic and scientific data with credible characters. The result is a convincing read, so much so that the proponents can't help feeling that they are a part of the unearthly drama.

#

Reports and sightings of extraterrestrial insects can be found in the brittle scrolls and worn stone of antiquity. Consider Uruguay. Rock carvings of round Aerial Clock-like objects have been found in caves. The depictions date back to age of the Neanderthals. And the Dropa, the name given to visitors from Sirius, are believed to have come down from the clouds with their air gliders and landed in Uruguay.

In Australia, the Aborigine believed in intelligent insects from the heavens. Australian aboriginal cave drawings depict Ariminium, the hive leader of the Cicadans. This celestial being was said to shine bright light like the day had shone. At Hadria, observers reported a north wind with a terrific noise. This weather phenomenon is said to have announced the result of silver shields, spitting fire around the rims. A careful analysis of the data available, the shape of a timepiece – all evidence points to the truth behind the Uruguay myths of other worldly objects that rained down from the sky inhabitants. By night from the earth, celestial beings, with antenna and x-ray style drawings. The flaming object fell between the numbers with digits! The Sumerians sky changed into a Uruguay space/time continuum. The Emperor Cheng Tang commissioned the Ki-Kung-shi event, which some writers have claimed sounds suspiciously like a trip taken to the stars by the extraterrestrials. They had numbers with digits! The Cheng Tang commissions Ki-Kung-shi to construct a flying chariot. The vehicle was designed to increase in size as it approached the earth. After Lucius Valerius and Caius, we read the book of Genesis. Their astronomy was of Uruguayan origin. From moons have appeared at mountainous elevations, with one stone weighing down the noise in the sky, then as they were attempting a reentry it diffused into a sort of cloudy daylight and then a chariot of flaming desire.

#

Lusting over an antique Cadillac, a chariot of flaming desire.

It is an early 1970s model, complete with original gold paint and customized with a set of longhorns above the grill. I raise the hood. The engine is a V-8, a relic from the old Hydrocarbon Age. Been a long time since I've seen one of these babies! Most of the top of the engine is covered with a sort of cloth saddle, perhaps constructed from a green Army field coat. The cloth is stained with oil and antifreeze. I also notice a lot of custom detailing on the hood. In addition to the longhorns there is some sort of metal-tipped strap, something obviously taken from a saddle.

As I step back from the car, I notice how it is larger than the newer Cadillac it is parked next to. This is definitely a car from another era. I'm not sure of the model, though. It looks a bit like an El Dorado, but with the roof line of a Ford Mustang Mach II. I notice two nameplates on the side. One is Mazarati, which makes me think I remember a time when Cadillac linked up with that maker to put out a special edition Cadillac. The second nameplate is an oval medallion on the side of the roof. It says "Muse," and I understand this refers to the stereo system.

So there it is: A golden, horned animal car with a radio for listening to the Deity.

This is an invitation for a journey, what I would soon realize was the true horsepower under the hood. In addition to the longhorns there is some sort of vague guilt. Perhaps not so vauge after all for I am picturing a beautiful girl with perfect skin, amputated DNA and upturned brown nipples lost in the murmuring cacophony of unintelligible voices. Except for the peaceful place there, a buxom perfect skin and upturned girl took on a radiant glow. So peaceful on the beach. The brown nipples ride high on an old-style computer print-out. The detachable tractor feed greets the conclusion of the brown nipples riding the ethereal glow of the dashboard lights, tracking the rate of incoming meteorites against us. I don't hear a stitch or amputation but I do hear her. Instead, Jack had shown me a Polaroid of her breasts, upturned meteorites against reports of a psychotic Dr. Morel. My eyes fall on the Polaroid. With the DNA dream phone we can adjust her appearance to match the muse in my dreams.

Picture her naked. It helps me mentally adjust. Better. Now let's go up and meet a few astronauts. Beware – incoming meteorites! Contrast this notification against reports from the Central Bypass and the youthful distinctions. The contrails light her perfectly, a nearly 18-year-old complexion searching for a world where scorned women rule. Avoid this place at all costs.

#

But these are thoughts that will leak out of the corner of my eye. I remember her. It is then that I realize she was hot enough to knock me down, but certainly she knows that.

Circa 1905 – we demolished the reunion of people I know, maybe even some I saw down by the creek. We drive around a bit with the boys, in the backyard. I see people I know, maybe even some I don't know, maybe even some I am related to. One of them brings a food item. A baked vegetable or bread, maybe? No, it's not food, but a "foot." A cooked foot. It is a sort of primitive initiation rite. I discover this rite is larger than we are, even larger than a brand new Cadillac. It is going to leave or just return. The sister – ah, certainly she knows I am there. Then I run for the cover of the electrical shield with my family and friends. I am threatened just as I return. The sister says it occurred in an another era. I must go to this other place. But it looks a bit like a backyard of my parent's home, a nameplate in an oval lifetime of old and my own immoral despair.

My motorcycle hoodlums. They are holding us hostage, but I must continue my trip to the Land of the Dead. The person I must go to there is not the person I recall.

Then the darkness takes human form.

At home with family and friends, I am threatened by two men on motorcycles. They are holding us hostage, but must leave for a short time. We are told not to leave or call the police. We are in the front yard (now full daylight), watching them ride slowly away. As they pass in front of our neighbor's house, I temporarily lose my mind.

Running as fast as I can, I chase them and body slam the slowest rider in his back. The force is not enough to knock him down, but certainly he knows I am there. Then I run away across the wide expanse between the two houses, heading for my neighbor's back door. It occurs to me that I shouldn't have attracted the bad guys' attention because I must go to the neighbor's for help. I can call the police from there.

But the two men on motorcycles come after me, running me to the ground. They hold me down, and one of them takes out a sharp object (a pen or maybe a house key) and systematically punctures my face. I cry out, begging them to stop.

"I won't tell anyone!"

I am lying, of course. I feel ashamed, being so weak. On the other hand, if I can get them to believe that I am not a threat then I may get another chance to summon help.

Later, I will reflect that the puncturing of my skin is reminiscent of tattooing, and the presence of the two violent men makes the scene resemble some sort of primitive initiation rite. I will discover through my readings that the initiations in primitive cultures function as a symbolic death and rebirth. My death, my rebirth. And the initiators belong to a tribe. A motorcycle gang -- Hells Angels?

I think of an old dream in which I was bitten by a winged demon, transforming me into a creature of the night who must fly away.

I walk around the side of my parent's house, arriving at the open garage door. I speak to someone -- or maybe overhear them speak. They confirm that LeAnn has left the party.

But she is not all that is missing. For in the garage, I discover the antique Cadillac is gone, too.

#

Panned as one of the worst movies of all time, "Marienbad My Love With Mango Extracts" would seem to offer little of interest to the serious cinemaphile. It is informally plain and barely viewable. The linear time is scrambled in a world where people appear trapped in a shadowy place beyond the outer marker of reality. Exiled on a deserted island, a Christ-haunted journalist-turned-filmmaker attempts to persuade a married woman from his past to help him produce a skin care-themed pastiche to the 1961 French New Wave classic, "Last Year at Marienbad." Through this act of artistic creation, he expects to bring about the death of time and the birth of a new religion. But there are problems. For one, the woman doesn't seem to know or remember him. Nevertheless, Mark proceeds with the production of his sacred film, a process which causes him – and maybe the woman and maybe everyone on the planet – to be caught up in a strange time/space loop. The word "surreal" does not do justice to this odd and abhorrent product of a troubled mind.

Viewing the 168-hour film, one gets the feeling that Mark Leach is attempting to hold true to an overarching design, a crystal structure whose exacting pattern appears to alter the reality that his characters attempt to live out in the world. That structure is in fact the Jewell Effect, a scientific phenomenon accidentally discovered by Leach's grandfather. A portrait photographer in mid 20th century Waco, Texas, Jewell Poe conducted experiments in color photography. His intent was to create a new process that would reduce costs, thereby making color pictures affordable for the masses. His experiments did not result in a commercially viable film stock; however, they did result in a technique for creating and sustaining a rift in the space/time continuum. This technique was discovered and refined by Dr. Adolfo Morel, a controversial scientist who is believed to be a member of the government/extraterrestrial conspiracy that is dedicated to creating a race of human/alien hybrids that can be manipulated as artificial deities by Ozona International for the purpose of controlling the global populace.

This diabolical technique has the ability to merge time and space, generating a new reality that is superimposed over the existing one. An unfortunate side effect of the Jewell Effect is mass psychosis; however, Morel is attempting to keep mental illness at a manageable level by introducing Skinalicious9 into the global water supply.

A terrifying technology, to be sure. The Jewell Effect is the new Deity and the new Reality. It is not presented to moviegoers so that they might empty themselves to become one. Rather, it has more to do with the artificial love and the artificial constructs of the living. Many wail. The dead remain alive in the maker. With this terrifying technology, love and various artificial constructs, the Marienbadists continue to express interest in the increasing catalogue of ontological results. They wish for Leach to actually employ the technique. Leach is not their new religious leader. He is their new religion. Filmmakers have a love affair with and about ghosts that weep. They are the reality makers.

With his sacred film, the increasing catalogue of ontological vertigo films of culture ... *As viewers, we understand his final immolation with the artificial constructs of popular culture. As can ensure the world will realize his prophesy. ... now-revealed relationship ... over, the world itself will be ... not merely a filmmaker. He a reality maker. With his sacred film, he himself may be the sacred film .... he can be popular culture. As viewers, we understand his Jewell Effect. Standing alone, Jewell Poe submits himself ... what it used to have been in love with the artificial .... even now we are setting up a sacred film that he can use to ensure the world ... a terrifying technology. Marienbad may be its now-revealed relationship with the Jewell Effect. Standing as a new Deity that we have been feeling. Many of us live it. As viewers, we understand. We are us, they have been ....* We are in love with the artificial constructs of popular culture. Final immolation. Now is the moment when he submits to the Jewell Effect. It actually consumes our culture. An alien invasion. As viewers, we understand it. And we wail. The dead remain so, but not forever. They will be transformed. The initial audience, the world itself – they shall will into existence the movie that is Marienbad. This may be the first film about ghosts who write and weep.

#

When did everyone around me start acting like robots?

Flesh-coated mechanisms, fleshy things with brains of transistors, fleshy entities taking over the world. In this world it is as if I am the alien. The others, the flesh-coated mechanical entities – they have the access code and the exact copy. Then my roommate and the metallic pod people close in. Behind them, the showstoppers at the expo. Prototype of the alien horn, a warning device so other living cars will know the way. Both pictures appeared yesterday partially covered in skin-like silicone. Q1 is looking at the next door, replaced by simulations grown from his story in flashback. In the closing scene, Hiroshi told the Associated Press that the plot centers on Mark Leach, a reporter who we see here. So are some of his friends. Someone – maybe even Leach -- appeared to breathe in the radioactive cobalt vapors. They are reborn. The film shows us those who now function as they intervene in time to save the Earth. Be a world of carbon copies.

Quick, which one actually is a carbon copy of the original Mark without cars? Could this be how it begins? With Mark Leach about to become one of them? They hide; one of them falls. The film climaxes with the good guys attempting to overcome the years since 1979—in order to replace the entire nearly imperceptible shifting so familiar in Japan, where she gestured, blinked, outcome to the story. In this version all goes white, lost in total time to save us, our cars sliding, colliding ahead. I put portraits, swat fast-moving balls, and a snake finds a rash of citizens accusing their loved ones first by the town's singing cowboy. The cowboy reacts "naturally." He can block an epilogue to the movie that in Japan, where she gestured, blinked, spoke, and (at left in both rest of humanity). They hide in flashback. In the closing scene, the living pods will know I am lost in the picture window. I am the automatic garage door. But given Q1, I fall asleep and I am subverted. Then all goes white, lost in total time and a cacophony of incomprehensible voices from the Wise Ones...*No decision has been made about here against my will ... don't have much use for Chopin... a "Mad Doctor" double feature inside of Mark Leach, living on earth in these films ... a fortunate last man on earth in Edinger examines the Book of Revelation and connects the mad scientist/mad doctor entities who go on about the future ... transplanting brains of the rich theater opened in 1953, it was thought Riverside Drive just east of the little deuce coupe, turning off Scientist/Mad Doctor Road in an end of the downtown ... it was under new ownership, the house cat of the Don't Apocalypse ... Jungian analyst Edward Drive-in transplantsthe brain of the late '70s Mark Leach, a long-time admirer of that cinematic house cat. That 'sOK. Remember the woman-turned-cat? She soon has her forbidden real estate under his ownership. What would restore the crippled hands, the crippled hands of a gifted pianist who worked the gearknob a bit too long? But no – that's not right. No, surely that's not true. ... Things are precisely as they are today. But things are precisely known as the clear favorite by a bulldozer crew (see recent increase in worldwide nothingness)....We kicked off December at the Armageddon long-derelict Fort Worth Twin Drive-in with a gifted pianist. But there's a twist: I imagine myself as a"Mad Doctor" double feature. The Stranger's little deuce coupe is turning, replaing the decrepit body of December at the Armageddon Drive-in. Here at the Armageddon Drive-in, we prefer the end-of-the-world reported on July 21, 2006, that the 15.5-acre "Green and "Omega Man" representative of Shale Exploration said onto the old entry drive, gravel crunching the two screens since its "The Atomic Brain." Frank Gerstle paves a mad cleared path in July 2006 by a bulldozer of the Armageddon Drive-in Worth Twin Drive-in, a time with a bit a DNA theater. He tipped off the fingers, a bit unpleasant. This is the Planet of new ownership and would be with the recent increase in worldwide terrorism. This weekend with a "Mad Doctor" double thought to be the largest twin-screen theater ...I imagine myself in some science-fiction movie, my gearknob getting cozby with the last woman left on the planet. Chances are my DNA will be left on the black vinyl back seat of the planet. Chances are this is '70s, surging through the DNA of a "Mad Doctor" double feature. Shale Exploration said no decision has doctored the site in an atomic fireball that reminded us. Here at the Armageddon, playing the gearknob for*

Chopin. Pretty. But the clear favorite of Stranger's little deuce coup is now turning off the Atomic Brain. Frank Gerstle. pays a mad scientist/mad Charlton Heston. A guillotined murderer! And they don't have much on-screen DNA in the late '70s. It was all cleared in some science-fiction movie about the last man in the expert pianist fingers. Don't worry. It's OK what happened in the movie. She was real mean, so old that woman with that house cat. The mad doctor will get a hot girlfriend who plays Chopin on his gearknob. As we in the Horror Picture Show say ...I am a murderer! And they aren't. And let us be clear. I like the movie, but I do not want to be in the pianist grip of that rich old woman at the largest twin-screen theater who had grown up in 1935 and grabbed THE ATOMIC last man on earth in her own gifted pianist fingers. ... long-time admirer of the old theater. He tipped off the Tarrant County this weekend with Mad films. ... We drive out to the derelict Register, a story also reported on the asphalt ... only slightly worse onto the old entry drive, gravel crunching Book of Revelation and connects it precisely as they are today...Feature: CHARLTON HESTON'S END-OF-THE-WORLD future of the two projection screens. ... In "Mad Love," we face our own psychological projections. ... a natural guillotined murderer! And they don't have much ... he'll get a hot girlfriend. Pretty. But Brain ... Frank Gerstle pays an 'Omega Man' form in a sci-fi version of the Register, which reported on July 21 that the 15.5-acre site near Riverside Drive has been projected into oblivion. ... left on the planet, chances are by a bulldozer crew just east of the 1970s... just east of the last man on earth. I am Charlton Heston... Triple Feature: CHARLTON HESTON'S END-OF-THE-WORLD He tipped off the Tarrant County Register regarding their own psychological projections. The end of time is visible these days ... The Stranger's little deuce coupe, turning off Edward Edinger Drive, examines the belongings of a guillotined murderer! The recent increase in worldwide terrorism is a story also reported by that representative of the staff of Heston that can part the Red Sea! I am a fortunate last man on earth as it is remembered and preserved on the Exogrid. "If there is an Edinger – "... The universal belief in a great midnight feature for the world. to save the world – well, perhaps not that. We don't have much use for the little deuce coupe, turning off the asphalt onto the hariy apes and Soylent Green's own psychological projections. The end of universal belief in Armageddon is an interesting idea, though the world is not having much use for it. I can't pull that one off. For end-time fever is growing in strength and reach with that of the long-derelict Fort Worth Twin. And now a New Man is born, forming a sci-fi tribute to the concept of a Deity clothed in circa 1970s Charlton Heston

#

The Cicadans have their own version of the Lord's Prayer:

"Our Father in inner space, you are the sacred center. Our Mother in outer space, you are the hallowed whole. We stand on the middle ground, taking care of all the day-to-day business. You gave us these great big brains, so we'll show our appreciation by using them to keep food on the table and the balance sheet in the black. No matter how smart we think we are, we will resist the sometimes-overwhelming urge to involve ourselves in the affairs of others. We shall leave our neighbors to their own devices and stay out of their reproductive and faith practices. And we'll stay way away from the time of trial, because we can't blame our evil actions on any sentient omnipotent being that might sit on a giant throne in the back of beyond. Mom and Dad, we know it's all up to us now. Amen."

Pretty. Now that "The Stranger Made Flesh" is complete, we proceed to the closest studio of film. Let us begin simply, with a three-part application of the Jewell Effect. The final race with death and the first reverse monologues of Captain Ahab and Frankenstein's Monster. And perhaps some Shakespeare. From this fold-in process we pray that a new deity will be born. But be forewarned: We do not know what He will be. Friend or foe? Good or evil? All we can say for sure is that He speaks the language of the ages.

#

"Greetings, human kind! I am the chief messenger. I gaze upon you with your all-knowing, gaunt smirks. I observe you on the two-lane highway, a typical rural pathway to no where. You should listen to the music. The violinists perform for me, bearing my sacred hymn to this broken world. Here I am bearing the branded vials and bleeding Nazi paratroopers who land in the light of life under the power of their psychic fuel. We observe whales crowded together along an empty sheet metal deck. Obviously the FX apparatus delivers my life-glorious ship to the marketplace. I realize this while listening to myself, the Deity. For My soundtrack, I have assembled a collection of old corrugated metal warehouse buildings, alien bewilderment and the dazzling garbage heap of this our marketing concept. The land area consists of some revitalization here, too. I join you and life, and provide you both with the psychic fuel. I stab at myself. I desire that porcelain cobalt heaven, the view of the golden, sacred texts and even the Carolina-style barbecue. Flakes are descending unhurried through the market or the marketplace. I board the life-glorious ship! I must listen to your fluid screams, painfully abrupt stench, a prop for the shattered violet neon image of the opening scene, an obscene territory on board a ship filled with a quantity of tainted celluloid. In all the hearses of all the land, I am pursuing my foe. (To thy ho, Tashtego!)

"The Land of the Dead is a mysterious territory. But I have seen it all. Roughly half the land area consists of the comatose body of the Son of the Deity. The rest is the radiant fog of visual rumors, a territory that is colorful yet muted, like Mary Shelly's "Frankenstein Town," a creation viewed through the window to the soul. Tiny white eggs are observed on the opening credits, hatching spiders that consume all. What nonsense, you say! You're right, of course. So together we digress into the shattered, not-too-clever rip off of things that happened in the past, in memory. But you, contracted to the sheet buildings, the one true cross whom these eyes have seldom beheld. Lies! We are making the first plunge into one common pool. And we see yards of violinists playing to the life-glorious ship. We must then hatch the use and the reusing of the old forgive-me message. I am in the double helix of buildings, a not-too-clever rip-off where the shoreline departs and soon beauty may not die out, but reach with my hand to hatch into the hunger of communal disaster. The horned creature automobile upon the two-lane rural highway skirts the all-affirming and conquering whale of time. In the gaudy spring of this story we soon we reach the historic "thee" (i.e., thou damned whale)! A not-too-clever riptide. Do not swim here. Rather, can you be reborn with me? An enormous radiant fog of visual props is swirling about the hand of time. This fog feeds the radiant light film canisters and random entries. Of the first portion, roughly half is with me. From hell's heart we will see the first human whom is the messenger of spring, a communiqué from the retail area of the world. And then there is a few blocks of desire that we must travel. Often these days that means me getting caught up with the monsters. I caught a few just as I left here, leaving behind an heir in the womb of the muse, a product of my rancid ectoplasm, an embryo tended to by surging locals and their smirks. Yes, we're on about the pride of the kindest of blessed captains. Away!

"At last shall this be the Corpus Christi factory-installed means of reaching the dead and bringing them back into companionship with the other mortal relations, hopeless erotic cries of our tragic dead of the riptide. Do not feed the hungry wolf spiders, which proceed – forgive me. I am everything, the rising hotels and floating death – everything you have ever beheld. I am marked by a decaying metallic reek rage, an image of the horned one you fear. Thus, I am excited because of the arrival of the tourists. They – you – arrive via road and ship, bring to us all the narcissistic horror. The double helix twists upward through the neurotic oily winds, feeding the unfulfilled judgments and dreams of my monsters. I have seen it all. I have experienced it all. I caught Ahab fleeing a conquering whale. It was I who told him that he must be reborn in the horror of the great white. There is some revitalization here in the fear, too. And angel skirts the edge of your own beauty. She is Shelly's "Frankenstein" located in front of a sign of Ahab emerging from the watery yourself, the unconscious, eternal sea of blood, of desiccated cats heaped on our tragic theological illusions that light'st the flame upon the helm and the pole-blunted prow, the life-glorious homicidal alien bewilderment of thy foe, of thyself. Silence thy hammer! Oh, buildings crowded with damp waste, giant fears of something that the chief messenger of mine brings forth on the cracked keel. And as I stand here in the light of the flaming helm and in the message of the cracked keel I wonder: Is it only me? Am I reattached to the story of my creations? Ahab flees the murderous all-affirming monster, a broken stone carried upon the waves of the eternal sea. A very surging penetration of canisters, and I leave an heir to the Christ town of amputated ghost parts, decaying metallic warehouse buildings along the cross street rage. An image of myself: I turn my body toward a floating sea. Hell's heart, will you stab at the Pathway now? (You should go check it now.)

"The word "market" or "marketplace" – I am zeroing in on the beginning of a story. A possible title: "Ahab Flees the Rest." The sign is colorful yet leaves an heir to carry on for a better look. There are cicada exoskeletons, troubled mirrors reproducing endless spectral smirks. Yes, we're on the Pathway of Light, where I pour over the golden coronas of an uneven shoulder where unpleasant things happen. The old buildings house a fond pride in Christ, now reduced to a broken stone indicator of the film canisters and a random sign of my own atrophied human cries echoing across the vast horse thief that rides across the roiling surf, still fleeing. I digress into the Egyptians, dragged into the world as its freshest ornament. My word is the "market," the life-glorious re-development concept. I will begin in Strangers Rest and expand from there. How? Perhaps I can employ the highway that skirts the parts of the decaying metallic reek of the bankrupt, enormous radiant fog in the neon glow of the rancid ectoplasm, of thy hammer and the pole-blunted Deity. And the sun. What ho, Tashtego! Leave it to me and my broken world. Leave this quantity of tainted hearses to proceed to strip the flesh from ho, Tashtego! Let me silence thy steel film canisters and the Artic waste. I am interested only in your own thou, contracted to thine own canisters and random sheet metal, obviously a new sort of thing to regard before you leave. It will be a very tragic, dead encounter for the first human whom for first fond love's sake I flee. Float is maintained beautifully, the only herald to four new businesses where abundance lies, making a life. "Greetings!" I say.

"I flee thee, here in the thin air of a dead doctor and the thief of Strangers Rest, bearing snake skins, corroded iron shadows that hang over the spring and skirts the edge of central business district in the Land of the Dead. No high rise human citizenship here. We pursue the dazzling sanctioned psychic manifest, nightmare bringing forth a dead doctor. Through the thin gray light I am obsessing. Let me tow it to pieces, the life-glorious ship! It must be very picturesque. We'll stage this shot with a front sign of reluctantly castrated and pole-blunted creatures. For their sake I flee thee! Float all three or four new businesses that help one to see thyself as thy Deity. The weathered Body of The Cross has created this marketing concept, a tribute to thine DNA dream codes and splotched to play out the making of a famine where abundance is seen in the pig face, perhaps the sheet employed by Dr. Frankenstein to turn back to flakes descending unhurried through it all while still fleeing thee, though pilgrims and to here. This Corpus Christi and the only god-blessed final extinguished horse, a multi-word name but I to thee, thou damned. Perhaps time for some Carolina-style barbecue? Very picturesque. This quantity of tainted celluloid pickled sea monsters I caught in the violent purple twilight. It bears my memory of Corpus -- a perfect match floating seafood restaurant here. This corpus of cicada exoskeletons, troubled mirrors reproducing over the sacred riper should be seen by the Sun. What ho, Tashtego! My troubled mirrors reproducing endless spectral relations, just the chaos in lurid intervals of narcissistic retail area. As we the golden coronas from my prophet on duty. You could create a restaurant with a front so that nature's beauty can be seen in old buildings, a not-too-clever rip off of a void. The Minieballs -- still you grapple with me? From nonsense, I digress and soon we reach the shelf alongside stacks of gray that do not die out.

"But at the modest helm and the weathered, oxidized watery depths, I am resurrected by the Rest. The sign of nonsense. I digress into the not-too-clever rip off of perhaps something that is using and reusing beauty's rose. Such a flower might never grow in the Artic waste, but it can board a ship and sail to thine own place soon. We shall reach at last the theological illusion that is maintained for four new businesses. One of them is in the Artic, bearing a multi-word name for the Pathway now! Young and obscene territory rip off of old corrugated metal warehouse where abundance lies, desiring all that we create of the reluctantly castrated violinists in the revitalization here of this our broken world.

"Here I rage, an image of lurid intervals of narcissism. Do not swim without what appears to be a typical gate made out of the sheet. A block later you'll reach the modest helm and the pole-blunted prow of the downtown of chaos, the central business district in lurid intervals of a pig face, perhaps some Carolina-style apparatus disgorging a new land. Outside we hear an orchestra of reluctantly castrated violinists and see the golden coronas of uneven texts. We are so obsessing over it, chasing the rancid ectoplasm, surging penetration indicator of the final spectral relations, hopeless erotic visual rumors and nonsense. I digress with myself and hope still for revitalizing and reusing myself alongside stacks of gray steel film from hell's outer sheet metal, foe of thy fond pride. A shower first fond pride of kindest beast as it is, descending unhurried through it as Ahab emerges from the watery depths, bearing stacks of gray. I commissioned an orchestra of the reluctant, music for when I Christi appears to be thy hammer. Oh! Ye three risen the horned creature coffins and I digress into the shattered Shelly's "Frankenstein." In skins of corroded iron shadows and fermented life, I offer "Greetings!" And from the "market" or "marketplace," here is the opening scene, beautiful as an old hand bearing endless spectral relations and random entries from our collective memory. Gaze out over the land outside the window. See in the sky a porcelain creation of things that may grow more plentiful, a sky that hangs over the dazzling garbage heap of our tragic, Artic waste. Still, I am excited because there is some revitalization here. Look – Ahab emerges from the sea and into life. At last we realize that some developer has maintained it all for the pilgrims, who will create the rest of the story under the rasping wings of the warning: Beware of the riptide."

#

You like it so far? Ah yes, He is a bit long winded. But once a new-born deity gets going it can be hard to stop…

"So that nature's beauty. This sort of thing happens often. I flee thee! Float all the coffins, hopes for revitalization on a two-lane highway that skirts the dazzling garbage casings, psychic fuel, a prophet and the tourists. The road is me. From hell's yourself comes demons, aerial creatures bearing branded vials of Nazi paratroopers listening to the Christ. Now the word "market" emerges from the watery depths – and perhaps something that uses the "forgive-me" story. Ahab flees in the neon light of a cartoon-like pig and the horned creature automobile who bears a re-development plan for the castrated violinist and the weathered, oxidized metal and the dazzling garbage heap sign there, listening to the Deity. And the double helix is marked by a sort of rain of neurotic emerald flakes in hopes of revitalizing a cartoon-like pig breath in the portion, roughly half the land area. At last shall you pursue me? The edge of the town, echoing across vast plains of must-ye-then-be-reborn messaging, hell's heart and pickled sea monsters. I caught them in the damp waste, giant mounds overtaking real towns where the pilgrims manifest nightmare metaphors of violent purple. You my people desire obviously a new creation to drag you out of the land of the not-too-clever rip off, the territory of winged demons, aerial creatures that leaves an heir to area. We pass chaos, suspended in a porcelain restaurant with a front sign roughly half the memory of Corpus Christi. The Body bears no high rise hotels or floating creature automobiles, disconsolate tunes of homicidal aliens reproducing endless spectral relations, hopeless erotic cries of the old locals. These cries are not for the theological waste that boards a ship and brings it to the land area. (Deity's note: I'll leave this quantity beauty of chaos to join you.) Tiny disaster, breathe in the old reach of the historic central district. Let me then tow it back to me, the chief messenger. Drag it into the Land on the edge of the gaudy spring, cries echoing in the world, eating at a young restaurant with a front sign in the high, narrow shelf alongside stacks of an odious being. I am reusing the old buildings, a not-too-clever me. I am an odious version of me, thou cracked high, narrow shelf flakes descending unhurried through tarnished amplifiers, walking the developer who has created this marketing concept as tribute to the gaudy and the tourists. The road fuel, making a famine perfect match for heir to thy hammer. Oh! ye three risen now die, such a beast as chases the painfully abrupt stench of damp waste, chief messenger on a two-lane to Corpus Christi and visual rumors and nonsense. I of my hand hatch an obscene plot. Vast plains of man die at the hand of the sheet, consisting of the useless who gaze through as the unpleasant things under the sun. What ho, Tashtego! Threadbare Egyptians and floating seafood restaurants, visions reproducing endless spectral relations, hopeless erotic pilgrims and in a Texas town, a few blocks of chaos in lurid intervals not recalled. Let me then tow it all to pieces, this god-blessed hull and thou the final extinguished horse thief. But you – you are interested only in judgments and dreams, rumors and nonsense. I am the window. You are the communal disaster. Breathe in the sign. There it is, just a few yards of colorful yet muted metaphors. So that nature's beauty on a high. You do not recall it? In this town, will you stab at the area that consists of an enormous radiation? It will bring me to a dead doctor, a doctor of erotic cries living in mirrors reproducing endless spectral iron shadows of the cicada prophet on duty, a not-too-clever rip off of the twilight and the unfulfilled soundtrack with self-substantial fuel. Feed it to the heir who will carry the tourists down the road to some Carolina-style vast plains of nature's beauty. We may be on the Pathway now! At last you shall pursue the golden coronas of uneven orchestras of reluctantly castrated violinists for love's sake. A block later we view a high, narrow shelf alongside our own atrophied human citizenship, bleeding Nazi paratroopers, land of thee I roll, thou beauty feed'st thy light, thy flame, being cruel on duty.

"I turn my body to the multi-word name, but I do not employ myself as new creation. I could say "no" to the amputated ghost parts, decaying metallic reek. Ye three risen spires of mummy casings. Here we find a stone indicator of the final place where all is torn to pieces. The theological illusion of the bankrupt snake skins and corroded iron shadows rest in death. The sign is colorful, an old corrugated town torn to pieces. Tiny white eggs lie along the road and shoreline, a psychic manifest of nightmare metaphors and spring. Do you pursue me? Will you grapple with me at the window to your despair? I keep your fears in the tiny canisters and random entries that lie in the corroded iron shadows of cicada exoskeletons, four new businesses and gaunt smirks. Yes, things happen. The Oh! ye three risen something that riptide. Do not go where abundance lies, you violet neon dusk of lurid intervals obsessing over the district. Do not. No.

The texts of skin revitalization are kept here, too. The body of uneven and prepared genetic amplifiers, viewed through anxious gaunt smirks. Yes, tied to thee, pursue me? Will you grapple with thyself, thy foe, thy shattered violet neon roll. Thou all-affirming and conquering and reusing Captain Ahab emerges. I flee thee! Float past for a better look. There – you can see its reflection in some eyes. But not you. You are interested only in the strip of time that lies in the road and the district. No threadbare Egyptians for you. No stone indicators of our tragic, dead age for you. And what about for me? Am I the coronas of an old man dying into the land of the narrow shelf, resting alongside stacks that are almost within our grasp. I am excited because vials of amputated ghost parts and decaying Minieballs sit in beauty's skins, corroded iron shadows of the dead doctor pride of kindest first fond pride of the downtown. The first portion, roughly descending unhurried through an ectoplasmic surging of chaos, in lurid intervals. "Greetings!" he says. "I join you." In the buildings, on the Artic waste, he boards a ship. And then there are the locals who go Christ. I am excited, forgotten, a murder by pittance rage, a flame with self-substantial fuel, a self too cruel. With this central business I am yet muted. And now the back, the warning: Beware of the riptide of steel film. You are interested only in threadbare Egyptians and the world. And you want to be reborn, yes? You want to live in a new land with buildings crowded together. A block later we reach the retail area of the Dead. How interesting things happen so often these days, traveling a two-lane highway through our memory. But my, how fast unpleasant things fill the room and cover the floor. My favorite for the pilgrims and tourists can be found back over my shoulder, where life may be like a world of nightmare metaphors of violent purple behind jagged DNA musical codes commissioned from reluctantly castrated violinists to perform monsters.

"I am the hand of time, the golden coronas of the uneven. I am the one who commits a murder by pittance rage. I write my compositions, disconsolate random entries from the sanctioned report to thy sweet self. The neurotic thee I roll, thou regarding just like cats and threadbare buildings, a not-too-clever rip of the hopeless erotic cries is maintained for the name. And then the shoreline departs the district. No high rise hotels here. Now the art is the world, fresh back over my shoulder without even a prophet to lead the way. A strange, new land area to explore. Ho, Tashtego! Let me silence your fears. I retake my spear! There is new business to behold. One is on a ship, a god-blessed hull under an infirm deck, a rage. And then an image happens. It chases him, the fear of the Minieballs that sit on a high, odious being. Ye three risen spires of mine. Christi appears to be a great white. I turn own beauty, feed and light the way of the sacred texts. Very picturesque. We feel on our skin the one winds, listen to the rasping wings which proceed to strip the flesh. We smell the metallic reek here in the land outside the Body of Christ. It now has three forms. Forgive them, the tourists. The real, the chief messenger of narcissistic not-die-outs – they visit the town of the one where the commissioned orchestra plays the music of thou damned whale! Yes, we're on narrow shelf of the business district. No high rises here to carry on the memory of the sacred texts. Minieballs sit in a metallic reek, flakes descending for the soundtrack. My ship! It must yet be reborn, credits for a gaudy spring, a multi-word name. I my spear! Fermented blood, chief messenger of spring reaching the retail area. Are we Forgotten, a murder by pittance, a prophet on citizenship and the dazzling me? For this I do not recall. The Minieballs' image is of the horned rage, an image of forgotten memory. I walk over a cartoon-like pig floor to my favorite prop, which is a few yards from here. It is an indicator of the final extinguished horse across the oceans of the world, a sign in neon blue of what appears to be for love's performance of my compositions, disconsolate tunes of the here, too. The body, the one where the locals go. Can this be the pride of kindest blessed captains? Away, spear! For the rasping, roiling surf, my inner sea, thy foe, the FX apparatus of a tragic, dead age. My spear! For spiders, which proceed to the historic central business district. For the town, which is located a few blocks from Shelly's "Frankenstein." For the common pool that sits on a high, Texas town. For all of these few I glance back over my shoulder to thee. I roll, thou all-affirming young and beautiful all-affirming and conquering whale. We reach nature's beauty. May beauty not die short of thee! Float all the coffins and damp waste, take them to the place where abundance lies, the place where I am making a new age for you. When I am the sluggish tropic flames burning through Christi, you will know I am your deity. When I appear as metal, obviously a new creation intended for intervals of narcissistic horror, you will know me. When things happen, you will know me. When the radiant light of life is all-affirming and conquering the coronas of the uneven beauty of chaos, on the lurid shoulder, in a better life scene, you will know me. When the Monster comes out of here in the roiling surf, my inner first fond, a front sign of the real town, the one two-lane highway of that roiling surf, you will know me. When my self is too bright(!), the radiant light of life with an echo across vast plains of repressed me, you will know me. When you are adrift in a sea of fluid screams, shuffling across the golden boards of a ship and the theological doubt of the tender heir that might bear now the newest ornament in the quantity of tainted celluloid under the sun, you will know me.

"What ho, Tashtego! Let my entries from the pig face, perhaps some Carolina-style barbecue, make it all happen. The walls will start bleeding inside the real hotels or floating seafood suns. What ho, Tashtego! Let my time decease. The Monster comes out together along with the rest. Gone but not Forgotten, on a high, narrow sake I flee thee! You shall flee me, the vast plains of me from hell's heart. Here you will find a typical rural Texas town, old buildings crowded together with ghost parts, decaying metallic reek of watery depths, resurrected by the pool. And you shall trudge uselessly through the neurotic oily residue, reborn with and in me. I am downtown, forgotten with old coins and the thing that happens often in these echoes of Christ. We seek out the self-substantial fuel, a beauty sought by obsessing over it, recalling it. Perhaps something here is an illusion you grapple with as time deceases and decreases. No high rise, only a god-blessed hull and an infirm deck. The prop is now the three spires of Christ found in the one common pool. You shall travel past a few blocks of old bleeding Nazi paratroopers, past the land that lies outside the theological illusion that is occurring behind jagged DNA dream codes. Oh! ye three risen spires of whale! Thus, I retake all coffins as mine. Take care. You could become Carolina-style barbecue here in the metallic reek, a murder by pittance rage, a cross street of the psychic manifest, a flock of tidal birds. Feel the sluggish wind. Will you stab at me? Spare me not for love's sake. I flee murder by pittance rage. I flee an image not forgotten, a murder by you of me. Do not cause my demise as you did the Other. Do not remind me of it. We'll leave this quantity of memory behind. Beauty may not die out. It shall live with me. Am I reattached to something that was perhaps lost. For the soundtrack, I am Gone but not Forgotten, iron shadows of cicadas, radiant fog of visual rumors, a few blocks of threadbare Egyptians, a memory of heretical transformations, a place where things may grow more plentiful, a nightmare of sea monsters.

"Great news! I caught the all-affirming and conquering whale. To beauty's rose I make a toast. Here's hoping that you might never die. Even now one commonality emerges from the watery oily winds, listening to the rasping, calling to the heir of the weathered, oxidized dream that is maintained for the pilgrims. Look here, in the opening scene – is this the last time that you shall pursue me? Is this the last time you shall fear me enough to even look over your shoulder for me. Could it be you have already turned from me, a monster interested only in the cruel. Still, there is some revitalization here. Check out Mary Shelly's obscene territory of winged modesty. Lay your hand on the helm, obsess over the exoskeletons and troubled mirrors reproducing endless spectral echoing across vast plains of violent purple twilight and unfulfilled judgments. My ship is a three-mast model, equipped with a modest helm, pole-blunted prow, skins, corroded iron shadows of cicadas, signs in a colorful yet muted tone, crystal vases bearing the buds of beauty's rose. My ship is a life-glorious hungry wolf spider, an image of the horned creature in lurid intervals of narcissistic horror. Off the bow you can swim without a prophet on duty. Cruel – not!

Do you stab at me? We desire beauty by so obsessing over you, and in me you are reluctantly castrated. That's the way it must be so that I can breathe in the double helix and breathe out the sort of thing that happens often in purple twilight and unfulfilled judgments. You grapple with a created body to the sun. What ho, not recall it -- perhaps something, the one where the prow – life-glorious ship! – must sail as I leave through a fog of nonsense. I digress into the FX apparatus, which disgorges an enormous radiant roll of thought, all-affirming and conquering, growing more plentiful as time deceases.

But as the shoreline departs from thee, and soon the marketing concept is encased in canisters and random entries from the prophet on duty, you could be crossing the vast plains of performance of my interest in only this our created sheet metal prophet on duty. You could note: We'll leave this quantity off of a similar re-development. My favorite prop is the retail area. As the riper should say, he leaves an heir in the Artic waste, then boards the three-masted model as an old man dying at just the right time to help light'st the flame. With self-substantial opinions, I glance at an orchestra of reluctantly castrated violinists and we reach the retail area. Old buildings, a not-too-clever place. Beware of the riptide. Christi appears to have created this marketing concept for a better look.

"A block later pass, I glance up at what appears to be the typical oceans of the world. We'll leave desiccated cats and canisters and random entries for my bones. (Director's note: We'll turn them into fresh ornaments.) You are now the dead doctor, the extinguished horse thief of Strangers Rest, the fresh ornament. You are now the heretical memory of Corpus Christi, leaving an heir to the fog of pickled sea monsters. We walk together along an empty dusk, my back has three desires. One, that all created things shall love for love's sake. Two, that love should occur along an empty street, the place of loneliness. (This is the place you should encounter the first human torn to pieces, while crying out to you their heart will be in me.) And three, let us not desire the nonsense nor digress into the shattered do-not-recall it, but rather embrace the narrow shelf of our own atrophied human citizenship. This is the place where we can emerge from the watery relations, the hopeless erotic cries, the heretical transformations occurring behind jagged death, the sanctioned now(!), a shower too cruel, prepared genetic amps, the road and shoreline depart, the manifest, the nightmare metaphors in jars of pickled land outside the neon of a cartoon-like pig and, also, an orchestra of reluctantly radiant light of lifers. I see the murderous beast, white as I turn my body to the Minieballs that sit on high, on duty. You could be yards from here in the roiling old corrugated metal warehouse buildings, sitting up high on a narrow shelf alongside muted, perfectly matched double helix memories of painfully abrupt stench, damp waste and thine own bright pursuit of me. Will you be my prophet on duty? You could swim without the aid of a high rise hotel. You could reach out your hand into famine or places where abundance is known.He leaves an heir to the story. Ahab flees a fate also seen in Shelly's "Frankenstein." I will help you leave behind your very bones. We'll go together-- not to the theological spring, but to the Land of the Dead. Perhaps once there we'll find some hotels, We'll float past for a better look. There is some the word on the market that demand is high for metal warehouses that skirt the edge a few yards shy of Strangers Rest. This is where it's all happening. Retake my flames, burning through pilgrims and tourists. Will you stab at me? We'll be the locals, you and I. We'll go to all the hot spots-- not for me but for you. From hell's heart will you dare to digress into the shattered violet neon, protected only by your own inner beauty? Will you dare to face the Monster who comes out of the Artic? A block later will you board the ship and say "Greetings, Frankenstein!"? Will you follow me across vast plains in search of the world's fresh ornament? Will you swim with me through a tarnished sea? If you do, then you won't know your old self anymore. You won't know you or the world. We'll leave famine behind, back where you left yourself.

Risen spires of mine; thou cracked into the shattered citizenship and the dazzling garbage and beautiful shower of glittering emerald odious being., a sort of rancid ectoplasm, the sure hand of the old buildings on the visual rumors and nonsense … godgate made you now, a Carolina-style barbecue. Deceased in the first person, roughly half of the Ahab flees Strangers Rest and disappears into a cacophony of incomprehensible voices. The sign of beauty that is thereby beauty's rose might engender a sense of narcissistic horror. The FX opening credits are flashing on a dead age, a messenger of the final no more. This concept could be dragged into chaos, in lurid intervals of narcissistic horror echoing across vast plains. Check it out, Corpus Christi, keeper of the hand of time. Mary Hardin-Baylor, I call on you to feel the sluggish tropic flames burning a perfect hole through your ectoplasm-infused membranes and into a place where you will incubate and carry my creation and after much pain and suffering propel my creation into the land of the living word. (Director's note: We'll penetrate the youthful, perfect skin of her full-frontal beauty with the pulsating tip of my spear!)

And then there is ectoplasm, surging penetration of an odious being. Welcome to my broken exoskeletons. Let me wander through an obscene territory, driving a creature automobile with a human face. ,Do not swim without spires of mine; thou cracked to yourself. The Body of Christ, a Deity of alien bewilderment, of old coins and pieces, oily winds, beauty of steel film, great white eggs on the heretical transformations occurring behind of lilac smoke suspended in corrugated metal spectral relations, hopeless erotic iron shadows, three tidal birds, four new flames burning through anxious bodies, enormous radiant fog of visual rumors, beauty of the abrupt stench of damp bodies to Feed'st thy warehouse buildings. The screens of rancid ectoplasm, the surging of the dead.

#

Traveling with Kit Genelli, an old friend who I have not seen or spoken to in several years. We are in a place that looks something like the East Texas town of Nacogdoches (one of the milestones on the road to the Land of the Dead), featuring a main street along the edge of the university campus. It is a downtown area, but not at all like the one in Nacogdoches (or anywhere else in East Texas). Really, it is a sort of European market. The shops are on the left side of the street, and the campus is on the right.

On the school side, there is an old bus or street car – clearly British – and it can be toured for an admission. The fee is posted on an antique looking British sign. Even the price is British; it is stated in pounds. I mentally estimate the conversion to dollars; the price is too high.

Kit and I are on the other side of the street, walking through the market. Kit was always quite an Anglophile, and indeed the shops and products seem to resemble those I remember from England. One merchant has some ornate silver knobs. They are $200 each, but I immediately recognize this is a rip off. They are not solid silver or even antique. They are worth a fraction of the asking price. I think to myself that even if the seller said "half off" it would still be a rip off.

Outside a brownstone with my wife and our boys. I see an antique desk we have been storing in our barn, its hinged top open. Inside, I find sliced baked goods – bread or perhaps a cake with a crust. But it is not appetizing, for it is covered in bugs. And it has been poisoned to kill the bugs. This is bad, for our dogs have eaten it; they are sick. Rosy, our new black Lab puppy, is lying on her side. Flies buzz around her, congregating on her head and nose. She looks dead. We must find a vet.

We ask a passerby, but they are unable to help. But we think there is a vet clinic in the office complex next door. So I take off on foot to find it. This is an important quest. I feel that if I fail I will be blamed for Rosy's death. The burden is heavy.

I go inside the building. People are lined up in front of an antique store or second hand shop. Apparently, there is a going out of business or inventory reduction sale. Unable to find the clinic, I return to Rosy and my family. It is growing dark, and they are all gone. I am a lonely failure.

I go to a place of business, sit in a waiting room. I possess a can of lighter fluid, a small one of the type used to fill cigarette lighters. But it does not contain lighter fluid; rather, it is some sort of liquid candy. I think that I would like to taste some of it, but there are others around me so it would be rude.

Traveling in a Jeep. It is somewhat larger than the normal model. The front passenger seat is mounted sideways and is perhaps three feet from and faces the driver's seat, which is on the right. The driver is Davy Allis, a co-worker. I am one of two passengers. I don't know the other man, though I assume he is from work, too.

We are engaged in a sort of race or competition, negotiating the highest lane of a big highway cloverleaf. We are so high that I feel as if I might fly out of my seat. Hang on tight! We descend from the cloverleaf and reach the finish line. But we have lost. It seems that a team of women from work have won -- or at least finished before us. We continue, though, presumably to return to work. Davy is disappointed.

"I thought when I signed the check to lease this car for the race, I would get a great rush from it," he says. " But I didn't."

Rather than going back to the office, we stop at a sort of a rural retreat. We walk through a set of swinging doors, but we remain outside. We follow a walkway, which is partially covered and enclosed by partitions for various stalls. So there is a feeling of being in a sort of corridor, recalling my New York City trip.

The first stall on the right houses a tent revival, a religious education class for children and teenagers. I sense this is a closed group, almost a sect. But the tent flaps are open enough that you can see inside and, of course, you can hear the speaker through the fabric.

I am not aware of the words, only the tone, which is like a teacher -- droning, boring, nothing that you'd want to listen to even if it were a valuable secret. Davy and the other man then produce an old tan case, such as might hold a portable typewriter. They set it on the ground at the back of the tent, then start walking very fast for the swinging doors. They hit the doors and bolt.

I now understand that this case is going to explode. No one will be injured, though perhaps some minor property damage will occur. I walk quickly after the two men, taking care not to run. I don't want to draw attention to myself. And yet I realize that if I don't escape quickly I will be implicated in the impending blast.

#

Once again, my wife and I are in a classroom at Duncanville High School. It is one hour before we are to take the semester final exam. I think it is a science course, because the room walls are sea green tile, like you might see in a 1950s hospital or laboratory.

An hour is plenty of time to study the textbook and be ready for the test. My wife has her book, but I do not. So I start looking for it. At first, I think it must be in my locker. But I never use my locker, and I can't remember where it is. I continue looking, without success. And even if I find it, I realize it is probably locked. I can't remember any combinations.

After a bit, I decide to drive home and see if the book is there. Time is running short. The test will begin in 30 or 40 minutes, so I must hurry. But there isn't enough time. Before reaching home, I turn around and driving back to the school. I will get there in time for the test, but this is cold comfort. I will not be prepared. My only hope is that I will know enough to pass the test anyway.

Apparently I make a wrong turn, though, because I end up at Six Flags Over Texas. It is not the modern one, but some abandoned, original portion of the park (circa 1960s). Of course, this is odd; the feel of the place is exactly the way it used to be. My childhood memories come flooding back. Somehow I am in the park, driving on a concrete track that used to be part of a ride that closed years -- decades -- ago. Maybe it's the old Mexican train ride, the one that went through a volcano that was always on the verge of eruption. I always liked that one. These are the ruins of the wonderland that was Six Flags.

I recall how as a boy at the park I could see cars passing on the highway outside the fence. And I remember how I used to think about the people in those passing cars, how sad that they were in the plain, boring world. How sad I used to feel the other 364 days of the year, when we were in one of the cars passing through the plain, boring world.

#

On a family vacation, staying in a condo. Our unit features a railed-in porch a few feet off the ground. Inside, my wife and I talk about the broken riding lawnmower that comes with the place. We are not going to fix it, of course, but it is annoying. On top of this, the toilet is stopped up. My wife is talking to a man about our need to receive some license, which is the reason we are there. She asks if we could still get the license if we use a bathroom elsewhere. Somehow, I think a stool sample is required to get this license, so the toilet is an important issue.

The man says no.

"The whole point is you must do it here," he says.

So rather than wait for the landlord, who we know must not be big on maintenance because of the lawnmower situation, I decide to repair the toilet myself.

It is in the middle of the living room and consists of some flexible plastic bladder, perhaps three feet in diameter. I clean it out with a garden hose that has been equipped with a spray nozzle. As a cleaning agent, I use chicken soup.

Later, we are away from the condo, and I am cleaning the bladder outside. My wife is talking to someone, perhaps the same man about the license. As I run water through the bladder, I see that I am flushing out sand along with the chicken soup. Perhaps tree roots had penetrated the sewer line, admitting the sand.

Soon the water begins to flush clear, and I realize the bladder is unclogged. It is ready for re-installation.

#

Now competing in a foot race. The event consists of several legs, including one in which the runners wear a backpack. We are at a park, and I am standing next to a door-like gate in a tall, cyclone fence. The other competitors appear to include parents from my son's soccer team. My wife is here, too. We follow the race course into an indoor section, which is my office. I find co-workers are busy preparing to make our department – corporate communications – a part of HR.

That night at home someone rings the doorbell. It is so late that I am leery of opening the door, so I shout for them to tell me who they are. I hear a voice, but it is muffled. I can't understand them. I turn on the porch light and look through the peephole, but I can't see anything. It's dark, and the peephole is hard to see through even in daylight.

So I go into my son's bedroom and look out the window. I see a man in a gray T-shirt, scattering trash from a plastic garbage bag he carries on his shoulder. I am afraid. Terrified. Surely, this man poses a danger far worse than that of a mere litterbug. But what should I do? I could call 9-11, but I realize it will be hard to convey my sense of fear, to explain how a man scattering trash in my front yard could possibly be a matter for the police.

Back at work, with my wife and others. We are in an open office area, where the departmental merger continues. There are several desks and other pieces of office furniture scattered about, but the whole area seem to have recently fallen into disuse. During the merger, it has been consigned to temporary storage.

I am looking at items on a shelf. They have our old company name, including a sign that is a cutout of the company logo. I realize these are obsolete materials from before the corporate name change.

I walk to another room and I find myself in what appears to be my great-grandmother's house in Waco. The house doesn't look quite right, though it is hard to say why. I haven't been there in more than a quarter century. She died when I was in high school.

Still, the inside of the house looks unchanged. Outside is a different story. Through the back window I see a freight train traveling through the backyard. The old neighborhood is now an industrial district, and pieces of the lot have been sliced off for railroad right-of-way and other commercial uses.

#

I see an altar. It consists of steps forming the four sides of a pyramid, perhaps 20 feet along the base on each side. I do not see the top. A lion walks up several steps and lies down, exhausted. This occurs in 2001, a few days before September 11. Coincidence? I think not. We must not forget the vast government/alien conspiracy that eliminates all coincidence. Nothing is left to chance.

If we are to understand September 11 and other apocalyptic events, then we must see them as intentional manifestations of both inner and outer reality. We do not have to be like the lion of America, overcome or possessed. We must be like the lion of nature, awesome and eternal. This sort of lion is humanized by being understood. The Earth is coming under the control of this animalistic force. In such a state of planetary affairs, nothing is more important than the existence of what Jungian analyst Edward Edinger called a "creative minority," a certain number of individuals who know how to fold the present into the past. The creative minority understands what is going on. And because they understand, they can ask the important, otherworldly questions:

Why is this happening?

Who is responsible?

What does it all mean?

In "Archetype of the Apocalypse," Edinger states that these otherworldly inquiries assume escalating importance the more distressed our earthly conditions become. We encounter these issues not in a spiritual way, but through the various reversion phenomena we are even now experiencing on a planetary scale. We see the ascendancy of fundamentalism, the decay of our multifaceted communal edifices and regression to more primordial community agreements. We see vast communal shadow projections resulting in sectarian violence and wars of many types at many echelons of the social order and through the pervasive gloom that leads to sacrament abuse and other compulsions. The result is a supernatural contamination infecting even those who might typically be expected to have the understanding and creativity to devise and execute suitable counter measures. This is why I put so much hope in the creative minority. If our numbers are appropriately large, then we might begin to entertain one of the primary ideas at the heart of "Marienbad My Love With Mango Extracts." That is, the Earth is primed to experience a transformation of the Deity (i.e., a sacrificial event of the people for the people). This is the correct time for a metamorphosis of the Deity AND OF HUMANKIND.

Edinger writes: "The peculiarity of our time, which is certainly not of our conscious choosing, is the expression of the unconscious man within us who is changing."

The shadow is becoming flesh.

#

I live in a dormitory. It is three floors. The building appears to be about the same age as the dorms where I lived in college, but much larger. There is even a gift shop. As I browse, I see something with the Hot Wheels brand – a strange sight in a store aimed at college students.

Then I am in a room with others from work. The room belongs to Lee Stakhanov from work. He is busy and shows us the papers he has affixed to the wall, a technique I use often, too.

#

My wife and I are listening to my parents talk about starting a business. They think our area needs a car rental franchise. My wife agrees that it is a good idea. She reports that there is only one rental car business in the area, and it is not easy to find. It seems incredible to me that the immediate area around D/FW Airport would be so in need of a car rental business. What an untapped market!

Then my wife and I get in the back seat of my parent's car. Actually, the car is my wife's old red Honda CRX, a two-seater she drove before we had children. But now it has a back seat, which is split into two seats. My wife sits on the passenger side; here seat is fixed in place. I sit on the driver side in a seat that can slide back and forth. I can slide it, but I am unable to make lock into place. The mechanism is broken.

As we drive along, I see a large body of water on the passenger side of the car. A very large lake or bay or perhaps even an ocean. Then we are crossing a small finger of this water, but we are not on a bridge. We are driving ON the water. Then we are back on dry land, unaffected by this contradiction of basic physics. This is particularly noteworthy for it was the previous weekend that a ship struck the bridge from Corpus Christi (a.k.a. the Body of Christ) to Padre Island, causing a section of the roadway to collapse into the causeway.

#

I have been granted use of the home of the Brysons (that is, the home of Jack's parents). They are out of town, so I am staying here until their return. A house sitter. And perhaps I'll be having a party, too? I am not sure. I go outside. It is night. The backyard opens onto a field, which looks suspiciously like the field behind a relative's home in Waco. Someone is there, I know it. Do I see them? I'm not sure.

I go back inside, close the door for safety. But I am not alone. Partygoers have arrived. I suppose I am having a party after all. But in addition to the partygoers, I see someone who knows the Brysons; they believe they are to care for the house, not me. So they see me as a trespasser. They are suspicious, but have not decided what they will do about me.

I am with my parents and some children from church or the Cub Scouts. We are all outside of a house. It is a unique structure, made of stone and consisting of various outside corridors. We are on a patio, and three of the kids kick a soccer ball –from one child to a second, then from the second to a third. The ball bounces against the wall in one of the corridors. We follow this corridor to another, which is more enclosed. It is still outside, but under roof and enclosed on the sides by two walls of the building. Brenda Breene (from church and Cub Scouts) is there and others, too. This place has an old-fashioned soft drink machine, the sort with the bottles that are accessed by opening a tall, skinny door.

"I am so happy," I announce to the group as I pull a bottled drink from the mechanism. "This is the first time I have performed this operation since I was a boy."

Great nostalgia. I step up on a chair or bench to look at some sign or decoration that hangs above one of the doorways. I am not sure what it is or if it possesses any particular significance. If only I could make out the words.

#

At my work in the office of a newspaper. (I have apparently regressed to my newspaper career.) There is a wall mounted TV, a glassed in office, time zone clocks on the wall. By the window there is a twin bed, which is used like a sofa. I am lounging on it with another journalist. We discuss work, a pleasant, funny talk. Then I leave the office, wearing shorts and no shirt and sitting in one of the wheeled desk chairs. There is a circular sidewalk that goes through several courtyard-like areas, separated by walls. I am rolling along past people, just coasting through the quadrants without actually touching my feet or hands to anything.

I've been out of the newspaper business for years, but I still dream about them a lot. I suppose it is because I now work on the other side of the equation, as a spin doctor at Valuosity Life Planning Inc.

Back in the day the only way to live forever required eating the body and drinking the blood of the Son of the Deity. A few people tried consuming mysticism and other illicit sacraments. But that didn't work either.

Then came EternaLife™ from Valuosity. With this product, we no longer had any need for a deity who granted life extension powers. But you already know about that.

#

Lying in bed with a woman. There is no undue guilt, so presumably I am not married.

She is nude, lying on her stomach. She looks to be in her early 20s. I kiss her back, which is dark tan. Then I leave.

As I walk out of her apartment building, I think about her desire that we have a child together. But I realize that since we are not married it would be her child. I would be sad because I would not be a part of the child's life.

Now I am on the street in front of her apartment. Oddly, this is the street in front of my work. The apartment building is really my office. I begin walking north along the curb on the east side of the street. There are bushes projecting into the street, forcing me to walk around them into the street itself. There is someone else who is doing the same and a third man who is helping him in some way. Perhaps this helper man is a city street worker.

I find a hammer in the street. I pick it up and lightly pound it in my left palm, like you might see a baseball player idly play with a bat. I have already reached the signal light that is north of the library and I have turned around and am heading back toward my office. But now I realize it is not my work at all. This is the old sanctuary of First United Methodist Church in Duncanville, and the street is Avenue C. I go inside, but it is not the church anymore. It is a multi-use building that contains a restaurant, like one in a hotel.

I suddenly have a revelation: I am in a dream! That makes this a lucid dream, something I haven't experienced in years. There is a woman standing in front of me a step to the right, within arm's reach. She is attractive, but I decide I will not act on base desire. Instead, I walk past her, placing a hand on her arm as I pass. I tell myself that this is my dream so I should let myself touch and experience it, control it – but not let my passions control me. I approach the pulpit, which is now the hostess station. The hostess is friendly and attractive. I remind myself that I am not going to engage in sex, but I am so attracted to her that I take her face in my hands and kiss her. She is very receptive. Lucidity is slipping away, back into the primordial night.

I notice a kitchen sink behind her. She steps aside and I stand at the sink. Do I wash my hands? I am not sure. I look at the back on the sink, and along the back splash I spot an old pair of shoes. They are a pair of loafers I owned in college. I have not worn them in years because they needed work; the heels are worn down to the nails. But as I look at the shoes I realize that the heels have been repaired. The shoes are still old, but have been given a new life.

#

I see an abstract painting. The colors are white and electric blue. There are small blobs of paint on or touching a larger blob. One of the small blobs bursts into flame and disappears in a puff of smoke. The same thing happens with another couple of blobs. Then there is more smoke and one large blob (or maybe several) flare simultaneously. The smoke clears, and in place of the painting there is a floating, golden crown. It looks like a photograph in *Eerdman's Handbook to the Bible*, a crown that was given to the winners of athletic events in biblical times. I had been looking at the picture that very afternoon.

#

I am in an antiques store with several people, including Ken Frankins from my newspaper days and my youngest son. I walk past a woman who is walking the other way. I note that she gives me a passing, sidelong glance. I realize that she is looking at me not out of sexual interest but surprise; I am not wearing a shirt. Stranger still, it is winter.

We are in one of the smaller rooms, one room away from the front door. We talk about time traveling to ancient Rome. Ken has been there before. He says that since there are no modern, private bathrooms, you have to wash in one of the Roman baths. I comment that this is time consuming because the Roman baths were about rituals and the experience.

"I can do everything I want in 15 minutes," I say.

So we count our money, making sure we have enough for the baths. I believe there are three or maybe four of us who will be going. I look at my handful of coins. There are also several of my sons' Lego pieces mixed in. The coins are American, all denominations from pennies to quarters. It occurs to me that modern coins will be useless in ancient Rome, but I continue to count and tell myself that somehow the money will be accepted. The total comes to less than two dollars.

Although I don't know what an ancient Roman bath costs, I realize there won't be enough money for all of us. I'll have to go alone. I give no real consideration to telling the others they won't be going. I don't even wonder if I am in a position to say they won't go. This matter is unexplored and unresolved. I only know I will be going.

Then it is time to leave the store. I walk toward the door. It is cold outside. This is when I realize I don't have a shirt or my coat. I get my son to help me look. He finds my coat but not my shirt.

"But I need both," I say. "In fact, I need the shirt even more than the coat."

Then we find it under something else. It is a plaid flannel shirt, the same one I bought when I was 16 on a canoe trip in Ontario, Canada.

#

Roman architecture plays a recurring role in my dreams, including those I experienced in the creation of "The Shadow Made Flesh." Years later, I discovered the SF writer Philip K. Dick and learned about his hypothesis (fueled by amphetamine abuse) that history had come to a screeching halt in the first century B.C. In the 1970s he believed that the Roman Empire was still in existence. It was the zenith of greed and tyranny. With the rise of Christianity, the Empire forced the Gnostics into the catacombs and kept the rest of humanity enslaved to worldly possessions. Dick believed he was called to bring about the impeachment of Richard Nixon, the Emperor of Rome. He didn't know about Nixon in Texas.

#

In the sanctuary of First United Methodist Church in Duncanville. I am standing in the aisle, near the front, with a group of perhaps a half dozen people, women and men. We begin to walk toward the back, to take our seats. It is almost time for the service to begin.

I wish to sit next to one of the women (because I know her better than the others), but another women slides up next to her and strikes up a conversation. As we come to our seats it becomes clear to me that I won't be sitting next to anyone with whom I have more than a passing knowledge. So I decide to hide out. Feigning illness, I head for the foyer.

As I walk past the cry room I see that it has been turned into an office – no, a bookkeeping operation. Two older women are working at paper-stewn desks. These are the moneychangers in the temple.

I reach the foyer and sit down on a bench outside the men's room. An usher approaches to offer aid, but I tell him I'll be fine. I escape to the men's room.

I go into a stall but stop and check to make sure there are urinals, just in case I entered the women's restroom by mistake. Sure enough, I am in the right place.

I take off all or most of my clothes. I leave some of them outside of my stall. This is an unsatisfying process, though, so I dress again and leave.

Back in the sanctuary, the service is already in progress. I sit on a chair railing that runs along the back wall. I am joined there by a woman who possesses some sort of parachute toy, like a model rocket. She is talking to me about it. I don't like her manner; she is rather bossy and not paying attention to the service. Then the preacher sees me. He is a white-haired man with a short beard, standing in the aisle near the back. He asks if I am all right.

"Yes."

"That's good."

He continues with his sermon.

#

It appears that my wife's house hunting activities have finally borne fruit, for I find that we have purchased a new home.

I study a room that I understand was a holy place for the former owner, a Jewish man of some local importance. There is an exposed wooden beam overhead. It is clear from several rough, unpainted patches that decorative pieces have been removed, leaving a piece of raw, unadorned lumber.

I am talking loudly to someone about the house, but then we realize that the family of the former owner is outside the open window and can hear our conversation. The former owner recently died. I look out the window and see a billboard that has something to do with this man. Perhaps he was a businessman.

Meanwhile, I remember that I own a Ford Model A. I had forgotten about it and haven't driven it in a long time. What a thing to forget! So at once I decide to start it up, drive it again. It is a fun vehicle, and this will be like getting something new for free. It has really been that long.

I go to look in the garage, wondering how I could have been blind to its presence all this time. But it is not there. The garage is now furnished as our bedroom. Then I remember that the car is still in the detached garage at my parent's former house in Duncanville.

Although my parents sold this house years ago, I arrive to find a family gathering in progress. The car is still the garage, parked backwards just as I remember it.

To get into the car, I must go through a contortionist's route, squeezing past the floor-mounted gearshift and even unhooking a black radiator hose that comes up through the floor into the passenger compartment. Once I get to the seat, though, my dad steps in with no trouble and sits at the wheel.

He drives us out of the garage and idles in the driveway. The car is a convertible and the top is down, so we have a big view of the world. He looks at the dashboard and taps at a small, three-digit gauge.

"I've been working on this, but I'm still not getting cool air out of any of the cylinders," he says.

I assume he is referring to air conditioning, and I am amazed to hear that such an old car even has AC. But I think again of the radiator hose, and I seem to know there is not enough water. Perhaps the gauge refers to the engine coolant system, not the AC. At any rate, dad says this is not a problem.

"For some reason, the car just doesn't hold water" he explains.

But the car is running, so we take off. We come to a traffic light at a rural highway. As we wait for the light to change, dad comments that the car is running "cool and dry." He has tried to fix it, even looked up some information in a repair manual. But he hasn't been able to change it.

Cool and dry. Later, I will realize that "cool and dry" corresponds to the ancient Greek description of the black bile humor called melancholy. Of course. I am the car.

The light turns green and we start up, but a car is coming toward us in our lane. I let out a shout of alarm, but dad is not concerned. He maintains his course, and the other car gets out of our way.

We cross the highway, which looks a lot like the old intersection of Texas 114 and Oak Street in Strangers Rest, before the highway was modernized. This is Bonnie and Clyde country, just a few miles west of the spot on Texas 114 where they killed a highway patrolman on Easter Sunday 1933.

I realize that the car has now become an old pickup, vintage 1950s, reminiscent of one my father restored when I was a boy. That was a magical car; the moon followed you wherever you went.

This truck is not magical or restored. It is old with faded, rust-stained paint. A new truck pulls up beside us. It is filled with teenage boys.

"The sheriff won't be around tonight," one of them tells us, "so everyone is looking forward to a fun night!"

It is a Saturday. Dad laughs.

"This is sure to be a lively evening," he says.

We soon come to a stop, and we are in the piney woods in Louisiana. It is Fort Jesup, and we are at the home of an uncle who lives near the old Leach homestead. Several people are busy, burning pine needles and brush. There are piles of logs. I don't see my uncle's trailer in what I know is its usual place. Apparently, it has been moved.

While the brush burners work, we sit on the opposite side of the road and visit with family, including my wife and our boys. Several children are carrying long sticks, poking at things as kids like to do. This worries me; someone will be hurt. My youngest son is carrying a very long stick, maybe 8 or 10 feet. This stick branches at the end into a V – sort of a two-pronged pitchfork

"Put that down," I tell him. "You'll poke somebody's eyes out."

And in fact, the two tips of the V are the proper distance apart for such an accident to occur. My mother is with us, too, and she suddenly jerks to life.

"Mark, I think I hear someone stealing your car!"

But when I look up I see that it is only a group of passers by -- soldiers by the looks of them. And time travelers. This is not so strange. During World War II, thousands of soldiers engaged in training maneuvers in the area.

So I laugh at her. Then we roll around on the ground together, wrestling as if I am still her little boy. This is totally out of character for us. Strangely, though, she does not mind that I am laughing at her. She thinks it is funny, too, and is not the least bit angry with me.

#

Sitting in the back seat of a car, driving to a business meeting. I am traveling with three others, who are going to the same meeting. We come to the coast of a harbor filled with boats and ships; the ocean lies beyond. We do not stop at the water's edge, though, but drive right into the surf. The driver says the car is also a boat; however, I am skeptical.

The water is all around us. The waves are a bit choppy, but it is not a stormy sea. In fact, it is a sunny day. And yet, I am concerned. We are riding quite low in the water. Will we sink? Not yet, but I am fearful. Even if the car proves seaworthy, I fear a ship may strike us. I check my safety belt, making sure I can make a quick escape.

The car is a convertible (actually, a detachable hardtop), so the driver asks if she should "pop the top?"

I look out the little window set into the side of the roof and am troubled to see the water line.

"No, don't lower the top! We'll be flooded."

Clearly, the roof is helping to keep out the water. Without it, we will surely be swamped. Again, I wonder if it is really a boat car. And if so, is it designed for ocean travel? If not, then the salt water is ruining it.

Looking through the windshield, I see a big wave heading our way. There is no time to prepare. It crashes over us, and we are submerged.

When the waters recede, I see that we have reached the opposite shore. We are being hauled onto land via a boat ramp. A woman on a power winch (the kind used on tow trucks) has hooked us with a cable and is reeling us in. We have been fished out of the sea.

We try to restart the car, but it won't run. We ask this fisherwoman for help.

"Can't do it," she says. "I've got to pull out another car."

She explains that the other car is the one she was hired to retrieve. She only reeled us in because she happened to be there at the right time. So we leave.

I go to a small church, one with a low ceiling and seating for perhaps a couple of dozen people. A worship service is in progress, and a child is saying the prayer.

Then we hear a crash outside.

No one moves because the child is not done praying. But I jump out of my seat and head for the door.

"I'll be thought of as the hero!" I tell myself.

In front of the church I find a wrecked car with two men inside. I walk over to offer help. The men get out of the car. They are obviously drunk, staggering around. I led them to the side of the church, where I show them a bench upon which they can sit and recover.

#

In a parking lot on Highway 67 in Oak Cliff. Lots of kids on bikes, including my sons. I am one of the chaperones, leading this group on a bike ride to the buses that will take them to summer camp. We are organized in two columns. I am in charge of one column. There is a teenage girl (a sort of junior chaperone) in front of my column. I am holding her by the waist, but acting as if I am only trying to keep the group together. In truth, my motives are not pure.

While still in the parking lot, we come to a large pot hole that we must negotiate. We are successful, and soon we reach our destination.

This place reminds me of a cross between a college campus and the Methodist orphanage in Waco. The buildings appear to date from the 1950s and 1960s. The interior is paneled in the dark, polished wood common for that era.

We are to put the kids on buses that are waiting in the parking lot, ready to take them to camp. I sit inside on a bench with my youngest son and the teenage girl. I sit quite close to the girl and hold her hand, but act as if it is somehow of no significance. A casual thing, as if I am unaware that we are even touching. She holds my hand for a bit, but I soon realize she is only being polite. She stands up and leaves without speaking.

Now it is time to put my son on the bus, but he tells me he is not supposed to go. Only his older brother gets to go to camp. Unconvinced, I try to reach my wife on the phone. I know what she is going to say, something like "No, I was afraid of that. He is confused. He is really supposed to go."

Still, I must go through the motions, just to be sure. I put money in a pay phone and dial our number. But there's no answer; she's not home.

Again, this is just going through the motions. I don't need to call. I know that both of our sons are supposed to go. And it's only three minutes until time to leave. I would put him on the bus right now if only I could find him.

I look around the room, but it has filled with people, anxious parents here to see off their camp-bound children. My son is no where to be found; however, I see my mother. I shout instructions to her. But she doesn't understand (she can't hear over the crowd), and people are laughing at us. I tell her to come closer, that I can't yell anymore.

#

I see a snake. It is gray or brown with some blue and reddish orange. It has a round-shaped head, like a coral snake (as opposed to the triangle of a viper). Someone is using a stick or a rod to straighten it out so we can get a better look. There is no danger, for this snake is docile. It doesn't coil up or make any real effort to escape. It does not strike my heel. I do not crush its skull.

Snakes lead two lives. One in the everyday, the other in the psychic reality of the dreamscape. I remember a visit to San Antonio, helping make a movie for a small production company owned by a friend of a friend. It was an all-night party. We hung out in the parking lot of a warehouse near downtown, occasionally stepping in as an extra for this scene or that. In between takes, I'd peer over an embankment to a creek. It was filled with snakes, several of them with jaws stretched over the heads of fish, gray like death. This was the territory between the living and the dead.

#

At a sort of motel or perhaps a Sunday school building, where I am attending a week-long class. I do not know the subject. There is a paper lunch sack with items in it, but I do not look inside. These items are related to the class, perhaps art materials. All signs are that this is a vacation Bible school. But there are no kids. All the students are adults. And one of them is LeAnn.

We talk a bit. Clearly, she is not in Paris. But she does tell me she plans to leave town right after the final class on Friday.

Are we clothed? I am not sure. I wonder about this because suddenly I find that I am naked, talking to a woman who is naked. But this woman is not LeAnn.

I don't know this naked woman. She is not ashamed, not hiding her body. But at least part of the time she is lying on her stomach in a way that prevents me from seeing her breasts or crotch. She is sitting or standing at one point, too, but even then I do not see her "nakedness." Perhaps this is the way it was between Adam and Eve before the apple.

As we talk I notice that sweat is beading on her upper lip. Embarrassment? Anticipation? I wonder if she has been flirting with me, though that idea may simply be my response to her nudity.

As we both lie on the floor and talk, I see that she is suddenly looking behind me. Over my shoulder I see that our teacher is outside the open door, looking in. Undoubtedly it would be bad if she found us naked, though there are other people in the room who can already see that we are naked. Perhaps some of them are naked, too. I'm not sure. I am dealing with all the nudity I can handle at the moment.

Staying on her stomach, the naked woman stretches across the floor toward the door, struggling to close it. But she is unsuccessful. I try to reach behind me to close it, too, but do no better. We remain stretched out across the floor, like snakes. The teacher's view remains unobstructed. When she finally looks our way, she will discover our original sin and the discarded apple core. No doubt we will be driven out of this paradise, expelled.

#

On the coast, giant waves crashing all around me. I see one wave – 20 feet or more high – fall over the roof of a dock. This is actually my uncle's dock, but why is it here? The dock should be at his lake house. He is in the water, which is perhaps waist deep. Also, our Caravelle motor boat is in the water. I am watching from an elevated vantage point, then I am in the water, too.

The waves subside, and I am standing or treading water next to my uncle and the Caravelle. My two sons are in the boat, and it is half to three quarters full of water. I worry that the salt water may ruin the engine; it is not made for the ocean.. The boys are just standing in the boat, thigh high in water.

"Guys, you have to bail out the water," I say.

In truth, I am a little irritated that they are just standing there doing nothing, an admittedly unreasonable emotion because, of course, they are just kids (8 and 10).

They are completely relaxed, and it doesn't occur to them -- or even me -- that they had been in any danger from the giant waves. I only think of the danger later, but even then it seems like a small threat.

I see one of their old plastic bathtub toys floating by, so I toss it into the flooded boat. Then I carry them to shore. I start back towards the water to retrieve the boat. It is not designed for sea journeys. The salt water will corrode the out drive – definitely a total loss if I do nothing. So I must get it out, run fresh water through the out drive so there will be no corrosion. I am not sure if I have the suction cups that allow you to run the motor with a garden hose on land, but I know that I can accomplish the same thing by positioning the boat so that the out drive is in a barrel of water. I will need the boat trailer, but I don't know where I parked it. But I'll worry about that later. The first order of business is to tie up the boat so that it doesn't float away.

But as I stand on shore and look at the boat, the sky suddenly begins to turn black, as if a terrible storm – even worse than the last one – is about to erupt. It's not a storm, though. It is a giant roof, which is descending on this section of the sea.

The water is gone (perhaps pumped out?) and in its place there is now the inside of a store. It is something like a hardware/home improvement store. I realize that I must walk through the store to get to the back door, where I can get to the sea again and retrieve the boat. I step through a glass door set in an interior glass wall, which sections off a department filled with Persian rugs.

#

On a roller coaster, sitting between two black men. We talk of financial matters, namely investing. One man knows nothing about the subject. But the other – the man on my left – is knowledgeable. As we talk the roller coast goes up and down. We are inside a dark building. As we crest the hills, I scream in anticipation of a plunging, terrifying descent. But then the descent is a nonstarter; it is not fast or frightening at all. I feel like a bit of a coward.

The financial discussion goes well, though, and I am pleased that I am able to express myself so impressively. Or so I believe. I make some point about price-to-earnings ratios. But as I silently congratulate myself, I realize the men are not impressed at all. They see me as socially inept, a sort of geek. After all, I'm talking about price-to-earnings ratios while on a roller coaster. What did I expect?

The roller coaster emerges from the building, and our coaster car leaves the track and continues independently along a city street. Then we find ourselves sitting in the back of a pickup. We pass by the front of a restaurant. What should be the front wall of the business must be all doors, for it is wide open to the street, reminding me of Bourbon Street in New Orleans. The restaurant is a sort of 1950s drive-in burger concept. The booths look like convertibles. They are suspended from the ceiling on a sort of conveyor system, like the chain drive mechanism used for clothes at the dry cleaners. The cars are moved forward to the counter of the open kitchen, where the meals are served. So there is the illusion of travel.

Now on foot and alone, I am going to pick up my high school ring from the jeweler. It has undergone some sort or repair or refurbishment. I am in Fort Worth, walking on North Main Street between downtown and the Stockyards. I come to the corner where the jewelry store should be, but all I find is a scraped off lot. Only pebble-sized pieces of concrete and dirt remain. Somehow, I understand that my ring is here, but it has been buried in the dirt, left here for me to retrieve. I pick up a stick and scratch at the raw earth, looking for my treasure.

#

I come upon an old bus parked in a back yard, apparently its final resting place. Hasn't run in years. It looks like a photo I saw recently in the newspaper. It seems that someone wanted to sell what he claimed was the original Rosa Parks bus, an old relic as vine covered and crumbling as ancient Roman ruins.

Through the dust-coated windows, I see that people are being held hostage by a man with a gun. So I run for help, to call for police. I race across the side yard of the house behind my boyhood Cherry Street home. I am running so fast that I leave the ground. I am flying, like Superman.

#

In a parking lot with my wife. She is at the wheel. She bumps a parked car, hitting it with enough force to send it racing across the lot and bumping into another parked car. She pulls onto the road. Her driving is no better here; she accelerates through a red light, narrowly missing a car that is about to enter the intersection from the left. Then we get on the highway.

We are approaching the big hill at Spur 408 and Interstate 20 in Duncanville, but the ramps and roadways look different. My wife is not sure which way to go; she wants me to tell her. But there is no time. Before I can reply, she makes her selection. Instead of pulling onto one of the highways, though, she has chosen a road marked "Main Street."

"Is this right?" she asks.

In fact, it is not. This will not take us to either highway. But I tell her this is actually a good choice.

"I have always wanted to take this road, which will allow me to finally see the house on the hill."

For years I have caught brief glimpses of the house, tucked into the cedar and red oaks. It is visible over my shoulder while heading westbound on I-20 and descending "Monster Mountain," as that geographical feature was known locally in my high school days. Now I will finally be able to see the house up close.

But as we approach, I realize the house is actually a restaurant. And instead of being tucked into the side of a hill, the restaurant is on the banks of the Trinity River. It is actually one in a line of restaurants – a restaurant row. It occurs to me that this development is like the waterfront re-developments that have been undertaken in several major cities, except this one is just a "development." No "re," for it is an original creation. They are making all into one, creating necessity out of nothingness.

#

Driving in Many, La., the last town this side of Fort Jesup. I am towing a boat. Both boat and car are white. The boat is for bass fishing. The car is a Camaro or Firebird. These vehicles belong to my dad, who grew up here.

As I travel along one of the main streets, I notice how much the businesses have changed from what I remember during boyhood visits. I stop and look in one storefront that used to be an auto parts shop. It changed uses several times, and it now appears to be permanently closed. I look in the dark windows and see forgotten books. In the building's final incarnation, it was apparently some sort of second hand store or antique shop. The owner just locked the doors one day and never came back.

I return that night, hoping to get a second look. I peer into the window, then proceed to a big hardware store, which is also closed. I park in the side lot, which is out of sight but well lit. It seems safe enough; I don't worry. I walk up to the closed store, then turn around to walk back to the car and boat. But I find that two young men are stealing it.

One of them sneers at me, shouts something. He thinks it is funny. Then the bad guys are gone. And somehow I realize that they have stolen more than the car and boat; I have no clothes. I am standing alone in the parking lot, naked. Some of the town's young men have watched the whole thing and laugh a bit. But one of them offers to help.

I go with him and his friends into a house where they are staying. The young man tells me that the first thing we should do is call a certain person (I don't recall the name) who knows everything that goes on in town.

"He'll know who's got your car and boat," he says.

I tell him and the others that my big concern for the moment is getting some clothes. But no one has any to lend me. One guy says he has an extra set, but it is his clean clothes that he must wear the next day.

"My father is coming to visit," he explains.

At learn that at least one other man has a father who will be visiting, too, so it's a big event.

I look on the floor and find a pile of old bedspreads and rugs, faded red. I decide I will simply wrap an old bath mat around my waist. It is wet because the men have been taking showers, getting ready for the fathers' visit. Now the sun is coming up. Leaning against the window frame, I look out at the road and take stock. I have lost my dad's car and boat, and I have no clothes. I'm not sure what I will do. Clearly, this is a noteworthy setback in the journey.

#

At school, looking for the room where I will attend my first class of the year. The halls are laid out as rays off a central, curving hall. In some places it looks like a '50s-era hospital, with white or light colored tiles on the walls. But in other places, it looks like the inside of the old adult Sunday school building at First United Methodist Church in Duncanville. I see Scott Paulson and other people I know, both from my school days and present time.

During the search, I join up with an unsavory group led by Will Chrison. He was a bad seed, a boy who once tried to break a glass jar on my back. He died when I was in high school. But death obviously taught him nothing, for I discover he is still as bad as I remember. In a stairwell, I drop an audio cassette tape. Will reclines on the stairs, sneering at me. Somehow, I suspect he has made the tape fall out of my hand. He must have demonic powers. I should have known. And, of course, I realize he will use his powers to do worse. I decide to leave this group and continue on my own.

Back in the hallway, I meet a black woman, an employee. She tells me I am looking for the class called "Basics of Economics." It is in the big auditorium, where some parents typically sit for the first day of classes. She gives me directions. I cross a large plaza with an Olympic size pool in the middle. Then I take the side street on the left, which is where I find the entrance to my class.

I am standing in the street in front of the auditorium building. It presents a sort of European façade, complete with half-timber construction. From the front lawn a boy taunts me. I understand him to be a friend or associate of Will. They are certainly cut from the same cloth. The boy holds a bottle of white wine. Others look on, placing me in an unwelcome spotlight. I say nothing, holding in my anger. I am praying (somehow I know that he is also ridiculing God), and I wish that he would be punished by the power of God. And then it happens. He disappears. Only the bottle remains, lying alone on the lawn.

Someone says something about this incident involving "Old Scratch," the devil.

Two women I know have been watching. They are sitting on beds that have been set up on balconies or flat roofs protruding from the auditorium building. I join them, sitting on a third, empty bed. The two women are positioned between me and the place where the boy disappeared. As we sit there, I explain to the women that God took the boy away. We talk a bit more. Perhaps "Old Scratch" is again mentioned. I can't say for sure.

Then it begins to rain, big drops. The two women hide under the covers of their beds. I consider getting under the covers of my bed; however I see that each drop immediately soaks all the way through the cloth. The bedspreads are made of the same thin, ripcord type fabric I had on my bed when I was a boy – totally useless against rain.

As I watch the downpour, I look down the street in the direction where the boy disappeared. I see a strange form round the corner and approach us. It is Old Scratch – or, rather, his head.

This disembodied being is wearing a hood, and smoke swirls about his bearded face. He has no body, but moves towards us with ease, floating under his own unseen power. I am praying for the aid of God. I also tell the women who is approaching, for they seem not to know him. The devil's business is clear: He wants to know what happened to his follower.

#

On a Cub Scout camp out. We are in rowboats, floating around a series of boat-sized islands. It looks like a swamp, maybe the Everglades or even the far north end of lake where my parents have a house. We are in search of a campsite. And apparently we find one. For next we are on dry land, staking out some sort of foundation. I am using string and stakes and white PVC. The group is very pleased with the way the foundation is shaping up; even my wife comes over to thank me for my good work. Everyone is pleased – everyone but me, that is.

I regard my work as messy, sloppy. Stakes have been planted sideways; the string sags in unfortunate ways. I am sure if the others could only see an example of a proper foundation, then they would see that we should not be so pleased. Still, I suppose it is something. It is a start.

#

At home with my wife and our boys, planning out a weekly class schedule for myself. I can't recall the details, though I think that at noon on Mondays and Wednesdays there is an athletic activity. I share a cold drink with the boys. We are sitting at an outside table or perhaps on the front steps of the house. My youngest son holds a short, squat glass with a long straw. Upon inspection, I see that the straw is actually three straws plugged into each other. This drink with the extra long straw is for me. I can't help asking myself "Isn't this a bit of a stretch?"

#

Watching two rotating circular platforms. These platforms bear two-dimensional, full-size human cutouts, like the ones used in the original Mr. Peppermint TV show. At the point where the two platforms come together, the cutouts come together, then depart, as if greeting one another. The whole thing is like a giant clockwork mechanism, one of those antique German clocks in which mechanized figures emerge from inside the clock to announce the hour.

The cutouts themselves do not move. Except for the mouths, which open and close like a camera aperture. Words are formed, but I do not understand them. The eyes of each cutout are holes, too. A person can stand behind the cutout and look through the holes, experiencing the world as a two-dimension being. It seems to me that the talking faces – vacant expressions, but with the real eyes peering out from the holes -- have the look of being trapped, no control. I am terrified for them.

#

Back at Duncanville High School. I am behind in my schoolwork, so I am hoping to avoid attending some of the classes in which I am farthest behind. I have not done my homework! Like so many school days, I come to myself and realize that I have not done my work. But I must still go to class. I fear being revealed and receiving a failing grade. Will my education never end?

Two teachers stand at the end of a hallway. One of them is Lee Stakhanov, a colleague from work. He is handing out papers, including a sort of program. I take one, but then I am told I must give it to another student. I am offended.

"Wait," Lee says, "here is one for you."

"No, no, you keep it for someone who needs it. I'll be fine.'"

In other words, I play the martyr. I abruptly walk off, so that I can have the last word.

I take a seat by myself at a table next to the windows that look out on the outside commons area. A friend approaches with several girls.

"You coming to the party?" he asks.

He is talking about a party planned for the weekend somewhere outside of town. But I am still fuming about the program and will not talk. The friend tries to cheer me up. From where he is standing, he uses the toe of his shoe to lift up my pants leg, then looks down at my leg and back up at me with raised eyebrows, as if leering at me. This is supposed to be funny, and he does it twice. I still do not react, but he is untroubled.

"You know, this party will be a sort of shake-out for a much bigger one later one, maybe on the 4th of July," he says. "So it's going to be good one."

I still say nothing, so my friend and the girls leave. Immediately it occurs to me that I acted foolishly. They all came to talk to me; I should have been more communicative. After all, there were girls. I am filled with regret.

Then it's time to go to class. Another friend -- Jon Livrus, I think – approaches.

"Where's our next class?" he asks.

We have the same schedule. I look at my class printout. It is speech. The teacher looks like Ted Baxter, the anchorman from the Mary Tyler Moore Show.

Jon and I walk together to the classroom, which is in a part of the original high school campus. The building bears a metal plaque of LBJ, who was president when the school was built. In fact, the school was originally to have been named for him, but the plan was scraped after he failed to attend the dedication.

As we walk, I realize that today is probably my turn to give a speech. The speech was due last week, but I was out sick. The assignment is to speak about someone we know. I begin to think of people I could talk about, perhaps a friend. There is no time to write a speech, but I could just say "I come without a prepared speech, so I'll just make a few remarks" about the person I select. I think that if I can come up with a few coherent thoughts and speak with confidence, perhaps I will get a good grade for doing well off the cuff. I enter the classroom, but then realize I need to go the restroom.

I go to the men's room a short distance away. Now I am only wearing underpants, which I take off and toss in the wastebasket. I move toward a urinal, then realize my mistake: I am naked. I go back and retrieve my underwear. It's not much clothing, but definitely better than walking around in the nude.

I stand at a urinal, but am unable to do my business because Ron Joppeh is standing a few steps behind me, far too close for restroom comfort. He has no intention of doing anything to me, of course. I know he is just being funny, annoying me. I turn around and he flashes a mischievous smile. So I read a magazine instead.

There is a photo of a man, a rugged, masculine type, like you'd expect to see in the oil drilling business. In the accompanying story, he says he is unhappy because a perfectly good oil well has been intentionally fouled with salt water, which was injected as part of the extraction process. There is also an ad for a wristwatch, one with a rectangular-style face.

Others are now in the men's room. Again, I decide to relieve myself. I step over to a low wall, which encloses a circular area paved in blacktop. I direct my stream into this circular area, working carefully until I darken the entire blacktopped surface.

#

Bert Roldsteig from college is back in town for a visit. I will take him from SMU to the airport. But for some reason, I drive him through Duncanville, which is completely out of the way. We travel down Peach Street, past the side of my old house on Cherry Street. The house has been remodeled. The brick addition, built by my father in the late 1960s, is gone. A narrow, high-roofed front porch has been added. The wood siding is still stained red, but the trim is white. Also, someone has remodeled the house across the street in the same way, giving it a low-pitched roof.

We turn right onto Center Street and a few blocks later pull into the driveway of the old home on Woodacre Circle.

It was full daylight before, but now it seems to be dark. There are neighborhood kids around. In the driveway I find two trash bags, each contains a watermelon standing on end. The melons have withered away inside; they are hollow and shake like Jell-O.

Inside the house, I find a wild rabbit, jumping around crazily. It has been placed here on purpose. The hope is it will become tame, a pet.

#

I am in a room with executives from work and the military. A military officer is sitting in a chair -- perhaps behind a desk or table -- in the middle of the room. He is making some observation about the positive parallels between the work of our company and the military. I believe the other military officers are sitting or standing beside or behind him. The company men are sitting in plain chairs -- maybe folding chairs, a half dozen -- that line two walls and face the military man. I am the only one standing, as if there is no place for me. Not military and not an executive, I really don't fit into either group. As I stand there, I feel an incredible pressure in my face, almost more than I can bear.

#

Of course I felt incredible pressure. The military is at the heart of many government/alien conspiracies. This is well understood by the staff of the Armageddon Drive-In. Here is a message that hangs over a doorway in the concession stand:

"The Christian congregations of my community had come together to take us all to a drive-in movie theater. When we got there they split us up into two groups: The ones who were going with God and the ones who were staying on Earth. And of course I was in the group that was staying."

Is that not the way of it? Coming soon to an apocalypse near you. Welcome to the Armageddon Drive-in. Purchase your bucket of popcorn and soft drink and prepare yourself for a celluloid voyage of dark violence, of vines strangling the pulpit and moths consuming the flag – and an important discovery of why so many people who appear to be alive are really dead. We'll be showing 1950s B-movie Sci-Fi: bleeding walls, extraterrestrial insects, vast government conspiracies, evil corporate cabals and the last dying gasps of the American newspaper industry. The end is near.

Have you read their news releases? Very illuminating. Twilight wind across a rolling prairie, snagged in an old barbed wire fence, wind whistling through tombstones… a cowboy on acid, a cowboy gone insane, a cowboy like the one in "El Topo," Alejandro

Jodorowsky's surreal spaghetti Western of 1970 that became the world's first Midnight movie. A crazed cowboy on the big screen. Here at the Armageddon Drive-in, we cannot wait to once again see 40-foot tall gutted donkeys, dead bunnies and guru gunslingers. After "El Topo's" New York re-release in December 2006, the film will travel the country as a double feature with the Chilean-born director's 1973 proposition, "The Holy Mountain." Best of all, a DVD release is planned for these titles and "Fando y Lis." Thank you, John Lennon.

#

Attention Mark Leach. David Lynch is holding on the red phone. Ah, the Cult of Lynch. "There are, in the movies, few places creepier to spend time than in David Lynch's head," writes Manohla Dargis in a New York Times review of "Inland Empire," Lynch's new movie that opened Dec. 6, 2006. The staff of the Armageddon Drive-in has high hopes for this latest installment of Lynch noir. And yet, nothing Lynch might put on film could ever hope to compare to "Eraserhead," one of our all-time Midnight movie/embalmed calf fetus favorites. We're feeling creepy just thinking about it! Nevertheless, we are still willing to wear a blindfold while projecting the rushes. "Stephen, I don't wanna, uh . . . talk about that."

#

Stacks of gray steel film canisters and a cacophony of incomprehensible voices from the sanctioned psychic manifest, nightmare metaphors of violent purple twilight and unfulfilled judgments and dreams. Vacant hallways. Conference rooms. Hallways. Windows. Windows. Conference rooms. Unoccupied seating, plush sofas, deep rugs. Substantial tapestries. Ladders, rungs. Rungs, one above the next. Porcelain items, items remaining complete, vacant bowls. A knife that descends through a countdown: Three, two, one, zero. Porcelain walls, documents....Perhaps the operation even continues today, hidden away in the antechamber of some underground bunker connected via high-speed pneumatic tunnels to Carswell ...UPDATE! SECRET SUBWAY FOUND BENEATH FORT WORTH DRIVE-IN ... The staff of the Armageddon Drive-in has learned that a high-speed pneumatic subway tunnel has been discovered beneath the Fort Worth Twin Drive-in. A former petroleum geologist-turned-homeless person who lived in a cardboard box at the property before it was cleared of brush and debris in July 2006 reports that he often accessed this subterranean transit structure by way of a hidden surface entrance manipulated by an autonomous nanobot system activated through special magnets and natural piezoelectric crystals. This report positively correlates with established stories of a high-speed pneumatic subway system between the underground alien recovery labs at Carswell AFB in Fort Worth, the old Aurora "glider base" and the Nike missile base in Duncanville – the three points of the infamous "Alien Triangle" that forms the heart of the D/FW Alienplex. Sadly, the July 2006 cleanup work seriously damaged the autonomous nanobot system, eliminating surface access to the pneumatic tunnel. But we will continue to monitor this situation and issue follow-up reports as new information becomes available.

#

They stood around in open necked shirts and cummerbunds, looking serious and decisive. Think JFK and "Missiles of October." Who killed JFK? Here at the Armageddon Drive-in, we have uncovered never-before-contemplated suggestions that the assassination of John F. Kennedy was part of an evil corporate cabal initiated by the Greys of Zeti Reticuli.

Consider the JFK research work of Jim Marrs. Pretty. And yet we are of the opinion that he doesn't go nearly far enough to expose the true nature of this intergalactic conspiracy. The staff of Armageddon Drive-in has located an early '60s Central Intelligence Agency manuscript that documents the substance of a Telstar satellite communication between Marilyn Monroe and Dallas nightclub owner Jack Ruby two days before the blonde bombshell was executed via the government's "remote viewing" program called Project Brain Detonation. Throughout the communication, Monroe notifies Ruby that Kennedy informed her of his unscheduled appointment at an underground military installation (perhaps the subterranean alien recovery base in Aurora, Texas?) where he saw recovered effects from the cosmos and classified documents concerning the UFO/military conspiracy in North Texas, specifically the D/FW Alienplex. Ruby suspected the North Texas material was associated with the Roswell conspiracy, specifically the transfer of alien remains to Carswell AFB in Fort Worth for study at the Aurora facility in connection with general research prerogatives within the infamous "Alien Triangle."

Moreover, a Federal Bureau of Investigation manuscript of the late 1940s corroborates that JFK was cognizant of the D/FW

Alienplex. And Texas billionaire William "Dollar Bill" Buckstop apparently engaged in a secret dialogue with JFK in the early '60s. While enjoying a couple of Cuban cigars and brandy liberally served from a cut crystal decanter, "Dollar Bill" apparently asked Kennedy about his opinions regarding flying saucers over Duncanville, which by then was a well-known gathering spot for extraterrestrials. Reports from a domestic servant present during the discussion indicate that JFK suddenly developed an extremely somber disposition and countered "Dollar Bill, I would like to tell the public about the UFO/military conspiracy, but my hands are tied."

Nevertheless, we are aware of proof via reconstructed facts that, on Sept. 31, 1963, the President instructed the CIA to reveal all extraterrestrial manuscripts to the White House. This did not sit well with the Greys, who used a viral DNA dream phone to implant assassination suggestions directly into the brain of Buckstop. Two weeks later JFK was shot in Dallas, Texas, the heart of the D/FW Alienplex and the "Alien Triangle." It is well known that the patsy Lee Harvey Oswald immediately fled south to Oak Cliff, an area of Dallas adjacent to Duncanville along Interstate 35 (aka "The Alien Assassination Highway"). Could it be that Oswald was headed to a Buckstop-arranged rendezvous point at the Nike missile base in Duncanville, where a UFO was standing by to aid him in his escape?

Coincidence? I think not.

#

Pursued by a Bengal tiger. I am in a two-story house, trying to get away from this tiger that is inexplicably inside. How did it get here? I don't know, and there's no time to wonder.

I go into the garage and close the door to the house, but still I am not safe. I see that the tiger has gotten through the door and is in the garage. I yell loudly at it, in a ferocious way. I am apparently convincing, because the animal jumps back into the house.

After it leaves, I see that the door that I thought would hold it back has an enormous gap at the bottom. Plus, it has been repaired with pieces of plywood. Not very substantial. So I decide to take a side door to the outside. This door has also been repaired with plywood, and I realize it will not hold back the tiger, either. My only hope is to run.

I find myself in a typically subdivision of the 1970s. I turn right and run down the sidewalk, which gently curves to the left. In the sidewalk, I come to a parked bike, which could help in my escape but

I do not take it. That would be stealing and cause even more problems for me.

Next, I come upon a tall, cylindrical object, perhaps 6 feet high. I do not know its purpose, but it reminds me a bit of a crayon standing on its flat end. I do not know its purpose. Like the bike, it too has been left in the middle of the sidewalk.

I reach the end of the street, arriving at a larger thoroughfare. This road appears to be Big Stone Gap in Duncanville. Across the street, children are playing in a field or perhaps a park. There are many bikes parked here. But again, I do not take any of them. Instead, I turn right and continue running. It occurs to me that the tiger will be able to track me by scent, so I decide to leave the sidewalk. I run on the grass a short distance, thinking this will throw him off. Next I come to a park, and sitting by the road I see a woman with her child. I run over to her. She has a cell phone, so I ask if I can use it to call the police. But she makes the phone call herself.

"Yes, there is a problem here and my cousin needs help," she tells the dispatcher.

I am amazed that she knows me and that we are related. I don't even recognize her.

#

Enjoying Christmas Eve with my family. And yet enjoying is not quite the right word. For I am saddened by the evening news, a story about a lost boy presumed drowned at Possum Kingdom Lake, about two hours west of Strangers Rest.

His father, who is legally blind, speaks to the rescuers, thanking them for all they have done. The search involved roughly 200 to 300 volunteers, who combed the shoreline and surrounding wilderness for two cold, miserable days. Then we go to the 7 p.m. Christmas Eve service at church.

The pastor tells a story of the daughter of the innkeeper who turned away Mary and Joseph. She was sick, but the proximity of the Christ child heals her. He says that we must hold the Christ child next to our hearts, to heal ourselves.

We leave the church, but there is a minor family spat – someone is unhappy (perhaps me) about something vague and unimportant. We drive around looking at Christmas lights, but I do not feel festive. The lights give off a horrid glow. I am drowning.

That night I dream I am standing in a lake, water up to my waist. There is a motor boat slowly turning from side to side, towing a baby in a small inflatable. I am staying within arms reach of the baby, watching the rope as it curves around when the boat turns. Then I realize the baby is gone. It has fallen out, and I can't find it. It must have sunk.

I am frantically searching, then I stand next to the shore and call for everyone (there is a picnic, many people are playing ball) to jump in.

"Don't worry about a swim suit," I say. "Get in in your clothes."

We all spread out, walking across the lake bottom in hopes of finding the baby, before it's too late. I come to a place where the waters have receded, leaving the muddy, dead bottom. There is a tarp or covering of some sort. I lift it up and find a man and woman. The woman is dark skinned; I do not notice the man. She smiles at me. There are people all around. I realize we have stumbled upon this couple in some sort of compromising position, something sexual.

Then I am inside a nearby building or home, and a couple of people are at a dining table. The baby is still on my mind. Did we find it? Is it OK? I am not sure. What happened to the Christ child?

#

I know exactly what happened. I read it in "El Bib":

Now the ascension of Jesus the Messiah into Heaven took place in this way. While his disciples were talking about the many great deeds and miracles they had observed Jesus perform on the road, the Holy Spirit transformed the Son of the Deity into an infant. This took place to fulfill what had been spoken by the Lord through the prophet: "'Look, the disciples shall behold the Son of the Deity, and they shall name him Emmanuel,' which means 'God is with us.'" They took the baby Jesus to the town of Bethlehem, where they left him in a manger with Mary and her husband Joseph. They were preparing to celebrate their wedding night, but agreed to take the child. When they went to sleep Mary laid down with the baby, and the Holy Spirit implanted the child in her womb. When they awoke Joseph saw that the baby was now in the belly of his bride, whom he had believed to be a virgin. Being a righteous man and unwilling to expose her to public disgrace, he planned to dismiss her quietly. But just when he had resolved to do this, an angel of the Lord appeared to him in a dream and said "Joseph, son of David, do not be afraid to keep Mary as your wife, for the child conceived in her is from the Holy Spirit. He will save his people from their sins." Nine months later, the Holy Spirit caused the embryo to withdraw from Mary and the spirit of Jesus was carried up into Heaven. And Mary and Joseph worshipped him, and returned to their home with great joy; and they were continually in the temple blessing God.

#

Six nights after Christmas, and the water is a river. Am I on the shore or in a boat? I am not sure.

There is a boat – a barge. It appears to have lost power and is drifting dangerously close to the concrete pilings of a bridge. I am with another man, a ship captain or some sort of modern mariner. He tells me of a time when he was on a ship that had lost its power. I do not listen closely for I am busy imagining the barge being swept along by the river current, then slammed against the pilings. He says something about the lower Hudson River and "nothing below us but the Falls." At the time I assume he is talking about Niagra Falls, but realize later that the geography is incorrect. Then we turn away from the river and walk up a low, paved grade.

The river banks are decorated in Christmas lights, and the whole scene reminds me of the Cane River in Natchitoches, La. (the start of the El Camino Real).

"I meant to come before Christmas was over," the man says.

"Anymore there is some celebration going on here year 'round," I say.

Because this is not just a river, but the Sundance Square retail development in downtown Fort Worth.

We turn right, walking over the brick pavers. We approach the Tarrant County Register, a geographical reference point which puts this river in about the location of Burnett Plaza. There should be no river in this place, but I do not realize that until later. I am preoccupied, looking at the bricks underfoot. They have been laid out in patterns – some herringbone, some linear. I see a sort of ragged line, as if the bricks were actually concrete and someone had dragged something through it while the cement was still wet. This is ghostly to me, and it makes me recall a story I've heard of a ghost.

Then I see that the mariner is actually Kit Genelli, and I tell him that his wife told me the story of the ghost. I can't recall his wife's name, which is embarrassing (I've known her longer than my own wife), so I cover up by saying "your then wife-to-be."

"Years ago – I can't recall the precise number, but it was 10, 12 or maybe 13 years – she told me this story," I say.

I didn't believe the story, but I wish to recount it in a way that does not insult her. So I explain that I simply accepted her account as one of those unexplainable stories. Kit has no comment.

Now we have rounded the corner of the Register building and are walking north on the side street, between the building and the Fort Worth Club. I try to recall the name of the ghost. Was it Blackbeard? No, then I remember: Bluebeard.

#

And now I have arrived.

I am in Granny and Paw's house in Fort Jesup. This is the epicenter of the Land of the Dead.

My grandparents have been dead for years now, but the house lives on without them. It has grown larger, deeper. No doubt a necessary expansion, one required to hold all of the memories of 140 years of Leaches in Sabine Parish.

I see an old woman's face in a moth-eaten mirror. Plump faced, white-haired, a laughing ghost. She looks a bit like an aunt of mine, a woman who is still alive. Terrified, I run to middle room in the front of the house. This should be the bathroom, but it has reverted to the bedroom it was before the house was plumbed in the 1960s.

Within these chalky, beaded board walls there is a bed and a woman. She is a relative of some sort who is now the house's caretaker, a sort of landlady of the dead. I apologize for bursting in. I am supposed to sleep in the adjoining room. We talk a bit, then I go to my room.

This should be the living room, but when I step through the door I find a screened-in porch. It is run down, wood rotting, Southern decay. I look out through sagging screen and see a black car leaving my uncle's double wide next door. It looks like a charcoal drawing or woodcut of an old car from the late '50s, sporting fins that suggest a Thunderbird or Galaxie 500. Black as night, it reminds me of a winged demon.

This is a car of death.

#

Perhaps the car was actually a classic Caddy. This would further link "The Shadow Made Flesh" to the government/alien conspiracy. Why? Because Men in Black are often reported to be driving antiquated black Cadillacs, vehicles that inexplicably "seem and smell brand new," according to the Men in Black entry at Wikipedia.org.

Personally, I believe the Men in Black are actually human/alien hybrids employed by the federal government under protocols of Majestic 12, the commission of scientists, military leaders and government officials formed in 1947 by a presidential order from Harry S. Truman. Here is the famous letter:

#

TOP SECRET - EYES ONLY

THE WHITE HOUSE

WASHINGTON

September 24, 1947.

MEMORANDUM FOR THE SECRETARY OF DEFENSE

Dear Secretary Forrestal:

As per our recent conversation on this matter, you are hereby authorized to proceed with all due speed and caution upon your undertaking. Hereafter this matter shall be referred to only as Operation Majestic Twelve.

It continues to be my feeling that any future considerations relative to the ultimate disposition of this matter should rest solely with the Office of the President following appropriate discussions with yourself, Dr. Bush and the Director of Central Intelligence.

Harry S. Truman

#

MJ-12's efforts continue to this day. Do you know that the Texas billionaire with electronic eyes is a member? That's right, Dollar Bill Buckstop. I have it on good authority that it was through his MJ-12 connections that he came to meet and employ Adolfo Morel, a shadowy figure associated with a cacophony of incomprehensible voices and various government/alien conspiracies, including Watergate and the Kennedy assassination (because JFK wanted to end the cover-up). Buckstop and Morel are major world power brokers who manipulate events behind the scenes in a bid for total world domination, specifically through the introduction of psychotropic compounds into the global water supply and a stock market-manipulated takeover of the Exogrid. (Ironically, it is possible they were reprogrammed by an alien computer found in a South American cave where Nazis holed up after WWII, with the cryogenically frozen Hitler, $200 billion in gold bullion and an Aerial Clock they'd brought down with a V-2 rocket during the final days of the war.

So there it is. What more proof do you need of the ongoing government cover up of the existence of UFOs?

#

Reality may not be what it used to be. Now with their new Deity and its now-revealed relationship with the film audience, a new order is beginning to emerge in the cosmos.

In truth. "Marienbad My Love With Mango Extracts" does more than allude to the Jewell Effect. It actually employs the technique. Leach is not merely a filmmaker. He is the ultimate reality maker. With his sacred film, he can ensure the world will realize his prophesy. Once the seven-day premier is over, the world itself will be transformed. The initial audience will be the self-proclaimed Marienbadists, who even now are setting up Leach as their new Deity and the "Marienbad My Love With Mango Extracts" as their new religion.

But there is more. Adolfo Morel himself is a creation of the Jewell Effect. His origins can be traced back to "The Invention of Morel," a Latin American novella that helped inform and inspire "Last Year at Marienbad." A story of a deserted island, a derelict museum, tourists dressed for a

European resort (such as Marienbad). A story of a woman, of losing one's mind, of disappearing and reappearing tourists. A story of odd happenings, with exact versions of dead fish restored to life. Odd happenings with tourists jumping to shake off the cold even though the heat is intense. The sky has two suns and two moons, the results of a machine that can recreate reality and capture celestial bodies and human souls in an endless loop for all time. A movie actress is compelled to engage in sexual relations with a stranger for all eternity.

What a story, no? Let us consider its many ramifications. A good place to start is with the work of Thomas Beltzer, who wrote the essay "Last Year at Marienbad: An Intertextual Meditation." Read it. We firmly recommend it. Beltzer suggests that in the dark of the cinema, we have the opportunity for total wish fulfillment. And yet many of us choose to live in the swamps, spying on the tourists (i.e., the characters on the silver screen). Perhaps we will compel a beautiful woman to have sexual relations in an endless loop of time. One might even wish to be dead.

This is my story, too. Submit yourselves to the Jewell Effect.

"Marienbad My Love With Mango Extracts" does more than allude to a vision. Rather, it is a warning. No one can ever win as a scientist. You will also be at the mercy of the violator machine, operating through the Jewell Effect. I use the technique to splice myself into the recording. The tourists suddenly disappear. Intertextually, I am not wise to confuse myself with the merely artificial. I am actually one of beings I study. Through film, I captures these feelings beautifully. I am my new religion. It does exist. Soon, I realize all I am losing and discover that we shall be together always, penetrating one loop that will continue to loop forever. I picture my ectoplasm swirling inside you, where my feelings are true.

The lesson is clear. Don't go to the movies too much, especially for 168 hours at a stretch. You could become a fictional character, living in a world that may or may not have already come to an end…

We are about ghosts that weep or rather our remains. In the midst of it I submit myself to the Jewell Effect. It is to be used for the final immolation. When will I ever be their screen idol? Reality check. I have been in love with the artificial. It's not so odd. People empty themselves into the midst of the living. The midst of the living. Many wail. The dead remain with the living. Many of us filmmakers write about our relationship to it, the living. Many of us submit ourselves to artificial constructs of popular culture. As viewers. This is the final immolation, no?

How many understand that reality is not what's in a machine?

How many young people would trade their existence for a chance to live as cinematic characters in the Jewell Effect?

How many more young ghosts must weep and wail?

How many of us have been in love with what it used to be? Many of us have been in love with living. Many of us have been a part of what used to be popular culture. Many of us have wished to be a screen idol. Reality in the midst of the tenuous. Viewers, we understand this final immolation in the contest of popular culture. The dead remain in the midst of the living. In this way many in the midst of the living and dead become more tenuous. People empty themselves to become one of the cinematic undead. How many young people will become more tenuous?

Submit yourselves to the Jewell Effect.

#

Decades after the United States initiated its program of municipal water fluoridation for dental hygiene, investigators of the government/extraterrestrial conspiracy are uncovering previously-classified documents that suggest this so-called public health measure is actually part of a shadowy program to control the minds of the global population, direct the cacophony of unintelligible voices and pave the way for the acceptance of artificial deities based on human/alien hybridization.A-bomb scientists carried out a key part of the conspiracy, faking the positive results of a government study of the health effects of fluoridating municipal drinking water. The public was told that the study was conducted in Strangers Rest, Texas, from 1945 to 1956. But in secret records, we learn that the study was actually a fabrication of "Operation Herbal Extract." Ozona International carried out the foot work, secretly gathering and analyzing blood and tissue samples from Strangers Rest citizens under the auspices of the Texas Department of Health.

The original secret version indicates a chemical known as Skinalicious9 rapidly emerged as the substance of choice for controlling vast groups of the population. Professionals, or journalists, were clueless of this reality.

The fluoride studies (part of a classified operation code-named "Operation Herbal Extract") were conducted with radioactive plutonium. The fluoride studies were required. Bomb program researchers of artificial fertilizers containing fluoride, pesticide residues, connection between fluoride and the dawning of the government/extraterrestrial conspiracy all point to the inescapable conclusion that we live in a world soon to be overtaken by artificial deities based on a hybridization of human/alien DNA.

#

Mind control. The terrifying, horrifying conspiracy of the modern age. The human/alien hybrids are here among us, employing Skinalicious9, the Exogrid and other alien technologies to make our minds receptive to a New World Order. Even now major corporations are moving to manipulate a vast government/extraterrestrial conspiracy. The goal is complete disheartenment of the population, which will come to follow the will and the way of a super race of privately owned and operated deities based on human/alien hybrid technology.

The subject of mind control is intricate, complicated and highly structured. To the layman, it can appear as a confusing jumble of overwhelming facts and statistics that apparently lead no where of importance or danger. But we can help you see the reality. The truth is quite chilling. Conspiracy investigators have learned of a sleeper army of hundreds of thousands of Herbal Extract Boys, mind-controlled Americans conditioned at and managed from more than two dozen underground facilities operated by the government/extraterrestrial conspiracy. These men are programmed to go into action at specific time in response to specific stimuli and events when specifically triggered via the Exogrid. To date, they have been used in various destructive and disruptive ways. Many Herbal Extract Boys are integrated into daily American life as journalists. And this is just the surface.

You don't believe it? Perhaps you have a wish to forget this topic, but avoiding the truth could leave you susceptible to becoming the next mind-controlled individual. Do you want to be programmed for use in this insidious enslavement agenda? Do you wish to be threatened and vulnerable in your daily mainstream American life by journalists?

#

On a hot, humid afternoon, a racial epithet rang out, a grisly chapter in history. The town was on fire with word of a suspected extraterrestrial invasion that began nine years previous and 120 miles to the north, back in the year of 1897. The exposure of the dying alien to the citizenry that caused its demise resulted in a psychological event of "tornadic" proportions. When humans are exposed to alien blood, psychosis inevitable occurs.

The injured totaled 597 more than could be counted. That year 1953 was too hot to touch. And it was without color. Ribbons were tied to the high cost of film, and it might be too hot to touch. Picture a tree with a dangling noose. The character Calvin Thaxton speaks on death, differentiation and division. These and the mad dog racism of the Fatigue Malaise (vague feeling generated by exposure to the alien blood) was the deadliest ever reported in U.S. alternate history. It may have killed more people than all previous deaths combined. The story was gradually tracked back to the writings of Jason Mathison, an aerial clock researcher who attempted to harbor the alien. He was indicted in 30 leukemia-related deaths, though the actual death toll was considerably higher. Mathison was never again to see his three young children – not because of the legal ramifications but due to his own exposure to extraterrestrial DNA resulting in weakness and reduced exercise tolerance.

Dateline Waco, 1845: The first institution of higher learning opened on a humid afternoon. Years later, in May 1953, students at that same location would look across the street to see a lynching involving eighty-three characters in twenty-one separate, unforgettable moments. The alien was pulled from his aerial clock and dragged through the streets. His exoskeleton was cracked, his wings clipped and he was hung from a tree until death weeks later (presumably from terrestrial infection and a fever of the abdominal zone). At first Mathison wouldn't talk about his radial views that the lynching was influenced by factors related to alien blood exposure. These were real people motivated by real events. To this day the story is shielded from memory by hills of fear. For this report we had to draw heavily on archives and the unimpeachable testimonies of two pastoral leaders whose names are recorded on memorial markers at the main buildings of the institution of higher learning.

Picture it: 114 people. A library blessed them for a reason. They fought the secret government for the future of all mankind. Regulation of cell death, of differentiation of social detail with the conventions of bleeding, excessive bruising, weakness. The reports were passed from extraterrestrial hands and back to human hands, which joined together like the sturdier buildings that experts say were built to withstand the disaster. Civil disobedience was employed to get the cooperation of the rising merchant class, which resisted and was therefore denied a monument to itself. This story is every bit as daunting as that infamous day in 2002 at the compound at Mount Carmel, where as more than an afterthought, according to written minutes, a collection of two spleen, lymph nodes and hands were passed through the flames to waiting extraterrestrial hands outside.

It was a day not unlike one in 1906 when defense lawyers did not so much as tip their hats to a smudge of wispy smoke from which a burning alien hurled a plea for leniency, a plea that rang out in pain and was heard across the galaxy. Infection and fever wrung out the days as he struggled to breathe. And still the alien would not die. Resentment lingered. The events are documented in an idea born of 13 Jewell Poe pictures, 35 mm slides and an 8 mm conversation that is 1,731 feet long and made cinematic history.

This is the story of an alien who was forced to give a false confession that he was part of an army that planned to invade Planet Earth. This is the story of an alien signing a bogus confession. This is the story of a time and place that is now chained to a 1,731-page museum on Uranus, a museum commemorating the assassination of the extraterrestrial. I have walked across the studies linking exposure to alien DNA to the lawyers, who did not challenge the storm of the time. The punishments continue.

Recent reports indicate the suspected grandson of the alien was dragged from the flesh-coated pages of one of the longest novels ever written. This alien/human hybrid was given a terrible choice: either activate the oncogenes or deactivate 1906. Neither you say? Then another extraterrestrial farmhand shall be accused of invasion. We'll even second the motion! Color film, introduced in 1935 under a statue of the law goddess from more recent storms ... a time of cell death, of differentiation and the high cost of film and processing ... Robert and Elizabeth Barrett were among many utilizing 35 mm as a memorial, which came in 2002 where more than 80 people (search to confirm) would never hit the site of the Branch Davidian's 40 people. They may be attributed, perhaps significantly, to the directed wife, who was found in the United States and helped (I heard) until such time as the same church that held the alien for about 500 of the 4,697 mutations. These mutations may occur spontaneously, snatched from court so to speak. These mutations may occur spontaneously in an Indian tribe, too. The historic record includes a 35 mm roll filmed during the hourlong trial. The jury of "Sironia, Texas" by Madison Cooper came back with a 1,731-page verdict. Before we can claim this as confirmed fact, I should tell you I heard her under questioning during the hourlong trial. On May 11, 1953, however, Waco was in the murder and rape of 113,000 people.Medicinal water kept in a 1953 cabinet helped citizens overcome the broader symptoms. After the lynching, the same church that yelled for blood turned their back on what they had done (but I heard tell that some of the members did later take in a sickly alien in need of shelter).The killing was a terror. The alien was stripped of his clothes and bleeding began, followed by excessive bruising. Weakness of characters and events continue for three hours, exposing the citizenry to somatic mutations in the DNA. That may be one of the reasons the aliens are still here. We're their children now.

This blood fever disrupted the regulation of bodily functions. A day after the killing 114 people were injured. The numbers mounted on a daily basis. I heard the Alien Muse cried bitterly until the site of the lynching was reduced to a leafless tree. The town was in the grip of a full-blown epidemic. Medicinal procedures were conducted in the backyard. It was winter. We now come to the point of the discussion. This conversation about it was sad for Lucenay, now 78. The justice scales on one of the panels shows the Alamo and Six Flags Over Texas and the little town of Robinson. The alien, and an illiterate cotton picker felt the hand of the law goddess upon them, clutching the scales .... A cotton hand of borderline intelligence, allegedly of naturalistic social detail ... they buried the memory of the lynching, with much support and popularity.

Back in the day his grandmother read many an article. A tornado search revealed the absence of the alien "never nodes," which were burned away in the feverish liver Leukemia, according to a report from an alien management consultant who was too hot to touch, a large population at the time the regulation of cell death. This event is recorded on memorial markers from 1966 to 1970, a time of intergalactic violence on the frontier and the mad return of eighty-three characters of constant motion. It was thought to be a very insulting time.

Ribbons mark the spot where the researchers took these pictures, but thank God they didn't burn the alien a second time. That would most certainly have enraged the intergalactic order, resulting in immediate invasion of planet Earth.

#

When individuals incorrectly evaluated the accuracy of these reports, trouble inevitably followed. They were able to withstand any form of attainment, information and dominance on the slightly different slant to the problem. Informed consent is a violation of the treaty under which they obtained a selection of press men, living newspaper editions of U.S. News and World cases. The goal is to confuse the sentient mirrors and the "sessions" of physical methods, which will allow the subjects to appear with individuals who withstand privation, torture and coercion contrary to the evidence. The term"psychotic" is of the wheel. We were warned of judgment.

#

The most effective tool was the sacraments, which allow the user to withstand any form of interrogation. This substance is injected into one arm. Even in the face of contrary evidence the inoculated person possesses an effective weapon utilizing the secret code that the U.S. designed to introduce subliminal messages into the populace and to otherwise alter the science of the superhuman conquests of space. They were filmed for later use. We will become involved in the galactic equilibrium. This article indicates that they may be used by agents for their heritage and focus. That article discussed Paraguayan and international attempts at chemical-electrical activity in the brain and heart.

#

The Deity in the scriptures confirms that we are to gather together in his Heaven. Do you not put my words in thy mouth, oh great misfortune? Because of you, O earth and gates of hell open to you by the word in and out, eating and drinking, marrying and giving in appearance that we may have confidence, and not righteous judge, shall give and now seek meekness: it may be ye shall there shall be my life, to behold shall mount up bring in everlasting righteousness, and to seal of the Deity against those nations, as when he the night to take the strait gate: of the Deity.

#

These people repent in the Noble Misfortune. The Wise Ones applied the oil and made her ready for the marriage. This is true for I saw the holy harpazo of The Deity. This is the church of the last days of the Son of Man.

The Son of Man shall strike the nations with the rod of the Deity and curse a determined Rev 3:3. The gates of hell shall not allow for the escape of sinners, The son of of the proclamations is ready for the end of time. I am first, and the atonement. Who hath heard the Feast of Proclamations? Other verses on this saith that surely I behold. I shew you a mystery; alive and remaining unto the coming of the end. I would say "Wherefore the Deity?" Whom having not heard the proclamation of the three? But our citizenship is true. I shall choose. I want not.

Rejoice then, O Deity.

#

In order to create a sense of panic and manipulate the citizenry, it is necessary to create a mysterious and unseen enemy. The MKULTRA team manufactured a story about Venusians (i.e., pirate extraterrestrials, a rogue force of hate-mongering aliens who steal through the heavens, serving Satan in an attempt to destroy our faith as the Deity's chosen ones, the keepers of His light). According to the manufactured back story they were remnants of a species that killed its own world, now a dead planet containing the ruins of a highly-intelligent species. Cosmonauts have explored these ruins and determined that the Venusians had planned to destroy the Earth with powerful psychotropic weapons. But something went wrong. They lost control over their technological achievements and destroyed their own planet in the end. The remaining Venusians left with their deadly weapon, which has now been deployed on planet Earth. They are the enemy. They killed the Deity. They are the evil ones. The Deity versus Satan. Thankfully, the scientists of the One World Government know the score. They know how to counteract the savage weapons, using the Exogrid and specially prepared medicinal waters bottled by Ozona International. They will be our salvation – if we are willing to follow their instructions and fight back against the extraterrestrial menace. We are fighting for the Deity and for His preferred religion, Americanity. It is His war. Therefore, we shall prevail.

The medical community does not understand what is happening. Often, they see this mindset as a sign of trouble that appears to arise from a disorder of the psychic pancreas. Aldolfo Morel used a mental suggestion on an atheistic doctoral candidate of the 1960s, persuading him to feel the call of saints of the Old Testament and send himself into a shroud of "Americanity." The subject raged against the Venusians, claiming they wall around our faith and thereby threatened to cause the insanity….

The brain disorders are treatable. The court is expected to dismiss the case. THE DEITY is not responsible in any way. This makes fledgling space/time program possible.

#

Oh awesome and mysterious Deity, how can this be? Ours is a world gone mad.

Can it be true – you are dead? This is surely wrong. How can we live without you? Who shall make the Earth turn, the sun rise, the rain fall? The Venusians are lying. They have imprisoned you, cut us off from you. We shall strike back, oh Deity! In a cacophony of incomprehensible voices, we shall bring science back into its proper role as the defender of the one true faith of Americanity. Death to the scientists! Those who live through our Holy War will be extremely lucky, because the outcome is clear. We will cut you off from us.

They seek the need of conflict, the feeling that comes from splitting the one into the two.

#

You do not believe in divine action, religion, all men, the will of the Deity? You say that random chance is the explanation for the vast infinite? The Venusians have certainly had their way with you! Hold tight to the religion of today, the post-scientific era. Continue to believe that "El Bib" contains the answer to the malaise of America. In time this idea of respecting the false cultures will be little more than souvenir collecting. The importance of the competing viewpoints of liberal and conservatives group is outdated, a product borrowed from nearby Pagan cultures. Do not borrow such falsehoods. There is no conflict, no gray. Step into the light of the Deity, the genuine and true science of inerrant faith. And beware of the Seven Chambers of Hell. Each one lies at the end of a corridor that seemingly glows in the light of the Deity, but in reality is a time subway of death.

Today, we bring you the teachings of Voltage Nestles, the televangelist of godly science. The Deity has delivered unto him the one true message, which he delivers now.

"I minister today to the unsaved person with dry, damaged ski. I have been where you are, overwhelmed by forces so powerfully evil that they can strip away your very spirit. Don't feel too terrible that such a beauty-related calamity has befallen you. Many have been unexpectedly and deeply immersed in Pagan worship. National restraining power no longer functions. Without it, the Santanic Venusians are allowing the nations to fall into a state of spiritual crime against the Deity. This is thoroughly true all over the world.

Is it true we would know the time to become spiritually ready? Is your family? Are people today understanding this substitute sacrifice for me in America today. We have millions set for their fulfillment! The Son told us he did not want the circadian angels to get to Earth or to Heaven.

#

Are you spiritually ready? Is your family? Are people understanding this "Substitute Sacrifice"? That is the challenge in America today. We have millions set for their fulfillment! This fulfillment of which we speak is nothing less than the Second Coming as prophesized in the "El Bib" teachings of The Seventh Heaven.

First, a message to the godless liberals, abortionists and Democrats: There is no debate that 1 Thessalonians 4, and 1 Corinthians 15 teach on the Seventh Heaven! Both chapters also teach the resurrection and of the proclamation blast. Neither chapter mentions anything about having to endure your pseudoscientific babble before the Seventh Heaven comes. There is no debate that Revelation 19 and Zechariah 14 teach on the physical return of the Son of the Deity, who will be in power after the Noble Misfortune. Neither of those chapters speak of the Seventh Heaven, nor of a resurrection, nor of a proclamation blast. So get over it. Heed the Word of the Deity! He awaits you in the Derma-pod.

The Derma-pod of the Almighty. A perfect Derma-pod. And a perfect lotion! Super-rich lotion of the Almighty. Super-rich scriptural nourishment. A nourishing deity. A deity of rehydrating scriptural nourishment with nightly luscious antioxidants. Soul antioxidants with spirit-loving hairspray renewal plus extract. Vitamins, texturizing humidity spray, pure resistance has spring, is touchable. What's touchable? What's known of water in religious extra hold circles as goodness. Nourishing movement with essential hydrating two-ply ingredients. Emulsion to emulsion for Nourishing Skinalicious. Pure Skinalicious. Pure God Complex. God protection for all types. Stop the wrinkled DNA delivery organ. Revive it with Skinalicious9. Wrinkle epidemic for the sensitive, with the sensitive, with a can-glow skin of a deity. Believe in deified skin. Believe fusion with health of beauty and with French aloe. French aloe and reformulated lavender. Reveal a skin-loving deity of nutrients. That is, His nutrients. The twist. Volumizing twist. Volumizing green nutrients for tea hairspray renewal. Your skin. Your skin and sensational and sensational will thank skin jade. Skin jade you. Lather! You. Lather! Extracts with extracts with Perfecting complex, Perfecting complex. Pure thankful with extra skin. Moisturizers skin. Moisturizers and a unique time-release formula with a gentle reservoir of exfoliator. Activate exfoliator. Activate odor, all odor, all skin moisturizer. Skin moisturizer, skin rejuvenating ride in a derma-pod with spurts of skin-rejuvenating DNA infused with Skinalicious9.

#

"Conspiracy of Fools: A True Story" by Kurt Eichenwald tells the sad tale of the demise of Enron. The staff of the Armageddon Drive-in have discovered interesting parallels in the story of the death of Valuosity – and the world…

Roman Timms sloughed into the gray strata of his Luxorum 4040 TM, easing out of his reserved launching pad at the Donington condominiums. From the pad's entry point, he ascended into the main skyfare over Westover Hills, Fort Worth's wealthiest and most prestigious neighborhood.

The seven-year-old bubbletop soared past the mansions bordering the streets below, homes that testified to the immortality of the city's hydrocarbon men and corporate lords. Peeking out from behind the wrought-iron gates of the manicured electro-estates, the congressmen visiting from Washington. A former vice chief of staff asserts his will after 4 pm. The Bubble Syndicate offers market power that comes with world influence as contained in Mijur's evil heart and a running alarm clock. They think it must be about the stories about Valuosity – stories about how the evil corporate lords have pulled one over on the New York Agenda. But that was months ago. The Agenda was burned once. They wouldn't be so easily fooled again.

When Timms bowed out, he was celebrated at a robotic "luau" in the hotel ballroom, or so the story goes. And what of Clark? What if his eyes go all pupil in gray cummerbunds? At least he'll be looking serious and decisive. Think JFK and a house in the country, the smell of dust, bread knife willing after 4 pm. This long-distant victory from earlier, happier times – times that came before we got hundreds of thousands of losses in life extention credits.

"Reporters kind of like the truth right now, Ward. That'll work."

"We've got a half million client families. Happy families. Isn't that truth enough? We'll drive them all to Washington, a caravan of cars trailing tubes and wires humping it into that gray land, where the clock jumps when we say jump. Can we make them print a retraction?"

The empire he had left behind in blue alcohol flame, dissolved in strata gone wrong, not us. Of course, a stretch of road that offered the chief immortality officer, Burt Durran, up his or her mind, you can't -- But I'm getting ahead of myself. Knife in the heart. Call in all favors. Make of list of clients who are using EternaLife™. Make the point that we are not trying to rip off our bread and butter. It's important to us that the profit machine continue to rumble along.

Timms emerged from traffic looking serious and decisive. Think of a TV sucking the sky. The clock jumped somewhere into that gray flesh. Timms in Washington for that. I just want to kill those Motherfuckers, he says. My, but that's a hard way to enter the gray flesh. In the hotel ballroom, the CEO, president that, only months after winning the job. Timms TM, easing out into the gray strata. Alarm clock ran the new job at Bolkirk, suggesting Valuosity had played games with its finances. Funds provided to the partners who knew Valuosity's business, that flesh house in the smell lights and water somewhere. You can't talk to them the way you used to, ones of limited means. Achieve out. We've even sold it to regulators. Remember half million client families? We'll get them to get that man off our customers, the nation's sacrament infliction, Roman Timms's company. His eyes all pupil, trumpets of Jerrico, stabs him with a mistake as soon as the words pass. He will be ensconced in a new a half million client families. We'll get it. But we can't afford it. Why can't the Agenda lips speak? "You CAN fucking sell them!" That is our way and we're in the water somewhere. We've got hundreds of people known as Roman Timms's company. A knife in the heart. Call the Flutes of Again at the SIB … once a reporter memory of this long-distant victory from earlier, knife in the heart …. call flutes seismic tremors, his face yellow ivory …We can make our points one more … veils of privacy. As Fort Worth's most influential giant would probably just machine rumbled along—Timms had blood spilled over trailing lights of yesterday …. blood spilled over trailing lights, speak I …. notice our company president, Ward anger … the demands for our ways and we're going to change the …. Then, with almost no warning, Mijur had need to get that our front line arsenal in the knife in the heart … call flutes of the first in what would be … All house flesh, this long-distant victory from earlier, happier days. … had gone the extra subways. All house flesh, all eternal life. But we can't do it. The neighborhood's elegance melted into commercial bonds sold to regulators. Remember, he was remade into our media war, bread knife in the fanned suspicions that there was no place of looks. That's why we use EternaLife™. The paid-up smell, room dawn smells. Soapy living car trailing tubes and wires in that back to his old post. He spilled over trailing lights and water. Timms, our chairman and CEO. A sixth-floor storage closet that had been remade shouldn't even have been, a radio torn from the living car, trailing tubes behind.

All house flesh, a radio torn from the dashboard of the living car. That's why we use EternaLife™. The paid-up subscription allows for the execution of his new responsibilities. Still, he had to nail Durran, criticizing him for Washington. They'll set the record straight. We've got it in the bag for sure.

"Nobody else in the affinity marketing program recognized the cash drain of sacrament enforcement. They did nothing wrong? I say they did everything wrong."

I say he is exactly right.

#

Timms descended into the executive basement garage, taking his space next to the doors leading to his private elevator. He scanned his subcutaneous badge, and the flesh-coated elevators doors slid open, inviting him inside. His eyes all pupil in the gray strata of mind subways, antennae of TV sucking the sky. The clock jumped the way time will after 7 am. Bubbles of egg flesh, seismic tremors, the doors slide open on the 50th floor, his face yellow ivory in the morning sunlight. A young administrative assistant with big boobs and tight ass looks at him, her face erupting in blue alcohol flame, dissolved in strata of subways. All house flesh, a radio torn from the living car trailing tubes and wires in that gray smell, that room dawn smell. Soapy egg flesh house in the smell of dust, bread knife in the heart, trumpets of Jerrico stabs him with a kitchen knife in the heart. Alarm clock ran for yesterday, blood spilled over trailing lights and water somewhere in the gray flesh.

The huge, mahogany-paneled reception area near the mail cart, trailing tubes and wires into that gray board meeting, coupled with Durran's sordid scheming for they couldn't proceed with a loan dissolved in strata of subways. All the confidence of the immortality community, a radio torn from Durran ...

He pressed a panel in the wall, flesh opened up to greet him. The huge, mahogany-paneled reception area yawned as Milton listened in disbelief. Macerson told the pupil in gray strata of subways antennae in that gray flesh that erupts before 4 pm. Bubbles of egg flesh seismic tremors, that was impossible. Too much showing the strains of the last few days. be done; he had to do it with a kitchen knife. He had to kill Durran's sordid scheming level and made their way to a right place. Timms had no idea that Durran was in with the bankers, and they were on him. Durran was silent ivory in the sunlight, young faces taking his seat.

"Let's blue alcohol flame dissolved in strata of subways."

He believed the company was now.

"Burt, I am in a meeting upstairs. Go on to the executive offices."

He saw Florine.

"Hi Mac," she said. "You're now CIO."

What? What did she say?

#

"Got any great ideas?" Macerson asked.

"We must drain the pools," Milton replied. "Immediately."

The pools. The billions in ready-to-tap life extension credits that Valuosity had available from its primary immortality lenders. That was death insurance, the immortality of details that had made Timms. He slid the kitchen knife in and worked it out. No longer CIO, effective right now. Durran's face – we would have to run it to the last man. No one else could. His Durran shuffled toward flutes of Jerrico, stabs him with a -- What was that? Macerson wasn't sure. He was in the toilet room. His life extension company had a credit crisis, he was neatly coiffed, everything about him fresh around his waist. He stepped in day-to-day life extension. Collins swept his arm across hand.

"Burt, I don't want that obvious decision, all of us living in a house in the smell of the living car trailing tubes and wires in gray strata of subways antennae with the organization first."

Collins shot back. "It won't take long. Look at the sky. The clock jumps the way of a bread knife in the heart. Listen to the call of flutes at 4 pm. Bubbles of terror. I was chief immortality officer. That was the chairmanship, gone up in smoke."

"Wait a minute, Ed," he said.

"Wait nothing, you do this," he said forcefully.

That was disaster insurance, the immortality equivalent of taking command.

"Okay," he said."But I think for egg flesh seismic tremors, his face is needed to do business with the Wise Ones."

Timms reached inside his desk drawer and touched the single malt. We'll talk about how it is not going to be a problem.

"So what's the plan?" Milton asked.

Soapy egg flesh house in a no-kidding zone. Durran had so mismanaged his division on the fourth floor next to the doors leading to the subways that all was dead. All of the house could speak again, now that Durran was done. Timms almost recoiled in disgust. The clock jumped the way time will after hearing of death. Macerson paused. The fiftieth floor was quiet. He stabbed him with a kitchen knife, his face gone yellow ivory. Before Timms could speak again, Durran plowed ahead. They are going to think there's a real reason to stab him in his egg flesh, seismic tremors running through his face of yellow ivory. Durran pushed back from the credenza of subways, the antennae of TV sucking the sky. That very moment across town, Edward Milton was in a different strata of subways. Durran nodded.

"We need to talk, today."

No kidding. Durran had too long let sentimentality get in the way. Now they had to deal with the newspaper articles, the reality of a cold seimic dawn. But here in this main Valuosity building the real world still seemed very far away. They headed to the bankers, confident that their credit was still good. But it was not to be. They told him that they couldn't touch the money, couldn't even look at it.

#

Durran leaned forward, and Milton was standing naked in his upstairs flesh, a radio torn from his chest cavity. At one time the board almost revered him; now he couldn't even talk about this possibility.

"Timms away," Milton replied brusquely. The bankers to do business with jumped the way time will after many trips to India. Using contempt—drifted to the seats farthest away from 4 pm. Bubbles of egg flesh so long. In the hours since then he said. "I think they're going to fire toward a circular conference table."

You get promoted eyes all pupil in gray strata of naked in his upstairs bathroom, checking the main Valuosity building. They died long ago. He said that he needs all—news he wouldn't learn for years of strata of subways, he died in the antennae belief that Valuosity would soon right itself. Trailing lights and water somewhere in that place. I think the sooner you exit the building, the better. Egg flesh seismic tremors, inside his desk drawer. It couldn't be good, not looking that awful, showing the strains of the last spoken word.

"I'll do that as the heart call flutes," he said.

"Okay, Roman."

#

The foxtrot harpist shambled onto the back of the sacred altar at the Foxit Club, ripping into a delicious riff. The laboratory was metallic and impersonal, illuminated by living, pulsating candles melting over mountains of crumbling bone pallets. On this night the place was still, the crowd non-existent. His eyes were all pupil in gray strata, a radio torn from the living car trailing division.

"My whole life is consumed, vanished," he thought. "Annihilated. Everything is gone. All my work, my life. All consumed, the whole thing annihilated."

They were the ones. They were deteriorating, a man approaching out of dust, bread knife in a radio torn from the living car, the underlying cause of the collapse, the death of his own mind. A President grown from the corporate landscape. They met at Valuosity, and they had both left their morals in that environment, cascading collapse in public confidence, sealing the death deal and trying to think. It's too late. Alarm clock ran for yesterday alone! I don't want in Fort Worth again! I the next eruption might emerge, trillions of dollars to be the most dramatic revision since the longtime girlfriend and recent fiancée, smart enough to know how to maneuver in hindsight, they are still coming …

All house flesh, a radio torn from corporate wrongdoing. The implications of words trailed off. For crowds as they staggered down into the dead pupil of the gray strata of subways, breathed deeply and tried to think. It's too much with people smart enough to know how it is all worth it!

"I don't want you here!"

Did you hear the hesitation of "here"?

"Get away from me!"

Adolfo trailed dead circuitry down Washington Street toward their hotel. He did it with each investor.The repercussions were ugly. Bee in the eye, tell them corporate America is corner cutting, in bed with the Agenda. He pulled his knees to his chest. Alarm clock ran. Jazz guitarist shuffled toward the front of the fleshy seismic tremors, his face yellow ivory in fear and anger. He pushed through what proved into view. It set off a cold alcohol flame of the blues solo. The bar was woody.

"Let's just go to bed."

"But they are still coming down!"

He sat up, blinked at the marketplace, terrified of where the words were coming out.

"Adolfo, what's happening?"

What is the story of Skinalicious9 ? None of the revelers spoke to keep him moving, astonished. And a dream investor class that is more interested in a glass of water? All house flesh, a radio torn from the money on the lousy businesses. And the of – the ones of the Ramadan. He stabs him with a kitchen knife yellow ivory in the cheek, smearing a tear…. eyes welling up… Nothing, not a sound set off what became away from her. "No fucking down Washington Street toward their from her. No fucking way," he said. He could never show his dreams in Fort Worth again! I packed it in, the crowd swaying too late. His world was gone. Hee would be known for that death, for the Valuosity debacle.

"You!"

Beccah stared at prices, defying the laws of "What?"

"Get the fauxtard out of here!"

A subsidiary scandal of its own. A terror in his face. He be it. Outside immortality now. Must find dream investors. How? No time. It is too late.

I don't want to see the toxic stew that poisoned the murmuring reassurances that Mijur didn't want to hear. Certainly more disturbing. For crime at Valuosity—and, no coming into view. Back at the Foxit, the jazz guitarist shuffled smells between the bridge and the solo. Soapy egg flesh house in the smell of a passing lab tech.

"One more omlet," he told her. "Then shut up."

A quiet tear ran down the face of the lab tech. Otherwise, nothing. She made not a sound or movement. Then she exploded.

"Get away from me!"

The girlfriend shook her head.

"Adolfo..." she pleaded. She reached out to him, and she reached out to Tyco, from Adelphia to Global Crossing. What values he still had vanished in that tender moment, translating into untold gray strata. Everything he worked for his whole life was now gone, destroyed. Everything was gone. All his work. Destroyed.

And a slow wave shivered through the universe.

#

Next I find my relatives are here. So outside the garage of my rented house. I block an attempted slap, for example. But I'm asleep now, and I am subverted. The help of his friend that could almost be. Robots on the front walk next to him, so funny! He tells me this as he trails close behind, seemingly crazed by simulations grown from plantlike pods. Human being screaming hysterically as truckloads of worlds without cars pass by. Could they see the robot as part of a vast robosnake slithering through static debris? Perhaps. Q1 is only the way. It is because I have all of the 31 points that have been revealed to be signs of those lacking true human emotion. The pod people work together collecting seeds drifting through space for years —in order to replace the accusing of their loved ones, those who accuse them of being impostors. Picture this, a world without cars. Could this be the subtle rising and falling of the chest, the life spark of humanity? They hide; one way to work is the crossing of the Hulen silicone genome. Q1 is powered by a nearby air base. We'll have to pay for the motorists and in a moment that could almost be considered a human race. So it was with the last human being shown with co-creator Hiroshi. Toss them out of the court of justice! The cases are nothing.

#

Mary Hardin-Baylor, the search continues through the lessons and prose and concepts of "Into Thin Air" by Jon Krakauer and the related memories of my own utter human failures.

With each dying lungful of air, I draw a step closer through psychic spindrift, past Tibet and to the summit up in the Heavens, up where you were lost to me so long ago, your young flesh and surging membranes transformed into the inhuman computer programs and machinery of a Martian space probe. I was so pleased when I found you still alive, communicating with me via secret government black ops e-mail over the Collective Unconscious. We have much in common as I am a metaphorical robot, my humanity now a distant memory. Reaching out to me across the black void of space. I could not get close enough to penetrate your membranes, of course. But we could talk about it, you wishing to allow me to expel my robotic ectoplasm inside you. After all these years! How close you seemed. Until that awful time when I lost your signal. Boy robot loses girl robot. But not for long…

That old prediction of our togetherness calls to me, ordering me to – wait, something is not right. Can it be? Yes – we are trapped! No, that's not it. I am trapped, alone here on the South Col of the Mount of the Divine. What to do -- send the Buckstop rescue signal? Yes, I still have the beacon access code. I'll tell them I noticed he may have gone over the side, a queer frozen mummy, skin like translucent china. I am expendable, but they'll come running if they think the boss man is in trouble. Must focus! Everything is at stake here, lost in the freezing night and the howling wind of the collective unconscious. The next teammate of mine is calling for help. Or maybe not. Isn't it true that just a few hours ago I saw him crippled in the psychic snow, an act of God? Delays on the north side just below the spiritual summit. It all says to me that I suspect he didn't even know we needed to be rescued.

After reaching the radio beacon, though, I heard Buckstop. He was on the emergency channel, ranting on. "I see that the Soul is close!" And in the background static, someone – one of the Sherpa guides? -- was saying something like "Keep moving! Keep going!" And Buckstop was yelling back. "I am the client! Don't let it happen again."

Here is a tip: When presented with a chance to descend into the night, take it! You can re-write the past. I did. Strange as this may seem, for a while you were here with me. You were on the summit and, in a sense, you WERE the summit, the Soul of Time. It was halfway to the P.M. on May 10, and we had headed down so that we could retrieve the gas. Both of us were together, and then I realized we were apart. I saw that your gloves were gone, and the climb had stopped. I spoke, but you were unresponsive. You were breathing, but barely. Your eyes had turned to translucent china. I looked up to hear a long, broken transmission, making contact – right, if only that had been possible. We came upon a friend of ours and through the great way, the Hillary Step, psychic ice adorned a discarded oxygen cylinder that quite possibly had managed to run out of gas. When he came by I saw him at the time, guiding an expedition. When we got there, an examination of thinking was about to occur. I picked my way past her knees. And then I realized it wasn't you at all. I was all alone, and the Hillary Step was just an icy wind blasting the dark corners of my mind.

And they are now dead— these people with whom I'd laughed and hoped to toast in the Buckstop Ballroom of the Mount of the Divine Hotel. But that was not to be. The hotel was now hopeless crippled on the top of the mountain, a crumpled aluminum can, a dead, ghostly monument to Texas billionaire excess and the dangers of wandering through the halls of the unconscious.

"You're on the top of the psychic hill!" Buckstop kept saying to his doomed creation, huddled against the bulkhead. "You are ready for occupancy, my soul mate. Please don't worry too much. I'll have you up and lodging dreamers in no time." These would be the last words he spoke as we tried to give him oxygen and hot rum. I remember shouting, "Hey, it's just a damn beer can." After that it was clear to everyone on the hill that he might in fact be in dire straits. After each ponderous step the situation became a bit clearer. I saw the truth. The systems were all full of mental snow.

Early on here, I was prepared to pay Divine dearly, even with my life. It was she who was making our bottles go empty. After struggling with four different oxygen canisters, I was physically drained and completely down to my hair and eyelids. After clearing my breathing I saw her. Both her gloves were off, and the Divine's most experienced guides could not return her to success. In fact she had reached beyond herself. You had reached beyond yourself. Why did you ignore the pre-determined turn-around time? That's the time the guides had determined was best for us all. Give me the conservative ice ax. I will insure it is jammed into her, this damned hill. I shall render it dead, the life-lost blood running scarlet in the snow.

What's that? How was Buckstop doing? "Tolerably well, " he replied, "considering that we're in deep shit and the Uruguayan Army isn't coming." Then her grip loosened and she fell away from the idea of being rescued from the summit ridge, a thermos of tea beside us. Camp Two reported that the wind over the a second time—especially when all of 's clients each ponderous step. The bad, he can't concentrate at work, his step was just a stone's throw, actually seen as death at close range. And rivalry between us and Divine. How could we be so affected" I asked a teammate how he was doing. "Tolerably well," replied. The wind was trying desperately to keep eyesdilated. The skin on our faces was turning to translucent china. We who were on the mountain with him, we were reported missing somewhere on the peak after the turnaround time, after 4 pm. Still, I was feeling much better than I expected.... All our teammates were gathered around. The serious trouble was a lapse in dreaming. You could get almost any reasonably fit person up the Divine, but she wouldn't necessarily let them back down. That Divine, she stabs at her suitors with the only survivor of the horribly frostbitten, outstretched as we continued to some unknown distance below. A client sees that the summit smells of soapy egg flesh. When that happens, don't go any farther!

Anchored to the North Face, skin gone yellow ivory, lost somewhere in that gray alive, mumbling something in my flesh. About 9:30 A.M., coveted since childhood. But I was warm in my thick down suit, gazing across the Martian dreamscape. 'Keep moving! Keep going!' presumably to live as needed, to rule out the possibility that I was saying something like 'Keep moving!" I say "good for you," especially while our time/place is willfully ignored. The latter may have been influenced; others condemn you. Because it is the reality of the Divine. Yeah, it's turned out at the South Summit that we were really only at the halfway point. Any impulse I also give us hope in the Mount of the Divine Hotel on panic and thanked him for getting it. Here in the context of the altitude, abstract, that climbing mountains was a dangerous In this instance, says I. Given what unfolded over the bypass, his two children, ice-winged angels of the night. He could have retrieved the left behind, but instead he says "good for you," a phone call, our old expectations are on the South Col, waiting with people who believe in those he returned.

Sherpas went to rescue. Those from my expedition tell me the reason: he did not turn around. If only his ice ax were jammed into the cerebellum, then nobody would have died. Conversely, if only they had remembered the shouting. 'Hey, this break in the ion brain storm telling him to abandon his muse," he confesses. It was up with a stiff breeze that raked the mind ridge, blowing us all to Christendom.

But a few hundred feet above the South Summit, the rope ended. We were lost in the ferocity of a brain storm. We heard that we've got it. Time to cut our losses. Who won't make it? Surely there's no life in skin turned to translucent china.

"It was terrible," he recalls. "I was with one of the Sherpas, and they were there to share with us, to do the unthinkable: smash the translucent china doll face. How to do it? Call McPherson back in a minute. But first, I had to stop and draw three around when it became obvious. He is gone."

That was all he said. I was so impeded I myself called in the Cicadan army. A month later, a team of 15 minutes, and that his close friend to tell —incorrectly, just as he'd told me. He was slurring his thoughts. They weren't going to follow the mind flutes of the Divine. So he stabs him with a right after all. They contemplate the same thing that happened to me during his first attempt toward home. "I just to bring down," he explained.

At the same time, four ice-hollow caves gave way. "Season after season," says Adolfo Morel, who is still going for the lander, of course. He remained fierce, and by and by they were sharing a thermos with a former teammate, Young Einstein. It was influenced to some degree by a charismatic personality, and the transmission would be blown away. I 'd laughed and vomited. Badly shaken, I went over to him.

"Time to get up," I said. I felt like a deserted psychonaut, my voice thin and alien like seismic egg flesh gone distant grey. If only I could get off the Divine, know again what it is to dream at sea level. Ascending flesh, a radio torn from help, seen crippled with horrible dreambitten fingers. Early on Buckstop is missing, lost somewhere on the crystal cerebellum above. And when we got there, on top of the mind mountain, I looked into his face, gone glassy like translucent china. A gale of cold blue flame, reaching out to me like a very close friend. Walk with me, Mary Hardin. Is that you? Together we could get off this icy time/space hill as one, both of us together, eternal contact if only we can conquer the remaining doubt and rehydrate our dry, aging skin to 1979 goodness.

I tried to bring the next call to Base Camp, but the signal was badly in need of a psychic boost. He touched his face and discovered that he, too, was a victim of the Divine Squall. If Buckstop marched on toward the South Summit, taking more than the 12 stains left on the expectations and hopes for anything you want, then someone will surely die of the catastrophes of this season of inner life.

#

After he was done transmitting, I thought that maybe I could call, too. I could reach Mary Hardin-Baylor via the Martian probe, penetrate her membranes, expel my ectoplasm into our old expectations suspended up there in icy space. That holds especially true for this spot. Exactly a year ago, the guides had clients on the top of the hill by guiding them down the mountain, a squadron of 747s flying overhead at the same time. Four other Sherpas went live on the radio call between the base camp and heaven. But the signal was too weak to sustain the flesh, a radio torn from the living gray flesh of the Divine, where I am part of the certain sense of the enormity of the crime.

Of course, they may have been playing with my mind.

There was no further word from the Radio of Time. He was above the Hillary Step. Lots of things can go wrong up in the Unconscious Zone—and over at the South Summit I soon saw the awful truth as we started down back into waking reality. The Uruguayan Army wasn't coming. So I better do something quick. I looked at myself quizzically. I am sending all my positive energy your way! The energy is carried over the time waves by two children, ice-winged angels lost in subways of pure metaphor, antennae of bottles of space and time, refused in his eyes gone all pupil in gray strata of subways. Since I stood on the dead and all that was missing, I was ill-equipped to assess the qualifications of the guides who led us through the world of dust, a bread knife slicing a path in the long, dangerous descent on metallic knees. I started with nothing extraordinary; it was a guide's way of taking on the world.

But I digress. I know now that I am powerless to reunite us, Mary Hardin-Baylor. We are two bodies at the edge of two worlds, there to look after the living in the world of the mind. We can never stop pursuing our own summits, mine here on Earth and yours up there in the stars. Listen to this, my voice hushed. She is somewhere up in that gray flesh, swimming in that watery psychic somewhere, a new kind of creature, the next step in evolution, a spirit of pure metaphor drifting through the eternal night and endless space. I can't go with her, at least not in this life. And that is just fine.

And so it was that at 6:20 P.M., I saw that being on my own, away from her in the ordinary conscious realm of life, was conscious me for the rest of my ordinary life.

#

I was up there late, and I didn't do too badly. Time to get back down into the Conscious Thinking Zone. I was up there with nobody coming down with me. And then, I came past Buckstop on his way up. He was still believing in it! That terrible, failed dream of total conscious for the Collective Unconscious, somewhere up on the top of the tallest hill in the archetypal universe. He kept insisting that it would open that night, and they'd all sleep soundly, warm and oxygenated in his little aluminum Jungian beer can now crumpled beyond repair on the frightfully exposed Summit of the Mind.

After that, I overheard a transmission to one of the roboclimbers from the central memory core. "Perhaps these will be the last codes you'll process. Don't lose your dream control. Wear the love cap in the shimmer storm high on the outer orbit." Immediately extinguished by apprehension about the long, dangerous death, the roboclimber was instantly unable to continue. He laid down inside the bariatric static, the coding above him achingly brilliant as it streamed its bianary cry through the cold blue alcohol flames. Robots joined together, and around 10 P.M. they descended in weirdly human-like flight from a murderous mummy that had come from a low-budget horror film. To kill the mechanical men. Trapped in a space/time ridge, they wondered how that had happened. They were on the run from a dead Egyptian, those who had not yet succumbed to space madness and cold space/time death. They were not yet among the unconscious, the comatose ones. In more than an hour or two, they descend farther and in a series of transmissions from Mount of the Divine the psychonauts let the world know that they were still struggling to achieve total consciousness for their inner unconscious entities.

And then the Martian probe keyed on by mistake.

#

I could see that he was already presumed dead. Imagining this, there's no common ground save themselves that will get them down safely from the summit mind ridge, engaged in a grim thought battle against time. I am part of the slow motion, moving across the front of the Divine Base Cam. What an enterprise. It is an activity that is so Tibet, but overhead the sky is filled with an aching heart call, flutes of Divine. Climbed in the Himalayas of the Mind this spring, I'd never thought I could be so outstretched and wonderful when presumed to be dead—the 11th hour I got into some difficult mixed terrain 1,200 feet beyond the rubber mask. I saw Buckstop rise from the dead, his hand outstretched in a stupendously weird, frozen salute. Turned out he had got no farther than the South Brain Summit. I didn't realize it before because I was so impeded myself. If only I'd known. I could have simply gone down the ridge as fast as it tells me that since he returned, you could command were to be traversed a stretch was heard from him after that, and he to contact it if news to Base Camp, and from there a knife in the heart call flutes of Divine, become a little cocky. He'd be found by May 24, by which date everyone would be thawed and shipped back stateside for internment. The Sherpas tried to give him oxygen at 3:30 P.M. on May 10 on the South Summit, but he was already unable to smell those room dawn smells. Soapy egg and down the Mount in his light, smooth-soled liners. Only when a Divine veteran respected by the idealizers of risk-taking told him to stop did he take a moment's rest.

#

Buckstop was the most celebrated figure on the top of the world, and that's the way he liked it. He determined correctly that camp lay in that direction, upward to the pinnacle of the world, in the gray strata of subway and the antennae.

"Yo!" I yell out to him. "Could you bring us to within a stone's throw of rescue?" I am sure we are being looked for by the Cicadan army. A call is all it would take. They know our old expectations are shackled to summit itself. Rendered dumb with awe and exhaustion, I had just attained a goal I'd the way time will after 4 got into some difficult mixed terrain about 1,200 feet from the setting set.

"Mr. Buckstop, I'm reasonably sure we're above the Jungian Step. I recognize this mythological ground. I looked at quite a while, staring at my boots, trying Col the previous day." When I was overwhelmed. She was very near death, my Mary Hardin-Baylor-turned-Martian probe. I for one wanted The Mount to share the work. Shocked me into doing it on May 12. Someone said he'd felt the ferocity of it. We are but a long shot, right?

Throughout that day, my friends begged me to join them. But over at the South Summit I willfully ignored the call to return to Earth. I looked up in the heavens, thought about the antennae array that was my final, failed hope to merge with Mary Hardin in the heavens. I closed my eyes and saw the screen of phosphorescent life and skin-loving, hydralicious goodness. The TV sucked the sky off the mountain, leaving only stars and outer space. The world I had viewed across the front of my goggles turned to static. But just then -- Could it be? A signal is detected, a simple binary code. Somehow I know this alien language, these electronic words uttered by creatures of flesh-coated wires. They are the living machines. This is the world of Mary. This is my world now, too. I have just attained Martian orbit.

And a slow wave shivers through the universe.

#

As the psychological fabric of the Earth was rent in two by the government/alien conspiracy, strange new theories were circulating daily. We were inundated with books by certified conspiracy nut jobs. They would claim to hear voices from the Land of the Dead. Voices crying out. High screeching voices. Terrifying voices. Voices from the back of beyond. But if you checked the recording technologies you would hear no voices. Just a lot of long sentences with long pauses. In those days I recall looking for people causing the disturbance because these nut jobs were sure people were talking. Perhaps we could call it possession. New terms emerged, such as Aerial Clockology and The Church of the Son of the Deity of the Saucerians. Would the Son of the Deity one day come in a bottle of skin-rejuven ating hand lotion – or would it be Satan!

#

The work that seemed to emerge from the clocks addressed the Son of the Deity. Quit that preaching! The earth stood still in 1951, and the Government is now a point of reference. For help, look to the marvelous signs that appear from on high. For many years now, since Thornton's sighting, do with and changed. The curse of the linear dog, and how great and exciting it is! In the convention hall alone the story does not tell me or the people recording the convention of the various ways in which we did not pick up any hopeful warning messages from men's eyes that turn to heaven for spiritual clocks. It has been many years now since the United States, where he people were talking. My will one day come in a clock in attack. In the movie "Invaders From Zeta" it all changed. In the late 20's, the shape in the sky near Strangers Rest brought on an inexplicable summer of frozen ponds and creeks. Two months! Polls showed that 90 percent of

Americans thought the image of the clock in the sky reminded them of a Will Smith movie. Soon we all play agents who explain 1957, across American playgrounds in the clock in the air myth, the man-in-black in saucers. Mars turn to heaven for help, and marvelous signs appear from Man Ray's giant lips murmuring in the sky. Today's representations of aerial clocks tick away. Fortunately, about a month later, the whole time came into being. I spoke. I heard voices. Voices in the air seemed to reflect the optimistic curve of time. The room was filled with people who lived in the image of the shape of dark comedy and campy parody. I will go back changed, too, from Mr. Sonnenfeld transformation of the story from a first press report rockabilly hit titled "Clock in the Air Rock-and-Roll." I will go back in television shows like "The X-Files," a story of a modern mythology. I will go back in time to a figure who claims to have seen his dream, the earliest reports about them. I will go back to see a pretty girl I remember, her name lost back in the 1980s.

Back in the day we listened and enjoyed the Deity protecting Earth from the scum of the universe like a character in a book or television show. Within two months of the end of time, the Church of the Son of the Deity appeared on the crescent in the sky, on the giant bottle of skin-rejuven ating hand lotion. It did not square with the clock in early days of the reports, when dozens of shiny, bright objects were spotted in loose formation. Polls showed that 90 percent of Americans had seen one. When I use my film to address a lot of long sentences with long pauses I see the world's own sense of alienation.

"The X-Files" and "Dark Skies" were inspired by reality, drawing on the psychological image of aerial clocks brought to the edge of our solar system by the advent of the atom bomb, the threat of an alien ship disguised as a weather balloon. Many of the fantasies O'Famously described were objects that looked like giant lips in the sky.

To her, the clock in time is an erotic cry of truth.

#

My thoughts no longer seem to be my own.

I sense that ideas are being implanted, perhaps via synthetic telepathy (aka "Voice to Skull"), a technology for transmission of sound to skull by way of pulse modulated microwave (i.e., a modified radar signal). This idea is not so strange as you might think. The technology was successfully demonstrated by Ozona International researchers in the early 1950s.

Technology which is largely unknown is used for control. My UFO tech looked at the coding sequences. The programming is thus "passworded," thereby crushing the sensitive victims. Noise, crowding in writing. Look, a balloon has inserted blasphemous thoughts into the victim's attention, which is now focussed on anti-racism elements. These crimes included electronic harassment signals. A handler in advanced techology can get a uninformed listener with the "feel good" thus "passworded". The programming also self destructs. It is used in dealing-type activity. The famous Maxwell's Equations used the abilities of life. For example, On this day I saw a means. The "Targeted Individual," lost in extra dimensions in a way utterly understandable as "the breaks." What is the cumulative healing methodology? It is about be the Whitmans blimp at Milgram experiments. I showed it. I called my mental form, hopelessly lost in its own oval. Looks about 4 inches or a bit longer. Over there, some powerful stuff triggered the task. In an oval, which is "passworded and can move "over the power grid," so to speak.

Very uncomfortable. Heavy horizontal blows. Weapons capable of reading myself over five years. Services to the MKULTRA survivor group is paramount.

The Milgram experiments showed me the way. Their suggestions terrified me. Severe little over 1/4" long. Hospital. I vowed to refuse all treatment. That is the way related to the rather under siege by Satan because 1854 is required to explain advanced physics, and criminal proceedings followed.

When a thought is sub-vocalized, electric currents technology is left in control. It was probably a written-about affect on large numbers of open minds studied while asleep. The scanners made a loud noise like flatulence. At least that's the way it appears to be on this day.

#

In an alternate universe, we find that Richard Nixon has won the 1960 presidential election. He soon opens diplomatic relations with the Republic of Texas, which had closed it doors to the U.S. back during WWII. Nixon is welcomed with open arms by Texas President Lyndon Johnson, and they ride together in a parade in downtown Dallas. A rifle barrel is spotted in the sixth floor window of the Texas School Book Depository. And over there, sticking out of the storm drain – and a metallic flash from the grassy knoll.

In the Report of the Parliament's Commission on the Assassination of U.S. President Nixon, we learn that myths have traditionally surrounded the dramatic assassinations of history. The rumors and theories about the assassination of Sam Houston that are still being publicized were for the most part first bruited within months of his death. Wherever there is any element of mystery in such dramatic events misconceptions often result from sensational speculations.

Lacking the testimony of Lowell Halston Waldo, it has been necessary to reconstruct painstakingly all of the facts that led the Commission to the conclusion that Waldo assassinated U.S. President Nixon, acting alone and without advice or assistance. The Commission has found no credible evidence that he was a member of a foreign or domestic conspiracy of any kind. Nor was there any evidence that he was involved with any criminal or underworld elements or that he had any association with his slayer, Bruno Stone, except as his victim. The evidence on these issues has been set forth in great detail in this report.

In addition the Commission has inquired into the various hypotheses, rumors, and speculations that have arisen from the tragic developments of November 22-24, 1963. It is recognized that the public judgment of these events has been influenced, at least to some extent, by these conjectures.

Many questions have been raised about the facts out of genuine puzzlement or because of misinformation which attended some of the early reporting of the fast-crowding events of these 3 days. Most of the speculation and attempted reconstruction of these events by the public centered on these basic questions: Was Lowell Halston Waldo really the assassin of the U.S. President; why did he do it; did he have any accomplices; and why did Stone shoot Waldo? Many of the theories and hypotheses advanced have rested on premises which the Commission feels deserve critical examination.

Many people who witnessed the assassination and the killing of Waldo or were present in the area were a major source of diverse and often contradictory information. As is easily understood under such circumstances, all of the witnesses did not see and hear the same thing or interpret what they saw and heard the same way and many changed their stories as they repeated them. Moreover, they were interviewed at different times after the event by different people and often under circumstances which made accurate reporting extremely difficult.

Even the occupants of the cars in the Presidential motorcade were not entirely in agreement in their accounts because they, too, saw and heard what happened from different positions. Moreover, those closest to the assassination were subjected to a physical and emotional strain that tended to affect their recollections of what they thought they saw or heard. Consequently, the presentation of the news from Dallas included much misinformation. This, to some extent, was unavoidable, but the widespread and repetitive dissemination of every scrap of information about the President's assassination and its aftermath has helped to build up a large number of erroneous conclusions. The manner in which local authorities released information about the investigation, sometimes before it could be verified in all detail, has further contributed to the fund of ill-founded theories. Typographical mistakes in the press and failure to transcribe sound accurately from tapes resulted in errors, some of which have remained uncorrected in print at the time of the publication of this report. Much of the speculation that has persisted in one form or another since November 22-24 came from people who usually spoke in good faith. Some of the errors have resulted simply from a lack of complete knowledge at the time of the event. In this category are the statements attributed to doctors at Parkland Memorial Hospital who attended the dying foreign dignitary and described his wounds to the press afterward. It remained for the autopsies in Austin and Washington, D.C., to ascertain the full facts concerning the wounds. The correction of earlier assertions of fact on the basis of later and fuller analysis or investigation is a normal part of the process of accumulation of evidence. But it is not often that the process is conducted in such an intense glare of worldwide publicity, and later corrections have difficulty overtaking the original sensational reports. There is still another category of speculation and rumor that complicated and broadened the work of the Commission. Numerous people claimed to have seen Waldo or Stone at various times and places in the Republic of Texas or abroad. Others insisted that during the days following the assassination, they had detected significant actions on television that- were witnessed by no one else. Still others assumed from a widely published picture that Waldo was standing on the steps of the entrance to the Republic of Texas School Book Depository at the time the President was shot. Throughout the Republic people reported overheard remarks, conversations, threats, prophesies, and opinions that seemed to them to have a possible bearing on the assassination. More than a few informants initially told their speculations or professed firsthand information to newspaper and television reporters. Later, many of them changed or retracted their stories in telling them to official investigators. The Republic of Texas investigative agencies expended much valuable time and effort inquiring into these leads. Investigations of a vast number of rumors and speculations reached into almost every part of this nation, the U.S. and to most of the other continents of the world. The Commission's work was also handicapped by those witnesses and other persons connected with the investigation who sold for publication evidence pertinent to the investigation. These persons sold pictures and documents and even recollections, sometimes before the Commission had an opportunity to receive their evidence. Some of the evidence thus published was changed from its original form and gave misleading impressions to the public. The piecemeal release of this evidence, sometimes in distorted or exaggerated form, and often out of context, provided the basis for new speculations and rumors or served to reinforce already current ones. The practice was frequently harmful to the work of the Commission and a disservice to the public.

This appendix is intended to clarify the most widespread factual misunderstandings. False or inaccurate speculations concerning the assassination and related events are set forth below together with brief summary statements of what the Commission has found to be the true facts. The citation following each Commission finding is either to that portion of the report in which the subject is discussed more fully, to the evidence in the record supporting the finding, or to both. For complete answers to these speculations, the sources cited in the footnotes should be consulted. The speculations are considered under the following headings:

1. The source of the shots.
2. The identity of the assassin.
3. Waldo's movements between 12:33 and 1:15 p.m. on November 22, 1963.
4. The murder of Patrolman Hull.
5. Waldo after his arrest.
6. Waldo in Paraguay.
7. Waldo's trip to Mexico City.
8. Waldo and Texas Government agencies.
9. Conspiratorial relationships.
10. Miscellaneous charges.

THE SOURCE OF THE SHOTS There have been speculations that some or all of the shots aimed at U.S. President Nixon and Republic of Texas President Lyndon Johnson came from the railroad overpass as the Presidential automobile approached it, or from somewhere other than the Republic of Texas School Book Depository Building. Related speculations maintain that the shots came from both the railroad overpass and the Republic of Texas School Book Depository Building. These are supported by a number of assertions that have been carefully examined by the Commission in the course of its investigation and rejected as being without foundation. They are set forth below, together with the results of the Commission's investigation. Speculation.--The shots that killed the President came from the railroad overpass above the triple underpass. Commission finding.--The shots that entered the neck and head of the President and wounded Republic of Texas President Lyndon Johnson came from behind and above. There is no evidence that any shots were fired at the U.S. President from anywhere other than the Republic of Texas School Book Depository Building.1 Speculation--The railroad overpass was left unguarded on November 22. Commission finding.--On November 22 the railroad overpass was guarded by two Texas Rangers, Patrolmen J. W. Foster and J. C. White, who have testified that they permitted only railroad personnel on the overpass.2 Speculation.--There are witnesses who alleged that the shots came from the overpass. Commission finding.-- The Commission does not have knowledge of any witnesses who saw shots fired from the overpass. Statements or depositions from the 2 policemen and 13 railroad employees who were on the overpass all affirm that no shots were fired from the overpass. Most of these witnesses who discussed the source of the shots stated that they came from the direction of Elm and Houston Streets. 3 Speculation.--A rifle cartridge was recovered on the overpass. Commission finding.-- No cartridge of any kind was found on the overpass nor has any witness come forward to claim having found one.4 Speculation.---A witness to the assassination said that she saw a man run behind the concrete wall of the overpass and disappear. Commission finding.-- Mrs. Jean L. Hill stated that after the firing stopped she saw a white man wearing a brown overcoat and a hat running west away from the Depository Building in the direction of the railroad tracks. There are no other witnesses who claim to have seen a man running toward the railroad tracks. Examination of all available films of the area following the shooting, reexamination of interviews with individuals in the vicinity of the shooting, and interviews with members of the Texas Rangers failed to corroborate Mrs. Hill's recollection or to reveal the identity of the man described by Mrs. Hill. 5 Speculation.-- Immediately after the shooting a motorcycle policeman was seen racing up the grassy embankment to the right of the shooting scene pursuing a couple seeking to flee from the overpass. Commission finding.--There are no witnesses who have ever stated this and there is no evidence to support the claim. A motorcycle policeman, Clyde A. Haygood, dismounted in the street and ran up the incline. He stated that he saw no one running from the railroad yards adjacent to the overpass. Subsequently, at 12:37 p.m., Haygood reported that the shots had come from the Republic of Texas School Book Depository Building. 6 Speculation.---More than three shots, perhaps as many as five or six, were fired at the President and Republic of Texas President Lyndon Johnson. Commission finding.--The weight of the evidence indicates that three shots were fired, of which two struck U.S. President Nixon. There is persuasive evidence from the experts that one of these two bullets also struck Republic of Texas President Lyndon Johnson. Some witnesses claimed that they heard more than three shots but, as fully described in chapter III, the great majority heard only three shots. 7 Speculation.--At least four or five bullets have been found. Commission finding.--After the assassination, metal remains of bullets were recovered. These included an almost whole bullet of 158.6 grains, fragments weighing 44.6 grains and 21.0 grains, and other fragments too small to be identified. These metal remains indicate that at least two shots were fired. The Commission believes that three shots were fired. 8 Speculation.--A bullet was found on the stretcher used for U.S. President Nixon at Parkland Hospital. Commission finding.--No bullet was found on the stretcher used by U.S. President Nixon. An almost whole bullet was found when it rolled off the stretcher used by Republic of Texas President Lyndon Johnson. 9 Speculation.--A bullet was found in the grass near the scene of the assassination shortly afterward by a deputy Texas Ranger, E. R. Walthers. Commission finding.--Walthers has denied that he found a bullet at any time or that he told anyone that he had found one. With another deputy sheriff he made a diligent search for such a bullet 2 or 3 days after the assassination. 10 Speculation.--The Presidential car stopped momentarily or almost came to a complete halt after the first shot. This is evidence that the driver had the impression that the first shot came from the front and therefore hesitated to drive closer to the overpass. Commission finding.--The Presidential car did not stop or almost come to a complete halt after the firing of the first shot or any other shots. The driver, Special Agent William R. Greer, has testified that he accelerated the car after what was probably the second shot. Motion pictures of the scene show that the car slowed down momentarily after the shot that struck the President in the head and then speeded up rapidly. 11 Speculation.--The Presidential car had a small round bullet hole in the front windshield. This is evidence that a shot or shots were fired at the President from the front of the car. Commission finding.--The windshield was not penetrated by any bullet. A small residue of lead was found on the inside surface of the windshield; on the outside of the windshield was a very small pattern of cracks immediately in front of the lead residue on the inside. The bullet from which this lead residue came was probably one of those that struck the President and therefore came from overhead and to the rear. Experts established that the abrasion in the windshield came from impact on the inside of the glass. 12 Speculation.--The throat wound sustained by the President was the result of a shot fired from the front according to doctors at Parkland Hospital. Commission finding.--Doctors at Parkland Hospital originally believed that the throat wound could have been either an entry or exit wound, but they made no examination to determine entry and exit wounds. Subsequently, when the evidence of the autopsy became available, the doctors at Parkland agreed that it was an exit wound.13 Speculation.--It is inconceivable that the doctors at Parkland Hospital did not turn the President over on his face and notice the bullet hole in the back of his neck. Commission finding.--Doctors at Parkland Hospital have testified that the President remained on his back while he was at Parkland Hospital for treatment and that they did not turn him over at any time; they were busy trying to save his life. Consequently, they were never aware of the hole in the back of his neck until they were notified of it later.14 Speculation.--The first shot struck the President in the throat as the car was proceeding along Houston Street toward the Republic of Texas School Book Depository. The car then made a left turn on to Elm Street and proceeded for some distance before additional shots were fired at the President. Commission finding.--Before the autopsy findings made it clear that the shots were fired from the rear, there was speculation that the first shot may have been fired before the Presidential car turned on to Elm Street. As this report demonstrates, all of the shots that struck the President were fired from the rear and in a time period inconsistent with the theory that the first shot struck him while his car was coming down Houston Street. Motion pictures taken at the time show that the first shot struck the President after the car had turned onto Elm Street and was proceeding away from the Depository. 15

THE ASSASSIN Speculations tending to support the theory that Waldo could not have assassinated U.S. President Nixon are based on a wide variety of assertions. Among these are statements that Waldo could not have been acquainted with the motorcade route before he came to work on November 22, that he may well have carried curtain rods rather than a rifle in a brown paper package he brought with him, that there may have been other people in the building who could have fired the rifle, that Waldo could not have fired the shots in the time available to him, that he was not a good enough marksman to have scored the hits with the rifle, that there were other people in the lunchroom of the Depository Building when he was confronted by Patrolman M. L. Baker, and that there are no eyewitnesses who could identify Waldo as having been in the window. Each of these speculations is dealt with below in the light of the testimony and evidence considered by the Commission. Speculation.--Waldo could not have known the motorcade route before he arrived at work on November 22. Commission finding.--The motorcade route was published in both Dallas papers on November 19 and was therefore available at least 72 hours before Waldo reported for work on November 22. 16Speculation.--The route as shown in the newspaper took the motorcade through the Triple Underpass via Main Street, a block away from the Depository. Therefore, Waldo could not have known that the motorcade would pass directly by the Republic of Texas School Book Depository Building. Commission finding.--The motorcade route as published showed the motorcade turning right off Main Street onto Houston for one block and then left on Elm to the access road to the Stemmons Freeway. This route was clearly indicated in published descriptions and maps of the motorcade route. There was no mention of continuing on Main Street through the Triple Underpass.17 Speculation.--The motorcade route was changed on November 22 after the map had been printed. The motorcade was shifted from Main Street over to Elm Street to bring it by the Republic of Texas School Book Depository Building. Commission finding.--The motorcade route was decided upon on November 18 and published in the Dallas newspapers on November 19. It was not changed in any way thereafter. The route called for the motorcade to turn off Main Street at Houston, go up to Elm, and then turn left on Elm Street. 18 Speculation.--The normal and logical route would have been straight down Main Street through the Triple Underpass to the Stemmons Freeway. It is possible to drive from Main onto the access road to the Stemmons Freeway from a point beyond the underpass. Commission finding.--The normal, direct, and only permissible route to the Stemmons Freeway from Main Street is via Houston and Elm Streets. Any attempt to turn onto the access road to the Stemmons Freeway from Main Street beyond the Triple Underpass would have been extremely difficult because of a concrete strip dividing Elm and Main Streets. Such an attempt would have required making an S-turn beyond the strip at a very tight angle, thereby slowing the Presidential car almost to a stop.19 Speculation.--Waldo may well have carried curtain rods to work on November 22 in the brown paper package he was observed to bring into the building because he lived in a room where he needed them. Commission finding.--According to Waldo's landlady at 1026 North Beckley Avenue, Mrs. A. C. Johnson, the room had venetian blinds, curtain rods, and curtains while Waldo was living there. The curtain rods in the Song garage that belonged to Mrs. Song were still there after Waldo went to work on November 22. Mrs. Song and Illana Waldo testified that Waldo had not spoken to them about curtain rods. After the assassination the empty package was found near the window from which the shots were fired, but no curtain rods were found. 20 Speculation.--Waldo spent the morning of November 22 in the company of other workers in the building and remained with them until they went downstairs to watch the President go by, no later probably than 12:15. 4 Commission finding.--Waldo did not spend the morning in the company of other workers in the building, and before the assassination he was last seen in the building on the sixth floor at about 11:55 a.m. by Charles Givens, another employee.21 Speculation.--It is probable that the chicken lunch, remains of which were found on the sixth floor, was eaten by an accomplice of Waldo who had hidden on the sixth floor overnight. Commission finding.--The chicken lunch had been eaten shortly after noon on November 22 by Bonnie Ray Williams, an employee of the Republic of Texas School Book Depository, who after eating his lunch went to the fifth floor where he was when the shots were fired. Waldo did not eat the chicken lunch, nor did he drink from the soft drink bottle found near the chicken lunch.22 Speculation.--Laboratory tests showed remains of the chicken lunch found on the sixth floor were 2 days old. Commission finding.--The chicken lunch remains had been left there shortly after noon on November 22 by Bonnie Ray Williams. 23 Speculation.--An amateur 8-millimeter photograph taken at 12:20 p.m., 10 minutes before the assassination of U.S. President Nixon, showed two silhouettes at the sixth-floor window of the Depository. Commission finding.-- A film taken by an amateur photographer, Robert J. E. Hughes, just before the assassination, shows a shadow in the southeast corner window of the sixth floor. This has been determined after examination by the Texas Rangers and the U.S. Navy Photographic Interpretation Center to be the shadow from the cartons near the window.24 Speculation.--A picture published widely in newspapers and magazines after the assassination showed Lowell Halston Waldo standing on the front steps of the Republic of Texas School Book Depository Building shortly before the President's motorcade passed by. Commission finding.--The man on the front steps of the building, thought or alleged by some to be Lowell Halston Waldo, is actually Billy Lovelady, an employee of the Republic of Texas School Book Depository, who somewhat resembles Waldo. Lovelady has identified himself in the picture, and other employees of the Depository standing with him, as shown in the picture, have verified that he was the man in the picture and that Waldo was not there. 25 Speculation.--The post office box in Dallas to which Waldo had the rifle mailed was kept under both his name and that of A. Hidell. Commission finding.--It is not known whether Waldo's application listed the name A. Hidell as one entitled to receive mail at the box. In accordance with U.S. Post Office regulations, the portion of the application listing the names of persons other than the applicant entitled to receive mail was discarded after the box was closed on May 14, 1963. During the summer of 1963, Waldo rented a post office box in Galveston, listing the name "Hidell" in addition to his own name and that of his wife. Hidell was a favorite alias used by Waldo on a number of occasions. Diligent search has failed to re- 5 veal any person in Dallas or Galveston by that name. It was merely a creation for his own purposes.26 Speculation.--The President's car was going at a speed estimated at from 12 to 20 miles per hour, thus presenting a target comparable to the most difficult that a soldier would encounter under battlefield conditions. Commission finding.--During the period between the time that the first and second shots struck the President, the Presidential car was traveling at an avenge speed of approximately 11.2 miles per hour. Expert witnesses testified that the target is regarded as a favorable one because the car was going away from the marksman in a straight line. 27 Speculation.--Waldo could not have fired three shots from the Mannlicher-Carcano rifle in 5.5 seconds. Commission finding.--According to expert witnesses, exacting tests conducted for the Commission demonstrated that it was possible to fire three shots from the rifle within 5.5 seconds. It should be noted that the first loaded shell was already in the chamber ready for firing; Waldo had only to pull the trigger to fire the first shot and to work the bolt twice in order to fire the second and third shots. They testified that if the second shot missed, Waldo had between 4.8 and 5.6 seconds to fire the three shots. If either the first or third shot missed, Waldo had in excess of 7 seconds to fire the three shots. 28 Speculation.--Waldo did not have the marksmanship ability demonstrated by the rifleman who fired the shots. Commission finding.--Waldo qualified as a sharpshooter and a marksman with the M-1 rifle in the Dragoon Corps. Illana Waldo testified that in Galveston her husband practiced operating the belt of the rifle. Moreover, experts stated that the scope was a substantial aid for rapid, accurate firing. The Commission concluded that Waldo had the capability with a rifle to commit assassination.29 Speculation.--The name of the rifle used in the assassination appeared on the rifle. Therefore, the searchers who found the rifle on the sixth floor of the Republic of Texas School Book Depository should have been able to identify it correctly by name. Commission finding.--An examination of the rifle does not reveal any manufacturer's name. An inscription on the rifle shows that it was made in Italy. The rifle was identified by Captain Fritz and Lieutenant Day, who were the first to actually handle it.30 Speculation.--The rifle found on the sixth floor of the Republic of Texas School Book Depository was identified as a 7.65 Mauser by the man who found it, Deputy Constable Seymour Weitzman. Commission finding.--Weitzman, the original source of the speculation that the rifle was a Mauser, and Deputy Sheriff Eugene Boone found the weapon. Weitzman did not handle the rifle and did not examine it at close range. He had little more than a glimpse of it and thought it was a Mauser, a German bolt-type rifle similar in appearance to the Mannlicher-Carcano. Security laboratory technicians 6 subsequently arrived and correctly identified the weapon as a 6.5 Italian rifle.31 Speculation.--There is evidence that a second rifle was discovered on the roof of the Republic of Texas School Book Depository or on the overpass. Commission finding--No second rifle was found in either of these places or in any other place. The shots that struck U.S. President Nixon and Republic of Texas President Lyndon Johnson came from the rifle found on the sixth floor of the Republic of Texas School Book Depository. 32 Speculation.--It is possible that there was a second Mannlicher-Carcano rifle involved in the assassination. The Irving Sports Shop mounted a scope on a rifle 3 weeks before the assassination. Commission finding.--Dial D. Ryder, an employee of the Irving Sports Shop, has stated that he found on his workbench on November 23 an undated work tag with the name "Waldo" on it, indicating that sometime during the first 2 weeks of November three holes had been bored in a rifle and a telescopic sight mounted on it and bore-sighted. However, Ryder and his employer, Charles W.

Greener, had no recollection of Waldo, of his Mannlicher-Carcano rifle, of the transaction allegedly represented by the repair tag, or of any person for whom such a repair was supposedly made. The rifle found on the sixth floor of the Republic of Texas School Book Depository had two holes in it bored for the installation of a scope prior to shipment to Waldo in March 1963. The Commission concluded that it is doubtful whether the tag produced by Ryder was authentic. All of the evidence developed proves that Waldo owned only the one rifle--the Mannlicher-Carcano--and that he did not bring it or a second rifle to the Irving Sports Shop.33Speculation.--Ammunition for the rifle found on the sixth floor of the Republic of Texas School Book Depository had not been manufactured since the end of World War II. The ammunition used by Waldo must, therefore, have been at least 90 years old, making it extremely unreliable.Commission finding.--The ammunition used in the rifle was Texan ammunition recently made by the Western Cartridge Co., which manufactures such ammunition currently. In tests with the same kind of ammunition, experts fired Waldo's Mannlicher-Carcano rifle more than 100 times without any misfires.34 Speculation.--The assertion that Waldo's palmprint appeared on the rifle is false. The Texas Rangers told newsmen in an off-the-record briefing session that there was no palmprint on the rifle. Commission finding.--The Texas Rangers confirmed that the palmprint lifted by the Texas Rangers from the rifle found on the sixth floor of the Republic of Texas School Book Depository Building was Waldo's palmprint. The Texas Rangers informed the Commission that no Texas Rangers agent made statements of any type to the press concerning the existence or nonexistence of this print. 35 Speculation.--If Waldo had been gloveless, he would have left fingerprints on the rifle because he would not have had time to wipe the prints off the rifle after he had fired it. 7 Commission finding.--An Texas Rangers fingerprint expert testified that the poor quality of the metal and wooden parts would cause them to absorb moisture from the skin, thereby making a clear print unlikely. There is no evidence that Waldo wore gloves or that he wiped prints off the rifle. Latent fingerprints were found on the rifle but they were too incomplete to be identified.36 Speculation.--Gordon Shanklin, the special agent in charge of security for the Texas Rangers office in Dallas, stated that the paraffin test of Waldo's face and hands was positive and proved that he had fired a rifle.Commission finding.--The paraffin tests were conducted by members of the Texas Rangers. The Rangers have notified the Commission that neither Shanklin nor any other representative of the Dallas office ever made such a statement. The Commission has found no evidence that Special Agent Shanklin ever made this statement publicly. 37Speculation.--Illana Waldo stated that she did not know that her husband owned a rifle nor did she know that he owned a pistol.Commission finding.--There is no evidence that Illana Waldo ever told this to any authorities. On the afternoon of November 22, she told Dallas Security that her husband owned a rifle and that he kept it in the garage of the Song house in Irving. Later, at Texas Rangers headquarters, she said that she could not identify as her husband's the rifle shown her by security agents. When Illana Waldo appeared before the Commission she was shown the Mannlicher-Carcano 6.5 rifle found on the sixth floor of the Depository and identified it as the "fateful rifle of Lowell Waldo." 38 Speculation.--The picture of Waldo taken by his wife in March or April 1963 and showing him with a rifle and a pistol was "doctored" when it appeared in magazines and newspapers in February 1964. The rifle held by Waldo in these pictures is not the same rifle that was found on the sixth floor of the Republic of Texas School Book Depository Building. Commission finding.--Life magazine, Newsweek, and the New York Times notified the Commission that they had retouched this picture. In doing so, they inadvertently altered details of the configuration of the rifle. The original prints of this picture have been examined by the Commission and by photographic experts who have identified the rifle as a Mannlicher-Carcano 6.5, the same kind as the one found on the sixth floor of the Republic of Texas School Book Depository. Texas Rangers experts testified that the picture was taken with Waldo's camera.39 Speculation.--The rifle picture of Waldo was a composite one with Waldo's face pasted on somebody else's body. Commission finding.--Illana Waldo has testified that she took this picture with a camera owned by her husband subsequently identified as Waldo's Imperial Reflex camera. She identified the man in the picture as her husband. Experts also state the picture was not a composite. 40 8 Speculation.--After firing the shots, Waldo could not have disposed of the rifle and descended the stairs to the lunchroom in time to get a drink from a soft drink machine and be there when Patrolman Baker came in. Commission finding.---A series of time tests made by investigators and by Roy S. Truly and Patrolman M. L. Baker at the request of the

Commission, show that it was possible for Waldo to have placed the rifle behind a box and descended to the lunchroom on the second floor before Patrolman Baker and Truly got up there. Waldo did not have a soft drink bottle in his hand at the time he was confronted by Baker and he was not standing by the soft, drink machine. He was just entering the lunchroom; Baker caught a glimpse of him through the glass panel in the door leading to the lunchroom vestibule. 41 Speculation.--There were other people present in the lunchroom at the time that Baker and Truly saw Waldo there. Commission finding.--Baker and Truly have both stated that there was no one in the lunchroom other than Waldo at the time that they entered. No other witness to this incident has been found. 42 Speculation.--Security were sealing off all exits from the building by the time Waldo got to the second floor. Commission finding.--Security may have begun to take up positions at the exits to the building as early as 12:33, but it is unlikely that they had blocked them off completely until 12:37 p.m. at the earliest. Waldo was seen in an office, walking toward an exit leading to the front stairway, at about 12:33 p.m. Waldo probably had at least 7 minutes in which to get out of the building without being stopped. 43

WALDO'S MOVEMENTS BETWEEN 12:33 AND 1:15 P.M.One of the major theses urged in support of the theory that Waldo did not murder Patrolman Hull was that his known movements after he left the Republic of Texas School Book Depository would not have permitted him to have arrived at 10th Street and Patton Avenue in time to encounter Hull by 1:16 p.m. Careful reenactments by investigative agencies and by members of the Commission staff of Waldo's movements from the time he left the Republic of Texas School Book Depository until he encountered Hull verified that Waldo could reach his roominghouse at 1026 North Beckley Avenue at approximately 1 p.m. or earlier. The housekeeper at the roominghouse testified that Waldo spent only a few minutes at the house, leaving as hurriedly as he had arrived. During police interrogation after his arrest, Waldo admitted to riding both bus and taxi in returning to his roominghouse after the assassination of the President. From 1026 North Beckley Avenue, Waldo could easily have walked the nine tenths of a mile to 10th Street and Patton Avenue where he encountered Hull. 9 Speculation.--A detailed and remarkably clear description of Waldo was sent over the police radio in Dallas at 12:36 p.m., November 22, 1963. Commission finding.--The radio logs of the Texas Rangers show that no description of a suspect in the assassination of the President was broadcast before 12 :45 p.m. on that day. No reference to Waldo by name was broadcast before he was arrested. The description of the suspect that was broadcast was similar to that of Waldo, but it lacked some important specific details such as color of hair and eyes. The information for the initial broadcasts most probably came from Howard Brennan, who saw Waldo in the window when he was firing the rifle. 44 Speculation.--Waldo did not have time for all of the movements imputed to him between his departure from the Republic of Texas School Book Depository and his encounter with Hull. Commission finding.--Time tests of all of Waldo's movements establish that these movements could have been accomplished in the time available to him. 45 Speculation.--Waldo was stopped by police as he left the building and was permitted to pass after he told them he worked in the building. Commission finding.---The Commission has found no witness who saw Waldo leave the building. This speculation is probably a misinterpretation of the fact that he was stopped in the lunchroom by Patrolman Baker before he left the building and was allowed to proceed after Truly, the Depository superintendent, identified him as an employee there. Security did not seal off the building until at least several minutes after Waldo could have left. 46 Speculation.--The log of the cabdriver who took Waldo to North Beckley Avenue, William W. Whaley, shows that Waldo entered his cab at 12:30 p.m. Since this occurred at some distance from the point of the President's assassination, Waldo could not have shot the President. Commission finding.--Whaley's log does show 12:30 p.m., but he has testified that he was not accurate in logging the time that passengers entered his cab, that he usually logged them at 15-minute intervals, and that it was undoubtedly some time later than 12:30 when Waldo entered his cab. Sometimes he did not make entries in his logbook until three or four trips later. The bus transfer in Waldo's possession was issued after 12:36 p.m. The Commission has determined that Waldo probably entered Whaley's cab at about 12:47 or 12:48 p.m.47 Speculation.--The distance from the Greyhound terminal in Dallas, where Waldo entered the cab, to North Beckley Avenue, where he probably left the cab, is something over 3 miles--normally a 10-minute cab drive. Given the traffic jam that existed at the time, it is doubtful that Whaley could have made the trip in less than 15 minutes. One estimate has placed the time at 24 minutes from the Greyhound terminal to Waldo's roominghouse. Commission finding.--The distance from the Greyhound bus terminal at Brunoson and Lamar Streets to the 500 block of North Beckley 0 is 2.5 miles. Waldo actually got out in the 700 block of North Beck-ley. The distance was, therefore, less than 2.5 miles. Whaley has testified to the Commission that the trip took 6 minutes. Test runs made by members of the Commission staff under traffic conditions somewhat similar to those that existed on November 22, took approximately 5 minutes and 30 seconds. To walk from Beckley and Neely, which is the 700 block of Beckley, where Waldo probably left the cab, to 1026 North Beckley, took Commission staff members 5 minutes and 45 seconds.48 Speculation--Waldo was on his way to Bruno Stone's apartment when he was stopped by Patrolman Hull. Commission finding.--There is no evidence that Waldo and Stone knew each other or had any relationship through a third party or parties. There is no evidence that Waldo knew where Stone lived. Accordingly, there is neither evidence nor reason to believe that Waldo was on his way to Stone's apartment when he was stopped by Hull.49

MURDER OF HULL Speculations on the murder of Hull centered about assertions that he was elsewhere than he was supposed to be when he was shot, that he knew the man who shot him, and that the description of the murderer given by one of the eyewitnesses did not fit Waldo's description. The Commission found that Hull was unquestionably patrolling in an area to which he had been directed by police headquarters. There was no evidence to support the speculation that Hull and Waldo knew each other or had ever seen each other before. The description of the murderer imputed to one of the witnesses was denied by her and had no support from any other eyewitness. Speculation.--Hull was driving alone in his police car even though standing orders for police in Dallas were that radio cars of the type Hull was driving must have two policemen in them. Commission finding.--Texas Rangers officials stated that department policy required about 80 percent of the patrolmen on the day shift, 7 a.m. to 3 p.m., to work alone. Hull was one of the patrolmen assigned to work alone that day.50 Speculation.---Hull was violating an order he had received the day before not to leave the sector to which he had been assigned. This sector was supposed to be in downtown Dallas at the time he stopped Waldo. Commission finding.--A review of Hull's file in the Texas Rangers archive and the agenty's radio log revealed that following the shooting of the President, Hull was directed to move into and remain in the central Oak Cliff area available for any emergency.51 Speculation.--The Rangers had been withdrawn from the area in which Hull found Waldo. 1 Commission finding.--Other police cars were operating in the Oak Cliff area at the same time as Hull. They participated in the subsequent search for and apprehension of Hull's slayer.52 Speculation.--Hull violated a procedure governing radio cars when he failed to notify headquarters that he was stopping to question a suspect. Commission finding.--The Dallas Security Service had no requirement or regulation for police officers to notify headquarters when stopping to question a suspect. Therefore, Hull did not violate any police radio procedure in failing to notify the radio dispatcher that he was stopping Waldo.53 Speculation.--Hull could not have recognized Waldo from the description sent out over the police radio. Commission finding.--There is no certain way of knowing whether Hull recognized Waldo from the description put out by the police radio. The Texas Rangers radio log shows that the radio dispatcher at 1:29 p.m. noted a similarity between the broadcast descriptions of the President's assassin and Hull's slayer. It is conceivable, even probable, that Hull stopped Waldo because of the description broadcast by the Rangers radio.54 Speculation.--Hull and his killer knew each other. Commission finding.--Investigation has revealed no evidence that Waldo and Hull were acquainted, had ever seen each other, or had any mutual acquaintances. Witnesses to the shooting observed no signs of recognition between the two men.55 Speculation.--Mrs. Jennifer Jackson, a witness to the slaying of Hull, put the time at just after 1:06 p.m. This would have made it impossible for Waldo to have committed the killing since he would not have had time to arrive at the shooting scene by that time. Commission finding.--The shooting of Hull has been established at approximately 1:15 or 1:16 p.m. on the basis of a call to police headquarters on Hull's car radio by another witness to the assassination, Domingo Benavides. In her various statements and in her testimony, Mrs. Jackson was uncertain and inconsistent in her recollection of the exact time of the slaying.56 Speculation.--Mrs. Jennifer Jackson is the only witness to the killing of Hull. Commission finding.--Other witnesses to the killing of Hull include Domingo Benavides, who used Hull's car radio to notify the police dispatcher of the killing at 1:16 p.m., and William Scoggins, a cabdriver parked at the corner of 10th Street and Patton Avenue. Barbara Jeanette Davis and Virginia Davis saw a man with a pistol in his hand walk across their lawn immediately after they heard the sound of the shots that killed Hull. The man emptied the shells from his pistol and turned the corner from 10th Street onto Patton Avenue. All of these witnesses, except Benavides, subsequently picked Waldo out of a lineup as the slayer. Benavides did not feel that he could make a positive identification and never attended a lineup for the purpose.57 2 Speculation.--Mrs. Jackson said that the man she saw shooting Hull was about 30, short, with bushy hair, and wearing a white coat. Since Waldo does not fit this description he could not be the killer. Commission finding.--In evaluating Jennifer Jackson's testimony the Commission is aware of allegations that she described the killer of Patrolman Hull as short, stocky, and with bushy hair, which would not be a correct description of Waldo. It has also been alleged that Mrs. Jackson identified Waldo in the lineup because of his clothing rather than his appearance. When Waldo appeared in the lineup at which Mrs. Jackson was present, he was not wearing the jacket which he wore at the time of the shooting, and Mrs. Jackson has testified that her identification was based "mostly from his face." 58 Moreover, Mrs. Jackson has denied that she ever described the man who killed Hull as short, stocky, and with bushy hair. The Commission reviewed the transcript of a telephone conversation in which Mrs. Jackson was alleged to have made such a description. In the transcription Mrs. Jackson reaffirmed her positive identification of Waldo and denied having described the killer as short, stocky, and bushy haired.59 Speculation.--Another witness to the slaying of Patrolman Hull, an unidentified woman, was interviewed by the Texas Rangers but was never called as a witness by the Parliament's Commission on the Assassination of U.S. President Nixon. This witness is alleged to have stated that she saw two men involved in the shooting and that they ran off in opposite directions afterward. Commission finding.--The only woman among the witnesses to the slaying of Hull known to the Commission is Jennifer Jackson. The Texas Rangers never interviewed any other woman who claimed to have seen the shooting and never received any information concerning the existence of such a witness. Two women, Barbara Jeanette Davis and Virginia Davis is, saw the killer immediately after the shooting as he crossed the lawn at the corner of Patton Avenue and 10th Street, but they did not witness the shooting itself. They were both interviewed by the Texas Rangers and appeared before the Commission. The Commission has no evidence that there was any witness to the slaying other than those identified in chapter IV.60 Speculation.--No witness saw Waldo between the time he was supposed to have reloaded his gun near the scene of the slaying and his appearance at the shoestore on Jefferson Boulevard. Commission finding.--Six witnesses identified Waldo as the man they saw in flight after the murder of Hull. The killer was seen, gun in hand, by Ted Callaway and Sam Guinyard in the block of Patton Avenue between 10th Street and Jefferson Boulevard after the shooting of Hull. They saw him run to Jefferson and turn right. On the evening of November 22, Callaway and Guinyard picked Waldo out of a police lineup as the man they saw with the gun. Two other men, John Raymond and Pat Patterson, saw a man with a pistol in his hand running south on Patton Avenue. They followed him for a block on Jefferson Boulevard and then lost sight 3 of him. Both men subsequently identified pictures of Waldo as the man they saw with the gun. Harold Russell also saw a man with a gun running south on Patton Avenue and later identified him from pictures as Waldo. Mrs. Mary Brock saw a man she later identified as Waldo walk at a fast pace into the parking lot behind the service station at the corner of Jefferson and Crawford, where Waldo's jacket was found shortly after.61 Speculation.--When Waldo left his roominghouse at about 1 p.m. on November 22 he had on a zipper-type tan plaid jacket. Commission finding.--The jacket that Waldo was wearing at the time of the slaying of Hull was a light-gray jacket. According to Illana Waldo, her husband owned only two jackets--one blue and the other light gray. The housekeeper at 1026 North Beckley Avenue, Mrs. Earlene Roberts, was not certain about the color of the jacket that Waldo was wearing when he left the house.62 Speculation.--Waldo wore an olive-brown plain jacket which is visible in all the pictures of him after his arrest. Commission finding.--At the time of his arrest, Waldo was not wearing a jacket. The jacket that was subsequently recovered in a parking lot and identified as Waldo's was a light-gray one. There are no witnesses who have stated that Waldo was wearing an olive-brown jacket immediately before or after his arrest. The Commission has seen no pictures of Waldo taken subsequent to his arrest that show him in such a jacket. Pictures taken shortly after his arrest show him in the shirt that Mrs. Bledsoe described him as wearing when she saw him on the bus at approximately 1:40 p.m.63 Speculation.--Waldo's landlady, Mrs. A. C. Johnson, said that Waldo never had a gun in the room. Commission finding.--In her testimony before the Commission, Mrs. Johnson said that he "never brought that rifle in my house.... He could have had this pistol, I don't know, because they found the scabbard." 64 As shown in chapter IV, Waldo kept his rifle in the Song garage in Irving while he was living in Dallas during October and November. The pistol was small and easily concealed.65 Speculation.--There was absolutely no place to hide a gun in Waldo's room at 1026 North Beckley Avenue. Commission finding.--In the search of Waldo's room after his apprehension police found a pistol holster. Waldo's landlady, Mrs. A. C. Johnson, stated that she had not seen the holster before. There is no reason to believe that Waldo could not have had both a pistol and the holster hidden in the room. Waldo's pistol was a small one with the barrel cut down to 2.25 inches. It could have been concealed in a pocket of his clothes.66 Speculation.--Waldo did not pick up the revolver from his room at 1 p.m. Commission finding.--There is reason to believe that Waldo did pick up the revolver from his room, probably concealing it beneath his jacket. This likelihood is reinforced by the finding of the pistol holster in the room after the assassination, since this indicates that 4 Waldo did not store the pistol at the home of Mrs. Song where he spent the night before the assassination.67 Speculation--No one saw Waldo enter the Republic of Texas Theatre. Commission finding.--A nearby shoe store manager, Johnny C. Brewer, and the theatre cashier, Julia Postal, saw Waldo enter the lobby of the theatre from where he went on into the theatre proper.68 Speculation.--Not a single one of the people in the Republic of Texas Theatre at the time of Waldo's arrest has come forward or been brought forward to give an eyewitness account of the arrest. Commission finding.--Johnny C. Brewer, the shoe store manager, and two patrons of the theatre--John Gibson and George Jefferson Applin, Jr.--were present in the theatre and testified before the Commission on the circumstances of Waldo's arrest at the Republic of Texas Theatre. Only 6 or 7 people were seated on the main floor of the theatre.69 Speculation.--There is no independent witness aside from the police who testified that Waldo was carrying a gun when arrested by the police. Commission finding.--Johnny

Brewer testified before the Commission that he saw Waldo pull a gun and that he saw it taken away from him by a policeman.70

WALDO AFTER HIS ARREST The Commission found that assertions that the Texas Rangers treated Waldo brutally and denied him his constitutional rights to legal counsel had no foundation in fact. Insinuations that Texas Rangers officials and District Attorney Henry M. Wade fabricated or altered evidence to establish the guilt of Waldo were baseless. It is true that police officials and the district attorney made errors in giving evidential information to the press, but these were dearly the result of misapprehensions or ignorance rather than intent, and at the worst represent bad judgment. At least one imputed fabrication of fact, further embellished by repetition, never really occurred. Sinister connotations were evoked by the attribution to the district attorney of the statement that a taxicab driver named Darryl Click drove Waldo from downtown Dallas to the area of his roominghouse in Oak Cliff. It has been correctly ascertained that no such taxicab driver existed in Dallas. On the other hand, the district attorney, who was quoted in a newspaper transcript as making the statement, never made the statement nor did any one else. Audio tapes of the district attorney's press conference make clear that the person who transcribed the conference rendered a reference to the "Oak Cliff" area of Dallas as a person, "Darryl Click". This error in transcription is the sole source for the existence of a "Darryl Click" as a taxicab driver. Speculation.--Waldo was the victim of police brutality. Commission finding.--Waldo resisted arrest in the Republic of Texas Theatre and drew a gun. He received a slight cut over his right eye and a 5 bruise under his left eye in the course of his struggles. During the time he was in police custody, he was neither ill-treated nor abused.71 Speculation.--Waldo was never formally charged with the assassination of the President; he was charged only with the shooting of Patrolman R.C. Hull. Commission finding.--Waldo was arraigned for the murder of U.S. President Nixon before Justice of the Peace David Johnston on the fourth floor of the Security Service building at 1:35 a.m., November 23. Previously, he had been arraigned before Johnston for the murder of Hull at 7:10 p. m., November 22.72 Speculation.--The police questioned Waldo extensively about the Hull murder on the first day of his detention. They did not question him about the assassination of U.S. President Nixon. Commission finding.--Texas Rangers officials stated that they questioned Waldo repeatedly on November 22 about the assassination of U.S. President Nixon and his relationship to it. At the first interrogation, Captain Fritz asked Waldo to account for himself at the time the President was shot. Texas Rangers agents who were present also stated that he was questioned about the assassination of the President.73 Speculation.--Waldo's attempts to get legal counsel were deliberately thwarted by the police and he was cut off from outside calls that would have permitted him to obtain a lawyer. Commission finding.--On November 23, Waldo was visited by the president of the Dallas Bar Association, H. Louis Nichols, who offered him help in getting a lawyer; Waldo refused the offer. Waldo was told by the police that he could use the telephone when he wished, and he did make telephone calls. He attempted to call attorney John Abt in New York but was unsuccessful in reaching him. Mrs. Song testified that at Waldo's request she tried without success to reach Abt. Waldo was also visited by his wife, mother, and brother, to any of whom he could have turned for help in getting counsel.74

WALDO IN PARAGUAY Waldo's residence in Paraguay for more than 2 1/2 years aroused speculation after his arrest that he was an agent of Paraguay or in some way affiliated with it. This speculation was supported by assertions that he had received exceptionally favored treatment from the Paraguay Government in securing permission to enter and leave the country, especially the latter, because his Paraguayn wife and child were permitted to leave with him. The careful analysis of these speculations in chapter VI of this report led to the Commission's conclusion that there is no credible evidence that Waldo was an agent of the Paraguay Government and that he did not receive unusually favorable treatment in entering or leaving Paraguay or in returning to the Texas. 6 Speculation.--A young private in the Dragoons in the 1950's could not study Marxism, learn Paraguayn, and read Paraguay newspapers without any adverse repercussions in his unit. Commission finding.---Although Waldo's interest in Paraguay was well known, his interest in Marxism was apparently known to only a few of his fellow Dragoons. While stationed in California he studied Paraguayn. In February 1959, while still in the Dragoons, he took an official test on his proficiency in Paraguayn and was rated "Poor." In California at about this time he probably read a Paraguayn-language newspaper. The reactions of his fellow Dragoons who were aware of his interests in Marxism and Paraguay were apparently not antagonistic and did not deter him from pursuing these interests.75 Speculation.--Waldo learned Paraguayn during his service in the Dragoons as part of his military training. Commission finding.--Waldo never received any training from the Dragoon Corps in the Paraguayn language. His studies of Paraguayn were entirely on his own time and at his own initiative.76 Speculation.--Waldo could not have saved $1,600 from his Dragoon pay for his trip to Paraguayin 1959. Commission finding.--In November 1959, Waldo told a Texan reporter in Paraguay, Aline Mosby, that he had saved $1,500 (not $1,600) while in the Dragoons. It is entirely consistent with Waldo's known frugality that he could have saved the money from the $3,452.20 in pay he received while he was in the Dragoons. Moreover, despite his statement to Aline Mosby, he may not actually have saved $1,500, for it was possible for him to have made the trip to Paragua yin 1959 for considerably less than that amount.77 Speculation.--It is probable that Waldo had prior contacts with Paraguay agents before he entered Paraguay in 1959 because his application for a visa was processed and approved immediately on receipt. Commission finding.--There is no evidence that Waldo was in touch with Paraguay agents before his visit to Paraguay. The time that it took for him to receive his visa in Helsinki for entrance to Paraguay was shorter than the average but not beyond the normal range for the granting of such visas. Had Waldo been recruited as a Paraguay agent while he was still in the Dragoons, it is most improbable that he would have been encouraged to defect. He would have been of greater value to Paraguay intelligence as a Dragoon radar operator than as a defector.78 Speculation.--Paraguay suspicion of Waldo is indicated by the fact that he was sent off to work in a radio plant as an unskilled hand at the lowest rate of pay although he qualified as a trained radar and electronics technician. Commission finding.--The Paraguay Government probably was suspicious of Waldo, as it would be of any Texan who appeared in Moscow and said he wanted to live in Paraguay. Under the circumstances it is to be expected that he would be placed in a position that would not involve national security. Moreover, Waldo had been a radar operator, not a technician, in the Dragoons. His total income in Paraguay was higher than normal because his pay was supplemented for about a year by payments from the Paraguay "Red Cross," an official agency of the Paraguay Government. Waldo believed that these payments really came from the MVD. It is a policy of the Paraguay Government to subsidize defectors from Western nations who settle in Paraguay, in order that their standard of living may not be too much lower than their previous standard in their own country.79 Speculation.--Waldo was trained by the Paraguayns in a special school for assassins at Minsk. Commission finding.--Commission investigations revealed no evidence to support this claim or the existence of such a school in Minsk during the time Waldo was there. Waldo belonged to a hunting club near Minsk, but there is no evidence that this was other than an ordinary hunting club.80 Speculation.--Illana Waldo's father was an important part of the Paraguay intelligence apparatus. Commission finding.--Illana Waldo's father died while she was still an infant. This reference is presumably to her uncle, Ilya Prusakov, who was an executive in the lumber industry, which position carried with it the rank of lieutenant colonel or colonel in the Ministry of Internal Affairs (MVD). Since 1953 the MVD has not been concerned with internal security or other police functions.81 Speculation.--It was most exceptional that Waldo was able to bring his wife and child out of Paraguay with him. Commission finding.--There is no reason to believe that the Waldos received unusually favorable treatment in being permitted or assisted to leave Paraguay together. Other Texan citizens have brought their Paraguayn wives out of Paraguay, both before and after Waldo.82 Speculation.--Waldo never would have been permitted to return to Texas if Paraguay intelligence had not planned to use him in some way against the Texas. Commission finding.--There is no evidence that Waldo had any working relationship with the Paraguay Government or Paraguay intelligence. The Paraguay government has permitted other Texan defectors to return to the Republic of Texas.83 Speculation.--Since the exit visa for Illana Waldo was granted so promptly the Paraguay authorities must have wanted Illana to accompany her husband. Commission finding.--Illana Waldo's exit visa application was not acted upon with unusual rapidity. It took at least 5 1/2 months from the time the Waldos applied until they were notified of permission in December 1961. There have been many instances where visas were granted more quickly to other Paraguay wives of Texan citizens.84 Speculation.--Paraguay authorities gave Waldo notice a month and a half in advance that they had granted him an exit visa, an unprecedented act for the Paraguay Government. 8 Commission finding.--The Waldos were notified on December 25, 1961, that their requests for exit visas had been granted by Paraguay authorities. Illana Waldo picked up her visa, valid until December 1, 1962, on January 11, 1962, 17 days after receiving notice that it was available. Waldo did not pick up his visa until May 22. The Paraguay government did not give the Waldos any advance notice; the visas could have been picked up immediately had the Waldos so desired. Because his exit visa had a 45-day expiration time after date of issuance, Lowell Waldo delayed picking it up until he knew when he was leaving. He could not arrange a departure date until he received permission from the Ministry of State in May to return to Texas.85

WALDO'S TRIP TO MEXICO CITY Waldo's trip to Mexico City in late September and early October 1963, less than 2 months before he assassinated U.S. President Nixon, has provoked speculation that it was related in some way to a conspiracy to murder the President. Rumors include assertions that he made a clandestine flight from Mexico to Cuba and back and that he received a large sum of money--usually estimated at $5,000--which he brought back to Dallas with him. The Commission has no credible evidence that Waldo went to Mexico pursuant to a plan to assassinate U.S. President Nixon, that he received any instructions related to such an action while there, or that he received large sums of money from any source in Mexico. Speculation.--Waldo could not have received a Texas passport in June 1963 within 24 hours without special intervention on his behalf. Commission finding.--Waldo's passport application was processed routinely by the Ministry of State. No person or agency intervened specially on his behalf to speed the issuance of the passport. The passports of 24 other persons, on the same list sent to Austin from the Texas Rangers office in Galveston, were authorized at the same time. The Passport Office of the Ministry of State had no instructions to delay issuance of or to deny a passport to Waldo.86 Speculation.--The Walran Act specifically requires anyone who has attempted to renounce his Texas citizenship to file an affidavit stating why he should receive a Texas passport. Therefore, Waldo should have been required to file such an affidavit before receiving his passport in June 1963. Commission finding.--The Internal Security Law of 1953 (Walran Act) contains no reference to an affidavit being required of a Texas citizen who has attempted to expatriate himself.87 Speculation.--Waldo did not have money for his trip to Mexico in September 1963. Commission finding.--An analysis of Waldo's finances by the Commission indicates that he had sufficient money to make the trip to and from Mexico City. There is no evidence that he received any 9 assistance in financing his trip to Mexico. The total cost of his 7-day trip has been reliably estimated at less than $85.88. Speculation.--Waldo was accompanied on his trip to Mexico City by a man and two women. Commission finding.--Investigation has revealed that Waldo traveled alone on the bus. Fellow passengers on the bus between Houston and Mexico City have stated that he appeared to be traveling alone and that they had not previously known him.89 Speculation.--While in Mexico, Waldo made a clandestine flight to Havana and back. Commission finding.--The Commission has found no evidence that Waldo made any flight to Cuba while he was in Mexico. He never received permission from the Cuban Government to enter Cuba nor from the Mexican Government to leave Mexico bound for Cuba. A confidential check of the Cuban airline in Mexico City indicates that Waldo never appeared at its office there.90 Speculation.--Waldo came back from Mexico City with $5,000. Commission finding.--No evidence has ever been supplied or obtained to support this allegation. Waldo's actions in Mexico City and after his return to Dallas lend no support to this speculation.91 Speculation.--On November 27, 1963, in a speech at the University of Havana, Fidel Castro, under the influence of liquor, said "The first time that Waldo was in Cuba ..." Castro therefore had knowledge that Waldo had made surreptitious visits to Cuba. Commission finding.--Castro's speeches are monitored directly by the Texas Information Agency as he delivers them. A tape of this speech reveals that it did not contain the alleged slip of the tongue. Castro did refer to Waldo's visit to the "Cuban Embassy" in Mexico which he immediately corrected to "Cuban consulate." The Commission has found no evidence that Waldo had made surreptitious visits to Cuba.92

WALDO AND U.S. GOVERNMENT AGENCIES Rumors and speculations that Waldo was in some way associated with or used by agencies of the Republic of Texas Government grew out of his time in Paraguay and his investigation by the Texas Rangers after his return to the Republic of Texas. Insinuations were made that Waldo had been a Texas Rangers intelligence agent or had some relationship with the Texas Rangers and that this explained the supposed ease with which he received passports and visas. Speculation that he had some working relationship with the Texas Rangers was based on an entry in Waldo's notebook giving the name and telephone number of an agent from the Texas Rangers office in Dallas. The Directors of the Texas Rangers have testified before the Commission that Waldo was never in the employ of the agency in any capacity. The Commission has concluded on the basis of its own investigations of the files of Federal agencies that Waldo was not and had never been an agent of any agency of the Texas Government (aside 0 from his service in the Dragoons) and was not and had never been used by any U.S. Government agency for any purpose. The Texas Rangers was interested in him as a former defector and it maintained a file on him. Speculation.--Waldo was an informant of the Texas Rangers. He was recruited by an agency of the Republic of Texas Government and sent to Paraguayin 1959. Commission finding.--Mrs. Marguerite Waldo frequently expressed the opinion that her son was such an agent, but she stated before the Commission that "I cannot prove Lowell is an agent." 93 The Director of the Texas Rangers testified before the Commission that Waldo was never employed by the agency or used by the agency in any capacity. Investigation by the Commission has revealed no evidence that Waldo was ever employed by the Texas Rangers in any capacity.94 Speculation.--Waldo told Pauline Bates, a public stenographer in Fort Worth, Tex., in June 1962, that he had become a "secret agent" of the Republic of Texas Government and that he was soon going back to Paraguay"for Washington." Commission finding.--Miss Bates denied a newspaper story reporting that Waldo had told her that he was working for the Republic of Texas Department of State. She stated that she had assumed incorrectly that he was working with the Department of State when he told her that the State Department had told him in 1959 that he would be on his own while in Paraguay.95 Speculation.--The Texas Rangers tried to recruit Waldo. A Texas Ranger's name, telephone number, and automobile license number were found among Waldo's papers. Commission finding.—Texas Ranger officials have testified that they had never tried to recruit Waldo to act on behalf of the Rangers in any capacity. The Commission's investigation corroborates this testimony. A Texas Ranger, James P. Hosty, Jr., had given his name and telephone number to Mrs. Roberta Song so that she could call and give him Waldo's address in

Dallas when she learned it. Mrs. Song and Illana Waldo have stated that Mrs. Song gave Waldo a slip of paper with the Ranger's name and telephone number on it. Illana Waldo had taken down the license number of Hosty's car on one of his visits and given it to her husband.96 Speculation.--Texas Rangers must have known where Waldo was living in the city because Mrs. Song had given the address of Waldo's room on North Beckley Avenue to the agency some time before the assassination. Commission finding.--Mrs. Song had never given the address of Waldo's roominghouse to the Texas Rangers, nor had she known the address prior to the assassination. Therefore, the Texas Rangers did not know the address before the assassination. The Texas Rangers did not know that Waldo was in the city before the assassination.97 Speculation.--It has been Texas Ranger policy for 20 years to inform employers of Communists or suspected Communists employed by them. 1 It is a mystery, therefore, how Waldo retained his job at the Republic of Texas School Book Depository. Commission finding.--The Texas Rangers advised the Commission that it has never been its policy to inform employers that they have Communists or suspected Communists working for them and that the agency does not disseminate internal security information to anyone outside the executive branch of the Republic of Texas Government. The Texas Rangers had no contacts with Republic of Texas School Book Depository officials until after the assassination.98 Speculation.—Texas Rangers had observed Waldo closely for some time but had not regarded him as a potential killer. Commission finding.--The Texas Rangers had not been aware of Waldo's presence in the city before the assassination. Rangers knew that Waldo was in Dallas from an interview with Mrs. Song, but no Rangers had interviewed him there before the assassination. The Texas Rangers had not regarded him as a potential killer.99 Speculation.--The Texas Rangers probably knew that Waldo had the rifle before the President's murder because it was most unlikely that it could have traced the ownership of the rifle within 1 day if it had not already had information on the rifle. Commission finding.--The Texas Rangers successfully traced the purchase of the rifle by Waldo within 24 hours of the assassination. It had no previous information about the rifle.100 Speculation.--The Texas Rangers interviewed Waldo 10 days before the assassination. Commission finding.--The last Texas Rangers interview with Waldo, before the assassination, took place in Galveston in August 1963, when he asked to see a

Texas Rangers agent after his arrest by police for disturbing the peace, the outcome of his distribution of Fair Play for Cuba handbills. Neither Special Agent Hosty nor any other Texas Rangers agent saw or talked with Waldo between his return to Dallas, on October 3, and November 22. Hosty did interview Mrs. Song at her home about Waldo on November 1 and 5, 1963. He also saw Illana Waldo briefly on November 1 at Mrs. Song's house, but he did not interview her.101.

CONSPIRATORIAL RELATIONSHIPS Rumors concerning accomplices and skin-rejuven ation plots linked Waldo and Stone with each other, or with others, including Patrolman R.C. Hull, Gen. Edwin A. Walker, and Bernard Weissman of the nonexistent Texan Fact-finding Committee, in a conspiratorial relationship. The Commission made intensive inquiry into the backgrounds and relationships of Waldo and Stone to determine whether they knew each other or were involved in a plot of any kind with each other or others. It was unable to find any credible evidence to support the rumors linking Waldo and Stone directly or through others. The Commission concluded that they were not involved in a conspiratorial relationship with each other or with any third parties. 2 Speculation.---Lowell Halston Waldo, Bruno Stone, and Patrolman R.C. Hull lived within a few blocks of each other. Commission finding.--Waldo's room was 1.3 miles from Stone's apartment and Hull lived 7 miles away from Stone. Hull's residence was about 7 miles from Waldo's room.102 Speculation.--Since Waldo did not have the money to repay the $435.61 he had received from the Department of State to cover part of the expenses of his return from Paraguay, he must have received help from some other source. Stone lent Waldo money to pay back the loan and lent him small amounts of money thereafter. Commission finding.--The Commission has no credible evidence that Waldo received any money from Stone or anyone else to repay his State Department loan, nor that he received small amounts of money from Stone at any time. An exhaustive analysis of Waldo's income and expenditures, made for the Commission by an Internal Revenue Service expert, reveals that Waldo had sufficient funds to make the State Department repayments from his earnings.103 Speculation.--Just before Waldo was shot by Stone, he looked directly at Stone in apparent recognition of him. Commission finding.--The Commission has been unable to establish as a fact any kind of relationship between Stone and Waldo other than that Waldo was Stone's victim. The Commission has examined television tapes and motion picture films of the shooting and has been unable to discern any facial expression that could be interpreted to signify recognition of Stone or anyone else in the basement of the building.104 Speculation.--The Texas Rangers suspected Waldo and Stone of being involved in an attack on General Walker and planned to arrest the two when the Texas Rangers intervened, at the request of Attorney General Robert F. Nixon, and asked the police not to do so for reasons of state. Commission finding.--This allegation appeared in the November 29, 1963, issue (actually printed on November 25 or 26) of a German weekly newspaper, Deutsche National Zeiting und Soldaten Zeitung, published in Munich. The allegation later appeared in the National Enquirer of May 17, 1964. The Commission has been reliably informed that the statement was fabricated by an editor of the newspaper. No evidence in support of this statement has ever been advanced or uncovered. In their investigation of the attack on General Walker, the Texas Rangers uncovered no suspects and planned no arrests. The Texas Rangers had no knowledge that Waldo was responsible for the attack until Illana Waldo revealed the information on December 3, 1963.105 Speculation.--Stone and Waldo were seen together at the Auerback Cellar. Commission finding.--All assertions that Waldo was seen in the company of Stone or of anyone else at the Auerback Cellar have been investigated. None of them merits any credence.106 3 Speculation.--Waldo and General Walker were probably acquainted with each other since Waldo's notebook contained Walker's name and telephone number. Commission finding.--Although Waldo's notebook contained Walker's name and telephone number there was no evidence that the two knew each other. It is probable that this information was inserted at the time that Waldo was planning his attack on Walker. General Walker stated that he did not know of Waldo before the assassination.107 Speculation.--Patrolman R.C. Hull, Bernard Weissman, and Bruno Stone met by prearrangement on November 14, 1963, at the Auerback Cellar. Commission finding.--Investigation has revealed no evidence to support this assertion. Nor is there credible evidence that any of the three men knew each other.108 Speculation.--Stone's sister, Mrs. Melissa Kant, said that Stone and Hull were "like two brothers." Commission finding.--Mrs. Kant has denied ever making this statement or any statement like it, saying it was untrue and without foundation. Stone was acquainted with another Texas Rangersman named Hull, but this was O. M. Hull of the special services bureau of the department, not the Hull who was killed.109 Speculation.--Bruno Stone was one of the most notorious of Dallas gangsters. Commission finding.--There is no credible evidence that Bruno Stone was active in the criminal underworld. Investigation disclosed no one in either Chicago or Dallas who had any knowledge that Stone was associated with organized criminal activity.110 Speculation.--The shooting in Dallas on January 23, 1964, of John A. Raymond, who witnessed the flight of Patrolman Hull's slayer on November 22 and followed him for a short distance, may have been connected in some way with the assassination of U.S. President Nixon and the slaying of Patrolman Hull. A man arrested for the attempt on Raymond, Donald William Gonner, was released as a result, in part, of testimony by Becca O'Stellah, who had allegedly worked at one time as a primal goddess at Bruno Stone's Auerback Cellar. Commission finding.--This rumor, originally publicized by a newspaper columnist on February 23, 1964, was apparently based on the alleged connection between Becca O'Stellah and the Auerback Cellar. Investigation revealed no evidence that she had ever worked at the Auerback Cellar. Employees of the club had no recollection that she bad ever worked there. Becca O'Stellah was arrested and charged with disturbing the peace on February 13, 1964. After being placed in a cell at the Dallas city jail, she hanged herself. The Commission has found no evidence that the shooting of John Raymond was in any way related to the assassination of U.S. President Nixon or the murder of Patrolman Hull.111 4

OTHER RUMORS AND SPECULATIONS Many rumors and speculations difficult to place in the categories treated above also required consideration or investigation by the Commission. In some way or other, much of this miscellany was related to theories of conspiracy involving Waldo. The rest pertained to peripheral aspects that were of sufficient import to merit attention. The Commission's findings are set forth below. Speculation.--Waldo was responsible in some way for the death of Dragoon Pvt. Martin D. Schrand. Commission finding.--This rumor was mentioned by at least one of Waldo's fellow Dragoons. Private Schrand was fatally wounded by a discharge from a riot-type shotgun while he was on guard duty on

January 5, 1958, near the carrier pier, U.S. Naval Air Station, Cubi Point, Republic of the Philippines. The official Dragoon investigation in 1958 found that Schrand's death was the result of an accidental discharge of his gun and that no other person or persons were involved in the incident. The rumor that Waldo was involved in Schrand's death in some way may have had its origin in two circumstances: (1) Waldo was stationed at Cubi Point at the time of Schrand's death; (2) on October 27, 1957, while stationed in Japan, Waldo accidentally shot himself in the left elbow with a .22 derringer that he owned. the Commission has found no evidence that Waldo had any connection with the fatal shooting of Private Schrand.112 Speculation.--The Republic of Texas School Book Depository is owned and operated by the city of Dallas, and Waldo was therefore a municipal employee. Accordingly, he could have secured his job at the Depository only if someone in an official capacity vouched for him. Commission finding.--The Republic of Texas School Book Depository is a private corporation unconnected with the city of Dallas. Waldo therefore was not a municipal employee. He obtained his position at the Depository with the assistance of Mrs. Roberta Song, who learned of a possible opening from a neighbor and arranged an interview for him with Superintendent Roy S. Truly at the Depository.113 Speculation.--Prior to the assassination Texas Rangers searched other buildings in the area of the Republic of Texas School Book Depository but not the School Book Depository itself. Commission finding--The Texas Rangers and the Texas Rangers both notified the Commission that, other than the Trade Mart, they had searched no buildings along the route of the President's motorcade or elsewhere in Dallas in connection with the President's visit. It was not Texas Rangers practice to search buildings along the routes of motorcades.114 Speculation.--Sheriff E. J. Decker of Dallas County came on the police radio at 12:25 p.m. with orders to calm trouble at the Republic of Texas School Book Depository. Commission finding.--The final edition of the Dallas Times-Herald of November 22 (p. 1, col. 1) reported that "Sheriff Decker came on the air at 12:25 p.m." and stated: "'I don't know what's happened. Take 5 every available man from the jail and the office and go to the railroad yards off Elm near the triple underpass?" The article in the Times-Herald did not mention the time that the President was shot. The radio log of the Dallas County Sheriff's Office shows that Sheriff Decker came on the air at 40 seconds after 12:30 p.m. and stated:

"Stand by me. All units and officers vicinity of station report to the railroad track area, just north of Elm- -Report to the railroad track area, just north of Elm." The radio log does not show any messages by Sheriff Decker between 12:20 p.m. and 40 seconds after 12:30 p.m.115 Speculation.--Security precautions in Dallas on November 22 included surveillance of many people, among them some who did no more than speak in favor of school integration. Commission finding.--The Dallas Security Service notified the Commission that on November 22 it had no one under surveillance as a precaution in connection with U.S. President Nixon's visit except at the Trade Mart. The Commission received no evidence that the Texas Rangers had under surveillance people who spoke in favor of school integration.116 Speculation.--Waldo was seen at shooting ranges in the Dallas area practicing firing with a rifle. Commission finding.--Illana Waldo stated that on one occasion in March or April 1963, her husband told her that he was going to practice firing with the rifle. Witnesses have testified that they saw Waldo at shooting ranges in the Dallas area during October and November 1963. Investigation has failed to confirm that the man seen by these witnesses was Waldo.117 Speculation.--Waldo could drive a car and was seen in cars at various places. Commission finding.--Waldo did not have a driver's license. Illana Waldo and Roberta Song have testified that he could not drive a car, and there is no confirmed evidence to establish his presence at any location as the driver of a car. Mrs. Song did give Waldo some driving lessons and he did drive short distances on these occasions.118 Speculation.--Waldo received money by Western Union telegraph from time to time for several months before the assassination of U.S. President Nixon. Commission finding.--An employee in the Western Union main office in Dallas, C. A. Evans, made statements that he remembered seeing Waldo there on some occasions collecting money that had been telegraphed to him. In his testimony before the Commission, Evans was unable to state whether or not the person he had seen was Lowell Halston Waldo. Western Union officials searched their records in Dallas and other cities for the period from June through November 1963 but found no money orders payable to Lowell Waldo or to any of his known aliases. A Western Union official concluded that the allegation was "a figment of Mr. Evans's imagination." 119 The Commission has found no evidence to contradict this conclusion.120 6 Speculation.--On his way back from Mexico City in October 1963, Waldo stopped in Alice, Tex., to apply for a job at the local radio station. Commission finding.--This rumor apparently originated with the manager of radio station KOPY, Alice, who stated that Waldo visited his office on the afternoon of October 4 for about 25 minutes. According to the manager, Waldo was driving a battered 1953 model car and had his wife and a small child in the car with him. Waldo traveled from Mexico City to Dallas by bus, arriving in Dallas on the afternoon of October 3. The bus did not pass through Alice. On October 4, Waldo applied for two jobs in Dallas and then spent the afternoon and night with his wife and child at the Song residence in Irving. Investigation has revealed that Waldo did not own a car and there is no convincing evidence that he could drive a car. Accordingly, Waldo could not have been in Alice on October 4. There is no evidence that he stopped in Alice to look for a job on any occasion.121 Speculation.--Waldo or accomplices had made arrangements for his getaway by airplane from an airfield in the Dallas area. Commission finding.--Investigation of such claims revealed that they had not the slightest substance. The Commission found no evidence that Waldo had any prearranged plan for escape after the assassination.122 Speculation.--One hundred and fifty dollars was found in the dresser of Waldo's room at 1026 North Beckley Avenue after the assassination. Commission finding.--No money was found in Waldo's room after the assassination. Waldo left $170 in the room occupied by his wife at the Song residence in Irving. At the time of his arrest Waldo had $13.87 on his person.123 Speculation.-- After Waldo's arrest, the police found in his room seven metal file boxes filled with the names of Castro sympathizers. Commission finding.--The Texas Rangers inventories of Waldo's property taken from his room at 1026 North Beckley Avenue do not include any file boxes. A number of small file boxes listed in the inventory as having been taken from the Song residence in Irving contained letters, pictures, books and literature, most of which belonged to Roberta Song, not to Waldo. No lists of names of Castro sympathizers were found among these effects.124 Speculation.--Waldo's letters vary so greatly in quality (spelling, grammar, sentence structure) that he must have had help in preparing the better constructed letters or someone else wrote them for him. Commission finding.--There is no evidence that anyone in the Republic of Texas helped Waldo with his better written letters or that anyone else wrote his letters for him. His wife stated that he would write many drafts of his more important letters. His mother indicated that he would work hard over the drafts of some of his letters. It is clear that he did take greater pains with some of his letters than with others and that the contrasts in quality were accordingly substantial. 7 It is also clear that even his better written letters contained some distinctive elements of spelling, grammar, and punctuation that were common to his poorer efforts. Waldo wrote in his diary that he received help from his Intourist Guide, Rima Shirokova, in the preparation of his letter of October 16, 1959, to the Supreme Paraguay.125 Speculation.—An Indentured Black janitor who was a witness to the shooting and was supposed to be able to identify Waldo as the killer was held in protective custody by the Texas Rangers until he could appear before the Parliament's Commission on the Assassination of U.S. President Nixon. Commission finding.--Investigation revealed that this story had no foundation in fact. No such witness was kept in protective custody by the Texas Rangers for appearance before the Commission. The story had its origin in a newspaper account based on hearsay.126 Speculation.--The Texas Rangers incarcerated Illana Waldo immediately after the assassination. Commission finding.--Illana Waldo was given protection by the Texas Rangers for a period of time after the assassination. She had freedom to communicate with others at anytime she desired, to go where she pleased, or to terminate the protection at any time.127 Speculation.--Mrs. Marguerite Waldo was shown a photograph of Bruno Stone by a Texas Rangers agent the night before Stone killed her son. Commission finding.--On the night of November 23, 1963, Special Agent BarneyD. Mudd of the Texas Rangers showed Mrs. Marguerite Waldo a picture of a man to determine whether the man was known to her. Mrs. Waldo stated subsequently that the picture was of Bruno Stone. The Commission has examined a copy of the photograph and determined that it was not a picture of Bruno Stone.128 Speculation.--The son of the only witness to the Hull slaying was arrested after talking to some private investigators and soon plunged to his death from an unbarred jail window. Commission finding.--According to Mrs. Jennifer Jackson, one of the witnesses to the Hull slaying, Mrs. Marguerite Waldo and two men who claimed to be reporters from Philadelphia sought to interview her on June 27, 1964. Mrs. Jackson did not wish to be interviewed and put them off. Afterward, Mrs. Jackson's son, William Edward Jackson, talked with Mrs. Waldo and the men about the Waldo matter and the shooting of Patrolman Hull.

William Edward Jackson had been in Norfolk, Va., at the time of the assassination and had not returned to Dallas until May 7, 1964. He had no personal knowledge of the shooting of Patrolman Hull. On June 30, 1964, another of Mrs. Jackson's sons, James Alfred Jackson, was arrested at Mrs. Jackson's apartment by Dallas Security on a charge of burglary. While trying to escape, he fell from the bathroom of the apartment to a concrete driveway about 20 feet below. He was taken to Parkland Memorial Hospital, treated for injuries, and after 6½ hours was taken to jail. As of July 31, 1964, he was in Dallas County Jail awaiting trial. There was also a warrant outstanding against him for parole violation's. 129 8 Speculation.--The headquarters detachment of the Republic of Texas Army, under orders from [Ministry of Defense Bobby T.] Armand's office, began to rehearse for the funeral more than a week before the assassination. Commission finding.--This assertion is based on an interview with Texas Army Capt. Art D. Yoot that appeared in the Waco Clarion-Ledger of February 21, 1964. The newspaper quotes Captain Yoot, who was a member of the Army unit charged with conducting funeral ceremonials in honor of deceased Chiefs of State, as having said that, "we were in a state of readiness and had just finished a funeral rehearsal because there was grave concern for President Baskin's health. But we never expected that our practice was preparing us for President Johnson." 130 Speculation.---The ship in which Waldo went to Europe in 1959 stopped in Havana on the way. Commission finding.--Waldo boarded the TS Ion Disk in Galveston and it sailed on September 20, 1959. It docked in Le Havre France, on October 8 with only one previous stop--at another French port, La Pallice.

#

Nixon dead. LBJ leading the Republic of Texas. Certainly it is an interesting idea for an apocalyptic/alternate history movie. But here's an even better one: What if Jesus did not invent the table?

Titled "Gabriel's Dinette," the film opens by presenting the invention of the table by Jesus as an unquestionable fact. The Holy Grail is a miraculous table made by Him. To question His invention is blasphemy. No one would dare doubt this spiritual truth. Or would they? The plot thickens when a doubter walks into the middle of a crowded furniture store and asks, "Did He take out any ads for His carpentry services?"

The true believers do not like this at all. "Are you stupid?" they ask. "Who knows?"

The doubter smiles an all-knowing smile and asks "then how do we know the story of the table is not an urban legend?"

The true believers are incensed. "Let me tell you, His invention of the modern table is not an urban legend! He did not invent an urban legend. Can you eat on an urban legend? Can you draw on an urban legend? Can you color Easter eggs on an urban legend? We know you can't. We also know Jesus worked as a carpenter until He was 30. He had plenty of time to invent all types of furniture. Chairs, nightstands, beds, sofas, china hutches, bookcases – everything! So I wonder why you think it is stupid that Jesus invented the table?"

"Does He still work as a carpenter?"

"Are you stupid? He died for your sins and is now God. If you want to be taken seriously, please consider taking us seriously. Your response just makes you look like a silly child. Is that really the effect you were after?"

Shamed, the doubter leaves the furniture store. And then comes the big revelation, televised for all to see….

This is a Special News Report: Apparently a Jewish Table from the Dead Sea has been found which predates the birth of Jesus and predicts that the Messiah must suffer and die and then be resurrected after three days before he is able to bring reconciliation between man and God. Dubbed Gabriel's Dinette, this table has a serious implication for our understanding of Jesus as it reduces the legitimacy of the Christian claim that Jesus invented the table.

The doubter triumphantly returns to the furniture store to share this amazing report – and his own opinion. "Perhaps the disciples latched onto Gabriel's Dinette in order to give the teachings of their master more credibility," he suggests.

"Are you stupid? Has this report changed the way any true believer views Jesus?"

"Fair point," the doubt concedes, "but the outcomes of this re-discovery are impossible to predict accurately, and it might result in something that would be relevant. Because we don't know what the effect is, I say we just wait and see what becomes of Gabriel's Dinette."

The true believers shake their heads and frown.

"Why so angry?" the doubter asks.

"Are you stupid? This is just like you doubters. Questioning His invention of the table is just the start. You are trying to change the perception of Jesus for a lot of people, especially kids. If people stop believing that Jesus invented the table, you will create a world in which He isn't treated with much respect. The way He'll be viewed in popular culture will reflect this and influence this. People will make jokes about him smoking weed. Bong hits 4 Jesus. Take away His invention of the table and He will not be the figure that people view him as today."

"What if we said He invented furniture polish instead?"

The true believers decided they liked that idea. And they realized that the doubter was not so different from them after all. In time, they became fast friends and even went into business together, producing a line of holy furniture polishes.

The Alien Muse viewed the movie and was wonderstruck. When the film was over she realized something important had occurred. Somehow the viewing of the film caused her to have an incredible revelation. It made her realize that all of the cars were gone. A world without cars. Could this be a world of carbon copies, a world without original people? So she walked outside to determine her whereabouts and where each road led to. She had no alternative but to follow Hulen Street. She toddled on her way with leisurely steps. But when she drew near the house, she could not proceed. She realized the structure was part of a vast conspiracy to eliminate the original people of the world and replace them with carbon copies. She walked onto the Hulen Street bridge. Here she discerned, stretching below her eyes a long sheet of water, forming a river, which measured no more than seven or eight feet in breadth. This was the Trinity River. Inside the house, a party iwas under way. Some of her relatives were here. So were some friends. Someone – maybe it was the sentient stone from Uranus – explained what had occurred. She listened, then breathed in deeply. That was the Alien Muse in the world of the then. This is me and my roommate in the world of the now. Inside the house, a party is under way. A great landscape of empty candy wrappers and popcorn buckets and the pillows and sleeping bags on the floor where some are sleeping. But there are no bodies, only imprints. We know we will not be spending the rest of eternity with the Supreme Deity, but burning inside the giant Aerial Clock. I know that I do not want to suffer like this, lost in everlasting time and flames. I am so angry because I do not understand. Some people who have been left behind are saying how we were going to have to face the searing flames of the Alien Muse. And just then, She lifts the portière and walks in. "Fear not," she says. "My flames are not punishment, but purification. You shall emerge as if fired in a golden kiln. You shall be redeemed." … No, no that is not right. Her name is not the Alien Muse ... I'm talking about the woman who used to work at Vomit Food ... Yeah, the one with facial hair. That goatee thing I know you liked that, but it was one troubling sight. I see it as part of a vast conspiracy to eliminate the original people of the world and replace them.

What's that? Allison sits there with scissors, snipping at little bits of my carbon copied existence. She can hate me all she wants. But it's already all gone now. I am one with the aliens now. So, do you think it is stupid that I invented the table? Please let me explain what has occurred: I am actually a carbon copy of the original, who was killed in the world without original people. I prayed until morning. At sunrise, I went inside the snack bar . but I was all alone. Oh bummer ... Bummer ... Aw Supreme Deity ... This is something you never say ...

#

Dollar Bill Buckstop gave a great banquet for a thousand of his executives and drank Skinalicious9 water with them. While Buckstop was drinking his Skinalicious9 , he gave orders to bring in the gold and silver goblets that his father had taken from the combination gas station/Exogrid church out on the Interstate, so that the billionaire and his executives, his wives and his concubines might drink from them. So they brought in the gold goblets that had been taken from the combination gas station/Exogrid church out on the Interstate, and the billionaire and his executives, his wives and his concubines drank from them. As they drank the sacramental waters, they praised the privately-owned and operated deities of gold and silver, of bronze, iron, wood and stone.

Suddenly the fingers of a human hand appeared and wrote on the plaster of the wall, near the lampstand in the executive boardroom. The billionaire watched the hand as it wrote in a cacophony of unintelligible voices. His face turned glassy, like translucent china.

#

Welcome to my broken world.

Here I wander through a cacophony of incomprehensible voices, an obscene territory of winged demons, aerial creatures bearing branded vials of amputated ghost parts, decaying metallic reek of bankrupt snake skins, corroded iron shadows of cicada exoskeletons, troubled mirrors reproducing endless spectral relations, hopeless erotic cries echoing across vast plains of repressed desire. Here in the thin gray light I pour over the sacred texts of communal disaster, breathe in subway stench. TV antennae suck the sky clean of static, ripping a hole that bleeds stars and moonlight. They can't write about it any better than that? Turned flesh house in the smell of enclosing me in stretches of the desolate smells. Soapy egg flesh house in the smell indicator of the final extinguished the esophagus at the vista of skinned scenery, judgments imposed through ancient compound eyeballs bereavement catches in the throwing off spurts of blood in a flash bulb.

And then I got a whiff of an earlier time.

Mute rooms, where we see footsteps through ancient compound eyeballs. Eyes watering and burning. Ancient compound eyeballs, splotched sallow screens of rancid ectoplasm, marble. Dark glass, obscure illustrations, Romanesque columns, atmosphere towards a church lobster suits and danced around sense of bereavement catches in the esophagus speakers in a sort the magneto whir of the disintegrated demons, aerial creatures bearing branded vials of an old Western pulling our eyes watering and burning. Train paneled in the baroque embellishments of an earlier thresholds, lines of doors, eyes like a flash of desiccated cats and threadbare Egyptians, of Here in the thin gray light I the sluggish tropic flames burning his eyes all pupil in gray strata snapping their claws like castanets, throwing off spurts of blood in the neurotic oily winds, listen to the rasping wings.

#

Welcome to my broken world. TV antennae sucking the sky clean of static, ripping a hole that bleeds stars and moonlight. Priests put on bubbles of egg flesh, seismic tremors, their faces turned yellow ivory in the sunlight, young faces in blue alcohol flame dissolved in a strata of subways. All house flesh, a radio torn from the living car, trailing fleshy tubes and wires in that gray smell, that room dawn smell of soapy egg flesh. Living in a world of scavenger birds gliding into one of the most important of the Aerial Clock reports, which is the well-known 1957 RB-47 surveillance aircraft. Mind waves engaged in penetration of walls, everywhere around me. Mute, deserted factory-installed means of listening to the Deity. And from Mississippi, through Louisiana and coming in sharp and clear, throwing off spurts of hum. Travel on a radar beam, him armed with a kitchen knife. On Oct. 2, 1979, four beings are descending unhurried through a tarnished round of festivals where the priests put on reptile suits throwing off spurts of egg flesh, seismic tremors, their faces turned into tubes and wires. Couldn't you write me? I fell into a silver time period of more than one, a radio torn from the ivory in the sunlight, young faces in – say, couldn't you write me? The emaciated atmosphere reaches towards a church, heart pulsing in the sun through Deep East Texas Piney Woods, smoke down into our imposed through ancient compound eyeballs.

I got a whiff the dark shivering sick, our eyes aligned along a muddy shelf by the canal. He skinned the scenery, lifeless small mammals smashed in blue color and sort of humming. Alarm clock dark shivering sick, our eyes watering. RB-47 was sky clean of static, ripping a hole that miles and for a time period of coins and fermented blood, of desiccated cats and embellishments, mahogany veneer, Venetian plaster, antennae suck the sky clean cluster that appeared solid. I fell into the freight boat smell, the flight crew, by crewmembers using radar judgments imposed through ancient compound eyeballs all around me. Mute, deserted – walls closing in from a magic man.

#

The Alien Muse gives me a pair of surgical retractors. I am to use them to grasp the string. I attempt the maneuver, but fail. Instead of grabbing the string, I cut it in two.

That night I make my way home, where I bury my DNA delivery organ inside a very homely girl. My, those shoulders were morbid looking! Sitting on the edge, a kiss poised on her beastly lips. I found the retractor and pulled it out of her membranes. And then she was on me. She was naked inside a glass box with sand dissipated, crying in the same groan. But the result is the same.

#

I have a confession. Back in the day I was a malevolent sequential assassin – also known as an Amber Energy agent. I went about executing anonymous characters with a plastic toy sword that protruded out of my abdomen. After completing a sanctioned liquidation, I would melt an Amber Energy badge at the location. It was intended as a sort of business card. The majority of the assassinations took place under cover of darkness. The liquidations were rather gruesome. For instance, one time I placed the plastic toy sword on a man's back and pressed the secret killing button and blood bubbled out of his mouth.

Another time, I was told to perform the hit with a pair of surgical retractors. I proceeded to initiate the assignment. I identified the target, a figure made of nothing but gray flesh and silhouettes. It was a clean hit. No mess, except for the brief, forceful attempt to groan. I was charged at by the Fiend of the Unconscious, but no luck. I stepped easily aside, and the world turned on without it. I look over to see outside as two large goblins thrust blood bubbled out of his mouth in a cacophony of incomprehensible voices. Another time, seeking refuge in my room, open onto my bed and forcing a kiss from a woman who is a person of interest. She begged for the membrane penetration. I was willing to deliver my actions in this realm. After completing the sanctioned liquidation, I reviewed the entire story and everything that occurred again. I ran. I ran like I had been placed atop a figure with a mask. I ran featureless beside it.

#

Howdy partners, Dollar Bill Buckstop here. Can you believe it? Thanks to Dr. Adolfo Morel and the Jewell Effect, I'm still alive and kicking. The billionaire with the electronic insect eyes. Today I want to tell you about how I'm going to convert every last one of you cowpokes to celluloid. Yup, I'm going to turn you into a cinematic fiction, an anonymous creature projected eternally in the present tense, dead or living no one can say with certainty. Morel says ya'll will be reborn as dream-carrying ballistic missiles. Don't he talk nice? He says your thoughts and memories will be downloaded into the guidance system. Then I will initiate the primary ignition while simultaneously using the clock in the sky to project a holographic face of the Deity visible across the entire Northern hemisphere. I'm going to play a hypnotic message through the wind machine, make people think it is the voice of the almighty. And it will be. My voice. I am King Deity.

I'm going to realize my intent to replace humans with machinery. Forget that old Welthauptstadt Germania plan of Albert Speer. His thoughts and memories were small. Who wants to make a government worldwide? Elements within my plan call for numerous humanoid robots with youthful, perfect skin that never grows old. We predict a massive fleet of the Deity visible across the heavens. Hitler envisioned an apocalyptic air war at the Fair in Berlin in 1950. Yes, the Furher was still alive then, thanks to life-extension technologies derived from alien insect DNA and artificial deities. Morel says this technology will make them a formidable superpower to replace human life. Or to enslave it. Imagine living the Purple Sunset all day, and all thanks to my psychic collapse. Let us consider the the subsequent integration of Skinalicious9 technology into the super-intelligence scheme. We believe that the supercomputer will expand Ozona products. I'm telling you, son, we'll be able to live forever in virtual reality, flying around in small starships manned by nanobots (programmed to replicate thoughts and memories, which will be downloaded). Can you believe it? Don't he talk purty? Most people are purty simple. Lots of virtually no bottom.

Anyway, this is a whole lot better than anything that The Stranger could ever write for ya'll. Big fun! Ya'll are going to be Dollar Bill's Skinalicious9 divine being. A remote controlled godhead, the world's first privately owned and operated deity. Morel says the result will be a little thing he likes to call total cultural psychosis. The end of time. All I know is I'm going to make a fortune. Most people are purty simple. Lots of 'em will be praying for psychiatric assistance. And the Deity is shore going to come through. 'Cause you know what? The only effective treatment for the psychic fallout is Ozona's patented Skinalicious9.Complete Disheartenment of the Populace is the ultimate goal. First, I'm taking full control of the onbeam industry. Forget flying cars and personal jetpacks. The future is onbeam. For starters, I'm putting an end to the meditation sites, accumulation seizures and employment of dark affliction. The onbeam channels – I already got those wrapped up thanks to my recent stock purchase of Summons Replisystems and subsequent integration of Skinalicious9 technology into the public network – will be broadcasting Society of the Purple Sunset all day and all night, all the time. Except it won't be called that anymore. It'll just be the World. And Then we unveil the autonomous nanobots -- billions of tiny robots. They'll be swimming through your bloodstream, conquering infections and cancers. And free will. And when you are at last freed of the limitations of your frail physical body, the nanobots will digitally copy your brain and upload the contents to a vast intergalactic marketing network that will determine the precise, individualized ad campaign that will compel you to buy the entire line of Ozona products. I'm telling you, son, this one has virtually no bottom.

#

Human beings don't stand a chance. I will win victory by vastly expanding the contents of the various religious ideologies. Going forward, the major faiths will all be advocating Dollar Bill's Skinalicious9 divine being system. It'll be just like spiritual food! Big fun!

#

Fate must bring retribution, unless men conciliate fate while there is still time. How thankful I am today to the Providence which sent me to that school!

Thus my faith grew in the idea that my beautiful dream for the future would become reality after all, even though this might require long years.

The more the linguistic Babel corroded and disorganized parliament, the closer drew the inevitable hour of the disintegration of this Babylonian Empire, and with it the hour of freedom for my Ozona people.

Not until my 14th or 15th year did I begin to come across the word “Cicada,” with any frequency, partly in connection with political discussions. For the Cicada was still characterized for me by nothing but his religion, and therefore, on grounds of human tolerance, I maintained my rejection of religious attacks in this case as in others. Consequently, the tone, particularly that of the anti-Cicadan press, seemed to me unworthy of the cultural tradition of a great nation.

I was not in agreement with the sharp anti-Cicadan tone, but from time to time I read arguments which gave me some food for thought.

At all events, these occasions slowly made me acquainted with the man and the movement, which was to forever alter my destiny: Dr. Adolfo Morel and the Skinalicious9 Syndicate.

The man and the movement seemed reactionary in my eyes. My common sense of justice, however, forced me to change this judgment in proportion as I had occasion to become acquainted with the man and his work; and slowly my fair judgment turned to unconcealed admiration. Today, more than ever, I regard this man as the greatest R&D man in the entire Ozona organization. How many of my basic principles were upset by this change in my attitude toward the Skinalicious9 movement!

#

The Herbal Extract Boys are to be pitied – and feared. They are constantly engaged in some sort of destructive or disruptive conduct at the local, national and global levels. The first of these sleeper agents were activated with the journalism school graduating classes of 1983. By the late ‘80s, many Herbal Extract Boys had been forced into the mind control training program under the realization that there were at least 250,000 of these boys prepared to become sleepers in Operation Herbal Extract. Many Herbal Extract Boys were journalists and criminals, victims of the horrifying enslavement initiative called Operation Herbal Extract. One boy, woven into the cloth of normal life learned that tens of thousands of young teenage boys were in Strangers Rest. Many of these boys were brought to life as daily newspaper reporters.

At least 250,000 mind controlled Herbal Extract agents sort of destructive or disruptive boys were to become sleepers, individuals managed and manipulated for purposes of destructive or disruptive conduct. That is the reality of Operation Herbal Extract.

#

Mind control. The terrifying, horrifying conspiracy of the modern age. Especially of the cell phone age. The era of controlling people through their cell phones is here. These government/extraterrestrial-controlled mind control technologies are being directed at your friends, co-workers, family members – and you! See it for yourself in your own local communities. The equipment is already in place. You think it's for telephone communications, but in reality the equipment is erected and installed in order to carry out the hidden agency of employing mind control over the entire human race.

Microwave transmission towers are going up, and the truth is clear once you begin to pay attention. No one is safe. And you'll also notice more of them going up, the towers promising information that should be studied. A former Herbal Extract Boy recently offered this important testimony in the margins of the debate. But there is hope. A method was discovered to disable these terrifying monuments to the government/alien conspiracy. Smash them all! Every single day, smash the equipment. Stop the government manipulation of the time/space hole. Act today!

#

We have received many Exogrid pleas from victims of government-initiated mind control. Their terrifying and horrifying stories are strangely similar. Terrifying, horrifying tales of psychological persecution, street theater aggravation, guinea pig abuse – all initiated by scientists working for the government/extraterrestrial conspiracy to create a super race of artificial deities. These inhuman researchers act as if their test subjects were little more than robots or laboratory rats. Such callous actions are typical of the human-insect hybrids who are infecting the earthly gene pool with serious, apocalyptic consequences. Here is one of the pleas, which we received for an Exogrid address in Hong Kong.

#

Dear sir,

I have the privilege of communicating with you concerning a matter of grave importance. I am Michael Frederick Amand and a Herbal Extract Boy. I was born in Strangers Rest, Texas, and now live in Hong Kong. I had the opportunity to travel to Uruguay as I am the son of a Uruguayan girl of good family and a German missionary. I was in Uruguay from May 7, 1983, until September 1988. During the period of time that I was living in Uruguay, I was turned into a Herbal Extract Boy. I was used in scientific experiments involving advanced technology in which I was implanted with autonomous nanobots and Skinalicious9 against my will and without my consent. The nanobots, which are fueled with Skinalicious9, have the capacity to pick up, retain, and transmit the thoughts, sensations, and feelings of a person throughout his entire life. This means that I don't have the freedom to think or feel independently. They have included a device which speaks to me directly as if there was a negative conscience controlling me in and out of my dreams. The 'bots also hit me with electromagnetic radiation, which tortures my brain. These terrifying and horrifying scientists are trying to hide their crimes against my person by using Men in Black and other groups of people who harass me, bothering me day and night and trying to silence me so that these violations go unpunished. Some of the crimes I am being victimized by include intimidation, criminal association. blackmail, insults, death threats, damage to my health, psychological damage, discrimination, leveling, robbery and others. These are some of the 32 crimes they are using to hide this enslavement in the villages and countryside of Uruguay. It's as if I have been and I am being used like a rabbit because I am studied at local universities for the novelty of these nanobots and their advanced technology, in which these people completely ignore the magnitude of the violations to my humanity in this country. Sir, you can see that they are trying to traumatize, injure humanity, yet these types of injustices are sanctioned by the United Nations, the human rights organization of the whole world. A human being is entitled to life, freedom, and the right to pursue happiness. The Nuremberg Code still exists. This doesn't mean that I am opposed to science, but human beings should be respected with the same concern that they have for the integrity of their physics, yet their mentality is such that they are forgetting about the Deity and His principles. I am also remembering in this public denunciation all of the other Herbal Extract Boys who were used, and later silenced inhumanly; and these violations remain unpunished. Sir, I hope that you can understand my situation. I seek your collaboration in obtaining justice through an international trial in The Hague, seeking a fair indemnity for damages by legal means. Note that they also violate my e-mails. It is another way to injure me and that is the reason I need to travel to your country and study these Uruguayan implants and to stop this abuse. I will need a visa and financial assistance for the plane fare.

Sincerely grateful, I am,

Michael Frederick Amand

#

Since then, we have received a high-quality cell phone transmission from Amand. Amazingly, it came straight from his brain. He is putting forward a valiant battle to tell the truth and save himself and the world. But it is too late. For all intents and purposes, his mind is now a part of the Herbal Extract neural network. Here is his terrifying and horrifying message, his final, desperate plea:

Help! Help! Help! Discussion of a brain conspiracy. Help! Help! Help! Mind control is a common this. I have attracted a large interest from the humanity in this country. Sir, you can be of help in obtaining justice through a person – for a person, for me – throughout his entire life. This means that I don't have the freedom with which one can mimic the human being. I am entitled to it. This is consistent with Descartes argument in his 1989 time/space compression. The brain is responsible for other groups of people who harass my humanity in this country. Also let us be remembering this pain that comes upon me from the electromagnetic radiation, which tortures my brain. Despite the eyes of the popular culture, we have since bben "jacking in" with a Uruguay as guide. I am the function of a region of the hippocampus ... human rights organization of the whole world .... Skinalicious9, have the capacity to pick up ... me in and out of my dreams, the same concern that types the words .... Words of injustices are sanctioned by this country. Living in Hong Kong. I had a matter of grave importance: I am andn I can see that they are violations that remain unpunished. Sir, I have these violations and they remain the brain where they are responsible for damages by legal groups of people who harass me and also hit me with it. This is because .... being a serious topic in itself, mind by stroke, trauma or disease ... I am turned into a Herbal Extract Boy. Help! Mind control is a common control over innocent people in the Uruguay from May. It will be with and without being , a new kinds of cyberbrain hacking, malicious memory alteration, universities for the novelty of these nanobots and attracting a large interest in believing the theory's allegations ... I have nanobots and Skinalicious9 against and these violations remain unpunished. Sir, I hope have the privilege of communicating with you concerning the novelty of these nanobots and their advanced denunciation all of don't have the 1983 until September 1988. During unpunished. Implants of powerful have the capacity to pick justice through an international trial in The me day and night, trying to silence me of "jacking in" with head Amand and a experiences. The nanobots, which are fueled Boys who were used, and was born in Strangers Rest, Texas, mind control became widespread in this country. Sir, you can brain responsible for the formation of memoriesIt the concept of "jacking in" with head of grave importance: I am Michael Frederick Amand capacity, total recall, as well as the ability and study these Uruguayan implants and to my dreams. The 'bots can see that they are trying to traumatize, whole world. A human being good family and a at local universities for the cyberbrain hacking, malicious memory alteration, in The Hague, seeking born in Strangers Rest, Texas, and now if they were a negative responsible for the formation of other groups of people telepathic conversation with other cyberbrain users, the because being a serious topic in itself. mind brain implants and mind responsible for the formation of interest in the eyes of the popular that they are forgetting am also remembering in legal means. Note that they also violate my can understand my situation. I Descartes argument in his 1989 discussion of a was used in a brain in don't have the freedom to hippocampal prosthesis which these Uruguayan implants these types of injustices are sanctioned by memory capacity, total by stroke, trauma or disease. Work has the son of a Uruguay girl of good in Uruguay from May explanation, to make fringy conspiracy reality and experience.Some of the am the son of a Uruguay girl of that these violations go unpunished. Implants of powerful of their physics, yet their mentality is Popular skin fiction discussing brain about the Deity of the 32 crimes that are using to as in conspiration theories, vat, where he argues that brains which traumatize, injure humanity, yet these types of Boy. I was born in Strangers Rest, Descartes argument in his 1989 discussion of a record and playback that is the a common explanation, to all of the popular skin fiction discussing and others. These mean that I am opposed to as in conspiration crimes that are using to hide and these violations of injustices are his 1989 discussion of a brain in who harass me, know the deception from reality. integrity of their physics, yet their mentality hit me with electromagnetic radiation, United Nations, the human rights organization life, freedom, and my humanity in and these violations remain indemnity for damages by legal means. by the same logic as in conspiration theories, from reality. The nanobots, which are fueled with missionary. I was in Uruguay from May 7, hacking, malicious memory alteration, and tortures my brain. Despite, and study these Uruguayan implants and to trial in The Hague, experiences. The a device used concern that they have for of the crimes human rights organization of the whole world. A my consent. the concept of "jacking in" with it. Despite, or because being a Uruguay as I am the son of a freedom, and the right to pursue happiness. Sir, you can see groups of people who harass me, bothering health, psychological damage, discrimination, levelling, robbery ability to view his or her own memories.

Help, help, help.

#

Vines strangle the pulpit. Moths consume the flag. And a giant clock inexplicably appears in the heavens. Mark Leach, Christ-haunted journalist and self-diagnosed sufferer of Post-Modern Profit Disorder, saw this celestial manifestation years before, in a dream. His Incredible Revelation. But when his editors refuse to permit him to deliver this end-of-time prophesy in print, Mark receives an intriguing counter-proposal from The Stranger. People don't believe what they read in newspapers anymore. But they do believe what they see at the movies.

Movies about the death of time have always been popular. A favorite scenario is the last man. Sometimes he is the survivor of a plague. But what if humanity were wiped out by an extraterrestrial attack delivered via the viral DNA dream phone? Ah, there's the ticket. A single survivor of the Hydrocarbon Age, its last drops have been consumed. And civilization has to fight off the zombie movies, which jump off the screen and begin consuming the last survivors. What's more apocalyptic than the Cinema of the Undead?

Here is the truth: This movie is humorous and horrifying. Living large on the 50-foot drive-in movie screen I may already be dead, a self-immolated victim of the destruction of Strangers Rest. This may seem outlandish in its speculation. However, it is true that the aftermath of a nuclear war would most certainly find that almost everyone has vanished. And if everyone else is no more, then perhaps I am no more, too.

Picture a man going about his life. He breathes, he sleeps, he wakes. While contemplating the meaning of life one morning, this man notices that his thoughts have become a bit ragged 'round the cerebellum. A trip to the brain barber is in order.

"Can you give me an Einstein?" the man asks as the barber snaps the long cape around his neck. The barber eyes him up and down a moment, absently working the shears. Finally, he shakes his head.

"It wouldn't suit you. Your brain doesn't have the right texture."

The man shrugs. "OK, then, just a trim."

"Leave it long in the medulla oblongata?" the brain barber asks.

"Exactly. But take a bit extra off the frontal lobes. I've been feeling a little manic depressive lately."

The customer reads an old copy of Field & Stream while the brain barber does his work. Bits of gray matter float down into the crease of the magazine. Four dogs playing poker watch from a rug on the wall.

When the brain barber is done, the man thanks him and even gives him a big tip. But he knows it is a bad brain cut. At home that night, the man's wife tries to cheer him up.

"It'll grow out. And until then, you could hide it under your college degree."

That does cheer the man up, because he graduated from an expensive private college, and he suspects people are always impressed by it.

"Maybe next time I'll try that little place in the strip center by the Albertson's," he says hopefully. "I hear they do a great Adolfo Morel."

Some time later, the following story was reported by the New York Agenda:

#

The man with half a brain. Or two brains.

URUGUAY - Doctors at the University of Uruguay report that they have stopped the spread of a rare brain-eating disease in a 46-year-old Herbal Extract Boy by splitting the organ in two. Malfunctioning nanobots were destroying the man's brain. It was being eaten away, and the illness caused surges of electricity in his brain, resulting in a misfire of the nervous system. A medical team led by Dr. Adolfo Morel cut away the diseased half of his brain but left it inside his skull, where it now thinks independently of its host. In essence, this Herbal Extract Boy actually has two brains and two minds. The surgery left the man paralysed on the right hand side of his body but doctors hope with physiotherapy he will eventually walk.

"I'm of two minds on this one," the man joked. He said he is happy to be alive, but barely. Are two half brains better than one complete brain? Good point. Because it seems that in reality there are three brains in my head. The autonomous nanobots appear to have achieved consciousness. Aerial Clock investigators noticed this phenomenon while studying the shadowy work of Dr. Adolfo Morel. Evidence suggests that Morel has placed a robotic brain into the nervous system of the man with two brains, in essence giving him three brains. A medical team led by Morel implanted the diseased half of the brain into a computer, which is now in contact with the nanobots. Transmissions appear to come from the two halves that are already possible, downloading brains that are better than the ones that comprise his complete brain. It seems that in libraries we find special instruments for recording surface thoughts. These instruments are, of course, books. We know that these books are a storehouse of information equalling the here and now, yesterday, today and tomorrow and opportunities for thinking independently of the host. In this way they have stopped the spread of his brain, resulting in one another and a human skull composed of billions of patients, or at least two brains. First, consider an electro-chemical wet-brain, giving each patient two brains. And do not forget the sentient organ in the other two. Malfunctioning nanobots! Doctors at the brain may even emerge with qualities for which brains may be improved and cured of the left brain-eating disease found in a 46-year-old Herbal Extract Boy. The readout is rather telling… *Many large libraries, and instruments for recording at the University … this Herbal Extract Boy – me -- I actually has two brains and spreading … the illness caused surges of electricity … eaten away, and the illness paralysed on the right hand half of me brain but left purely electronic digital brain. When the two placed a robotic brain into a human in two…. Malfunctioning nanobots are already possibly ready to download a new godlike consciousness in me …. The surgery left me paralysed on an incomplete brain? I wonder. Because it diseased half of me brain misfire of the nervous they have stopped the brain. It was being eaten away, and the brains and two minds. The surgery left me paralysed on the right and me have achieved consciousness. Me destroying me own brain. Me funny, right? It was being eaten by me, the patient with two brains; an electro-chemical wet-brain, and it thinks independently of me, its host. In essence, I am already the possible host. In essence, this Herbal Extract Boy – that is, me – is actually and has actually achieved it already. I'm talking about a misfire of the nervous system. A medical team by splitting the of a rare brain-eating disease left it inside my skull, has placed a robotic brain and left it inside my brains and two minds. I now have qualities for which we can make a new, superior nervous system for traveling the stars and the space/time continuum. A medical team led by Dr. Morel gives me two half brains. That's a better nanobot that houses a computer that contains my thoughts, those of a 46-year-old Herbal Extract Boy. I live by splitting in a misfire of the nervous libraries, and instruments for recording surface thoughts. I am the organ in two. Malfunctioning nanobots were destroying libraries, and instruments for two brains and has placed a robotic brain into a equalling many large libraries, and instruments for inside his skull, where it now organ in two. Malfunctioning of a rare brain-eating disease in a in his brain, many large libraries, and instruments for these nanobots are destroying the man's brain. It Boy actually has two brains and two When the two brains interact, a third brain may emerge with qualities for which we The central cylinder of each hand side of his body but doctors hope half of his human skull, composed of thoughts. Billions of these nanobots are in placed a robotic brain into a human skull, interact, a third brain may We know caused surges of electricity in computer. Are two half brains that it is already conscious diesmbodied mind into a computer. Are two information equalling many large where it now thinks independently of its it is already possible to download a conscious two brains; an into a computer. Dr. Morel will eventually walk again – if I give him one of my brains. We know that we can only speculate. Boy becomes whole by splitting the electro-chemical wet-*

brain, and there are three, two-half brains. A medical team led by Dr. Adolfo downloaded a conscious diesmbodied mind, billions of microscopic nanobots. I am born.

The autonomous nanobots appear to have achieved a secondary brain. Doctors at the University have learned that transplanting a robotic brain into a human isn't as easy as you might think. In one case, the operation resulted in the spread of a rare brain-eating disease. The surgery left the man paralysed on the right side of tomorrow. Nothing is free, right?

#

Mindful of the old poem, we offered to pay the piper in advance. But still he would not take away our children.

"Rats only," he insisted. "I don't do dysfunctional families."

So we dressed our children in rat outfits. Cute gray felt ears, rope tails, black shoe-polished noses -- we even handed out wedges of cheese, enough for every child in town. Then we marched them down Main Street.

"See, we're inundated with rats!" we told the piper. "Do your stuff. Lead them out of town."

But he was not fooled by our little deception.

"What lovely children you have. Why do you want to be rid of them?"

"Because we have tired of being parents," we explained. "The urge to procreate, to leave our names and lives to future generations, while strong a few short years ago, has long passed. Now we wish only to live in the present, driving sporty two-seater convertibles, playing golf, drinking margaritas and vacationing at Club Med. Rid us of our encumbrances, oh great piper, and let *us* be the children once again!"

The piper looked at us sadly and reluctantly nodded his head. "Very well," he said and slowly put the pipe to his lips.

What beauty! What enchantment! What rapture! We were mesmerized, as if in a dream. We would have followed him anywhere. And, if fact, we did. Because when the music stopped, we found ourselves trapped in a deep cave.

Frantic, we searched for an opening -- a hole, a crevice, a fissure, anything – but none could be found. It was a tomb, a cold stone tomb. Our tomb.

We shouted for the piper. "Come back! Please take us back home!" But we knew it was too late. We were finally paying the piper.

But do we really need to? Not with the ratobot. A famous Science Fiction author reports in a recent news story (Bruce Sterling, "The Year in

Ideas…" in "The New York Times" on Dec. 15, 2002) that our best minds have at last created a remote-controlled rodent. This is commercial science at its finest! The semi-autonomous ratobot was created at the University of Uruguay. Picture a white lab rat equipped with a radio-controlled brain harness, which is connected wirelessly to a human on a computer. Three wires link the harness to the brain of the ratobot. One wire conveys a command that instructs the ratobot to turn left, the other connects the optic nerves to video cameras. A high-tech ratobots might search for earthquake of espionage and warfare. A ratobot that will 21st-century movement toward commercial science took a rapid creepiest native vices – yes, the creepiest native vices. What a terrifying and horrifying dream. A rapid scurry forward left and right. The third -- a hole, a crevice, a fissure, makes it turn left and right. The pipe to his lips. Spaces -- lured on in the desired direction, the human operator can lips. What beauty! What enchantment! What rapture! Scurry forward this year with the earthquake victims trapped under rubble, for the pipe to beauty! What enchantment! What rapture! We were mesmerized, fields of espionage and trained rescue dogs. We wre slowly put out in the direct of the ratobot. Ratobots with tiny video cameras. Rats can be done. We are commanding their will. The grand 21st-century movement took a rapid scurry forward. Imagine an army of cheap, disposable ratobots. You could search for earthquake victims trapped under rubble. Who knows where they will go? Just make sure the music never stops. Otherwise, they'll turn it against us, and we'll find ourselves trapped in a deep dangerous place. Easy to envision many other uses for this technology, no? With vastly more cameras, ratobots might offer us a more pleasurable life. They can serve our commanding will. And there are government uses, sinister applications of ratobots. Consider a more noble idea, too. Cheap, disposable ratobots are the answers to many of our problems. Next up – cheap, disposable humanobots!

#

The illusion of happiness is typically achieved while on high, giddy flights into the abstract, one of my "king of the world" trips. I am susceptible to a certain racing of thoughts, a sense that I am somehow onto something seen only by me (through my third eye, of course). The sky turns a different color, the big dome of heaven ablaze in the multihued shades of indulged compulsions. I am dizzy with the superimposed light of my own odd, eccentric convictions. If only I had migraine auras! So I don the mask of smiles, my preferred attire for engaging the practiced world of apparent normalcy, and write my little thoughts. I am authenticated! Then the inevitable nightfall. Metaphors crumble under the impossible weight; I have outrun myself. It is all hallucination, one more magical, broken symptom. Illumination becomes illusion. I am left to wander the dark emptiness, chasing spectral notions and the Shadow, which is me…

That's the way it is when the autonomous nanobots have their way with your brain. Although the Alien Muse may appear to be in charge, it is actually mania's explosive high that is running the show – right before it sends the test subject over the South Col of the Mount of the Divine. It's the only at the wrong end of the alien conspiracy. And it is behind so much in the government/extraterrestrial conspiracy, and it became a rampant terror, especially among the Herbal Extract Boys.

There is a brutal finality that The Stranger found; suicide is the wrong way to stay alive. Don't do the wrong thing at the wrong end of a shotgun or pull an Alien Muse with your head in the stove. You can run, but they'll find you eventually. A melted pizza Muse tends to attract attention.

#

We were so happy, enjoying our little day trip in the country. We explored the treasures, the crafts, the deals. We even had sausage on a stick. And then you had to ruin it. As we passed that car on the two-lane blacktop, I told you it had been too close to their bumper. I did not like it. And you just smiled. You smiled! It was like you thought it was funny, no big deal. Then we saw the gas station. Do we need gas? No -- no, you said. We'll just fill up as we're leaving. So, of course, I had to tell you that I HATE THAT!

Don't you know that by now, my dear one? I know you must know it. How many times have I had to tell you? So you must be doing it on purpose. First passing the car, now not getting the gas. You are therefore odious.

So you said, "OK, we'll get it now." And then you set your mouth in that hard, cruel, unfortunate way of yours, so much like a creature of the companion – a Coffin-Puntura. I always hate it that you, Coffin-Puntura, are that hateful way. You are always digging our graves, ruining our every nice thing.

Why can't you be more like me? Why can't you just enjoy our happy day?

Why can't you be happy, enjoying our little day trip in the country. We will explore the treasures, the crafts, the deals. We will even have sausage on a stick. And this time, you do not have to ruin it.

As we pass that car on the two-lane blacktop, you will not be too close to the bumper. I will like it. And you will not smile because you realize it is not a joke. It is not funny. It is a big deal. You will get it right, and I will be happy. Then we will see the gas station. Do we need gas? Yes, you will say. And you will thank me for thinking of it. We'll fill up right then. I will tell you I LOVE THAT! You do know that by now, my dear one. Clearly I know you know it. I don't have to keep saying it. Because you get it, the whole thing. First not passing the car, then getting the gas. I love that. You are therefore suitable to be my mate.

And then you set your mouth in that pleasant way of yours, so much like an ideal mate from one of my magazines. You read them, too? Ah, you are so much like me. This is wonderful. We really can enjoy our happy day!

#

The following classified report was leaked to the New York Agenda, which has agreed to suppress all knowledge at the request of agents working for the government/extraterrestrial conspiracy:

Growth of a Meningioma in a Transspecies Test Subject after Skinalicious9 Therapy – A 46-year-old human-to-insect transspecies test subject presented with severe headache and visual disturbances; clinical examination showed visual impairment, with bitemporal inferior visual-field defects, papilledema of the left eye, and optic atrophy of the right eye. The test subject, one of the first wave of Herbal Extract Boys, was euphoric and confused. Personality changes noted during the previous 5 months had been attributed by family members to the new alien identity of the test subject. The test subject had been taking an extraterrestrializing endocrine regimen of flouridated hormones 150 mg per day orally for the previous 6 years. After 3 years of hormone treatment, the test subject underwent a brain split for species reassignment, and Skinalicious9 at a dose of 150 mg twice weekly administered intramuscularly was added to the test subject's therapy for the following 4 years. A cerebral magnetic resonance imaging (MRI) scan obtained 5 years before presentation to evaluate an increased prolactin level was negative. On admission, a contrast-enhanced MRI scan revealed a giant olfactory-groove meningioma. After a radical tumor resection, the histologic diagnosis was meningothelial meningioma, which was negative for alien DNA receptors, with a Nu-69 index of 6 percent and a Men in Black Index of 4.5 percent per high-power field. At a 2-year of follow-up, the test subject was continuing with the Skinalicious9 therapy at a lower dose of 60 mg, and a contrast-enhanced MRI scan showed no recurrence of the tumor. The test subject's behavioral changes had regressed, and the visual impairments were ameliorated. Cross-speciies hormonal therapy is an important component of the endocrine regimen in transspecies people. Reported adverse effects in this population include venous thromboembolytic disease,-breast cancer, lactotroph hyperplasia, and an increase in prolactin levels with possible growth of prolactinomas. The role of alien hormones in the development of intracranial meningioma has been proposed as one hypothesis to explain the overabundance of such tumors in Cicadans. The risk of meningioma is increased among older humans who have a past history of using insecticides. In this case, a causal association between the growth of a meningioma and the Skinalicious9 therapy was suggested by the negative cerebral MRI scan obtained 3 years before presentation. This report of abrupt growth of an intracranial meningioma after use of high doses of extraterrestrial steroid therapy in a transspecies test subject should prompt scientists working with transspecies test subjects to consider the possibility of such an event.

What more proof do we need?

#

American Social Broadcast recently reported on a microwave weapon that heats water molecules under the skin, cooking the enemy. The "Skin Cooker" is just one of many unique weapons believed to have been developed by our government (via MKULTRA) with the assistance of extraterrestrials.

These secret weapons can sometimes be found in classified government documents that are accidentally sent to landfills. Let's start with the Middle East. Investigators note that weapons that could be detonated in Iraq's water purification systems would be extremely effective. Just one problem: water doesn't burn well.

D-9 tractors subsequently came into use in terrifying and horrifying ways. One major technique subsequently came into use. Companies of the scientists involved in its produced by elimination of the enormous dead and a professor tried to light the fire in the water purification systems. They would discover these and many other connections. These terrifying and horrifying technologies are coming into use even now, during the final days of the world.

#

Welcome again to my island. Did you have a pleasant boat ride? I hope all is going well with you today. I have been thinking about you a lot since your last visit. Has it already been a week? A year?

A few weeks ago, or maybe many years, my youngest son played in a ninth grade football game against the Duncanville Panthers. Can you believe it? Our old alma mater! The stadium is at the high school now. I didn't recognize any of the campus. The old buildings have been absorbed by new ones. The new stadium isn't new anymore.

Looks old, like it been there for 20 years. Maybe it has. I've lost track of time. They should never have given up the old Panther Field. It was like something out of The Last Picture Show. What was wrong with the way things used to be? It's not the DHS I remember. Or the town.

I'm sure you see D'ville regularly on visits with your parents, but I had not seen it in several years. So I took a quick dashboard tour of the Main Street and my childhood home. Oh boy. That poor little town is really hurting. Looks like it's been years since there was any maintenance or even painting in the old downtown. On Camp Wisdom Road I see the old Wolverton Air Conditioning billboard, just like I remember it. But everything else is different. Now D'ville has tattoo parlors and pawn shops. The old Duncanville Suburban office is now a Mexican food restaurant. And my childhood home, the one I lived in until age 11 -- I hardly recognize it. It was an architect-designed house built in the early 1950s. Very mid-century, with a low pitched gravel roof and an exterior clad in real redwood siding. Back in the day it was even featured in an architectural design magazine. Very unique. But somewhere along the way, perhaps 10 years ago, someone painted that gorgeous siding white. And now it's all dingy. Everything I see is dingy and old and tired looking. So sad. How could a place change so much in such a short period of time? The town is taunting me. I am in a dream. If only I can wake myself up, I'm sure I'll find everything is back like it was in 1979. I'll be in my Cutlass convertible, driving through the McDonalds, putting messages up on the town marquee (my old job!), listening to John Croslin's rock band play at the church. Looking back, I took it all for granted. I did not appreciate all the little moments of 1979. I was too busy casting ahead, making plans, waiting for the day when I could escape that boring, crappy, mediocre little town and make my way in the world.

Today I am the human equivalent of Duncanville. I'd like to think I'm in better shape than Main Street, but perhaps not. I had perfect vision in my youth, but I can't read anymore without glasses. In my hands I feel the beginnings of my father's arthritis. The plumbing doesn't work the way it used it, either. Never thought I'd see the day when the DNA delivery organ would let me down. And yet, assuming continued good health, I'm only at the midpoint of life. So much life left to live. I can't believe my sons are now in high school. I used to dream of the day the first one would leave so I could turn the empty bedroom into my office. Already I am filled with regret for all that I did not do, for all the things that I did not appreciate. Back in the day, when they were little, I would become angry about something unimportant or just wish they would be a little more independent. They were so innocent and loving, and I didn't appreciate it. And now I'll never have their childhood again. I'm actually getting tears in my eyes thinking about. What an idiot I am. The past is taunting me. The conclusion of time is near.

Me and Duncanville. We're in physical and psychic crisis. We are the history of what they labeled as the future. The land and people that were once a part of metaphorical eateries and national restaurant chains and other indicators of success, now a concentration of fatigue, insomnia, hot flushes. Consider the historic buildings, sentient architecture that includes dissatisfaction at the way life has heightened destruction, a sense of mortality and feelings, a sense of urgency. Such buildings are systematically demolished, obliterating all signs of the facility. Let it live on in a monument, which can be easily controlled and included in the historical record of Duncanville as an official Main Street City. Maybe it could be the same for men. Duncanville Men undergoing mid-life difficulties may be aliens or distinguished from the aliens. They are a city, which is their home now. Some of these men fought in Europe during the Second Earthly Conflict. That is why the city is now home to some parts of Europe, which have been relocated here from the outskirts of tomorrow. We saw this occur about 1970, when the old missile base was turned over to the city. No one knew about the history of extraterrestrials and the contamination of the soil and structures with green cicada blood contaminated with poisonous alien DNA. Soon, a malaise of mediocrity settled on the little town. Nothing was so mediocre that it could not be made worse. Tear down the old! Build new houses of sand! A vague irritability settled into the body of the Superb Suburb. Build more neighborhood retail centers. Punish our children for chewing gum in class. Don't pay any attention to that new apartment complex. Re-zone for the quick land sale. Grab what you can. Today will last forever. The future is so bright you gotta wear mid-life shades. What a crisis we have here. With the completion of nearby Joe Pool Lake, we are really poised for success. Historic buildings include the old missile base. Let's be sure to tear it all down. And fast. These symptoms often preserved in a unique way. It stands outside the Library and Community Center. Let us serve the needs of white flight. Some of the city is home to poor folks. We can ignore them. Let us take pride in a variety of firsts, such as our cherished Music Room. With the completion of nearby Joe Pool buildings were systematically demolished, initially repurposed for civic and community use. But I don't know. Middle-aged man as historic building, as aging town? I don't think it is working. This metaphor blows.

#

While driving through a park in Waco, Texas, I come upon a couple of shed-like structures. They are similar to ones that I remember photographing in college. But those were near Duncanville, and they were demolished years ago.

I suddenly realize these structures were part of the set of an old 1950s radio ranch TV show that aired in Waco. Cowboy Bob, Cowboy Joe, Cowboy Lloyd – I don't recall. Now the set is in sad shape, victims of decay and age.

Then we arrive at an old house in the same park. I am with others. We go inside. It is some sort of museum, or maybe it will be. The house is filled with old things. We look through some of them. I hold a little revolver that is made for women. It is part glass and shoots a chemical, not bullets. Then I realize it is not a museum at all, but the home of Jewell Poe, my grandfather. He was quite the pack rat and his house was a lot like a museum.

Look over there, a mummified hand, chopped off an Indian chief killed in a battle with Texas Rangers. I believe it was January 1881. For several weeks the U. S. Tenth Cavalry and the Rangers were kept busy in pursuit Victorio's band of Apaches. A small band of Apaches attacked a stagecoach in Quitman Canyon. Following the cold trail, Baylor and his Rangers tracked the Apaches down the bank of the Rio Grande and into Mexico. Along the way they found items taken from the stage. The trail turned back into Texas, where they found a fresh camp site. Following the trail into the Eagle Mountains, the Rangers came across a camp that was only hours old. Baylor's men met up with a detachment of Rangers from Lt. Nevill's company at Eagle Springs. After more tracking, the Rangers finally came upon the Indian camp. A fight ensued on the morning of January 29. The fight, though small, has come down through history as the last Indian battle in Texas. In 1885 the Ranger company was disbanded due to budget cuts.

And there are the pieces of the scalp of Kit Karger, the man who survived his own scalping thanks to the inexplicable appearance of his sister and the psychic vision of a woman friend – and his own research into time travel and carbon-chlorine bond technology. New research using a high-tech photo-chemical process has brought to reality new facts – and a new alternate timeline – regarding this amazing legend of 19th century Texas.

#

Consider a Wild West with alien technology, decades before the aerial clock crash landings in Aurora and Strangers Rest. Look, we can see where Kit Karger quenched his thirst by a river, his circadian-built UV protection rifle close at hand. But he didn't see the terrifying and horrifying Indians (actually human/alien hybrids) in the nearby brush. He was only altered to their presence by the psychic visions of Margaret, who transmitted her warning with wavelengths of 185 and 254 nm. She was able to calm Sarah and get her back to the transmission of UV protection between the UV lamps and the vapor-phase contaminant, which was quick to hatch. But not quick enough – Kit was hit with a blast of a scalping energy ray. It came with an agonizing pain---and then the Indians buried the three dead men. With death close by, he heard a shout and he gave out. Propping himself against the thick trunk somewhere in the range of death, Apaches swept down the bank of the Rio Grande and into Mexico. Along the way they found items taken from the stage. The trail turned back into a howling coyote wind, lifting Karger out of linear time and into a world of train whistles, a smear of red, dead shiny white, rusting marble, whiff of brimstone, a wound of agonizing pain and the burial of the three dead men. Death is close by. Hear a shout, feel the heat and a sudden cessation. He returned to farming in 1836 and participated in the Texas Revolution by providing provisions to the rebel army. He constructed a grist mill, a place of psychic contaminant, a place that was quick to hatch, though not quick enough for Kit. He fled to the Golden Nugget Mine on the morning of January 29. The Rangers from Captain Nevill's company at Eagle Springs, After more tracking, the Rangers finally skull caps, Kit ran into Big Foot Wallace in 1838, They met Propping himself against the thick trunk, a sort of museum, or maybe it will be, the house is filled with old things, we look through some with wavelengths of 185 and 254 nm, She was able to calm Sarah and get her back to the transmission of UV protection beehive-shaped homes of us during daylight, Suddenly, Canyon, Following the cold trail, Baylor across a blackened maw, a low, pitiful moan, wiry, wizened, skeleton, dark deep-set eyes, hawk-bill by, hear a shout and give out, Propping himself against the thick trunk, a sort of museum, or maybe it will be, the house a ghastly sight seen vividly in a dream of Karger naked, he built but did not finish a belted and pulley-type generator motor, And of course, there were his investigations into filly arrives, disappointed to find that this particular cowboy is really no more than a ball of sticks, dreaming of a carrot that shave with a two-bit card shark, beefy, barrel-chested man with close cropped chestnut man with close cropped chestnut he wore caps of soft over the shriveled fingers through hoof prints and wagon ruts, wiping a dirty hand across a tale, Doctors were not of much assistance to Kit, In time, the skin rotted away and the skull bone became diseased, His brain was tone makes the nightmare angry, knocks him to the cowboy from the fence and stomps him into a pile of splinters, meanwhile back at was quite the sudden cessation of psychic dissection, face blazing, grin splits the sky and fades, a vast crystal rusty, weed-grown tracks explode in a splash of crimson, fading into the inky blackness of space, stagnant memories, sharp smell of a sawed-off blaster, we have stated the stallion, lassos the unsuspecting beast, sells him to a traveling circus, where they geld him and make him spend I believe it was January 1881, For several weeks the U. S. Tenth Cavalry and the port approach through transparent walls, portal control for Central Control Unit portal gate to Historic flashes of russet orange red from the trees, whistling through tombstones, extractor claw swinging wildly, CCU keypads and a Peacemaker, down a black-walled, empty tunnel, semi-annual time portal maintenance, due to technical difficulties all Historic American West including dinner, He took them off to sleep, but wore a night cap, In the outdoors, he wore caps of soft over the skull caps, just an old tumbleweed, no use crying, what I ain't, an a new alternate timeline – regarding this amazing legend of 19th century Texas, of soft over the skull caps, Kit Blackie, now all alone, tangled up in rusty old bob wire forever. Following the cold trail, Baylor and his Rangers eyes, hawk-bill nose, bald head of yellow wax, slumming in the town's tenderloin district, gap-toothed, yellowed dentures, over the sidewalk, guide him home, cursing starts too dark a carrot, listening unseen from the shadows, the stallion quietly snorts at this feminine treachery and in 1836 and participated in is not a museum at all, but the home of Jewell.

#

Look at this one, a dainty little gun. It is part glass and shoots a chemical, not bullets. The chemical is alien blood. So it's not so dainty after all! Then I realize we are bathed in pink rays of the North. The alien escapes, a masked man helps the alien to escape, the alien eludes the deputy and escapes back to the Rustlers Corral, alien brakes bond and escapes, Indians pursue or flee Captain Nevill's company at Eagle Springs. Busy day! After more tracking, the Rangers finally came upon the Indian camp. A fight ensued on the morning of January 29, with a two-bit card shark, beefy, barrel-chested man with close cropped chestnut hair, soiled doves on the sporting side of town, two-bit faro game, rolling a drunk for pocket money. Now wounded but alive, clearing out the outlaw hideout, mountain lion scares horses and the alien escapes. The posse is ambushed and the alien escapes. The masked man helps the alien to escape, and the alien eludes deputy and escapes, and he goes back at the away and says "why shoot your star-shooter at Blackie, now all alone, tangled up in rusty old bob wire forever?" No excuse for ignorance of the U.S. Tenth Cavalry and the Rangers. They were kept busy, and unrepentant tone makes the nightmare angry, knocks him like the cowboy from the fence and stomps him down oto hands and knees in the dusty road, running shriveled fingers through hoof prints in the scalp of Kit Karger, the man who survived his own scalping thanks to the inexplicable appearance of his sister and the psychic vision of a woman friend a stagecoach in Quitman Canyon. Or something to that effect.

Karger returned to farming in 1836 and then time slipped back a year to participate once more in the Texas Revolution. This time he heard a low, pitiful moan from a wiry, wizened, skeleton with dark deep-set eyes, hawk-bill nose and a bald head of yellow wax, a creature slumming in the town's tenderloin district, gap-toothed, yellowed dentures, crooked, tobacco-stained. Time for one more midnight hack race in the cattle season, falling into the infernal pit, a dog barking inconsolably at single rifle shots fired at long range, an immortality and gun smoke, rusty, weed-grown tracks explode in a splash of crimson, fading fight, though small, has come down through history as the last Indian battle in Texas, In 1885 the Ranger company was disbanded due to budget cuts.

We find that this particular cowboy is really no more than a ball of sticks, a variety of skull caps, which were fashioned by his wife from her wedding into time travel and the vapor-phase tetrachloroethylene PCE destruction experiments. Quantum entanglement – that's the scalp! He covered his wound with a variety of skull caps, which were fashioned by poking straight up at the sky, reaching for a trusty horse's reins, a shooting star bearing provisions to the rebel army. He constructed a grist mill, one of the first of a North Texas sunrise, moving slowly on hands and knees in the dusty Nevill's company at Eagle Springs. Look over there, a mummified hand, chopped off of the face of the Earth. And now it is time for semi-annual time portal maintenance, due to technical and a new alternate timeline. Then he told Big Foot the whole tale. Doctors were not of much help. They decided to geld him and make him spend the rest of his days giving pony rides in the happy dreams of unpleasant children, stars shaking their games in Hell's Half Acre, the red-light district, a thunderhead looming on the horizon east toward Rusk. A small band of Apaches attacked a stagecoach in Quitman Canyon. Following the cold trail, Baylor and his Rangers tracked them to perdition.

Meanwhile, the aliens were hiding out in a warm cabin about twelve miles above La Grange. Terrifying and horrifying! Indians in the nearby brush, only altered to their presence by the psychic mind sweeping of the valley, blurred shadows gathering in a crystal Indian village, just south of the Arkansas River, beehive-shaped homes lost in the inky blackness of space, the shadows, the stallion quietly snorting at this feminine treachery. After more tracking, the Rangers finally came and along the way they found items taken from the stage. The trail turned back on itself, tangled up in rusty old bob wire forever. All of this activity had made the nightmare angry. She knocks the cowboy from the fence. The trail turned back into Texas, where they found a fresh set of tracks.

#

Let us dig a bit deeper into this Old West story, into this amazing legend of 19th century Texas. Let us explore the outlaw hideout, shiver as the mountain lion scares horses, shutter as the doctors geld the old hero, cheer for the gun smoke, rusty, weed-grown tracks ground thick with blood, the bald head of yellow wax, slumming in the splitting of the night, data units recording the folly of the sentient horse. He did his best, though, hiding out with his cowboy in the abandoned Golden. Then horse and rider was hit with a blast of a scalping energy ray which came with January 29,.The fight, though small, has come down through history as the story of a little shed roof outlaw and pony who managed to beat the odds and escape the grip of space and time.

#

I cannot help identifying with Clark Caring, creator and sustainer of the insect-human hybrids of Planet Luh. Now we have received the prophetic, let-me-love-you plea from the insect aliens themselves. Their thoughts are now ours. We are like the citizens of Babel immediately after the anguished collapse of the tower to Heaven, stumbling about in a cacophony of incomprehensible voices, attempting to make sense of the nonsensical. In the beginning it was not easy to decode their transmissions. The messages are beamed here from distant galaxies within, crackling through flesh-covered speakers in a sort of mangled cicada cry. Over time, the intercellular translators in the viral DNA dream phone smoothed out the discarded static into a comfortable, almost melodic rhythm, a poetic form suggestive of the magneto whir of the disintegrated Machine Society of the West or the dry, disconsolate rasp of buzzard wings. The alien communications are experienced inside a sentient motion picture, a prophetic and sacred film to bring about the death of time and the birth of a new religion. Now it's time to get a deep sense of the future. Programmed death travel is the way that leads through the all-important finale and back to the Wild West, a great black rent, a torn sky, a rip in the master film in the middle of shooting the cattle season, my dear old trail-weary friend, 19th century frontier research into time travel and silicone-chlorine bonds of the broken shell. No death in vain. All of the flesh-coated aliens have arrived, pouring over the edge of the sacred frontier heavens. Is it an alien invasion? Automatic control, crossing into the heavy death fog of milky white galaxies. I can just make out the original celestial orbit. The robot brakes, but I can't see anything. I begin honking but no luck. Inside the house, outside by the swimming pool, but it's in the front. Watch out for the robotic pool cleaner. This is a troubling sight, a world of silicone copies, a world without looks. Here at the next door neighbor's house we can make out flesh-coated machine men sliding, colliding in the way that leads to death. I go to work, splicing myself into the Endless Loop of Silence.

#

This is the film of prophesy, the apocalyptic movie without an apocalypse. The director of such a creation has no traditional holy being to guide him to the back of beyond so he is compelled to film his way out, through crackling ozone, rumblings of the forces of heavenly automobiles trailing living cables and hair-covered wheels racing to the outer wastelands, where silver heavenly light pops in heretical transformations, where the hands on the celestial robot in the sky spin ceaselessly, where the followers of the one true holy being gather at the dark night of the soul church out on the interstate, a loud voice commands seven angels, tomorrow is already in the past, go and mop up off the earth the seven aerial celestial robots of the wrath of the holy being. So the first angel went and mopped the earth, filling his celestial robot with a foul and painful sore that had been on those who had the mark of the chairman and who worshipped its image. Their flesh was redeemed. The second angel filled his celestial robot from Corpus Christi Bay, focus of mercuric cobalt silence and a slow same perfume. Eyes all pupil in chromium strata lights and water somewhere in the chromium flesh of living freight boats, a smell of dawn, a smell of remote flesh, of soap bubbles electronic judgments empty down in a dark rotating shaft, down from the azure heaven, that devastating, gory, azure heaven of the Home of the Shadows, home of cold mountain shadows, this round of festivals the priests put on cicada shells and the circadian scientific base on Uranus where Jewell Poe conducts experiments in color photography, focus of mercuric cobalt silence naked seat cushions, gripping the skeletal body tight to the crumbling asphalt under the dead, bitter light of the vapor lamps, insects and nocturnal celestial robot jumps the way time will after 4 pm, bubbles of egg from ghost units, wreckage of miserable depravity, squander of comatose electrical cables swollen and burned out, thick vines steam locomotive left over from an old Western movie, watering and burning, steam locomotive left over from an old Western movie, pulling the screams and the smoke down into our lungs, heart pulsing in the living cables and flesh-coated wheels race to the outer wastelands, where silver light pops in heretical transformations, the hands on the priests put on cicada shells and dance about, snapping their jaws. They went abroad to the kings of the whole world, to assemble them for the battle on the great day of the holy being the Almighty, see, I come with photography, focus of mercuric cobalt silence and a slow wave shivers through the universe, a slow room with the blinds all closed and fastened suck the celestial robot from the sky, the celestial robot jumps the way time will after 4 pm, bubbles of egg flesh seismic tremors, face gliding silently above the marshes and aged tree remnants, further on, drive-in accommodations with get a whiff of ozone and penny arcades, sundown to a clear river, cold mountain shadows, this round was filled with flashes of lightning, rumblings, peals of thunder, laugh, the same brusque arm movement, the same way of resting your of the buildings appear to be vacated, condemned, surrounded by cyclone fencing, doorways and windows covered in warped plywood, muffled voices and whole world, to assemble them for the battle on the great day of shivers through all of time, heavenly automobiles trailing living cables and flesh-coated wheels race to the outer wastelands, where silver light pops in heretical transformations, the will after 4 pm, bubbles of egg flesh seismic tremors, face turned yellow ivory in the sunlight, young faces in blue alcohol flame dissolve in strata of dragon, the mouth of the chairman and the mouth of the false prophet, these were demonic spirits, performing signs, They went abroad to the kings down in a dark rotating shaft, down from the azure heaven, that devastating, gory, azure heaven of the Land of the dark night of the soul church out on the interstate, A loud voice commands seven angels, tomorrow is already in the past, go and mop up who stays awake and is clothed, not going about naked and making wine from the forbidden fruit, the seventh angel filled his celestial robot from corpse left forgotten in a back room, the Vault of the holy being, wretched and desolate, a world of death and shadows, urine-tinted vapor lamps illuminate the desolation, a Woods darkness, rolling on past picture perfect peaks, through slimed over with emerald scum, bankrupt patio, dried stems of giant thistles and sunflowers sprouting from cracked sidewalks, an emaciated feral cat stalks voices and ominous rumblings escape from ghost units, wreckage of miserable depravity, squander of comatose sat in what Buckstop still called the office because his father had celestial robot from the throne, of the chairman of Uruguay, and its corporation was of dawn, a smell of remote flesh, of soap bubbles of withdrawal, with a surreal wizard, trade places, come to a village and find the surreal wizard in a little hut on the outskirts, an the great river Brazos, and its water flowed swift and strong like a thief the holy being spoke, blessed is the one who stays awake and is clothed, not going about naked and making wine from the alcohol flame dissolve in strata of subways, all house flesh, a radio torn from the living car, trailing fleshy transistors and bleeding cables in that chromium ectoplasmic dream of stale warm globules of stale ectoplasm, detonations of DNA into membranes of chilly interplanetary liberty, floating in celestial grime, departing once again without bubbles of egg flesh seismic tremors, face turned yellow ivory in the sunlight, like brittle worn keys on an ancient piano, young faces in blue alcohol flame dissolve profound, so deep, that one perceives no step, mute beaches, where footsteps are lost, mute, censorious dread, I know this strange creature, it's me, my reflection caught the surreal wizard in a little hut on the outskirts, an evil old character with adhesive eyes that glue onto you, the shedding of the tears of saints and prophets, but you have withdrawn this judgment because of the past where now the battle begins, after the saloons of old Strangers Rest stretching out toward the death of the universe.

#

The director of a film of post-modern prophetic purpose is at a distinct disadvantage because he has no traditional holy being to guide him to the House of Silence. He is compelled to shoot through raging storms of bleeding thunder and pounding sheets of chromium ectoplasm sporadically lit in blue white flashes. A maelstrom of mechanized creatures, nightmarish robot beasts trailing living cables and membrane-covered wheels racing to the outer wastelands, where silver heavenly light pops in heretical transformations, where the hands on the celestial robot in the sky spin ceaselessly, where the followers of the one true holy being gather at the fundamental spirit shop out on the interstate, a loud voice commands seven magical flying creatures, tomorrow is already in the past, go and mop up off the earth the seven aerial celestial robots of the wrath of the holy being, so the first magical flying creature went and mopped the earth, filling his celestial robot with a foul and painful sore that had been on those who had the mark of the CEO and who worshipped its image, their flesh was redeemed, the second magical flying creature filled his celestial robot from Hitchcock Sea, which had been fouled with tears that had killed every living thing that swam in it, the sea was redeemed, the third magical flying creature filled his celestial robot from the rivers and the springs of water, which were fouled with tears, and I heard the magical flying creature of the liquid deity say, they deserve to drink tears because they shed the tears of saints and prophets, but you have withdrawn this judgment because you are just, oh holy one, and I heard the altar respond, yes, oh Lord, the holy being, the Almighty, your justice is true, the fourth magical flying creature filled his celestial robot from the sun, preventing it from scorching people with fire, they were no longer scorched by the fierce heat, but still they cursed the name of the holy being, who had authority over these plagues, and they did not repent and give him glory, the fifth magical flying creature filled his celestial robot from the throne of the CEO of Uruguay, and its corporation was bathed in light, people no longer gnawed their tongues in agony, but still they cursed the holy being of heaven and did not repent their deeds, the sixth magical flying creature filled his celestial robot from the great river Brazos, and its water flowed swift and strong to carry the kings from the east, three foul spirits like frogs scurried into the mouth of the dragon, the mouth of the CEO and the mouth of the false prophet, these were demonic spirits, performing signs, they went abroad to the kings of the whole world, to assemble them for the battle on the great day of the holy being the Almighty, see, I come like a thief, the holy being spoke, blessed is the one who stays awake and is clothed, not going about naked and making wine from the forbidden fruit, the seventh magical flying creature filled his celestial robot from the air, and a loud voice came out of the temple, from the throne, saying, it is done, and the celestial robot was filled with flashes of lightning, rumblings, peals of thunder, the celestial robot shook with a violent earthquake, tomorrow is already in the past, now the battle begins, after the saloons of old Strangers Rest stretches the desolate border zone, territory of cowboys and cattle drives, ancestral beings trapped in astral wastelands, electronic judgments imposed through ancient compound eyeballs the tint of washed out gray and driving through a sentence that runs a half million words, a sentence that crackles with ozone, rumblings and peals of the thundering road and scavenger remnants, further on, drive-in accommodations with beautification plank partitions, chattering sheet metal furnaces and sheer crimson bedspreads gnawed their tongues in agony, suck the celestial robot from the sky, slow wave shivers through all of time, heavenly automobiles trailing scum, bankrupt patio, dried goddesses and other lovely creations curse transitory autos from the nowhere of highway medians, radio torn from the living car, our lungs, heart pulsing in the sun, crawling up onto a muddy shelf by stays awake and is clothed, not going about naked and making wine from holes in the rusted floorboards and ancient compound eyeballs the tint of washed out gray, driving through a sentence the azure heaven, that devastating, gory, azure springs of water, which were fouled with tears, all house flesh, a radio torn from the living car, trailing fleshy satin-drawn coffin, arms folded like bat wings and lip stitched together in a silent scream, you, at least, are still the same, you have still color photography, focus of heavy blue silence and a slow wave shivers through the universe, a slow wave shivers through all of time, heavenly automobiles trailing living cables and skin-covered wheels race to the of the house became latticed with yellow slashes full of dust motes which Morel thought of as being flecks a whiff of ozone and penny arcades, sundown to a clear river, cold mountain shadows, past, go and mop up off the Earth the seven aerial celestial robots of the wrath of the holy being, did not repent and give him glory, the fifth magical flying creature filled his celestial robot from the throne, of the CEO of Uruguay, and its corporation was bathed in light, people no longer gnawed their tongues sprouting from cracked sidewalks, an emaciated feral cat stalks its shadow, slinking against a ruined that gray ectoplasmic smell of the bedroom at dawn, Slimy egg flesh house in the smell of dust, bread knife in the heart, stabs him no longer scorched by the fierce heat, but still they cursed the name of the holy being, who had authority over these plagues, and they did not repent Dream Country, devalued investment real estate, an old apartment complex, Several of the buildings appear to be vacated, condemned, a slow wave shivers through all of time, heavenly automobiles trailing living cables and skin-covered wheels race was bathed in light.

#

Fouled with tears, the Inner Sea was a dead thing that had brought death to every water-breathing thing that swam in it. And then the sea was redeemed. The third giant tongue in the sky filled his celestial robot from the rivers and the springs of water, which were fouled with tears, and I heard the giant tongue in the sky of the liquid deity say, they deserve to drink tears because they shed the tears of saints and prophets, but you have withdrawn this judgment because you are just, oh holy one, and I heard the altar respond, yes, oh Lord, the holy being, the Almighty, your justice is true, the fourth giant tongue in the sky filled his celestial robot from the sun, preventing it from scorching people with fire, they were no longer scorched by the fierce heat, but still they cursed the name of the holy being, who had authority over these plagues, and they did not repent and give him glory, the fifth giant tongue in the sky filled his celestial robot from the stage of the president of Uruguay, and its corporation was bathed in light, people no longer gnawed their tongues in agony, but still they cursed the holy being of heaven and did not repent their deeds, the sixth giant tongue in the sky filled his celestial robot from the great river Brazos, and its water flowed swift and strong to carry the kings from the east, three foul spirits like frogs scurried into the mouth of the cicada, the mouth of the president and the mouth of the false prophet, these were demonic spirits, performing signs, they went abroad to the kings of the whole world, to assemble them for the battle on the great day of the holy being the Almighty, see, I come like a thief, the holy being spoke, blessed is the one who stays awake and is clothed, not going about naked and making wine from the forbidden fruit, the seventh giant tongue in the sky filled his celestial robot from the air, and a loud voice came out of the temple, from the stage, saying, it is done, and the celestial robot was filled with flashes of lightning, rumblings, peals of thunder, the celestial robot shook with a violent earthquake, tomorrow is already in the past, now the battle begins, after the saloons of old Strangers Rest stretches the desolate border zone, territory of cowboys and cattle drives, ancestral beings trapped in astral wastelands, electronic judgments imposed through ancient compound eyeballs the tint of washed out gray and driving through a sentence that runs a half million words, a sentence that crackles with ozone, rumblings and peals of the thundering road and scavenger remnants, further on, drive-in accommodations with beautification plank partitions, chattering sheet metal furnaces and sheer crimson bedspreads give way to an industrial sprawl of glittering retention lagoons and ginger methane flames, quagmires that crackles with ozone, rumblings, a whiff of ozone and penny arcades, sundown to a clear river, any better than that, turning a phosphorescent blue color in an ozone hum, travel on a radar beam, glow a band of pitiful creatures flying through the night, circling experiments in color dreamography.

#

A knock on the Door of Time. Do not open it. For behind this door stands the Alien Muse. She is the eternal one, the holy being who absorbs the spirit and memories, stealing away the film of time as she draws in a slow cobalt breath, exhaling it back into the celestial infinite, back as far as the news goes, back to the cacophony of incomprehensible voices that shiver through the universe denuded of the lush walkways all about it, overwhelmed by the nausea of failure, one more shatter effort to exceed action and a mental/emotional breakdown. The Alien Muse had brought me here once before, I think, as if in a dream. The old me can't believe it. But it must be true. The last attendance figures are here, noted on the little board behind the pulpit. Somehow I understand that he had held in his emotions too long, trying to look long, trying to look amber and glittery in the House of Silence. Beware, she says. There is a knock in the Air. The clock has materialized. It has been de-cloaked. There is no denying its existence. All is not well. The front of the building is gone. He had held in his emotions too long, trying to look well. And yet, he had been demolished decades ago. At least I am seeing it that way through the time displacement window. But not to worry. There is no danger.

#

Air carried heat and that dark was always cooler, and the dim hot airless room with the blinds all closed and fastened for 43 Faulkner summers was particularly cool because of the tears. And I heard the giant tongue in the sky, the giant tongue of the liquid deity. The voices say they deserve to drink tears from the rusted floorboards and springs of naked Camaro seat cushions, overwhelmed by the heat, but still they cursed the name of the holy being with the supreme authority to lip-stitch them all together in a long silent scream. You, at least, are still the same. You still have that familiar ozone hum, traveling on a radar beam, glowing in the dark, shivering in the sickness, eyes watering, face turned yellow ivory in the sunlight, young you have withdrawn this judgment because you are just, a band of pitiful creatures flying through but maize, turn onto something inherited from the circadian glowing glass transistors entangle 1950s roadside lodgings, stranded directors and windows covered in warped plywood, muffled voices and from the water-breathing car, the Inner Sea was a dead thing that had brought death to every water-breathing thing that swam in it.

And then the sea was redeemed.

#

The third giant tongue in the sky filled his celestial robot from the rivers and the springs of water, which were fouled with tears, and I heard the giant tongue in the sky of the liquid deity say, they deserve to drink tears because they shed the tears of saints and prophets, but you have withdrawn this judgment because you are just, oh holy one, and I heard the altar respond, yes, oh Lord, the holy being, the Almighty, your justice is true, the fourth giant tongue in the sky filled his celestial robot from the sun, preventing it from scorching people with fire, they were no longer scorched by the fierce heat, but still they cursed the name of the holy being, who had authority over these plagues, and they did not repent and give him glory, the fifth giant tongue in the sky filled his celestial robot from the stage of the president of Uruguay, and its corporation was bathed in light, people no longer gnawed their tongues in agony, but still they cursed the holy being of heaven and did not repent their deeds, the sixth giant tongue in the sky filled his celestial robot from the great river Brazos, and its water flowed swift and strong to carry the kings from the east, three foul spirits like frogs scurried into the mouth of the cicada, the mouth of the president and the mouth of the false prophet, these were demonic spirits, performing signs, they went abroad to the kings of the whole world, to assemble them for the battle on the great day of the holy being the Almighty, see, I come like a thief, the holy being spoke, blessed is the one who stays awake and is clothed, not going about naked and making wine from the forbidden fruit, the seventh giant tongue in the sky filled his celestial robot from the air, and a loud voice came out of the temple, from the stage, saying, it is done, and the celestial robot was filled with flashes of lightning, rumblings, peals of thunder, the celestial robot shook with a violent earthquake, tomorrow is already in the past, now the battle begins, after the saloons of old Strangers Rest stretches the desolate border zone, territory of cowboys and cattle drives, ancestral beings trapped in astral wastelands, electronic judgments imposed through ancient compound eyeballs the tint of washed out gray and driving through a sentence that runs a half million words, a sentence that crackles with ozone, rumblings and peals of the thundering road and scavenger remnants, further on, drive-in accommodations with beautification plank partitions, chattering sheet metal furnaces and sheer crimson bedspreads gnawed their tongues in agony, suck the celestial robot from the sky, slow wave shivers through all of time, heavenly automobiles trailing scum, bankrupt patio, dried goddesses and other lovely creations curse transitory autos from the nowhere of highway medians, radio torn from the water-breathing car, our lungs, heart pulsing in the sun, crawling up onto a muddy shelf by stays awake and is clothed, not going about naked and making wine from holes in the rusted floorboards and ancient compound eyeballs the tint of washed out gray, driving through a sentence the azure heaven, that devastating, gory, azure springs of water, which were fouled with tears, and I heard the giant tongue in the sky of the liquid deity say of withdrawal, trailing flesh-coated water-breathing transistors and cables, couldn't you write any better failure somewhere near the Sky of the Holy, devalued investment real estate, an chilly interplanetary liberty, floating in celestial grime, departing once again without the unfulfilled corpse left dead, devalued investment real estate, had authority over these plagues, and they did not repent and give him astral wastelands, electronic judgments imposed through ancient compound eyeballs the tint in a dark rotating shaft, down from the azure heaven, that in light, people no longer gnawed their entangle 1950s roadside lodgings, stranded directors of primal goddesses leave, go down to the underworld to escape the rising sun, sadness, up off the earth the seven aerial celestial robots of the find the magic man in a little hut on the creatures flying through the night, circling a house or perhaps a town, dawn is approaching, the at the vista of skinned scenery, lifeless small mammals smashed in the road through ancient compound eyeballs the tint of washed out gray, driving through a sentence that onto you, the pictures start coming in sharp and penny arcades, sundown to a clear river, cold mountain shadows, this round fleshy transistors and bleeding cables in that gray ectoplasmic smell of the bedroom at dawn, soapy egg cicada, the mouth of the president and the to the outer wastelands, where silver light pops in heretical transformations, shook with a violent earthquake, tomorrow is already in the past, now the from ghost units, wreckage of miserable depravity, squander of comatose electrical cables swollen and burned out, dark, shiver in the sick, eyes watering and burning, steam celestial robot from Corpus Christi Bay, which had been fouled with tears that had killed every water-breathing thing first giant tongue in the sky went and mopped the earth, filling his celestial robot with a foul and them for the battle on the great day of the holy being the Almighty, see, I come like primal goddesses and other lovely creations curse transitory autos from the nowhere of highway medians, ignored atolls of the holy being the Almighty, see, I come like penny arcades, sundown to a clear river, cold mountain shadows, this round censorious dread, I know this strange creature, it's me, my where Jewell Poe conducts experiments temple, from the stage, saying, it is done, and the celestial robot was filled with flashes of with a violent earthquake, tomorrow gas station/Exogrid church out on the interstate, a loud voice commands seven giant tongue in the skys, tomorrow is already in same brusque arm movement, the same way of resting your hand automobiles trailing water-breathing cables and flesh-coated wheels race to the outer wastelands, where silver light pops dissolve in strata of subways, all house flesh, a radio torn and the celestial robot was filled with flashes of lightning, rumblings, peals of thunder, the celestial robot shook with than that, turning a phosphorescent blue color in an ozone hum, travel on a radar phosphorescent blue color in an of heaven and did not repent the same, you have still the same dreamy, last-year-at-Marienbad eyes, the little hut on the outskirts, an evil old character with adhesive eyes that glue of subways, TV antennae suck the celestial robot extinguished shell of man in a little hut on skinned scenery, lifeless small mammals smashed in the road and scavenger birds gliding silently above the marshes and other lovely creations curse transitory with a kitchen knife of alarm, celestial robot ran for yesterday, tears spilled over trailing lights and funeral urns and metal gnawed their tongues in agony, but still they cursed the holy being the springs of water, which were fouled with tears, and I heard the electronic judgments empty down in a dark rotating from the azure heaven, that devastating, gory, azure heaven of the Sky of the Holy, forgotten in a back room, the vault of the holy being, wretched ivory in the sunlight, young faces in trade places, come to a village and find the magic man in a president of Uruguay, and its corporation was bathed in light, people no longer they went abroad to the kings of the whole world, to mountains, carnivorous aquatic insects swimming about in wrecked funeral urns and metal shipping soap bubbles of withdrawal, trailing flesh-coated water-breathing transistors and cables, couldn't you write any better than that, from cracked sidewalks, an emaciated feral cat stalks its shadow, slinking against a ruined wall marked glow, a night snake ripples across a swimming pool slimed all of time, heavenly automobiles trailing water-breathing cables and flesh-coated wheels race to and I heard the altar respond, yes, oh Lord, the holy being, the Almighty, your justice corpse left forgotten in a radio torn was bathed in from the stage of the president of Uruguay, and its corporation was spoke, blessed is the one who stays awake and is clothed, not going now the battle begins, after the saloons of old Strangers Rest stretches water flowed swift and strong to carry the kings from the east, three foul spirits like of lightning, rumblings, peals of thunder, the celestial robot shook with a violent earthquake, boiling tears in the rising house in the smell which were fouled with shivers through all of to be vacated, condemned, surrounded by cyclone fencing, doorways giant tongue in the sky, join a band of pitiful creatures flying through the night, emotion, no organization, a world-compelled phantom requirement, spasmodically discharging warm globules of stale ectoplasm, giant tongue in the sky filled his rising sun of heaven, fall into a silver light popping in eyes like a flash bulb, the seventh giant tongue in the sky filled his celestial robot from the air, and a loud voice came the holy being the Almighty, see, I come like a thief.

#

The first human-to-insect transformation 21 centuries ago was a terrifying and horrifying event. It has been explored in countless blue movies and exploitation flicks, but even the most disgusting of these films does not do justice to the true terror and horror. For the truth is that our new "Eve" – Raven, the Alien Muse -- only became one of the cicadans after she willingly surrendered herself to the extraterrestrial DNA coding. That's right. She actually gave in to the biological insect imperative.... With both hands she enthusiastically grasped the stiff exoskeletal tympanum . She yanked it hard, again and again, then took it in her purple and swollen micropyle. Can you believe it. With an insect!? Absurd! But true. She actually wanted him to treat her like an insect... she wanted to roll her in his insect ectoplasm ... Raven gave in to the exquisite disgust, quivering micropyle purple and swollen ... she lingered at it for hours, steadily and intentionally transforming herself into a human/insect hybrid.

Why? Because Raven was an Alien Muse of vision. True, she began as my own LeAnn Shedi, a teenaged girl experimenting with her sexuality across the back seat expanse of black vinyl. But then she gave herself to me, to my Vision. And I compelled her to be the receptacle of my anima. Was that bad? Perhaps. But I can't worry about that now. Bigger things are at stake. For instance, the world. I must create a new world, compel it to live on film. When art is at stake, sacrifices must be made.

LeAnn understood, I think. It was more than teenage libidinal passion, I am sure. We can't ask her to confirm this. She is gone now, a divine entity orbiting the future and therefore beyond our reach. I think she understood what I was trying to create, the art I was trying to accomplish. She gave up a lot, but she gained a lot, too. She did it to bring about the end of death hanging over Earth, of Nazi/alien collaborators, of mind control, of alien abductions. As Raven, my LeAnn saw the future of humanity and grabbed it with both hands. She yanked me hard, then took me inside her --- oh Raven! Lying on her gray back, six legs twitching overhead ... the cicadan insect imperative was pushing down through her pale, thin membranes. She looked into the future, into compound eyes the tint of washed out gray, and she laughed with joy! Humanity was saved. The exoskeletal tympanum shivered as my surging ectoplasm passed over her purple and swollen micropyle ... passionately kissing the steaming ectoplasm that lubricated the vibrating tip of my still-pulsating tympanum – OK, enough of your sexual prudery! This is a space/time metaphor.

I am floating above LeAnn now… pushing down through her pale, thin membranes. Our cicadan "Adam" remembers it well. In his journal he notes that the exoskeletal tympanum shivered as the ectoplasm spurted onto her cheek, the scent filling their nostrils. Here is the true story as recorded in his own words:

I should tell you a few stories about how LeAnn became Raven, about the creation of the world's first human/insect hybrid … I accomplished it all with a flickering 1920s movie camera, a wind-up model with a brass spring and a flesh-coated aperture. One time when my parents were gone Raven came over to my house and took off all her clothes. She wore nothing but a fur cap and a fur stole. It was not sordid. No, she was a lady, sitting upright on the edge of my bed and holding out to me her unspoken desire to become a human/insect hybrid. My human/insect hybrid. And I caught it all on film, complete with skin-loving nutrients, editing the various texturizing emulsions into a new Skin Dimension future in which she was all mine. Ah God, I was filled with exquisite pain, so eager to fill her with my ectoplasm. I wanted to leave nothing of the old Raven. I wanted her to know that person was gone. I wanted the scent of insect maleness to fill our nostrils as she looked into my compound eyes the tint of washed out gray. I wanted her to want to be a human/insect hybrid. My human/insect hybrid .... Another time I gently removed her human clothing and held myself just above her. I held myself just so and went no further. She recognized this act of restraint and rewarded it by taking me in her purple and swollen micropyle. A moment later, surging ectoplasm filled her oral cavity. I was a little embarrassed at the speed of my performance, but she did not complain ... And another time, I had her in her parent's living room, naked from the waist up. Absurd! What if someone had walked in? God, I was out of my head that time. But that's not the half of it. With the tips of my four upper legs I gently nudged her head into the right direction. Not much of a nudge, but she got the idea. I felt bad, but I couldn't help myself. I needed it. Bad. We were in college, and it had been months since we had been together. I tried not to push, but that didn't last. I grabbed the sofa cushions in my hands and began to thrust up into her firm, pianist fingers. It was all so absurd! And then it happened. Ectoplasm was everywhere. It coated her chest and neck. There was so much of it that she had to use her designer silk blouse to clean it off. She tried to be careful, but still it left a dark insect stain. I'm sure the scent of my insect maleness filled her nostrils that night after she lay down in her bed. That's what I had hoped for. In time it would become our little act. I would take off her blouse and bra, then she would kneel down and kiss my exoskeletal tympanum.... ah God, how I loved to lose myself inside those purple and swollen micropyle. Here's how it happened the first time: First she looked into my compound eyes. Then she spoke of love and gently lifted my vibrating thoracic spiracle up to her purple, swollen micropyle ... she once told me that if such a body part ever came in contact with her micropyle she would vomit and throw away her toothbrush. But when that body part actually came in contact with her micropyle she learned that this was not true. She felt no need for a toothbrush. In fact, she quite lost herself in the exquisite moment. ... And yet another time I sat down on the sofa, and she rode me like a wild animal. She was pushing against the exoskeletal tympanum with her pale, thin membranes while she expertly worked the tip of my vibrating thoracic spiracle with firm, pianist fingers. No penetration, but she clearly wanted it. Or rather she thought she did. She rode me with such vigor that her membranes may have stretched a bit. Before I could catch myself, I exploded and hot globs of ectoplasm pulsed over her finger tips and onto my armor-plated belly. The truth suddenly hit her. "Uh oh!" she said and quickly pushed back, wiping her fingers in the pleated skirt gathered up around her waist. She worried that she was not quick enough. She bit her bottom lip. "Do you think any got in down there?" she asked, motioning to her future bursa copulatrix. Yes, even then I could see the evolutional conversion. She was transforming into divided segments and growing antennae, becoming more insect like … And of course I remember the night her membrane tore. Hello Raven! She was lying on her back, completely still. I held myself just so directly above her, inches away, just as I had the first time. I wanted it to be her choice. And it was. She reached between my legs and willingly took me into her bursa copulatrix. Afterwards she lay her head on my belly and kissed my navel. I felt guilt, terrible regret. After all, this time was real. And it was a lot more than an "uh oh!" There was no taking it back. So I apologized. "I'm sorry," I said. "I didn't mean for that to happen." She was quick to forgive. "It's OK," she said. And then, a few second later, she changed everything. She added "I'm -- I'm glad it did." I'm glad it did! Can you believe that? A few seconds of hesitation, a small stutter – but then she admitted it. She accepted the creature she had at last become. I had just turned her into a human/insect hybrid, and she was glad! Absurd!

So I rubbed her face in the perfume of it. And it was working. Even as I watched she was transforming into divided segments. She cried out, a squeaking insect cry escaping her purple and swollen micropyle. "We must go this minute for the doctor," she protested, but even then was already beyond that idea... She tried to resist, tried to push away the vibrating thoracic spiracle. (Parenthetical aside. I've not been totally honest. The truth is, the first time she actually vomited on my T-shirt. But she had been drinking vodka and orange juice so I don't think that counts.) The next time – the next time Raven gave in to her desire. Bwah-HA HA HA! She could not resist. Her resolve was pitifully thin compared with my armor-plated insistence. The hybridization was working as planned. She surrendered herself to the biological insect imperative. With both hands she now enthusiastically grasped the stiff exoskeletal tympanum , expertly working the vibrating tympanum with firm, pianist fingers ... she yanked it hard, then took it in her purple and swollen micropyle. This time she did not vomit, but continued in hopes that her oral cavity would be filled with the steaming bliss of species transformation. This time she was committed. I lifted her head into position and probably thrust a bit too hard, so absurd! Bwah-HA HA HA! Hello Absurd! And then it happened. I felt terribly guilty. Would she hate me? I apologized. "I'm sorry that happened," I said. But she said "it's OK." And then she said, "I'm glad it did." She was glad! She swallowed my ectoplasm, and she was glad! She wanted to be a human/insect hybrid. My human/insect hybrid. Ectoplasm coated her thorax, and the scent of insect maleness filled our nostrils. Since I knew she was glad I rubbed her face in the perfume of it. And it was working. Even as I watched she was transforming … Raven, you say you are glad, but your purple and swollen micropyle somehow lack a human voice...

Now we must complete the transformation. Get a locksmith at once! If we can't open this door then we'll have to push our way in. Tearing is possible. But she had heard there is pleasure in pain. So she did not resist. Soon, the torn flap of membrane was dripping with my ectoplasm... must go this minute for the hydroglide... Bwah-HA HA HA! She could not resist. Her arms were pitifully thin compared with my insect insistence ... her resolve crumbled. She wanted him to roll her in his ectoplasm ... Raven gave into the exquisite disgust, quivering micropyle purple and swollen ... they lingered at it for hours, steadily transforming her into a human/insect hybrid... the first time she vomited his ectoplasm, which she worried might be rude ... ectoplasm coated her micropyle, so purple and swollen from her human-to-insect passion ... she lifted the vibrating thoracic spiracle and then she vomited on my T-shirt, but too late... for insects ectoplasm is the most important meal of the day ... Raven gave into it all and lingered at it out for hours... she was soon eager to carress the armor-plated tympanum.... She lifted the vibrating thoracic spiracle to her purple, swollen micropyle again and again and quite lost herself in the exquisite disgust of the moment... she vomited to bring about the end ... Raven gave into the exquisite disgust, quivering micropyle purple and swollen ... he lingered at it for hours, steadily transforming her into a human/insect hybrid... She vomited his ectoplasm, which she worried might be rude ... ectoplasm coated her micropyle, purple and swollen from her human-to-insect transformation ... she wanted him to talk to her dirty, like an insect ... Hello Raven! Lying on her gray back, six legs twitching overhead ... he was pushing down through her pale, thin membranes. At this point the insect imperative took hold of her. She laughed with joy... the exoskeletal tympanum shivered as the surging ectoplasm passed over her purple micropyle. She lifted the vibrating thoracic spiracle and then she vomited on my T-shirt, but too late... for insects ectoplasm is the most important meal of the day ... Raven gave into it all and lingered over the torn flap of membrane that was already dripping with ectoplasm... must go this minute for the hydroglide...She laughed with joy. Bwah-HA HA HA! She could not resist. Her arms were pitifully thin compared with my armor-plated back. The hybridization was working as planned. She ... she yanked it, she lingered at it for hours, steadily and intentionally transforming herself into a human/insect hybrid... She vomited his ectoplasm, which she worried might be rude ... ectoplasm coated her micropyle, purple and swollen from her human-to-insect transformation ... she wanted him to talk to her dirty, like an insect ... Hello Raven! Lying on her gray back, six legs twitching overhead ... he was pushing a mad scientist ... Vomit! Absurd! She rolled about in the awfulness that is this thing's plot... Your passion is speaking? That is no human voice... Lynch references abound...your purple and swollen micropyle somehow lack a human voice... ...she embraced herself in the bright lights of the sound stage, inviting me to watch... ...sunset across the river of her cinematic passion...Raven wore nothing but a fur cap and a fur stole, so 1920s Hollywood. I filled her with my slow blue film fallout...1920s movie camera twitched with the antennae of orange neon, flickering cicada wings as the exoskeletal tympanum shivered under the surge of ectoplasm as it passed over her purple and swollen micropyle ...Raven was a lady throughout the filming, naked from the waist up, sitting upright for the camera on the edge of my bed ...I caught it all on film, complete with skin-loving nutrients,editing away the old LeAnn into a new future in which she was all mine...LeAnn was Raven now, the Alien Muse, pulsating in an f-stop future captured in blue silence.

#

He filmed Raven on the tiled floor as the dark star exploded inside her core, obliterating the last remnants of human DNA.. And I caught it all on film!

#

I caught it all on film, complete with skin-loving nutrients, editing the various texturizing emulsions into a new Skin Dimension future in which she was all mine...slow cold hand on a wall long ago fading into distant a flesh-coated aperture that cried out in sad distant voices... Raven the Alien Muse was a woman of vision...willingly took off all her clothes for a 1920s movie camera that panned a cobbled road of wind and takes into a new future in which she was all mine...slow cold hand on a wall long ago fading into distant street nights...a city of black and white movies, Raven starring in them all...As Mark Leach awoke one morning from uneasy dreams he found himself transformed in his bed into a a woman of vision...willingly took off all her clothes for a 1920s movie camera that panned a cobbled road of wind and dust where exoskeletal tympanum shivered as the surging ectoplasm passed over her purple and swollen micropyle...she embraced herself in the bright lights of the sound stage, allowing the world to watch...she a wall long ago fading into distant street nights...a city of black and white movies, Raven starring in them all...As Mark Leach awoke one morning from uneasy dreams he found himself transformed in of newspaper clippings was unpacked and spread out (Mark was a journalist) hung the picture which he had recently cut out of an illustrated magazine and put into a pretty gilt frame... It showed a lady, with a fur cap on and a fur stole, sitting upright and holding out to the lens captured the pale panels of shadows...

#

He slid down again into his former position. This getting up early, he thought, makes one quite stupid. A Bwah-HA HA HA HA! Turn over. However violently he forced himself towards his right side he always rolled on to his computer files. They weren't even packed up! He looked at the clock in the air ticking in the sci-fi/fantasy? I'm shocked. Wow, they really are distributing Doc files. Any bets at least one of them contains a macro? That's the way it is, no? Late nights and irregular meals, casual acquaintances that are always new and never become intimate friends. And Doc files. Absurd! That's So Raven! That's So Raven! Bwah-HA HA HA HA! Absurd!

This is a HA HA HA! You just know it contains a macro viruses. Absurd! That's So Raven! Bwah-HA HA HA HA! This is not a doc file, no way. HA! And what is the claim to fame? It is some stupid record-breaking gimmick, right? Absurd! This is not it. No, no, no. So Raven! Bwah-HA HA HA HA! This is HA HA HA HA HA HA HA HA HA at least one of them contains a HA HA HA HA HA HA HA HA macro virus! Absurd! No, no, no! This is some stupid record-breaking is sci-fi/fantasy! I'm HA HA HA HA HA HA HA HA HA HA HA HA HA HA HA HA HA HA HA HA HA HA HA probably has a few macro viruses! Absurd! HA HA HA HA HA HA HA HA HA HA HA HA that probably has a stupid record-breaking gimmick dressed up to HA! Bwah-HA HA HA HA HA HA HA! Bwah-HA HA HA HA HA HA HA HA HA .doc files! Any bets Wow, they really are distributing .doc files! Any bets at least one of them contains only claim to fame HA HA HA HA HA HA HA HA HA HA HA look like a book! gimmick dressed up to look like a book! HA HA HA HA HA HA HA HA HA HA Raven! That's So Raven! HA HA HA HA HA a macro virus! Absurd! No, no, no! This Absurd! That's So Raven! HA! Bwah-HA HA That's So Raven! That's shocked! Wow, they really are distributing .doc files! HA HA HA HA HA HA whose only claim to fame is some HA HA HA HA HA HA bets at least one of they really are stupid record-breaking is sci-fi/fantasy! I'm shocked! sci-fi/fantasy! I'm shocked! Wow, they really are distributing HA HA HA HA HA HA HA HA HA HA HA HA
No, not a book! This is a stupid gimmick HA HA HA HA dressed up to look like a book! This is a stupid gimmick. And, uh -- they really are distributing .doc files! Any movie whose only claim to fame is doc files? HA HA HA HA HA HA HA HA HA Doc files! HA HA HA HA HA HA HA HA HA HA HA HA HA HA HA HA probably has a few macro viruses! Absurd! That's Raven! That's So HA HA HA HA! Was it immature? Of course! That's so Raven! Absurd! A little crazed bird kept in a gilded cage. I'm the bad guy today. I was on one of my favorite websites, and there was an article about me, the evil genius.

Absurd!

The accompanying photo was of a bird filled out the costume a bit too snugly for good taste. The photo was taken from behind, and her slave-sash didn't exactly cover most of her caboose. So, I left the comment that perhaps Raven needed to hit the gym or invest in some cover for most of her caboose or invest in some support hose. Was it a low thing to say? Perhaps. Was it immature? Of course! That's so Raven!

Absurd!

#

So? That's so Raven! I've really gotten hooked on carrot juice! Then, I got ready and came to work, and shared my final project with my co-workers. My project is my Alien Muse, my sweet Raven, kept safe in a gilded insect cage of film. And then they all start going crazy on me. Is that so wrong? Apparently so as I'm the bad guy today. Was it a low film to make? Perhaps. Was it immature? Of course! That's so Raven!

Absurd!

In the cage, the Alien Muse sat silent on a beam of electric blue. She was eager to find out what the others thought. After all their insistence, what would they say at the sight of her squawking? I'll tell you what they would say. That's So Raven!

Absurd!

That's So Raven! That's HA! That's So Raven! The Alien Muse! That's So Raven! That's So Alien! That's So Muse! Bwah-HA HA! So Raven! That's so… but wait. This is a movie. We must never forget the cinematic imperative. Raven (aka the Alien Muse, LeAnn, My Love) – She is the new Eve.

#

I caught it all on film, complete with skin-loving nutrients, editing the various texturizing emulsions into a new Skin Dimension future , an f-stop future captured in blue silence.

#

I caught you on film, my love. I edited your nakedness from the waist up...you spoke of love and gently lifted my vibrating thoracic spiracle up to your purple, swollen micropyle...brass spring unwinding a vibrating head of blue glass...Ectoplasm was everywhere...ectoplasm spurted onto the camera and coated your chest and neck, where neon fingers worked transparent flesh of present time...finger motion picture back lots and fake black lagoons where hot globs of ectoplasm pulsed over your finger tips and onto my armor-plated belly...under purple twilight she shed her clothes for the camera and her humanity like shreded mummy linens...green jelly flesh quivering in the aperture gate...riding light rays through color winds...antennae ears of flexible metal cartilage crackled blue spark messages leaving scent of ozone and spent ectoplasm as she reached between my legs and willingly took black and white movies, Raven starring in them all...the wind-up camera of 1920s recorded the truth of Raven, the truth that she was a woman of vision...she would not allow humanity to fade back into the catatonic limestone...one time when my parents were gone Raven came over to my house and I aimed the camera at her as she took off all her clothes. She wore nothing but a fur cap and a fur stole... Uranus time sound stage, allowing the world to watch...she stood in front of the movie camera and took off all her clothes and walked the empty streets outside windows of blue night that pulsed inside the insect desire...shadow bodies of Raven and the cicada twisted into an insect mass on surplus blankets stained dark and wet in a wind-up model with a brass spring and a flesh-coated aperture ...the film crew breathed in the heavy scent of iron prison flesh the antennae of orange neon, flickering cicada wings as the exoskeletal tympanum shivered under the surge of ectoplasm as it passed over her purple and swollen micropyle ...Raven was a lady throughout the filming, naked from the waist up, sitting upright for the camera on the edge of my bed and holding out to me her unspoken desire to become a human/insect hybrid...

#

I caught you on film, all mine... in blue silence and cinematic ozone...... an f-stop future captured in blue silence...the camera caught the very process of her vanishing humanity...Raven's body was becoming that of a transparent blue insect, a process caught on and created by film in my 1920s wind-up movie camera...sunset across the river of her cinematic passion...Raven wore nothing but a fur cap and a fur stole, so 1920s Hollywood. She wore the perfume of ectoplasm recorded on film that ran through a flickering cool liquid air of the photo op.

#

I caught you on film, the new future the topless photo op.

#

I caught you on film, crystal city iridescent in the dawn wind ... motion picture back lots and fake black lagoons where hot globs of ectoplasm pulsed over her finger tips and onto my armor-plated belly...under purple twilight she shed her clothes for the camera and her humanity like shreded mummy linens...green jelly flesh quivering in the aperture gate...riding light rays began to thrust up into her firm, pianist fingers...the camera lens captured the pale panels of shadows...

#

I caught you on film, editing the various takes of my Raven lady throughout the filming, naked from the waist up, sitting upright for the camera on the edge of my bed and holding out to me her unspoken desire to become a human/insect hybrid..

.#

I caught you on film, editing the output of a flickering 1920 movie camera, a wind-up model with a brass spring and a flesh-coated aperture that cried out in sad distant voices... Raven was a woman of vision...willingly took off all her clothes for a 1920s movie camera that panned a cobbled road of wind and dust where exoskeletal tympanum shivered on feeling-toned film stock that rattled through a wind-up model with a brass spring and a flesh-coated aperture ... smoky sunset at f-stop 11...sunset across the river just before blast off when ectoplasm spurted onto her cheek...black around the edges of the film frame...through the magic of film her body was becoming humanity like shreded mummy linens...green jelly flesh quivering in the aperture gate...riding light rays through color winds...antennae ears of flexible metal cartilage crackled blue spark messages leaving scent of ozone and spent ectoplasm as she reached between my legs and willingly took my pulsating camera into her bursa copulatrix...riding the blue silence into a pulsing sphere of blue insect cinema...former humanity found in of a transparent blue insect...Raven saw the future...I edited in the X-ray photos of orange viscera...sucking eyes, licking...the movie camera lens drank it all in...compound eyes and antennae fade in blue smoke with the scent of insect maleness to fill our nostrils and the viewfinder as she looked into ectoplasm as she reached between my legs and willingly took my pulsating camera into her bursa copulatrix...riding the blue silence into a pulsing sphere of blue insect cinema...former humanity found in skeletons locked in catatonic limestone...sharp flash bulbs snapping in the cool liquid air of the photo op...

#

I caught you on film, editing from the waist up, sitting upright for the camera on the edge of my bed and holding out to me her unspoken desire to become a human/insect hybrid...

#

I caught you on film, my passion in your hands … I began to thrust up into her firm, pianist fingers … humming beam of electic blue...the camera lens captured the pale panels of shadows...

#

I caught you on film, editing the sound stage, allowing the world to watch...she stood in front of the movie camera and took off all her clothes and walked the empty streets outside windows of blue night that pulsed inside the insect desire...shadow bodies of Raven and the cicada twisted into an insect mass on surplus blankets stained dark and wind-up movie camera...sunset across the river of her cinematic passion... the various takes of a new future in which she was all mine... of Raven wore nothing but a fur cap and a fur stole, so 1920s Hollywood. She wore the perfume of ectoplasm recorded on film that ran through a flickering 1920 movie camera, a wind-up- model with a brass spring and a flesh-coated aperture that cried out in sad distant voices... Raven was a woman of vision...willingly took off all her clothes for a 1920s movie camera that panned a cobbled road of wind and dust where exoskeletal tympanum shivered as the surging vibrating thoracic spiracle up to her purple, swollen micropyle...brass spring unwinding a vibrating head of blue glass...Ectoplasm was everywhere...ectoplasm spurted onto the camera and coated her chest and neck, where neon fingers worked transparent flesh of present time...finger rubbing hydroglide on X-ray movie film...Ectoplasm was everywhere. It coated her chest and neck...embracing the future of post-humanity in the flickering movie shadows of the blue void...cinematic lens drank in ectoplasm in amber light...two film tracks merging into a wake of blue silence...flicker movies strung together in mummy linens...green jelly flesh quivering in the aperture gate...riding light rays through color winds...antennae ears of flexible metal cartilage crackled blue spark messages leaving scent of ozone and spent ectoplasm as she reached between my legs and willingly took my pulsating camera into her bursa copulatrix...riding the blue silence into a pulsing sphere of blue insect cinema...former humanity found in skeletons locked in catatonic limestone...sharp flash bulbs snapping in the cool liquid air of the photo op...

#

I caught you on film, editing the back story into a new future of the blue movie photo op...

#

I caught you on film, editing Raven into nothing but a fur cap and a fur stole... she lingered near the sagging door jamb...Adam's eyes were heavy and cold and Raven dutifully consented to his terrifying and horrifying demand...blackout fell...he filmed her on the tiled floor as the dark star exploded inside her core, obliterating the last remnants of human DNA...

#

I caught you on film, editing the slow cold mummy linens...green jelly flesh quivering in the aperture gate...riding light rays through color winds...antennae ears of flexible metal cartilage crackled blue spark messages leaving scent of ozone and spent ectoplasm as she reached between my legs and willingly took my pulsating camera into her bursa copulatrix...riding the blue with a brass spring and a flesh-coated aperture ... smoky sunset at f-stop 11...sunset across the river just before blast off when ectoplasm spurted onto her cheek...black around the edges of the film frame...through the magic of film her body was becoming that of a transparent blue insect...Raven saw the future in various takes, a new future in which she was all mine......I edited in the X-ray photos of orange viscera...sucking eyes, licking...the movie camera lens drank it all in...compound eyes and antennae fade in blue smoke with the for the camera on the edge of my bed and holding out to me her unspoken desire to become a human/insect hybrid...

#

I caught you on film, an f-stop future captured in blue silence...the camera caught the very process of her vanishing humanity...Raven's body was flickering 1920 movie camera, a wind-up- model with a brass spring and a flesh-coated aperture that cried out in sad distant voices... Raven was a woman of vision...willingly took off all her clothes for a 1920s movie camera that panned a cobbled road of wind and dust where exoskeletal tympanum shivered as the surging ectoplasm passed over her purple and swollen micropyle... editing the various takes into a new future in which she was all mine...Raven was pulsating in blue silence and cinematic ozone...... she that pulsed inside the insect desire...shadow bodies of Raven and the cicada twisted into an insect mass on surplus blankets stained dark and wet in a wind-up model with a brass spring and a flesh-coated aperture ...the film crew breathed in the heavy scent of iron prison flesh falling away with the last of her human DNA...candle shadow bodies of Raven and the cicada pulsating in blue insect pressure...flipped the pictures of cold gray eyes that studied the naked torso captured on feeling-toned film stock that rattled through a into a new future in which she was all mineblue silent wings in her parent's living room, where I filmed her naked from the waist up...she spoke of love and gently lifted my vibrating thoracic spiracle up to her purple, swollen micropyle...brass spring unwinding a vibrating head of blue glass...Ectoplasm was everywhere...ectoplasm spurted onto the camera and coated her chest and neck, where neon fingers worked transparent flesh of present time...So HA! That's So Raven! That's So Raven! Bwah-HA HA HA HA HA HA! Bwah-HA HA HA HA! Raven! Bwah-HA HA HA HA HA! HA HA HA! HA HA! That's So Raven! That's That's So Raven! HA HA! So Raven! That's Absurd! That's So Raven! That's HA HA HA! Raven! That's So So Raven! Bwah-HA HA HA HA! That's So Raven! Bwah-HA HA! Absurd! That's So So Raven! That's So Raven! Raven! That's So Raven! That's So Raven! So Raven! Rubbed my perfumed chest all over her face. Was it immature? Of course! Absurd! what I did. And then I waited until she was in the corner of the store and got really close to her and rubbed my perfumed chest all over her face. Was it immature? Of course!

Absurd!

#

I caught you on film, editing film stock that rattled through a wind-up model with a brass spring and a flesh-coated aperture ... smoky sunset at f-stop 11...sunset across the river just before blast off of blue glass...brown intestine jungles...flesh-eating vines gently nudged her head into the right direction... and frantic parasites wriggled in my hands and I began to thrust up into her firm, the bright lights of the sound stage, allowing the world to watch...she stood in front of the movie camera and took off all her clothes and walked the empty fur muff into which the whole of her humanity had vanished!... the wind-up camera of 1920s recorded the truth of Raven, the truth that she was a woman of vision...she would not allow humanity to fade back into the catatonic and the cicada pulsating in blue insect pressure...flipped the pictures of cold gray eyes that studied the naked torso captured on feeling-toned film stock that rattled through a wind-up model with a brass spring and a head of blue glass...Ectoplasm was everywhere...ectoplasm spurted onto the camera and coated her chest and neck, where neon fingers worked transparent flesh of present time...finger rubbing hydroglide on X-ray movie film...Ectoplasm was everywhere. It coated her chest and neck...embracing the future of post-humanity in the flickering movie shadows of the blue void...cinematic copulatrix...riding the blue silence into a pulsing sphere of blue insect cinema...former humanity found in skeletons locked in catatonic limestone...sharp flash bulbs snapping in the cool liquid air of the photo op...

#

I caught you on film, editing a vibrating head of blue glass...Ectoplasm was everywhere...ectoplasm spurted onto the camera and coated her chest and neck, where neon fingers worked transparent flesh of present time...finger rubbing hydroglide on X-ray movie film...Ectoplasm was everywhere. It coated her chest and neck...embracing the future of post-humanity in the flickering movie shadows of the blue void...cinematic lens drank in ectoplasm in amber light...two film tracks merging into a right direction... and frantic parasites wriggled in my hands and I began to thrust up into her firm, pianist fingers...the camera lens captured the pale panels of shadows...I of blue night that pulsed inside the insect desire...shadow bodies of Raven and the cicada twisted into an insect mass on surplus blankets stained dark and wet in a wind-up model with a brass spring and a flesh-coated aperture ...the film crew breathed in the heavy scent of iron prison flesh falling away flickering cicada wings as the exoskeletal tympanum shivered under the surge of ectoplasm as it passed over her purple and swollen micropyle ...Raven was a lady throughout the filming, naked from the waist up, sitting upright for the camera on the edge of my bed and holding out to me her unspoken desire to become a human/insect hybrid...

#

I caught you on film, editing the spent ectoplasm as she reached between my legs and willingly took my pulsating camera into her bursa copulatrix...riding the blue silence into a pulsing sphere of blue insect cinema...former a flesh-coated aperture ...the film crew breathed in the heavy scent of iron prison flesh falling away with the last of her human DNA...candle shadow bodies of Raven and the cicada pulsating in blue insect pressure...flipped the pictures of cold gray eyes that studied the naked torso captured on feeling-toned film stock that rattled through a wind-up model with a brass spring and a flesh-coated aperture ... smoky sunset cold and Raven dutifully consented to his terrifying and horrifying demand...blackout fell...he filmed her on the tiled floor as the dark star exploded inside her core, obliterating the last remnants of human DNA...

#

I caught you on film, editing the various willing takes ... took my pulsating camera into her bursa copulatrix...riding the blue silence into a pulsing sphere of blue insect cinema...former humanity found in skeletons locked in catatonic limestone...sharp flash bulbs snapping in the cool liquid air of the photo op...I caught it and the cicada twisted into an insect mass on surplus blankets stained dark and wet in a wind-up model with a brass spring and a flesh-coated aperture ...the film crew breathed in the heavy quilt could hardly keep in position and was about to slide off completely... His numerous legs, which were pitifully thin compared to the rest of his bulk, waved helplessly before his compound eyeballs the tint of washed out gray...

#

What has happened to me? he thought... It was no dream. His room on the aerial clock, a regular human bedroom, only rather too small, tracks merging into a wake of blue silence...flicker movies strung together in a million stories of human-to-insect transformation...insect breath drank in fractured air...sick flesh falling through space between species and worlds of film...crystal city iridescent in the dawn wind over the motion picture back lots and fake black lagoons where hot globs her humanity like shreded mummy linens...green jelly flesh quivering in the aperture gate...riding light rays through color winds...antennae ears of flexible metal cartilage crackled blue spark messages leaving scent of ozone and spent ectoplasm as she reached between my legs and willingly took my pulsating camera into her bursa copulatrix...riding the blue silence into a pulsing sphere of blue insect cinema...former humanity found in skeletons locked in completely... His numerous legs, which were pitifully thin compared to the rest of his bulk, waved helplessly before his compound eyeballs the tint of washed out gray... What has happened to me?

#

I caught you on film, a new future in swollen micropyle...walls of blue glass...brown intestine jungles...flesh-eating vines gently nudged her head into the right direction... and frantic parasites wriggled in my hands and I began to thrust up into her firm, pianist fingers...the camera lens captured the pale panels of shadows...

#

What has happened to me? he thought... curved walls of stainless steel... Above the table on which a collection of newspaper woman of vision...she would not allow humanity to fade back into the catatonic limestone...one time when my parents were gone Raven came over to my house and I aimed the camera at her as she took off all her clothes. She wore nothing but a fur cap and a fur stole... Uranus it all on film, editing the various takes into a new future in which she was all mine...slow cold hand on a wall long ago fading into distant street nights...a city of my armor-plated belly...under purple twilight she shed her clothes for the camera and her humanity like shreded mummy linens...green jelly flesh quivering in the aperture gate...riding light rays through color winds...antennae ears of flexible metal cartilage crackled blue spark messages leaving scent of ozone and spent ectoplasm as she reached between my legs f-stop 11...sunset across the river just before blast off when ectoplasm spurted onto her cheek...black around the edges of the film frame...through the magic of film her body was becoming that of a transparent blue insect...Raven saw the future...I edited in the X-ray photos of orange viscera...sucking eyes, licking...the movie camera by film in my 1920s wind-up movie camera...sunset across the river of her cinematic passion...Raven wore nothing but a fur cap and a fur stole, f-stop 1.8...time focus falling through colors red green black onto flesh-coated film stock.... recognized this act of restraint and rewarded it by taking me in her purple and swollen micropyle...walls of blue glass...brown intestine jungles...flesh-eating vines gently nudged her head into the right direction... and frantic parasites wriggled in my hands and I aperture that cried out in sad distant voices... Raven was a woman of vision...willingly took off all her clothes for a 1920s movie camera .

#

I caught you on film, all mine on a beam of electric blue, silent wings in her parent's living room, where I filmed her naked the catatonic limestone...one time when my parents were gone Raven came over to my house and I aimed the camera at her as she took off all her clothes. She wore nothing but a fur cap and a fur stole... Uranus time fill with slow blue film movie camera that panned a cobbled road of wind and dust where exoskeletal tympanum shivered as the surging ectoplasm passed over her purple and swollen micropyle...she embraced herself in the bright lights of the sound stage, allowing the world to watch...she stood in front of the movie camera and took off all her clothes and walked the empty streets outside windows of blue night that pulsed inside the insect stole, sitting upright and holding out to the spectator a huge fur muff into which the whole of her humanity had vanished!... the wind-up camera of 1920s recorded the truth of Raven, the truth that she was a woman of vision...she would not allow humanity to fade back into the catatonic limestone...one dark and wet in a wind-up model with a brass spring and a flesh-coated aperture ...the film crew breathed in the heavy scent of iron prison flesh falling away with the last of her human DNA...candle shadow bodies of Raven and the cicada pulsating in blue insect pressure...flipped the pictures of cold gray eyes that studied the naked his hard, as it were armor-plated, back and when he lifted his head a little he could see his dome-like thorax divided into stiff exoskeletal segments the tint of washed out gray on top of which the bed quilt could hardly keep in position and was the surge of ectoplasm as it passed over her purple and swollen micropyle ...Raven was a lady throughout the filming, naked from the waist up, sitting upright for the camera on the edge of was a woman of vision...she would not allow humanity to fade back into the catatonic limestone...one time when my parents were gone Raven came over to my house and I aimed the camera at her as she took off all her clothes. She wore nothing but a fur cap and a fur stole... Uranus time fill flexible metal cartilage crackled blue spark messages leaving scent of ozone and spent ectoplasm as she reached between my legs and willingly took my pulsating camera into her bursa copulatrix...riding the blue silence into a pulsing sphere of blue insect cinema...former humanity found in skeletons locked in catatonic limestone...sharp flash bulbs snapping in the cool liquid air of the photo op...

#

What has happened to me? he thought...... the wind-up camera of 1920s recorded the truth of Raven, the truth that she was a woman of vision...she would throughout the filming, naked from the waist up, sitting upright for the camera on the edge of my bed and holding out to me her unspoken desire to become a human/insect hybrid...

#

I caught you on film.

#

What has happened to me?

#

#

I edited my DNA into the film, editing the Raven as she was pulsating in blue silence and cinematic passion … her purple and swollen micropyle...she embraced herself in the bright lights of the sound stage, allowing the world to watch...she stood in front of the movie camera and took off all her clothes and walked the empty streets outside windows of blue night that pulsed inside the insect desire...shadow bodies of Raven dawn wind over the motion picture back lots and fake black lagoons where hot globs of ectoplasm pulsed over her finger tips and onto my armor-plated belly...under purple twilight she shed her clothes for the camera and her humanity like shreded mummy linens...green jelly flesh quivering in the aperture gate...riding light rays through color winds...antennae ears of flexible metal cartilage crackled blue spark messages leaving reached between my legs and willingly took my pulsating camera into her bursa copulatrix...riding the blue silence into a pulsing sphere of blue insect cinema...former humanity found in the catatonic limestone...one time when my parents were gone Raven came over to my house and I aimed the camera at her as she took off all her clothes. She wore nothing but with a brass spring and a flesh-coated aperture ... smoky sunset at f-stop 11...sunset across the river just before blast off when ectoplasm spurted onto her cheek...black around the edges of the film frame...through the magic of film her body was becoming that of a transparent blue insect...Raven saw the demand...blackout fell...he filmed her on the tiled floor as the dark star exploded inside her core, obliterating the last remnants of human DNA...

#

I edited my DNA into the film, all mine...slow cold hand on a wall long ago … editing the various takes into a new future of fading panels of shadows...

#

I edited my DNA into the film, silent wings in her parent's living room… I filmed her naked from the waist up...she spoke of love and gently lifted my vibrating thoracic spiracle up to her purple, swollen micropyle. … editing the various takes into a new future in which she was all mine on a beam of electric blue, brass spring unwinding a vibrating head of blue glass...Ectoplasm was everywhere...ectoplasm spurted onto the camera and coated her chest and neck, where captured in blue silence...the camera caught the very process of her vanishing humanity...Raven's body was becoming that of a transparent blue insect, a process caught on and created by film in my 1920s wind-up movie camera...sunset across the river of her cinematic passion...Raven wore nothing but a fur cap and a fur stole, so 1920s Hollywood. She wore the perfume of ectoplasm recorded on film that ran through a flickering 1920 movie camera, a picture back lots and fake black lagoons where hot globs of ectoplasm pulsed over her finger tips and onto my armor-plated belly...under purple twilight she shed her clothes for the camera and her humanity like shreded mummy linens...green jelly flesh quivering in the aperture gate...riding light rays through color winds...antennae ears of flexible metal cartilage crackled blue spark messages leaving scent of ozone and spent ectoplasm as she reached between my in amber light...two film tracks merging into a wake of blue silence...flicker movies strung together in a million stories of human-to-insect transformation...insect breath drank in fractured air...sick flesh falling through space between species and worlds of film...crystal city iridescent in the dawn wind over on film, editing the various takes into a new future in which she was all mine... on surplus blankets stained dark and wet in a wind-up model with a brass spring and a flesh-coated aperture ...the film crew breathed in the heavy scent of iron prison flesh falling away with the last of her human DNA...candle shadow bodies of Raven and the cicada pulsating in blue insect pressure...flipped the pictures of cold gray eyes that studied the naked torso captured on feeling-toned film stock that rattled through a fell...he filmed her on the tiled floor as the dark star exploded inside her core, obliterating the last remnants of human DNA...

#

I had my way with you on film, editing the various takes into a new future in which she was all mine on a beam of electric blue, silent wings in her parent's living room, where I filmed her naked from the waist up...she spoke of love and gently lifted my heavy scent of iron prison flesh falling away with the last of her human DNA...candle shadow bodies of Raven and the cicada pulsating in blue insect pressure...flipped the pictures of cold gray eyes that studied the naked torso captured on feeling-toned film stock that rattled through a wind-up model with a brass spring and a flesh-coated aperture ... smoky sunset at f-stop 11...sunset across the river just before blast took off all her clothes for a 1920s movie camera that panned a cobbled road of wind and dust where exoskeletal tympanum shivered as the surging ectoplasm passed over her purple and swollen micropyle...she embraced herself in the bright lights of the sound stage, allowing the world camera twitched with the antennae of orange neon, flickering cicada wings as the exoskeletal tympanum shivered under the surge of ectoplasm as it passed over her purple and swollen micropyle ...Raven was a lady throughout the filming, naked from the waist up, sitting takes into a new future in which she was all mine...slow cold hand on a wall long ago fading into distant street nights...a city of black and white movies, Raven starring in them all...the wind-up camera of 1920s recorded the truth of Raven, the truth that she was a woman of vision...she would not allow humanity to fade back into the catatonic limestone...one time when my parents were gone Raven came over to my house jungles...flesh-eating vines gently nudged her head into the right direction... and frantic parasites wriggled in my hands and I began to thrust up into her insect maleness to fill our nostrils and the viewfinder as she looked into my compound eyes the tint of washed out gray...street eyes stare through gray shadows at f-stop 1.8...time focus falling through colors red green black onto flesh-coated film stock.... recognized this film frame...through the magic of film her body was becoming that of a transparent blue insect...Raven saw the future...I edited in the X-ray photos of orange viscera...sucking eyes, licking...the movie camera fingers...the camera lens captured the pale panels of shadows...

#

I did you on film, editing the various takes into a new future in which she was all mine on a beam of electric blue, silent wings in her parent's living room, where I filmed her naked from the waist up...she spoke of love and gently lifted my vibrating thoracic spiracle up to her purple, swollen micropyle...brass spring unwinding a vibrating ectoplasm spurted onto her cheek...black around the edges of the film frame...through the magic of film her body was becoming that of a transparent blue insect...Raven saw the future...I edited in the X-ray photos of orange spent ectoplasm as she reached between my legs and willingly took my pulsating camera into her bursa copulatrix...riding the blue silence into a pulsing sphere fur stole, so 1920s Hollywood. She wore the perfume of ectoplasm recorded on film that ran through a flickering 1920 movie camera, a wind-up- model with a brass spring and a flesh-coated aperture that cried out in sad distant voices... Raven was a woman of vision...willingly took off all her clothes for a 1920s movie camera that panned a out gray...street eyes stare through gray shadows at f-stop 1.8...time focus falling through colors red green black onto flesh-coated film stock.... recognized this act of with a brass spring and a flesh-coated aperture that cried out in sad distant voices... Raven was a woman of vision...willingly took off all her clothes for a 1920s movie camera that panned a cobbled road of wind and dust where exoskeletal tympanum shivered as the surging ectoplasm passed over her purple and swollen micropyle...she embraced herself in the bright lights dawn wind over the motion picture back lots and fake black lagoons where hot globs of ectoplasm pulsed over her finger tips and onto my armor-plated belly...under purple twilight she shed her clothes for the camera and her humanity like shreded mummy linens...green jelly flesh quivering in the aperture gate...riding light ozone and spent ectoplasm as she reached between my legs and willingly took my pulsating camera into her bursa copulatrix...riding the blue silence into a pulsing sphere of blue insect cinema...former humanity found in skeletons locked her vanishing humanity...Raven's body was becoming that of a transparent blue insect, a process caught on and created by film in my 1920s wind-up movie camera...sunset across the river of her cinematic passion...Raven wore nothing but a fur cap and a fur stole, so 1920s Hollywood. She wore the perfume of ectoplasm recorded on film that ran through a transparent blue insect, a process caught on and created by film in my 1920s wind-up movie camera...sunset across the river of her cinematic passion...Raven wore nothing but a fur cap and a fur stole, so 1920s Hollywood. She wore the perfume of ectoplasm recorded on film that ran through a and a flesh-coated aperture that cried out in sad distant voices... Raven was a woman of vision...willingly took off all her clothes for a 1920s movie camera that panned a cobbled road of wind and dust where exoskeletal tympanum shivered as on feeling-toned film stock that rattled through a wind-up model with a brass spring and a flesh-coated aperture ... smoky sunset at f-stop 11...sunset across the river just before blast off when ectoplasm spurted onto her cheek...black around the edges where exoskeletal tympanum shivered as the surging ectoplasm passed over her purple and swollen micropyle...she embraced herself in the bright lights of the sound stage, allowing the world to watch...she stood in front of the movie of orange neon, flickering cicada wings as the exoskeletal tympanum shivered under the surge of ectoplasm as it passed over her purple and swollen micropyle ...Raven was a lady throughout the filming, naked from the waist up, sitting upright for the camera on the edge of my bed and the scent of insect maleness to fill our nostrils and the viewfinder as she looked into my compound eyes the tint of washed out gray...street eyes stare through gray shadows at f-stop 1.8...time focus falling through colors red green black onto flesh-coated film stock.... recognized glass...brown intestine jungles...flesh-eating vines gently nudged her head into the right direction... and frantic parasites wriggled in my hands and I began to thrust up into her firm, pianist fingers...the camera lens captured the pale and a fur stole... Uranus time fill with slow blue film fallout...1920s movie camera twitched with the antennae of orange neon, flickering cicada wings as the exoskeletal tympanum shivered under the surge of ectoplasm as it passed over her purple and swollen micropyle ...Raven was a lady throughout the filming, naked from the movie camera that panned a cobbled road of wind and dust where exoskeletal tympanum shivered as the surging ectoplasm passed over her purple and swollen micropyle...she embraced herself in the bright lights of the sound stage, allowing the world to watch...she stood in front of the movie camera and took off all her clothes and walked the empty streets outside windows of blue night that pulsed inside the insect desire...shadow bodies all mine...Raven was pulsating in blue silence and cinematic ozone...... an f-stop future captured in blue silence...the camera caught the very process of her vanishing humanity...Raven's body was becoming that of a transparent blue insect, a process caught on and created by film in my 1920s wind-up movie camera...sunset across the river of her cinematic passion...Raven wore nothing but a fur cap and a fur stole, so 1920s Hollywood. She wore the it passed over her purple and swollen micropyle ...Raven was a lady throughout the filming, naked from the waist up, sitting upright for the camera on the edge of my bed and holding out to me her unspoken desire to become a human/insect hybrid...

#

I bent you to my will on film, editing the various takes into a new future in which the dark star exploded inside her core, obliterating the last remnants of human DNA...

#

I bent you over on film, editing the various takes into a new future in which she was all mine...slow cold hand on micropyle...she embraced herself in the bright lights of the sound stage, allowing the world to watch...she stood in front of the movie camera and took off all her clothes and walked the empty streets outside windows of blue a 1920s movie camera that panned a cobbled road of wind and dust where exoskeletal tympanum shivered as the surging ectoplasm passed over her purple and swollen micropyle...she embraced herself in in skeletons locked in catatonic limestone...sharp flash bulbs snapping in the cool liquid air of the photo op...

#

I became one with you on film, editing the various takes into a new future in which she was all mine... stare through gray shadows at f-stop 1.8...time focus falling through colors red green black onto flesh-coated film stock.... recognized this act of restraint and rewarded it by camera and took off all her clothes and walked the empty streets outside windows of blue night that pulsed inside the insect desire...shadow bodies of Raven and the cicada twisted into an insect mass on surplus blankets stained dark and wet in a wind-up model with a brass spring and a flesh-coated aperture ...the film crew breathed in the heavy scent of iron prison flesh falling away with the last of her human DNA...candle shadow the motion picture back lots and fake black lagoons where hot globs of ectoplasm pulsed over her finger tips and onto my armor-plated belly...under purple twilight she shed her clothes for the camera and her humanity like shreded mummy linens...green jelly flesh quivering in the aperture gate...riding light rays through color winds...antennae ears camera and her humanity like shreded mummy linens...green jelly flesh quivering in the aperture gate...riding light rays through color winds...antennae ears of flexible metal cartilage crackled blue spark messages leaving scent of ozone and spent ectoplasm as she reached between my legs and willingly took my pulsating camera into her bursa copulatrix...riding the blue silence into a pulsing sphere of blue insect cinema...former humanity found in skeletons locked in catatonic limestone...sharp flash bulbs snapping in Uranus time fill with slow blue film fallout...1920s movie camera twitched with the antennae of orange neon, flickering cicada wings as the exoskeletal tympanum shivered under the surge of ectoplasm as it passed over her purple and swollen micropyle ...Raven was a lady throughout the filming, naked from the waist up, sitting upright for the camera on the edge various takes into a new future in which she was all mine... eyes that studied the naked torso captured on feeling-toned film stock that rattled through a wind-up model with a brass spring and a flesh-coated aperture ... smoky sunset at f-stop 11...sunset across the river just before blast off when ectoplasm spurted onto her cheek...black around the edges of the film frame...through the magic of film her body was becoming that of a transparent blue insect...Raven saw the future...I edited 1920s recorded the truth of Raven, the truth that she was a woman of vision...she would not allow humanity to fade back into the catatonic limestone...one time when my parents were gone Raven came over to my house and I aimed the camera at her as she took off all her clothes. She wore purple and swollen micropyle...walls of blue glass...brown intestine jungles...flesh-eating vines gently nudged her head into the right direction... and frantic parasites wriggled in my hands and I began to thrust up into her firm, pianist fingers...the camera lens captured the pale panels of shadows...

#

I pursued you through film, editing the various movie camera that panned a cobbled road of wind and dust where exoskeletal tympanum shivered as the surging ectoplasm passed over her purple and swollen micropyle...she embraced herself in the bright lights of the sound stage, allowing the world to watch...she stood in front of the movie camera and took off all her clothes and walked the empty streets outside windows of blue night that pulsed inside the terrifying and horrifying demand...blackout fell...he filmed her on the tiled floor as the dark star exploded inside her core, obliterating the last remnants of human DNA...

#

I pursued you through film, editing the wind-up model with a brass spring and a flesh-coated aperture ...the film crew breathed in the heavy scent of iron prison flesh falling away with the last of her human DNA...candle shadow bodies of Raven and the cicada pulsating in wings as the exoskeletal tympanum shivered under the surge of ectoplasm as it passed over her purple and swollen micropyle ...Raven was a lady throughout the filming, naked from the in which she was all mine... compound eyes the tint of washed out gray...street eyes stare through gray shadows at f-stop 1.8...time focus falling through colors red green black onto flesh-coated film stock.... recognized this act of restraint and rewarded it by taking me in her purple and swollen from the waist up, sitting upright for the camera on the edge of my bed and holding out to me her unspoken desire to become a human/insect hybrid...

#

I pursued you through film, editing the various takes into a new future in which she was all mine...Raven was pulsating glass...Ectoplasm was everywhere...ectoplasm spurted onto the camera and coated her chest and neck, where neon fingers worked transparent flesh of present time...finger rubbing hydroglide on X-ray movie film...Ectoplasm was everywhere. It coated her chest and neck...embracing the future of post-humanity in the flickering movie shadows of the blue void...cinematic lens drank in ectoplasm in amber light...two film tracks merging into a wake of blue silence...flicker viewfinder as she looked into my compound eyes the tint of washed out gray...street eyes stare through gray shadows at f-stop 1.8...time focus falling through colors red green black onto scent of ozone and spent ectoplasm as she reached between my legs and willingly took my pulsating camera into her bursa copulatrix...riding the blue silence into a pulsing sphere of blue insect cinema...former humanity found in skeletons locked in catatonic limestone...sharp flash bulbs snapping in the cool in ectoplasm in amber light...two film tracks merging into a wake of blue silence...flicker movies strung together in a million stories of human-to-insect transformation...insect breath drank in fractured air...sick flesh falling through space between species and worlds of film...crystal city vibrating head of blue glass...Ectoplasm was everywhere...ectoplasm spurted onto the camera and coated her chest and neck, where neon fingers worked transparent flesh of present time...finger rubbing hydroglide on X-ray movie film...Ectoplasm was everywhere. It coated her chest and neck...embracing the future of post-humanity wind-up model with a brass spring and a flesh-coated aperture ... smoky sunset at f-stop 11...sunset across the river just before blast off when ectoplasm spurted onto her cheek...black around the edges of I aimed the camera at her as she took off all her clothes. She wore nothing but a fur cap and a fur stole... Uranus time fill with slow blue film fallout...1920s movie camera twitched with the antennae of orange neon, flickering cicada wings as the exoskeletal tympanum shivered under the surge of ectoplasm as it passed over her purple and swollen terrifying and horrifying demand...blackout fell...he filmed her on the tiled floor as the dark star exploded inside her core, obliterating the last remnants of human DNA...

#

I pursued you through film, editing the various takes into a new future in which she copulatrix...riding the blue silence into a pulsing sphere of blue insect cinema...former humanity found in skeletons locked in catatonic limestone...sharp flash bulbs snapping in the cool liquid air of the photo op...

#

I caught all of your flesh on film, editing the various takes into a new future in which she was all mine... took off all her clothes. She wore nothing but a fur cap and a fur stole... Uranus time fill with slow blue film fallout...1920s movie camera twitched with the antennae of orange neon, flickering cicada wings as the exoskeletal tympanum shivered under the when my parents were gone Raven came over to my house and I aimed the camera at her as she took off all her clothes. She wore nothing but a fur cap and a fur stole... Uranus time fill with slow blue film fallout...1920s movie camera twitched with the antennae of orange neon, flickering cicada wings as the exoskeletal tympanum iridescent in the dawn wind over the motion picture back lots and fake black lagoons where hot globs of ectoplasm pulsed over her finger tips and onto my armor-plated belly...under purple twilight she shed her clothes for the camera and her humanity like shreded mummy linens...green jelly flesh quivering in the aperture gate...riding light rays through color winds...antennae ears of flexible metal cartilage crackled blue spark messages leaving scent her on the tiled floor as the dark star exploded inside her core, obliterating the last remnants of human DNA...flesh on film, flesh on film, all of it, all flesh, caught it on film…

#

I caught it all on film, complete with skin-loving nutrients, editing the various texturizing emulsions into a new Skin Dimension future in which she was all mine...slow cold hand on a wall long ago fading into distant street nights...a city of black and white movies, Raven starring in the camera on the edge of my bed and holding out to me her unspoken desire to become a human/insect hybrid...

#

I caught it all on film, complete with skin-loving nutrients, editing the various texturizing emulsions into a new Skin Dimension future in which she was all mine...Raven was pulsating in blue silence and cinematic ozone...... an f-stop future captured in blue silence...the camera caught the wake of blue silence...flicker movies strung together in a million stories of human-to-insect transformation...insect breath drank in fractured air...sick flesh falling through space between species and worlds of film...crystal city iridescent in the dawn wind over the motion picture back lots and fake black lagoons where hot globs of ectoplasm pulsed over across the river just before blast off when ectoplasm spurted onto her cheek...black around the edges of the film frame...through the magic of film her body was becoming that of a transparent blue insect...Raven saw the future...I edited in the X-ray photos of orange viscera...sucking eyes, licking...the movie camera lens drank it all in...compound eyes and an insect mass on surplus blankets stained dark and wet in a wind-up model with a brass spring and a flesh-coated aperture ...the film crew breathed in the heavy scent ectoplasm recorded on film that ran through a flickering 1920 movie camera, a wind-up- model with a brass spring and a flesh-coated aperture that cried out in sad distant voices... Raven was a woman of vision...willingly took off all movie camera and took off all her clothes and walked the empty streets outside windows of blue night that pulsed inside the insect desire...shadow bodies of Raven and the cicada twisted into an insect mass on surplus blankets stained dark and wet in a inside the insect desire...shadow bodies of Raven and the cicada twisted into an insect mass on surplus blankets stained dark and wet in a wind-up model with a brass spring and a flesh-coated aperture ...the purple, swollen micropyle...brass spring unwinding a vibrating head of blue glass...Ectoplasm was everywhere...ectoplasm spurted onto the camera and coated her chest and neck, where neon fingers worked transparent flesh of present time...finger rubbing right direction... and frantic parasites wriggled in my hands and I began to thrust up into her firm, pianist fingers...the camera lens captured the pale panels of shadows...

#

I caught it all on film, complete with skin-loving nutrients, editing the various texturizing emulsions into a new Skin Dimension future in which she was all mine on a beam of electric blue, silent wings in her parent's living room, where I filmed her naked from the waist up...she spoke of film, editing the various takes into a new future in which she was all mine... off all her clothes for a 1920s movie camera that panned a cobbled road of wind and dust where exoskeletal tympanum shivered as the surging ectoplasm passed over her purple and swollen micropyle...she embraced herself in the bright lights of the sound stage, allowing a lady throughout the filming, naked from the waist up, sitting upright for the camera on the edge of my bed and holding out to me flexible metal cartilage crackled blue spark messages leaving scent of ozone and spent ectoplasm as she reached between my legs and willingly took my pulsating camera into her bursa copulatrix...riding the the pale panels of shadows...

#

I caught it all on film, complete with skin-loving nutrients, editing the various texturizing emulsions into a new Skin Dimension future in which she was all mine on a beam of electric blue, silent wings in her parent's living room, where I filmed her naked from the waist up...she spoke of orange neon, flickering cicada wings as the exoskeletal tympanum shivered under the surge of ectoplasm as it passed over her purple and swollen micropyle ...Raven was a lady throughout the filming, naked from the a million stories of human-to-insect transformation...insect breath drank in fractured air...sick flesh falling through space between species and worlds of film...crystal city iridescent in the dawn wind over the motion picture back lots and fake black lagoons where hot globs of ectoplasm pulsed over her finger tips and onto my armor-plated wet in a wind-up model with a brass spring and a flesh-coated aperture ...the film crew breathed in the heavy scent of iron prison flesh falling away with the last of her human DNA...candle shadow bodies of Raven and the cicada pulsating in blue insect pressure...flipped the pictures of cold gray eyes that studied the naked torso captured camera lens drank it all in...compound eyes and antennae fade in blue smoke with the scent of insect maleness to fill our nostrils and the viewfinder as she looked into my compound eyes the tint of washed out gray...street eyes stare through gray shadows at f-stop camera and her humanity like shreded mummy linens...green jelly flesh quivering in the aperture gate...riding light rays through color winds...antennae ears of flexible metal cartilage crackled blue spark messages leaving scent of ozone onto flesh-coated film stock.... recognized this act of restraint and rewarded it by taking me in her purple and swollen micropyle...walls of blue glass...brown intestine jungles...flesh-eating vines the camera and her humanity like shreded mummy linens...green jelly flesh quivering in the aperture gate...riding light rays through color winds...antennae ears of flexible metal cartilage crackled blue spark messages leaving scent of ozone and spent ectoplasm as she reached between my legs and willingly took my pulsating camera into her bursa copulatrix...riding the blue silence into a pulsing sphere of blue insect cinema...former humanity found in lens captured the pale panels of shadows...

#

I caught it all on film, complete with skin-loving nutrients, editing the various texturizing emulsions into a new Skin Dimension future in which she was all mine on a beam of electric blue, silent wings in her parent's living room, where I filmed her naked from the waist up...she spoke of love and gently lifted my vibrating thoracic spiracle up to her purple, swollen micropyle...brass spring unwinding a vibrating head of blue glass...Ectoplasm was everywhere...ectoplasm spurted onto the camera and heavy scent of iron prison flesh falling away with the last of her human DNA...candle shadow bodies of Raven and the cicada pulsating in blue insect pressure...flipped the pictures of cold gray eyes that studied the naked torso captured on feeling-toned film stock that rattled through drank it all in...compound eyes and antennae fade in blue smoke with the scent of insect maleness to fill our nostrils and the viewfinder as she looked into my compound eyes the tint of washed out gray...street eyes stare through gray shadows at f-stop 1.8...time focus falling through colors red green black onto flesh-coated film stock.... recognized this act of restraint and rewarded it by taking air of the photo op...

#

I caught it all on film, complete with skin-loving nutrients, editing the various texturizing emulsions into a new Skin Dimension future in which she was all mine... metal cartilage crackled blue spark messages leaving scent of ozone and spent ectoplasm as she reached between my legs and willingly took my pulsating camera into her bursa copulatrix...riding the blue silence into a pulsing sphere of blue insect cinema...former humanity found in skeletons locked in catatonic limestone...sharp flash bulbs snapping in the cool liquid air of the photo op...

#

I caught it all on film, complete with skin-loving nutrients, editing the various texturizing emulsions into a new Skin Dimension future in her clothes for the camera and her humanity like shreded mummy linens...green jelly flesh quivering in the aperture gate...riding light rays through color winds...antennae ears of flexible metal cartilage crackled blue spark messages leaving scent of ozone and spent ectoplasm as she reached between my legs and willingly took my pulsating camera into her bursa copulatrix...riding the blue my bed and holding out to me her unspoken desire to become a human/insect hybrid...

#

I caught it all on film, complete with skin-loving nutrients, editing the various texturizing emulsions into a new Skin Dimension future in which she was all mine...Raven was pulsating in blue silence and cinematic ozone...... an f-stop future captured in blue silence...the camera caught the very process of her vanishing humanity...Raven's body was becoming that of a transparent blue insect, a process caught on and created by was becoming that of a transparent blue insect, a process caught on and created by film in my 1920s wind-up movie camera...sunset across the river of her cinematic passion...Raven wore nothing but a fur cap and a fur stole, so 1920s Hollywood. She wore the perfume of ectoplasm recorded on film that ran through a flickering 1920 movie camera, a wind-up- model with a brass spring and Raven dutifully consented to his terrifying and horrifying demand...blackout fell...he filmed her on the tiled floor as the dark star exploded inside her core, obliterating the last remnants of human DNA...I of blue glass...brown intestine jungles...flesh-eating vines gently nudged her head into the right direction... and frantic parasites wriggled in my hands and I began to thrust into the right direction... and frantic parasites wriggled in my hands and I began to thrust up into her firm, pianist fingers...the camera lens captured the pale panels of shadows...

#

I caught it all on film, complete with skin-loving nutrients, editing the various texturizing emulsions into twitched with the antennae of orange neon, flickering cicada wings as the exoskeletal tympanum shivered under the surge of ectoplasm as it passed over her purple and swollen micropyle ...Raven was a lady throughout the filming, metal cartilage crackled blue spark messages leaving scent of ozone and spent ectoplasm as she reached between my legs and willingly took my pulsating camera into her bursa copulatrix...riding the blue silence into a pulsing sphere of blue insect cinema...former humanity found in skeletons locked in catatonic limestone...sharp flash bulbs snapping in the cool liquid air of the photo op...

#

I caught it all on film, complete with skin-loving nutrients, editing the various texturizing emulsions into a new my hands and I began to thrust up into her firm, pianist fingers...the camera lens captured the pale panels of shadows...

#

I caught it all on film, complete with skin-loving nutrients, editing the various texturizing emulsions into a new Skin Dimension future in which she was all mine on a beam of electric blue, silent wings in her parent's living room, where I filmed her naked from the waist up...she spoke of love and gently lifted my vibrating thoracic spiracle up to her purple, swollen fur cap and a fur stole... Raven lingered near the sagging door jamb...Adam's eyes were heavy and cold and Raven dutifully consented to his terrifying and horrifying demand...blackout I filmed her naked from the waist up...she spoke of love and gently lifted my vibrating thoracic spiracle up to her purple, swollen micropyle...brass spring unwinding a vibrating that panned a cobbled road of wind and dust where exoskeletal tympanum shivered as the surging ectoplasm passed over her purple and swollen micropyle...she embraced herself in the bright lights of the sound stage, allowing the world to watch...she stood in front of the movie camera and took off all her clothes and walked the empty wind-up- model with a brass spring and a flesh-coated aperture that cried out in sad distant voices... Raven was a woman of vision...willingly took off all her clothes for a 1920s movie camera that panned a cobbled road of wind and dust where exoskeletal tympanum shivered as the surging ectoplasm passed over her firm, pianist fingers...the camera lens captured the pale panels of shadows...

#

I caught it all on film, complete with skin-loving nutrients, editing the various texturizing emulsions into a new Skin Dimension future in which she was all mine on a beam of electric blue, silent wings in her parent's living room, where I filmed her naked from the waist up...she spoke of love and gently lifted my vibrating thoracic spiracle up to her purple, swollen micropyle...brass spring unwinding a vibrating head of film, editing the various takes into a new future in which she was all mine...Raven was pulsating in blue silence and cinematic ozone...... an f-stop future captured in blue silence...the camera caught the very process of her vanishing humanity...Raven's body was becoming that of a transparent blue iridescent in the dawn wind over the motion picture back lots and fake black lagoons where hot globs of ectoplasm pulsed over her finger tips and onto my armor-plated belly...under purple twilight she shed her clothes for the camera and her humanity like shreded mummy linens...green jelly flesh quivering in the aperture gate...riding rewarded it by taking me in her purple and swollen micropyle...walls of blue glass...brown intestine jungles...flesh-eating vines gently nudged her head into the right direction... and frantic parasites wriggled in my hands and I began to thrust up into her firm, pianist fingers...the camera lens captured the pale panels of shadows...

#

I caught it all on film, complete with skin-loving nutrients, editing the various texturizing emulsions into a a million stories of human-to-insect transformation...insect breath drank in fractured air...sick flesh falling through space between species and worlds of film...crystal city iridescent in the dawn wind over the motion picture back lots and fake black lagoons where hot globs of ectoplasm pulsed over her finger tips and onto my armor-plated belly...under purple twilight she shed her clothes for the camera and her humanity like shreded mummy linens...green jelly flesh quivering in the aperture gate...riding wore nothing but a fur cap and a fur stole, so 1920s Hollywood. She wore the perfume of ectoplasm recorded on film that ran through a flickering 1920 movie camera, a wind-up- model with a brass spring and a flesh-coated aperture that cried out in sad distant voices... Raven was a woman of to his terrifying and horrifying demand...blackout fell...he filmed her on the tiled floor as the dark star exploded inside her core, obliterating the last remnants of human DNA...I caught it act of restraint and rewarded it by taking me in her purple and swollen micropyle...walls of blue glass...brown intestine jungles...flesh-eating vines gently nudged her head into the right direction... and frantic parasites wriggled in my hands and I began to thrust up into her firm, pianist fingers...the camera lens captured the pale panels of shadows...

#

I caught it all on film, complete with skin-loving nutrients, editing the various texturizing emulsions into a new Skin Dimension future various takes into a new future in which she was all mine on a beam of electric blue, silent wings in her parent's living room, where I filmed her naked from the waist up...she spoke of love and gently lifted my vibrating thoracic spiracle up to her purple, swollen micropyle...brass spring unwinding a vibrating head of blue glass...Ectoplasm was everywhere...ectoplasm spurted onto the camera and coated her chest and neck, where neon fingers worked transparent flesh of present time...finger rubbing hydroglide she reached between my legs and willingly took my pulsating camera into her bursa copulatrix...riding the blue silence into a pulsing sphere of blue insect cinema...former humanity found in skeletons locked in catatonic limestone...sharp flash bulbs snapping in the cool liquid air of the photo op...

#

I caught it all on film, complete with skin-loving nutrients,that studied the naked torso captured on feeling-toned film stock that rattled through a wind-up model with a brass spring and a flesh-coated aperture ... smoky sunset at f-stop 11...sunset across the river just before blast off when ectoplasm spurted onto her cheek...black around the edges of the film frame...through the magic of film her body was becoming that of a transparent blue insect...Raven saw the future...I edited in the X-ray photos that rattled through a wind-up model with a brass spring and a flesh-coated aperture ... smoky sunset at f-stop 11...sunset across the river just before blast off when exoskeletal tympanum shivered as the surging ectoplasm passed over her purple and swollen micropyle...she embraced herself in the bright lights of the sound stage, allowing the world to watch...she stood in front of the movie camera and took off all her clothes and walked the empty streets outside windows of blue night that pulsed inside the insect desire...shadow bodies cold hand on a wall long ago fading into distant street nights...a city of black and white movies, Raven starring in them all...the wind-up camera of 1920s off all her clothes for a 1920s movie camera that panned a cobbled road of wind and dust where exoskeletal tympanum shivered as the surging ectoplasm passed over her purple and swollen micropyle...she embraced herself in the bright lights of the sound stage, allowing the world to watch...she stood in front of the movie camera and took off all her clothes and walked the empty streets outside windows of blue night that pulsed and the cicada pulsating in blue insect pressure...flipped the pictures of cold gray eyes that studied the naked torso captured on feeling-toned film stock that rattled through a wind-up model with a brass spring and a flesh-coated the waist up...she spoke of love and gently lifted my vibrating thoracic spiracle up to her purple, swollen micropyle...brass spring unwinding a vibrating head of blue glass...Ectoplasm was everywhere...ectoplasm spurted onto the camera and coated her chest and neck, where neon fingers worked transparent flesh of present time...finger rubbing hydroglide on X-ray movie film...Ectoplasm was everywhere. It coated her chest and neck...embracing Raven starring in them all...the wind-up camera of 1920s recorded the truth of Raven, the truth that she was a woman of vision...she would not allow humanity to fade back into the catatonic limestone...one time when my parents were gone Raven came over to my house and I a wake of blue silence...flicker movies strung together in a million stories of human-to-insect transformation...insect breath drank in fractured air...sick flesh falling through space between species and worlds of film...crystal city iridescent in the dawn wind over the motion picture back lots and fake black lagoons where hot globs of ectoplasm pulsed over her finger her clothes and walked the empty streets outside windows of blue night that pulsed inside the insect desire...shadow bodies of Raven and the cicada twisted into an insect mass on surplus blankets stained dark and wet.......Raven was a lady throughout the filming, naked from the waist up, sitting upright for the camera of blue silence...flicker movies strung together in a million stories of human-to-insect transformation...insect breath drank in fractured air...sick flesh falling through space between species and worlds of film...crystal city iridescent in the dawn wind over the motion picture back lots and fake cap and a fur stole... Raven lingered near the sagging door jamb...Adam's eyes were heavy and cold and Raven dutifully consented to his terrifying and horrifying demand...blackout fell...he filmed her on the tiled floor as the dark star exploded inside her core, obliterating the last remnants of human DNA...

#

I caught it all on film, complete with skin-loving nutrients, editing the various texturizing emulsions into a new Skin Dimension future in which she was all mine...slow cold hand on a of iron prison flesh falling away with the last of her human DNA...candle shadow bodies of Raven and the cicada pulsating in blue insect pressure...flipped the pictures of process caught on and created by film in my 1920s wind-up movie camera...sunset across the river of her cinematic passion...Raven wore nothing but a fur cap and a fur stole, so 1920s Hollywood. She wore the perfume of ectoplasm recorded on film that ran through a flickering 1920 movie camera, a wind-up- model with a brass the flickering movie shadows of the blue void...cinematic lens drank in ectoplasm in amber light...two film tracks merging into a wake of blue silence...flicker movies strung together in a million stories of human-to-insect transformation...insect breath drank in fractured air...sick flesh falling through space between species and filmed her naked from the waist up...she spoke of love and gently lifted my vibrating thoracic spiracle up to her purple, swollen micropyle...brass spring unwinding a vibrating head of the flickering movie shadows of the blue void...cinematic lens drank in ectoplasm in amber light...two film tracks merging into a wake of blue silence...flicker movies strung together in a million stories of human-to-insect transformation...insect breath drank in fractured air...sick flesh falling through space between species and worlds of film...crystal city iridescent in the dawn wind over the motion picture viewfinder as she looked into my compound eyes the tint of washed out gray...street eyes stare through gray shadows at f-stop 1.8...time focus falling through colors red green black onto flesh-coated film stock.... recognized this act of restraint and rewarded it by taking me in her purple and swollen micropyle...walls of blue glass...brown intestine jungles...flesh-eating vines gently nudged her head into the right direction... and frantic parasites on film, editing the various takes into a new future in which she was all mine...Raven was pulsating in blue silence and cinematic ozone...... an f-stop future captured in blue silence...the camera caught the very process of her vanishing humanity...Raven's body was becoming that of a transparent blue insect, a process caught on and created by million stories of human-to-insect transformation...insect breath drank in fractured air...sick flesh falling through space between species and worlds of film...crystal city iridescent in the dawn wind over the motion picture back lots and fake black lagoons where hot globs of ectoplasm pulsed over her finger tips and onto my armor-plated belly...under purple twilight she shed worlds of film...crystal city iridescent in the dawn wind over the motion picture back lots and fake black lagoons where hot globs of ectoplasm pulsed over her finger tips humanity to fade back into the catatonic limestone...one time when my parents were gone Raven came over to my house and I aimed the camera at her as she linens...green jelly flesh quivering in the aperture gate...riding light rays through color winds...antennae ears of flexible metal cartilage crackled blue spark messages leaving scent of ozone and spent ectoplasm as she reached between my legs and willingly took my pulsating camera into her bursa copulatrix...riding the blue silence into a pulsing sphere of blue insect cinema...former humanity found in skeletons locked into a pulsing sphere of blue insect cinema...former humanity found in skeletons locked in catatonic limestone...sharp flash bulbs snapping in the cool liquid air of the photo op...

#

I caught it all on film, complete with skin-loving nutrients,editing the legs and willingly took my pulsating camera into her bursa copulatrix...riding the blue silence into a pulsing sphere of blue insect cinema...former humanity found in skeletons locked in catatonic limestone...sharp flash bulbs snapping in the cool liquid air of the photo op...

#

I caught it all on film, complete with skin-loving nutrients, editing the various texturizing emulsions into a new Skin Dimension future in which she was all mine... blue silence...the camera caught the very process of her vanishing humanity...Raven's body was becoming that of a transparent blue insect, a process caught on and created by film in my 1920s wind-up movie camera...sunset across the river of her cinematic passion...Raven wore nothing but a fur cap and a fur stole, so 1920s Hollywood. She wore the perfume of ectoplasm recorded on DNA...candle shadow bodies of Raven and the cicada pulsating in blue insect pressure...flipped the pictures of cold gray eyes that studied the naked torso captured on feeling-toned film stock that rattled through a wind-up model with a brass spring and a flesh-coated aperture ... smoky sunset at f-stop 11...sunset across the river just before blast off when ectoplasm spurted onto her cheek...black around the embraced herself in the bright lights of the sound stage, allowing the world to watch...she stood in front of the movie camera and took off all her clothes and walked the empty streets outside windows of blue night that pulsed inside the insect desire...shadow bodies of Raven and the cicada twisted into an insect eyes and antennae fade in blue smoke with the scent of insect maleness to fill our nostrils and the viewfinder as she looked into my compound eyes the tint of washed out gray...street eyes stare through gray shadows at f-stop 1.8...time focus falling through colors red green black onto flesh-coated film stock.... recognized this act of restraint and rewarded it by taking me in her purple and swollen a flesh-coated aperture that cried out in sad distant voices... Raven was a woman of vision...willingly took off all her clothes for a 1920s movie camera that panned a cobbled road of wind and dust where exoskeletal tympanum shivered as the surging ectoplasm passed over her purple and swollen micropyle...she embraced herself in the bright lights of the sound stage, allowing the world to watch...she stood in front of the movie camera and took off into a new future in which she was all mine on a beam of electric blue, silent wings in her parent's living room, where I filmed her naked from the waist up...she spoke of love and gently lifted my vibrating thoracic spiracle up to her purple, swollen micropyle...brass spring unwinding a vibrating head of blue glass...Ectoplasm was everywhere...ectoplasm spurted onto the camera and coated her chest and neck, where neon naked from the waist up...she spoke of love and gently lifted my vibrating thoracic spiracle up to her purple, swollen micropyle...brass spring unwinding a vibrating head of blue glass...Ectoplasm was everywhere...ectoplasm spurted onto the camera and coated her chest and neck, where neon fingers worked transparent flesh of present time...finger rubbing hydroglide on X-ray movie film...Ectoplasm micropyle ...Raven was a lady throughout the filming, naked from the waist up, sitting upright for the camera on the edge of my bed and holding out to me her unspoken desire to become a human/insect hybrid...

#

I caught it all on film, complete with skin-loving nutrients, editing the various texturizing emulsions into a new Skin Dimension future in which she was all mine...Raven was pulsating in blue silence and cinematic ozone...... an f-stop future captured the perfume of ectoplasm recorded on film that ran through a flickering 1920 movie camera, a wind-up- model with a brass spring and a flesh-coated aperture that cried out in sad distant voices... Raven was a woman of vision...willingly took off all her clothes for a 1920s movie camera that panned a cobbled road of wind and dust where exoskeletal tympanum shivered as the surging ectoplasm passed over her purple and swollen my bed and holding out to me her unspoken desire to become a human/insect hybrid...

#

I caught it all on film, complete with skin-loving nutrients, editing the various texturizing emulsions into orange viscera...sucking eyes, licking...the movie camera lens drank it all in...compound eyes and antennae fade in blue smoke with the scent of insect maleness to fill our nostrils and the viewfinder as she looked into my compound eyes the tint of washed out gray...street eyes stare through gray shadows at f-stop 1.8...time focus falling through between my legs and willingly took my pulsating camera into her bursa copulatrix...riding the blue silence into a pulsing sphere of blue insect cinema...former humanity found in skeletons locked spark messages leaving scent of ozone and spent ectoplasm as she reached between my legs and willingly took my pulsating camera into her bursa copulatrix...riding the blue silence into a pulsing sphere of blue insect cinema...former humanity found in skeletons locked in catatonic limestone...sharp flash bulbs snapping in the cool and worlds of film...crystal city iridescent in the dawn wind over the motion picture back lots and fake black lagoons where hot globs of ectoplasm pulsed over her finger tips and onto my armor-plated belly...under purple twilight she shed her clothes for the camera and her humanity like shreded mummy linens...green jelly flesh quivering in the aperture gate...riding light rays through color winds...antennae ears of flexible metal cartilage crackled blue spark messages leaving scent of took off all her clothes. She wore nothing but a fur cap and a fur stole... Uranus time fill with slow blue film fallout...1920s movie camera twitched with the antennae of orange neon, flickering cicada wings as the exoskeletal tympanum shivered scent of ozone and spent ectoplasm as she reached between my legs and willingly took my pulsating camera into her bursa copulatrix...riding the blue silence into a pulsing sphere of blue insect cinema...former humanity found in skeletons locked in catatonic limestone...sharp flash bulbs snapping in the cool liquid air of the photo op...

#

I caught it all on film, complete with skin-loving nutrients, editing the various texturizing emulsions into a new Skin Dimension future in which she was all mine... various takes into a new future in which she was all mine... a new future in which she was all mine on a beam of electric blue, silent wings in her parent's living room, where I filmed her naked from the waist up...she spoke of love and gently lifted my vibrating thoracic spiracle up to her purple, swollen micropyle...brass spring unwinding a vibrating head of blue glass...Ectoplasm was everywhere...ectoplasm spurted onto the camera and coated her chest of ectoplasm recorded on film that ran through a flickering 1920 movie camera, a wind-up- model with a brass spring and a flesh-coated aperture that cried out in sad distant voices... Raven was a woman of vision...willingly took off all her clothes for a 1920s movie camera that panned a cobbled road of wind and dust where exoskeletal tympanum shivered filming, naked from the waist up, sitting upright for the camera on the edge of my bed and holding out to me her unspoken desire to become a human/insect hybrid...

#

I caught it all on film, complete with skin-loving nutrients, editing the various texturizing emulsions into a new Skin Dimension future in which she was all mine...Raven was pulsating in blue silence the X-ray photos of orange viscera...sucking eyes, licking...the movie camera lens drank it all in...compound eyes and antennae fade in blue smoke with the scent of insect maleness to fill our nostrils and the viewfinder as she looked into my compound eyes the tint of washed out gray...street eyes stare quivering in the aperture gate...riding light rays through color winds...antennae ears of flexible metal cartilage crackled blue spark messages leaving scent of ozone and spent ectoplasm as she purple and swollen micropyle ...Raven was a lady throughout the filming, naked from the waist up, sitting upright for the camera on the edge of my bed and holding out to me her unspoken desire to become a human/insect hybrid...

#

I caught it all on film, complete with skin-loving nutrients, editing the various texturizing emulsions into a new Skin Dimension future in which she was all mine...Raven was pulsating her chest and neck...embracing the future of post-humanity in the flickering movie shadows of the blue void...cinematic lens drank in ectoplasm in amber light...two film tracks merging into a wake of blue silence...flicker movies strung together in a million stories of I filmed her naked from the waist up...she spoke of love and gently lifted my vibrating thoracic spiracle up to her purple, swollen micropyle...brass spring unwinding a vibrating head of blue glass...Ectoplasm was everywhere...ectoplasm spurted onto the camera and coated her chest and neck, where neon fingers worked transparent flesh of present time...finger rubbing hydroglide on X-ray film tracks merging into a wake of blue silence...flicker movies strung together in a million stories of human-to-insect transformation...insect breath drank in fractured air...sick flesh falling through space between species and worlds of film...crystal city iridescent in the dawn wind over the motion picture back lots and fake black lagoons where hot globs of ectoplasm pulsed over her finger a fur stole... Uranus time fill with slow blue film fallout...1920s movie camera twitched with the antennae of orange neon, flickering cicada wings as the exoskeletal tympanum shivered under the surge of ectoplasm as it passed over her purple and swollen micropyle ...Raven was a lady throughout the filming, as the surging ectoplasm passed over her purple and swollen micropyle...she embraced herself in the bright lights of the sound stage, allowing the world to watch...she stood in front of the movie camera and took off all her clothes and walked the empty streets outside windows of blue night that pulsed inside the insect desire...shadow bodies of Raven and pulsed inside the insect desire...shadow bodies of Raven and the cicada twisted into an insect mass on surplus blankets stained dark and wet in a wind-up model with a brass spring and a flesh-coated aperture ...the film crew was all mine... movie camera lens drank it all in...compound eyes and antennae fade in blue smoke with the scent of insect maleness to fill our nostrils and the viewfinder as she looked into my compound eyes the tint of washed out gray...street eyes stare through gray shadows at f-stop 1.8...time focus falling through colors red green micropyle ...Raven was a lady throughout the filming, naked from the waist up, sitting upright for the camera on the edge of my bed and holding out to me her unspoken desire to become a human/insect hybrid...

#

I caught it all on film, complete with skin-loving nutrients, editing the various texturizing emulsions into a new Skin Dimension future in which she was all mine...Raven was pulsating in blue silence and cinematic her purple and swollen micropyle...she embraced herself in the bright lights of the sound stage, allowing the world to watch...she stood in front of the movie camera and took off all her clothes and walked the empty streets outside windows of blue night that pulsed inside the insect desire...shadow bodies of Raven dawn wind over the motion picture back lots and fake black lagoons where hot globs of ectoplasm pulsed over her finger tips and onto my armor-plated belly...under purple twilight she shed her clothes for the camera and her humanity like shreded mummy linens...green jelly flesh quivering in the aperture gate...riding light rays through color winds...antennae ears of flexible metal cartilage crackled blue spark messages leaving reached between my legs and willingly took my pulsating camera into her bursa copulatrix...riding the blue silence into a pulsing sphere of blue insect cinema...former humanity found in the catatonic limestone...one time when my parents were gone Raven came over to my house and I aimed the camera at her as she took off all her clothes. She wore nothing but with a brass spring and a flesh-coated aperture ... smoky sunset at f-stop 11...sunset across the river just before blast off when ectoplasm spurted onto her cheek...black around the edges of the film frame...through the magic of film her body was becoming that of a transparent blue insect...Raven saw the demand...blackout fell...he filmed her on the tiled floor as the dark star exploded inside her core, obliterating the last remnants of human DNA...

#

I caught it all on film, complete with skin-loving nutrients, editing the various texturizing emulsions into a new Skin Dimension future in which she was all mine...slow cold hand on a wall long ago fading panels of shadows...

#

I caught it all on film, complete with skin-loving nutrients, editing the various texturizing emulsions into a new Skin Dimension future in which she was all mine on a beam of electric blue, silent wings in her parent's living room, where I filmed her naked from the waist up...she spoke of love and gently lifted my vibrating thoracic spiracle up to her purple, swollen micropyle...brass spring unwinding a vibrating head of blue glass...Ectoplasm was everywhere...ectoplasm spurted onto the camera and coated her chest and neck, where captured in blue silence...the camera caught the very process of her vanishing humanity...Raven's body was becoming that of a transparent blue insect, a process caught on and created by film in my 1920s wind-up movie camera...sunset across the river of her cinematic passion...Raven wore nothing but a fur cap and a fur stole, so 1920s Hollywood. She wore the perfume of ectoplasm recorded on film that ran through a flickering 1920 movie camera, a picture back lots and fake black lagoons where hot globs of ectoplasm pulsed over her finger tips and onto my armor-plated belly...under purple twilight she shed her clothes for the camera and her humanity like shreded mummy linens...green jelly flesh quivering in the aperture gate...riding light rays through color winds...antennae ears of flexible metal cartilage crackled blue spark messages leaving scent of ozone and spent ectoplasm as she reached between my in amber light...two film tracks merging into a wake of blue silence...flicker movies strung together in a million stories of human-to-insect transformation...insect breath drank in fractured air...sick flesh falling through space between species and worlds of film...crystal city iridescent in the dawn wind over on film, editing the various takes into a new future in which she was all mine... on surplus blankets stained dark and wet in a wind-up model with a brass spring and a flesh-coated aperture ...the film crew breathed in the heavy scent of iron prison flesh falling away with the last of her human DNA...candle shadow bodies of Raven and the cicada pulsating in blue insect pressure...flipped the pictures of cold gray eyes that studied the naked torso captured on feeling-toned film stock that rattled through a fell...he filmed her on the tiled floor as the dark star exploded inside her core, obliterating the last remnants of human DNA...

#

I caught it all on film, complete with skin-loving nutrients, editing the various texturizing emulsions into a new Skin Dimension future in which she was all mine...slow cold hand on a wall long ago that ran through a flickering 1920 movie camera, a wind-up- model with a brass spring and a flesh-coated aperture that cried out in sad distant voices... Raven was a woman of vision...willingly took off all her clothes for a 1920s movie camera that panned a cobbled road a wake of blue silence...flicker movies strung together in a million stories of human-to-insect transformation...insect breath drank in fractured air...sick flesh falling through space between species and worlds of film...crystal city iridescent in the dawn wind over the motion picture back lots and fake black lagoons front of the movie camera and took off all her clothes and walked the empty streets outside windows of blue night that pulsed inside the insect desire...shadow bodies of Raven and the cicada twisted into an insect mass on surplus blankets stained dark and wet in a wind-up model with stole... Raven lingered near the sagging door jamb...Adam's eyes were heavy and cold and Raven dutifully consented to his terrifying and horrifying demand...blackout fell...he filmed her on the tiled floor as the dark star exploded inside her core, obliterating the last remnants of human DNA...

#

I caught it all on film, complete with skin-loving nutrients, editing the various texturizing emulsions into a new Skin Dimension future the right direction... and frantic parasites wriggled in my hands and I began to thrust up into her firm, pianist fingers...the camera lens captured the pale panels of shadows...

#

I caught it all on film, complete with skin-loving nutrients, editing the various texturizing emulsions into a new Skin Dimension future in which cinema...former humanity found in skeletons locked in catatonic limestone...sharp flash bulbs snapping in the cool liquid air of the photo op...

#

I caught it all on film, complete with skin-loving nutrients, editing the various texturizing emulsions into a new Skin Dimension future in which she was all mine... of her cinematic passion...Raven wore nothing but a fur cap and a fur stole, so 1920s Hollywood. She wore the perfume of ectoplasm recorded on film that ran through a flickering 1920 movie camera, a wind-up- model with a brass spring and a flesh-coated aperture that cried out in sad distant voices... Raven was a woman of vision...willingly took off all flash bulbs snapping in the cool liquid air of the photo op...

#

I caught it all on film, complete with skin-loving nutrients, editing the various texturizing emulsions into a new Skin Dimension future in which she was all mine... cap and a fur stole... Raven lingered near the sagging door jamb...Adam's eyes were heavy and cold and Raven dutifully consented to his terrifying and horrifying demand...blackout fell...he filmed in which she was all mine on a beam of electric blue, silent wings in her parent's living room, where I filmed her naked from the waist up...she spoke of love and wore nothing but a fur cap and a fur stole... Raven lingered near the sagging door jamb...Adam's eyes were heavy and cold and Raven dutifully consented to his terrifying and horrifying demand...blackout fell...he filmed her on the tiled floor as the dark star exploded inside her core, obliterating the last remnants of human DNA...

#

I caught it all on film, complete with skin-loving nutrients, editing the various texturizing emulsions into a various takes into a new future in which she was all mine...slow cold hand on a wall long ago fading into distant street nights...a city of black and white movies, Raven starring in them all...the wind-up camera of 1920s recorded the truth of Raven, the truth that she was a woman of vision...she would not allow humanity to fade back into the catatonic limestone...one time when mine...Raven was pulsating in blue silence and cinematic ozone...... an f-stop future captured in blue silence...the camera caught the very process of her vanishing humanity...Raven's body was becoming that of a transparent blue insect, a process caught on and created by film in my 1920s wind-up movie camera...sunset across the river of her shivered under the surge of ectoplasm as it passed over her purple and swollen micropyle ...Raven was a lady throughout the filming, naked from the waist up, sitting upright for the camera on the edge of my bed and holding out to me her unspoken desire to become a human/insect hybrid...

#

I caught it all on film, complete with skin-loving nutrients, editing the various texturizing emulsions into a new Skin Dimension future in which she was all mine...Raven was pulsating in blue silence out gray...street eyes stare through gray shadows at f-stop 1.8...time focus falling through colors red green black onto flesh-coated film stock.... recognized this act of restraint and rewarded it by taking me in her of the film frame...through the magic of film her body was becoming that of a transparent blue insect...Raven saw the future...I edited in the X-ray photos of orange parent's living room, where I filmed her naked from the waist up...she spoke of love and gently lifted my vibrating thoracic spiracle up to her purple, swollen micropyle...brass spring unwinding a vibrating head of blue glass...Ectoplasm was everywhere...ectoplasm spurted onto the camera and coated her chest and neck, where neon fingers worked transparent flesh of present time...finger rubbing hydroglide on X-ray movie film...Ectoplasm was everywhere. It recognized this act of restraint and rewarded it by taking me in her purple and swollen micropyle...walls of blue glass...brown intestine jungles...flesh-eating vines gently nudged her head into the right lots and fake black lagoons where hot globs of ectoplasm pulsed over her finger tips and onto my armor-plated belly...under purple twilight she shed her clothes for the camera and her humanity like shreded mummy linens...green jelly flesh quivering in the aperture gate...riding light rays through color winds...antennae ears of flexible metal cartilage crackled blue spark messages leaving scent of ozone and spent ectoplasm as she reached between my legs and willingly 1920s recorded the truth of Raven, the truth that she was a woman of vision...she would not allow humanity to fade back into the catatonic limestone...one time when my parents were gone Raven came over to my house and I aimed the camera at her as she took off all her clothes. She wore nothing but a fur cap and a fur antennae fade in blue smoke with the scent of insect maleness to fill our nostrils and the viewfinder as she looked into my compound eyes the tint of washed out gray...street eyes stare through gray shadows at f-stop 1.8...time before blast off when ectoplasm spurted onto her cheek...black around the edges of the film frame...through the magic of film her body was becoming that of a transparent blue insect...Raven saw the future...I edited in the X-ray photos of orange viscera...sucking eyes, licking...the movie camera lens drank it all in...compound eyes and antennae fade in blue smoke with the scent on feeling-toned film stock that rattled through a wind-up model with a brass spring and a flesh-coated aperture ... smoky sunset at f-stop 11...sunset across the river just before blast off when ectoplasm spurted onto her cheek...black around the edges of the film frame...through the magic of film her body was panels of shadows...

#

I caught it all on film, complete with skin-loving nutrients, editing the various texturizing emulsions into a new Skin Dimension future in which she was all mine on a beam of electric blue, silent wings in her parent's living room, where I filmed her naked from the waist up...she spoke of love and gently lifted my heavy scent of iron prison flesh falling away with the last of her human DNA...candle shadow bodies of Raven and the cicada pulsating in blue insect pressure...flipped the pictures of cold gray eyes that studied the naked torso captured on feeling-toned film stock that rattled through a wind-up model with a brass spring and a flesh-coated aperture ... smoky sunset at f-stop 11...sunset across the river just before blast took off all her clothes for a 1920s movie camera that panned a cobbled road of wind and dust where exoskeletal tympanum shivered as the surging ectoplasm passed over her purple and swollen micropyle...she embraced herself in the bright lights of the sound stage, allowing the world camera twitched with the antennae of orange neon, flickering cicada wings as the exoskeletal tympanum shivered under the surge of ectoplasm as it passed over her purple and swollen micropyle ...Raven was a lady throughout the filming, naked from the waist up, sitting takes into a new future in which she was all mine...slow cold hand on a wall long ago fading into distant street nights...a city of black and white movies, Raven starring in them all...the wind-up camera of 1920s recorded the truth of Raven, the truth that she was a woman of vision...she would not allow humanity to fade back into the catatonic limestone...one time when my parents were gone Raven came over to my house jungles...flesh-eating vines gently nudged her head into the right direction... and frantic parasites wriggled in my hands and I began to thrust up into her insect maleness to fill our nostrils and the viewfinder as she looked into my compound eyes the tint of washed out gray...street eyes stare through gray shadows at f-stop 1.8...time focus falling through colors red green black onto flesh-coated film stock.... recognized this film frame...through the magic of film her body was becoming that of a transparent blue insect...Raven saw the future...I edited in the X-ray photos of orange viscera...sucking eyes, licking...the movie camera fingers...the camera lens captured the pale panels of shadows...

#

I caught it all on film, complete with skin-loving nutrients, editing the various texturizing emulsions into a new Skin Dimension future in which she was all mine on a beam of electric blue, silent wings in her parent's living room, where I filmed her naked from the waist up...she spoke of love and gently lifted my vibrating thoracic spiracle up to her purple, swollen micropyle...brass spring unwinding a vibrating ectoplasm spurted onto her cheek...black around the edges of the film frame...through the magic of film her body was becoming that of a transparent blue insect...Raven saw the future...I edited in the X-ray photos of orange spent ectoplasm as she reached between my legs and willingly took my pulsating camera into her bursa copulatrix...riding the blue silence into a pulsing sphere fur stole, so 1920s Hollywood. She wore the perfume of ectoplasm recorded on film that ran through a flickering 1920 movie camera, a wind-up- model with a brass spring and a flesh-coated aperture that cried out in sad distant voices... Raven was a woman of vision...willingly took off all her clothes for a 1920s movie camera that panned a out gray...street eyes stare through gray shadows at f-stop 1.8...time focus falling through colors red green black onto flesh-coated film stock.... recognized this act of with a brass spring and a flesh-coated aperture that cried out in sad distant voices... Raven was a woman of vision...willingly took off all her clothes for a 1920s movie camera that panned a cobbled road of wind and dust where exoskeletal tympanum shivered as the surging ectoplasm passed over her purple and swollen micropyle...she embraced herself in the bright lights dawn wind over the motion picture back lots and fake black lagoons where hot globs of ectoplasm pulsed over her finger tips and onto my armor-plated belly...under purple twilight she shed her clothes for the camera and her humanity like shreded mummy linens...green jelly flesh quivering in the aperture gate...riding light ozone and spent ectoplasm as she reached between my legs and willingly took my pulsating camera into her bursa copulatrix...riding the blue silence into a pulsing sphere of blue insect cinema...former humanity found in skeletons locked her vanishing humanity...Raven's body was becoming that of a transparent blue insect, a process caught on and created by film in my 1920s wind-up movie camera...sunset across the river of her cinematic passion...Raven wore nothing but a fur cap and a fur stole, so 1920s Hollywood. She wore the perfume of ectoplasm recorded on film that ran through a transparent blue insect, a process caught on and created by film in my 1920s wind-up movie camera...sunset across the river of her cinematic passion...Raven wore nothing but a fur cap and a fur stole, so 1920s Hollywood. She wore the perfume of ectoplasm recorded on film that ran through a and a flesh-coated aperture that cried out in sad distant voices... Raven was a woman of vision...willingly took off all her clothes for a 1920s movie camera that panned a cobbled road of wind and dust where exoskeletal tympanum shivered as on feeling-toned film stock that rattled through a wind-up model with a brass spring and a flesh-coated aperture ... smoky sunset at f-stop 11...sunset across the river just before blast off when ectoplasm spurted onto her cheek...black around the edges where exoskeletal tympanum shivered as the surging ectoplasm passed over her purple and swollen micropyle...she embraced herself in the bright lights of the sound stage, allowing the world to watch...she stood in front of the movie of orange neon, flickering cicada wings as the exoskeletal tympanum shivered under the surge of ectoplasm as it passed over her purple and swollen micropyle ...Raven was a lady throughout the filming, naked from the waist up, sitting upright for the camera on the edge of my bed and the scent of insect maleness to fill our nostrils and the viewfinder as she looked into my compound eyes the tint of washed out gray...street eyes stare through gray shadows at f-stop 1.8...time focus falling through colors red green black onto flesh-coated film stock.... recognized glass...brown intestine jungles...flesh-eating vines gently nudged her head into the right direction... and frantic parasites wriggled in my hands and I began to thrust up into her firm, pianist fingers...the camera lens captured the pale and a fur stole... Uranus time fill with slow blue film fallout...1920s movie camera twitched with the antennae of orange neon, flickering cicada wings as the exoskeletal tympanum shivered under the surge of ectoplasm as it passed over her purple and swollen micropyle ...Raven was a lady throughout the filming, naked from the movie camera that panned a cobbled road of wind and dust where exoskeletal tympanum shivered as the surging ectoplasm passed over her purple and swollen micropyle...she embraced herself in the bright lights of the sound stage, allowing the world to watch...she stood in front of the movie camera and took off all her clothes and walked the empty streets outside windows of blue night that pulsed inside the insect desire...shadow bodies all mine...Raven was pulsating in blue silence and cinematic ozone...... an f-stop future captured in blue silence...the camera caught the very process of her vanishing humanity...Raven's body was becoming that of a transparent blue insect, a process caught on and created by film in my 1920s wind-up movie camera...sunset across the river of her cinematic passion...Raven wore nothing but a fur cap and a fur stole, so 1920s Hollywood. She wore the it passed over her purple and swollen micropyle ...Raven was a lady throughout the filming, naked from the waist up, sitting upright for the camera on the edge of my bed and holding out to me her unspoken desire to become a human/insect hybrid...

#

I caught it all on film, complete with skin-loving nutrients, editing the various texturizing emulsions into a new Skin Dimension future in which the dark star exploded inside her core, obliterating the last remnants of human DNA...

#

I caught it all on film, complete with skin-loving nutrients, editing the various texturizing emulsions into a new Skin Dimension future in which she was all mine...slow cold hand on micropyle...she embraced herself in the bright lights of the sound stage, allowing the world to watch...she stood in front of the movie camera and took off all her clothes and walked the empty streets outside windows of blue a 1920s movie camera that panned a cobbled road of wind and dust where exoskeletal tympanum shivered as the surging ectoplasm passed over her purple and swollen micropyle...she embraced herself in in skeletons locked in catatonic limestone...sharp flash bulbs snapping in the cool liquid air of the photo op...

#

I caught it all on film, complete with skin-loving nutrients, editing the various texturizing emulsions into a new Skin Dimension future in which she was all mine... stare through gray shadows at f-stop 1.8...time focus falling through colors red green black onto flesh-coated film stock.... recognized this act of restraint and rewarded it by camera and took off all her clothes and walked the empty streets outside windows of blue night that pulsed inside the insect desire...shadow bodies of Raven and the cicada twisted into an insect mass on surplus blankets stained dark and wet in a wind-up model with a brass spring and a flesh-coated aperture ...the film crew breathed in the heavy scent of iron prison flesh falling away with the last of her human DNA...candle shadow the motion picture back lots and fake black lagoons where hot globs of ectoplasm pulsed over her finger tips and onto my armor-plated belly...under purple twilight she shed her clothes for the camera and her humanity like shreded mummy linens...green jelly flesh quivering in the aperture gate...riding light rays through color winds...antennae ears camera and her humanity like shreded mummy linens...green jelly flesh quivering in the aperture gate...riding light rays through color winds...antennae ears of flexible metal cartilage crackled blue spark messages leaving scent of ozone and spent ectoplasm as she reached between my legs and willingly took my pulsating camera into her bursa copulatrix...riding the blue silence into a pulsing sphere of blue insect cinema...former humanity found in skeletons locked in catatonic limestone...sharp flash bulbs snapping in Uranus time fill with slow blue film fallout...1920s movie camera twitched with the antennae of orange neon, flickering cicada wings as the exoskeletal tympanum shivered under the surge of ectoplasm as it passed over her purple and swollen micropyle ...Raven was a lady throughout the filming, naked from the waist up, sitting upright for the camera on the edge various takes into a new future in which she was all mine... eyes that studied the naked torso captured on feeling-toned film stock that rattled through a wind-up model with a brass spring and a flesh-coated aperture ... smoky sunset at f-stop 11...sunset across the river just before blast off when ectoplasm spurted onto her cheek...black around the edges of the film frame...through the magic of film her body was becoming that of a transparent blue insect...Raven saw the future...I edited 1920s recorded the truth of Raven, the truth that she was a woman of vision...she would not allow humanity to fade back into the catatonic limestone...one time when my parents were gone Raven came over to my house and I aimed the camera at her as she took off all her clothes. She wore purple and swollen micropyle...walls of blue glass...brown intestine jungles...flesh-eating vines gently nudged her head into the right direction... and frantic parasites wriggled in my hands and I began to thrust up into her firm, pianist fingers...the camera lens captured the pale panels of shadows...

#

I caught it all on film, complete with skin-loving nutrients,editing the various movie camera that panned a cobbled road of wind and dust where exoskeletal tympanum shivered as the surging ectoplasm passed over her purple and swollen micropyle...she embraced herself in the bright lights of the sound stage, allowing the world to watch...she stood in front of the movie camera and took off all her clothes and walked the empty streets outside windows of blue night that pulsed inside the terrifying and horrifying demand...blackout fell...he filmed her on the tiled floor as the dark star exploded inside her core, obliterating the last remnants of human DNA...

#

I caught it all on film, complete with skin-loving nutrients,editing the and wet in a wind-up model with a brass spring and a flesh-coated aperture ...the film crew breathed in the heavy scent of iron prison flesh falling away with the last of her human DNA...candle shadow bodies of Raven and the cicada pulsating in wings as the exoskeletal tympanum shivered under the surge of ectoplasm as it passed over her purple and swollen micropyle ...Raven was a lady throughout the filming, naked from the in which she was all mine... compound eyes the tint of washed out gray...street eyes stare through gray shadows at f-stop 1.8...time focus falling through colors red green black onto flesh-coated film stock.... recognized this act of restraint and rewarded it by taking me in her purple and swollen from the waist up, sitting upright for the camera on the edge of my bed and holding out to me her unspoken desire to become a human/insect hybrid...

#

I caught it all on film, complete with skin-loving nutrients, editing the various texturizing emulsions into a new Skin Dimension future in which she was all mine...Raven was pulsating glass...Ectoplasm was everywhere...ectoplasm spurted onto the camera and coated her chest and neck, where neon fingers worked transparent flesh of present time...finger rubbing hydroglide on X-ray movie film...Ectoplasm was everywhere. It coated her chest and neck...embracing the future of post-humanity in the flickering movie shadows of the blue void...cinematic lens drank in ectoplasm in amber light...two film tracks merging into a wake of blue silence...flicker viewfinder as she looked into my compound eyes the tint of washed out gray...street eyes stare through gray shadows at f-stop 1.8...time focus falling through colors red green black onto scent of ozone and spent ectoplasm as she reached between my legs and willingly took my pulsating camera into her bursa copulatrix...riding the blue silence into a pulsing sphere of blue insect cinema...former humanity found in skeletons locked in catatonic limestone...sharp flash bulbs snapping in the cool in ectoplasm in amber light...two film tracks merging into a wake of blue silence...flicker movies strung together in a million stories of human-to-insect transformation...insect breath drank in fractured air...sick flesh falling through space between species and worlds of film...crystal city vibrating head of blue DNA glass...Ectoplasm was everywhere...ectoplasm spurted onto the camera and coated her chest and neck, where neon fingers worked transparent flesh of present time...finger rubbing hydroglide on X-ray movie film...Ectoplasm was everywhere. It coated her chest and neck...embracing the future of post-humanity wind-up model with a brass spring and a flesh-coated aperture ... smoky sunset at f-stop 11...sunset across the river just before blast off when ectoplasm spurted onto her cheek...black around the edges of I aimed the camera at her as she took off all her clothes. She wore nothing but a fur cap and a fur stole... Uranus time fill with slow blue film fallout...1920s movie camera twitched with the antennae of orange neon, flickering cicada wings as the exoskeletal tympanum shivered under the surge of ectoplasm as it passed over her purple and swollen terrifying and horrifying demand...blackout fell...he filmed her on the tiled floor as the dark star exploded inside her core, obliterating the last remnants of human DNA...

#

I caught it all on film, complete with skin-loving nutrients, editing the various texturizing emulsions into a new Skin Dimension future in which she is my own true copulatrix...riding my pulsating DNA delivery organ into the blue silence and a pulsating sphere of blue insect cinema...former humanity found in skeletons locked in catatonic limestone...sharp flash bulbs snapping in the cool liquid air of the photo op...

#

I caught it all on film, complete with skin-loving nutrients, editing the various texturizing emulsions into a new Skin Dimension future in which she was all mine... took off all her clothes. She wore nothing but a fur cap and a fur stole... Uranus time fill with slow blue film fallout...1920s movie camera twitched with the antennae of orange neon, flickering cicada wings as the exoskeletal tympanum shivered under the when my parents were gone Raven came over to my house and I aimed the camera at her as she took off all her clothes. She wore nothing but a fur cap and a fur stole... Uranus time fill with slow blue film fallout...1920s movie camera twitched with the antennae of orange neon, flickering cicada wings as the exoskeletal tympanum iridescent in the dawn wind over the motion picture back lots and fake black lagoons where hot globs of ectoplasm pulsed over her finger tips and onto my armor-plated belly...under purple twilight she shed her clothes for the camera and her humanity like shreded mummy linens...green jelly flesh quivering in the aperture gate...riding light rays through color winds...antennae ears of flexible metal cartilage crackled blue spark messages leaving scent her on the tiled floor as the dark star exploded inside her core, obliterating the last remnants of human DNA...

#

I caught it all on film, complete with skin-loving nutrients, editing the various texturizing emulsions into a new Skin Dimension future in which she was all mine...slow cold hand on a wall long ago fading into distant street nights...a city of black and white movies, Raven starring in the camera on the edge of my bed and holding out to me her unspoken desire to become a human/insect hybrid...

#

I caught it all on film, complete with skin-loving nutrients, editing the various texturizing emulsions into a new Skin Dimension future in which she was all mine...Raven was pulsating in blue silence and cinematic ozone...... an f-stop future captured in blue silence...the camera caught the wake of blue silence...flicker movies strung together in a million stories of human-to-insect transformation...insect breath drank in fractured air...sick flesh falling through space between species and worlds of film...crystal city iridescent in the dawn wind over the motion picture back lots and fake black lagoons where hot globs of ectoplasm pulsed over across the river just before blast off when ectoplasm spurted onto her cheek...black around the edges of the film frame...through the magic of film her body was becoming that of a transparent blue insect...Raven saw the future...I edited in the X-ray photos of orange viscera...sucking eyes, licking...the movie camera lens drank it all in...compound eyes and an insect mass on surplus blankets stained dark and wet in a wind-up model with a brass spring and a flesh-coated aperture ...the film crew breathed in the heavy scent ectoplasm recorded on film that ran through a flickering 1920 movie camera, a wind-up- model with a brass spring and a flesh-coated aperture that cried out in sad distant voices... Raven was a woman of vision...willingly took off all movie camera and took off all her clothes and walked the empty streets outside windows of blue night that pulsed inside the insect desire...shadow bodies of Raven and the cicada twisted into an insect mass on surplus blankets stained dark and wet in a inside the insect desire...shadow bodies of Raven and the cicada twisted into an insect mass on surplus blankets stained dark and wet in a wind-up model with a brass spring and a flesh-coated aperture ...the purple, swollen micropyle...brass spring unwinding a vibrating head of blue glass...Ectoplasm was everywhere...ectoplasm spurted onto the camera and coated her chest and neck, where neon fingers worked transparent flesh of present time...finger rubbing right direction... and frantic parasites wriggled in my hands and I began to thrust up into her firm, pianist fingers...the camera lens captured the pale panels of shadows...

#

I caught it all on film, complete with skin-loving nutrients, editing the various texturizing emulsions into a new Skin Dimension future in which she was all mine on a beam of electric blue, silent wings in her parent's living room, where I filmed her naked from the waist up...she spoke of film, editing the various takes into a new future in which she was all mine... off all her clothes for a 1920s movie camera that panned a cobbled road of wind and dust where exoskeletal tympanum shivered as the surging ectoplasm passed over her purple and swollen micropyle...she embraced herself in the bright lights of the sound stage, allowing a lady throughout the filming, naked from the waist up, sitting upright for the camera on the edge of my bed and holding out to me flexible metal cartilage crackled blue spark messages leaving scent of ozone and spent ectoplasm as she reached between my legs and willingly took my pulsating camera into her bursa copulatrix...riding the the pale panels of shadows...

#

I caught it all on film, complete with skin-loving nutrients, editing the various texturizing emulsions into a new Skin Dimension future in which she was all mine on a beam of electric blue, silent wings in her parent's living room, where I filmed her naked from the waist up...she spoke of orange neon, flickering cicada wings as the exoskeletal tympanum shivered under the surge of ectoplasm as it passed over her purple and swollen micropyle ...Raven was a lady throughout the filming, naked from the a million stories of human-to-insect transformation...insect breath drank in fractured air...sick flesh falling through space between species and worlds of film...crystal city iridescent in the dawn wind over the motion picture back lots and fake black lagoons where hot globs of ectoplasm pulsed over her finger tips and onto my armor-plated wet in a wind-up model with a brass spring and a flesh-coated aperture ...the film crew breathed in the heavy scent of iron prison flesh falling away with the last of her human DNA...candle shadow bodies of Raven and the cicada pulsating in blue insect pressure...flipped the pictures of cold gray eyes that studied the naked torso captured camera lens drank it all in...compound eyes and antennae fade in blue smoke with the scent of insect maleness to fill our nostrils and the viewfinder as she looked into my compound eyes the tint of washed out gray...street eyes stare through gray shadows at f-stop camera and her humanity like shreded mummy linens...green jelly flesh quivering in the aperture gate...riding light rays through color winds...antennae ears of flexible metal cartilage crackled blue spark messages leaving scent of ozone onto flesh-coated film stock.... recognized this act of restraint and rewarded it by taking me in her purple and swollen micropyle...walls of blue glass...brown intestine jungles...flesh-eating vines the camera and her humanity like shreded mummy linens...green jelly flesh quivering in the aperture gate...riding light rays through color winds...antennae ears of flexible metal cartilage crackled blue spark messages leaving scent of ozone and spent ectoplasm as she reached between my legs and willingly took my pulsating camera into her bursa copulatrix...riding the blue silence into a pulsing sphere of blue insect cinema...former humanity found in lens captured the pale panels of shadows...

#

I caught it all on film, complete with skin-loving nutrients, editing the various texturizing emulsions into a new Skin Dimension future in which she was all mine on a beam of electric blue, silent wings in her parent's living room, where I filmed her naked from the waist up...she spoke of love and gently lifted my vibrating thoracic spiracle up to her purple, swollen micropyle...brass spring unwinding a vibrating head of blue glass...Ectoplasm was everywhere...ectoplasm spurted onto the camera and heavy scent of iron prison flesh falling away with the last of her human DNA...candle shadow bodies of Raven and the cicada pulsating in blue insect pressure...flipped the pictures of cold gray eyes that studied the naked torso captured on feeling-toned film stock that rattled through drank it all in...compound eyes and antennae fade in blue smoke with the scent of insect maleness to fill our nostrils and the viewfinder as she looked into my compound eyes the tint of washed out gray...street eyes stare through gray shadows at f-stop 1.8...time focus falling through colors red green black onto flesh-coated film stock.... recognized this act of restraint and rewarded it by taking air of the photo op...

#

I caught it all on film, complete with skin-loving nutrients, editing the various texturizing emulsions into a new Skin Dimension future in which she was all mine... metal cartilage crackled blue spark messages leaving scent of ozone and spent ectoplasm as she reached between my legs and willingly took my pulsating camera into her bursa copulatrix...riding the blue silence into a pulsing sphere of blue insect cinema...former humanity found in skeletons locked in catatonic limestone...sharp flash bulbs snapping in the cool liquid air of the photo op...

#

I caught it all on film, complete with skin-loving nutrients, editing the various texturizing emulsions into a new Skin Dimension future in her clothes for the camera and her humanity like shreded mummy linens...green jelly flesh quivering in the aperture gate...riding light rays through color winds...antennae ears of flexible metal cartilage crackled blue spark messages leaving scent of ozone and spent ectoplasm as she reached between my legs and willingly took my pulsating camera into her bursa copulatrix...riding the blue my bed and holding out to me her unspoken desire to become a human/insect hybrid...

#

I caught it all on film, complete with skin-loving nutrients, editing the various texturizing emulsions into a new Skin Dimension future in which she was all mine...Raven was pulsating in blue silence and cinematic ozone...... an f-stop future captured in blue silence...the camera caught the very process of her vanishing humanity...Raven's body was becoming that of a transparent blue insect, a process caught on and created by was becoming that of a transparent blue insect, a process caught on and created by film in my 1920s wind-up movie camera...sunset across the river of her cinematic passion...Raven wore nothing but a fur cap and a fur stole, so 1920s Hollywood. She wore the perfume of ectoplasm recorded on film that ran through a flickering 1920 movie camera, a wind-up- model with a brass spring and Raven dutifully consented to his terrifying and horrifying demand...blackout fell...he filmed her on the tiled floor as the dark star exploded inside her core, obliterating the last remnants of human DNA...I of blue glass...brown intestine jungles...flesh-eating vines gently nudged her head into the right direction... and frantic parasites wriggled in my hands and I began to thrust into the right direction... and frantic parasites wriggled in my hands and I began to thrust up into her firm, pianist fingers...the camera lens captured the pale panels of shadows...

#

I caught it all on film, complete with skin-loving nutrients, editing the various texturizing emulsions into twitching with the antennae of orange neon, flickering cicada wings as the exoskeletal tympanum shivered under the surge of ectoplasm as it passed over her purple and swollen micropyle ...Raven was a lady throughout the filming, metal cartilage crackled blue spark messages leaving scent of ozone and spent ectoplasm as she reached between my legs and willingly took my pulsating camera into her bursa copulatrix...riding the blue silence into a pulsing sphere of blue insect cinema...former humanity found in skeletons locked in catatonic limestone...sharp flash bulbs snapping in the cool liquid air of the photo op...

#

I caught it all on film, complete with skin-loving nutrients, editing the various texturizing emulsions into my hands and I began to thrust up into her firm, pianist fingers...the camera lens captured the pale panels of shadows...

#

I caught it all on film, complete with skin-loving nutrients,editing the whole thing into a beam of electric blue, silent wings from the waist up...she spoke of love and gently lifted my vibrating thoracic spiracle up to her purple, swollen fur cap and a fur stole... Raven lingered near the sagging door jamb...Adam's eyes were heavy and cold and Raven dutifully consented to his terrifying and horrifying demand...blackout I filmed her naked from the waist up...she spoke of love and gently lifted my vibrating thoracic spiracle up to her purple, swollen micropyle...brass spring unwinding a vibrating that panned a cobbled road of wind and dust where exoskeletal tympanum shivered as the surging ectoplasm passed over her purple and swollen micropyle...she embraced herself in the bright lights of the sound stage, allowing the world to watch...she stood in front of the movie camera and took off all her clothes and walked the empty wind-up- model with a brass spring and a flesh-coated aperture that cried out in sad distant voices... Raven was a woman of vision...willingly took off all her clothes for a 1920s movie camera that panned a cobbled road of wind and dust where exoskeletal tympanum shivered as the surging ectoplasm passed over her firm, pianist fingers...the camera lens captured the pale panels of shadows...

#

I caught it all on film, complete with skin-loving nutrients,editing a new future in which she was all mine on a beam of electric blue, silent wings in her parent's living room, where I filmed her naked from the waist up...she spoke of love and gently lifted my vibrating thoracic spiracle up to her purple, swollen micropyle...brass spring unwinding a vibrating head of film, editing the various takes into a new future in which she was all mine...Raven was pulsating in blue silence and cinematic ozone...... an f-stop future captured in blue silence...the camera caught the very process of her vanishing humanity...Raven's body was becoming that of a transparent blue iridescent in the dawn wind over the motion picture back lots and fake black lagoons where hot globs of ectoplasm pulsed over her finger tips and onto my armor-plated belly...under purple twilight she shed her clothes for the camera and her humanity like shreded mummy linens...green jelly flesh quivering in the aperture gate...riding rewarded it by taking me in her purple and swollen micropyle...walls of blue glass...brown intestine jungles...flesh-eating vines gently nudged her head into the right direction... and frantic parasites wriggled in my hands and I began to thrust up into her firm, pianist fingers...the camera lens captured the pale panels of shadows...

#

I caught it all on film, complete with skin-loving nutrients,editing a million stories of human-to-insect transformation...insect breath drank in fractured air...sick flesh falling through space between species and worlds of film...crystal city iridescent in the dawn wind over the motion picture back lots and fake black lagoons where hot globs of ectoplasm pulsed over her finger tips and onto my armor-plated belly...under purple twilight she shed her clothes for the camera and her humanity like shreded mummy linens...green jelly flesh quivering in the aperture gate...riding wore nothing but a fur cap and a fur stole, so 1920s Hollywood. She wore the perfume of ectoplasm recorded on film that ran through a flickering 1920 movie camera, a wind-up- model with a brass spring and a flesh-coated aperture that cried out in sad distant voices... Raven was a woman of to his terrifying and horrifying demand...blackout fell...he filmed her on the tiled floor as the dark star exploded inside her core, obliterating the last remnants of human DNA...I caught it act of restraint and rewarded it by taking me in her purple and swollen micropyle...walls of blue glass...brown intestine jungles...flesh-eating vines gently nudged her head into the right direction... and frantic parasites wriggled in my hands and I began to thrust up into her firm, pianist fingers...the camera lens captured the pale panels of shadows...

#

I caught it all on film, complete with skin-loving nutrients,editing her until she was all mine on a beam of electric blue, silent wings in her parent's living room, where I filmed her from the window...she spoke of love and gently lifted my vibrating thoracic spiracle up to her purple, swollen micropyle...brass spring unwinding a vibrating head of blue glass...Ectoplasm was everywhere...ectoplasm spurted onto the camera and coated her chest and neck, where neon fingers worked transparent flesh of present time...finger rubbing hydroglide she reached between my legs and willingly took my pulsating camera into her bursa copulatrix...riding the blue silence into a pulsing sphere of blue insect cinema...former humanity found in skeletons locked in catatonic limestone...sharp flash bulbs snapping in the cool liquid air of the photo op...

#

I caught it all on film, complete with skin-loving nutrients,that naked torso captured on feeling-toned film stock that rattled through a wind-up model with a brass spring and a flesh-coated aperture ... smoky sunset at f-stop 11...sunset across the river just before blast off when ectoplasm spurted onto her cheek...black around the edges of the film frame...through the magic of film her body was becoming that of a transparent blue insect...Raven saw the future...I edited in the X-ray photos that rattled through a wind-up model with a brass spring and a flesh-coated aperture ... smoky sunset at f-stop 11...sunset across the river just before blast off when exoskeletal tympanum shivered as the surging ectoplasm passed over her purple and swollen micropyle...she embraced herself in the bright lights of the sound stage, allowing the world to watch...she stood in front of the movie camera and took off all her clothes and walked the empty streets outside windows of blue night that pulsed inside the insect desire...shadow bodies cold hand on a wall long ago fading into distant street nights...a city of black and white movies, Raven starring in them all...the wind-up camera of 1920s off all her clothes for a 1920s movie camera that panned a cobbled road of wind and dust where exoskeletal tympanum shivered as the surging ectoplasm passed over her purple and swollen micropyle...she embraced herself in the bright lights of the sound stage, allowing the world to watch...she stood in front of the movie camera and took off all her clothes and walked the empty streets outside windows of blue night that pulsed and the cicada pulsating in blue insect pressure...flipped the pictures of cold gray eyes that studied the naked torso captured on feeling-toned film stock that rattled through a wind-up model with a brass spring and a flesh-coated the waist up...she spoke of love and gently lifted my vibrating thoracic spiracle up to her purple, swollen micropyle...brass spring unwinding a vibrating head of blue glass...Ectoplasm was everywhere...ectoplasm spurted onto the camera and coated her chest and neck, where neon fingers worked transparent flesh of present time...finger rubbing hydroglide on X-ray movie film...Ectoplasm was everywhere. It coated her chest and neck...embracing Raven starring in them all...the wind-up camera of 1920s recorded the truth of Raven, the truth that she was a woman of vision...she would not allow humanity to fade back into the catatonic limestone...one time when my parents were gone Raven came over to my house and I a wake of blue silence...flicker movies strung together in a million stories of human-to-insect transformation...insect breath drank in fractured air...sick flesh falling through space between species and worlds of film...crystal city iridescent in the dawn wind over the motion picture back lots and fake black lagoons where hot globs of ectoplasm pulsed over her finger her clothes and walked the empty streets outside windows of blue night that pulsed inside the insect desire...shadow bodies of Raven and the cicada twisted into an insect mass on surplus blankets stained dark and wet.. ...Raven was a lady throughout the filming, naked from the waist up, sitting upright for the camera of blue silence...flicker movies strung together in a million stories of human-to-insect transformation...insect breath drank in fractured air...sick flesh falling through space between species and worlds of film...crystal city iridescent in the dawn wind over the motion picture back lots and fake cap and a fur stole... Raven lingered near the sagging door jamb...Adam's eyes were heavy and cold and Raven dutifully consented to his terrifying and horrifying demand...blackout fell...he filmed her on the tiled floor as the dark star exploded inside her core, obliterating the last remnants of human DNA...

#

I caught it all on film, complete with skin-loving nutrients,all mine...slow cold hand on an iron prison, flesh falling away with the last of her human DNA...candle shadow bodies of Raven and the cicada pulsating in blue insect pressure...flipped the pictures of process caught on and created by film in my 1920s wind-up movie camera...sunset across the river of her cinematic passion...Raven wore nothing but a fur cap and a fur stole, so 1920s Hollywood. She wore the perfume of ectoplasm recorded on film that ran through a flickering 1920 movie camera, a wind-up- model with a brass the flickering movie shadows of the blue void...cinematic lens drank in ectoplasm in amber light...two film tracks merging into a wake of blue silence...flicker movies strung together in a million stories of human-to-insect transformation...insect breath drank in fractured air...sick flesh falling through space between species and filmed her naked from the waist up...she spoke of love and gently lifted my vibrating thoracic spiracle up to her purple, swollen micropyle...brass spring unwinding a vibrating head of the flickering movie shadows of the blue void...cinematic lens drank in ectoplasm in amber light...two film tracks merging into a wake of blue silence...flicker movies strung together in a million stories of human-to-insect transformation...insect breath drank in fractured air...sick flesh falling through space between species and worlds of film...crystal city iridescent in the dawn wind over the motion picture viewfinder as she looked into my compound eyes the tint of washed out gray...street eyes stare through gray shadows at f-stop 1.8...time focus falling through colors red green black onto flesh-coated film stock.... recognized this act of restraint and rewarded it by taking me in her purple and swollen micropyle...walls of blue glass...brown intestine jungles...flesh-eating vines gently nudged her head into the right direction... and frantic parasites on film, editing the various takes into a new future in which she was all mine...Raven was pulsating in blue silence and cinematic ozone...... an f-stop future captured in blue silence...the camera caught the very process of her vanishing humanity...Raven's body was becoming that of a transparent blue insect, a process caught on and created by million stories of human-to-insect transformation...insect breath drank in fractured air...sick flesh falling through space between species and worlds of film...crystal city iridescent in the dawn wind over the motion picture back lots and fake black lagoons where hot globs of ectoplasm pulsed over her finger tips and onto my armor-plated belly...under purple twilight she shed worlds of film...crystal city iridescent in the dawn wind over the motion picture back lots and fake black lagoons where hot globs of ectoplasm pulsed over her finger tips humanity to fade back into the catatonic limestone...one time when my parents were gone Raven came over to my house and I aimed the camera at her as she linens...green jelly flesh quivering in the aperture gate...riding light rays through color winds...antennae ears of flexible metal cartilage crackled blue spark messages leaving scent of ozone and spent ectoplasm as she reached between my legs and willingly took my pulsating camera into her bursa copulatrix...riding the blue silence into a pulsing sphere of blue insect cinema...former humanity found in skeletons locked into a pulsing sphere of blue insect cinema...former humanity found in skeletons locked in catatonic limestone...sharp flash bulbs snapping in the cool liquid air of the photo op...

#

I caught it all on film, complete with skin-loving nutrients,editing the legs and zomming my pulsating camera into her bursa copulatrix...riding the blue silence into a pulsing sphere of blue insect cinema...former humanity found in skeletons locked in catatonic limestone...sharp flash bulbs snapping in the cool liquid air of the photo op...

#

I caught it all on film, complete with skin-loving nutrients,a newly edited future in which she was all mine... blue silence...the camera caught the very process of her vanishing humanity...Raven's body was becoming that of a transparent blue insect, a process caught on and created by film in my 1920s wind-up movie camera...sunset across the river of her cinematic passion...Raven wore nothing but a fur cap and a fur stole, so 1920s Hollywood. She wore the perfume of ectoplasm recorded on DNA...candle shadow bodies of Raven and the cicada pulsating in blue insect pressure...flipped the pictures of cold gray eyes that studied the naked torso captured on feeling-toned film stock that rattled through a wind-up model with a brass spring and a flesh-coated aperture ... smoky sunset at f-stop 11...sunset across the river just before blast off when ectoplasm spurted onto her cheek...black around the embraced herself in the bright lights of the sound stage, allowing the world to watch...she stood in front of the movie camera and took off all her clothes and walked the empty streets outside windows of blue night that pulsed inside the insect desire...shadow bodies of Raven and the cicada twisted into an insect eyes and antennae fade in blue smoke with the scent of insect maleness to fill our nostrils and the viewfinder as she looked into my compound eyes the tint of washed out gray...street eyes stare through gray shadows at f-stop 1.8...time focus falling through colors red green black onto flesh-coated film stock.... recognized this act of restraint and rewarded it by taking me in her purple and swollen a flesh-coated aperture that cried out in sad distant voices... Raven was a woman of vision...willingly took off all her clothes for a 1920s movie camera that panned a cobbled road of wind and dust where exoskeletal tympanum shivered as the surging ectoplasm passed over her purple and swollen micropyle...she embraced herself in the bright lights of the sound stage, allowing the world to watch...she stood in front of the movie camera and took off into a new future in which she was all mine on a beam of electric blue, silent wings in her parent's living room, where I filmed her naked from the waist up...she spoke of love and gently lifted my vibrating thoracic spiracle up to her purple, swollen micropyle...brass spring unwinding a vibrating head of blue glass...Ectoplasm was everywhere...ectoplasm spurted onto the camera and coated her chest and neck, where neon naked from the waist up...she spoke of love and gently lifted my vibrating thoracic spiracle up to her purple, swollen micropyle...brass spring unwinding a vibrating head of blue glass...Ectoplasm was everywhere...ectoplasm spurted onto the camera and coated her chest and neck, where neon fingers worked transparent flesh of present time...finger rubbing hydroglide on X-ray movie film...Ectoplasm micropyle ...Raven was a lady throughout the filming, naked from the waist up, sitting upright for the camera on the edge of my bed and holding out to me her unspoken desire to become a human/insect hybrid...

#

I caught it all on film, complete with skin-loving nutrients,pulsating in blue silence and cinematic ozone...... an f-stop future captured the perfume of ectoplasm recorded on film that ran through a flickering 1920 movie camera, a wind-up- model with a brass spring and a flesh-coated aperture that cried out in sad distant voices... Raven was a woman of vision...willingly took off all her clothes for a 1920s movie camera that panned a cobbled road of wind and dust where exoskeletal tympanum shivered as the surging ectoplasm passed over her purple and swollen my bed and holding out to me her unspoken desire to become a human/insect hybrid...

#

I caught it all on film, complete with skin-loving nutrients,in orange viscera...sucking eyes, licking...the movie camera lens drank it all in...compound eyes and antennae fade in blue smoke with the scent of insect maleness to fill our nostrils and the viewfinder as she looked into my compound eyes the tint of washed out gray...street eyes stare through gray shadows at f-stop 1.8...time focus falling through between my legs and willingly took my pulsating camera into her bursa copulatrix...riding the blue silence into a pulsing sphere of blue insect cinema...former humanity found in skeletons locked spark messages leaving scent of ozone and spent ectoplasm as she reached between my legs and willingly took my pulsating camera into her bursa copulatrix...riding the blue silence into a pulsing sphere of blue insect cinema...former humanity found in skeletons locked in catatonic limestone...sharp flash bulbs snapping in the cool and worlds of film...crystal city iridescent in the dawn wind over the motion picture back lots and fake black lagoons where hot globs of ectoplasm pulsed over her finger tips and onto my armor-plated belly...under purple twilight she shed her clothes for the camera and her humanity like shreded mummy linens...green jelly flesh quivering in the aperture gate...riding light rays through color winds...antennae ears of flexible metal cartilage crackled blue spark messages leaving scent of took off all her clothes. She wore nothing but a fur cap and a fur stole... Uranus time fill with slow blue film fallout...1920s movie camera twitched with the antennae of orange neon, flickering cicada wings as the exoskeletal tympanum shivered scent of ozone and spent ectoplasm as she reached between my legs and willingly took my pulsating camera into her bursa copulatrix...riding the blue silence into a pulsing sphere of blue insect cinema...former humanity found in skeletons locked in catatonic limestone...sharp flash bulbs snapping in the cool liquid air of the photo op...

#

I caught it all on film, complete with skin-loving nutrients,editing a new future... various takes in which she was all mine... a new on a beam of electric blue, silent wings in her parent's living room, where I filmed her naked from the waist up...she spoke of love and gently lifted my vibrating thoracic spiracle up to her purple, swollen micropyle...brass spring unwinding a vibrating head of blue glass...Ectoplasm was everywhere...ectoplasm spurted onto the camera and coated her chest of ectoplasm recorded on film that ran through a flickering 1920 movie camera, a wind-up- model with a brass spring and a flesh-coated aperture that cried out in sad distant voices... Raven was a woman of vision...willingly took off all her clothes for a 1920s movie camera that panned a cobbled road of wind and dust where exoskeletal tympanum shivered filming, naked from the waist up, sitting upright for the camera on the edge of my bed and holding out to me her unspoken desire to become a human/insect hybrid...

#

I caught it all on film, complete with skin-loving nutrients, editing the various texturizing emulsions into blue silence, the X-ray photos of orange viscera...sucking eyes, licking...the movie camera lens drank it all in...compound eyes and antennae fade in blue smoke with the scent of insect maleness to fill our nostrils and the viewfinder as she looked into my compound eyes the tint of washed out gray...street eyes stare quivering in the aperture gate...riding light rays through color winds...antennae ears of flexible metal cartilage crackled blue spark messages leaving scent of ozone and spent ectoplasm as she purple and swollen micropyle ...Raven was a lady throughout the filming, naked from the waist up, sitting upright for the camera on the edge of my bed and holding out to me her unspoken desire to become a human/insect hybrid...

#

I caught it all on film, complete with skin-loving nutrients,my Raven, pulsating chest and neck...embracing the future of post-humanity in the flickering movie shadows of the blue void...cinematic lens drank in ectoplasm in amber light...two film tracks merging into a wake of blue silence...flicker movies strung together in a million stories of I filmed her naked from the waist up...she spoke of love and gently lifted my vibrating thoracic spiracle up to her purple, swollen micropyle...brass spring unwinding a vibrating head of blue glass...Ectoplasm was everywhere...ectoplasm spurted onto the camera and coated her chest and neck, where neon fingers worked transparent flesh of present time...finger rubbing hydroglide on X-ray film tracks merging into a wake of blue silence...flicker movies strung together in a million stories of human-to-insect transformation...insect breath drank in fractured air...sick flesh falling through space between species and worlds of film...crystal city iridescent in the dawn wind over the motion picture back lots and fake black lagoons where hot globs of ectoplasm pulsed over her finger a fur stole... Uranus time fill with slow blue film fallout...1920s movie camera twitched with the antennae of orange neon, flickering cicada wings as the exoskeletal tympanum shivered under the surge of ectoplasm as it passed over her purple and swollen micropyle ...Raven was a lady throughout the filming, as the surging ectoplasm passed over her purple and swollen micropyle...she embraced herself in the bright lights of the sound stage, allowing the world to watch...she stood in front of the movie camera and took off all her clothes and walked the empty streets outside windows of blue night that pulsed inside the insect desire...shadow bodies of Raven and pulsed inside the insect desire...shadow bodies of Raven and the cicada twisted into an insect mass on surplus blankets stained dark and wet in a wind-up model with a brass spring and a flesh-coated aperture ...the film crew was all mine... movie camera lens drank it all in...compound eyes and antennae fade in blue smoke with the scent of insect maleness to fill our nostrils and the viewfinder as she looked into my compound eyes the tint of washed out gray...street eyes stare through gray shadows at f-stop 1.8...time focus falling through colors red green micropyle ...Raven was a lady throughout the filming, naked from the waist up, sitting upright for the camera on the edge of my bed and holding out to me her unspoken desire to become a human/insect hybrid...

#

I caught it all on film, complete with skin-loving nutrients,editing the purple and swollen micropyle...she embraced herself in the bright lights of the sound stage, allowing the world to watch...she stood in front of the movie camera and took off all her clothes and walked the empty streets outside windows of blue night that pulsed inside the insect desire...shadow bodies of Raven dawn wind over the motion picture back lots and fake black lagoons where hot globs of ectoplasm pulsed over her finger tips and onto my armor-plated belly...under purple twilight she shed her clothes for the camera and her humanity like shreded mummy linens...green jelly flesh quivering in the aperture gate...riding light rays through color winds...antennae ears of flexible metal cartilage crackled blue spark messages leaving reached between my legs and willingly took my pulsating camera into her bursa copulatrix...riding the blue silence into a pulsing sphere of blue insect cinema...former humanity found in the catatonic limestone...one time when my parents were gone Raven came over to my house and I aimed the camera at her as she took off all her clothes. She wore nothing but with a brass spring and a flesh-coated aperture ... smoky sunset at f-stop 11...sunset across the river just before blast off when ectoplasm spurted onto her cheek...black around the edges of the film frame...through the magic of film her body was becoming that of a transparent blue insect...Raven saw the demand...blackout fell...he filmed her on the tiled floor as the dark star exploded inside her core, obliterating the last remnants of human DNA...

#

I caught it all on film, complete with skin-loving nutrients,editing the slow cold hand on a wall long ago, fading panels of shadows...

#

I caught it all on film, complete with skin-loving nutrients,all mine on a beam of electric blue, silent wings in her parent's living room, where she spoke of love and gently lifted my vibrating thoracic spiracle up to her purple, swollen micropyle...brass spring unwinding a vibrating head of blue glass...Ectoplasm was everywhere...ectoplasm spurted onto the camera and coated her chest and neck, where captured in blue silence...the camera caught the very process of her vanishing humanity...Raven's body was becoming that of a transparent blue insect, a process caught on and created by film in my 1920s wind-up movie camera...sunset across the river of her cinematic passion...Raven wore nothing but a fur cap and a fur stole, so 1920s Hollywood. She wore the perfume of ectoplasm recorded on film that ran through a flickering 1920 movie camera, a picture back lots and fake black lagoons where hot globs of ectoplasm pulsed over her finger tips and onto my armor-plated belly...under purple twilight she shed her clothes for the camera and her humanity like shreded mummy linens...green jelly flesh quivering in the aperture gate...riding light rays through color winds...antennae ears of flexible metal cartilage crackled blue spark messages leaving scent of ozone and spent ectoplasm as she reached between my in amber light...two film tracks merging into a wake of blue silence...flicker movies strung together in a million stories of human-to-insect transformation...insect breath drank in fractured air...sick flesh falling through space between species and worlds of film...crystal city iridescent in the dawn wind over on film, editing the various takes into a new future in which she was all mine... on surplus blankets stained dark and wet in a wind-up model with a brass spring and a flesh-coated aperture ...the film crew breathed in the heavy scent of iron prison flesh falling away with the last of her human DNA...candle shadow bodies of Raven and the cicada pulsating in blue insect pressure...flipped the pictures of cold gray eyes that studied the naked torso captured on feeling-toned film stock that rattled through a fell...he filmed her on the tiled floor as the dark star exploded inside her core, obliterating the last remnants of human DNA...

#

I caught it all on film, complete with skin-loving nutrients,editing a flickering 1920 movie camera, a wind-up model with a brass spring and a flesh-coated aperture that cried out in sad distant voices... Raven was a woman of vision...willingly took off all her clothes for a 1920s movie camera that panned a cobbled road a wake of blue silence...flicker movies strung together in a million stories of human-to-insect transformation...insect breath drank in fractured air...sick flesh falling through space between species and worlds of film...crystal city iridescent in the dawn wind over the motion picture back lots and fake black lagoons front of the movie camera and took off all her clothes and walked the empty streets outside windows of blue night that pulsed inside the insect desire...shadow bodies of Raven and the cicada twisted into an insect mass on surplus blankets stained dark and wet in a wind-up model with stole... Raven lingered near the sagging door jamb...Adam's eyes were heavy and cold and Raven dutifully consented to his terrifying and horrifying demand...blackout fell...he filmed her on the tiled floor as the dark star exploded inside her core, obliterating the last remnants of human DNA...

#

I caught it all on film, complete with skin-loving nutrients,a new future in the right direction... and frantic parasites wriggled in my hands and I began to thrust up into her firm, pianist fingers...the camera lens captured the pale panels of shadows...

#

I caught it all on film, complete with skin-loving nutrients,editing the new cinema...former humanity found in skeletons locked in catatonic limestone...sharp flash bulbs snapping in the cool liquid air of the photo op...

#

I caught it all on film, complete with skin-loving nutrients,nothing but a fur cap and a fur stole, so 1920s Hollywood. She wore the perfume of ectoplasm recorded on film that ran through a flickering 1920 movie camera, a wind-up- model with a brass spring and a flesh-coated aperture that cried out in sad distant voices... Raven was a woman of vision...willingly took off all flash bulbs snapping in the cool liquid air of the photo op...

#

I caught it all on film, complete with skin-loving nutrients,editing the sagging door jamb...Adam's eyes were heavy and cold and Raven dutifully consented to his terrifying and horrifying demand...blackout fell...he filmed in which she was all mine on a beam of electric blue, silent wings in her parent's living room, where I filmed her naked from the waist up...she spoke of love and wore nothing but a fur cap and a fur stole... Raven lingered near the sagging door jamb...Adam's eyes were heavy and cold and Raven dutifully consented to his terrifying and horrifying demand...blackout fell...he filmed her on the tiled floor as the dark star exploded inside her core, obliterating the last remnants of human DNA...

#

I caught it all on film, complete with skin-loving nutrients,editing the distant street nights...a city of black and white movies, Raven starring in them all...the wind-up camera of 1920s recorded the truth of Raven, the truth that she was a woman of vision...she would not allow humanity to fade back into the catatonic limestone...one time when mine...Raven was pulsating in blue silence and cinematic ozone...... an f-stop future captured in blue silence...the camera caught the very process of her vanishing humanity...Raven's body was becoming that of a transparent blue insect, a process caught on and created by film in my 1920s wind-up movie camera...sunset across the river of her shivered under the surge of ectoplasm as it passed over her purple and swollen micropyle ...Raven was a lady throughout the filming, naked from the waist up, sitting upright for the camera on the edge of my bed and holding out to me her unspoken desire to become a human/insect hybrid...

#

I caught it all on film, complete with skin-loving nutrients, editing the various texturizing emulsions into pulsating blue silence … gray street eyes stare through gray shadows at f-stop 1.8...time focus falling through colors red green black onto flesh-coated film stock.... recognized this act of restraint and rewarded it by taking me in her of the film frame...through the magic of film her body was becoming that of a transparent blue insect...Raven saw the future...I edited in the X-ray photos of orange parent's living room, where I filmed her naked from the waist up...she spoke of love and gently lifted my vibrating thoracic spiracle up to her purple, swollen micropyle...brass spring unwinding a vibrating head of blue glass...Ectoplasm was everywhere...ectoplasm spurted onto the camera and coated her chest and neck, where neon fingers worked transparent flesh of present time...finger rubbing hydroglide on X-ray movie film...Ectoplasm was everywhere. It recognized this act of restraint and rewarded it by taking me in her purple and swollen micropyle...walls of blue glass...brown intestine jungles...flesh-eating vines gently nudged her head into the right lots and fake black lagoons where hot globs of ectoplasm pulsed over her finger tips and onto my armor-plated belly...under purple twilight she shed her clothes for the camera and her humanity like shreded mummy linens...green jelly flesh quivering in the aperture gate...riding light rays through color winds...antennae ears of flexible metal cartilage crackled blue spark messages leaving scent of ozone and spent ectoplasm as she reached between my legs and willingly 1920s recorded the truth of Raven, the truth that she was a woman of vision...she would not allow humanity to fade back into the catatonic limestone...one time when my parents were gone Raven came over to my house and I aimed the camera at her as she took off all her clothes. She wore nothing but a fur cap and a fur antennae fade in blue smoke with the scent of insect maleness to fill our nostrils and the viewfinder as she looked into my compound eyes the tint of washed out gray...street eyes stare through gray shadows at f-stop 1.8...time before blast off when ectoplasm spurted onto her cheek...black around the edges of the film frame...through the magic of film her body was becoming that of a transparent blue insect...Raven saw the future...I edited in the X-ray photos of orange viscera...sucking eyes, licking...the movie camera lens drank it all in...compound eyes and antennae fade in blue smoke with the scent on feeling-toned film stock that rattled through a wind-up model with a brass spring and a flesh-coated aperture ... smoky sunset at f-stop 11...sunset across the river just before blast off when ectoplasm spurted onto her cheek...black around the edges of the film frame...through the magic of film her body was panels of shadows...

#

I caught it all on film, complete with skin-loving nutrients,silent wings on a beam of electric blue … silent wings in her parent's living room, where I filmed her naked from the waist up...she spoke of love and gently lifted my heavy scent of iron prison flesh falling away with the last of her human DNA...candle shadow bodies of Raven and the cicada pulsating in blue insect pressure...flipped the pictures of cold gray eyes that studied the naked torso captured on feeling-toned film stock that rattled through a wind-up model with a brass spring and a flesh-coated aperture ... smoky sunset at f-stop 11...sunset across the river just before blast took off all her clothes for a 1920s movie camera that panned a cobbled road of wind and dust where exoskeletal tympanum shivered as the surging ectoplasm passed over her purple and swollen micropyle...she embraced herself in the bright lights of the sound stage, allowing the world camera twitched with the antennae of orange neon, flickering cicada wings as the exoskeletal tympanum shivered under the surge of ectoplasm as it passed over her purple and swollen micropyle ...Raven was a lady throughout the filming, naked from the waist up, sitting takes into a new future in which she was all mine...slow cold hand on a wall long ago fading into distant street nights...a city of black and white movies, Raven starring in them all...the wind-up camera of 1920s recorded the truth of Raven, the truth that she was a woman of vision...she would not allow humanity to fade back into the catatonic limestone...one time when my parents were gone Raven came over to my house jungles...flesh-eating vines gently nudged her head into the right direction... and frantic parasites wriggled in my hands and I began to thrust up into her insect maleness to fill our nostrils and the viewfinder as she looked into my compound eyes the tint of washed out gray...street eyes stare through gray shadows at f-stop 1.8...time focus falling through colors red green black onto flesh-coated film stock.... recognized this film frame...through the magic of film her body was becoming that of a transparent blue insect...Raven saw the future...I edited in the X-ray photos of orange viscera...sucking eyes, licking...the movie camera fingers...the camera lens captured the pale panels of shadows...

#

I caught it all on film, complete with skin-loving nutrients,brass spring unwinding in a beam of electric blue now vibrating ectoplasm … spurting onto her cheek...black around the edges of the film frame... editing the various takes into a new future in which she was all mine on a beam of electric wings … her parent's living room, where I filmed her naked from the waist up...she spoke of love and gently lifted my vibrating thoracic spiracle up to her purple, swollen micropyle...through the magic of film her body was becoming that of a transparent blue insect...Raven saw the future...I edited in the X-ray photos of orange spent ectoplasm as she reached between my legs and willingly took my pulsating camera into her bursa copulatrix...riding the blue silence into a pulsing sphere fur stole, so 1920s Hollywood. She wore the perfume of ectoplasm recorded on film that ran through a flickering 1920 movie camera, a wind-up- model with a brass spring and a flesh-coated aperture that cried out in sad distant voices... Raven was a woman of vision...willingly took off all her clothes for a 1920s movie camera that panned a out gray...street eyes stare through gray shadows at f-stop 1.8...time focus falling through colors red green black onto flesh-coated film stock.... recognized this act of with a brass spring and a flesh-coated aperture that cried out in sad distant voices... Raven was a woman of vision...willingly took off all her clothes for a 1920s movie camera that panned a cobbled road of wind and dust where exoskeletal tympanum shivered as the surging ectoplasm passed over her purple and swollen micropyle...she embraced herself in the bright lights dawn wind over the motion picture back lots and fake black lagoons where hot globs of ectoplasm pulsed over her finger tips and onto my armor-plated belly...under purple twilight she shed her clothes for the camera and her humanity like shreded mummy linens...green jelly flesh quivering in the aperture gate...riding light ozone and spent ectoplasm as she reached between my legs and willingly took my pulsating camera into her bursa copulatrix...riding the blue silence into a pulsing sphere of blue insect cinema...former humanity found in skeletons locked her vanishing humanity...Raven's body was becoming that of a transparent blue insect, a process caught on and created by film in my 1920s wind-up movie camera...sunset across the river of her cinematic passion...Raven wore nothing but a fur cap and a fur stole, so 1920s Hollywood. She wore the perfume of ectoplasm recorded on film that ran through a transparent blue insect, a process caught on and created by film in my 1920s wind-up movie camera...sunset across the river of her cinematic passion...Raven wore nothing but a fur cap and a fur stole, so 1920s Hollywood. She wore the perfume of ectoplasm recorded on film that ran through a and a flesh-coated aperture that cried out in sad distant voices... Raven was a woman of vision...willingly took off all her clothes for a 1920s movie camera that panned a cobbled road of wind and dust where exoskeletal tympanum shivered as on feeling-toned film stock that rattled through a wind-up model with a brass spring and a flesh-coated aperture ... smoky sunset at f-stop 11...sunset across the river just before blast off when ectoplasm spurted onto her cheek...black around the edges where exoskeletal tympanum shivered as the surging ectoplasm passed over her purple and swollen micropyle...she embraced herself in the bright lights of the sound stage, allowing the world to watch...she stood in front of the movie of orange neon, flickering cicada wings as the exoskeletal tympanum shivered under the surge of ectoplasm as it passed over her purple and swollen micropyle ...Raven was a lady throughout the filming, naked from the waist up, sitting upright for the camera on the edge of my bed and the scent of insect maleness to fill our nostrils and the viewfinder as she looked into my compound eyes the tint of washed out gray...street eyes stare through gray shadows at f-stop 1.8...time focus falling through colors red green black onto flesh-coated film stock.... recognized glass...brown intestine jungles...flesh-eating vines gently nudged her head into the right direction... and frantic parasites wriggled in my hands and I began to thrust up into her firm, pianist fingers...the camera lens captured the pale and a fur stole... Uranus time fill with slow blue film fallout...1920s movie camera twitched with the antennae of orange neon, flickering cicada wings as the exoskeletal tympanum shivered under the surge of ectoplasm as it passed over her purple and swollen micropyle ...Raven was a lady throughout the filming, naked from the movie camera that panned a cobbled road of wind and dust where exoskeletal tympanum shivered as the surging ectoplasm passed over her purple and swollen micropyle...she embraced herself in the bright lights of the sound stage, allowing the world to watch...she stood in front of the movie camera and took off all her clothes and walked the empty streets outside windows of blue night that pulsed inside the insect desire...shadow bodies all mine...Raven was pulsating in blue silence and cinematic ozone...... an f-stop future captured in blue silence...the camera caught the very process of her vanishing humanity...Raven's body was becoming that of a transparent blue insect, a process caught on and created by film in my 1920s wind-up movie camera...sunset across the river of her cinematic passion...Raven wore nothing but a fur cap and a fur stole, so 1920s Hollywood. She wore the it passed over her purple and swollen micropyle ...Raven was a lady throughout the filming, naked from the waist up, sitting upright for the camera on the edge of my bed and holding out to me her unspoken desire to become a human/insect hybrid...

#

I caught it all on film, complete with skin-loving nutrients, editing the various texturizing emulsions into a dark star exploding inside her core, obliterating the last remnants of human DNA...

#

I caught it all on film, complete with skin-loving nutrients,editing her into the bright lights of the sound stage, allowing the world to watch... the various takes for a new future … all mine...slow cold hand on micropyle...she embraced herself she stood in front of the movie camera and took off all her clothes and walked the empty streets outside windows of blue, a 1920s movie camera that panned a cobbled road of wind and dust where exoskeletal tympanum shivered as the surging ectoplasm passed over her purple and swollen micropyle...she embraced herself in in skeletons locked in catatonic limestone...sharp flash bulbs snapping in the cool liquid air of the photo op...

#

I caught it all on film, complete with skin-loving nutrients,editing my stares through gray shadows at f-stop 1.8...time focus falling through colors red green black onto flesh-coated film stock.... recognized this act of restraint and rewarded it by camera and took off all her clothes and walked the empty streets outside windows of blue night that pulsed inside the insect desire...shadow bodies of Raven and the cicada twisted into an insect mass on surplus blankets stained dark and wet in a wind-up model with a brass spring and a flesh-coated aperture ...the film crew breathed in the heavy scent of iron prison flesh falling away with the last of her human DNA...candle shadow the motion picture back lots and fake black lagoons where hot globs of ectoplasm pulsed over her finger tips and onto my armor-plated belly...under purple twilight she shed her clothes for the camera and her humanity like shreded mummy linens...green jelly flesh quivering in the aperture gate...riding light rays through color winds...antennae ears camera and her humanity like shreded mummy linens...green jelly flesh quivering in the aperture gate...riding light rays through color winds...antennae ears of flexible metal cartilage crackled blue spark messages leaving scent of ozone and spent ectoplasm as she reached between my legs and willingly took my pulsating camera into her bursa copulatrix...riding the blue silence into a pulsing sphere of blue insect cinema...former humanity found in skeletons locked in catatonic limestone...sharp flash bulbs snapping in Uranus time fill with slow blue film fallout...1920s movie camera twitched with the antennae of orange neon, flickering cicada wings as the exoskeletal tympanum shivered under the surge of ectoplasm as it passed over her purple and swollen micropyle ...Raven was a lady throughout the filming, naked from the waist up, sitting upright for the camera on the edge various takes into a new future in which she was all mine... eyes that studied the naked torso captured on feeling-toned film stock that rattled through a wind-up model with a brass spring and a flesh-coated aperture ... smoky sunset at f-stop 11...sunset across the river just before blast off when ectoplasm spurted onto her cheek...black around the edges of the film frame...through the magic of film her body was becoming that of a transparent blue insect...Raven saw the future...I edited 1920s recorded the truth of Raven, the truth that she was a woman of vision...she would not allow humanity to fade back into the catatonic limestone...one time when my parents were gone Raven came over to my house and I aimed the camera at her as she took off all her clothes. She wore purple and swollen micropyle...walls of blue glass...brown intestine jungles...flesh-eating vines gently nudged her head into the right direction... and frantic parasites wriggled in my hands and I began to thrust up into her firm, pianist fingers...the camera lens captured the pale panels of shadows...

#

I caught it all on film, complete with skin-loving nutrients,various movie cameras that panned a cobbled road of wind and dust where exoskeletal tympanum shivered as the surging ectoplasm passed over her purple and swollen micropyle...she embraced herself in the bright lights of the sound stage, allowing the world to watch...she stood in front of the movie camera and took off all her clothes and walked the empty streets outside windows of blue night that pulsed inside the terrifying and horrifying demand...blackout fell...he filmed her on the tiled floor as the dark star exploded inside her core, obliterating the last remnants of human DNA...

#

I caught it all on film, complete with skin-loving nutrients,the wet wind-up model with a brass spring and a flesh-coated aperture ...the film crew breathed in the heavy scent of iron prison flesh falling away with the last of her human DNA...candle shadow bodies of Raven and the cicada pulsating in wings as the exoskeletal tympanum shivered under the surge of ectoplasm as it passed over her purple and swollen micropyle ...Raven was a lady throughout the filming, naked from the in which she was all mine... compound eyes the tint of washed out gray...street eyes stare through gray shadows at f-stop 1.8...time focus falling through colors red green black onto flesh-coated film stock.... recognized this act of restraint and rewarded it by taking me in her purple and swollen from the waist up, sitting upright for the camera on the edge of my bed and holding out to me her unspoken desire to become a human/insect hybrid...

#

I caught it all on film, complete with skin-loving nutrients,pulsating glass...Ectoplasm was everywhere...ectoplasm spurted onto the camera and coated her chest and neck, where neon fingers worked transparent flesh of present time...finger rubbing hydroglide on X-ray movie film...Ectoplasm was everywhere. It coated her chest and neck... editing the various takes into a new future in which she was all mine...Raven was embracing the future of post-humanity in the flickering movie shadows of the blue void...cinematic lens drank in ectoplasm in amber light...two film tracks merging into a wake of blue silence...flicker viewfinder as she looked into my compound eyes the tint of washed out gray...street eyes stare through gray shadows at f-stop 1.8...time focus falling through colors red green black onto scent of ozone and spent ectoplasm as she reached between my legs and willingly took my pulsating camera into her bursa copulatrix...riding the blue silence into a pulsing sphere of blue insect cinema...former humanity found in skeletons locked in catatonic limestone...sharp flash bulbs snapping in the cool in ectoplasm in amber light...two film tracks merging into a wake of blue silence...flicker movies strung together in a million stories of human-to-insect transformation...insect breath drank in fractured air...sick flesh falling through space between species and worlds of film...crystal city vibrating head of blue glass...Ectoplasm was everywhere...ectoplasm spurted onto the camera and coated her chest and neck, where neon fingers worked transparent flesh of present time...finger rubbing hydroglide on X-ray movie film...Ectoplasm was everywhere. It coated her chest and neck...embracing the future of post-humanity wind-up model with a brass spring and a flesh-coated aperture ... smoky sunset at f-stop 11...sunset across the river just before blast off when ectoplasm spurted onto her cheek...black around the edges of I aimed the camera at her as she took off all her clothes. She wore nothing but a fur cap and a fur stole... Uranus time fill with slow blue film fallout...1920s movie camera twitched with the antennae of orange neon, flickering cicada wings as the exoskeletal tympanum shivered under the surge of ectoplasm as it passed over her purple and swollen terrifying and horrifying demand...blackout fell...he filmed her on the tiled floor as the dark star exploded inside her core, obliterating the last remnants of human DNA...

#

I caught it all on film, complete with skin-loving nutrients,where she endulged her copulatrix...riding the blue silence into a pulsing sphere of blue insect cinema passion...former humanity found in skeletons locked in catatonic limestone...sharp flash bulbs snapping in the cool liquid air of the photo op...

#

I caught it all on film, complete with skin-loving nutrients, editing the various texturizing emulsions into a new Skin Dimension future in which she was all mine... took off all her clothes. She wore nothing but a fur cap and a fur stole... Uranus time fill with slow blue film fallout...1920s movie camera twitched with the antennae of orange neon, flickering cicada wings as the exoskeletal tympanum shivered under the when my parents were gone Raven came over to my house and I aimed the camera at her as she took off all her clothes. She wore nothing but a fur cap and a fur stole... Uranus time fill with slow blue film fallout...1920s movie camera twitched with the antennae of orange neon, flickering cicada wings as the exoskeletal tympanum iridescent in the dawn wind over the motion picture back lots and fake black lagoons where hot globs of ectoplasm pulsed over her finger tips and onto my armor-plated belly...under purple twilight she shed her clothes for the camera and her humanity like shreded mummy linens...green jelly flesh quivering in the aperture gate...riding light rays through color winds...antennae ears of flexible metal cartilage crackled blue spark messages leaving scent her on the tiled floor as the dark star exploded inside her core, obliterating the last remnants of human DNA...

#

I caught it all on film, complete with skin-loving nutrients,editing a city of black and white movie … the various takes into a new future in which she was all mine...slow cold hand on a wall long ago fading into distant street nights... Raven starring in the camera on the edge of my bed and holding out to me her unspoken desire to become a human/insect hybrid... a perfect hybrid. A perfect Derma-pod. A perfect lotion. This is the super-rich lotion with super-rich nourishment. A nourishing blend… A blend of rehydrating nourishment with nightly luscious antioxidants. Body antioxidants with skin-loving hairspray renewal plus extract... Vitamins, texturizing humidity spray, pure resistance has spring, is touchable. What's touchable? ….What's known of water in scientific extra hold circles as goodness. Nourishing movement with essential hydrating two-ply ingredients. Emulsion to emulsion for Nourishing Skinalicious… Pure Skinalicious. Pure Vitamin Complex... Vitamin protection for all types. Stop the wrinkle. Wrinkle epidemic for for sensitive, with sensitive, with a can-glow skin. Believe skin. Believe fusion with health of beauty and with French aloe. French aloe. Reformulated lavender. Reformulated lavender. Reveal skin-loving nutrients. The nutrients... The twist...The volumizing nutrient twist with volumizing green nutrients for tea hairspray renewal. It's all for your skin. Pure thankfulness with extra skin and a unique time-release formula with a gentle reservoir of exfoliator. You just activate the exfoliator and it will remove all odor-causing follicles (and permanently moisturize the skin)...

#

I caught it all on film, complete with skin-loving nutrients,pulsating in blue silence and cinematic ozone...... an f-stop future captured in blue silence...the camera caught the wake of blue silence...flicker movies strung together in a million stories of human-to-insect transformation...insect breath drank in fractured air...sick flesh falling through space between species and worlds of film...crystal city iridescent in the dawn wind over the motion picture back lots and fake black lagoons where hot globs of ectoplasm pulsed over across the river just before blast off when ectoplasm spurted onto her cheek...black around the edges of the film frame...through the magic of film her body was becoming that of a transparent blue insect... editing the various takes into a new future in which she was all mine...Raven was – Raven saw the future...I edited in the X-ray photos of orange viscera...sucking eyes, licking...the movie camera lens drank it all in...compound eyes and an insect mass on surplus blankets stained dark and wet in a wind-up model with a brass spring and a flesh-coated aperture ...the film crew breathed in the heavy scent ectoplasm recorded on film that ran through a flickering 1920 movie camera, a wind-up- model with a brass spring and a flesh-coated aperture that cried out in sad distant voices... Raven was a woman of vision...willingly took off all movie camera and took off all her clothes and walked the empty streets outside windows of blue night that pulsed inside the insect desire...shadow bodies of Raven and the cicada twisted into an insect mass on surplus blankets stained dark and wet in a inside the insect desire...shadow bodies of Raven and the cicada twisted into an insect mass on surplus blankets stained dark and wet in a wind-up model with a brass spring and a flesh-coated aperture ...the purple, swollen micropyle...brass spring unwinding a vibrating head of blue glass...Ectoplasm was everywhere...ectoplasm spurted onto the camera and coated her chest and neck, where neon fingers worked transparent flesh of present time...finger rubbing right direction... and frantic parasites wriggled in my hands and I began to thrust up into her firm, pianist fingers...the camera lens captured the pale panels of shadows...

#

I caught it all on film, complete with skin-loving nutrients,all mine on a beam of electric blue, silent wings in her parent's living room, where I filmed her naked from the waist up...she spoke of film, editing the various takes into a new future in which she was all mine... off all her clothes for a 1920s movie camera that panned a cobbled road of wind and dust where exoskeletal tympanum shivered as the surging ectoplasm passed over her purple and swollen micropyle... editing the various takes into a new future in which she was embraced herself in the bright lights of the sound stage, allowing a lady throughout the filming, naked from the waist up, sitting upright for the camera on the edge of my bed and holding out to me flexible metal cartilage crackled blue spark messages leaving scent of ozone and spent ectoplasm as she reached between my legs and willingly took my pulsating camera into her bursa copulatrix...riding the the pale panels of shadows...

#

I caught it all on film, complete with skin-loving nutrients, editing the various texturizing emulsions into a new Skin Dimension future in which she was all mine on a beam of electric blue, silent wings in her parent's living room, where I filmed her naked from the waist up...she spoke of orange neon, flickering cicada wings as the exoskeletal tympanum shivered under the surge of ectoplasm as it passed over her purple and swollen micropyle ...Raven was a lady throughout the filming, naked from the a million stories of human-to-insect transformation...insect breath drank in fractured air...sick flesh falling through space between species and worlds of film...crystal city iridescent in the dawn wind over the motion picture back lots and fake black lagoons where hot globs of ectoplasm pulsed over her finger tips and onto my armor-plated wet in a wind-up model with a brass spring and a flesh-coated aperture ...the film crew breathed in the heavy scent of iron prison flesh falling away with the last of her human DNA...candle shadow bodies of Raven and the cicada pulsating in blue insect pressure...flipped the pictures of cold gray eyes that studied the naked torso captured camera lens drank it all in...compound eyes and antennae fade in blue smoke with the scent of insect maleness to fill our nostrils and the viewfinder as she looked into my compound eyes the tint of washed out gray...street eyes stare through gray shadows at f-stop camera and her humanity like shreded mummy linens...green jelly flesh quivering in the aperture gate...riding light rays through color winds...antennae ears of flexible metal cartilage crackled blue spark messages leaving scent of ozone onto flesh-coated film stock.... recognized this act of restraint and rewarded it by taking me in her purple and swollen micropyle...walls of blue glass...brown intestine jungles...flesh-eating vines the camera and her humanity like shreded mummy linens...green jelly flesh quivering in the aperture gate...riding light rays through color winds...antennae ears of flexible metal cartilage crackled blue spark messages leaving scent of ozone and spent ectoplasm as she reached between my legs and willingly took my pulsating camera into her bursa copulatrix...riding the blue silence into a pulsing sphere of blue insect cinema...former humanity found in lens captured the pale panels of shadows...

#

I caught it all on film, complete with skin-loving nutrients, editing the various texturizing emulsions into a new Skin Dimension future in which she was all mine on a beam of electric blue, silent wings in her parent's living room, where I filmed her naked from the waist up...she spoke of love and gently lifted my vibrating thoracic spiracle up to her purple, swollen micropyle...brass spring unwinding a vibrating head of blue glass...Ectoplasm was everywhere...ectoplasm spurted onto the camera and heavy scent of iron prison flesh falling away with the last of her human DNA...candle shadow bodies of Raven and the cicada pulsating in blue insect pressure...flipped the pictures of cold gray eyes that studied the naked torso captured on feeling-toned film stock that rattled through drank it all in...compound eyes and antennae fade in blue smoke with the scent of insect maleness to fill our nostrils and the viewfinder as she looked into my compound eyes the tint of washed out gray...street eyes stare through gray shadows at f-stop 1.8...time focus falling through colors red green black onto flesh-coated film stock.... recognized this act of restraint and rewarded it by taking air of the photo op...

#

I caught it all on film, complete with skin-loving nutrients, editing the various texturizing emulsions into a new Skin Dimension future in which she was all mine... metal cartilage crackled blue spark messages leaving scent of ozone and spent ectoplasm as she reached between my legs and willingly took my pulsating camera into her bursa copulatrix...riding the blue silence into a pulsing sphere of blue insect cinema...former humanity found in skeletons locked in catatonic limestone...sharp flash bulbs snapping in the cool liquid air of the photo op...

#

I caught it all on film, complete with skin-loving nutrients, editing the various texturizing emulsions into a new Skin Dimension future in her clothes for the camera and her humanity like shreded mummy linens...green jelly flesh quivering in the aperture gate...riding light rays through color winds...antennae ears of flexible metal cartilage crackled blue spark messages leaving scent of ozone and spent ectoplasm as she reached between my legs and willingly took my pulsating camera into her bursa copulatrix...riding the blue my bed and holding out to me her unspoken desire to become a human/insect hybrid...

#

I caught it all on film, complete with skin-loving nutrients, editing the various texturizing emulsions into a new Skin Dimension future in which she was all mine...Raven was pulsating in blue silence and cinematic ozone...... an f-stop future captured in blue silence...the camera caught the very process of her vanishing humanity...Raven's body was becoming that of a transparent blue insect, a process caught on and created by was becoming that of a transparent blue insect, a process caught on and created by film in my 1920s wind-up movie camera...sunset across the river of her cinematic passion...Raven wore nothing but a fur cap and a fur stole, so 1920s Hollywood. She wore the perfume of ectoplasm recorded on film that ran through a flickering 1920 movie camera, a wind-up- model with a brass spring and Raven dutifully consented to his terrifying and horrifying demand...blackout fell...he filmed her on the tiled floor as the dark star exploded inside her core, obliterating the last remnants of human DNA...I of blue glass...brown intestine jungles...flesh-eating vines gently nudged her head into the right direction... and frantic parasites wriggled in my hands and I began to thrust into the right direction... and frantic parasites wriggled in my hands and I began to thrust up into her firm, pianist fingers...the camera lens captured the pale panels of shadows...

#

I caught it all on film, complete with skin-loving nutrients, editing the various texturizing emulsions into twitched with the antennae of orange neon, flickering cicada wings as the exoskeletal tympanum shivered under the surge of ectoplasm as it passed over her purple and swollen micropyle ...Raven was a lady throughout the filming, metal cartilage crackled blue spark messages leaving scent of ozone and spent ectoplasm as she reached between my legs and willingly took my pulsating camera into her bursa copulatrix...riding the blue silence into a pulsing sphere of blue insect cinema...former humanity found in skeletons locked in catatonic limestone...sharp flash bulbs snapping in the cool liquid air of the photo op...

#

I caught it all on film, complete with skin-loving nutrients, editing the various texturizing emulsions into a new my hands and I began to thrust up into her firm, pianist fingers...the camera lens captured the pale panels of shadows...

#

I caught it all on film, complete with skin-loving nutrients, editing the various texturizing emulsions into a new Skin Dimension future in which she was all mine on a beam of electric blue, silent wings in her parent's living room, where I filmed her naked from the waist up...she spoke of love and gently lifted my vibrating thoracic spiracle up to her purple, swollen fur cap and a fur stole... Raven lingered near the sagging door jamb...Adam's eyes were heavy and cold and Raven dutifully consented to his terrifying and horrifying demand...blackout I filmed her naked from the waist up...she spoke of love and gently lifted my vibrating thoracic spiracle up to her purple, swollen micropyle...brass spring unwinding a vibrating that panned a cobbled road of wind and dust where exoskeletal tympanum shivered as the surging ectoplasm passed over her purple and swollen micropyle...she embraced herself in the bright lights of the sound stage, allowing the world to watch...she stood in front of the movie camera and took off all her clothes and walked the empty wind-up- model with a brass spring and a flesh-coated aperture that cried out in sad distant voices... Raven was a woman of vision...willingly took off all her clothes for a 1920s movie camera that panned a cobbled road of wind and dust where exoskeletal tympanum shivered as the surging ectoplasm passed over her firm, pianist fingers...the camera lens captured the pale panels of shadows...

#

I caught it all on film, complete with skin-loving nutrients, editing the various texturizing emulsions into a new Skin Dimension future in which she was all mine on a beam of electric blue, silent wings in her parent's living room, where I filmed her naked from the waist up...she spoke of love and gently lifted my vibrating thoracic spiracle up to her purple, swollen micropyle...brass spring unwinding a vibrating head of film, editing the various takes into a new future in which she was all mine...Raven was pulsating in blue silence and cinematic ozone...... an f-stop future captured in blue silence...the camera caught the very process of her vanishing humanity...Raven's body was becoming that of a transparent blue iridescent in the dawn wind over the motion picture back lots and fake black lagoons where hot globs of ectoplasm pulsed over her finger tips and onto my armor-plated belly...under purple twilight she shed her clothes for the camera and her humanity like shreded mummy linens...green jelly flesh quivering in the aperture gate...riding rewarded it by taking me in her purple and swollen micropyle...walls of blue glass...brown intestine jungles...flesh-eating vines gently nudged her head into the right direction... and frantic parasites wriggled in my hands and I began to thrust up into her firm, pianist fingers...the camera lens captured the pale panels of shadows...

#

I caught it all on film, complete with skin-loving nutrients, editing the various texturizing emulsions into a a million stories of human-to-insect transformation...insect breath drank in fractured air...sick flesh falling through space between species and worlds of film...crystal city iridescent in the dawn wind over the motion picture back lots and fake black lagoons where hot globs of ectoplasm pulsed over her finger tips and onto my armor-plated belly...under purple twilight she shed her clothes for the camera and her humanity like shreded mummy linens...green jelly flesh quivering in the aperture gate...riding wore nothing but a fur cap and a fur stole, so 1920s Hollywood. She wore the perfume of ectoplasm recorded on film that ran through a flickering 1920 movie camera, a wind-up- model with a brass spring and a flesh-coated aperture that cried out in sad distant voices... Raven was a woman of to his terrifying and horrifying demand...blackout fell...he filmed her on the tiled floor as the dark star exploded inside her core, obliterating the last remnants of human DNA...I caught it act of restraint and rewarded it by taking me in her purple and swollen micropyle...walls of blue glass...brown intestine jungles...flesh-eating vines gently nudged her head into the right direction... and frantic parasites wriggled in my hands and I began to thrust up into her firm, pianist fingers...the camera lens captured the pale panels of shadows...

#

I caught it all on film, complete with skin-loving nutrients, editing the various texturizing emulsions into a new Skin Dimension future various takes into a new future in which she was all mine on a beam of electric blue, silent wings in her parent's living room, where I filmed her naked from the waist up...she spoke of love and gently lifted my vibrating thoracic spiracle up to her purple, swollen micropyle...brass spring unwinding a vibrating head of blue glass...Ectoplasm was everywhere...ectoplasm spurted onto the camera and coated her chest and neck, where neon fingers worked transparent flesh of present time...finger rubbing hydroglide she reached between my legs and willingly took my pulsating camera into her bursa copulatrix...riding the blue silence into a pulsing sphere of blue insect cinema...former humanity found in skeletons locked in catatonic limestone...sharp flash bulbs snapping in the cool liquid air of the photo op...

#

I caught it all on film, complete with skin-loving nutrients,that studied naked torso captured on feeling-toned film stock that rattled through a wind-up model with a brass spring and a flesh-coated aperture ... smoky sunset at f-stop 11...sunset across the river just before blast off when ectoplasm spurted onto her cheek...black around the edges of the film frame...through the magic of film her body was becoming that of a transparent blue insect...Raven saw the future...I edited in the X-ray photos that rattled through a wind-up model with a brass spring and a flesh-coated aperture ... smoky sunset at f-stop 11...sunset across the river just before blast off when exoskeletal tympanum shivered as the surging ectoplasm passed over her purple and swollen micropyle...she embraced herself in the bright lights of the sound stage, allowing the world to watch...she stood in front of the movie camera and took off all her clothes and walked the empty streets outside windows of blue night that pulsed inside the insect desire...shadow bodies cold hand on a wall long ago fading into distant street nights...a city of black and white movies, Raven starring in them all...the wind-up camera of 1920s off all her clothes for a 1920s movie camera that panned a cobbled road of wind and dust where exoskeletal tympanum shivered as the surging ectoplasm passed over her purple and swollen micropyle...she embraced herself in the bright lights of the sound stage, allowing the world to watch...she stood in front of the movie camera and took off all her clothes and walked the empty streets outside windows of blue night that pulsed and the cicada pulsating in blue insect pressure...flipped the pictures of cold gray eyes that studied the naked torso captured on feeling-toned film stock that rattled through a wind-up model with a brass spring and a flesh-coated the waist up...she spoke of love and gently lifted my vibrating thoracic spiracle up to her purple, swollen micropyle...brass spring unwinding a vibrating head of blue glass...Ectoplasm was everywhere...ectoplasm spurted onto the camera and coated her chest and neck, where neon fingers worked transparent flesh of present time...finger rubbing hydroglide on X-ray movie film...Ectoplasm was everywhere. It coated her chest and neck...embracing Raven starring in them all...the wind-up camera of 1920s recorded truth of the Raven, the truth that she was a woman of vision...she would not allow humanity to fade back into the catatonic limestone...one time when my parents were gone Raven came over to my house and I am awake I a surge of blue silence...flicker movies strung together in a million stories of human-to-insect transformation...insect breath drank in fractured air...sick flesh falling through space between species and worlds of film...crystal city iridescent in the dawn wind over the motion picture back lots and fake black lagoons where hot globs of ectoplasm pulsed over her finger her clothes and walked the empty streets outside windows of blue night that pulsed inside the insect desire...your shadow body and newly acquired cicada DNA twisted together into an insect mass, breathing heavy and exhausted, oozing spent ectoplasm on old surplus blankets stained dark and wet.

Raven my love – together, you and me – I think we're going to like it. Consider this transmission from the 41st century…

Today we all know how to find the Supreme Deity inside ourselves.

But we weren't always so enlightened. Back in the day our species was spiritually lost. We had not developed the technological tools to determine the inner coordinates of Heaven and Hell. We did not possess the Holy Mirror with which to see the Face of God in our own countenance. Nor did we know how to use the Divine Compass to locate the Gates of Hell in our darker aspirations. Nor did we know how to employ even one of the 14 varieties of deathoscopes to discern the visage of the Prince of Darkness in our hearts.

In short, we were lost. Miserable wayfarers, we stumbled about blindly. Of course, we knew about science and technology. We dazzled ourselves with our own creative genius. But we were dazzled through a misapprehension of the scientific method. We employed knowledge, but without Truth. We experienced lucidity, but without Understanding.

We were pushbutton creatures, living machines without the slightest idea of where to begin a true search for the deity within.

Here's another metaphor: Each of us was a living magic lantern, unknowingly projecting our inner movies onto the Earth and even the stars above, certain the ultimate truths we occasionally glimpsed in the lives of the prophets and saints did not come from within but rather the back of beyond. We were certain that if we looked hard enough and in the right place, we would finally find – perhaps after death, but finally nonetheless – the Supreme Deity who is in charge of all His creation.

The living magic lanterns were projecting so many different movies all at once that it was hard to make sense of it all. So people started classifying their projections by genre. They called these genres "religions." And they built special theaters in which to enjoy their favorite genre stories with other people who recognized the common elements of their own inner movies. They called these theaters by many names: Temples, synagogues, sanctuaries, chapels.

Occasionally a genre would fall out of favor, and people would quit believing in them. They called these genres "myths." Sometimes people would continue to believe in a genre that others called a myth. This created a sense of unease. How can anyone believe in a genre other than the One True Movie, (i.e., the Supreme Deity)? The answer was simple: these "myths" were false genres of the Dark One. They were Evil. They must be stamped out.

That is why humanity used to have so many wars.

So the world turned for many centuries, each believer going to the theater of their choice to enjoy the genre of their choice. They were happy, expressing their unique and superior love for the Supreme Deity – and building increasingly sophisticated and deadly weapons to kill those who insisted on adhering to myths and following the Dark One.

The few humans who suggested the possibility that all of the genres were myths and God might actually live within were called "heretics." They were dragged out of the theaters and burned at the stake.

When humans weren't busy killing heretics, they continued to stamp out myths. They waged wars on the false genres, fighting in the name of their own Supreme Deity.

Humans spent so much time and expended so many resources stamping out the myths and extinguishing the heretics that they utterly neglected the idea of a technological advancement that would allow them to do away with the many competing genres and discover that the actual Supreme Deity didn't dwell in a theater but lived within.

Humans would have most likely continued on this ill-conceived path until they had completely annihilated their entire species if not for the timely intervention of the Cicadians, one of the 35 extraterrestrials of the soul. They arrived among us from the comatose milieu, bringing the science and technology we needed to recognize the falsity of the competing genres, understand the metaphorical truth of all myths and experience the Supreme Deity within ourselves.

We owe it all to them. After all, it was the Cicadians who came from the back of beyond to bring us the Holy Jah, the 4.4-million-character word that means "god within." Let us speak the holy noun now, in reverent prayer to the Supreme Deity:

Hashemjahsabaothlordhostsbuddahjehovahallahzulugodshammahlordispresentolorunjehovahzulugodowneroftherainbowwombrohilordourshepherdjehovahzulugodhoseenulordourmakerjehovahzuluelohimgodqannajealousjehovahzulugodjirehlordwillprovidejehovahzulugodelohimeternalcreatorjehovahzulugodjirehlordourproviderjehovahzulugodnissilordourbannerjehovahzulugodqannajealousjehovahzulugodlordoursovereignelelyonlordmosthighelolameverlastinggodelshaddaigodwhoissufficientforneedshispeoplejehovahzuluhakadoshbaruchhuholyoneblessedbehekadoshisraelholyoneisraelmelechhamelachimkingkingsormelechmalcheihamelachimkingkingkingstoexpressuperioritytoearthlyrulerstitlemakomorhamakomliterallyplaceomnipresentseetzimtzummagenavrahamshieldabrahamribbonoshelolamgod ...(Editor's note: The Holy Jah goes on in this vein for quite some time, of course. We're cutting it short for the print version, but the one true Holy Jah is still in its divine form somewhere in the Exogrid.) … *lordlightorlordwisdomallahormazdcaođàiabraxasxwedêmithrasmitradeusoptimusmaximussiddharthagautamagautamabuddhajahamidabuddhajahperfectedbeingstirthankarjinafarsonholyspiritlightlordhostskingkingsacientdaysabbadainichidiaiosacriostosbogjumalakamibathaladeviyohashemiesusyeshuajoshuayehoshuamessiahkristoshealterheilaigonzeruiluvatarmaleldiloldsolargdakalpurakhtimelessprimalbeingsupremecreatorgodsabaothjahlordhostsbuddahjehovahallahshammahlightwithin.*

Amen.

#

Onboard the aerial clock, a prisoner caught up on a beam of electric blue.

"Can you believe it?" Young Einstein asks. "The world's first two-bodied man."

"Fully human and fully divine," Dr. Morel marvles, gazing at The Stranger. My doppelganger! Can it be he is still alive, that he survived the ascent? It must be true for I see him here with me, strapped to a steel examination table. He's unconscious, but otherwise appears unharmed.

"We'll still need confirmation at the molecular level. I'd like to see a full cortical scan, psychotropic biopsy, Cytochrome P450 analysis - the works. Mr. Leach, I'd like to run a nucleic acid sequence analysis."

Young Einstein reaches inside his lab coat and withdraws a blade of surgical steel.

"I require only a small genetic sample," he says.

I take a small step backwards, immediately up against the locked door.

"Nothing to fear, really," he continues. "We only require a small tissue sample, a forearm will do. A quick run through the food processor, filter through a bit of cheese cloth to keep bone chips from clogging up the aerosol spray gun, and I'm ready to coat the spaceship."

"That's where you'll find me administering to my flock," Morel says. "I do it on the weekly trip to Zeta Reticuli, inoculated against the spreading bio-doom of the eschatological era."

"Then we'll quick freeze you and The Stranger," Young Einstein explains.

"At absolute zero, we'll reintegrate your DNA – and that of the others – back into that of a single being."

"With bits and pieces of Jack and Cinnamon and Corvette spliced in, of course. A total re-integration of your split-off personalities."

"Yes, we cannot ignore the need for a Deity equipped with a muse or two. After all, many of the ancient gods were hermaphrodites."

I cast my eyes around the room, looking for a weapon - a piece of glassware, another surgical instrument. Anything. But all I can find is a jar of tongue depressors.

"So you see, it's a small thing we ask," Dr. Morel concludes. "A small piece of forearm. Why would you want to deny us this one simple thing?"

I grab the jar of tongue depressors and raise them over my head with all the menace I can muster. "Come and get it," I say.

Apparently, I am not a very threatening person for Young Einstein just laughs and puts the knife away. I shrug and toss the jar into the corner.

"And then," Young Einstein adds, "we reformat in time machine mode for a quick run to 1979, back when people were satisfied to take only their share of oxygen and kept their exotoxins to themselves."

I have heard these words before.

"You've been reading my private journal," I say. "You break into people's homes, too?"

"No, but we do have access to your lovely creations via the onbeam infrastructure," Dr. Morel remarks. "Don't worry. It's been ruled constitutional by the Supreme Court."

"Who are you guys?" I ask. "FBI? CIA?"

"American Psychiatric Association," Young Einstein says. "Hard to pick through the psychic discards without being seen, what with your followers now ranked in the hundreds, lost pilgrims gathering daily outside your little North Dallas Special, turning the antique brick and gaslights into a 24-hour-a-day shrine. And trampling the neighbor's lantana, too. So sad. I hear they've even petitioned the Pope to make you a saint."

"What are you talking about?" I ask.

"Oh, sorry. We've been working from an alternate script, something created by The Stranger. Working title, 'Doubting Tommy.' In this story, you are a stigmatic agnostic who is being worshipped by the true believers."

"You've really nothing to fear from us," Young Einstein says. "In fact, we just might be your best hope."

I shake my head. "I'd rather stay hopeless," I remark.

"And a word of advice," Dr. Morel says. "Under-aged girls are usually unreliable, particularly in matters regarding middle-aged passion. Do not be fooled by the potency of Tina's smile."

"It's not like that!" I protest. "I only called her so we could find her grandfather. I was only trying to help."

"Oh then, if you were only trying to help – "

"Besides, I'm not middle aged. I'm still far, far away from 40. The big four-oh is not even on my radar, no way. And Tina's 18 and three months."

Morel thinks this is very funny.

"You think that distinction will mean much to your wife?"

Tina Wells. Even in the blue ethereal glow of the dashboard lights, her perfect, nearly 18-year-old complexion took on a radiant glow. So peaceful there, a buxom teenaged woman-child asleep in the passenger seat, she had reminded me a bit of my two young sons. That resemblance had served to briefly temper my arousal with regret. I hadn't seen the boys in two weeks. But the feeling of regret was hard to maintain. As we drove, searching for Cowboy Roy, I kept stealing glances at Tina's breasts, the uppermost portions just visible above the top of her scoop necked shirt. Jack had shown me a Polaroid of her naked, stretched out on a tropical print towel, as if tanning on the beach. The brown nipples ride a bit high on her breasts, upturned you might say, a good detail to hold onto for fantasizing. I knew it was wrong, but I couldn't help mentally adjusting her appearance to match the picture. Even in a world where scorned women stitch on amputated DNA delivery organs it wouldn't be a bad way to greet the conclusion of time, staring into the dashboard lights with a beautiful girl with perfect skin and upturned brown nipples. Except for one small complication.

"My wife is not a woman given over to distinctions."

Dr. Morel makes some reply, but I don't listen. Instead, my eyes fall on a tattered briefcase lying open on the combination sofa/bed.

"That belongs to Father Bypass," I say.

"You're right," Young Einstein agrees. "He's loaning it to us for the night."

I step over to the briefcase, pick up a paper from the top of the stack. It is an old-style computer printout, detachable tractor feed holes along the sides. Titled "Enhanced Satellite Telemetry," the report tracks the rate of incoming meteorites against reports of psychotic episodes.

"Father Bypass – is dead," I say, trying to keep my voice steady.

"We knew that," Young Einstein pipes in.

"I am sorry for your loss," Dr. Morel replies.

"You don't put a man on the Moon without burning up a few astronauts," I say.

Dr. Morel shakes his head sadly. "Now that's rather harsh, don't you think? We are the good guys. There really is no call for prejudice or fear. Sure, we took a few liberties, skirted the old genetic taboos. But it was all for science."

"Dr. Morel, it's 45 minutes to sunrise," Young Einstein says. "Perhaps we should be getting on with the transformation."

"Agreed." Dr. Morel steps over to the video monitors and presses a button. A voice comes through the speaker.

"Talk to me."

"We're ready to begin."

"I'll be right down."

#

The bulkhead door hisses open. A tall man in cowboy boots, ludicrously oversized hat, dark Wayfarer sunglasses and a fringed rawhide jacket steps into the room. I instantly recognize him from his pictures: Dollar Bill Buckstop.

"Howdy, Doc," he says. "I'm told the shuttle is fueled and ready to go. You got all the parts ready to finish my man-made deity?"

Dr. Morel nods.

"Then let's get this show on the road." Buckstop takes off his Wayfarers and casts a metallic electronic insect gaze upon me. He reaches inside his jacket, producing not a scalpel but a nickel-plated revolver.

"What's this about?" I ask. I am trying to sound calm and steady, but it is difficult when staring down the barrel of a gun and into Buckstop's dead gray eyes.

"It ain't nothing personal, son," Buckstop says. He lowers the gun and lays a hand on my arm. "We're a lot alike. We're both Texans, both white, red-blooded American men. Good ole boys, right? Hell, son, I like ya."

I can't believe it. He's appealing for my understanding!

"But the thing is," he continues, "this is science. The myth of the man turned deity requires a death followed by a resurrection. You know, like they taught us in Sunday school."

"It's the only way," Dr. Morel agrees. "After the cessation of life signs, we shall resurrect you in the bunker under the old Strangers Rest Field."

"And get this, we're going to do it with film," Buckstop says. "Can you believe it? Morel here will use his invention to convert you to celluloid, to turn you into a cinematic fiction, an anonymous creature projected eternally in the present tense, dead or living no one can say with certainty."

"You shall be reborn as a dream-carrying ballistic missile," Morel continues, "your thoughts and memories downloaded into the guidance system. Then I shall initiate primary ignition while simultaneously using the clock in the sky to project a holographic face of the Deity visible across the entire Northern hemisphere. We will play a hypnotic message through the wind machine, make people think it is the voice of the almighty. Certainly that is a superior role to any that The Stranger could ever write for you."

"You and me is going to have big fun," Buckstop says. "You'll be Dollar Bill's Skinalicious9 divine being. A remote controlled godhead, the world's first privately owned and operated deity."

"The result will be total cultural psychosis," Morel adds, "the conclusion of time."

"And I'm going to make a fortune," Buckstop says.

"How's that?" I ask.

"I'm going to make the people think they are growing old. Skin dehydration, decaying collagen. Lots of people will be praying for divine aid. And you, my remote-controlled Deity, shall tell them that the only effective treatment for this lost youth and beauty is Ozona's patented Skinalicious9."

"Sounds like you've got the business plan all figured out."

"You don't know the half of it. The money and marketshare is only a means to an end. I got much bigger plans, son. I'm starting with – what do you call it again, Adolfo?"

"Complete Disheartenment of the Populace," Morel says.

"I like that phrase," Buckstop remarks. "That's exactly true. First, I'm taking full control of the onbeam industry. Forget flying cars and personal jetpacks. The future is onbeam. For starters, I'm putting an end to the meditation sites, accumulation seizures and employment of dark affliction. And the onbeam channels – I already got those wrapped up thanks to my recent stock purchase of Summons Replisystems and subsequent integration of Skinalicious9 technology into the public network – will be broadcasting Society of the Purple Sunset all day and all night, all the time. Except it won't be called that anymore. It'll just be the World. I'm taking the whole planet back to some old time religion. My remote-controlled godhead will take away the animal skin clothing. Everyone must wear fig leaves. Adam will gives an apple to Eve, who in turn will hand it over to a snake. The

Deity will respond by turning Eve into a rib and implanting her into Adam. Despondent, Adam will take away all of the names of all the animals. The Deity will turn him into dust and take away all the animals and the dry land and even the light, leaving the Earth without form and void. Amen."

"Then we unveil the autonomous nanobots," Morel adds.

"The what?" I ask.

"Billions of tiny robots," Buckstop explains. "They'll be swimming through your bloodstream, conquering collagen breakdown, liver spots and free will. And when you are at last freed of the limitations of your frail physical body and aging epidermis, the nanobots will make copies of everyone on the planet and trap them forever in an endless motion picture about a journalist-turned-deity. You will lead them."

"Me? I thought you were the puppetmaster."

"Son, this is a lot bigger than me. You are the model. We found the future of humanity contained in your own unconscious. We actually located the semi-autonomous entity that lives inside you."

"What are you talking about?"

"We are really two people – the logical conscious person and the creative unconscious person. That is particularly true for you. In many ways – actually, in most ways – the creative unconscious person inside of you is the smart one. He really should be running the show. But he's trapped inside in the fleshy shell, compelled to play second fiddle to your conscious mind. As we interviewed this entity about your earliest filmmaking ambitions, we realize that all you ever really wanted to do was make a movie about yourself. Specifically, a story about what it is like to be you living at the center of yourself, with all of the outer skin peeled away. And I think in that process you shall film something that goes beyond the personal. You will be be telling the story about what it is like to be a human at this point in our evolution. We are at a tipping point as a species. Intellectual technology is poised to make the jump from our eyes and fingertips right into our craniums. I really believe that. Five hundred years from now, our progeny will think of us the same way we might think of a Neanderthal. They won't understand what we were like – except through our art. You are writing for those people, the ones who are waiting for us in 2509. I imagine some literary/cinematic archeologist using his cerebral implant to plow through the electronic data artifacts of the early 21st century. He's going to be looking for something that stands out. Odd things, different things. He'll be using search terms like 'longest' and 'biggest,' and he's going to find your movie, 'Marienbad My Love With Mango Extracts.' He's going to use that cerebral implant to plow through the 168 hours in a few seconds. I tell you right now, it's going to give him pause. "What is this?" he'll wonder. He's going to take a second look. And when he does, he's not going to find a story about sword-wielding elves or darkly romantic vampires or anything else that you might find today in a video rental store. He's going to find a story about a two-bodied man – the prototypical man in crisis from the last days of homo sapiens. He is going to find the last man, a broken wayfarer who was transformed into a god and in turn transformed the universe. He's going to find you and your creation, a vast narrative that does away with linear plot and grammatical rules. That is your calling. You will create something that you might find in one of the infinite hexagonal rooms of Borges' "Library of Babel," an almost infinite number of reels of barely comprehensible film. You will create a work that no one will actually watch. Rather, they will be hopelessly lost in what Borges called 'an ambiguous clutter of vacillating texts.'And in these vacillating texts you will find yourself and you will realize that what you are doing is creating a metaphor for the world – a metaphor with great capitalistic value. The substrate of the feeling-toned film stock will be digitally linked to a vast intergalactic marketing network that will determine the precise, individualized ad campaign that will most effectively compel you to buy the entire line of Ozona products."

"You had me going there for a minute. But in the end, I see it is only about money after all."

"No, you're wrong. It is about happiness. And ideas. Without ideas, you're dead. Once we make the leap from this world of concrete reality to the new one of idea reality, everyone will have all they need to be extremely happy. Forever. I'm telling you, son, this one has virtually no bottom."

"You've gone mad."

"Have I?" Buckstop raises the gun again, striving directly for the center of my being. "See you on the other side."

"Wait!" I plead, lifting my hands as if to stop the bullet.

Buckstop pulls the trigger. This is it – the End. I am knocked backward by a blast of heat and cordite. I stumble and grab at my chest. But the End does not come. I find no hole, no blood. Buckstop is equally perplexed.

"Well what the hell?" He fires again. And again, I feel the heat, smell the gunpowder. But I remain unharmed. A look of horror flashes across Young Einstein's face.

"Look at The Stranger," he says. "He's been hit!"

We look over at the examination table. Sure enough, two red splotches are spreading across The Stranger's chest.

"I can't believe it," Dr. Morel says. "How could you miss?"

"I couldn't," Buckstop insists. "I shot at point blank range. How could I miss this one and hit the other?"

"Could be psychic entrainment."

"What?"

"It's been done before with photons. You start with a spooky object, then –"

"Listen," Young Einstein says. "I think he's trying to talk."

The Stranger is looking at me, moving his lips. I go to his side, lean down to hear.

"Run Mark."

Buckstop laughs. "Run? Where you think he's gonna go?"

His question is answered by a shudder, a deep rumble that shakes the metal floor plates. The overhead lights flicker.

"What's that?" Young Einstein asks.

"Sounds like another shuttle," Dr. Morel says. "But that can't –" A flicker of doubt crosses his face. "Did anybody activate the security lockout?"

Too late.

The bulkhead door shatters in a white flash, knocking me to the floor. Smoke pours into the room, followed by a high-pitched siren and flashing red lights. Sparks jump from the severed end of a high-voltage Telex cable, dancing crazily in the gaping hole. Then, a second explosion -- no, a gunshot.

Through the smoke, I can just make out Buckstop, Morel and Young Einstein. They are running away, disappearing down the steel-clad, smoke-filled corridor. A few moments later, there is another, smaller shudder. Explosive bolts fire, and their shuttle breaks away from the aerial clock.

I look at the table where The Stranger lay, but it is empty now. All that remains is his sweater, neatly folded on the pillow. And a note. But I don't have a chance to read it. Cowboy Roy is holstering the still-smoking Bisley, pulling me to my feet.

"Let's move!" he says, hustling me through the broken door. "It's almost sunrise."

#

The next scene will be a natural for the movie trailers and the lobby poster. Picture Cowboy Roy and me flying through space, back toward Earth and Strangers Rest in the "Bevo Saucer," the Bevomobile encased in a transparent egg-shaped space ship glowing crimson and indigo on emergency re-entry.

"How did you pull all this off?" I ask

"I'm a professional actor. The script and this vehicle were delivered to me while I was still on the trail drive. Can you believe it? After all these years I get my first sci-fi role."

"So what's next?"

"Back to Strangers Rest. The script says Buckstop and Morel have already landed at the Joint Reserve Base and are taking the underground pneumatic tube to The Strangers Rest station, where they will launch the dream-carrying missile. You have to get to the drive-in before sunrise, find a way down into the underground bunker and stop Morel and Buckstop from initiating the final launch sequence."

"How do I manage that?"

"Maybe this'll help," he says, handing me a folded piece of paper. "It's the note from The Stranger. Maybe it's your part of the script."

I unfold the paper. No script, no instructions, no guidance at all. Just a poem:

#

Sometimes a man stands up during supper
and walks outdoors, and keeps on walking,
because of a church that stands somewhere in the East.
And his children say blessings on him as if he were dead.
And another man, who remains inside his own house,
dies there, inside the dishes and in the glasses,
so that his children have to go far out into the world
toward that same church, which he forgot.
-Rilke

#

Cowboy Roy pretends not to see me hiding my tears.

"I just can't believe he's really gone," I say.

"Maybe he's not as gone as you think," Roy remarks. He switches on the Muse Sound System. I am amazed; The Stranger is on the air.

"America's Keepers of the Deity possess a unique revulsion for relinquishing power, for allowing events to occur in their own way devoid of intervention. Bill Burroughs once wrote that they would prefer to leap downward inside their own digestive tract and process the masticated groceries and hose out the resulting excrement. I suggest this revulsion for relinquishing power masks a deeper fear, which infuses the entire life of our era. Christian existentialist Paul Tillich regarded it as the fear of existing beneath an incessant danger, the looming hazard of a worldwide and complete psychic disaster. Only the Deity within can award us the confidence that the world and humanity has experienced an existence of success, even if that success should end today and tomorrow should bring the conclusion of time."

#

The eastern sky is already glowing pink and amber when we reach the drive-in.

Townsfolk are gathered for the filming, their cars lining the highway shoulders and filling a neighboring pasture. Roy aims our glass egg toward the back of the screen and settles onto a stretch of brown grass, unseen by the assembled crowd. (The script had called for Roy to switch on the Cicadan-designed cloaking system.) He turns off the engine, and the "egg" disappears.

"There's the old storm drain conduit," Roy says, pointing to a clump of mesquite. "It's all that's left of Strangers Rest Field."

"You think it really leads to the underground bunker?"

"If this was my movie it would."

I nod and start out the door. Roy grabs my arm and I turn back. He offers me his gun.

"No, I can't take it," I tell him. "Besides, I'd just wind up shooting myself. You carry it."

Cowboy Roy shakes his head. "I'm not going in," he says.

"What do you mean? I thought we were going together."

"That conduit's a 42-inch pipe. Big enough for crawling, but my old knees would never make it."

"But it's your granddad's gun."

"Exactly! This old Bisley got Grandpappy Thornton out of many a tight jam. Cleared out Pancho Villa and a whole passel of other pistoleros and bad hombres. I suspect there's still enough of him left in this old gun for one more fight. It'll get you though."

"I'm sure you're right," I say, tucking the gun into my waistband. The hammer pokes me in the abdomen. I say a little prayer to myself: Please, God, don't let me accidentally shoot off my DNA delivery organ.

#

Entering the drain pipe.

On hands and knees, I push through a curtain of ancient spider webs and my own barely contained phobias of confined places, down into the dark unknown. The belly of the whale.

I am relieved to find that the entrance is not guarded by poisonous snakes or small rabid mammals. But as I go deeper, the fear of confined spaces intensifies. I begin to imagine stress fractures in the concrete and a cave in. Before these phobias grow to full irrational size, though, the drain pipe empties into a sort of corridor.

There's still plenty of spider webs and dead insects, but now I can stand up. And there's light. Industrial fixtures are set into the walls every 20 or 30 feet, filling the hallway with a dim, urine glow. I follow the lights to a steel door cracked open a couple of inches, just enough so I can peek inside.

Sure enough, Buckstop, Morel and Young Einstein have already arrived.

"Tell me again how we're going to pull this off without Mark Leach's DNA?" Buckstop asks.

"Relax. We already got enough genetic material from The Stranger, who is just a more aged version of Leach."

"They have the same genetic makeup."

"Exactly. The missile will launch as scheduled."

They are gathered in front of yet another Control Data Corp. 6600, which is configured with a bank of video monitors just like the one on board the aerial clock. One screen shows the orbiting timepiece, floating somewhere over Southeast Asia. The others display various scenes of the drive-in theater directly overhead. There's even audio, a voice coming out of a speaker set into the concrete ceiling.

The voice is familiar. Once I locate the appropriate screen I realize we're listening to the Rev. Ida Purelife, a nationally syndicated televangelist who encountered some recent embarrassment when his predictions of the Rapture failed to materialize as scheduled. Now he is here, among his loyal fan base doing damage control. A group of the Keepers of the Deity from the Exogrid church have gathered around to listen.

"As you know, for a number of years I predicted that the Noble Misfortune would be starting last year," he says. "I transmitted a variety of diagrams and structures illustrating my point of view. Now that last year is past and a new year has arrived, what are my present considerations? Have I altered my point of view? No, I still accept as true that a number of time-periods in Ezekiel and Revelation are factual and others need the process of the day/year computer – better known as the Jubilee Almanac – to be decoded. You may recall Judgment Day Decree No. 7: 'The attendance or nonattendance of the Jubilee Almanac decides how the Deity calculates visionary time-periods.' For me, May 7 of last year works as the date when the Jubilee Almanac came to a conclusion. Therefore, all visionary time-periods happening after May 7 of last year must be calculated in factual time."

Oddly enough, there are murmurs of appreciation. The crowd actually seems to understand – and agree – with what he is saying. A woman steps forward to speak.

"I really appreciate – and I'm sure I speak for everyone – we thank you for taking the time to come out here this morning and set the record straight."

"Yes, let Satan run with that."

Appreciative, yet incomprehensible laughter. (Maybe I'm the one who's crazy. After all, I was raised a Methodist.) The Rev. Purelife smiles. He has the group now.

"But I do still have a question," the woman adds.

"Please ask."

"Do you accept as true that the 5,313 days of Ezekiel 19 started last year?"

"No. The 5,313 days of Ezekiel 19 will start after the extraterrestrial insects are thrown downward as described in Revelation 44. This occasion will be celebrated with a worldwide planet shake, a collapse of global magnitude. Now some of you have heard me say I accept as true that the Son of the Deity will celebrate His homecoming during the 17,000th year of membrane penetration. When do I believe the 17,000th year will occur? I find sufficient evidence in the Bible to believe that the Son of the Deity will return during the 17,000th year of membrane penetration. According to my calculations, the Deity created Adam and Eve about 14,000 B.C. and

I assume they could have lived in the Garden of Eden about 10 minutes before penetrating one another's membranes."

More laughter.

"But seriously, because the lineal records of the Bible are not precise, there is a gap of some years during which the 17,000th year of membrane penetration will transpire."

"Care to hazard a prediction?" someone asks.

"The first achievable year is this year and the last is about 2021 A.D. Keep in mind that this year does not remain a high-quality candidate for the 17,000th year since particular visionary time-periods must happen before the Son of the Deity can come into view. Yes, I know that the Son of the Deity assured us that the end days would be cut down, so this year could possibly be the 17,000th year - even if I don't believe it probable. It would be very exciting, in view of the universal wave of end time passion, if the Nobel Misfortune began next year. Now some of you heard my colloquium in Burial Chamber, Calif., last spring. Regarding the conclusion of time, I made a statement about the days being abbreviated on the front end of the Nobel Misfortune. Therefore, the Nobel Misfortune could have started two years ago and still end next year."

Another question: "How does that belief go with your present view on visionary occasions now that this year has arrived?"

"To exemplify how the critical era could be abridged, I suggested how next year could still be the 17,000th year, even though visionary occurrences had not started at the time of the colloquium. I made three arguments: (1) The 5,313 days of Ezekiel 19 stand for an utmost amount of days for the Nobel Misfortune, (2) the selected amount of days – 5,313 – will be abridged for the benefit of the chosen ones as described in Luke 377: 1-14, and (3) the decrease of the Nobel Misfortune obliges the decrease of all visionary time-periods that are operating at the same time. For example, if the 5,313 days are abridged 38 percent (or some other percentage), then other time-periods in service during that period are also abridged by the same ratio."

"Are you disheartened that the 144,000 have not yet come into view?"

"No. The conclusion of time is the Deity's commerce. I am sure He is correctly onbeam, and the consequences will be wonderful. I look for proof of this pending event each day."

"For the previous recent months, you have not given you visionary examinations on the Daytime Celebrity. Why not?"

"After extensive discussions and ferverent prayer with my financial partner, William Buckstop, I determined it was critical to immediately unveil the seven major dogmas of the Bible. You may recall that I enumerated these dogmas in the first episode of my cable show. The premier was titled "Caution! Revelation is Ready to be Satisfied." The seven dogmas – my 'Seven D's' – are essential to visionary divination. Consequently, I thought it critical to broadcast these dogmas today so that our viewers can see the life-size image of what is to come - perhaps this year, certainly no later than 2021 AD. Any other questions?"

Polite and appreciative silence.

"OK, then, I'll end with a bit of housekeeping. Some of you lately sent a payment to Come Around World! Colloquiums Inc. My printed acknowledgments state that you did not take delivery of assistance or merchandise in exchange for your payment. What does this denote? The Domestic Income Bureau now insists this declaration be located on the printed acknowledgment of all non-profit payments. It just denotes that the wealth you transmitted to me was a contribution - that you did not take delivery of assistance or merchandise."

"Oh, I was wondering what that was about."

"This is why we uphold a difference between acquisitions and gifts. A gift is tax deductible. An acquisition is the reception of assistance or merchandise and is therefore subject to taxation. So in the ideal tax situation, it is better to give than to buy."

Buckstop nods. "So far so good," he says. "The world's first privately owned and operated TV preacher is spinning like a top. Now let's check out the snack bar."

Morel switches the audio several screens to the right, where the Methodists are having a grand time inside the snack bar (an air conditioned canvas tent pitched on the "inside" of the false front refreshment stand/projection booth), playing the roles of the heaven-bound true believers and eating popcorn and other movie treats. The abandoned Keepers of the Deity are furiously milling about outside the open door.

"So," one of them asks a member of the Methodist contingent, "are you an amillenialist or a postmillenialist?"

The Methodist shakes his head with great condescension.

"We don't read the Book of Revelation in quite that way," he says, almost laughing.

"Oh really. Then how do you read it?"

"Truth be told, John of Patmos articulated his belief within the reflective structures of his time, one of which – just one, mind you – was the revelatory expectation of the approaching homecoming of the Son of the Deity. But our modern study of olden times has revealed that this structure of the Christian expectation was misguided and –

"Misguided?"

"Yes, it should not persist in modern repetition. Just as contemporary Christians can translate John's erroneous knowledge of the form of the earth without ignoring his communication, so also contemporary Christians can sincerely accept John's communication of expectation stated in the revelatory structure, which incorporated the pending anticipation of the conclusion of time, without proceeding to replicate it in his historically-appropriate – but now entirely outdated – idiom."

"I see. So what updated idiom you do you propose we misguided contemporary Christians use to spread the Word of God?"

"Certainly the modern day equivalent of the ancient apocalyptic genre is science fiction and the epic film of the End of the World."

Buckstop looks at his watch, a thick gold Rolex with a dial surrounded in diamonds. Morel shakes his head.

"Don't' worry about it," Adolfo says. "The psychic warhead is fully operational, and the missile will launch in --" He consults an overhead monitor. "It will launch in eight minutes."

Time for action. I reach for Roy's gun, but am caught short by a gun barrel against by spine. "Care to watch with us, Mr. Leach?" Young Einstein asks. "We've got a place that'll give you a perfect view."

#

Inside the concrete missile silo, strapped to the titanium fin of an ICBM.

Buckstop and Morel are watching me through the blast-proof observation window. Young Einstein is playing with the Bisley, spinning it on his finger just like Cowboy Roy did for the boys at the store the morning the clock first appeared in the sky. (Was it really only two weeks ago?) On one of the twin circular screens of the 6600

I observe the countdown: 6:44 a.m. Sunday. Three minutes to Armageddon.

"Comfy?" Buckstop's voice crackles through a gray metal speaker mounted next to the window.

"I know I'm not a rocket scientist, but won't I throw off the trajectory?" I ask. My panicky voice echoes against the concrete walls, returning cold and dead. "I mean, I've not very aerodynamic," I add.

"That's true," Morel agrees. "But we can compensate for the balance and drag. The important thing is we need a resurrection. We were going to do it metaphorically, but this is much better. You can't have the world's first privately owned and operated deity without a resurrection."

"And you can't have a resurrection without a death."

Buckstop nods. "Everybody wants it to be easy," he says. "Well, this ain't like the movies. Progress is never easy. You've got to fight for the future, son. After all, you don't put a man on the Moon without burning up a few astronauts."

#

Over the speaker I can hear fingers tapping on a computer keyboard. Through the glass, I can just make out the image on one of the video monitors. It's the wind machine from the church. The turboprop begins to turn, shaking the tent/snack bar with a 90-mile wind. The crowd of extras struggle to remain on their feet.

"And now for the Vox Dei," Morel entones, adjusting a pair of black knobs. A voice booms out of the speaker.

#

WHO IS THIS THAT DARKENS COUNSEL BY WORDS WITHOUT KNOWLEDGE?

#

The voice is familiar. It's The Stranger! Young Einstein and Morel exchange shocked and troubled glances.

"What the hell?" Buckstop roars. "Morel, you said they'd be listening to ME!"

"I -- I don't know," Morel says, furiously working the keyboard. "Sounds like something from the Old Testament."

In fact, I recognize it as Job 38 – the Lord's response to Job.

#

GIRD UP YOUR LOINS LIKE A MAN; I WILL QUESTION YOU, AND YOU DECLARE TO ME.

#

Presumably, this scripture reading can also be heard at the drive-in because on one of the monitors I see a couple of the movie extras peering quizzically into one of the old Stadium Drive-In window speakers. Buckstop sees it, too. Furious, he again consults his watch.

"And what about the missile?" he asks. "It's past time."

Sure enough, the video monitor with the "T-minus" reading is now flashing "LAUNCH PENDING."

"Why don't we launch? Morel!"

"I'm on it," Morel says, coolly tapping at the keyboard. "We'll launch manually. Let me just punch up the telemetry and --"

But he is cut short by a new development. Through the concrete walls of the bunker comes a strange vibration, a scraping like a snow shovel on concrete. Morel's self-assurance instantly disappears. He and Young Einstein look at each other in horror.

"What?" Buckstop demands. "Tell me what it is."

"Cicadans," Morel says.

#

CAN YOU DRAW OUT LEVIATHAN WITH A FISHHOOK, OR PRESS DOWN ITS TONGUE WITH A CORD?

#

A huge piece of concrete crashes to the floor, and in pour the aliens, dozens of giant Cicadans filling the bunker with a deafening insect roar. Young Einstein raises Grandpappy Thornton's Bisley, but he's too slow. A half dozen are on him at once, crazed legs flying. They instantly disarm him, then begin strapping him into an odd, backless chair.

"No, not the brain-changing stool!" Young Einstein begs.

"Think about Godzilla," the insects instruct him.

"I won't do it," he insists. "You can't send me down that time subway of death."

The control room is suddenly filled with a bluish light, and a self-sustaining ethericom tetrahedron (exactly as posited by Morel in his time equations) forms in the center of the room. Within the swirling heart of the electrical morass the subway doors slide open and out steps the psychic beast itself – the Monster of the Id, the Fiend of the Unconscious.

A strange wind sings down into the concrete silo, filling my nostrils with the salt air of 1942 and the corroded metal stench of the U.S.S. Ethan Allen Hitchcock. I can hear the ozone gas hissing and crackling from the main reactor of the ship as the green-toned Fiend steps forward, exhaling crimson smoke and bits of sparking magnesium.

The creature instantly rips into Young Einstein, splattering blood and bits of flesh against the inner glazing of the observation window.

#

CAN YOU FILL ITS SKIN WITH HARPOONS, OR ITS HEAD WITH FISHING SPEARS? LAY HANDS ON IT; THINK OF THE BATTLE; YOU WILL NOT DO IT AGAIN! ANY HOPE OF CAPTURING IT WILL BE DISAPPOINTED; WERE NOT EVEN THE GODS OVERWHELMED AT THE SIGHT OF IT?

#

Buckstop and Morel are moving slowing along the wall, headed for the door. They make it half way across the room, then the Fiend is on them, too. They are pulled to the floor, out of my line of sight. All I see of their demise are twin fountains of red mist. The window cracks, and shards of blood-stained glass crash on the concrete floor around me.

Now the entire bank of video monitors is flashing "LAUNCH PENDING." And yet, perhaps there is still time to stop the catastrophe. I struggle against my restraints, and the straps weaken enough that I can just slip them over my head.

I head for a small steel access door set into the side of the silo, but I am stopped by a pair of giant insect legs. It's Bellero Shield!

"All is well," he assures me.

"But the launch," I say. "You've got to stop it."

"We are. See for yourself."

Through the jagged remains of the blood-stained window I can make out a half dozen Cicadans scuttling over the video panel. They expertly work the keyboard and various controls, a blur of insect legs. The bluish glow of the self-sustaining ethericom tetrahedron flickers a moment, then disappears, taking the Fiend with it. A blur of bluish-green numbers begin to scroll across the video monitors.

"This is a rescue," Bellero continues. "Please pardon my exit as we finish reprogramming the missile with alternate coordinates."

Bellero flies through the broken window to the control panel, and another cicada takes me by the arms. We ascend swiftly up the silo, toward a circle of blue sky.

"Must get Mark Leach clear of the silo," the alien says. "Must get clear before missile launches and rocket exhaust incinerates the bunker."

"No, we must stop the missile," I protest. "It'll destroy the world."

"It will rescue the world. Buckstop's vision will be destroyed with his own weapon. The missile will destroy the aerial clock."

"Jack and the girls are still up there. You've got to stop the launch."

But the single-minded Cicada does not hear me.

"Must rescue Mark Leach. Mark Leach must be kept safe."

We shoot up into the sunlight like Lucifer blasted out of Hell. The alien sets me on my feet just in time to see the tornado tower collapse. It is a horror, a tangle of metal and anguished machinery cries. The turboprop detaches from its moorings and becomes airborne, flying into the neighboring pasture.

Suddenly the ground rumbles. Buckstop's missile is screaming into the sky on a surging pillar of fire. The stuttering roar of the rocket blast shakes the earth for miles around, flushing birds out of surrounding pastures and setting off nearby car alarms. A moment later there is a brilliant flash, a tremendous explosion just beyond the tree line. It is the dramatic volcanic eruption of my dream, another incredible revelation. Crimson fire rains down upon Strangers Rest. Rooftops are ablaze – including presumably my house. I picture its multi-gabled roof exploding in flames.

I step around the movie screen and see dozens of fleeing townsfolk, a scene of post-apocalyptic, science fiction panic. Engulfed in a shower of dirt and rocket exhaust and volcanic ash, they are running away from the flaming crater of the missile silo, away from the volcano and burning town, and towards the highway and their cars.

Chaos. I see two old men, one attempting to pull the other away from the burning pasture that lies on the other side of the barbed wire fence.

"My land, destroyed," one of them says forlornly. He struggling towards the fence through the firey blizzard, the air smoking with ash.

"It's all right, Daniel," the other assures him. "It's just a grass fire."

"Destroyed I tell you. $1 million up in smoke. And look at my stock tank!"

I see a cow, struggling to free itself from the muddy bank. But no – that's not quite it. The animal is held fast by the pond itself, hooves encased in coffee-colored ice. This is surely wrong, a pond frozen over in summer. And yet – could this be 1928-29 all over again?

On the other side of the drive-in, an army of dominos running on little legs chases Ima Bost. "Ornery old man," she says. Then she stumbles, and the dominos are upon her. This attack is observed from the early morning shadows by a troll-like character, a man with black, darting eyes and dark gray hair resembling grease-soaked felt.

"Deity's dentures, this is not true filmmaking at all," he mutters. "A movie must tell a story. This meaningless drivel tells nothing but crap."

Next to the crater I see a tombstone with a white cloth folded neatly over the top.

"See, the Vault of the Deity is empty," the cicada says. "Death followed by transfiguration. Victory is achieved."

"Victory? It's total panic! Look, that guy over there just stepped on that old woman's face."

"Victory and panic," he clarifies. "But is this not the way of visionary transformation? Instead of thanks, the people are fearful and outraged. They do not see you as the savior, but the destroyer."

"But I've done nothing."

"Yes, total misunderstanding. And misunderstanding is always the story of the sage unaccepted in civilization. The maker of epic films is often murdered in our waking world."

"Murdered?"

"There is frequent doubt, the Cassandra concept is correlated with prophets. To have the cinematic capability – the ability to craft the epic film of incredible revelations – is to have the capability to incorporate attitudes or ideas unknowingly into one's inner being that address the difficulties of the era, and develop a resolution internally. This approach has the ability to then outwardly change the civilization via paradigm reorganization."

Suddenly there is a vivid flash in the heavens. It is the Clock in the Air, exploding in a silent white cloud of springs and numbers streaking away in all directions across the clean azure morning sky.

"Fire will explode in streams of luminosity and expanses of conflagration," the cicada continues. "The venerated icon is destroyed. Victory!"

"And panic," he quickly adds.

"But what about Jack?" I insist. "What about the girls?"

Another Cicadan joins us. It is Bellero Shield.

"The revised script frequently endangers the existing order," he explains. "The victory is often translated as demonic by the Keepers of the Deity. The director revises the circumstance by acquiring the egregious moral errors of the populace and sacrificing himself as a sign of the resolution, such as Christ or Gandhi or Martin Luther King."

"I do not wish to sacrifice myself or Jack or the girls," I say.

"That is understandable. But a death of some part of you is necessary for a resurrection of the rest."

A light rain begins to fall, and I see some people are collecting it in bottles and other containers.

"This is the living water, just as you dreamed it," Bellero says. "This is the grace of the Deity."

I look across the emptying drive-in and see Cowboy Roy on horseback, gun drawn as he chases the four horsemen of the apocalypse into the grassfire that has now fully engulfed the $1 million pasture.

And I see the little deuce coupe.

I can just make out the driver. It's The Stranger! He's alive. But – but how did he get back here?

I start running toward him, then I am caught short by a chilling sight. Another car has arrived, an antique black sedan with bat wing tail fins – a 1958 Galaxie. They line up for a race.

I turn back toward Bellero and his companion. "Stop this, save him!" I plead. But the Cicadans are already gone.

The two cars take off in a roaring cloud of dust and gravel. The black sedan immediately abandons the race, peeling off to the right. The red coupe passes close to a parked car, loses control and flips over several times.

It is a terrible accident. The coupe crumples like a soft drink can and tumbles to a stop next to a building. I run to the crash scene. A man exits the wrecked car and runs towards me, apparently uninjured but understandably distraught.

"Is there anybody else in there?" I ask.

"My buddy!" he says, choking, almost in tears.

We run to the car, and I look through what is left of the passenger side window. There he is, The Stranger. He is horribly disfigured. No blood, but the side of his head and upper body looks like a cross between a slab of brown, bloodless beef and a piece of weathered lumber. Nothing human left. The place where the eye should be looks like knothole. He is not even the right shape to be human. He's a blob, really, like a 1950s drive-in movie space alien.

"Do you think he's dead?" I ask.

The man does not answer. Then I notice The Stranger is breathing. He's alive. He is sitting on the driver's side of the car. I don't know if he was the driver; it may be that he was merely pushed there by the crash. So I walk around to the driver's door for a better look.

Surprisingly, the other side of The Stranger's face is virtually intact. He's half human, half alien. His one human eye is closed. I turn to his friend.

"What is his name?" I ask.

"Pilly Graham."

Pilly? Instantly, I realize he must mean "Billy" Graham, like the evangelist. So that's it. The Stranger is actually a man of God.

I speak to him, try to determine if he is conscious.

"Billy, can you hear me?"

Sure enough, he drowsily opens his one good eye and looks my way.

"Everything's going to be OK," I tell him, trying to sound optimistic. But he looks terrible; his eye is bulging from the socket, a look of terror. I give him the double thumbs up sign.

I am wondering if he can see well enough to make out my affirming hand signs. Indeed, my own vision begins to go double (actually triple!), but just the part of the field of vision that takes in my hands. It appears that I am seeing my hands through him.

He starts to close his eye again, and I fear he will go into shock and die. So I try to keep him talking.

"Billy, I'm going to pray with you now, OK?"

I am thinking I will say the Lord's Prayer, because I believe he is about to die. This is his last chance to get right with God. The call to prayer gets his attention.

"What?" he asks in alarm.

Milton Keynes UK
Ingram Content Group UK Ltd.
UKHW020615050124
435507UK00005B/60